Politics In Context:

Assimilation and Conflict
in Urban Neighborhoods

Politics In Context:

Assimilation and Conflict in Urban Neighborhoods

**Robert Huckfeldt,
Indiana University**

Agathon Press, Inc.
New York

© 1986 Agathon Press

Agathon Press is an imprint of
ALGORA PUBLISHING
222 Riverside Drive. New York. NY 10025

Library of Congress Cataloging-in-PublicationData

Huckfeldt, R. Robert.
  Politics in context

  Bibliography: p.
  Includes index.
  1. Neighborhood — New York (State) — Buffalo — Case
  Studies. 2. Neighborhood — Michiga — Detroit — Case
  studies. 3. Political participation — New York (State) —
  Buffalo — Case studies. **4.** Political participation —
  Michigan — Detroit — Case studies. 5. Social
  interaction — New York (State) — Buffalo — Case studies,
  6. Social interaction — Michigan — Detroit — Case studies.
  I. Title.
  HN80.B9H83 1986   307.3'362   85-28771

  ISBN: 0-87586-067-2 cloth
  ISBN: 0-87586-068-0 paper

Printed in the U.S.A

CONTENTS

ACKNOWLEDGMENTS

This book is part of a continuing preoccupation that dates at least to my second year of graduate school, and thus I have produced a trail of intellectual debts that begins at Washington University in St. Louis during the middle 1970s.

First things first: John Sprague introduced me to contextual theories of politics in a graduate seminar on mathematical modeling in the spring of 1975. In addition to signing off on my dissertation, he has always been available for trying out ideas, for help with problems of all sorts, for encouragement when things do not seem to be working, and for an unlimited supply of theoretical insight regarding the nature of social influence in politics. He is, in short, the model of an unselfish teacher.

A number of colleagues in St. Louis, Baton Rouge, South Bend, and Bioomington have generously responded to my musings regarding context and politics, as well as giving me fresh insights regarding a range of related intellectual problems. They include Carol Kohfeld, Michael Wolfe, Thomas Likens, Courtney Brown, Michael MacKuen, David Leege, Ronald Weber, Calvin Jillson, Cecil Eubanks, Ted Carmines and Gerald Wright. I am also grateful to Lyman Kellstedt for providing the Buffalo survey data, originally collected by Professor Kellstedt in collaboration with Everett Cataldo, Richard Johnson, and Lester Milbrath. The Detroit survey data were collected as part of the 1966 Detroit Area Study under the direction of Edward Laumann, and distributed by the Interuniversity Consortium for Political and Social Research. Neither the Consortium nor the original collectors of either data set bear any responsibility for the analyses or interpretations offered here.

At its best, the university is one of the true wonders of western civilization, and this research has been supported by three of them: Louisiana State University, the University of Notre Dame, and Indiana University. The National Science Foundation supported much of the research through grants SES 80-14321 to LSU, SES 81-18597 and SES 83-18899 to Notre Dame, and SES 84-15572 to IU. I have also benefitted greatly from the help of people connected with Agathon Press: Burton Lasky, Paul Hoeber, and my editor, James Kuklinski of the University of Illinois.

Parts of this book have appeared elsewhere. An earlier version of Chapter 3 was published in the *American Journal of Sociology* (1983b). Chapter 5 is taken from an article that appeared in *American Politics Quarterly* (1983a). Earlier forms of Chapters 7 and 8 appeared in the *American Journal of Political Science* (1979, 1984). Finally, a previous incarnation of Chapter 9 appeared as an article in *Political Behavior* (1980).

I am grateful to the editors of these journals for publishing in the first place, and to the publishers for allowing the integration of the work into this book.

Finally, I would like to thank Rachel, Peter, Christopher and especially Sharon. They have not exactly made these tasks easier, but they have certainly made them more interesting, and everyone knows that "interesting" is much to be preferred over "easy. -- Quite simply, they keep me sane and make me human.

R.R.H.
Bloomington, Indiana
April, 1985

CHAPTER 1

AN INTRODUCTION TO POLITICS IN CONTEXT

The group formed by associated individuals has a reality of a different sort from each individual considered singly.

Emile Durkheim, *Suicide,* p. 320

Voting is essentially a group experience. People who work or live or play together are likely to vote for the same candidates.

Paul Lazarsfeld, Bernard Berelson,
and Hazel Gaudet, *The People's Choice,* 3rd ed., p. 137

The motivating thesis of this book is simply stated: the political opinions and behavior of individuals cannot be explained apart from the environments within which they occur. Individual characteristics alone do not determine political actions and opinions. Rather, political behavior must be understood in terms of the actor's relationship to the environment, and the environmental factors that impinge on individual choice.

An individual's environment can be defined at varying degrees of spatial inclusiveness: Missouri, St. Louis, the Central West End. The neighborhood environment is especially important, however. Missourians can avoid St. Louis, and St. Louisans can avoid the Central West End, but residents of the Central West End have a more difficult time avoiding each other. A neighborhood's residents walk its streets, share its facilities, depend upon it for security, and frequently encounter other neighborhood residents. Further, associational patterns are influenced by spatial proximity: it is often easier to initiate and maintain an active friendship with someone who lives nearby.

Various features of neighborhood environments are important to politics and political behavior, and a variety of environmental properties are considered in this book. Personalized social interactions within the environment serve as important sources of political information and guidance. Casual and impersonal contacts contradict or reinforce social and political identities, beliefs, and opinions. Locationally specific events provoke dramatic political responses.

One aspect of the neighborhood environment will receive special attention: the neighborhood social context, or the social composition of the neighborhood's spopulation. Attention centers upon (1) the manner in which social relations and patterns of social interaction are structured by neighborhood social contexts, and **(2)** the consequences of these contextually structured interactions for political behavior. This study does not equate the neighborhood with a cohesive community of friends and acquaintances. Such cohesive communities sometimes exist, but they are tangential to the present argument and cannot be measured with the kinds of data that are available. The neighborhood, **as** it is conceived here, refers to the shared geographic locale of a residential grouping, and the neighborhood social context refers to the population composition of the people who live in the neighborhood. This neighborhood definition subsumes the cohesive community but does not depend upon it. The definition is designed to capture the inescapable social relations of any geographically based social collectivity. Thus, the neighborhood is of interest as a structural factor in the lives of its residents, rather than as a well-articulated social organization.

This study explores several questions regarding neighborhood social contexts and residents' political behavior using surveys of residents from the Buffalo, New York metropolitan area and from the Detroit, Michigan metropolitan area. How does the neighborhood social context influence political behavior? Which political behaviors and activities are most affected? How **is** the neighborhood social context translated into political influence? Are individual attributes and contextual properties mutually influential in explaining political behavior, or is one set of factors more influential than the other? Are the effects of neighborhood social contexts and individual attributes independent, or does the influence of factors at one level depend upon factors at the other level?

DEMONSTRATIONS OF
CONTEXTUAL INFLUENCE

Social scientists have demonstrated the political impact of the residential social environment in a wide range of temporal and cultural settings. In a study of 55 Stockholm election districts, Tingsten (1963) showed that vote choice was affected by the social composition of the election district. The proportional vote for socialist parties within a district fell short of the working class proportion when the working class was in a small minority, but approached and then exceeded the working class proportion as working class densities increased, This nonlinear (s-curve) relationship between the socialist share of the vote and the working class share of the population indicates that the individual probability of voting for a socialist party varied as a function of the social context (see Przeworski and Soares, 1971).

On the other side of the Atlantic, David Segal and Marshall Meyer (1974) analyzed a survey of residents from nine northeastern United States towns, and found that the neighborhood's social composition (in this case a voting ward) and the town's political climate had important effects upon individual partisan identifications. Low socioeconomic status (SES) respondents living in low SES neighborhoods were less likely to support the Republican Party than low SES respondents living in high SES neighborhoods. Similarly, high SES respondents living in low SES neighborhoods were less likely to support the Republican Party than high SES respondents living in high SES neighborhoods. In the authors' words, ". . . the local community can serve as an important means of political orientation for a person, regardless of whether or not he shares the social status of his neighbors" (1974: **220).** Segal and Meyer also demonstrated an important interaction between social and political factors in the respondent's residential environment: the effect of the neighborhood social context was most pronounced in towns which lacked a clear-cut political climate. Even in towns with clear partisan leanings, however, the effect of the social context was still evident. Both environmental factors were important sources of political influence that helped explain individual political partisanship.

Butler and Stokes (1974) analyzed the effect of local environments upon party support among British voters. A comparison of individuals living in heavily working class mining areas with individuals living in heavily middle class resort areas showed that support for the Conservative Party was higher in resort areas among both working class and middle class individuals. This same finding was substantiated in other areas with high working class and high middle class population concentrations (1974: 130–132). In short, an area's class composition seemed to be associated with the level of support given to political parties by a particular social class.

The social environment's importance is not limited to Europe or the United States. Chilean workers have been shown to be sensitive to the composition of their social environments as well. In their study of the 1964 Chilean election, Langton and Rapoport (1974) illustrated the importance of the social context as a determinant of subjective class identification, political cognition, and voting choice. Santiago workers living in more homogeneous working class environments were more likely to identify as workers, recognize Salvador Allende as being favorable toward workers' interests, and vote for Allende in the 1964 election.

In one of the first attempts to show environmental effects using national survey data, Warren Miller (1956)demonstrated that local political environments (measured as the Democratic percentage of a county's 1952 two-party presidential vote) had important mediating influences upon the relationships between factors influencing partisan choice and the 1952 presidential votes of nonsouthern survey respondents. The relationships between various partisan motivations and the vote were less pronounced among people who belonged to a partisan minority within the counties: Democrats in Republican counties, or Republicans in Democratic counties. These motivations included party identification, issue position or orientation, and candidate orientation.

> Just as the minority party seldom elects its "fair share" of candidates for office, so in the phenomenon with which we are concerned the minority fails to receive its "fair share" of votes if the relative incidence of supporting motivations is used as the criterion of fairness. (1956: 715)

Miller also showed that members of the minority demonstrated less unity and more heterogeneity than members of the majority (p. 717).

Robert Putnam also studied the effects of the county level political environment, measured as the Democratic percentage of the 1952 two-party presidential vote, upon nonsouthern survey respondents' 1952 vote choices. He found that (1) people more involved in secondary associations were more susceptible to community influence, (2) the political composition of respondents' primary groups partially reflected the political composition of the county, (3) members of secondary groups were more apt to have friendship groups which reflected the county political environment, and (4) members of secondary organizations seemed more susceptible to the opinions of friends (1966: 646–652).

Putnam's effort points to the social basis for politics that was well-established by the early empirical work of Columbia sociologist Paul Lazarsfeld and his associates. Their 1940 study of the presidential race in Erie County, New York identified the importance of social groups based on status, religious affiliation, and residence (1968: 138). The authors suggested that the vote decision was at least in part a social experience:

> people who live together under similar external conditions are likely to develop similar needs and interests. They tend to see the world through the same colored glasses; they tend to apply to common experiences common interpretations. . . . But this is only part of the picture. There may be many group members who are not really aware of the goals of their own group. And there may be many who, even if they were aware of these goals, would not be sufficiently interested in current events to tie the two together consciously.

They acquiesce to the political temper of their groups under the steady, personal influence of their more politically active fellow citizens. (pp. 148–149)

Their findings on primary group influence are summarized in the "two-step flow of communication" (pp. 151–152). This formulation suggests that most individuals do not directly digest information disseminated through the media and other direct sources. Rather they depend upon "opinion leaders," usually face-to-face acquaintances, as interpreters upon whose summaries they base their own views. In his elaboration of the two-step flow, Katz (1957: 77) suggested that these interpersonal interactions serve as "(1) channels of information, (2) sources of social pressure, and (3) sources of social support."

The findings of the Erie County study were built upon by the work of Berelson, Lazarfeld, and McPhee in their 1948 study of the presidential campaign in Elmira, a small city in upstate New York. The authors again found primary group interaction to be an important determinant of individual voting decisions (1954: 88—101). They also determined that "when the voter's immediate personal environment is split in political preference, he is more likely to vote in line with the majority of the larger community" (p. 116). In this way, the larger political environment makes its influence felt when the individual's immediate social environment does not clearly dictate an alternative.

In summary, social groups are politically relevant not only because members share common characteristics, but also because social interaction within the group makes the members aware of their commonalities. Thus, *group membership is not simply a function of individual characteristics; it is determined by social experience.* The findings of Lazarsfeld and the other Columbia sociologists demonstrate the importance of social contacts for individual political behavior. The important point for contextual research is that these contacts might be affected by the population composition of an individual's environment, an issue that is directly addressed in the present effort.

THE TRADITIONAL NEGLECT OF CONTEXT

These previous studies notwithstanding, most explorations of political behavior ignore the social context. One important reason for this neglect is the predominant research strategy used to study political behavior. National election studies effectively foreclose many opportunities for considering the social environment by employing large-scale sample surveys. Such a research strategy obscures the social context by randomizing it. Rather than explicitly isolating variables which are specific to a given residential environment, the national survey disregards political and social factors in the environment by sampling from many separate and radically different social milieus, i.e., by intentionally divorcing the individual from a unique social setting. Every research methodology contains its own set of biases; the national sample survey is biased against any theory of political behavior relying upon contextual factors. [1]

Even studies of urban political behavior and politics often fail to consider the social context within which the behavior occurs. When consideration has been given to an environmental factor, the analysis often focuses upon city versus suburban residence. Wirt and his associates, in an attempt to show that suburbanization has no effect upon political behavior, argued that residents are immune to any influence based upon their place of residence.

> Our failure to find measurable independent locale effects on attitudes, once we have "partialled-out" the effects of individual attributes, suggests that the dynamics of attitude formation in urban and suburban populations are the same. ...Surburbanites' attitudes are different from those of their urban counterparts because of the kinds of people they are, *not* [italics in original] because of where they live. **(1972: 129–130)**

The authors were substantially correct in suggesting that attitude formation **is** the same in city and **suburb**.[2] They were incorrect in suggesting that attitude formation is a function of individual attributes apart from the residential environment. Their analysis ignored important contextual and environmental properties and focused instead upon a relatively unimportant one — city versus suburban residence.

Urbanism and Social Disintegration

Perhaps the most important reason for this neglect of context is a fundamental intellectual ambivalence regarding the relationship between individuals and environments. One prevalent viewpoint suggests that modern society, and particularly urban society, results in an atomistic individual who is *divorced* from the environment.

In an early and influential article, Louis Wirth characterized the social contacts of urban dwellers as impersonal, superficial, transitory, and segmental. **He** linked these aspects of urban social life to specific factors in the structure and organization of urban society: the size, density, and heterogeneity of urban populations. According to this view, urbanization leads to a disintegration of social groups and group life. Even though cities are honeycombed with residential areas marked by social homogeneity, these settlement patterns are seen as being insignificant for the maintenance of durable social bonds (1938: 20–21).

Wirth clearly recognized the political consequences of the socially disintegrative process that he described. The individual finds "it difficult to determine what is in his own 'best interests' and to decide between the issues and leaders presented to him by the agencies of mass suggestion" (1938: **20**). Individuals are set adrift politically: without a social group with which to identify, they have no standard of judgment for evaluating political issues and leaders. Thus, urban society is marked by socially isolated individuals, highly susceptible to political appeals, and highly unstable in their political preferences and loyalties.[3]

The City and Social Intensification

While Wirth emphasized the depersonalization, anonymity, and disintegration of social institutions in urban areas, Park's classic analysis (1925) gave attention to other aspects of the urban experience, and arrived at different conclusions regarding its social potential. In particular, he viewed the social life of the group as being predicated upon geographical location within the city.

> The easy means of communication and of transportation, which enable individuals to distribute their attention and to live at the same time in several different worlds, tend to destroy the permanency and intimacy of the neighborhood. On the other hand, the isolation of the immigrant and racial colonies of the so-called ghettos and areas of population segregation tend to preserve and, where there is racial prejudice, to intensify the intimacies and solidarity of the local and neighborhood groups. *Where individuals of the same race or of the same vocation live together in segregated groups, neighborhood sentiment tends to fuse together with racial antagonisms and class interests.* (1925:9–10, emphasis added)

Wirth argued that the increased size, population density, and social heterogeneity of urban areas produce a breakdown of many social institutions and relationships, including the neighborhood. As a result, urban areas are populated by isolated atomized individuals. In contrast, Park and his associates argued that these same factors, and the residential segregation which results from them, have very different implications for individual behavior. For example, Park identified a phenomenon he believed to be social contagion in socially deviant neighborhoods: "'social contagion tends to stimulate in divergent types the common tempermental differences and to suppress characters which unite them with the normal types about them" (1925: 45). Wirth sees urban dwellers as being socially isolated and independent, while Park sees them as being solidly imbedded in, and influenced by, a social environment that is often locally based.[4]

More recent considerations of the city have suggested that the importance of social groups is *intensified* in an urban setting. Not only do urban areas possess a great number and variety of social groups, but also group members often demonstrate more intense group loyalties. Large urban populations often include large subpopulations capable of forming their own group identities, supporting their own institutions, and entering into intensive interaction within the group. The large size of the groups, fostered by an urban setting, allows internal consciousness to develop in ways that would be impossible with smaller numbers of group members (Fischer, **1976:37**).

Group loyalties are also intensified by interaction outside the group. Because of social diversity in urban areas, interaction often takes place between populations that are far different from each other, and this interaction between groups often results in either subtle or overt hostility and conflict. According to Coser (1956: **38**): "conflict serves to establish and maintain the identity and boundary lines of societies and groups." Thus, group boundaries and loyalties are not only maintained through integrative processes of assimilation and social support, but also through social processes rooted in conflict and hostility.

Social Life in Spatially Defined Contexts

How important are spatially defined social contexts to the encouragement and maintenance of social groups in urban settings? Are social groups dependent upon geographical proximity, or have they been freed from a reliance upon shared residential locations? Not only does disagreement occur regarding the effects of urbanism upon social groups, but disagreement also occurs regarding the role of neighborhoods in sustaining group life.

In large part echoing Wirth, many contemporary writers on the urban neighborhood minimize its importance as a social unit. A principal argument in support of this view is that spatial mobility within the modem city has undermined the integrity of urban neighborhoods. This increased mobility provides residents with increased freedom of association. A social group need not live together in order to enter into a rich social life. Urban residents may travel anywhere within a city to associate with whomever **they** please. This mobility frees residents' associational patterns in a way which severs their social ties to the residential neighborhood (Fischer, **1976: 118–119**). In short, the neighborhood is viewed as a gathering place for independent transients.

This argument suffers from several failings. Urban residents' mobility allows them freedom of residence as well as freedom of association; they are no longer required to live in areas nearby their places of employment. Residential locations can be chosen for other reasons. Hawley and Zimmer found that " . . . central cities and suburban areas attract residents who are closely similar to their indigenous populations" (Hawley and Zimmer, 1970: 38). However, this sort of self-perpetuating residential homogeneity may not be simply or completely a function of residential preferences. The primary motivation in selecting a residence is frequently the dwelling itself (Hawley and Zimmer, 1970: 32), and private industry practices in constructing and marketing housing often encourage segregation according to not only racial, but also social and economic criteria (Judd, 1979). In other words, residential choice operates within severe constraints that are imposed by the realities of urban housing markets. Thus, residential "freedom" often results in neighborhoods segregated according to racial, ethnic, occupational, economic, and family stage criteria. Although it is not predicated on a political basis, this segregation has important consequences for the integrity of social groups, for patterns of social interaction, for the formation of friendship groups, and for the political behavior of urban residents.

THE DATA BASE FOR THIS STUDY

In contrast to the traditional neglect of context, this study is explicitly concerned with the political influence of neighborhood social contexts. The data base for the study builds upon surveys of residents living in two metropolitan areas: Buffalo, New York and Detroit, Michigan. The Buffalo survey was conducted in the spring of 1968 by four members of the political science department at State University of New York at Buffalo, and the Detroit survey was conducted in 1966 as part of the Detroit Area Study program by Edward Laumann and his associates at the University of Michigan.[5] Census tract data have been matched and merged to the surveys; these tract data were obtained from the 1960 and 1970 Censuses of Population and Housing conducted by the United States Bureau of the Census.

Thus the operational definition for the neighborhood is a census tract, and that working definition requires some justification. Once again, the neighborhood is not being conceived as a cohesive community, and the reader need not believe in any mythical qualities related to neighborhood life. Some neighborhoods are socially organized in such a way that they sustain a rich neighborhood-based social life; other neighborhoods are socially disorganized or unorganized. The important point for this study is that any neighborhood presents a distinctive set of possibilities for social interaction at both intimate and impersonal levels. A census tract is a poor approximation of a cohesive community, but it is a reasonable surrogate for the environmentally circumscribed opportunities and constraints operating upon social interaction.

The census tract population mean for Detroit respondents is approximately ten thousand, and the census tract population mean for the Buffalo respondents is approximately eleven thousand.[6] Thus, the average census tract is much larger than a city block, but smaller than most municipalities, approximating the "macro-neighborhood" described by **Marans** and **Rodgers** (1975). No assumption is made that most neighborhood residents get to know each other, or that they identify the area as their neighborhood, or that the area is a self-contained social unit. The main importance of the neighborhood for this study is that its composition affects the social and political content of personal and impersonal social interactions for its residents.

Given this definition for the neighborhood, the Buffalo and Detroit surveys are valuable for several reasons. First, most mass survey data collection efforts have, in recent years, been concerned with the national population. For reasons previously discussed, the national sample survey is poorly suited to the present theoretical purpose. Second, taken together these surveys provide a range of information on various political loyalties and behaviors, social group memberships, neighborhood attitudes and evaluations, ethnic backgrounds, ethnic loyalties, friendship group composition, and social class loyalties. Finally, and importantly, each survey includes the respondents' 1960 census tract numbers, thereby making it possible to combine information on each respondent's behavior together with information on the respondent's social environment. **Thus,** individual behavior can be examined specific to a particular social setting.

In some ways it would be rewarding to employ more recent surveys for this study. For several reasons, however, the 1960s time frame proves to be advantageous. First, the questions motivating this analysis are not time bound. The neighborhood social context should not be more influential in the late 1960s than it was in the late 1950s or will be in the late 1980s. Furthermore, the spring of 1968 is an especially interesting time to observe Buffalo. Riots took place in Buffalo during the summer of 1967, and these disturbances are central to the analysis of residential satisfaction and white flight undertaken in Chapter 6. The spring of 1968 was a time of important presidential primary campaigns, and that factor is taken into account in Chapter 4. Buffalo has experienced a vigorous variety of ethnic politics that was in full bloom during 1968, and Chapter 5 is devoted to ethnic politics and the social context. Finally, the version of Detroit that was in place during the middle 1960s epitomizes American industrial society, thereby creating an excellent site for analyses of class loyalties, political loyalties, and social interaction patterns that are undertaken in Chapters 3 and 8.

For both substantive and methodological reasons, only white respondents are considered in the analyses conducted here. First, blacks are deleted from Chapters 4, 7, and 9 in a methodologically conservative effort at avoiding artificial exaggerations of contextual effects. Blacks are usually Democrats and they engage in some participatory activities at different rates than whites. In many instances blacks also live in lower status neighborhoods, but the relationships between their political behavior and their neighborhoods is largely spurious—other factors are quite obviously responsible for these differences. Second, blacks are deleted from the analyses of Chapter 5 and 6 for substantive reasons: the concern in these chapters is with white flight and various white ethnic groups. Finally, the Detroit survey, which serves as the data base in Chapters 3 and 8, only includes interviews with white males. Thus, while social contexts are important to blacks as well as to whites, an analysis of the role of social contexts in shaping the political behavior of blacks awaits some other investigation.

In *summary,* Buffalo in 1968 and Detroit in 1966 provide good laboratories for this investigation; the census tract is a reasonable approximation of the neighborhood as it is defined here; and the surveys being used include a range of important data for approaching the questions at hand.

CONCLUSIONS

The central argument of this book is that neighborhood social contexts have important political consequences, not only for individual behavior, but also for the political vitality of groups in the political process. This argument has *nothing* to do with suburbanization, or with the embourgeoisement thesis as it is traditionally constructed. The embourgeoisement explanation for the disappearance of class politics argues that improved working conditions, better pay, and suburban living create a working class that is infused by middle class values and a middle class lifestyle. Especially in terms of residential location, a suburban residence produces changed values and, along with these changed values, an entirely different set of political viewpoints.

The embourgeoisement viewpoint has been attacked on a number of fronts. Goldthorpe et al. (1968), in their study of affluent British workers, found little evidence to support the argument using *individual* affluence as a criterion. They did, however, discover a change toward a political orientation that was "instrumental" rather than "solidaristic collectivism''(1968: 76). Other investigators such as Wirt et al. (1972) and Berger (1960) also showed that the move to suburbia did not necessarily result in the inculcation of middle class values, or in the rise of Republicanism, or in the diminution of class loyalty.

The present effort does not dispute these results: there is no reason to believe that individual affluence or suburban residence should necessarily diminish class loyalties or political differentiation along class lines. It *is* argued that: (1) social class politics is, first and foremost, group politics (Hamilton, 1972); **(2)** group politics cannot be explained on the basis of individual interests and predispositions alone; and thus **(3)** the social contexts of group members must be taken into account in order to explain group politics.

The important point is that group membership and group politics should not be wholly conceived as the consequence of individual characteristics and individual circumstances. *Belonging to a group involves patterns of relations that bind the individual to the group: the very words provoke an image of strong social ties.*

CHAPTER 2

ASSIMILATION AND CONFLICT
IN URBAN CONTEXTS

What is the social context, and what constitutes a contextual effect? Influences arising from the actor's social environment have been termed structural, compositional, and contextual effects. Blau **(1957)** used the term "structural effect" to describe the individual level influences resulting from the distribution of some social property within a population.

> The general principle is that if ego's X affects not only ego's *Y* but also alters *Y,* a structural effect will be observed, which means that the distribution of X in a group is related to *Y* even though the individual's X is held constant. Such a finding indicates that the network of relations in the group with respect to X influences *Y.* It isolates the effects of X on *Y* that are entirely due to or transmitted by the processes of social interaction (1957: 64).

Davis, Spaeth, and Huson **(1961: 216)** pointed out that "there is only partial overlap between these relationships and what sociologists consider to be social structure. . . ." They substitute the label "compositional effects," but the phenomenon they are addressing is the same: instances in which individual behavior is affected by the presence of a social property in a population regardless of whether the individual possesses the property in question.

The term "contextual effect" has been used to describe a variety of behavioral influences arising from sources external to the individual. Eulau **(1976)** suggested a distinction between environmental and contextual effects that establishes the second as a subset of the first. Contextual effects are environmental influences that arise through social interaction within the environment, and it is through these social interaction patterns that social contexts are created. This study adopts Eulau's distinction to consider a range of environmental properties: population composition, riot activity, housing characteristics. The terms "contextual effect" and "social context" are reserved to describe and consider the influence of population composition as it structures opportunities for social interaction.[1] This convention underscores the importance of social densities in the neighborhood environment, and it builds upon a tradition established by Durkheim, and sustained by Blau and Davis.

If Blau's formulation is used, then a contextual effect—his structural effect—is present if the distribution of a population characteristic influences the behavior of individual population members regardless of the members' own characteristics. Blau asserted that such an effect must be a function of social interaction because it cannot be attributed to individual characteristics. A central goal of this study is to identify more clearly the relationship between social composition and social interaction. Many contextual studies *assume* an underlying mechanism of social interaction that ties together population composition and political behavior. This study will attempt to *demonstate* the social interaction mechanisms, and to establish the relationship between population composition and social interaction.[2]

Davis and his associates expanded upon Blau's work and identified a variety of potential effects that rely upon three possibilities: individual-level differences, group-level differences, and interaction effects between the two (1961: 216–222). Only an individual-level difference exists if the probability of a population member exhibiting some behavior depends upon individual characteristics but does not depend upon aggregate characteristics. In an example that will be considered again, suppose that identifying as a Democrat depends upon an individual's status, but does not depend upon the status of an individual's neighbors. As the fabricated data of Figure 2.1(a) show, the probability that an individual with a given status level will identify as a Democrat does not vary as a function of neighborhood status, but does vary as a function of the individual's own status level.

Now suppose that both individual- and group-level status differences exist: the probability of being a Democrat depends upon an individual's own status and the status of the individual's neighbors. Once again, the bogus data of Figure 2.1(b) show that low status individuals are more likely to be Democrats regardless of neighborhood status composition. In this example, however, people are also more likely to be Democrats if they live in neighborhoods more densely populated by low status residents. Further, the neighborhood effect is the same for both high and low status individuals.

Finally, imagine that the two factors' effects are interactive—that each factor's effect depends upon the other. The fabricated data of Figure 2.1(c) show that low status individuals are affected, but high status individuals are not. Only low status individuals are more likely to be Democrats if they live in low status neighborhoods. As a result, individual level

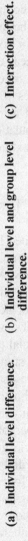

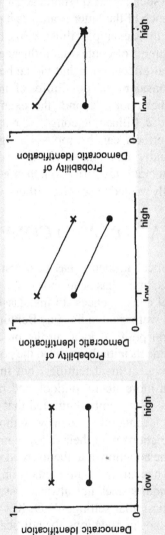

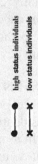

(a) Individual level difference.

(b) Individual level and group level difference.

(c) Interaction effect.

Percent of Neighborhood Residents Who Are High Status

high status individuals
low status individuals

Figure 2.1. Examples of individual level differences, group level differences, and interaction effects using fabricated data: the probability of individual Democratic identification as a function of both individual social status and the social status of neighborhood residents.

differences are present in low status neighborhoods, but they are absent in high status neighborhoods. Thus, the social context is capable of affecting politics in two different ways: (1) by influencing individual behavior, and **(2)** by altering the extent to which politics is structured by individual characteristics.

The neighborhood social context is unrelated to political behavior in the first example, but in each of the latter examples it provides a powerful explanatory factor. These three examples illustrate the basic components to contextual effects, but patterns of contextual influence can be much more complex. First, contextual effects upon individual behavior need not be linear, and Chapter 9 considers the possibility of nonlinear contextual effects upon individual behavior. Second, the examples of contextual influence shown in Figure **2.1** illustrate congenial responses to the social context, but contextual effects can be rooted in discord as well. For example, if higher status individuals react to lower status populations with a *lower* probability of Democratic identification, then a contextual effect is identified which is centrally related to social conflict.

ASSIMILATION AND CONFLICT

The social context's political influence has been established in diverse settings and circumstances, and it has been shown to produce qualitatively different types of political consequences. In his classic study, Newcomb (1957) showed that young women attending tiny Bennington College in the late 1930s acquired liberal political ideas in the process of acquiring a liberal education. Most students initially reflected the political views of their predominantly conservative, affluent families, but the social context at Bennington encouraged a more liberal outlook and many students soon converted to these views. Newcomb suggested that ''non-conservative attitudes are developed at Bennington primarily by those who are capable and desirous of cordial relations with their fellow community members" (1957: **148–149**). Thus, the adoption of a liberal creed was part of an effort at gaining acceptance and becoming assimilated within a social group.

Residential propinquity does not always foster cordial relations, however. In a radically dissimilar setting, V. O. Key also found that the social context had important implications for political behavior, but the contextual effects that he observed were far different in their consequences. Key argued that black population predominance in some southern counties heightened the political consciousness of whites.

The hard core of the political south—and the backbone of southern political unity — is made up of those counties and sections of the southern states in which Negroes constitute a substantial proportion of the populaton. In these areas a real problem of politics, broadly considered, is the maintenance of control by a white minority. (1949: 5)

Building upon the work of Key, Wright (1976a, 1977) showed that the level of support among southern rural whites for the 1968 presidential candidacy of George Wallace was higher in counties with more heavily concentrated black populations. Thus, counties with higher black densities were associated with higher levels of white support for a candidate who symbolized hostile attitudes toward blacks.

Newcomb's work demonstrated that a shared residential environment sometimes leads to political assimilation and conversion; Key and Wright demonstrated that shared residential environments sometimes lead to political conflict and competition. These two examples illustrate polar opposite contextual effects: contextual assimilation and conflict, or divergent and convergent political responses to the presence of social groups. This study is not, however, concerned with the contexts of southern counties or liberal arts colleges for affluent young women. Congenial and uncongenial responses to context must be defined and illustrated relative to urban neighborhoods.

Congenial Responses to Neighborhood Contexts

People exposed to neighborhood environments where particular characteristics predominate frequently adopt social and political sympathies that are congruent with these environments. *Assimilation, as it is defined here, refers to the adoption of political viewpoints and practices through a process of social transmission.* Assimilation is consensual, favorable response to a social context that can be empirically identified as an instance in which the individual probability of engaging in a behavior sympathetic toward a group, or predominant within a group, *increases* as a function of that group's concentration, or density, within the population.

Most explorations of the social context's political consequences have been concerned with assimilation, and many efforts have related neighborhood-level social contexts to the assimilation process. For example, Segal and Wildstrom (1970) found that residents of Wayne County, Michigan (Detroit) living in higher status locales were more likely to be Republicans, independent of individual status. Cox (1974) showed that the partisan composition of the local area (the precinct) had a positive effect upon the partisan identifications of Columbus, Ohio residents. Foladare (1968) demonstrated that a higher density of working class residents in Buffalo neighborhoods had a positive effect upon the individual probability of voting for Kennedy in the 1960 presidential election. Prysby (1975) found that a higher concentration of working class residents in Santiago, Chile voting districts had a positive effect upon the individual probability of voting for Allende in the 1958 Chilean presidential election. Similar findings have been presented using data from Great Britain (Butler and Stokes, 1974), Stockholm (Tingsten, 1963), Los Angeles (Weatherford, 1980), and other locations as well.

These studies share an important commonality: they show that individuals surrounded by particular viewpoints and social groups often demonstrate political preferences that are congruent with these groups and viewpoints. However, this sort of convergence need not always be the case.

Dissonant Reactions to Neighborhood Contexts

Politics, social interaction, and the social context are not simply matters of assimilation; they are also centrally related to conflict. Everyone is not assimilated into every neighborhood in the same way or at the same rate, and some people are not assimilated at all. People exposed to neighborhood environments where particular characteristics predominate sometimes display social and political behaviors that reflect discordant reactions to these environments. *The dejinition of conflict used here points to the adoption of political viewpoints and practices as the result of adverse social reactions and encounters.* Conflict, in this sense, is a dissonant reaction to context that can be identified empirically as an instance in which the individual probability of engaging in a behavior sympathetic toward a group, or predominant within a group, *decreases* as a function of that group's density in the population.

Not surprisingly, the most commonly observed instance of con-textually based conflict in American urban neighborhoods involves shared living space by blacks and whites. Orbell and Sherrill (1969) found evidence in Columbus, Ohio that some white survey respondents' racial and residential attitudes were influenced by the residential proximity of blacks. Whites living in low income neighborhoods were more likely to be racially intolerant if a higher proportion of blacks lived in their neighborhoods, and racially hostile whites were more likely to consider moving if blacks lived nearby. Wilson (1971) explored relationships between racial mixtures and feelings of anomie in three northeastern United States neighborhoods. He found that anomie among blacks increased in integrated neighborhoods. This reaction by blacks to a racially mixed environment points toward an underlying pattern of discord between racial groups that is contextually based.

Contextually based neighborhood conflict is not provoked solely by racial factors, however. Other factors, such as social class, also result in

exclusion or hostility between groups. Berger (1960) examined the migration of one hundred working class families that moved from an old industrial community to a new suburban environment in order to maintain their
jobs at a transplanted automobile factory. The new suburb was dominated
by working class families and individuals who found opportunities for
personal interaction that nurtured and sustained a sense of class consciousness. "In appraising the amount of turnover in the tract many [of the
workers] were quick to point out 'It isn't any of the Ford workers who **are**
moving' or 'The ones who moved out were the snobs'" (1960: 25). Thus,
according to the report of working class residents, higher status individuals
found the working class environment distasteful, and the workers were
happy to see them leave.

In his study of a new middle class suburban development, Gans
(1967: 49) found similar social processes. The newly arrived population
was rapidly stratified into several social groupings; area minorities—working class individuals, Jews, older people, upper middle class individuals—
were the first to be sorted into their own social subsystems. Gans further
argued that behavioral changes associated with the move could be traced to
the "population **mix**."

> The homogeneity of that mix was the major source of social life and benefits
> to morale that followed; its heterogeneity was largely responsible for **the**
> social isolation and resulting emotional costs. (1967: 283)

A final and important point must be made before proceeding.
Democratic or Republican party affiliations, opinions favoring a particular
political candidate, racially hostile attitudes, political participation, and
feeling of anomie do not in themselves constitute either contextual assimilation or contextual conflict. The pattern and direction of variation in these
behaviors across context *do* constitute evidence of assimilation or conflict.
Stated in a different manner, it is not the incidence or extent of a behavior
that serves as evidence of contextual assimilation or conflict, but rather the
direction of change in the behavior as a function of context.

MECHANISMS OF
CONTEXTUAL INFLUENCE

These divergent responses to context—assimilation and conflict—require an
elaboration of the mechanisms that are responsible for translating the social
context into a source of political influence. A first likely candidate is the
effect of context upon the content of informal social relations. The political
persuasiveness of primary groups and interpersonal contacts is nothing new

to political scientists, but the work of Putnam and others has demonstrated that the individual's configuration of personal contacts is subject to variation as a direct function of population composition. Putnam (1966) showed that the political composition of primary groups is a function of the county level political context: people living in counties with more Democrats are more likely to associate with Democrats. The survey respondents he considered did not entirely pick their friends at random with respect to political characteristics, but neither did they choose friends who were mirror images of their own political viewpoints. As a result, primary groups served as vehicles for community influence, and individuals were often assimilated by the predominant groups within social contexts. Similarly, in his study of Jewish voting in the 1952 presidential election, Fuchs (1955) argued that Jews living in predominantly Jewish environments were more likely to interact with other Jews and, as a result, were also more likely to vote Democratic.

The explanation for contextual influence offered by Langton and Rapoport (1975) in their study of Santiago working class support for Allende suggests an alternative mechanism through which the social context is translated into political influence. While not contradicting the importance of primary groups or interpersonal interaction, the authors suggested a flow of political influence that emphasizes different social factors. The environment, they asserted, is influential in shaping social loyalties, which in turn influence political perceptions, thereby affecting political behavior. This reference group explanation rests upon the social context, but it constitutes a significant variation from explanations relying upon primary groups and intimate social interaction. The reference group argument suggests, at least implicitly, that the social context and primary group interaction can be influential even if their content is seemingly apolitical—even if no one ever discusses politics. The social context affects political loyalties and behavior by affecting the social loyalties upon which these political actions and preferences are based. Further, the effect of the social context upon social and political loyalties might be realized in ways other than primary group interaction. Casual and impersonal interactions within a context might also be influential if they affect social loyalties, identities, and comparisons.[3]

Consider the individual whose involvements in politics are limited to voting in the presidential election every four years, and weakly identifying with a political party. This less than model citizen seldom reads beyond the sports page, and almost never discusses politics with acquaintances. If contextual influence operates solely through interpersonal interactions, and the transmission of political guidance through these interactions, then such an apolitical individual might be free from such influence, typifying the classic "massman" of scholarly literature (Komhauser, 1959).

The reference group explanation suggests that the potential for contextual influence extends beyond political discussions with friends. When apolitical men and women shop at the local supermarket, stand in line at the local post office, sit in line at the local gas station, mow their lawns, walk in their neighborhoods, and engage in other everyday activities, they are also experiencing a form of casual social interaction with politically important consequences. People who frequently encounter workers, for example, develop ideas regarding the working class, and structure their own social loyalties, identities, and perspectives accordingly.

These contextually influenced social attitudes are important to political behavior, even among antisocial, apolitical individuals. Parties and candidates are often chosen or supported because they are identified, however loosely, with workers, or small businessmen, or the middle class, or some other social grouping. Thus, the neighborhood social context might be important even for individuals who never discuss politics with close friends, and even for social isolates who *have* no friends.

Building upon these observations, a framework can be developed for analyzing the way in which people are assimilated by the social groups within their neighborhoods. This framework, which is summarized in Figure 2.2, rests upon several assumptions. First, the social context of a neighborhood is important because people's social contacts are influenced by residential proximity. These social interactions include both impersonal and interpersonal encounters. Casual interactions inevitably occur among a neighborhood's population, and residential propinquity supports the formation and maintenance of friendship groups as well. Thus, the social and

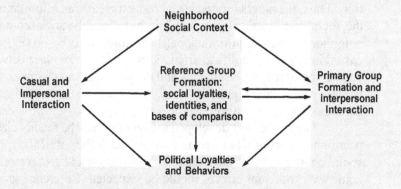

Figure 2.2. A framework for considering contextual effects.

political composition of primary groups tends to reflect the composition of the area in which an individual lives. An alternative way to view these relationships is that the social context structures casual encounters, which in turn provide opportunities for friendship formation and more personal relationships. (This particular formulation is used in the mathematical treatment of social contexts and social networks that is presented in Chapter 3.)

Second, both types of interaction have important consequences for social identities, loyalties, and comparisons. People surrounded by members of a group are more likely to view themselves in terms of that group, and this formation of a reference group has important implications for political behavior. People often base political responses upon perceptions of social groups, and the relationship of the groups to politics. In this way the social composition of a neighborhood influences political behavior by altering the social basis of reference within which the behavior is rooted.

Notice also that the relationship between reference group formation and primary group formation is reciprocal. Close associates and friends affect basic social loyalties, but basic social loyalties also play a role in determining friendship choice. Any social context provides a set of opportunities and constraints operating upon patterns of personal interaction, but individuals are not passive bystanders, and the social context does not produce a deterministic outcome. Individuals exercise discretion in their choices of associates—discretion that is rooted in fundamental social loyalties and identities. The important point is that individual discretion is circumscribed by context: the social context establishes an agenda for individual choice.

Finally, the social context of an urban neighborhood influences political loyalties and behavior in a more direct manner as well. A great deal of political information and guidance is transmitted through social interaction. Thus, the neighborhood social context creates an informational bias if the social composition of primary groups reflects the social composition of neighborhoods. An informational bias might also be produced through casual interactions: political discussions need not take place between close friends in order to be influential, and the yard signs and bumper stickers on neighborhood lawns and cars may turn even casual acquaintances into sources of political advice.

The framework developed in Figure 2.2 can be readily elaborated to accommodate conflict as well as assimilation. If the political response to the social context is contingent upon social loyalties and group memberships, complex contextual effects should be expected. Reference groups serve two functions: establishing and transmitting norms, and serving as a basis for social comparison (Kelley, 1952). In the first instance they are most likely to serve as agents of assimilation by incorporating individuals within social groups. In the second instance they are capable of producing hostility, intimidation, or exclusion. For example, a long-time resident of an area undergoing population transition may compare his own status to the lower status of the new arrivals, find them deficient, and form judgments accordingly. A new arrival may aspire to the higher status of residents already living in the neighborhood, and adopt social and political opinions that are perceived as being dominant among them. (Alternatively, Berger's class conscious workers *resented* the status comparison between themselves and their uppity middle class neighbors.) In short, people who fail to adopt a sympathetic attitude toward a particular group may respond in a conflictive manner to the increased presence of that group in a population.

The social interaction explanation for contextual influence asserts that the content of primary groups, as well as the configuration of other encounters and associations, is shaped by spatially defined environments. Intimate social interaction certainly cannot account for the full range of contextual effects, however. Some effects due to population composition are obviously *not* the result of social interaction at an intimate level. When the presence of blacks provokes racial hostilities among whites, it is not because whites and blacks associate at an interpersonal level and develop antagonisms. Social interaction that stimulates hostility, exclusion, or intimidation is certainly at an *impersonal* level and represents a significantly different process. It might well be argued that such hostility occurs because intimate contacts do *not* occur. Indeed, Finifter (1974) showed that the *formation* of primary groups *can* be rooted in an unsympathetic response to a social context. She considered the associational patterns of Detroit autoworkers in the context of the factory, and found that minority Republicans rejected association with Democrats who were in the vast majority. In this instance the primary group served as a retreat from the larger environment, and the social composition of the primary group was inversely related to the social composition of the larger environment.

An important implication of this framework is that the political influence of the social context is involuntary and inescapable. Even if people choose *all* their friends from outside the neighborhood, or, alternatively, *never* discuss politics with friends, they are destined to experience some form of social interaction at a casual and impersonal level.

The conceptual framework presented in Figure 2.2 is not offered as a fully specified model of contextual influence. Rather it is aimed at providing a theoretical vocabulary for the chapters that follow. At the moment this conceptual framework is only a set of general expectations largely unsupported by empirical evidence. The framework is subject **both** to elaboration and *to* empirical scrutiny, however, and it will prove to be a useful tool for considering the contextual dependency of political behavior and group politics in the remainder of this book.[4]

CHAPTER 3

CONTEXTUAL CONSTRAINTS ON FRIENDSHIP CHOICE

Selecting a friend is among the most personal of human choices, and thus it is not surprising that friendship groups tend toward social class homogeneity. Members of the working class usually associate with other workers, and middle class individuals generally choose friends who are middle class. But are these friendship choices wholly dependent upon the characteristics and preferences of the individual making the choice, or are they also constrained by the availability of socially similar individuals within the environment?

Studies of contextual assimilation establish a basic empirical relationship between individual behavior and the social context: individual behavior tends to move in the direction of a surrounding population's social makeup, even when individual characteristics are taken into account. For example, middle class people are more likely to support parties of the left if they reside in contexts that are heavily working class in their aggregate composition. Two assumptions are generally incorporated within the explanations for these relationships: (1) people are influenced through social interaction, and (2) social interaction patterns are structured by the social composition of the relevant environment. The remainder of this chapter ignores the first assumption in order to examine the second. To what extent is intimate social interaction, defined as friendship choice, structured by the social context?

SPATIAL BOUNDARIES AND SOCIAL CONTEXTS

Contextual research efforts typically use spatially bounded population data to obtain a measure of the social context. This means that the social context is made operational as a county, a voting precinct, a census tract, a workplace, or some other population aggregate. The imposition of these boundaries presents problems related to the relevance of the boundaries for associational patterns, and to the exercise of individual discretion over the choice of associates within a particular set of boundaries.

First, the boundaries used to circumscribe a social context are frequently criticized as being either too large to capture rich internal variation in social worlds, or too small to be treated as self-contained environments with the potential for structuring social interaction. Thus, a person's social context is often seen as being individually unique, because it is created from the particular set of environments within which that person resides. Next door neighbors live in the same neighborhood context, but they are employed by different enterprises, worship at different churches, and drink at different taverns. Each of these environments creates its own unique social context, and these neighbors may therefore encounter very different population mixes. As a result, they have vastly different opportunities for friendship formation, regardless of a shared neighborhood environment.

A second objection to assertions of contextually structured patterns of association points to the individual capacity for choosing associates. Even when people share the *same* set of contexts — neighborhoods, taverns, churches, laundromats — their personal preferences are still enforced upon their environment. They are able to choose associates who are socially attractive and personally agreeable and to avoid individuals who are either socially or personally obnoxious. For example, Berger (1960) showed that middle class residents of a newly established working class suburb were resented by working class residents, isolated from community life, and less likely to increase their levels of social interaction in the new environment. Finifter (1974) showed that Republican autoworkers who were employed in a workplace social context that was heavily Democratic chose to associate with other workers who were also Republicans. They enforced their preferences upon the context by constructing friendship groups that served as "protective environments."

A strict emphasis upon individual control over associational patterns and social network content produces its own set of problems, however. The militant contextualist may be in danger of ignoring the effect of individual preference upon associational patterns and friendship choice, but the focus upon personal control may ignore important external constraints upon supply. The available pool of socially similar individuals varies as a function of context, so that *the same set of preferences might produce different friendship groups in different environments.*

This chapter is concerned with one environment, the neighborhood, and the resulting task is thus twofold. First, I consider the relevance of the neighborhood as a social context that imposes constraints upon friendship choice, and second, I examine the interplay between individual choice and contextual constraint in the friendship selection process. Since little information is available regarding the qualitative nature of the search for compatible associates, the process is conceived abstractly, as the logical outcome of individual preferences that are constrained by context. Before proceeding with this analysis, however, two preliminary descriptive issues are addressed: the homogeneity and location of friendship groups.

Geographical Source and Homogeneity of Friendship Groups

This section examines the homogeneity of friendship groups by comparing the occupational class memberships of Detroit respondents to the occupational classes of their three closest friends. The geographical proximity of respondents and friends is also examined to determine whether the neighborhood environment is relevant to the composition of social networks. If the respondents do not have friends who live nearby, then the neighborhood social context is clearly meaningless to the content of friendship groups.

Each respondent to the survey was asked to name his three closest friends. Any relative included on the list was replaced by a nonrelative. The resulting three choices serve to make the concepts of friendship group and social network operational.[1] Our concern is only with the content of social networks, not with their form. As a result the analysis ignores issues of connectedness — the extent to which respondents' friends are associated with each other.

The homogeneity of friendship groups is well established in social science research, and the friendship groups of the Detroit respondents bear out that homogeneity. Table 3.1 shows that the working class respondents and both groups of middle class respondents (professional-managerial and clerical-service-sales) are socially integrated; tnat is, their friendships are more heavily concentrated within their own occupational group.[2] A member of one group is more likely than a nonmember to associate with other members. Thus, for example, clerical-service-sales respondents are more likely to have clerical-service-sales friends than are either working class or professional-managerial respondents.

Due in part to limited numbers of respondents, the middle class categories are combined later in the analysis. This practice, combining middle class categories, raises a question: Does the concept of a single middle class have any meaning, given the extent of the social fracture between the two groups of middle class respondents? The clerical-service-sales respondents occupy an intermediate position between the working class and professional-managerial respondents, not only in terms of individual status, but also in terms of friendship patterns. They are more likely

Table 3.1. Occupational Homogeneity of Friendship Groups among White Men

		Respondent's Occupational Status			
		Professional-Managerial	Clerical-Service-Sales	Working Class	All
Number of	3	5.1%	9.2%	40.0%	23.1%
working class	2	9.2	18.3	30.8	21.3
friends	1	28.7	31.7	20.0	24.8
	0	57.0	40.8	9.2	30.8
Number of	3	1.0	2.8	.4	1.0
clerical-	2	11.8	25.4	4.3	10.2
service-sales	1	24.5	40.8	23.6	26.7
friends	0	62.7	31.0	71.7	62.1
Number of	3	32.2	9.2	2.7	13.9
professional-	2	33.8	19.0	13.5	21.4
managerial	1	22.6	38.7	29.9	28.6
friends	0	11.5	33.1	53.9	36.0
	$N =$	3 14	142	445	905

Data Source: 1966 Detroit *Area* **Study.**

than the working class respondents to have professional-managerial friends and are more likely than the professional-managerial respondents to have working class friends. They are also the least socially introverted of the three occupational groups. However, their social ties to the professional-managerial group are clearly stronger. Professional-managerial respondents are more likely to have clerical-service-sales friends than are the working class respondents. And clerical-service-sales respondents are equally likely to have working class or professional-managerial friends, *even though the working class is more numerous in the population.*[3] Finally, approximately two-thirds of the clerical-service-sales respondents identify themselves as middle class (see note **2**). Thus, while it is necessary to take account of internal diversity, it is also meaningful to think of a single middle class.

A second characteristic of friendship groups, their geographical location, is displayed in Table **3.2(A)**. Respondents were asked whether each of their friends lived (1) in their own neighborhood, defined as a ten minute trip; (2) beyond their neighborhood but within the Detroit area; or (3) beyond the Detroit **area.**[4] The number of friends living inside the

Table 3.2. Geographical Location of Friendship Groups among White Men

A. Number of Neighborhood Friends by Respondent's Occupational Status

Number of Friends in Neighborhood	Respondent's Occupational Status		
	Professional- Managerial	Clerical- Service-Sales	Working Class
3	15.2%	18.7%	19.1%
2	23.7	18.0	21.7
1	30.7	32.0	31.5
0	30.4	31.3	27.6
$N =$	329	150	460

B. Percent of Respondents with a Majority of Neighborhood Friends by Neighborhood Proportion Working Class and by Respondent's Occupational Class[a]

Respondent's Status	Neighborhood Working Class Proportion[b]			
	Low	Medium Low	Medium High	High
Professional- managerial	40.0% (120)	36.4% (77)	33.3% (57)	44.7% (38)
Clerical- service-sales	36.8 (38)	40.0 (45)	40.0 (25)	36.0 (25)
Working class	48.2 (56)	37.1 (97)	40.3 (129)	41.7 (151)

[a] N sizes are shown in parentheses.
[b] Cutting points are chosen on the basis of quartile divisions for the sample: low = .058–.448; medium low = .448–.558; medium high = .558–.638; high = .638–.823.
Data Source: 1966 Detroit Area Study.

respondent's neighborhood is shown for each of the three occupational categories. Between **36** and **41** percent of all three groups have a majority of friends living in their neighborhoods, and less than a third of each group do not have any friends in the neighborhood. The working class respondents are only slightly more prone to have locally rooted friendship groups.

Thus, Table **3.2(A)** qualifies an analysis **of** urban neighborhoods that characterizes them as a place for neighborly relations, but not as a place for forming friendships. The neighboring role may not necessitate close interpersonal association (Keller, **1968:** 10–11), but it is a mistake to ignore the close physical proximity of neighborhood residents **as** a factor in the formation of friendship groups. This evidence also calls into question a distinction between locally oriented city dwellers, who are socially anchored in the local area, and more cosmopolitan city dwellers, who are oriented toward the city in a way that erases social ties to the neighborhood. An assumption frequently underlying these categories is that lower classes tend to be more local in their orientations (Keller, 1968: 116–123), but the evidence in Table 3.2(A) does not support such an assertion.

Finally, people might be expected to have more local friends in an area where their own social group is more heavily represented. In a previous discussion, it was noted that individual freedom in the choice of associates allows individuals to look beyond the neighborhood if they do not find neighborhood residents to be socially compatible. Table 3.2(B) does not support this expectation, however. No clear pattern is revealed in the number of local friends across context for any single occupational class.[5]

In summary, several empirical relationships have been demonstrated. First, in keeping with a substantial body of empirical research, friendship groups tend toward social class homogeneity. Second, regardless of individual social class, friendship groups are often rooted in the local area. These empirical relationships are suggestive, but reveal little regarding the process of associational choice, or the interplay between individual preference and environmental constraint in affecting that process. In order to consider these issues a mathematical representation of the friendship selection process is developed and applied to the Detroit respondents.

A MODEL OF FRIENDSHIP SELECTION

Any process occurs through time, and thus a process can best be understood in dynamic terms even when observation occurs at a single point in time. Such a procedure is employed here: Even though the social composition of a respondent's friendship group is observed as part of a static cross section, the friendship selection process is conceived as a search for compatible associates that occurs through time as one individual encounters other individuals in the environment. An analytical distinction is thereby drawn between (1) encounters and (2) friendships or associations. A basic assumption of the model is that the environment controls the likelihood of encounters within and between social classes, but that individuals exercise discretion in deciding whether to turn an encounter into an association. In other words, a middle class individual can hardly avoid encountering his working class neighbor when they are both mowing their lawns, but the middle class individual can decide whether or not to invite this neighbor to dinner, and the working class individual can decide whether or not to accept.

People use numerous criteria when they consider the possibility of turning an encounter into a friendship, but this analysis gives deliberate attention only to one: the social class of individuals involved in the encounter. Thus, the process being specified is necessarily an abstraction that ignores many important facets of friendship selection—shared interests, compatible personalities, similar political views, and so on. In ignoring these other criteria for associational discretion, it is assumed that (1) a member of a given social class will not reject association with another member of the same social class on the basis of a social class criterion, but that *(2)* a member of a given social class might reject a member of a different social class based upon a social class criterion. As with any simplifying assumption, exceptions abound. For example, a working class social climber might indeed reject association with other workers on the basis of a social class criterion, but ignoring these sorts of exceptions does not fundamentally compromise the analysis.

The model of friendship choice is presented graphically in Figure 3.1.[6] The concepts of environmental constraint and individual choice are incorporated within the model as S_j and r_{ij}, respectively. The parameter r_{ij} is the probability that a member of group i will reject association with a working class individual in context j, having encountered one at an opportunity for friendly association. Conversely, $1-r_{ij}$ is the probability that a member of group i will form a friendship with a working class individual in context j, having encountered one at an opportunity for friendly association. S_j is the proportion of context j that is composed of people who belong to group i, or the probability of encountering a member of group i at an opportunity for friendly association. Conversely, $1-S_j$ is the proportion of context j that is composed of people who do not belong to group i, or the probability of encountering a nonmember of group i at an opportunity for friendly association.

For illustrative purposes assume that (1) group i denotes the middle class, *(2)* the friendship search is being carried out by a member of the middle class, and (3) the entire population belongs to either the middle class or the working class. According to the abstraction of Figure 3.1, a middle class individual either encounters a middle class individual with probability S_j or a working class individual with probability $1-S_j$. If a middle class encounter occurs, a friendship is formed and the search ends. If a working class encounter occurs a decision must be made to either accept friendship (with probability $1-r_{ij}$) or to reject friendship (with probability r_{ij}). If friendship is accepted the search ends. If it is rejected the person continues the search, and the process is repeated.

Thus, as long as the middle class individual fails to encounter another middle class individual at an opportunity for association, and as long as this individual continues to reject association with the working class, the friendship search continues. The process ends either when (1) **a** middle class individual is encountered, or when **(2)** a working class individual is encountered and ***accepted*** as a friend. Thus, higher values for r_{ij} and smaller values for S_j tend to produce a longer search; smaller values for r_{ij} and larger values for S_j produce a shorter search.

A number of assumptions are crucial to the model, and therefore warrant restatement. First, a difference is assumed between encounters and associations. Encounters occur randomly and they take place on a daily

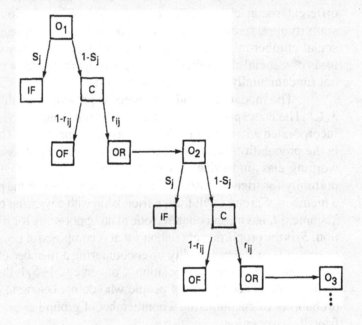

Figure 3.1. A model of friendship choice, incorporating environmental constraint and individual choice. The symbols are defined **as follows:**

O_t = opportunity for forming a friendship that occurs at time t
S_j = probability of encountering a member of own class at opportunity for forming a friendship, in context j
$1\text{-}S_j$ = probability of encountering a member of opposite class at opportunity for forming a friendship, in context j
IF = formation of friendship with another class member
C = individual discretion in deciding whether to associate with member of opposite class
OF = formation of friendship with member of opposite class
OR   = rejection of friendship with member of opposite class
r_{ij} = probability of rejecting friendship opportunity with member of opposite class, in context j by member of group or class i

basis in many different social situations: taking walks in a neighborhood, talking across backyard fences, and so on. Friendships do not occur randomly; they are subject to random encounters, but they are also subject to the preferences of those involved in the associations.

Second, the model specifies that a member of a given social class will use a social class criterion to reject association with another member of the same class, given an encounter, with a probability of zero. Third, the outgroup rejection probability is specific both to particular groups and to particular contexts. Thus, the rejection probability might **vary** across groups in a particular context, and across contexts for a particular group. Finally, the social density of a particular group within a particular context is assumed to be constant across associational opportunities.

The model shown in Figure 3.1 depicts a social process in time, where time is measured according to the metric of social encounters. At any point in time — after any given number of encounters — algebraic expressions are available to express either the probability of forming a friendship with another member of the middle class, or the probability of forming a friendship with a member of the working class. As time passes, the person has numerous opportunities for social encounters, and the algebraic expressions converge toward the following simple forms:

$$F_{ij} = \frac{S_j}{1 - {}_{ij}(1 - S_j)} \tag{3.1}$$

$$G_{ij} = \frac{(1 - S_j)(1 - r_{ij})}{1 - r_{ij}(1 - S_j)} \tag{3.2}$$

where F_{ij} is the probability that a member of group i in context j will form a friendship with another member of group i, and where G_{ij} is the probability that a member of group i in context j will form a friendship with a person who is not a member of group i.

It can be shown that the sum of the right-hand sides of equations 3.1 and **3.2** is unity. Thus, G_{ij} can be expressed as $1 - F_{ij}$, and attention will henceforth be restricted to equation **3.1**. Over the long haul this model suggests that individuals form friendships, even if they are part of an extreme minority that strenuously resists association with the majority. The third possibility entertained in Figure 3.1, continuation of the search and abstention from friendship, is self-extinguishing. Men and women are, according to this model, inevitably social.

Equation 3.1 **is** a causal statement based upon time ordered logic. It portrays the dynamic interplay, at equilibrium,[7] between individual discretion and contextual constraint in affecting the process of friendship choice. The discretion parameter, r_{ij}, deserves more careful scrutiny. If r_{ij} equals zero, then F_{ij} equals S_j. That is, if a group member does not resist association with nonmembers, then the probability of associating with a nonmember is equal to the probability of encountering a nonmember. Conversely, when r_{ij} equals one, F_{ij} equals one. This is the pure case of contextual isolation: a group member who rejects all nonmembers as associates will exclusively associate with members, regardless of the social context.

Clearly, r_{ij} is a theoretically abstract concept that cannot be directly observed. It sets forth one dimension of the class or group consciousness held by a particular collectivity. By not incorporating a rejection term for the members of one's own group, the model ignores the problems posed by individuals whose associational preferences lie beyond the boundaries of their own group. This is, however, a *conservative* assumption: if the model is altered so that individuals reject members of their own class with some probability, then the outgroup rejection parameter must necessarily *increase* in size to produce the same ingroup association probability (F_{ij}) at the same contextual density (S_j).[8]

Applying the Model to Detroit Respondents

The model of associational choice, as expressed in equation 3.1, can be usefully applied to a consideration of the Detroit respondents, but the mathematical language of the model must first be translated into measurable, operational terms. First, the value for F_{ij} is best interpreted as the probability that a single friend will be a member of the respondent's occupational class. Furthermore, in the ensuing analysis a distinction is drawn between local and nonlocal friends. A locally rooted network might extend beyond the neighborhood *so* that the local population composition could have consequences for the social class of nonlocal friends, but the neighborhood effect would be mediated by the point of origin—the local friend. Thus, in applying the model attention is restricted to respondents who have at least one local friend, and consideration is given to the probability that the first mentioned local friend is a member of the respondent's social class. (In Chapter 8 more general consideration is given to the social class composition of the friendship group as a whole.)

As a second step, "ingroup" and "outgroup" densities must be defined relative to each of the occupational classes. In order to make the modeling task manageable, neighborhood social densities are separated into the working class proportion and its complement.[9] This complement comes very close to being an exact measure of the middle class proportion, and it is treated as such. The ingroup density (S_j) for working class respondents consists of the neighborhood working class proportion, and the outgroup density $(1-S_j)$ consists of the neighborhood middle class proportion. Conversely, the ingroup density (S_j) for professional-managerial and clerical-service-sales respondents consists of the neighborhood middle class proportion, and the outgroup density $(1-S_j)$ consists of the neighborhood working class proportion. Thus, r_{ij} is the probability that working class individuals reject middle class individuals as associates, or the probability that middle class individuals reject working class individuals, depending upon the definition for S_j and $1-S_j$, and the particular occupational class of respondents being considered.

Equation 3.1 can be algebraically rearranged to express r_{ij} solely as a function of F_{ij} and S_j:

$$r_{ij} = \frac{F_{ij} - S_j}{F_{ij}(1-S_j)} \tag{3.3}$$

Thus, given a sequence of coupled values for F_{ij} and S_j, a matched sequence of values for r_{ij} can be produced, and the first task is to estimate F_{ij} as a function of S_j. Whether a friend belongs to the same social class as the respondent is a qualitative condition, and its analysis requires specially designed techniques. One appropriate strategy is the logit for microdata that is more fully explained in Appendix D (also see Hanushek and Jackson, 1977: Chap. 7). The coefficients produced by the logit model are useful to the task of estimating the contextually contingent probability that a local friend belongs to the respondent's social class (F_{ij}), but they do not estimate the probability as a linear function. Rather, they provide a linear estimate of the "logit" — a nonlinear transformation of the probability. As a result, the *magnitude* of a coefficient cannot be directly assessed. In order to determine the magnitude of an effect due to an explanatory variable, predicted probabilities are calculated across the range of that variable with all other explanatory variables held constant.

Table 3.3 shows the logit coefficients that are obtained when having a local friend who belongs to the respondent's own class is estimated as a function of context for each social class. To compensate for the combination of the two middle class categories, two additional variables are included in the middle class equation: a dummy variable for clerical-service-sales status, and an interaction variable formed by the product of this dummy variable and neighborhood social composition. These two variables allow for both individual level differences and contextual responsiveness differences between the two middle class categories. Additionally,

Table 3.3. Logistic Estimations of Having a Local Friend Who Belongs to Same Social Class as a Function of Individual Income and Education, Self-Perceived Social Class Identification, and Neighborhood Working Class Density, for Each Occupational Group[a]

$$P = 1/(1+e^{-f})$$

$$f = a_1 + a_2E + a_3I + a_4ID + a_5CSS + a_6INT + a_7S$$

		Respondent's *Social Class*	
		Middle Class[b]	Working Class
Constant	a_1	−2.88	− .40
		(3.48)	(.41)
E	a_2	.18	− .19
		(1.84)	(1.75)
I	a_3	.07	− .06
		(.51)	(.46)
ID	a_4	.58	− .24
		(1.77)	(.87)
CSS	a_5	.81	
		(.70)	
INT	a_6	− 1.36	
		(.58)	
S	a_7	4.74	3.59
		(3.52)	(3.20)
	$N =$	285	313

P = 1 if first mentioned local friend belongs to respondent's social class; 0 otherwise

E = respondent's education: 1 = 0–8 grades; 2 = some high school; 3 = high school graduate or nongraduate with vocational training; 4 = high school graduate with vocational training; 5 = some college; 6 = college graduate; 7 = college graduate with graduate training

I = respondent's income: 1 = under \$3,000; 2 = \$3,000–\$4,999; 3 = \$5,000–\$6,999 4 = \$7,000–\$9,999; 5 = \$10,000–\$14,999 6 = \$15,000–\$19,999 7 = \$20,000–\$24,999; 8 = \$25,000 and over

ID = 1 if respondent identifies as upper or middle **class**; 0 if respondent identifies as working class

CSS = 1 **if** respondent is clerical-service-sales; 0 otherwise

INT = the product **of** ingroup density and clerical-service-sales dummy variable: (CSS)(S)

S = proportion of employed neighborhood men who belong to the same social class as the respondent

[a] The t-ratio is shown in parentheses.
[b] The middle class category combines clerical-service-sales and professional-managerial respondents.
Data Source: 1966 Detroit Area Study.

controls are included for individual income and education, and for the respondent's self-perceived class identification. These additional controls are included because (1) the choice of friends is influenced by individual status considerations other than occupational class, and (2) the composition of each class is likely to vary across context in a manner that might compromise the results.[11]

The logit coefficients of Table 3.3 are used to estimate F_{ij}, the contextually contingent probability that respondents from each social class will have a friend who is from the same social class, while holding all other individual status measures constant. In order to draw a direct comparison between the two social classes, Figure 3.2(a) shows the probabilities that a local friend is *working* class, across neighborhood contexts for respondents from each social class. For both social classes, the probability that a local friend is working class increases significantly as a function of increased working class densities, even though pronounced individual level differences in the probability exist *between* the occupational classes.

The outgroup rejection parameter is shown specific to particular working class contexts for each occupational class in Figure 3.2(b). Combining the two parts of Figure 3.2 produces a startling picture. In spite of the high rates of change in the probabilities of having a working class friend, there are also some very high levels of resistance to association across class boundaries. The predicted probability that a working class respondent has a working class friend increases significantly across the observed range of working class densities, from .24 in a 6 percent working class neighborhood to .83 in an 82 percent working class neighborhood. The outgroup parameter *decreases* across that same range, from .80 at the lowest working class density to .07 at the highest working class density. A greater supply of working class residents also produces an increase in the probability of working class association for middle class respondents, from .04 at the lowest working class density to .62 at the highest. For these middle class respondents, however, the outgroup rejection parameter *increases* overall, from .35 at the lowest working class density to .64 at the highest. Thus, for both working class and middle class respondents, the tendency to reject friendships across class lines is generally higher when (1) the social density of the opposite class is higher, and (2) the probability of friendship with a member of the opposite class is also higher! Regardless of strong associational preferences, the formation of friendships is circumscribed by the opportunities and constraints of context. Individual preference is overwhelmed by factors related to supply.

Figure 3.2(b) can be usefully compared to Table 3.2(B): while minority status within a neighborhood does not necessarily force individuals to look elsewhere for friends, it is a mistake to ignore the forceful

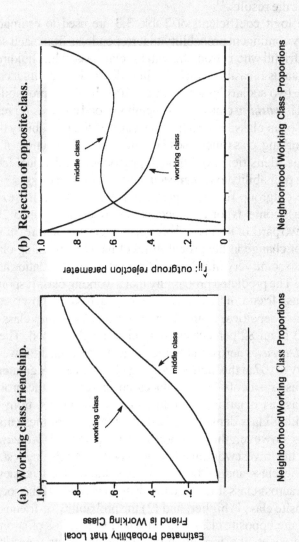

Figure 3.2. Probabilities of working class friendship and rejection of opposite class across working class contexts. Individual income and education are controlled at the sample means—4.6 and 3.5, respectively; subjective social class identification is controlled at the objectively defined membership. *Source:* The logit model of Table 3.3.

expression of social class preference in the formation of friendship groups. The clear implication is that people in a minority must look more diligently *within* the context for socially similar associates, and their search is often unsuccessful. Further, the process specified in Figure 3.1 takes more time to reach equilibrium because the search for associates must be extended. This analysis has assumed that respondents' friendship groups are at equilibrium, but in this sense the minority is more likely to be at disequilibrium: socially unstable and divorced from any strong social ties within the context. At the very least, this sort of social equilibrium will take longer to achieve for members of the minority.

Finally, Figure 3.2(b) also shows that resistance to the outgroup varies as a function of context. As an occupational class approaches minority status, the probability generally increases that members will reject association with nonmembers. Equation 3.1 shows that when S_j equals one, r_{ij} is mathematically undefined: in substantive terms, there is no one available to reject. Between these extreme values, any value for r_{ij} that lies between zero and one is *mathematically* possible. For example, an outgroup rejection parameter of .01 is possible at an ingroup density of .01, but it would produce an ingroup friendship probability (F_{ij}) of only .0101. These results, and the logic of the model, suggest that people resist this sort of social domination by increasing their level of resistance toward outgroup friendships. Conversely, an outgroup rejection parameter of .99 would be possible at an ingroup density of .99, producing an ingroup friendship probability of .9999. But if r_{ij} is reduced to .1, the ingroup rejection probability would *still* equal .9901. The logic of the model suggests that the additional investment in a higher level of resistance (r_{ij}) is simply not worth the effort, and these results indicate that people tend to relax their resistance toward the outgroup when their own group is ascendant. Thus, to the extent that the model adequately portrays the search for friends, groups naturally turn inward when they occupy a more pronounced minority status. As a result, F_{ij} considerably exceeds S_j at low ingroup densities, but the two values are more nearly equal at high ingroup densities.[12]

Empirical documentation of this inward search for associates on the part of minority status social groups is presented in a number of case studies. In her study of friendship groups in an automobile factory, Finifter (1974) demonstrated a turn inward on the part of minority status Republican autoworkers, but associational openness on the part of majority status Democratic autoworkers. Berger's (1960) study of a working class suburb documents the turn inward and residential relocation of upper class residents. And Gans (1967) showed a turn inward on the part of people who did not "fit in" at middle class, suburban Levittown: Jews, older people, the working class. The qualitative nature of this inward turn differs across groups and environments, but the underlying logic is the same.

CONCLUSIONS

Evidence presented here shows that the social class content of friendship groups is influenced by associational opportunities and constraints imposed by the neighborhood social context. A person residing in a social context where a particular class is more dominant is more likely to have a friend from that class, regardless of his or her own class membership. The interplay between associational preference and the social context in producing a social network is probably more important than the relationship between contexts and networks, Even though individuals demonstrate strong associational preferences, the contextually structured set of associational opportunities makes itself felt in the composition of friendship groups. Thus, the social content of social networks is not solely a function of either the social context or individual choice; *it is the complex product of individual preference operating within the boundaries of a social context.*

This chapter has constructed a demanding test for the efficacy of social contexts in structuring social interaction. The analysis has only considered the role that neighborhood contexts play in altering the construction of intimate friendship groups, but the social context is likely to affect other interactions as well. In particular, the content of social encounters (as opposed to associations or friendships) is likely to be much more responsive to the social composition of an environment. By showing that the context structures the formation of friendship groups this analysis does not encapsulate contextual influence, but it does show that even intimate social interactions are structured by associational opportunities and constraints that are contextually imposed.

How do the results of this chapter apply to the earlier discussions of social groups and urban neighborhoods? Do social groups thrive and become more cohesive in urban settings, or does urbanism disintegrate the social bonds that tie these groups together? At least when social groups are defined in terms of class, group members tend to seek out fellow group members as associates. To the extent that urban areas make this search easier by bringing together sufficient members of the same group and segregating them within a common social space, urbanism fosters the development of strong group ties and a cohesive group membership. To the extent that urban areas make this search more difficult by encouraging the diffusion of group members across an urban area, urbanism fosters a breakdown of group boundaries. In short, the basis for residential segregation within an urban area determines the effect of urbanism upon the boundaries, cohesiveness, and vitality of particular groups.

This chapter has shown that the neighborhood is much more than a social container: it is an important social force for individual behavior and group relations. Not only does the locally defined social context circumscribe the opportunities for social interaction by acting as a constraint upon associational choice, but it also affects relations between and within groups. The minority-majority status of a particular group within a local population has important consequences for the tendency of group members to turn inward in their search for friends, and for the likelihood that members will resist association outside the group.

The social and political significance of urban neighborhoods is frequently discounted because neighborhoods are measured against an excessive standard of intimacy and social cohesiveness. The neighborhood is seldom a cohesive unit, but that does not negate its importance as part of a residential sorting process that takes place in urban areas. This sorting process is built upon a set of informal rules that restricts movement within the city and has important consequences for urban social life (Suttles, 1972: 31–32). This process takes on special significance because a neighborhood's residents often and inescapably come into contact. In Suttles' words, "the most obvious reason for centering in on locality groups is that their members cannot simply ignore one another" (1972: 7). The only alternative to neighborly contact is extreme isolation—an alternative with its own social and political consequences (Sprague and Westefield, 1977). This sorting process is, of course, perpetually incomplete. The extent to which most social groups are residentially segregated varies radically across an urban setting, and thus becomes important for understanding group boundaries, social relations, and political behavior.

CHAPTER 4

INDIVIDUAL AND CONTEXTUAL BASES
OF PARTISAN **ATTACHMENT**

Discussions of American politics often link particular social groups to particular political loyalties. Members of some groups, such as blacks, ethnics, blue collar workers, and the poor, are likely to be Democrats. Members of other groups, such as the middle class, white Protestants, and the affluent, are likely to be Republicans. While linkages between social groups and political loyalties are frequently asserted, the substance of these linkages is just as frequently shrouded in ambiguity. For example, if group members adopt political preferences on the basis of their own individual calculations regarding self-interest, then the group is merely a collection of individuals with coincidental interests. Alternatively, if the political preferences of group members are either produced or supported by a social dynamic, then the group becomes important as a vehicle for the transmission of political reinforcement or persuasion, *apart* from individual calculations regarding self-interest.

This chapter takes a first step toward establishing the social context as a connecting tie between individual group members and the political loyalties of the group. Two questions are addressed: First, how **does** the political influence of individually defined group membership compare to the political influence of living among group members? Second, how and why do contextual effects on partisan behavior vary as a function of (1) the behavior being affected and (2) the individual being affected? The discussion initially focuses upon the manner in which continuing social experiences form and re-form political orientations, before the political loyalties of Buffalo survey respondents are considered within the contexts of their urban neighborhoods.

THE SOCIAL BASIS OF POLITICAL LOYALTY

Most considerations of mass politics stress the stable, enduring nature of political ties. The authors of the *American Voter* asserted that the develop-

42

ment of party identification is "characterized more by stability than by change" (1960: 146). Assertions such as these usually point to the deeply ingrained social basis for these loyalties. The family and other early and intimate social experiences are given responsibility for the transmission of basic political orientations (Dawson, Prewitt, and Dawson, 1977:49).

This focus upon the stable, deep-seated social basis of fundamental political loyalties sometimes ignores the fact that these orientations must be sustained **as** well **as** being transmitted. In a classic study using a sample stratified to include a large proportion of respondents who had forsaken the political party of their parents, McClosky and Dahlgren (1959) showed that later primary group influences beside the parental family have important consequences for political loyalties. In particular, marriage partners and peer groups affect both the stability and direction of individual **party** preference. Thus, political loyalties owe their birth *and* their sustenance to social stimuli. People who experience an alteration in their circle **of** closest associates may receive a dramatically different mix of political cues and information. This may lead, in **turn**, to alterations in political allegiances.

Langton (1969:20) outlined a process which he called "resocialization" in which an individual learns new patterns and modes of behavior. This resocializing is most likely to occur when individuals are thrust into new social settings. The social context of a new workplace or a new neighborhood has important implications for the individual if cues emanating from the context are significantly different from those previously received. If political socialization is a continuing process, then an investigation **of** the social contexts that undergird partisan attachments is an important undertaking.

POLITICAL LOYALTIES
IN BUFFALO NEIGHBORHOODS

Residents of New York State have a variety of parties to choose from: Democratic, Republican, Conservative, Liberal, and others. Residents of the Buffalo area, however, are especially apt to choose the Democrats. The Democratic party has been powerful in city politics, winning elections and controlling city government on a regular basis. In comparison, much smaller proportions of Buffalo area residents **are** Republicans, Independents, or identifiers with any other party. Given this political environment, it makes **good** sense to speak **of** Democrats and everyone else. Therefore, the dependent variable for this analysis is identification **as** a Democrat versus nonidentification **as** a Democrat, and the task is to relate this political loyalty (or lack **of** loyalty) to both individual and contextual social status.

Individual and contextual effects upon the Democratic loyalties of the survey respondents are directly compared in Figure 4.1. Each part of the figure considers a different social status indicator that is often linked to Democratic identification; Democrats are more likely to be lower income, less educated, blue collar workers. This figure differs from many considerations because it gives attention to social status at two different levels: individual and contextual.

The figure gives a clear picture of important contextual differences in party loyalties that are independent of individually defined status.

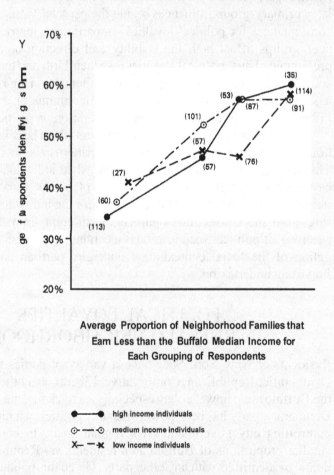

Average Proportion of Neighborhood Families that
Earn Less than the Buffalo Median Income for
Each Grouping of Respondents

●——● high income individuals
⊙——⊙ medium income individuals
✗——✗ low income individuals

Figure 4.1(a). The percentage of white respondents identifying as Democrats by individual family income and the proportion of neighborhood families earning less than the Buffalo median income. Cutting points on the horizontal axis for the proportion of neighborhood families earning less than the median are chosen as quartile divisions for the entire white sample. The *N* sizes for each grouping of respondents are shown in parenthesis. *Data source:* 1968 Buffalo survey.

For seven out of nine individually defined social groupings, lower status neighborhoods are rather consistently related to higher levels of Democratic identification, independently of individual status.

In contrast, individual-level status characteristics have an impact upon party identification that is less consistent and less pronounced, and varies across the different status attributes. Figure 4.1(a), which considers individual and neighborhood income, shows only minor differences among individual income categories within any contextual category. Similarly, Figure 4.1(b) shows **only** minor differences among individuals with low

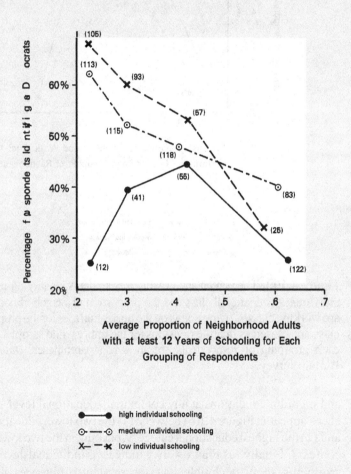

Figure 4.1(b). The percentage of white respondents identifying as Democrats by individual education and the proportion of neighborhood adult residents (25 years and over) with high school educations. Cutting points on the horizontal axis for the proportion with 12 years of schooling are chosen as quartile divisions for the entire white sample. The N sizes for each grouping of respondents are shown in parentheses. Data source: 1968 Buffalo survey.

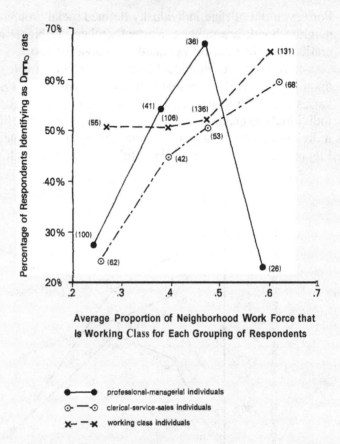

Figure 4.1(c). The percentage of white respondents identifying as Democrats by individual occupational class and the proportion of neighborhood residents who are working class. Cutting points on the horizontal axis for the proportion working class are chosen as quartile divisions for the entire white sample. The N sizes for each grouping of respondents are shown in parentheses. *Data source:* 1968 Buffalo survey.

and medium educations at any contextual educational level. Larger differences appear in Figure 4.1(b) between (1) the two lower educational categories and (2) the highest educational category, but only in the two lowest educational contexts. Finally, as Figure 4.1(c) indicates, individual-level occupational groupings show negligible and inconsistent differences in Democratic identification at intermediate working class densities, but these differences become sizable at extreme levels of working class concentration — in neighborhoods with either very low or very high working class densities.

Figure 4.1 indicates several things. First, individual status attributes fall far short of adequately accounting for differences in Democratic identification—the social context is also important. Second, the figure demonstrates important interaction effects between individual and contextual social status; some individual-level differences vary as a function of context, and the effect of context sometimes varies across individual status categories.[1] These interaction effects will be given further attention later in this chapter and in Chapter 9, but a more careful consideration of contextual and individual effects is warranted before they are pursued.

Comparing Individual and Contextual Differences

What is the best predictor of partisan loyalty: an individual's characteristics or the characteristics of others in the individual's social context? Stated somewhat differently, is the social context or individual status more influential in shaping political allegiances? Figure **4.1** provides a useful contrast between the two sets of factors, but a more direct and summary comparison can be obtained using the logit model for microdata.

Table 4.1 displays the logit coefficients that are obtained when the effects of individual and contextual social status are compared for each of the three Figure 4.1 status attributes: occupation, education, income. A quick inspection of the table indicates that (1) the signs of the coefficients for the three contextual measures all lie in the expected direction, and **(2)** the t-values for the same coefficients are large in magnitude. Indeed, each logit coefficient is more than four times the size of its respective standard error. (The t-value equals the coefficient divided by its standard error.)[2]

The coefficients for the individual status measures present a more ambiguous picture. Part A of Table 4.1 shows that individual income produces a small t-value, a result that is entirely consistent with the negligible individual differences appearing in Figure 4.1(a). In contrast, the coefficient obtained for individual education in Table **4.2** produces a strong t-value and lies in the expected direction, as does the coefficient for individual working class status shown in Table 4.1(C). The coefficient for individual clerical-service-sales status does not attain a strong t-value, however. Thus, the only individual-level attributes worthy of further consideration here are educational attainment and working class versus nonworking class occupational standing.

To compare the effects of individual and contextual education, I divide the sample into two equally sized groupings based upon neighborhood educational levels and then calculate group probabilities of Democratic identification based upon (1) the mean neighborhood educational level within each group and (2) the individual-level educational mean for the entire sample. These two probabilities, which vary as a function of neighborhood status, can be compared to similarly derived probabilities,

Table 4.1. Logistic Estimations of Democratic Identification as a Function of Individual and Contextual Social Status

$$D = 1/(1+e^{-f})$$

A. Democratic identification as a function of individual and neighborhood income: $f = a_1 + a_2 IN + a_3 I$

		Coefficient	t-ratio	
Constant	(a_1)	1.28	3.59	
IN	(a_2)	2.60	4.72	N = 871
I	(a_3)	− .005	.27	

B. Democratic identification as a function of individual and neighborhood education: $f = a_1 + a_2 EN + a_3 E$

		Coefficient	t-ratio	
Constant	(a_1)	2.04	7.44	
EN	(a_2)	−2.22	4.44	N = 939
E	(a_3)	− .11	4.50	

C. Democratic identification as a function of individual and neighborhood occupation: $f = a_1 + a_2 WN + a_3 CSS + a_4 W$

		Coeficient	t-ratio	
Constant	(a_1)	−1.19	5.15	
WN	(a_2)	2.14	4.26	N = 856
CSS[a]	(a_3)	.04	.20	
W[a]	(a_4)	.44	2.42	

D	= 1 if respondent identifies as a Democrat; 0 otherwise
IN	=proportion of neighborhood families who are low income, earning less than the Buffalo median
I	=respondent's family income in thousand dollar intervals (the three highest intervals are $15,000–$19,999, $20,000–$24,999, $25,000 and above)
EN	=proportion of neighborhood adults (25 years and over) with 12 years of schooling or more
E	=respondent's schooling in years (the highest category, 17, is college postgraduate)
WN	=proportion of neighborhood residents who are working class
CSS	= 1 if respondent is clerical-service-sales; 0 otherwise
W	= 1 if respondent is working class; 0 otherwise

[a] The uncoded third category which serves as a baseline is professional-managerial.
Data Source: 1968 Buffalo Survey.

Table 4.2. The Predicted Probabilities of Democratic Identification as a Function of Neighborhood Education, Controlling for Individual Education, and as a Function of Individual Education, Controlling for Neighborhood Education

	Democratic Identification as a Function of Neighborhood Education		*Democratic Identification as a Function of Individual Education*	
	Low Education Neighborhoods	High Education Neighborhoods	Low Educated Individuals	High Educated Individuals
Mean years of individual schooling	11.0[a]	11.0[a]	8.4[b]	13.3[b]
Mean proportion of neighborhood residents with high school educations	.266[b]	.513[b]	.387[a]	.387[a]
Probability of Democratic identification	.56	.42	.56	.43
Difference	.14		.13	

[a] This figure represents a mean for the entire sample.

[b] This figure represents a mean for half the entire sample, divided on the basis of the respective educational characteristic.

Source: Table 4.1 logit model.

which vary as a function of individual status. This time the sample is divided into approximately equal groups based upon *individual* education, and predicted probabilities of Democratic identification are calculated on the basis of (1) the mean level of individual education with each group and (2) the neighborhood educational mean for the whole sample.

This procedure is employed in Table 4.2, which shows almost identical effects for individual and contextual education. The difference in the probability as a function of the neighborhood context at the mean of individual education is .14. The difference in the probability as a function of individual educational status at the mean of neighborhood education is .13.

A closely related method is used to compare the political influence of individual and contextual occupational status in Table 4.3. In this instance, the individual-level groupings are defined for us, but the sample is almost equally divided between working class and non-working class respondents. Still, because it is inappropriate to calculate a mean of work-

Table 4.3. The Predicted Probabilities of Democratic Identification as a Function of Neighborhood Working Class Concentrations, Controlling for Individual Working Class Status, and as a Function of Individual Working Class Status, Controlling for Neighborhood Working Class Concentrations

	Low Working Class Neighborhoods: .314[a]	High Working Class Neighborhoods: .542[a]	Difference Due to Neighborhood
Working class individuals	.48	.60	.12
Nonworking class individuals	.37	.49	.12
Difference due to individual status	.11	.11	

[a] This figure represents a mean working class concentration in the neighborhood for half the sample, divided on the basis of working class concentrations in the neighborhood.
Source: Table 4.1 logit model.

ing class and nonworking class, four "difference measures" must be calculated instead of two. Once again, the effects of individual and contextual status are almost identical. Both of the predicted individual probability differences are .11, and both of the predicted contextual probability differences are .13.

This exercise shows that the social status of other neighborhood residents is at least **as** politically influential in predicting political loyalties as the social status of the individual. None of the social status attributes are more important at the individual level, and one attribute, income, makes no appreciable difference at the individual level when it is controlled at the contextual level. Why is income less important, controlling for the neighborhood social context, than the other individual-level attributes?

Quite simply, individually defined education and occupation are much more than characteristics of individuals; they are also indicators of a wide range of social experience. In other words, education and occupation are related to a variety of social contexts beside the neighborhood context. A person's occupation and education determine workplace associates, associates for recreational pursuits, perhaps even associates in marital relationships. In addition to being important individual-level determinants of political preferences, these two variables are directly related to a multiplicity of social experiences. Rather than downplaying the neighborhood context and its importance, these results point to other important contexts and social experiences: friendship groups, daily interaction patterns, workplace contexts. Education and occupation are more influential in the shaping of political loyalties when the neighborhood is controlled because they point to experiences beyond the neighborhood in a way that income probably does not. This is important because income would be expected to be most directly related to political behavior if an individualistic, self-interest conception of human motivation provided an accurate and complete portrayal of politics and political preferences.

Multiple Individual Characteristics

One criticism of contextual research centers on inadequate considerations of alternative explanations based upon individual-level characteristics (Hauser, 1974). Carried to its logical extreme this argument suggests that controlling *each* individual-level characteristic would eliminate any observed contextual differences. In other words, contextual differences are due to the type of people living in a context, not due to any direct effect of the social context operating independently of individual characteristics. For example, workers who live in higher status contexts might be more likely to support the Republican party because they are more highly educated and have higher incomes than workers living in lower status contexts.

This possibility is examined in Table 4.4, which uses the logistic model to estimate the probability of Democratic identification as a function of neighborhood education as well as individual income, occupation, and education. Only two variables have coefficients with adequate t-values: individual and neighborhood education. More important, the introduction of the individual-level controls does not compromise the influence of the neighborhood social context.

If individual income and education are controlled at their sample means (7.7 and **11.0**, respectively), Table 4.4 predicts a .56 probability of Democratic identification for professional-managerial respondents living in low status neighborhoods (with a mean high school educated proportion of .266), and a .40 probability for professional-managerial respondents living in high status neighborhoods (with a mean high school educated proportion of .513), for a difference of. **16.** This contextual effect is comparable to the contextual effect shown in Table 4.2, and it is as important as the individual-level effect of education predicted by Table 4.4. If individual income and neighborhood educational composition are controlled at the sample means, Table 4.4 suggests a .57 probability of Democratic identification for low educated professional-managerial respondents, and a .4 1 probability of Democratic identification for high educated professional-managerial respondents, for a difference of .16. (The mean number of school years completed for low educated respondents is 8.4, and the mean for high educated respondents is **13.3**.)

These results show that the observed contextual effect cannot be

Table 4.4. A Logistic Estimation of Democratic Identification as a Function of Individual Education, Individual Income, Individual Occupational Class, and the Proportion of Neighborhood Residents Who Are High School Educated

$$D = 1/(1+e^{-f})$$

$$f = a_1 + a_2 EN + a_3 E + a_4 I + a_5 CSS + a_6 W$$

		Coefficient	t-ratio	
Constant	(a_1)	2.11	4.77	
EN	(a_2)	−2.53	4.43	
E	(a_3)	− .13	4.05	N = 783
I	(a_4)	.03	1.55	
CSS	(a_5)	− .19	.80	
W	(a_6)	.12	.58	

Data Source: 1968 Buffalo Survey

explained by resorting to individual-level status attributes. Introducing individual income and occupational considerations does not compromise the contextual effect either in terms of its absolute magnitude, or in relationship to the effect of individual schooling.

VARIATIONS IN CONTEXTUAL INFLUENCE

Thus far attention has focused upon the magnitude of neighborhood effects in relationship to individual effects. At this point concern shifts to the second research question posed in the chapter introduction: how and why do contextual effects vary as a function of (1) the behavior being affected and (2) the individual being affected? The framework developed in Chapter 2 for considering the influence of the neighborhood social context (see Figure 2.2) emphasizes the importance of social interactions within the neighborhood. If the political influence of the neighborhood is realized through social interaction, then political behaviors and opinions that are more sensitive to influence through social encounters should be more affected by the social context than those that are not. While some work has been done on the varying intensities of relationships between the social context and various political behaviors, the explanations offered have not been based on social interaction arguments.

Foladare (1968) surveyed Buffalo residents four days prior to the 1960 election and found a stronger neighborhood contextual effect on voting intentions than on party identification. Based upon this finding, he argued that the effect of the social environment is more important for

Table 4.5. Ordinary Least Squares Estimates of the Individual Status Effects and Neighborhood Contextual Effects upon White Respondents' Opinions toward Hubert Humphrey and Richard Nixon[a]

$$C = a_1 + a_2EN + a_3E + a_4I + a_5W + a_6CSS$$

		Humphrey	Nixon
Constant	(a_1)	4.40 (19.68)	3.11 (12.41)
EN	(a_2)	− .537 (1.84)	−.002 (.00)
E	(a_3)	− .06 (3.54)	− .002 (.10)
I	(a_4)	.005 (.41)	.02 (1.70)
W	(a_5)	. 12 (1.08)	.09 (.75)
CSS	(a_6)	.06 (.48)	.02 (.14)
N =		756	750

[a] C = opinion toward candidate: (1) oppose very much; (2) oppose somewhat; (3) neither favor nor oppose; (4) favor somewhat; (5) favor very much. T-values are shown in parentheses. Data *Source:* 1968 Buffalo Survey.

"immediate decisions" than for the "more remote party identification." Similarly, Prysby (1975) found that residents of Santiago were more likely to prefer Allende in the 1958 Chilean election if they lived in working class areas of the city, regardless of individual occupational status. Because the respondents' social class self-identifications did not covary with residential social composition when objectively defined class membership was controlled, and because partisan identification was less strongly related to neighborhood social composition than candidate preference, Prysby concluded that "... the contextual effect under study operates primarily, though not exclusively, by influencing more superficial political orientations" (p. 238). Both studies point toward the deep-seated nature of the political behavior: superficial opinions are more likely to be affected than deeply embedded elements of the political psyche.

Opinions toward political figures and personalities are certainly more transitory and peripheral than party identification. If the works of Prysby and Foladare are correct, even more pronounced contextual effects upon these opinions should appear among the Buffalo respondents. Table 4.5 uses an ordinary least squares model to estimate the effects of individual education and neighborhood educational composition upon the opinions of respondents toward two political candidates: Hubert Humphrey and Richard Nixon. At the time of the survey, both men were candidates for the **1968** presidential nominations of their respective parties.[3]

The pattern of relationships exhibited among the respondents is exactly opposite the explanatory logic of Foladare and Prysby. While the neighborhood has a clear and statistically crisp effect upon the respondents' party loyalties, its effect is less clear for their candidate opinions. The neighborhood effect is completely absent for the opinion regarding Nixon, and it is relatively weak for the opinion regarding Humphrey. (The t-value for the coefficient estimating the neighborhood effect on the Humphrey opinion is only of moderate size.)

An even more rigorous test for the direct effect of the neighborhood upon these opinions includes an individual-level control for party identification. Figure **2.2** suggests that the neighborhood social context should have both a direct and an indirect effect upon the opinions. The direct effect operates through socially transmitted information, and the indirect effect operates through social and political loyalties that are contextually influenced. Thus, a rigorous comparison of contextual effects upon opinions and contextual effects upon loyalties should separate out the indirect effect of context upon opinions that occurs through loyalties.

Table 4.6 displays the regression coefficient and t-values that are obtained when the indirect effect of the social context via party identification is controlled. These results show even weaker neighborhood effects. The sign for one of the neighborhood coefficients lies in an unexpected direction: lower status neighborhoods are associated with higher levels of support for Richard Nixon; and the t-values for both neighborhood coefficients fail to achieve respectable magnitudes.

These findings—strong contextual effects on partisan identification and, at most, very weak contextual effects on candidate opinions—are clarified by a social interaction argument. The opinions of the Buffalo respondents toward political candidates are less affected by context than by individual factors because the social context had not, in the late spring of 1968, fully mobilized in support of any candidate, and political attention and discussion had not reached the fever pitch of the final campaign phase. In short, biased information cannot be socially transmitted unless the relevant topic becomes an object of concern during social interaction.

The findings of Foladare and Prysby are subject to reinterpretation

Table 4.6. Ordinary Least Squares Estimates of the Individual Status Effects, Party Identification Effects, and Neighborhood Contextual Effects upon White Respondents' Opinions toward Hubert Humphrey and Richard Nixon[a]

$$C = a_1 + a_2 EN + a_3 E + a_4 I + a_5 W + a_6 CSS + a_7 D$$

		Humphrey	Nixon
Constant	(a_1)	3.89	3.95
		(16.79)	(15.81)
EN	(a_2)	− .22	− .52
		(.77)	(1.68)
E	(a_3)	− .04	− .02
		(2.71)	(1.44)
I	(a_4)	.001	.03
		(.11)	(2.27)
W	(a_5)	.11	.11
		(1.03)	(.97)
CSS	(a_6)	.08	− .03
		(.73)	(.27)
D	(a_7)	.51	− .86
		(6.37)	(10.05)
N =		756	750

[a] T-values are shown in parentheses. *Data Source:* 1968 Buffalo Survey.

using the same social interaction argument. Indeed, Foladare's results can be readily explained. Since an individual's presidential vote is a highly salient topic four days before the election, it is frequently discussed and susceptible to the effects of biased information received through social interaction.

Prysby's finding regarding the resistance **of** subjective social identification to contextual influence cannot be readily explained with a social interaction argument, but research on the contextual basis of social class loyalties has generally produced mixed results (see Fitton, **1974;** Langton and Rapoport, **1976;** Jackman and Jackman, **1983;** and Chapter **8** of this monograph). A social interaction model *can* be used to explain Prysby's other findings: candidate choice is more affected by the social context than either party identification or two policy opinions regarding land reform and worker participation in management. Again, candidate preference during the latter stages of an election campaign is highly salient and frequently discussed and thus is especially susceptible to contextual influence. While party identification is a more deep-seated behavior, it frequently becomes obvious during many political discussions and social encounters, and contextual effects on party loyalties are likely to be cumulative over the long term. Although opinions on specific policy issues are not deep-seated, they are probably least discussed and considered during most social encounters. As a result, these opinions are less affected by the social context.

The conclusion is somewhat ironic: many superficial political opinions are *least* likely to be influenced by the social context. For example, housing policy is directly related to class and party, but it is unlikely to be a frequently discussed topic among most people. Thus, social influence is unlikely to have much effect upon these sorts of opinions.[4] The social context might have an indirect effect upon these opinions by way of contextually structured political and social loyalties, but this assumes that individuals efficiently translate such loyalties into policy opinions without the benefit of informal guidance and political discussion. That assumption is at variance with much of what is known regarding the formation of political opinions (Berelson, Lazarsfeld, and McPhee, 1954), and thus *many policy opinions remain individually idiosyncratic.*

In a politically inert environment, the social context is more important for the shaping of political loyalties than for the shaping of political opinions. This pattern of relationships suggests that the social context is influential for reasons besides the bias it introduces into socially transmitted political information. The social context is also influential through a more generalized milieu effect upon political and social loyalties, and this effect is likely to operate through impersonal as well as interpersonal processes of interaction. Thus, contextual effects upon basic political orientations may be long-term, diffuse, and cumulative; while contextual effects upon opinions may be specific, short-term, transitory, and dependent upon the salience of the particular opinion.

Election Campaigns and Contextual Influence

More direct longitudinal evidence has been presented by Huckfeldt and Sprague (1983) to support the campaign-related effects of the social context. The Center for Political Studies at the University of Michigan interviews a national sample of the eligible electorate both before and after presidential elections. Using these data for the 1976 election, each respondent's vote preference is ascertained before the election, and the reported vote of each respondent is determined after the election. By merging these survey data with contextual data at the level of counties and neighborhoods (census tracts), contextual effects on vote preference can be compared at two points in time: early in the campaign and later in the campaign at the time of the final vote decision. The analysis shows that pre-election vote preference is not structured by either the political composition of the county or the social composition of the neighborhood. In contrast, the respondents' post-election *reported* votes are structured *both* by the county environment *and* by the social context. In the spirit of Segal and Meyer (1974), this analysis allows for **an** interdependence between neighborhood and county, showing that respondents who live in higher status neighborhoods are relatively insulated from the county environment, but respondents in lower status neighborhoods show preferences that are highly responsive to the county environment. Conversely, in strongly Democratic counties, the effect of neighborhood status is strong and lies in the expected direction: higher status contexts discourage support for Carter. In strongly Republican counties the effect of the neighborhood context is much less pronounced and even lies in the opposite direction: higher status contexts slightly encourage support for Carter.

    For present purposes the important point is as follows: contextual effects upon voting preferences reflect a social influence process that is activated by the political stimulus of **an** election campaign. During the early stages of the campaign, before the social influence process is fully mobilized, contextual effects are not present because social influence is not realized. By the end of the campaign, however, voters have been brought into line with the social groups that surround them, and strong contextual effects consequently appear. Thus, even superficially held opinions will be unaffected by the social context if they are not subject to social influence. This reinforces the importance of a long-term and short-term component to contextual influence. The long-term effects of context are more generalized and related to the entire milieu—personal as well **as** impersonal social encounters and experiences. The short-term effects are highly dynamic and subject to the stimulus of campaigns and political events, and thus they are more difficult to assess in the cross section.

Variation in Influence across Individuals

The influence of the social context not only varies as a function of the behavior being affected, but also **as** a function of individual characteristics.

Table 4.7. Classification Scheme for Discussants and Nondiscussants[a]

Keep Informed about Politics	Engage in a Political Discussion			
	Not at all	Seldom	Fairly often	Regular
Not at all	0	1	1	1
Seldom	0	1	1	1
Fairly often	0	0	1	1
Regular	0	0	0	1

[a] Discussants = 1: nondiscussants = 0.

Using the terminology of Chapter 2, individual attributes interact with the social context so that the effect of factors at one level depends upon factors at the other level.

People might be differentially susceptible to contextual influence depending upon the means they use to obtain and process political information. If the social context affects opinions regarding candidates through the social transmission of political information and viewpoints, then people who are more reliant upon these informal communications should be more affected by the social context. More specifically, people who discuss politics should be more susceptible to contextual influence than either (1) people who do not discuss politics, or *(2)*people who are more reliant upon information received through formal sources—the media. Reliance upon alternative types of information is measured using the responses to two survey questions: the extent to which people report that they "engage in a political discussion," and the extent to which they "keep informed about politics." (Possible response categories are: not at all, seldom, fairly often, and regularly.) The first question serves to measure dependence upon informal, social communication, and the second serves to measure dependence upon formal, media communication.

Using the replies to these questions, a variable is constructed that separates respondents into two groups:

1. The *nondiscussants:* people who either never discuss politics, or people who keep informed more than they discuss.
2. The *discussants:* people who *both* discuss politics seldom, fairly often, or regularly, *and* who discuss as much or more than they keep informed.

Thus, the discussants are separated on the basis of two criteria. First, they report discussing politics. Second, they discuss with at least much frequency as they keep informed about politics. By including both criteria an attempt is made to separate out the opinion leaders who discuss politics, but whose discussion is aimed at influencing others rather than obtaining information. (See Table 4.7.)

Table 4.8 is a re-creation of Table 4.6 with one important alteration. The effect of the neighborhood social context is measured separately for the two previously described groups. As this table shows, the neighborhood's effect is stronger in the expected direction upon the opinion toward Humphrey among the "discussants," and the t-value for the neighborhood effect among the discussants is of respectable magnitude. The neighborhood effect upon the Humphrey opinion among nondiscussants lies in an unexpected direction, and its t-value fails to achieve respectable size. In contrast, both neighborhood effects upon the opinion toward Nixon are in an unexpected direction and the t-values fail to achieve satisfactory magnitudes for either discussants or nondiscussants. Thus, at least in relationship to the opinion regarding Humphrey, these expectations are fulfilled: discussants are more susceptible to the influence of the social context?

Why does the pattern fail to persist as strongly for the opinion regarding Richard Nixon? The Buffalo area is predominantly Democratic, and the spring of 1968 was primary season. Republican candidates were less salient to a Democratic population, and were undoubtedly discussed less, even among active discussants in higher status contexts.

Finally, conducting the same analyses for two other candidates, Nelson Rockefeller and Robert Kennedy, produces mixed results. As expected, the opinion toward the Republican, Rockefeller, does not vary as a function of the social context for either discussants or nondiscussants, but neither does the opinion toward the Democrat, Kennedy. This latter result becomes more understandable in light of the overall level of support for Kennedy during this period. As Table 4.9 shows, support for Kennedy surpasses considerably the levels of support for the other three candidates. (Part of this popularity was probably due to the fact that his assassination occurred during the period that interviews were being conducted.) Very little negative discussion is likely to have occurred regarding Kennedy in *any* context.

The observed effects are, overall, less impressive than the effect of the social context upon party identification. Why? At this early stage in a presidential campaign, before the Democratic candidate has been chosen, political discussants receive mixed cues regarding the abilities and merits of candidates. That ambiguity decreases once a candidate has been chosen. Not only do the cues become straightforward and clear, but also the contextually reinforced party loyalty is now activated in support of a single Democratic candidate.[6] In short, these are the early stages of a political mobilization process that is rooted in the social context. As the campaign progresses, so does the mobilization process.[7]

Table 4.8. Ordinary Least Squares Estimates of the Individual Status Effects, Party Identification Effects, and Neighborhood Contextual Effects upon White Respondents' Opinions toward Hubert Humphrey and Richard Nixon, with the Contextual Effect Measured Conditionally as a Function of Individual Reliance upon Political Discussion as a Source of Information.[a]

$$C = a_1 + a_2 EN1 + a_3 EN2 + a_4 E + a_5 I + a_6 W + a_7 CSS + a_8 D + a_9 DIS$$

		Humphrey	*Nixon*
Constant	(a_1)	3.71	3.98
		(15.09)	(14.84)
EN1	(a_2)	*.42*	*− .57*
		(1.13)	*(1.42)*
E N 2	(a_3)	− .94	− .47
		(2.44)	(1.13)
E	(a_4)	− .04	− .02
		(2.31)	(1.10)
I	(a_5)	.002	.03
		(.24)	(2.40)
W	(a_6)	.08	.10
		(.79)	(.83)
CSS	(a_7)	.03	− .05
		(.29)	(.37)
D	(a_8)	.52	− .86
		(6.52)	(9.99)
DIS	(a_9)	.25	− .22
		(1.22)	(.99)
N =		749	745

EN1 = proportion of neighborhood adults (*25* years and over) with *12* years of schooling or more for respondents who are nondiscussants; 0 for all others

EN2 = proportion of neighborhood adults (25 years and over) with **12** years of schooling or more for respondents who are discussants; 0 for all others

DIS = 1 if respondent is **a** discussant; 0 if respondent is a nondiscussant

[a] T-values are shown in parentheses. **Data Source:** *1968* Buffalo Survey.

Table 4.9. Percentage of White Respondents Holding Various Opinions toward Hubert Humphrey, Richard Nixon, Nelson Rockefeller, and Robert Kennedy

Opinion	Humphrey	Nixon	Rockefeller	Kennedy
Oppose very much	5.7%	9.5%	19.4%	4.9%
Oppose somewhat	9.2	14.9	18.6	8.8
Neither favor nor oppose	24.1	27.9	22.4	17.2
Favor somewhat	36.6	31.0	27.0	26.5
Favor very much	24.3	16.7	12.6	41.6
N =	929	927	934	918

Data Source: **1968** Buffalo Survey.

Self-Selection and Variations in Contextual Influence

This and the following chapter present contextual arguments that are rooted in assimilation, and assimilation is especially vulnerable to counterarguments asserting self-selection. Self-selection is the Achilles heel of contextual research, but it is also part of a common problem in establishing causal direction that plagues any cross-sectional research design. The problem goes beyond the competing explanation based upon multiple individual attributes that was discussed earlier in this chapter. Two individuals with the same demographic characteristics may have different social ambitions that encourage them to live in different neighborhoods and adopt different political identities. According to this scenario, social ambition produces both behaviors; living in a particular neighborhood covaries with the adoption of a political identity but does not cause it.

The cross-sectional results of this chapter offer no direct empirical evidence with which to refute the self-selection argument, (It would, however, be difficult to develop a self-selection explanation that could account persuasively for the results of Huckfeldt and Sprague, **1983).** Inferential evidence *does* exist to support the existence of contextual influence. This chapter shows that contextual effects vary systematically across individuals and behaviors, and explanations are offered to account for these patterns of variation. If self-selection accounted for the relationships between neighborhoods and political loyalties, these systematic differences in contextual influence should not appear. There would be no reason to expect that candidate opinions should be affected less than party identification, or that the candidate opinions of political discussants should be more affected than the candidate opinions of nondiscussants. Indeed, if the self-selection argument is accurate, roughly uniform effects should appear across behaviors and individuals.

Thus, self-selection is not plausible to the extent that an explanation for contextual influence accurately accounts for variations in contextual effects. The self-selection argument is less than satisfying for additional reasons, which are considered in the chapters that follow.

CONCLUSIONS

This chapter has presented several findings. First, the social context **is** at least as important as individual characteristics in predicting partisan identification. Second, the effect of the social context is more pronounced for party identification than it is for opinions toward candidates during the early stages of an election campaign. However, the opinions of people who rely upon discussion as a source of information about politics appear to be affected more than the opinions of people who are less reliant. Finally, while the social context appears to have negligible effects upon candidate preference early in the campaign, the political stimulus of the campaign serves to mobilize social influence, and strong patterns of contextual influence appear at the campaign's end. Taken **as** a whole, the evidence presented in this chapter provides strong support for the importance of contextual influence upon political behavior, and for the role of social interaction as the mechanism that translates the social context into a source of political influence.

CHAPTER 5

THE CONTEXTUAL BASIS FOR ETHNIC POLITICS

Ethnic communities in American cities constitute social subsets within the larger population in a manner that belies the myth of the melting pot. Ethnic groups have resisted complete assimilation, providing alternative social environments in a variegated social and cultural milieu. Whereas the previous chapter focused upon class and status and the contextual basis for these political cleavages, the primary focus of this chapter is upon systems of social support underlying the political cohesion of ethnic groups. I will examine several different explanations for ethnic politics and argue that the political persistence of the ethnic group often depends upon the extent of social contact within the group. The political integrity of the group, and the maintenance of a separate group identity, frequently rely upon the group's ability to structure the social interaction patterns of group members.

Questions central to this effort are: How important are social contacts with other ethnics to the persistence of a self-conscious ethnic identity, and to the persistence of ethnic politics? In particular, do ethnic concentrations within urban neighborhoods, and the proximity of familial ties to ethnic groups, affect the political behavior of first, second, and third generation ethnics? How does the political influence of ethnicity compare to the influence of class and social status?

EXPLANATIONS FOR ETHNIC POLITICS

An individualistic conception of human behavior has frequently dominated treatments of ethnic politics in American cities. The classic statement of ethnic politics portrays the ethnic as an individual who sells his vote to the highest bidder. Political bosses prey upon the uninformed ethnic who is all too willing to trade his vote for a sack of groceries or a hod of coal. Political machines secure the ethnic vote by lavishly distributing patronage. The underlying assumption of this traditional formulation is that group behavior and solidarity can be explained on the basis of individual rewards received from the political system. This view strains the imagination. A job per vote, or a sack of groceries per vote, is a high price to pay, even for a political machine with vast resources. The following discussion presents three different perspectives toward the factors that sustain ethnic politics in American cities. These perspectives differ in the emphasis they place upon individualistic determinants of group cohesiveness, and in the prospects they offer for the survival and continuation of ethnic politics.

The Social Status Explanation for Ethnic Politics

An important explanation for ethnic politics, which is generally individualistic in focus, gives attention to the shared social status concerns of individual group members. One statement of this perspective is contained in Robert Dahl's *Who Governs?* (1961). According to Dahl, the greatest potential for a lively ethnic politics occurs when members of a particular ethnic group are newly arrived in the United States. At this stage in the life of the group, members are most homogeneous in terms of socioeconomic positions and political attitudes:

> Policies that will help an individual to cope with the problem of his status as a first- or second-generation immigrant are not much different from policies that appeal to him as a wage-earner, a resident of a tenement in a ghetto, a member of a family with a low and uncertain income, a victim of unemployment, a person of little social prestige, or an object of discrimination by middle class citizens of Anglo Saxon stock (Dahl 1961: 35).

Thus, the ties that bind ethnics together in a self-conscious group are, first and foremost, related to the common social and economic concerns of group members. Dahl acknowledged that "ethnic ties are partially responsible," but the ultimate source of political cohesiveness is the individual well-being of group members.

This viewpoint naturally leads to Dahl's conclusion regarding the persistence of ethnic politics: Ethnic politics becomes less important and vital as the ethnic group has more time for its members to stake out claims to higher status positions in the larger society. In a sense, the ethnic group puts itself out of business as it successfully assists its members in achieving social and economic well-being.

Raymond Wolfinger developed an important critique of Dahl's position that is directly related to the factors underlying the political cohesiveness of ethnic groups. According to Wolfinger, ethnic politics develops more slowly than Dahl suggested. Ethnic politics cannot thrive until an ethnic group develops sufficient human capital for the provision of political leadership. Only when this leadership is present does the ethnic group develop a self-conscious identity (1965: 905). Wolfinger agreed with Dahl's position that social mobility reduces the political importance of ethnicity, not only because it creates heterogeneous interests within the group, but also because it exposes the upwardly mobile ethnic to a wider range of social contacts.

The Neighborhood View of Ethnic Politics

The Dahl and Wolfinger viewpoints toward ethnic politics were developed within a larger concern regarding political power in the city, and alternative sources of influence in urban politics. Thus, the city is seen as a single system, while other viewpoints see the city as an ecology of interacting but largely self-contained subsystems.

One tradition in social science research uses a case study method to understand the role of neighborhoods and social groups in urban settings. A number of classic neighborhood studies have demonstrated the contextual basis to the vitality of ethnic groups. Whyte (1955) and Gans (1962) gave attention to Italian areas in the city of Boston, and both stressed the crucial role played by social contacts within the group to the group's self-conscious survival. By fostering and encouraging these social ties, the neighborhood served as an important basis of social support to the ethnic community.

Kornblum was a more recent participant observer in an area contiguous to the steel mills in South Chicago. The area is marked by its reliance upon the mills for employment, and a diversity of racial-ethnic groups: blacks, Mexicans, Italians, Poles, and South Slavs—Serbians, Croatians, and Slovenes. The area is fragmented into a number of ethnic territories. Within the territorial fragments, a number of socially integrative processes are at work creating self-conscious identities within the groups:

> **The basic unit of this community solidarity is the** primary **group that is reconstructed throughout the life cycle of residents of the community. The primary groups are developed on multiple principles of affiliation: ethnic and neighborhood descent, common participation in a street corner gang, patronage of a local tavern, participation in a precinct organizations or union caucases, and friendship in the mills. Sometimes a single group will combine members who are all related to one another through separate circumstances (1974:32).**

In short, extensive social interaction within the ethnic group, encouraged in neighborhoods where group members predominate, creates a group cohesiveness and fosters the adoption of political loyalties that correspond to group sentiment.

The Geographically Independent Ethnic Group

A final perspective toward factors that encourage the persistence of ethnic politics views a system of social interaction as being primarily responsible, but denies the spatial dependence of these associational patterns. According to this general view, the urban social landscape is made up of a variety of social groups that are internally cohesive without sharing a common residential location (Fischer, 1976: 35–38). Parenti discounted the importance of ethnic neighborhoods in the maintenance of social interaction patterns within the ethnic grouping: ·· . . . residential segregation is not a necessary prerequisite for the maintenance of an ethnic sub-societal structure; a group can maintain ethnic cohesion and identity, while lacking an ecological basis" (1967: 721).

Parenti further argued that occupational and educational mobility do not necessarily result in decreased ethnic consciousness. Several factors work toward the maintenance of ethnic awareness, independently of geographic or social mobility (1967: 73). Early familial experiences deeply imbed the ethnic identity in an individual's psyche. Even thoroughly acculturated ethnics may still be rejected by a WASP-dominated social system, thereby reinforcing the ethnic identity **of** even the most "Americanized" ethnic. Finally, Parenti argued that "the vast pluralistic parallel systems of ethnic social and institutional life show impressive viability" (1967: 724).

Thus, ethnic politics may be the outgrowth of an ethnic consciousness deeply rooted within individual personalities and vigorously reinforced by nongeographically based associational patterns. According to this view, ethnic politics has been freed from the ethnic neighborhood. When an ethnic resident of an ethnic neighborhood graduates from the state university, takes a job with a major bank, and moves to the suburbs, she is still likely to maintain an ethnic consciousness rooted in a network of personal associates that is structured by an individually defined ethnic group membership.

A Summary of the Explanations

Each of the three explanations is typically offered as a partial account of the factors underlying ethnic politics. The reconstructions put forth here are not intended as criticisms of any previously mentioned scholarly work. These explanations are not necessarily competing; all three might add to an understanding of ethnic politics and its persistence. Still, it is useful to summarize the perspectives in a rigorous, "ideal type" fashion that allows their empirical evaluation.

1. The social status explanation portrays ethnic politics as the product of an identifiable group sharing common social and economic positions. Ethnic ties can be explained on the basis of class and status, and the real significance of ethnic politics lies in the social status concerns of individual ethnics. As members of the group realize varying degrees of economic and social mobility, the ability of the group to maintain its internal cohesiveness necessarily suffers, and ethnic politics begins to decline.
2. The neighborhood explanation for ethnic politics emphasizes the importance of a shared residential location that structures the social interaction patterns of individual ethnics, sustains a range of ethnic dominated secondary institutions, and fosters the development of a shared group identity. Ethnic ties are social ties, held in place by the geographically bounded social interaction patterns of individual ethnics. As members of the ethnic group become geographically dispersed, group consciousness and ethnic politics necessarily decline.
3. The geographical independence view of ethnic politics sees the self-consciousness of the group as being virtually irrepressible. The ties of the ethnic group are social and cultural, but they are also mobile, extending beyond the boundaries of the ethnic neighborhood. In spite of social or geographic mobility, ethnic self-awareness and ethnic politics persist because ethnically dominated secondary institutions and ethnic patterns of social interaction are able to endure.

ETHNIC POLITICS IN BUFFALO

The persistence of ethnic politics is considered here using the 1968 Buffalo survey data. The Buffalo survey presents several unique advantages for the study of ethnic politics. Few surveys record the countries of birth for all the respondents' parents and grandparents, as well as information regarding respondents' subjective ethnic identifications. Even when this information is recorded, surveys seldom produce sufficient interviews within a single ethnic group to allow any detailed analysis of the group. Fortunately, the Buffalo survey produces an adequate number of interviews for such analyses, both among Italian and Polish ethnics. Only white respondents to the Buffalo survey are considered, because this analysis is particularly concerned with the comparison between white ethnics and white nonethnics. For a variety of reasons discussed earlier, including black respondents in the analysis might produce misleading results.

Several behaviors centrally related to ethnic politics are considered: identification as a Democrat, identification with a particular ethnic group, and support for an ethnic politician. All these qualitative behaviors are measured on a binary scale (identification versus nonidentification, support versus nonsupport), and the logit for microdata is therefore used in the statistical analyses of this chapter. As before, the magnitude of a logit coefficient is not directly assessed in the analyses that follow. In order to determine the magnitude of an effect due to an independent variable, predicted probabilities are calculated across the range of a particular independent variable with all other independent variables held constant.

Ethnic Loyalties to the Democrats

In addition to being the dominant political party in Buffalo, the Democrats have generally managed to maintain the allegiances of ethnic groups within the city. *(An* exception to Democratic hegemony among ethnics is considered later in this chapter.) The party has incorporated and supported political candidates from various ethnic groups in a largely successful effort at building a broad-based coalition of ethnic support in city politics. As a result, Democratic politicians have a mixture of ethnic names, and ethnic politics in Buffalo has been primarily contained within the Democratic party.

The importance of these ties between the Democratic party and Buffalo ethnics is supported in Figure 5.1, which expresses Democratic identification as a function of individual ethnicity. Fifty-five percent of first and second generation ethnics identify as Democrats, while only 34 percent of white nonethnics—individuals with four grandparents born in the United States—identify as Democrats. *An* especially interesting pattern of Democratic identification appears among third generation ethnics. These individuals are more likely to identify as Democrats if a higher proportion of their grandparents are foreign born. Democratic support is lowest among third generation ethnics with only one foreign born grandparent (27 percent), and consistently increases to the highest level (56 percent) among third generation ethnics with four foreign born grandparents.

These results speak directly (if not decisively) to the importance of social bonds for the maintenance of ethnic politics. Democratic affiliation varies as a direct function of the family's ethnic composition. The third generation appears to be a crucial stage in the maintenance of loyalties toward the ethnic party: third generation ethnics who have stronger familial ties to the immigrant past are more likely to maintain appropriate political loyalties.

Several other possibilities must be considered as well, however. Especially in light of social status interpretations of ethnic politics, the importance of ethnicity must be evaluated in relationship to several status

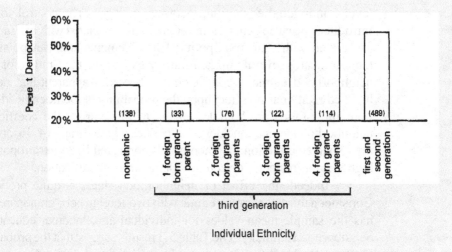

Figure 5.1. The percentage of respondents identifying as Democrats by individual ethnicity, calculated to the third generation. *N* sizes are shown in parentheses. *Data source:* 1968 Buffalo survey.

indicators. The social status view suggests that individual mobility is the nemesis of ethnic solidarity: ethnic politics is able to flourish only if ethics share a common set of interests and concerns at the individual level. Thus, introducing individual status controls should reduce the political role of ethnicity: ethnicity should have no effect upon partisan loyalty independent of social status.

Further, two different neighborhood-level explanations might account for the relationship between individually defined ethnicity and Democratic loyalties. First, in keeping with the analysis of Chapter 5, ethnics may adhere to the Democratic party because they reside in lower status neighborhoods where they frequently interact with lower status people who are more likely to be Democrats. These interactions with lower status individuals may encourage Democratic loyalties, independently of the interactions' ethnic content. Second, ethnic ties to the Democrats may be sustained because ethnic individuals reside in ethnic neighborhoods where they frequently interact with other ethnics. These interactions with ethnics might, in turn, encourage loyalties, both toward the ethnic group and toward the Democratic **party,** independently from their social status content.

Table 5.1 considers these possibilities by using the logit model to express Democratic identification as a function of neighborhood ethnicity[1] and individual ethnicity with controls for neighborhood education levels, individual education, income, and age. (The control for age is introduced because generational ethnicity is associated with age, and age is associated with numerous political involvements and viewpoints.) The table indicates several things. First, by examining the t-ratios for the two neighborhood ethnicity coefficients, it becomes apparent that neighborhood ethnicity has no effect upon the probability of Democratic identification: the t-ratios are both less than **.6.** In contrast, the coefficient for neighborhood educational levels generates a large t-ratio **(4.46)** and lies in the expected direction: neighborhoods populated by larger proportions of higher status residents discourage Democratic identification.

Indeed, the effect of neighborhood status is quite pronounced. Consider a third generation ethnic with two foreign born grandparents who has the sample mean values for individual age, income, education and neighborhood ethnicity. The Table 5.1 results suggest that the probability of Democratic identification for such an individual varies from .58 in a neighborhood where **17** percent of the adult residents are high school educated, to **.20** in a neighborhood where **79** percent are high school educated. (These high school educated percentages, **17** and **79** percent, represent the range for the respondents' neighborhoods.)

The effects of individually defined status and ethnicity present a different pattern. The coefficients for individual income and education lie in opposite directions, but both generate respectable t-ratios. The coefficient for the variable measuring the number of foreign born grandparents lies in the expected direction and also produces a t-ratio of respectable magnitude.[2] With all other variables controlled at their means, the probability of Democratic identification for nonethnics and third generation ethnics with one, two, three, and four foreign born grandparents are, respectively: **.30, .36, .44, .51,** and .58. Clearly, the effect of ethnicity, measured in terms of ethnic dominance within the family, has a strong and persisting influence even when individual status and neighborhood status are taken into account.

The evidence presented here fails to support the social status explanation for the persistence of ethnic politics. Social status is clearly important in its own right, both at the individual level and at the contextual level, but it does not eclipse the importance of the ethnic group. Ethnicity has an effect that extends beyond individual or corporate concerns regarding class or status. Further, individual ethnicity is not an "either-or" phenomenon. Ethnic political loyalties are encouraged and sustained as a direct function of ethnic densities within the extended family. A third generation ethnic with four foreign born grandparents is more likely to

Table 5.1. A Logistic Estimation of Democratic Identification as a Function of Neighborhood Education and Ethnicity, and Individual Education, Income, Age, and Ethnicity

$$D = 1/(1 + e^{-f})$$
$$f = a_1 + a_2 EN + a_3 ETHN1 + a_5 E + a_4 ETHN2$$
$$+ a_6 I + a_7 AGE + a_8 ETHR1 + a_9 ETHRGP$$

		Coefficients (a_i)	t-ratios
Constant	(a_1)	1.51	2.13
EN	(a_2)	−2.78	4.46
ETHN1	(a_3)	.66	.59
ETHN2	(a_4)	−.28	.36
E	(a_5)	−.12	3.66
I	(a_6)	.05	2.14
AGE	(a_7)	−.005	1.01
ETHR1	(a_8)	−.22	.99
ETHRGP	(a_9)	.30	2.60

$$N = 795$$

D = 1 if respondent identifies as a Democrat; 0 otherwise

EN = proportion of neighborhood adults (25 years and over) with 12 years of schooling or more.

ETHN1 = proportion of neighborhood residents who are first or second generation ethnics for nonethnics; 0 otherwise

ETHN2 = proportion of neighborhood residents who are first or second generation ethnics for first, second, or third generation ethnics; 0 otherwise

E = respondent's schooling in years

I = respondent's family income in thousand dollar intervals (the three highest intervals are: $15,000–$19,000, $20,000–$24,999, $25,000 and over)

AGE = respondent's age in years

ETHR1 = 1 if respondent is a first or second generation ethnic; 0 otherwise

ETHRGP = number of foreign born grandparents for respondents—first and second generation ethnics are scored as having four foreign born grandparents

Data Source: 1968 Buffalo Survey.

receive political cues encouraging the maintenance of ethnic political perspectives than a third generation ethnic with only one foreign born grandparent.

These results give tentative and partial support to the geographical independence view of ethnic politics, while they discredit the ethnic neighborhood explanation. The maintenance of ethnic political loyalties appears to be geographically independent, even if the loyalties are intimately related to a network of social reinforcement, in this case the family. Thus, while ethnic support for the Democratic party is geographically independent, it is not independent from a system of social support, and it tends to diminish as direct familial ties to the ethnic group disappear. Several other behaviors must be considered, however, before dismissing either the neighborhood perspective or the social status perspective.

Ethnic Identities and the Neighborhood Context

An important component of ethnic politics is a self-conscious ethnic awareness among ethnic group members. In order for any group to act cohesively in the electoral arena, group members must acknowledge their membership in the group. Gabriel (1972) displayed a strong simple relationship between ethnic voting and ethnic consciousness.[3] People who identify themselves as members of a particular ethnic group are more likely to vote as members of the group.

This self-conscious awareness is considered among objectively defined Polish- and Italian-American respondents to the Buffalo survey. The respondents were asked a question regarding what they considered their nationality background to be; this variable is treated as their subjective ethnic identification. If their answer to the question is Polish, their self-identification is defined to be Polish, and any other answer is classified as not Polish. Similarly, if their answer is Italian, they are considered to be subjective Italian identifiers, and any other answer is treated as not Italian. The respondents were also asked a series of questions regarding the countries of birth of their parents and grandparents. Objective measures of Italian and Polish ethnicity are based upon these batteries of questions, calculated to the third generation.[4]

Figure 5.2 shows the relationship between subjective Polish identification and both individual Polish ethnicity (objectively defined) and the Polish ethnic composition of the respondent's neighborhood context. The figure shows minimal differences in Polish identification between Polish ethnic generations when the neighborhood's Polish ethnic composition is controlled. Significant variation in Polish identification occurs within objectively defined Polish ethnic categories across neighborhood contexts, however. Slightly less than 54 percent of the objectively defined, first and second generation Polish ethnics classify themselves as Polish at the lowest level of Polish concentration, but this level of Polish awareness increases to more than 85 percent at the highest Polish concentration. Slightly more than

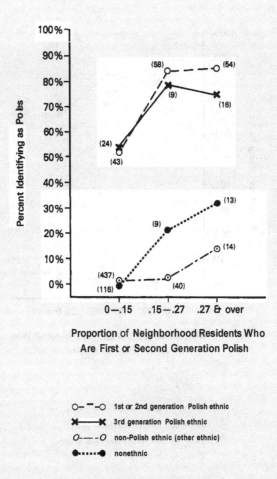

Figure **5.2.** Percent of whites who subjectively identify as Poles by the proportion of neighborhood residents who are first or second generation Polish ethnics, and by individual Polish ethnicity. The *N* sizes are shown in parentheses. Cutting points on the horizontal axis are chosen to maximize the equal distribution of Polish ethnics across the contextual categories. *Data* source: 1968 Buffalo survey.

54 percent of objectively defined third generation Polish ethnics identify **as** Poles at the lowest level of Polish concentration, but this increases to 75 percent at the highest level. Thus, a fairly strong relationship appears to be present between geographical residence in a Polish neighborhood, and a sense of Polish identification among individual Polish-Americans.[5]

Figure 5.3 gives the same sort of consideration to subjective Italian awareness. As the figure shows, however, there are no systematic differences between Italian ethnic generations when the neighborhood's Italian

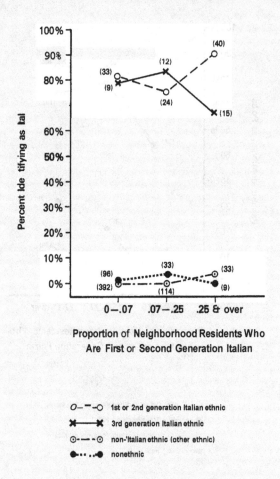

Figure **5.3.** Percent of whites who subjectively identify as Italians by the proportion of neighborhood residents who are first or second generation Italian, and by individual Italian ethnicity. *N* sizes are shown in parentheses. Cutting points on the horizontal axis are chosen to maximize the equal distribution of Italian ethnics across the contextual categories. Data source: 1968 Buffalo survey.

ethnic composition is controlled. Further, no significant or systematic relationship appears between the neighborhood social context and subjective Italian identification. In short, the sense of Italian awareness among Italian-American ethnics does not appear to be dependent upon residence in Italian neighborhoods, or upon individual generational differences within the ethnic group.

Two logit models are used to give further consideration to the subjective ethnic identifications of objectively defined Polish- and Italian-American ethnics in Table 5.2. Part **A** of the table shows that neighborhood Polish concentrations are positively related to the subjective awareness of Polish ethnicity even when controls are introduced for individual age, income, and education. The coefficient measuring the independent effect of third generation Polish ethnicity (apart from first or second generation ethnicity) fails to achieve a t-ratio of respectable magnitude. Thus, the predicted probability of Polish identification among Polish ethnics varies from .5 in a 1 percent Polish neighborhood, to .9 in a **36** percent Polish neighborhood, with controls for individual income and education set equal to the sample means. (These percentages, 1 and **36** percent, estimate the range of first and second generation Polish densities in respondents' neighborhoods.)

Part B of Table *5.2* confirms the conclusion reached on the basis of Figure **5.3**: subjective Italian identification is not conditioned on the basis of either the neighborhood density of Italian ethnics, or according to Italian ethnicity defined on the basis of objective, generational criteria. T-ratios for coefficients measuring the effects of neighborhood ethnicity and individual third generation ethnicity fail to satisfy commonly accepted criterion values.

These findings raise several questions. First, why is group awareness geographically dependent for Polish ethnics, but not for Italians? It may have been that Polish ethnicity in **1968** was less socially acceptable than Italian ethnicity. The Polish people have a distinguished history, but for a variety of reasons Polish-Americans have felt the brunt of ethnic jokes and slurs in American society. A socially supportive environment might offset this impediment to group solidarity among Polish ethnics.

Another possible explanation is the differing role played by kinship networks in the two ethnic groups. Various commentators have argued that Italians, both here and in Italy, have a strong sense of loyalty to family. The maintenance of these familial bonds and extended social networks within the ethnic group, coupled with a more socially acceptable ethnic identity, may account for the geographical independence of group awareness among Italian ethnics. These two explanations are supported by the relatively high overall level of subjective awareness among the Italian-American respondents: **81.2** percent of the Italian respondents identify **as** Italian but only **74.5** percent of the Polish respondents identify **as** Polish. Furthermore, notice in Table 5.2 that higher individual educational levels have a depressing effect upon group awareness among the Polish ethnics, but no effect among Italian ethnics! The depressing effect of education upon Polish identification is consistent with the social status perspective, which sug-

Table 5.2. Logistic Estimations of Subjective Ethnic Identification among Objectively Defined Polish and Italian Ethnics as a Function of Individual Ethnicity, Neighborhood Ethnicity, Individual Education, Individual Income, and Individual Age

A. Subjective Polish Identification among Objectively Defined Polish Ethnics

$$P = 1/(1 + e^{-f})$$

$$f = a_1 + a_2 POLN + a_3 POLR3 + a_4 AGE + a_5 E + a_6 I$$

		Coefficients (a_i)	t-ratios
Constant	(a_1)	1.25	.92
POLN	(a_2)	6.37	3.43
POLR3	(a_3)	− .09	.18
AGE	(a_4)	− .01	.80
E	(a_5)	− .17	2.18
I	(a_6)	.14	2.50

$$N = 186$$

B. Subjective Italian Identification among Objectively Defined Italian Ethnics

$$I = 1/(1 + e^{-f})$$

$$f = a_1 + a_2 ITLN + a_3 ITLR3 + a_4 AGE + a_5 E + a_6 I$$

		Coefficients (a_i)	t-ratios
Constant	(a_1)	1.57	.89
ITLN	(a_2)	− .52	.21
ITLR3	(a_3)	− .18	.27
AGE	(a_4)	.01	.70
E	(a_5)	.04	.43
I	(a_6)	− .003	.05

$$N = 120$$

P = 1 if respondent identifies as a Pole; 0 otherwise
I = 1 if respondent identifies as an Italian; 0 otherwise
POLN = proportion of neighborhood residents who are first or second generation Polish ethnics
POLR3 = 1 if respondent is a third generation Polish ethnic; 0 otherwise
AGE = age of respondent in years
E = respondent's schooling in years
I = respondent's family income in thousand dollar intervals (the three highest intervals are: $15,000–$19,999, $20,000–$24,999, $25,000 and over)
ITLN = proportion of neighborhood residents who are first or second generation Italian ethnics
ITLR3 = 1 if respondent is a third generation Italian ethnic; 0 otherwise

Data Source: 1968 Buffalo Survey

gests that ethnic cohesion is undermined by the social mobility of individual ethnics.[6] In contrast, the bonds of Italian ethnicity not only overcome the dissolution of Italian neighborhoods, but also overcome the individual mobility inherent in higher educational levels.

A second question raised by these findings relates to the differential effects of ethnic neighborhoods upon Democratic identification and Polish identification. Why do neighborhood contexts populated more heavily by Polish ethnics encourage group awareness among Polish ethnics, if neighborhood contexts more heavily populated by ethnics in general do not encourage Democratic identification among ethnics? A reciprocal relationship usually exists between political parties and ethnic groups: ethnic group membership encourages support for a particular party, and political parties learn to encourage ethnic support through mechanisms such as the ethnically balanced ticket (Pomper, 1966). As a result, ethnic politics often becomes strongly identified with a particular party over time, and it is frequently neutralized as a force independent of party. Prevailing political cleavages point toward a single party that is the ethnic party, and ethnics, as *ethnics,* have no other political home.

Within this set of ethnic cleavages, issues related to class and status generally provide the dynamic behind politics. Politics as usual is played out on the basis of these class-related issues and symbols, but it is always subject to other social loyalties and cleavages, such as ethnicity. Ethnicity is related to Democratic loyalty at the individual level because individual ethnicity, measured on the basis of direct familial ties to the ethnic groups, is directly related to social and political loyalties acquired through a political socialization process that occurs within the family. Neighborhood ethnicity is immaterial to Democratic loyalties because politics does not usually mobilize the population on the basis of ethnicity, and thus the *ethnic composition of neighborhood contexts does not tap the source of social influence that is politically relevant to party loyalties.* This is not to suggest that politics is never structured on the basis of ethnicity, however. The next section considers the way in which the same neighborhood factors that encourage Polish identification also mobilize the Polish ethnic population in support of a politician with a direct appeal to that group.

In summary, the geographical independence explanation is supported by the analysis of Italian ethnics, but not by the analysis of Polish ethnics. Italian ethnics demonstrate a high level of subjective identification with their ethnic group that is unaffected by the demise of ethnic neighborhoods, or by a decrease in direct family ties to the ethnic group, or by individual social mobility. The neighborhood and social status explanations do a better job of accounting for the persistence of Polish ethnicity.

Objectively defined Polish ethnics are less likely to identify with the Polish ethnic group if they live in non-Polish neighborhoods, or if they have attained higher educational levels.

Polish Support for a Polish Republican Politician

Are Polish neighborhoods only important for the group awareness of individual Polish ethnics, or do they also have political consequences for their residents? The argument offered above suggests that ethnic politics and ethnic cleavages are normally subsumed by a system of party cleavages. Ethnicity does not always lie dormant, however. In some instances ethnicity outweighs class and party as a factor influencing political behavior. Lorinskas, Hawkins, and Edwards (1969) showed that a candidate's ethnicity is more important than a candidate's party label in determining vote choice among a sample of ethnic residents in urban Chicago, but party is more important for a sample of ethnic respondents in rural Illinois. Pomper (1966) showed that party outweighs ethnicity as an explanatory factor for voting behavior in a partisan Newark election, but, in a nonpartisan Newark election, ethnicity is more important than either candidate issue positions or implicit party labels. The moral to be gained is twofold. First, any system of cleavages is peculiar to a place, time, and environment; generalizations are necessarily tentative and dependent upon situational specifics. Second, ethnicity may be important in some instances and for some behaviors, but unimportant for others.

Alfreda Slominski has been a controversial and outspoken Buffalo politician, a member of the city council, and an unsuccessful candidate for mayor. Her Polish surname suggests that at least part of her political support is based upon ethnic group loyalties among Polish ethnics. Further, that support might be encouraged in neighborhoods where these loyalties are encouraged, neighborhoods where larger proportions of the population are composed of other Polish ethnics. This offers an especially interesting test of the contextual argument because Ms. Slominski is a Republican, and 65 percent of the first, second, and third generation Polish ethnics in our sample identify as Democrats. (Only 16 percent identify as Republicans.)

Figure 5.4 shows that favorable opinions toward Slominski are encouraged by more heavily Polish neighborhoods, especially among objectively defined Polish ethnics and other ethnics. The level of support for Slominski increases from slightly less than 46 percent among third generation Polish ethnics who live in neighborhoods with low concentrations of Polish ethnic residents, to 75 percent among third generation Polish ethnics in neighborhoods with high Polish concentrations. The level of support

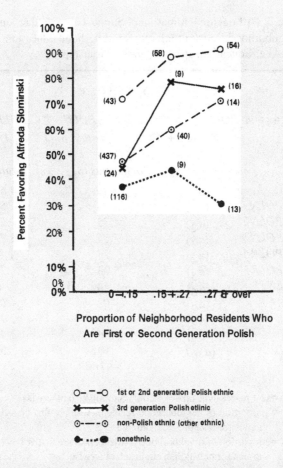

Figure 5.4. Percent of whites who favor Alfreda Slominski by the proportion of neighborhood residents who are first or second generation Polish ethnics, and by individual Polish ethnicity. *N* sizes are shown in parentheses. Cutting points on the horizontal axis are chosen to maximize the equal distribution of Polish ethnics across the contextual categories. *Data source:* 1968 Buffalo survey.

among first and second generation Polish ethnics increases from **72** percent in the low concentration Polish neighborhoods, to 91 percent in the high concentration Polish neighborhoods. **Thus,** not only do fairly consistent neighborhood effects appear, but consistent individual level differences between Polish ethnic categories are also present.

A logit model is used to consider the effects of individual and neighborhood ethnicity upon respondents' opinions toward Slominski, with controls introduced for individual age, education, income, and party

Table 5.3. A Logistic Estimation of **Support** for Alfreda Slominski **as** a Function of Neighborhood Polish Ethnicity, Neighborhood Education and Individual Ethnicity, Age, Education, Income, and Partisanship

$$S = 1/(1 + e^{-f})$$

$$f = a_1 + a_2 POLN1 + a_3 POLN2 + a_4 POLN3 + a_5 POLR1 + a_6 POLR3 + a_7 EN + a_8 AGE + a_9 E + a_{10} I + a_{11} D$$

		Coefficients (a_i)	t-ratios
Constant	(a_0)	-2.49	4.65
POLN1	(a_1)	1.06	.57
POLN2	(a_2)	4.25	2.79
POLN3	(a_3)	7.32	3.75
POLR1	(a_4)	.73	1.80
POLR3	(a_5)	.08	.17
EN	(a_6)	$-.44$	**.64**
AGE	(a_7)	.02	4.61
E	(a_8)	.07	2.07
I	(a_9)	.06	2.42
D	(a_{10})	.10	.58

$$N = 760$$

S	= 1 if respondent favors Alfreda Slominski; 0 otherwise
POLN 1	= proportion of neighborhood residents who are first or second generation Polish ethnics for nonethnics; 0 otherwise
POLN2	= proportion of neighborhood residents who are first or second generation Polish ethnics for non-Polish ethnics; 0 otherwise
POLN3	= proportion of neighborhood residents who are first or second generation Polish ethnics for first, second, and third generation Polish ethnics; 0 otherwise
POLR1	= 1 if respondent is first or second generation Polish ethnic; 0 otherwise
POLR3	= 1 if respondent is third generation Polish ethnic; 0 otherwise
EN	= proportion of neighborhood adults (25 years and over) with 12 years of schooling or more
AGE	= age of respondent in years
E	= respondent's schooling in years
I	= respondent's family income in thousand dollar intervals (the three highest intervals are: $15,000–$19,999, $20,000–$24,999, $25,000 and over)
D	= 1 if respondent identifies as a Democrat; 0 otherwise

Data Source: 1968 Buffalo Survey.

identification, as well **as** for the educational level of other neighborhood residents (See Table 5.3). The effect of neighborhood ethnicity is measured separately for (1) objectively defined Polish ethnics of **any** generation, **(2)**

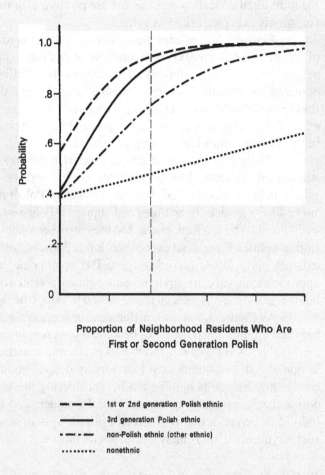

Proportion of Neighborhood Residents Who Are
First or Second Generation Polish

— — — 1st or 2nd generation Polish ethnic
———— 3rd generation Polish ethnic
— · — · non-Polish ethnic (other ethnic)
·········· nonethnic

Figure 5.5. Predicted probabilities of favoring Alfreda Slominski as a function of the proportion of neighborhood residents who are first or second generation Polish ethnics, with neighborhood education, and individual age, education, and income controlled at their mean values, and **with** partisanship controlled at Democratic identification. *Source:* The logit model of Table 5.3.

other ethnics, and (3) nonethnics. The t-ratios for the coefficients measuring the effect of these three variables show that the neighborhood has a statistically stable effect for Polish ethnics and for other ethnics. Among Polish ethnics, first and second generation Poles are more likely to favor Slominski, while third generation Polish ethnics are no more likely to favor Slominski, at the *individual level,* than the population **as** a whole.[7] The effects of social status are mixed: The coefficient for neighborhood education is negative but fails to produce a satisfactory t-ratio. The coefficients for individual education and income are positive with t-ratios that surpass commonly accepted criterion values.

Figure 5.5 translates these coefficients into predicted probabilities of support for Slominski as a function of both individual ethnicity and neighborhood Polish ethnicity. The neighborhood effects are quite pronounced for objectively defined Polish ethnics. Even if the deficient t-ratio for the neighborhood effect among the nonethnics is ignored the contextual effect for these individuals is very weak, and the contextual effect for other (non-Polish) ethnics is also less pronounced.[8]

These findings give dramatic support to the important relationships among ethnic group loyalty, political loyalty, and the social contexts of ethnic neighborhoods. Polish ethnics living in Polish neighborhoods are more likely to identify as Poles and support a Polish-surnamed politician, even though she is a Republican and they are overwhelmingly Democratic. Ethnic politics is not dead even when it lies dormant within the confines of existing party labels and cleavages. The appropriate candidate with the appropriate appeal can reinvigorate the political potential of the ethnic group, but the group itself is a social phenomenon held together by social bonds.

As Figure 5.5 shows, differences in support for Alfreda Slominski between ethnics and nonethnics become more pronounced as a function of the neighborhood context. Individual ethnic status matters relatively little in non-Polish neighborhoods. Individually defined ethnicity is important, but its importance is highlighted by considering the social context. The political role of ethnicity cannot be fully understood by focusing upon individual behavior that is divorced from the system of social support that sustains the actor, and this system of social support is neighborhood based.

Polish Consciousness and Self-Selection

Before concluding, consideration must be given to a self-selection explanation for some of these findings. Do Polish ethnics who identify as Poles and support a Polish-surnamed politician possess a set of individual level predispositions that also guides them in the choice of a neighborhood? Identification as a Pole and support for a Polish Republican politician might be caused by these predispositions, rather than by any independent neighborhood effect. Thus, residence in a Polish neighborhood might covary with these political behaviors without having any effect upon them.

This self-selection argument is certainly plausible. The militant ethnic who chooses to remain in the central city ethnic neighborhood is at least a potential factor in the persistence of ethnic politics (Wolfinger, 1965; Parenti, 1967). Further, if this is an either-or situation, either self-selection or contextual influence, there is little empirical basis for making a choice.

The self-selection argument is less than wholly satisfactory as a

repudiation of contextual influence, however. Some Polish ethnics undoubtedly choose to live in Polish neighborhoods, but that does not negate
the importance of the neighborhood. Indeed, self-selection actually constitutes a rather complex contextual argument. People choose to live in
neighborhoods (when they have the freedom to choose) because they are
attracted to them or because they are repelled by other residential alternatives. Both the attraction and the repulsion are, at least in part, contextually
based. Thus, this is *not* an either-or situation. Individual-level characteristics and contextual factors are both important to an understanding of
political behavior: their interaction produces a complex web of choices and
reactions rooted in the personality of the actor, and in the characteristics of
others in the actor's environment.

CONCLUSIONS

On the basis of this analysis several conclusions are warranted regarding the
persistence of ethnic politics. First, the survival (or demise) of ethnic
politics cannot be explained entirely on the basis of individually defined
ethnic status, or on the basis of individually defined social and economic
concerns. Class and status outweigh the importance of ethnicity for many
issues and in many circumstances, but the ethnic group is more than a
collection of individuals with similar social positions. The ethnic group is
not subsumed by the individual status characteristics of group members,
even though ethnic loyalties are frequently weakened by individual social
mobility. *Also,* ethnic politics does not eclipse the importance of class,
status, or party. Rather, it serves as an additional line of cleavage that will,
under appropriate circumstances, mobilize the relevant population.

Second, the persistence of ethnic politics is frequently rooted in a
supportive social environment. Two different social contexts have been
shown to be important: the family and the neighborhood. Third generation
ethnics are more likely to profess Democratic loyalties if ethnic ties within
their families are stronger—if more of their grandparents are foreign born.
Polish ethnics, but not Italian ethnics, are more likely to express an
identification with their ethnic group if they live in neighborhoods where
the group predominates. Polish ethnics living in Polish ethnic neighborhoods are also more likely to support a Polish-surnamed politician. Thus,
for some groups, ethnic loyalties appear to be independent from the ethnic
neighborhood and even from the ethnic context of the extended family,
corresponding to the geographic independence view of ethnic politics. For
other groups ethnic loyalties are rooted in a supportive context that is, at
least partially, neighborhood based.

What do these findings suggest regarding the future of ethnic
politics? The persistence of some ethnic groups is well explained by the

geographical independence view of ethnic politics. The Italians in this analysis, regardless of individual status and the ethnic composition of their families or neighborhoods, demonstrate a high level of subjective identification with the group. Thus, group cohesiveness might be expected to persist through time, regardless of the ethnic neighborhood's dissolution and the onward march of successive ethnic generations. Other groups, however, appear to be more dependent upon a system of social support for their survival. The persistence of such groups must be injured by the weakening of these ethnic social ties. In **this** analysis the same group whose identity was dependent upon social support—the Polish ethnics—was also vulnerable to dissolution based upon individual social status considerations,

In summary, several different forces work both to sustain and to weaken the political role of ethnic groups in American urban politics. Upward social mobility diminishes loyalty toward some groups. Increased levels of social support from the ethnic group strengthen these loyalties, thereby offsetting the disintegrating effects of individual social mobility for ethnics who receive such support. Finally, the social structures of some ethnic groups seem to make them invulnerable, either to the effects of individual status and mobility, or to the dissolution of ethnic neighborhoods and the attenuation of direct ethnic ties within the family.

This analysis has considered factors that strengthen or weaken ethnic politics, but many of the same factors also transform the nature of the ethnic group. As the group evolves in time, its political role evolves as well. Regardless of this evolution, however, ethnic politics and ethnic political loyalties are notable for their persistence rather than their decline. **As a** result, the ethnic group is still an important source of political resources. Failures at mobilizing ethnic groups are typically blamed upon the demise of ethnic politics. Instead, these failures should probably be blamed upon the inability of political organizations and entrepreneurs to appreciate the evolving role of ethnic groups in urban politics, as ethnic groups and their members continue to mature within the political system.

A Final Note Regarding the Persistence of Ethnic Politics

During the early **1980s** racially based political competition has frequently dominated the news in American electoral politics. In two major American cities, Chicago and Philadelphia, a black candidate and a white candidate struggled to gain control of the mayor's office, and the black candidate succeeded. In California, a black man and a white man competed for control of the governor's mansion, and the white man won. A black man entered the race for the **1984** Democratic presidential nomination, and many Democrats shuddered when they considered the political implications.

The current era of black-white competition builds upon an earlier established competitive tradition between various white ethnic groups, and between ethnics and nativists, for the control of city politics. Robert Dahl (1961) wrote persuasively regarding the competition that occurred between ethnic groups in New Haven politics. That competition began between the "patricians" and the new arrivals—the Irish ethnics who were attracted to New Haven by the promise of readily available industrial jobs during the nineteenth century. This competitive relationship was, in turn, displaced by twentieth-century competition between the ascendant Irish and the newly arrived Italians. The same sort of competition between white ethnic groups, or between nativists and ethnics, has occurred again and again in city after city (Stabrowski, 1984).

Thus, competitive political relationships between ethnic groups are a recurring phenomenon in American urban politics, and the most recent manifestations of ethnic politics continue to demonstrate a contextual dimension in which the political behavior of group members is interdependent. The political choices of individuals are circumscribed by the potential for social interaction within and beyond the boundaries of the group, and by the nature of the interactions that occur across group boundaries. The main disjuncture between the current black-white ethnic competition and the earlier ethnic competition within the white population relates to the permeability of the boundaries separating groups. The current basis for competition is more durable because the boundaries separating these groups are more substantial. This chapter has demonstrated the vitality of ethnic divisions within a white population, but these divisions are insignificant in comparison to those that persist between black and white, and even between Anglo and Hispanic.[9]

CHAPTER 6

NEIGHBORHOOD INFLUENCES ON WHITE FLIGHT AND RESIDENTIAL SATISFACTION

Like many other American cities, the city of Buffalo, New York has experienced large-scale white flight. From 1930 through 1970 the nonwhite percentage of Buffalo's population grew from 3 to 22 percent while the remainder of Erie County experienced a slight decline in the nonwhite percentage of its population. During the same period that the nonwhite percentage of Buffalo's population was growing rapidly, the city's total population underwent a significant decline in size. Buffalo's 1970 population declined to less than 81 percent of its 1930 level at the same time that the remainder of Erie County experienced a population increase of over 343 percent. The population decrease occurred because a large part of Buffalo's white population deserted the city. By 1970 the city's white population had declined to approximately 65 percent of its 1930 level and 79 percent of its 1960 level. The present chapter addresses this question: What are the neighborhood factors that best help to explain this sort of large-scale population movement?

EXPLANATIONS FOR WHITE FLIGHT

Various explanations have been offered for white flight and residential satisfaction. Some explanations focus upon conflict: whites object to the presence of blacks within their living space and react accordingly. Other explanations focus upon assimilation: some people are attracted to neighborhoods with higher status residents, and ethnic neighborhood are attractive to their ethnic residents. Still other explanations focus upon individual characteristics as determinants of residential choice.

Individual-Level Factors

Residential satisfaction, as well as the decision to move or stay within a residential environment, can be influenced by individual-level considerations. Gans **(1967: 33)** showed that most residents of a new suburban housing development left their old residences because they wanted or needed better housing. Hawley and Zimmer (1970: **32)** demonstrated that the most important motivations for urban to suburban moves among their Buffalo and Milwaukee area survey respondents were related to housing considerations. This sort of impetus is potentially unrelated to factors in neighborhood social environments. People evaluate an environment on the basis of their own immediate circumstances, not on the basis of their neighbors or neighborhoods.

Most individual-level explanations for residential satisfaction and mobility are intimately related to individual affluence. People with more resources purchase more pleasing homes in better neighborhoods, and people with higher incomes are able to move away from environments that are not satisfactory to them. Not only are well-off people more satisfied, but they are also capable of doing something about their dissatisfaction. Thus, white flight has an upper class bias: only well-off people are able to participate.

Social Factors in **the** Neighborhood

Social factors at the neighborhood level are also cited **as** motivating factors behind white flight and the residential satisfaction of urban residents. Even informal observers of urban population dynamics recognize the contagious quality of locally-based population movements. Population change is never uniform across a city; instead the movement is sporadic and uneven. Some neighborhoods experience rapid and nearly complete population turnover while others maintain a stable population base.

The most commonly cited neighborhood impetus for white flight is the presence of blacks. Orbell and Sherrill (1969) showed that Columbus whites living in low income areas are more likely to be racially intolerant if a higher proportion of blacks live in the same area. The authors also put forth evidence which suggests that racially hostile whites **are** more likely to be considering a move if they live in **areas** with higher concentrations of black residents. Sears and Kinder (1970), in their investigation of white racial attitudes in suburban San Fernando Valley, demonstrated that residents living nearer a small suburb with a concentrated black population are more likely to expect black instigated violence in their neighborhoods. The residents' ''appraisal of their personal danger from Negro violence is tied to their distance from any concentrations of blacks'' (p. **23).**

Other neighborhood explanations for residential satisfaction and relocation focus upon physical and social attractiveness. Gans (1967: **284)** suggested the importance of social factors in **his** analysis of residential satisfaction in Levittown: the homogeneous, lower middle class population of the new suburban development resulted in a social life that appealed to residents sharing the same characteristics. Zehner and Chapin (1974: 121-128) showed that a variety of similar factors are related to residential orientations: "a good class of people," nice neighbors, and physical upkeep.

Thus, explanations focusing upon the social attractiveness of neighborhood residents point toward at least two different compositional properties: the extent to which a neighborhood is populated by higher status people, and the extent to which the status composition of a neighborhood matches the individual resident's own status. One explanation asserts that individuals desire to live among higher status people. The other asserts that individuals desire to live among people similar to themselves.

Neighborhoods as Sources of Security

An alternative perspective toward the neighborhood focuses upon its functional role as a source of social organization for urban residents.

> The necessity for this additional basis for the social organization of cities lies in their very nature, since cities inevitably bring together populations that are too large and composed of too many conflicting elements for their residents to find cultural solutions to problems of social control. The result seems to be a partitioning of the city into several village-like areas where the actual groupings of people are of more manageable proportions (Suttles, 1972: 28-29).

Conceived in this manner, the neighborhood becomes a socially (and politically) functional institution that helps assure residents of their security. Many types of urban neighborhoods serve this function. Suttles (1972: 21) defined the defended neighborhood as a "residential group which seals itself off through the efforts of delinquent gangs, by restrictive covenants, by sharp boundaries, or by a forbidding reputation." The basis for a neighborhood's social organization may be social homogeneity, but it need not be. Neighborhoods are more than social containers, even though neighborhood social life may be profoundly influenced by varying social mixtures. Any neighborhood provides an important set of functions related to social organization, regardless of its social mix. Residents form neighborhood orientations based upon the performance of these functions, including the provision of safety and security.

RESIDENTIAL ORIENTATIONS IN BUFFALO

The effect of neighborhood social contexts upon white flight is examined here using the 1968 survey of the Buffalo metropolitan area. Two different residential orientations are considered: neighborhood evaluations and plans to move or stay at a particular residence. Moving intentions are measured with a survey question soliciting a positive or negative response as to whether respondents have serious thoughts of moving. The respondents' neighborhood evaluations are based upon three factors. A favorable evaluation requires that respondents (1) are satisfied or very satisfied with their neighborhoods, (2) believe their neighborhoods are good places to raise children, and (3) feel their neighborhoods are better than most others in the Buffalo area.

White Flight and White Fright

As was stated earlier, the most obvious neighborhood-level factor that might arouse the displeasure of white residents is the presence of blacks. Whites' objections to sharing living space with blacks have been well documented, and white emigration from neighborhoods experiencing racial change has been a common urban sight. On this basis it might be expected that whites would be less favorably disposed toward neighbor-

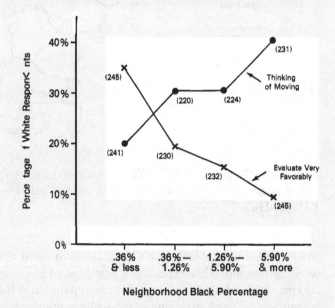

Figure 6.1. The percent of white respondents who evaluate their neighborhoods very favorably and who seriously think about moving by the estimated percentage of residents in their neighborhoods who are black. The sample sizes for the percentages are shown in parentheses. Cutting points for neighborhood black percentages are chosen on the basis of quartiles. *Data source:* 1968 Buffalo survey.

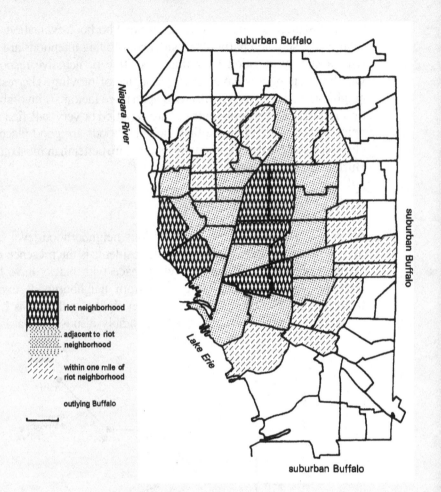

Figure 6.2. The proximity of Buffalo census tracts to the 1967 Buffalo riots (1960 census tract boundaries). *Source:* F. Besag and **P. Cook,** *The Anatomy of a Riot: Buffalo, 1967.*

hoods with higher black population concentrations and more likely to consider moving. This expectation is supported in Figure 6.1. The figure also provides a dramatic picture of racial separation in Buffalo; the median percentage of black residents in the white respondents' neighborhoods is only **1.26** percent. Even the presence of a minimal black population seems to have a dramatic effect upon the two orientations.

A relatively direct test can be made to determine whether neighborhood safety plays an important role in the formation of white residential attitudes. Race riots occurred in Buffalo during the summer of **1967.** These

riots were not on the same scale as disturbances in Watts, Newark, or
Detroit, but because they occurred within one year of the survey, their
relevance should be apparent among survey respondents. (A categorization
of Buffalo census tracts relative to the location of noting is graphically
displayed in Figure 6.2).

　　As Figure 6.3 shows, white respondents' residential locations with
respect to the riot activity are strong predictors of their neighborhood
evaluations and moving plans. People living closer to the riot areas are
more likely to be seriously considering a move, and less likely to evaluate
their neighborhoods favorably. These data suggest that people learn from
experience. White residential attitudes are not only related to the presence
of blacks; they are also affected by events—in this case the occurrence of
race riots.

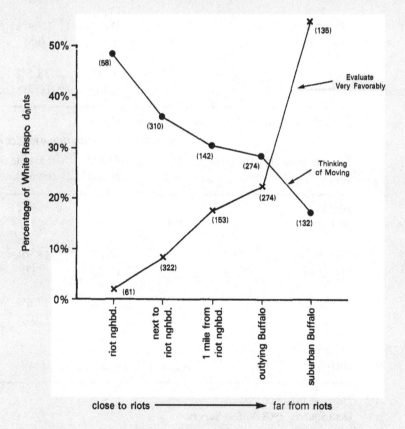

Figure 6.3. The percent of white respondents who evaluate their neighborhoods
very favorably and who seriously think about moving by the proximity of their
neighborhoods to the **1967** Buffalo race **riots.** The sample sizes for the percentages
are shown in parentheses. *Data source:* 1968 Buffalo survey.

Table 6.1. The Percent of White Respondents Who Are Planning to Move and the Percent Who Evaluate Their Neighborhoods Favorably by the Proximity of Their Neighborhoods to Riots and to Black Neighborhoods

A. Percent Seriously Considering a Move

| Neighborhood Proximity to Black Neighborhood | *Proximity of Neighborhood to Riot Activity* | | | |
	Riot nbd. [a]	Next to riotnbd.	Within mile of riotnbd.	Outlying Buffalo
Black nbd.	42.9% (7)	52.9% (17)		
Next to black nbd.		33.8% (231)	35.3% (34)	46.2% (13)
Within mile of black nbd.	59.3% (27)	38.5% (52)	27.4% (95)	12.0% (25)
Other Buffalo	37.5% (24)	50.0% (10)	38.5% (13)	28.7% (237)

B. Percent Evaluating Neighborhood Favorably

| Neighborhood Proximity to Black Neighborhood | *Proximity of Neighborhood to Riot Activity* | | | |
	Riot nbd.	Next to riot nbd.	Within mile of riot nbd.	Outlying Buffalo
Black nbd.	0.0% (8)	0.0% (17)		
Next to black nbd.		8.7% (242)	18.9% (37)	5.4% (17)
Within mile of black nbd.	0.0% (28)	3.8% (53)	17.6% (102)	1.5% (26)
Other Buffalo	4.0% (25)	10.0% (10)	7.1% (14)	23.6% (242)

[a] nbd. = neighborhood.
Data *Source:* 1968 Buffalo Survey.

One potential explanation for these results is that whites do not react to the proximity of race riots but rather to the proximity of blacks, and the proximity of blacks is closely related to the presence of race riots. Table 6.1 entertains this explanation by considering both neighborhood riot proximity and the proximity of neighborhoods that are more than 50 percent black. The table clearly indicates that the two factors are closely related: people living closer to black neighborhoods also live closer to riot areas.

Regardless of the close relationship between the two proximity measures, the independent effect of riot proximity is still demonstrated. Part A of Table 6.1 considers the effects of both factors upon moving intentions. The third row, composed of respondents living within one mile but not adjacent to black neighborhoods, contains cells with at least 25 respondents. This row shows that neighborhood riot proximity has a pronounced effect upon moving intentions even when the other spatial proximity factor is controlled. While none of the other rows or columns in Part A allow similar tests, the third row of Table 6.1 (B) also supports the effect of neighborhood riot proximity. Respondents living closer to riot areas are generally less likely to evaluate their neighborhoods favorably. Thus, while the effect of the two factors cannot be entirely separated, neighborhood riot proximity appears to have an effect that is independent of the proximity to black neighborhoods.

Relative Effects of Contextual and Individual Factors

Neighborhoods with higher black densities are more likely to be near the riot areas, and both of these neighborhood conditions are related to a variety of other factors at the individual and contextual levels. Table 6.2 uses the logit for microdata to give simultaneous consideration to several factors: individual income and education, the status composition of neighborhood residents, neighborhood black densities, and neighborhood riot proximity, Neighborhood riot proximity is entered in the logistic equation as a set of dummy variables. Each riot proximity category is dummy coded with the exception of suburban Buffalo. Thus, the coefficient for each category represents a change in the predicted "logit" from the suburban baseline.

The table shows that neighborhoods closer to riot areas tend to be associated with progressively less favorable residential orientations: they are less favorably evaluated, and people are most likely to be considering a move from these neighborhoods. The t-ratios for the coefficients surpass generally accepted criterion values in the neighborhood evaluations equation, but they lie below commonly accepted values in the moving plans equation.

Although the signs on the coefficients for neighborhood black densities lie in the expected directions, they fail to achieve respectable t-values in either the moving plans equation, or in the neighborhood evaluations equation. Two individual-level measures are included, education and family income, but they also fail to produce adequate t-values in either equation. The directions of the coefficients for family income sug-

Table 6.2. Logistic Estimations of the Residential Orientations as a Function of Neighborhood and Individual Factors[a]

$$\text{Neighborhood Orientations} = 1/(1+e^{-f})$$
$$f = a_0 + a_1 PR1 + a_2 PR2 + a_3 PR3 + a_4 PR4 + a_5 DS + a_6 BLK + a_7 IN + a_8 I + a_9 E$$

		Neighborhood Evaluation	Moving Plans
Constant	(a_0)	.82 (1.32)	−3.28 (5.75)
PR1	(a_1)	−2.24 (2.04)	1.08 (2.07)
PR2	(a_2)	−1.38 (3.38)	.59 (1.53)
PR3	(a_3)	− .67 (1.85)	.50 (1.36)
PR4	(a_4)	− .60 (2.12)	.49 (1.53)
DS	(a_5)	.22 (.34)	.98 (2.00)
BLK	(a_6)	− .46 (.44)	.49 (1.50)
IN	(a_7)	−4.21 (3.86)	1.71 (1.76)
I	(a_8)	.048 (1.81)	.023 (1.05)
E	(a_9)	.00042 (.01)	.038 (1.12)
N =		866	834

PR1 = 1 if neighborhood is a not neighborhood; 0 otherwise
PR2 = 1 if neighborhood is next to a riot neighborhood; 0 otherwise
PR3 = 1 if neighborhood is within a mile of a riot neighborhood; 0 otherwise
PR4 = 1 if neighborhood is in Buffalo but not included above; 0 otherwise
DS = proportion of neighborhood residents who are high school graduates for respondents who are **not** high school graduates; proportion of neighborhood residents who are not high school graduates
BLK = proportion of neighborhood residents who are black
IN = proportion of neighborhood families earning less than $9,000 per year in 1969 ($9,000 = the approximate median family income in Buffalo)
I = respondent's family income in thousand dollar intervals
E = respondent's years of schooling

[a] The t-values are shown in parentheses. Data Source: 1968 Buffalo Survey.

gest an opposite effect upon the two orientations: higher income people are more likely to be planning a move, but they are also more likely to evaluate their neighborhoods favorably. If the deficient t-values are momentarily ignored, higher income appears to result in a greater degree of satisfaction and an increased ability to respond to sources of dissatisfaction.

Finally, two different variables are included to measure the status composition of neighborhood populations. A social distance explanation for residential satisfaction is tested by constructing the following measure: the variable is set equal to the proportion of neighborhood adults who are high school graduates for respondents who are not high school graduates, and it is set equal to the proportion of neighborhood adults who are not high school graduates for respondents who are high school graduates. Thus, a higher proportion indicates a larger population that is dissimilar to the respondent in terms of social status. As Table 6.2 shows, this measure fails to produce an adequate t-value in the neighborhood evaluation equation, but it does produce a strong t-value in the moving plans equation, and in this latter case the coefficient lies in the expected direction.

The second measure of status compositon tests the more straightforward assertion that people prefer to live in higher status neighborhoods. Table 6.2 shows that higher neighborhood densities of families earning less than the median income produce less positive neighborhood evaluations, and a higher likelihood of moving. The variable produces a crisp t-value in the neighborhood evaluations equation, but a marginal t-value in the moving plans equation. Thus, people appear to evaluate higher status neighborhoods more favorably, and may be more likely to consider moving from lower status neighborhoods. However, these results suggest that they are also more likely to move from neighborhoods with higher levels of social distance — from neighborhoods where they are in a minority social status position. This interpretation complements the argument of Chapter 3: a minority social group is more likely to resist or to be excluded from association across social boundaries, and this exclusion may produce a higher probability of departure, quite apart from any evaluation of the neighborhood.

In summary, Table 6.2 supports the importance of neighborhood status levels and neighborhood riot proximity in affecting the residential orientations of neighborhood residents. Figure 6.4 demonstrates the magnitudes of these effects. In view of the observed range for the four neighborhood variables, the effects of riot proximity and low income densities are especially pronounced. In contrast, neighborhood black densities demonstrate a minimal effect upon moving plans, even if the marginal t-value of Table 6.2 is ignored. (The effects of social distance and black densities upon neighborhood evaluations are not plotted due to the extremely small t-values of Table 6.2.)

Racial Hostility and White Flight

Is white flight rooted in the racist attitudes of white urbanites, or is it a racially neutral response *to* a dangerous, deteriorating city? The data put forth here suggest that a neighborhood's potential for reassuring its residents of their security is a more important determinant of residential

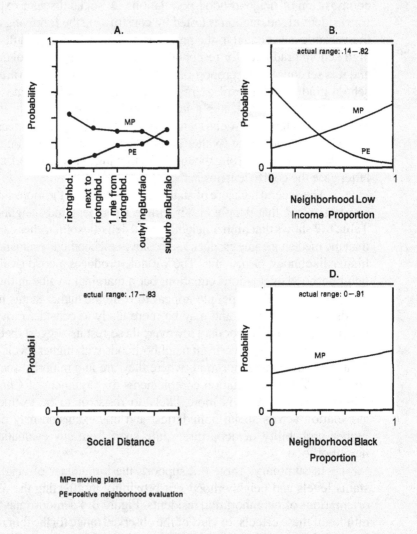

Figure 6.4. Estimated probabilities of moving plans and positive neighborhood evaluations across various neighborhood properties. *Source:* The logit model of Table 6.2. In Part A, all other independent variables are controlled at the sample means. In Parts B, C, and D, all other independent variables are controlled at the sample means except for not proximity, which is controlled at "one mile from riot neighborhood."

satisfaction than the presence of blacks in the neighborhood. Thus, white flight might be more fundamentally predicated upon individual calculations regarding security rather than prejudicial or discriminatory impulses. A further test of the motivation for residential dissatisfaction can be constructed by examining which individuals are most affected by neighborhood decline. If only racially hostile whites are affected by neighborhood riot proximity, then white flight and residential dissatisfaction are racially hostile responses that can be triggered by a concrete event or series of events.

In Table 6.3 the effect of riot proximity upon neighborhood evaluations is measured separately for racially antagonistic and for racially nonantagonistic respondents. Two different variables are used as surrogate measures for racial antagonism: the respondents' evaluations of Martin Luther King, Jr., and the respondents' attitudes toward neighborhood integration. In the first column of the table, the effect of not proximity is considered among respondents who favor King, and among respondents who either oppose him or who are ambivalent toward him. In the second column, the effect of riot proximity is considered among respondents who favor and who oppose neighborhood integration. In both instances, the two neighborhood categories closest to riots are collapsed into a single category due to limited numbers of respondents,

The first column of the table indicates that the effect of riot proximity is more pronounced among respondents who oppose or are ambivalent to King, even though the effect is also basically maintained among respondents who favor King. The pattern is less clear when respondents are compared on the basis of their attitudes toward neighborhood integration: respondents who favor neighborhood integration and live close to riot areas are less likely to evaluate their neighborhoods favorably than those who live close to the riot areas and oppose neighborhood integration. Furthermore, separate analyses not shown here produce an even less conclusive pattern of effects upon moving plans.

While these results are quite obviously mixed, there is at least some reason to believe that the effects of riot proximity upon neighborhood evaluations are slightly more pronounced among respondents who oppose or are ambivalent toward King. Table 6.3 suggests that respondents who favor King and live in, or next to, riot areas evaluate their neighborhoods favorably with a probability of .12; anti-King respondents evaluate the same neighborhoods favorably with a probability of .06.[1] These differences are slight, and no evidence has been presented to suggest that the riot effect is absent among those do not demonstrate racial antagonism. Thus, the adverse reaction to neighborhoods near the riot areas may be heightened by racially hostile attitudes, but it is not simply or wholly a response rooted in overt racial antagonism.[2]

Table 6.3. Logistic Estimations of the Neighborhood Evaluations as a Function of Neighborhood Riot Proximity[a]

Neighborhood Evaluation $= 1/(1+e^{-f})$

$$f = a_0 + a_1 PR1P + a_2 PR3P + a_3 PR4P + a_4 PR1A + a_5 PR3A + a_6 PR4A + a_7 DS + a_8 BLK + a_9 IN + a_{10} I + a_{11} E$$

		By the Respondents' Attitudes toward:	
		Martin Luther King, Jr.	Neighborhood Integration
Constant	(a_0)	1.06	.84
		(1.64)	(1.08)
PR1P	(a_1)	− 1.18	−1.31
		(2.60)	(2.20)
PR3P	(a_2)	− .43	− .22
		(1.05)	(.40)
PR4P	(a_3)	− .56	− .21
		(1.76)	(.54)
PR1A	(a_4)	−1.94	− .99
		(3.54)	(1.76)
PR3A	(a_5)	− 1.06	− .31
		(2.26)	(.60)
PR4A	(a_6)	− .78	− .41
		(2.33)	(.99)
DS	(a_7)	.35	−.092
		(.54)	(.12)
BLK	(a_8)	− 1.25	.42
		(1.00)	(.37)
IN	(a_9)	−4.20	−4.48
		(3.78)	(3.39)
I	(a_{10})	.052	.039
		(1.91)	(1.21)
E	(a_{11})	−.024	.0039
		(.57)	
N =		804	569

$PR1P$ = 1 if neighborhood is a not neighborhood or next to not neighborhood, and if respondent is not racially antagonistic; 0 otherwise

$PR3P$ = 1 if neighborhood is within a mile of a riot neighborhood, and if respondent is not racially antagonistic; 0 otherwise

$PR4P$ = 1 if neighborhood is in Buffalo but included above, and if respondent is not racially antagonistic; 0 otherwise

$PR1A$ = 1 if neighborhood is a riot neighborhood or next to a not neighborhood, and if respondent is racially antagonistic; 0 otherwise

$PR3A$ = 1 if neighborhood is within a mile of a riot neighborhood, and if respondent is racially antagonistic; 0 otherwise

$PR4A$ = 1 if neighborhood is in Buffalo but not included above, and if respondent is racially antagonistic; 0 otherwise

$1969(\$9,000)$ = the approximate median family income in Buffalo)

---

[a] In terms of Martin Luther King, a racially antagonistic respondent is defined as one who either opposes or is ambivalent toward King; a nonantagonistic respondent is defined as someone who favors King. In terms of neighborhood integration, a racially antagonistic respondent is defined as one who is opposed to neighborhood integration; a nonatnagonistic respondent is defined as someone who favors neighborhood integration. The t-values for coefficients are shown in parentheses.

Data Source: 1968 Buffalo Survey.

Exit and Loyalty as Responses to Decline

In *Exit, Voice, and Loyalty,* Albert Hirschman (1970) argues that cost-calculating individuals faced with deterioration in a product, service, or institution have two choices: exit or voice. They can quit purchasing a product, consuming a service, or belonging to an organization or institution. Alternatively, they can exercise voice by complaining, writing letters, attending meetings, or voting. Loyalty is an important factor in the individual calculation because it affects the choice of alternatives. Individuals sometimes decide against exit because they feel a sense of loyalty to the declining product or institution.

An important instance of loyalty to a declining institution is frequently cited in many American cities. The ethnic neighborhood may endure because ethnic residents feel a sense of loyalty to it. But what does it mean to assert that ethnics are loyal to their neighborhoods? If Hirschman's analysis is used as a guide, loyalty exists when people tolerate decline without exercising exit. Loyalty affects people's response to decline, but it does not affect their evaluations of decline. Thus, the essence of loyalty, and its true test, is that loyal individuals choose against exit *regardless* of decline, and *in spite* of their dissatisfaction. An important question becomes: can any evidence of residential loyalty be demonstrated among these Buffalo respondents?

Table **6.4** explores several potential sources of residential loyalty. First, loyalty toward the ethnic neighborhood is considered by constructing separate neighborhood ethnicity measures for respondents who are first or second generation ethnic, third generation ethnic, and nonethnic —fourth

Table 6.4. Logistic Estimations of the Residential Orientations as a Function of Neighborhood and Individual Factors[a]

Neighborhood Orientations = $1/(1+e^{-f})$

$$f = a_0 + a_1 PR1 + a_2 PR2 + a_3 PR3 + a_4 PR4 + a_5 DS + a_6 BLK + a_7 IN + a_8 I + a_9 E + a_{10} ETO + a_{11} ET1 + a_{12} ET3 + a_{13} RES + a_{14} AGE$$

		Neighborhood Evaluation	Moving Plans
Constant	(a_0)	.037 (0.04)	−.49 (.59)
PR 1	(a_1)	−2.26 (2.16)	1.60 (2.58)
PR2	(a_2)	−1.42 (2.99)	.96 (2.03)
PR3	(a_3)	−.69 (1.78)	.60 (1.44)
PR4	(a_4)	−.64 (1.98)	.70 (1.92)
DS	(a_5)	.39 (.58)	.78 (1.45)
BLK	(a_6)	−.85 (.64)	.73 (.84)
IN	(a_7)	−3.56 (3.09)	1.47 (1.35)
I	(a_8)	.059 (2.19)	.0030 (.12)
E	(a_9)	.015 (.36)	−.020 (.51)
ET0	(a_{10})	.34 (.23)	−1.04 (.76)
ET1	(a_{11})	−.12 (.09)	−1.46 (1.16)
ET3	(a_{12})	−.06 (.04)	−1.40 (1.08)
RES	(a_{13})	−.28 (1.44)	−.11 (.66)
AGE	(a_{14})	.0080 (1.17)	−.030 (5.19)
N =		793	762

ETO = proportion of neighborhood residents who are ethnics if respondent is nonethnic; 0 otherwise

$ET1$ = proportion of neighborhood residents who are ethnics if respondent is first or second generation ethnic; 0 otherwise

$ET3$ = proportion of neighborhood residents who are ethnics if respondent is third generation ethnic; 0 otherwise

RES = 1 if respondent has always lived in neighborhood; 0 otherwise

AGE = respondent's age in years

---

[a] The t-values are shown in parentheses
Data *Source:* **1968** Buffalo Survey.

generation or beyond. Each variable measures the proportion of neighborhood residents who are first or second generation ethnics for the relevant individual-level category. Thus, these variables make it possible to measure the effect of neighborhood ethnicity upon the residential orientations within each ethnic category among the respondents.

A second potential source of loyalty is also examined: long-term residence. People who have lived in a neighborhood for a large part of their lives might be less willing to move. In this case longevity would be its own reward: neighborhoods might endure because residents have lived in them for long periods of time, and developed loyalties as a result.

Finally, the durability of some urban neighborhoods may not be a matter of free choice on the part of residents. Rather, neighborhood survival may be a function of the age composition of neighborhood residents. For example, ethnic neighborhoods often contain large concentrations of older residents, and these older inhabitants may be less likely to move because they have a lessened capacity for tolerating the stress and physical exertion often associated with residential relocation. In this instance neighborhood survival is less due to loyalty than it is to the high cost of exit for older inhabitants.

As Table 6.4 shows, the only one of these variables that generates a crisp t-value is the respondent's age, and then only for moving plans. Older people are less likely to consider moving (see Figure 6.5), even though they are not more likely to evaluate their neighborhoods favorably. The coefficients measuring the effects of neighborhood ethnicity upon moving plans lie in the expected directions, and their magnitudes meet substantive expectations — the effect is most pronounced among ethnics. Their t-values, however, fail to achieve satisfactory levels. Thus, it would appear that the survival of ethnic neighborhoods under stress is not predicated primarily upon sentiment. Rather, the decision to move or stay in a particular neighborhood is best explained on the basis of neighborhood riot proximity and individual age. Notice that the introduction of age has served

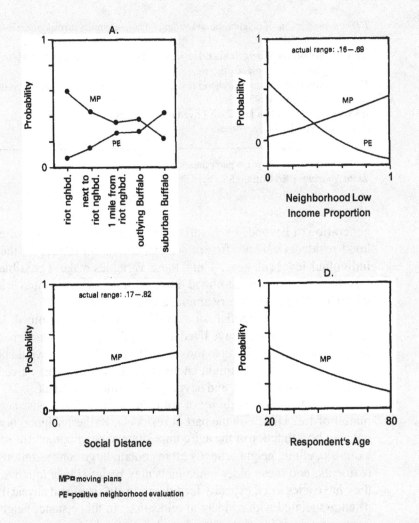

Figure 6.5. Estimated probabilities of moving plans and positive neighborhood evaluations across various neighborhood properties and individual age. Source: the logit model of Table 6.4. In Part A, all other independent variables are controlled at the sample means for nonethnic individuals. In Parts B, C, and D, all other independent variables are controlled at the sample means for nonethnic individuals, except for riot proximity, which is controlled at "one mile from riot neighborhood."

to produce weaker t-values for coefficients measuring the effects of social and racial composition upon moving plans, but stronger t-values for **riot** proximity (see the second column of Table 6.4). In other words, when the contaminating effects of age are controlled — the effects of being unable to move—the importance of riot proximity becomes even more apparent. (Compare Part A of Figure **6.4**with Part A of Figure **6.3.**)

These **data** present a clear and obvious public policy challenge. First, the stability of neighborhoods under **stress** is very fragile and may depend upon an aging population that is unwilling or unable to make a move. Neighborhood longevity is not its own reward, since neighborhood stability depends upon an aging population that is likely to be self-extinguishing. Second, objective conditions in the neighborhood, in particular riot proximity, are important in explaining neighborhood evaluations and white flight. And these factors are, at least in principle, subject to the manipulation of political leaders.

CONCLUSIONS

White flight is not simply the racist response of whites who resist living among blacks, even if it is accelerated by racially hostile attitudes. Black densities within neighborhoods have only weak effects upon neighborhood satisfaction and exit when the effects of neighborhood not proximity and neighborhood affluence are taken into account. These results support an interpretation of white flight that lays the blame on political factors. The **rise** of disorder in the city points to fundamental political failures, and it is to these failures that many emigres are responding.

None of *this suggests that whites are not racists.* Indeed, the extreme separation of racial groupings in Buffalo neighborhoods points to an unwillingness on the part of whites to share living space with blacks. [3] These results do suggest that racist attitudes alone are not the best explanations for white flight. Rather, white flight is a complex response growing out of security needs, social attraction and assimilation, as well as social conflict.

CHAPTER 7

THE SOCIAL CONTEXT OF POLITICAL PARTICIPATION

Previous chapters have been concerned with the neighborhood social context as it affects the direction of a behavior: whether or not people support a party or candidate, whether people associate across class boundaries, whether people support an ethnic politician, whether they decide to move from their residence. Attention now **shifts** to the *extent* of activity: **Does** the social context of an urban neighborhood affect the level of individual residents' political participation? Which acts and which individuals are most affected? What **are** the directions of the effects, and how do the effects depend upon (interact with) individual-level attributes?

SOCIAL STATUS, SOCIAL CONTEXT, AND PARTICIPATION

Many explorations have consistently shown that individual level social status is **an** excellent predictor of political participation: higher status individuals are more likely to perform most political acts than lower status individuals (Milbrath and Goel, 1977: Chap. **3,** pp. 90–106). The mechanisms that lie between social status and Participation are not always as clearly demonstrated. This effort first considers (1) the translation of higher status into more extensive participation, and **(2)** the effect **of** incongruous social environments upon participation. Then, using the Buffalo data in light of these considerations, relationships between the neighborhood social context and various types of participatory activity are examined empirically.

The Links between Status and Participation

Explanations for the greater political activity of higher status individuals usually rest upon individualistic assertions. Intrinsic characteristics of higher status individuals are usually held responsible. Although the indi-

vidual attributes associated with higher social status are certainly important, conditions in higher status social environments are also related to these
behavioral differences.

Verba and Nie (1972: 133) outlined several of the potential connecting links between higher status and more extensive participation:

> Many connective links have been suggested. Some depend on the social
> environment of upper-status citizens: They are more likely to be members
> of organizations, and they are more likely to be surrounded by others who are
> participating. Some connecting links depend on the availability of resources
> and skills: Upper-status citizens have the time, the money, and the knowledge
> to be effective in politics. Other connecting links depend on the psychological
> characteristics of upper-status citizens: They are more likely to be concerned
> with general political problems, and they are more likely to feel efficacious.

The second connective link discussed by Verba and Nie, available resources and skills, is composed of individual attributes that are largely
divorced from the social context. Regardless of the stimuli an individual
receives from the environment, many acts require time, money, and skills—
all of which are individually possessed. In contrast, the other two factors
discussed are more closely tied to an individual's social environment.

First, the extent of individual participation might depend upon the
participation of others in the person's environment. In discussing their
finding that older people generally participate more than younger people,
Verba and Nie suggested that "the data seem compatible with a gradual
learning model of political activity. The longer one is exposed to politics,
the more likely one is to participate" (1972: **148).** The same authors also
found that organizational membership intensifies the relationship between
social status and participation. Organizational memberships encourage
political participation and higher status people are more likely to belong to
organizations (1972: chap. 11). In short, people are more likely to participate if they are around others who participate. A process of imitative
behavior, fostered in more homogeneous higher status environments, can
accelerate the increased propensity to participate that results from greater
individual resources.

Second, Verba and Nie demonstrated that much of the relationship
between individual social status and political participation depends upon
intervening civic orientations (1972: 133-136). These orientations—
psychological political involvement, political efficacy, information about
politics, and a sense of contribution to the community—encourage participation, and higher status individuals are more likely to hold these orientations. Although Verba and Nie treated these orientations as individually
possessed characteristics, they might partially result as a function of the

social environment. Being around people with higher levels of interest, efficacy, and information might foster similar attitudes, habits, and interest. In **this** way a higher status social environment could indirectly stimulate participation by affecting the attitudes that encourage involvement.

In both instances an imitative learning process occurs in which individuals adopt group-based norms. *So,* a higher status social grouping can serve **as** a reference group that sets normative standards for behavior. People might participate more because they adopt the habits and norms that predominate within the higher status grouping to which they belong or aspire (Kelley, 1952).

Incongruous Social Environments

This imitative learning process may not occur at the same rate for **all** individuals. Individual attributes and contextual properties might produce interdependent effects, *so* that the effect of one set of factors depends upon the other set of factors. In particular, the congruence between individual-level social attributes and the social characteristics that predominate within a given environment might be especially important.

In their investigation of the 1940 presidential election in Erie County, New York, Lazarsfeld and his associates discovered strong relationships between: (1) nonvoting and a lack of political interest and (2) **a** lack of political interest and social cross pressures (Lazarsfeld, Berelson, and Gaudet, 1968: 46ff; 61-64). A cross pressure results when sources of political influence push an individual in opposite directions, thereby creating uncertainty and ambiguity regarding an appropriate political response.

Cross pressures need not result from factors in the social environment. Politically incongruous individual-level attributes often work at cross purposes in affecting political preferences and decisions. Affluent blacks and Republican autoworkers are the victims of cross pressures, *independent* of their associates and social environments. However, many cross pressures arise because individuals are located in environments where people of dissimilar attributes predominate. Liberal Democrats who belong to the local Kiwanis chapter are likely to be surrounded at Kiwanis meetings by people emitting political and social cues far different from their own predispositions.

According to the Erie County study, political interest is discouraged by the uncertainty that results from conflicting cues, but incongruities between individual attributes and the social environment might discourage participation in more direct ways **as** well. Occupying a minority status within a social context could exclude minority individuals from positions of real or symbolic influence, discourage group consciousness, and create feelings of political inferiority among minority group members. A lower status individual might be hesistant to engage in political activities dominated by higher status people, and higher status control might discourage or exclude lower status participation. Relying upon the work of Kelley (1952), higher status groups can serve as comparative reference groups for lower status individuals; seeing that higher status individuals dominate politics and realizing the status differential that exists might discourage lower status people from participating.

Expectations Regarding Contextual Influence

Several expectations can be advanced on the basis of this discussion:

1. Individual social status attributes play important roles in determining the extent of political participation. Many participatory acts require the intellectual, financial, and temporal resources generally possessed by higher status individuals.
2. Many participatory acts are, at least to some extent, socially learned and stimulated behaviors. As a result, higher status contexts populated by politically active individuals can encourage individual participation.
3. While being surrounded by politically active individuals can encourage participation, that effect is mediated by individual-level attributes. Individual level characteristics can interact with contextual properties in influencing the extent of participation.

POLITICAL PARTICIPATION IN BUFFALO

The following discussion considers the relationship between individual and contextual social status and the political participation of adult, white, Buffalo area survey respondents.[1] The measures of participation were obtained through a card sort interviewing technique. Interviewers gave respondents the following instructions:

> As you know, every citizen has some kind of relationship to government but people differ in what they think their relationships are or ought to be. On these cards we have listed some things people tell us they do politically. Please sort the cards into four piles, (1) those things you do regularly; (2) those things you do fairly often; (3) those things you seldom do; and (4) those things you never do at all.

Individual Versus Social Activity

While participation in politics often brings people into contact with other participants, some political acts are performed by individuals acting alone. Acts such as these should be less subject to contextual influence. For

POLITICS IN CONTEXT

108

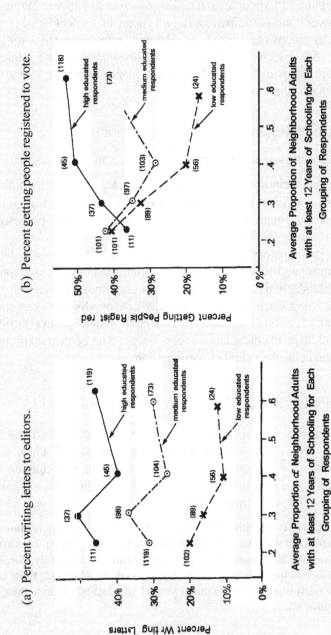

(a) Percent writing letters to editors.

(b) Percent getting people registered to vote.

Figure 7.1. The percentages of white respondents who engage in two different political activities by the proportion of neighborhood adult residents (25 years and over) with high school educations and by individual education. Cutting points on the horizontal axis for the proportion with 12 years of schooling are chosen as quartile divisions for the entire white sample. The N sizes for each grouping of respondents are shown in parentheses. Data source: 1968 Buffalo survey.

instance, writing letters to newspaper editors is an individually based activity carried out in isolation, and the data displayed in part (a) of Figure 7.1 show that individual education is a better predictor of letter writing than the educational levels of other neighborhood residents. A slight contextual relationship does exist among lower educated respondents: higher status neighborhoods are related to lower levels of letter writing. The difference in the proportion writing letters, however, is only 7 percent across contextual categories for the lower educated respondents, while the difference between individually defined status groupings averages 30 percent. Letter writing appears to depend primarily upon individual status characteristics rather than the social status attributes of other neighborhood residents.

In contrast to individually based activities like letter writing, many political activities require that participants either become involved within an organization, interact with other participants, or both. These sorts of acts should be more heavily influenced by the neighborhood social context. For example, the possibility of getting people registered to vote without coming into contact with other people, either the target population or co-workers, seems fairly remote. As part (b) of Figure 7.1 shows, whether or not people engage in the activity is dramatically dependent both upon individual attributes and the social context of their neighborhoods. [2]

Several relationships illustrated in Figii 7.1(b) are especially important and require more careful attention. First, higher status contexts are related to more active participation among high status respondents: higher educated individuals living in high education neighborhoods are 20 percent more likely to work at getting people registered than higher educated individuals living in low education neighborhoods. Second, the effect of higher status contexts is exactly opposite among low status respondents: lower educated individuals living in high education neighborhoods are over 20 percent less likely to work at getting people registered than lower educated individuals living in low education neighborhoods. Finally, considering individual status and political participation apart from the neighborhood context produces a misleading picture. Fifty percent of the 211 higher educated respondents and 32 percent of the 270 lower educated respondents have worked at getting people registered, but this difference overestimates (and even reverses) individual-level differences in low status neighborhoods and underestimates the same differences in high status neighborhoods. Not only does the effect of the social context depend upon individual status attributes, but also the extent to which political activity is structured by individual status depends upon the social context.

Other Participatory Acts

While these findings illustrate the importance of the social context for the performance of two participatory acts, they are slender reeds upon which to

Table 7.1. Item-Index Correlations (Pearson's R) for Measures of Socially and Individually Based Political Participation[a]

Item	Index of individually based participation		Index of socially based participation	
$X(1)$	.50	(825)	.28	(803)
$X(2)$	.69	(825)	.45	(820)
$X(3)$	.64	(825)	.49	(819)
$X(4)$	.56	(825)	.36	(822)
$X(5)$	.42	(817)	.68	(823)
$X(6)$	.34	(821)	.58	(823)
$X(7)$	.41	(822)	.64	(823)
$X(8)$	.44	(823)	.69	(823)
$X(9)$	.44	(818)	.52	(823)
$X(10)$	.43	(821)	.60	(823)
$X(11)$	.44	(821)	.63	(823)

Items for index of individually based participation:
$X(1)$ = vote in elections
$X(2)$ = send protest messages to political leaders when they are doing badly
$X(3)$ = make my views known to public officials
$X(4)$ = write letters to the editors of newspapers

Items for index of socially based participation:
$X(5)$ = participate in a political party between elections as well as at election time
$X(6)$ = give money to help party or candidate
$X(7)$ = work to get people registered to vote
$X(8)$ = take an active part in a political campaign
$X(9)$ = join groups working to improve community life
$X(10)$ = inform others in my community about politics
$X(11)$ = join and support a political party

[a] The numbers shown in parentheses represent the sample sizes upon which the item-index correlations are based.
Data Source: 1968 Buffalo Survey.

generalize. Other political activities must be considered as well. Two indices are used here to measure the extent of participation in both individually and socially based political activities. The items included in each index, along with item-index correlations, are shown in Table 7.1. A respondent's score on an index is determined by summing the reported frequency of participation in each component activity; acts that are never, seldom, fairly often, and regularly performed are scored 0,1,2, and 3 respectively. While the indices suffer from some degree of conceptual and empirical overlap (R = .63), they represent sets of activities that require different levels of social interaction by the participants. Acts included in the index of individually based activity can be socially stimulated, but they are carried out in isolation. Conversely, acts included in the index of socially based participation involve interaction with others. For example, giving money to a party or candidate is part of a cooperative venture; people seldom give money without being asked. Perhaps more important, other people know when and what they give.

Previous discussions and results suggest that individual levels of political activity are affected by individual status attributes, the social context, and an interaction between the two. That is, both individual and contextual social status affect participation, but each factor's effect depends upon the other factor. Part A of Table 7.2 displays the coefficients that are obtained using ordinary least squares to estimate the three factors' effects upon individually based participation. (The interaction between individual and neighborhood education is calculated as the product of the two variables.) While the effect of individual education is relatively slight—the standardized coefficient equals .13—the other two factors' effects are only slightly more pronounced. A standardized coefficient of −.20 shows that higher status neighborhoods are related to lower levels of participation, but this depressing effect is offset among higher educated respondents by the positive effect (.29) of the interaction between individual and neighborhood social status.

While these results meet substantive expectations, the coefficients are not particularly crisp. The t-ratios for the coefficients fail to satisfy commonly accepted levels of statistical significance. This problem is not encountered, however, when the three factors' effects upon socially based participation are considered in part B of Table 7.2. Once again, the standardized coefficient for individual education is of minimal size (.05). The Coefficient for the neighborhood context, however, is strong and negative (−.35), and the coefficient for the interaction between individual and neighborhood education is strong and positive (SO). Further, the coefficients' t-ratios meet any commonly accepted statistical criteria for null hypothesis testing and rejection.[3]

The Table 7.2(B) results become more meaningful when predicted participation levels for two individually defined groupings are compared. The raw score coefficients predict that a sixth grade educated individual would have a socially based participation index score of 3.9 in a neighborhood where 20 percent of residents are high school graduates and an index score of 1.2 in a neighborhood where 70 percent of residents are high school educated. In contrast, a college graduate would have an index score of 6.3 in the same sort of low status neighborhood, but a score of 8.0 in the high status neighborhood.

Table 7.2. Ordinary Least Squares Estimates of Individually and Socially Based Participation among White Residents by the Educational Composition of Residents in the Respondent's Neighborhood, the Respondent's Education Level, and the Interaction between the Educational Level of the Respondent and the Educational Composition of Neighborhood Residents

$$\text{A.} \quad IBP = a_1 + a_2 EN + a_3 INT + a_4 E$$

		Standardized coeficient	Raw score coeficient	t-ratio
Constant	(a_1)		3.19	
EN	(a_2)	− .20	−3.07	1.36
INT	(a_3)	.29	.25	1.39
E	(a_4)	.13	.09	1.28

$$N = 825$$

$$\text{B.} \quad SBP = a_1 + a_2 EN + a_3 INT + a_4 E$$

		Standardized coefficient	Raw score coefficient	t-ratio
Constant	(a_1)		4.51	
EN	(a_2)	− .35	−10.51	2.39
INT	(a_3)	.50	.87	2.48
E	(a_4)	.05	.07	.50

$$N = 823$$

IBP = index of individually based participation
SBP = index of socially based participation
EN = proportion of neighborhood adults *(25* pears and over) with *12* years of schooling or more
E = respondent's schooling in years
INT = $E(EN)$, the product of E and EN

Data Source: 1968 Buffalo Survey.

These results are consistent with those initially displayed in Figure 7.1(b). **High** status social contexts encourage participation among high status individuals, but discourage participation among low status individuals. As a result, political activity is more highly structured by individual status in **high** status contexts **than** in low status contexts. The results lend credibility to the assertion that socially based participation is more subject to contextual influence than individually based participation, but this inference must be made with caution. Variables that vary more are often easier to explain statistically than variables that vary less. The different metrics of two indices may be partially responsible for the different results.[4]

Alternative Explanations

Several alternative explanations that might account for the observed relationships should be considered. First, the relationship between socially based participation and the interaction between individual and contextual social status may be a spurious by-product of an important but unconsidered interaction between individual political identities and the social context. Regardless of individual status levels, Republicans may feel politically and socially at home in high status contexts while Democrats may feel politically and socially at home in low status contexts. As a result, the effect of the social context might be mediated by individual political loyalties rather than by individual-level status. This explanation is not supported, however, in part A of Table 7.3. The effect of the interaction between the social context and Democratic identification is slight in comparison to the interaction between individual and contextual social status, even though its t-ratio is adequately large. Furthermore, the effect is positive—a reflection of the strongly Democratic character of Buffalo politics.

The second alternative explanation has been considered in previous chapters. The relationship between individual participatory levels and the social context might actually be the spurious result of unconsidered individual-level attributes. This possibility is tested in part B of Table 7.3 where controls are introduced for the respondent's family income and the occupation of the respondent's household head, as well as individual education. The controls do little to alter the previously established effect of the social context; coefficients for the contextual factor and for the interaction between contextual and individual social status are maintained.

Finally, it is possible to refute at least partially the frequently voiced criticism of contextual research which argues that relationships between the social context and individual behavior are the result of people choosing reinforcing social environments. For this argument to be valid, it would be necessary to argue that low status people who participate very little choose high status neighborhoods, and high status people who participate very much also choose high status neighborhoods. The second half of this argument may be worthy of consideration, but the first half is not. If higher individual status encourages participation, why would higher status neighborhoods be chosen by the lower status people who are *least* likely to participate? The self-selection argument is at least plausible when a con-

Table 7.3. Tests of Alternative Explanations Concerning Factors that Are Responsible for Socially Based Participation Among White Respondents (Ordinary Least Squares)

A. $SBP = a_1 + a_2EN + a_3INT + a_4E + a_5D$

		Standardized coeficient	Raw score coeficient	t-ratio
Constant	(a_1)		4.42	
EN	(a_2)	− .39	−11.72	2.66
INT	(a_3)	.54	.94	2.68
E	(a_4)	.04	.06	.43
D	(a_4)	.09	2.09	2.61

$$N = 823$$

B. $SBP = a_1 + a_2EN + a_3INT + a_4E + a_5I + a_6PM + a_7W$

		Standardized coefficient	Raw score coefficient	t-ratio
Constant	(a_1)		5.27	
EN	(a_2)	− .39	−11.75	2.38
INT	(a_3)	.50	.88	2.20
E	(a_4)	−.03	− .04	.25
I	(a_5)	.08	.09	1.80
PM	(a_6)	.12	1.36	2.62
W	(a_7)	.01	.14	.34

$$N = 688$$

D = respondent's party identification (1 if Democrat; 0 otherwise) multiplied times EDN
I = respondent's family income in thousand dollar intervals
PM = 1 if respondent is professional-managerial; 0 otherwise
W = 1 if respondent is working class; 0 otherwise

[a] The uncoded third category is clerical-service-sales.
Data Source: *1968* Buffalo Survey.

textual argument rests upon assimilation—when the effect of a contextual property is in the same direction as the related individual-level attribute. The self-selection argument is not plausible when a contextual explanation rests upon conflict, that is, when the effect of a contextual property is in the opposite direction from the related individual-level attribute. People might prefer neighborhoods where they are surrounded by people who share a common viewpoint and ethos, but they are unlikely to prefer a neighborhood where they will be excluded or intimidated. On the basis of the self-selection argument low status individuals living in high status neighborhoods would be expected to participate more, but instead they participate less.

The Giles and Dantico Replication

Giles and Dantico (1982) undertook a contextual analysis of political participation using national survey data which replicated most of this chapter's results. They showed that socially based activity was more susceptible to contextual influence, and higher status neighborhoods were shown to encourage socially based activity among high status people. However, their evidence was mixed regarding a contextual effect among low status people, and they concluded that no contextual effect was present. Thus, while the interaction effect on participation that occurs between individual and contextual status was maintained, the nature of the interaction was modified.

Regardless of the differences that are present between the findings of this chapter and those of Giles and Dantico (1982), their work is a strong statement in support of contextual effects on political participation. They demonstrated important contextual effects that (1) vary systematically across participatory acts, (2) vary systematically across different individuals, and **(3)** produce a relationship between individual status and participation that varies systematically across context.

CONCLUSIONS

This chapter shows that the neighborhood social context is an important connecting tie between individual social status and political participation. Strong evidence exists to reaffirm a familiar finding: higher status individuals generally participate more than lower status individuals. More important, living in a neighborhood context surrounded by higher status people encourages several types of political activity among some individuals. In particular, higher status neighborhoods encourage socially based political activity among higher status individuals. A far different phenomenon occurs among lower status people. Rather than being encouraged to participate in higher status contexts, lower status people are discouraged. Socially based participation is less extensive among low status people living in high status contexts than among low status people living in low status contexts. Higher status social groupings serve distinctly different functions for high and low status individuals, assimilating higher status people at the same time that they exclude lower status people.[5]

As a result of these interactions between the social context and individual social attributes, explaining political participation apart from the social context often misspecifies its relationship to individual-level factors. Such a procedure overestimates individual-level participatory differences in low status neighborhoods, and underestimates individual differences in high status neighborhoods. Thus, the neighborhood social context influences both (1) the extent of individual participation, and *(2)*the relationship between participation and individual social status.

CHAPTER 8

ASSIMILATION, CONFLICT, AND THE MECHANISMS OF CONTEXTUAL INFLUENCE

Two different explanations for contextual influence have been put forward in earlier chapters: (1) the social context as a source of social loyalty and group membership, and **(2)** the social context **as** a structural factor that transforms the content of social interaction. In this chapter the contextual influence mechanisms are compared to each other in a more systematic fashion, and their potential for producing either convergence or divergence — assimilation or conflict — between individuals and groups is established. This analysis uses the Detroit survey data and addresses several issues related to class-based political loyalties: How do contextual effects upon friendship group composition compare to contextual effects upon social class loyalties? Are contextual effects upon political loyalties mediated by the composition of friendship groups and by the formation of social loyalties, or do contextual effects operate independently through other channels and mechanisms? What are the political consequences that derive from "choosing out" of a social context? Can people shield themselves from contextual influence by controlling the content of social interaction?

Mechanisms and Responses: A Short Review

A common finding in contextual research is a politically convergent relationship between individuals and a surrounding social group. Regardless of individual social position, numerous studies have shown that Democratic environments encourage residents to become Democrats, Republican environments produce Republican sympathies, socialist environments generate more socialists, and *so* on. The common unifying theme of these studies is a tendency toward congruence between individual preference and the preferences that are associated with surrounding social groups.

117

Politics is not simply a matter of harmony and congruence between groups and individuals, however. Politics is also related to conflict and discord: people sometimes react in a manner unsympathetic to groups other than their own (Berger, 1960). Social relations such as these are unlikely to produce the political congruence that is so often cited in the contextual research literature. Thus, while some individuals demonstrate political preferences that lie in the direction of the dominant social group, other individuals are likely to respond in a divergent manner.

Two different explanations were constructed in Chapter 2 to account for these sorts of contextual effects: the social context as a factor affecting reference group formation, and the social context as a structural factor affecting social interaction. The first explanation asserts that the political influence of context operates indirectly through its impact upon basic social loyalties and comparisons. The second explanation asserts that the effect of context upon politics is the direct consequence of the manner in which it transforms the pattern and content of social interaction. (See Figure 2.2 and its discussion.)

The social interaction and reference group explanations both assume that the environment affects behavior. A self-selection reinterpretation asserts that individuals seek out compatible environments. Any correspondence between context and political preference is a by-product of individual choice: the social context occupies a socially and politically supportive role that is antecedent and subordinate to the formation of political preferences. A self-selection revision of the reference group model suggests that people with middle class loyalties choose environments to support these loyalties. The self-selection revision of the social interaction model suggests that people exercise discretion in their choice of associates by selecting environments that expose them to the people with whom they wish to associate.

Direct evidence regarding the direction of causation in contextual relationships of political congruence is often difficult to obtain.[1] The present effort has only circumstantial evidence to use in addressing this issue, and thus its discussion must be speculative in nature. Notice however, that the self-selection argument is logically inconsistent with contextual relationships that involve political divergence between groups and individuals. People do not choose environments where they will be politically and socially ill at ease: Wright's (1976a, 1977) southern whites did not choose to live among blacks, and Berger's (1960) class conscious workers did not choose to live among the middle class neighbors whom they resented.

Further, even if self-selection did wholly account for convergent relationships between groups and individuals, the political importance of context would still persist. If people choose environments where they will be socially and politically at ease, then they will be uneasy in other environments. The political role of context would be antecedent to individual choice and political predispositions, but its political significance would still be substantial.

No expectations are developed here regarding the factors that might produce either sympathetic or unsympathetic responses to the social context. Instead, the goal of this chapter is to consider (1) the channels through which these responses are produced—the connecting ties between social classes and political loyalties, and (2) the relationship between these mechanisms and the nature of the political response to context.

POLITICS AND CLASS IN DETROIT

A social interaction measure is constructed based upon a battery of questions that solicits the occupations of each Detroit respondent's three closest friends. Thus, the measure of social interaction is linked to friendship groups and intimate associations. Such a measure has both substantive and theoretical implications that will be more fully considered. Social interaction is measured on a dichotomous scale: Individuals who have only "ingroup" associates are separated from individuals who associate at least partially with members of the "outgroup", where ingroup and outgroup are measured according to ''objective'' occupational criteria. For objectively defined working class respondents, individuals with all working class friends are separated from individuals who have at least one middle class friend. For middle class respondents (professional-managerial or clerical-service-sales), individuals who have all middle class friends are separated from individuals who have at least one working class friend.

A "subjective" measure of class membership is based upon each respondent's self-perceived class identification. Respondents were asked to identify the social class to which they belonged, and their responses to this question serve to identify their own perceived class memberships. The measure is constructed as a dichotomy: working class versus middle or upper class. (For ease of exposition these two categories are referred to as working class and middle class.)

Finally, the social context is measured as the proportion of neighborhood residents who are objectively (occupationally) defined as working class, and the dependent political behavior is measured as Democratic identification versus any other identification or nonidentification. Thus, all dependent behaviors for this analysis—friendship group composition, class loyalties, and party loyalties—are qualitative in nature, and the logit for microdata is therefore employed in the statistical analysis.

Social Class Loyalties and the Neighborhood Context

One explanation for contextual influence points toward social loyalty and individual identification with a group. A second explanation points toward the pattern and content of social interaction. A first step in examining the validity of these explanations is to determine whether group loyalties and social interaction patterns are empirically related to context. Are people who live in working class neighborhoods more likely to identify with the working class? Are they more likely to have working class friends? If neither of these questions can be answered in the affirmative, then either the connecting ties between individuals and groups would not appear to be contextually based, or the contextual linkage between groups and individuals lies elsewhere.

The analysis begins by relating the social context of respondents' neighborhoods to their perceived class identities. Table 8.1 shows the results of a logit analysis that introduces controls in this relationship for individual income and education. The relationship is estimated separately for three objectively defined occupational groups: working class, clerical-service-sales, and professional-managerial. Several features of the table are important. First, notice that the effects of individual income and education are consistently negative across all three groups. Further, the coefficients are large in relationship to their standard errors, with t-ratios that vary from 2.3 to 3.3. Second, the coefficients for neighborhood working class densities lie in the direction of contextual convergence—higher working class densities produce higher probabilities of working class identification—but the coefficients are inconsistent in terms of statistical stability, with t-ratios that vary from .84 to 4.06. Thus, even without calculating the actual magnitudes of effects, the social context does not seem to offer a satisfactory explanation for social class loyalties.

The main exception to this pattern is found among professional-managerial respondents, who demonstrate a strong contextual effect. Within this group, respondents living in working class neighborhoods are much more likely to identify as working class: the estimated contextual effect predicts a probability that varies from .05 to .68 across the observed range of working class densities, with individual income and education controlled at their mean values. Why should the relationship be so much stronger for this higher status group?

A positive relationship between the density of working class residents and the probability of identifying as working class suggests that either: (1) individuals choose an environment based upon their own perceived status and loyalty, or (2) their context encourages the adoption of a congruent self-identification. As was stated earlier, no direct evidence is

Table 8.1. Logistic Estimations of Subjective Class Identification as a Function of Individual Status and the Social Context[a]

$$WID = 1/(1 + e^{-f})$$

$$f = a_1 + a_2E + a_2I + a_3WN$$

		Working Class[b]	Clerical-Service-Sales[b]	Professional-Managerial[b]
Constant	(a_1)	1.71	2.57	− .67
		(2.23)	(1.79)	(.63)
E	(a_2)	− .29	− .39	− .28
		(3.30)	(2.32)	(3.05)
I	(a_3)	− .25	− .60	− .36
		(2.30)	(2.88)	(2.65)
WN	(a_4)	1.29	1.25	4.98
		(1.51)	(.84)	(4.06)
N =		453	139	293

WID = 1 if respondent identifies as working class; 0 otherwise

E   = individual education: 1 = 0–8 grades; 2 = some high school, 9–11 grades; 3 = high school graduate or nongraduate with vocational training; 4 = high school graduate with vocational training; 5 = some college; 6 = college graduate; 7 = college graduate with graduate training

I   = individual income: 1 = under $3000; 2 = $3,000–$4,999,3 = $5,000–$6,999; 4 = $7,000–$9,999; 5 = $10,000–$14,999; 6 = $15,000–$19,999; 7 = $20,000–$24,999; 8 = $25,000 and over

WN = proportion of neighborhood (census tract) residents who are working class

[a] The t-ratios are shown in parentheses.
[b] Defined by respondent's occupational classification.
Data Source: 1966 Detroit Area Study.

available for choosing between these alternatives. It may well be that the relationship works in both directions: the choice of an environment is predicated upon a particular configuration of social loyalties, and the outcome of the choice helps to reinforce those predispositions. However, the presence of a strong contextual relationship within the high status group that is probably best able to exercise residential choice strongly suggests that professional-managerial respondents who identify as workers may live in working class contexts because they are attracted to them.

What are the implications of these findings for contextual influence? Among these Detroit males, self-perceived class membership is most clearly determined on the basis of individual status attributes and individual choice (also see Jackman and Jackman, 1983). However, this is not necessarily the case for other group memberships (see Chapter 5), and class membership in other cultures may not be so wholly tied to individual-level status determinants (Langton and Rapport, 1975). Further, this analysis shows that these findings do not mean that the social context is without social or political consequence, or that contextual influence operates independently from social class loyalties.

Social Interaction and the Social Context

The second explanation for contextual influence points toward patterns of social interaction that are structured by the social context. Thus, attention focuses upon the relationship between the occupational composition of the neighborhood, and the occupational composition of the respondent's three-member friendship group. Are individuals more likely to have friends from the opposite social class if they live in a context where the opposite class is relatively more numerous? This analysis parallels the analysis of friendship choice undertaken in Chapter 4, but more general attention is given to nonlocal as well as local friends. Table 8.2 considers the relationship between the class composition of the social context and the class composition of friendship groups for each of the three occupational groupings. In addition to the individual-level controls for education and income, a control is also included for subjective identification with the working class.[2]

The magnitudes of these contextual effects are calculated by controlling income and education at the sample means, and by controlling subjective class identification at working class for occupationally defined working class respondents, and at middle class for respondents who are occupationally defined as clerical-service-sales or professional-managerial. Using this procedure, the probability that working class respondents have only working class friends varies from .05 at the lowest working class density (.06) to .6 at the highest working class density (.82). The probability that clerical-service-sales respondents associate exclusively with middle class friends varies from .69 to .10 across the same range, and this probability varies from .82 to .22 for professional-managerial respondents. Thus, the effect is quite pronounced for each group.

These are not primarily *casual* encounters that occur across backyard fences, or in lines at the local grocery store, or while taking walks in the neighborhood. More commonplace interactions are quite obviously related in an even more direct way to local population composition, and unless an individual becomes a total recluse, they are nearly impossible to

Table 8.2. Logistic Estimations of Friendship Group Composition as a Function of Individual Status and the Social Context for Various Subjective and Objective Class Groupings[a]

$$H = 1/(1 + e^{-f})$$

$$f = a_1 + a_2 WID + a_3 E + a_4 I + a_5 WN$$

		Working Class[b]	Clerical-Service-Sales[b]	Professional-Managerial[b]
Constant	(a_1)	−2.12	−2.89	.80
		(2.56)	(1.66)	(.87)
WID	(a_2)	.14	.99	− .69
		(.64)	(1.82)	(2.01)
E	(a_3)	− .22	.25	.30
		(2.33)	(1.51)	(3.57)
I	(a_4)	− .10	.67	− .02
		(.96)	(2.92)	
WN	(a_5)	4.42	−4.02	−3.71
		(4.46)	(2.40)	(3.75)
N =		411	122	266

H   = 1 if respondent has 3 ingroup friends; 0 otherwise
WID = 1 if respondent identifies as working class; 0 otherwise
E   = individual education: 1 = 0–8 grades; 2 = some high school, 9–11 grades; 3 = high school graduate or nongraduate with vocational training; 4 = high school graduate with vocational training; 5 = some college; 6 = college graduate; 7 = college graduate with graduate training
I   = individual income; 1 = under $3,000; 2 = $3,000–$4,999; 3 = $5,000–$6,999; 4 = $7,000–$9,999; 5 = $10,000–$14,999; 6 = $15,000–$19,999; 7 = $20,000–$24,999; 8 = $25,000 and over
WN = proportion of neighborhood (census tract) residents who are working class

[a] The t-ratios are shown in parentheses.
[b] Defined by respondent's occupational classification.
Data Source: 1966 Detroit Area Study.

avoid or control. As these Detroit data show, however, even the pattern and content of intimate associations are structured by the social context.

In summary, these results give tentative support to the social interaction explanation for contextual influence. Either because the social context has a direct effect upon interaction patterns, or because people choose contexts on the basis of associational preference, this important tie between groups and individuals is contextually based.

Party Loyalties and the Social Context

As a second step in evaluating these mechanisms of contextual influence, the manner in which they mediate the relationship between the social context and politics is examined. For example, if the relationship between political loyalties and context is wholly explained in terms of friendship group composition, then the relationship should disappear among people with similarly constructed friendship groups. Alternatively, even though the relationship between social class self-identification and the context is problematic, a person's context-independent social class loyalty may determine the response to context. That is, self-identified working class and middle class individuals may respond in different ways to a concentrated working class population.

The Democratic party has been traditionally allied with the working class in the Detroit area. This is reflected in the survey data: **64** percent of working class respondents identify as Democrats, but only 36 percent of middle class respondents do the same. Thus, a common contextual argument suggests that both working class and middle class individuals would be more likely to hold Democratic loyalties in working class contexts, but this effect might be mediated either by individually perceived group membership, or by the content of friendship groups, or by both. Does the social context have any effect on political loyalties after class identifications and the composition of friendship groups are taken into account? Does the effect vary as a function of either friendship group composition or subjective identification with a social class?

Table 8.3 estimates the relationship between the social context and Democratic identification for four combinations of objectively and subjectively defined social classes. The effect of context is estimated separately for middle class and working class identifiers, both among the objectively defined working class respondents and the objectively defined middle class respondents. Due to sample size limitations, the *two* objectively (occupationally) defined middle class categories are combined, but an individual-level control is introduced for clerical-service-sales status in the middle class equation.

For three of the four categories, the direction of the coefficient measuring the effect of the social context upon party identification lies in the direction of assimilation. In these three instances the t-ratios are of respectable magnitude: the coefficients vary between **1.93** and 3.41 times the size of their standard errors. For one group—workers who identify as workers—the effect of context is in a slightly opposite direction, but its t-ratio is only .36, thereby indicating a statistically meaningless relationship.

Table 8.3. Logistic Estimations of Democratic Identification as a Function of Individual Status and the Social Context, for Various Subjectively and Objectively Defined Class Groupings[a]

$$D = 1/(1+e^{-f})$$

$$f = a_1 + a_2 CSS + a_3 WID + a_4 E + a_5 I + a_6 WN_w + a_7 WN_m$$

		Working Class[b]	Middle Class[b]
Constant	(a_1)	− .55 (.54)	− .71 (.93)
CSS	(a_2)		− .36 (1.52)
WID	(a_3)	2.13 (2.09)	− .22 (.22)
E	(a_4)	− .05 (.56)	− .04 (.55)
I	(a_5)	− .14 (1.29)	− .17 (1.84)
WN_w	(a_6)	− .38 (.36)	2.99 (1.93)
WN_m	(a_7)	2.96 (2.09)	2.87 (3.41)
N =		446	424

D = 1 if respondent identifies as a Democrat; 0 otherwise
CSS = 1 if respondent is clerical-service-sales; 0 otherwise
WID = 1 if respondent identifies as working class; 0 otherwise
E = individual education: 1 = 0–8 grades; 2 = some high school, 9–11 grades; 3 = high school graduate or nongraduate with vocational training; 4 = high school graduate with vocational training; 5 = some college; 6 = college graduate; 7 = college graduate with graduate training
I = individual income; 1 = under $3,000; 2 = $3,000–$4,999; 3 = $5,000–$6,999; 4 = $7,000–$9,999; 5 = $10,000–$14,999; 6 = $15,000–$19,999; 7 = $20,000–$24,999; 8 = $25,000 and over
WN_w = proportion of neighborhood (census tract) residents who are working class for respondents who identify as working class; 0 otherwise
WN_m = proportion of neighborhood (census tract) residents who are working class for respondents who identify as middle class; 0 otherwise

[a] The t-ratios are shown in parentheses.
[b] Defined by respondent's occupational classification.
Data Source: 1966 Detroit Area Study.

The magnitudes of the Table 8.3 estimated contextual effects are considered in Figure 8.1, with income and education controlled at the sample means, and with subjective class identification set equal to objectively defined class membership. Working class respondents with working class loyalties show a high level of Democratic identification that is not diminished by middle class contexts. In contrast, the other three groups show pronounced contextual effects: people who live among the working class are more likely to identify as Democrats.

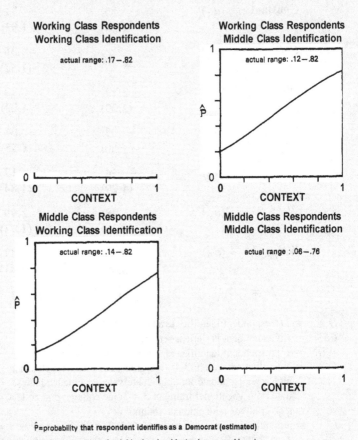

$\hat{P}$=probability that respondent identifies as a Democrat (estimated)

Context=proportion of neighborhood residents who are working class

Figure 8.1. Probability that respondents identify as Democrats, across neighborhood contexts, by occupational class membership and by respondents' self-perceived class identification. *Source:* The logit model of Table 8.3, with education and income controlled at the sample means, with clerical-service-sales status set equal to zero for middle class respondents, and with subjective class identification controlled as indicated.

Why are working class respondents who identify as workers not affected? The Democratic party in Detroit is the ascendant party in an area where the working class is the ascendant class. In their articulation of the breakage effect, Berelson et al. (1954) suggest that political dissonance in the individual's immediate environment produces a situation in which the community environment becomes influential. In other words, a person can only resist the community's political environment if more immediate stimuli point in a uniform and opposite direction. Thus, when workers who identify as workers are surrounded by nonworkers, the community's political environment may be enough to maintain Democratic loyalties.

Consider the opposite case of the middle class respondents who identify as middle class. When they are surrounded by workers in their neighborhood, they are more likely to identify as Democrats. In this instance, the dissonance in their immediate environment exposes them to a climate of opinion that moves them toward the Democratic party.

Social Interaction as a Mediating Factor

Even though the social context structures the content of social interaction, individuals are far from powerless in choosing their own intimate associates. As Finifter (1974) showed, even Republican autoworkers in an overwhelmingly Democratic workplace are able to find Republican friends. The ability of people at least partially to control their own associational patterns, and the potential importance of social interaction as the vehicle for contextual influence, raises several additional questions. First, does the social context have any political influence beyond its ability to structure the choice of personal associates? Second, what are the political consequences for people who "choose out" of a social context by constructing a friendship group that protects them from its composition?

Table 8.4 shows the estimated relationship between the social context and Democratic identification for working class respondents with (1) all working class friends and (2) at least one middle class friend, and for middle class respondents with (3) all middle class friends and (4) at least one working class friend. For all four categories, the coefficient measuring the effect of the social context has a healthy t-ratio: the coefficients vary from 2.16 to 3.13 times the size of their standard errors. The coefficients for three groups lie in the direction of contextual convergence, but for working class respondents with homogeneous working class friendship groups, the probability of Democratic identification increases in contexts where workers are less dominant in the population.

The magnitudes of the Table 8.4 estimated contextual effects are displayed in Figure 8.2, with appropriate controls for the other explanatory

Table 8.4. **Logistic Estimations of Democratic Identification as a Function of Individual Status and the Social Context, for Objective Class Groupings with Differing Friendship Group Compositions**[a]

$$D = 1/(1+e^{-f})$$
$$f = a_1 + a_2CSS + a_3WID + a_4H + a_5E + a_6I + a_7WN_i + a_8WN_o$$

		Working Class[b]	Middle Class[b]
Constant	(a_1)	− .41	−1.31
		(.48)	(1.35)
CSS	(a_2)		− .39
			(1.54)
WID	(a_3)	.24	− .21
		(1.07)	(.75)
H	(a_4)	4.47	.95
		(3.41)	(1.15)
E	(a_5)	− .02	− .04
		(.16)	(.54)
I	(a_6)	− .12	− .18
		(1.14)	(1.79)
WN_i	(a_7)	−4.82	2.26
		(2.67)	(2.24)
WN_o	(a_8)	2.37	4.07
		(2.16)	(3.13)
N =		405	381

D = 1 if respondent identifies as a Democrat; 0 otherwise
CSS = 1 if respondent is clerical-service-sales; 0 otherwise
WID = 1 if respondent identifies as working class; 0 otherwise
H = 1 for respondents whose friends are all from their own social class; 0 otherwise
E = individual education: 1 = 0–8 grades; 2 = some high school, 9–11 grades; 3 = high school graduate or nongraduate with vocational training; 4 = high school graduate with vocational training; 5 = some college; 6 = college graduate; 7 = college graduate with graduate training
I = individual income; 1 = under $3,000; 2 = $3,000–$4,999; 3 = $5,000–$6,999; 4 = $7,000–$9,999; 5 = $10,000–$14,999; 6 = $15,000–$19,999; 7 = $20,000–$24,999; 8 = $25,000 and over
WN_i = proportion of neighborhood (census tract) residents who are working class, for respondents whose friends are from their own social class; 0 otherwise
WN_o = proportion of neighborhood (census tract) residents who are working class, for respondents whose friends are not all from their own social class; 0 otherwise

[a] The t-values are shown in parentheses.
[b] Defined by respondent's occupation classification.
Data *Source:* 1966 Detroit Area Study.

variables. All four groups show significant variation in the probability of Democratic identification across context. For working class respondents who associate exclusively with other workers, however, the effect lies in the opposite direction of contextual divergence. How can these patterns of influence be explained?

It would appear that the social context (1) bears an inconsistent relationship to social class self-identification, (2) shows a pronounced correspondence to friendship group composition, but (3) demonstrates a relationship to political loyalties that persists even when intimate associa-

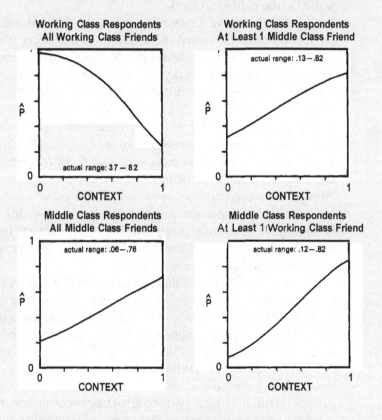

$\hat{P}$=probability that respondent identifies as a Democrat (estimated)

Context=proportion of neighborhood residents who are working class

Figure **8.2.** Probability that respondents identify as Democrats across neighborhood contexts, by occupational class and friendship group composition. Source: The logit model of Table **8.4,** with education and income controlled at the sample means, with clerical-service-sales status set equal to zero for middle class respondents, with subjective class identification controlled at occupationally defined class membership, and with friendship group composition controlled as indicated.

tion and social class loyalties are controlled! This persistent political effect might be explained as a self-selection component to the contextual relationship. That is, because the contextual relationships persist even after social class identification and friendship group composition are taken into account, an aspect to the contextual relationship may be isolated that is due to a tendency of individuals to choose social environments that fit their own political and social predispositions and preferences. **This** individual-level explanation is less than satisfactory: these predispositions would seem to be tapped by the consideration of friendship selection and class loyalty, but the contextual relationships are maintained even when both factors are con-, trolled at the individual level.

An alternative explanation is that the political influence of social interaction extends beyond the interactions that occur within friendship groups. That is, the less intimate interactions that have been ignored in this discussion — talks over backyard fences, casual encounters while taking **walks** or standing in line at the grocery, and so on—may be politically influential even though they do not occur between close and intimate associates. Indeed, Sprague **(1982)** argues that social interaction may be persuasive not because it is intensive or intimate, but rather because it is frequent and recurring: *the most important social learnings are those that are reinforced continually.* In short, the context may become influential through a more generalized milieu effect that occurs because individuals are imbedded within distinctive social and political worlds. Such an effect **is** impossible to measure *independently* of the context. Indeed, it points toward a contextual effect that is not captured by other surrogate measures: social networks, class loyalties, etc.

A second feature of these relationships that deserves attention is the unsympathetic response to context among workers who exclusively associate with other workers. An increased middle class presence has a reverse effect upon the political loyalties of these workers, encouraging a *higher* level of Democratic identification. Thus, we are witnessing a variation of the Finifter (1974) effect. This group has chosen out, or been forced out, of their social context. Whether by their own choice, or by the choice of upper status individuals who rejected them as associates, these men have constructed friendship groups that serve as "protective environments" in middle class contexts. The political implication is clear: overcompensation by a higher level of adherence to working class political norms. Rather than being assimilated by the prevailing sentiments of their neighborhoods, they react on the basis of social discord. [3]

Why is the same negative effect not present among middle class men who exclusively associate with middle class friends? Once again, the political environment of Detroit rewards the Democrats and punishes the

Republicans. **As** Miller has shown (1956), a minority party generally receives less than its "fair share" of political support. Given the political climate of Detroit, middle class adherence to the Democratic party has a very different significance than the rejection of Democratic loyalties among working class individuals. Viewed in slightly different terms, the survey data show that it is far more acceptable for middle class men to be Democrats (36 percent) than it is for working class men to be Republicans (16 percent).

CONCLUSIONS

This chapter **is** motivated by several theoretical expectations regarding the contextually based linkages between groups and individuals. Mechanisms of contextual influence have been constructed to explain both political convergence and divergence between groups and individuals. These mechanisms have also been employed to examine the contextual dependence of political loyalties. The analysis adds to an impressive body of evidence suggesting that groups in politics are not merely collections of individuals with coincidental interests. Depending upon the social context, people with similar social characteristics have very different political loyalties. The relationship between political loyalties and context is complex, however, and requires an understanding of the linkages between individuals and groups. Several findings related to these social bonds stand out.

First, the social context is more clearly related to the social class composition of friendship groups than it is to self-perceived social class memberships. Persons living among workers may or may not be more likely to identify as members of the working class, and their social class loyalties are more obviously affected by *individual* social status attributes. Persons living among workers *are* more likely to have working class friends, even when both objectively and subjectively defined class membership are taken into account.

Second, when both self-perceived and objectively defined social class identification are treated as simultaneous mediating influences, greater working class densities increase the probability of Democratic identification for everyone except working class individuals who identify as workers. These class conscious workers demonstrate a high probability of Democratic identification *regardless* of the social context. When both objectively defined social class and friendship group composition are treated as simultaneous mediating influences, a greater working class concentration in the neighborhood increases the probability of Democratic identification for everyone except working class individuals who associate exclusively with other workers. For these individuals, the probability of

Democratic identification is increased by a greater density of *middle* class neighborhood residents.

These findings have several implications for explanations of the social context's political influence. At least in terms of class and politics in Detroit, the social context fails to show a strong and consistent relationship to social class loyalties. It seems more likely that the political influence of context is realized through social interaction processes. The importance of contextual influence is not subsumed by its effect upon patterns of *intimate* association, however. Thus, it may be that the social context is important not only because it affects patterns of intimate association, but also because it affects the casual, less personal, and nearly inescapable encounters that occur with greater frequency and regularity.

Finally, the political response to context varies across different groups and individuals in a way that emphasizes (1) the importance of the larger political environment for a theory of contextual influence, and (2) the potential for both politically sympathetic and unsympathetic responses to the increased presence of a social group. This analysis shows that social groups are sometimes resistant to influence by other social groups, and this resistance appears to be supported by the larger political environment. Furthermore, some working class respondents appear to withdraw from middle class contexts by exclusive association with other workers, and by a higher level of Democratic identification,

CHAPTER 9

ASSIMILATION, CONFLICT, AND TIPPING POINTS

Politically convergent and divergent responses to the social context are not wholly separate and independent ways of responding to the presence of a social group in the population. Rather, both responses are rooted in a common social process that produces a high level of interdependence between assimilation and conflict in urban contexts. This chapter capitalizes upon the variability of contextual effects across context to consider an explanation that ties together assimilation and conflict. The effort is admittedly speculative in nature, and is based upon a pattern of relationships that may be idiosyncratic to a single data set. This does not compromise the value of what follows, however, or foreclose the opportunity to work toward more sophisticated explanations for contextual influence.

Systematic patterns of variation in contextual influence are central to this chapter's arguments. The political influence of the neighborhood social context not only varies across individuals and behaviors, but also across neighborhood contexts. Different individuals and behaviors are differentially influenced by variations in context, and both the magnitude and direction of contextual influence are conditioned by the social context.

The focus of this chapter is upon the pattern of contextual influence demonstrated previously among Buffalo respondents in Figure 4.1(c). Several questions guide the consideration of its theoretical significance: **How** does the effect of the neighborhood social context, measured as working class densities in the neighborhood, vary across context within individually defined occupational classes? How are these patterns of variation across context related to processes of conflict and assimilation? What consequences do these interdependent processes of conflict and assimilation have for individual behavior, and for the structure of politics?

VARIATIONS IN CONTEXTUAL RESPONSES ACROSS CONTEXT

Before considering the Buffalo data, it is useful to establish a framework for analyzing the interdependence of conflict and assimilation. This framework is built upon two concepts: differential susceptibility to contextual influence as a function of social densities, and tipping points.

Differential Susceptibility and Tipping Points

In Chapter 2 the concepts of assimilation and conflict were defined relative to the political consequences of the social context. Assimilation involves the adoption of a political practice or orientation through a process of social transmission: it is a consensual, favorable response to a social group within the population. In contrast, conflict is a dissonant response to a social group: it points to the adoption of political practices and orientations as the result of discordant social reactions and encounters. The political response to context is not always a uniform simple function of either conflict or assimilation, however. More complex responses to context also occur.

Using a data set that included British respondents living in residential areas with a wide array of social class mixtures, Butler and Stokes (1974: 134-135) displayed important nonlinear relationships between an area's class composition and the proportional party support given by members of a class. Even in solidly middle class areas, working class support for the Labour Party did not fall below 40 percent. Working class support for the party increased slowly from that level as a function of greater working class densities, but the rate of change in the increase *kept* increasing as working class densities grew. The authors also showed a nonlinear relationship between middle class support for the Conservatives and middle class residential concentrations. Both findings suggest complex patterns of differential susceptibility to contextual influence that result in variable reactions across context within a single individually defined grouping.

Along these same lines, it is useful to review the Finifter effect. In her study of the workplace social environment, Finifter (1974) discovered that Republican workers at an automobile plant with an overwhelmingly Democratic work force were likely to seek out other Republicans as associates, while Democrats were not as selective in their choice of friends. She regarded the friendship group as a "protective environment for political deviants." Finifter's work is suggestive: processes of group conflict appear to occur simultaneously with processes of group assimilation. The assimilation process predominates up to the point that group members are in a minority position threatening to their own identity or status. At that "tipping point," members of the minority turn inward in an attempt at preserving their own identities.

The Detroit data analyzed earlier in this monograph shed further light on the problem. Two findings stand out:

1. Individuals are more likely to resist association across social class boundaries if their own social class occupies an extreme minority position within the context. (See Chapter 3.)
2. Working class individuals who associate exclusively with other working class individuals demonstrate higher levels of Democratic identification in *middle class* contexts. Thus, at least among workers, individuals who are secluded from the context by the composition of their friendship groups are more likely to demonstrate political loyalties that diverge from the context. (See Chapter 8.)

By putting these two findings together, an important expectation emerges: *the potential for a politically conflictive response to context should increase among groups that occupy minority status.* And, theoretically at least, a tipping point should exist that marks the transition between politically congenial and conflictive responses to context.

In summary, assimilation and conflict occur within social contexts, and sometimes both processes occur simultaneously. Individuals are frequently assimilated by the groups that claim them as members ("ingroups"), but they can also be assimilated by groups to which they do not belong ("outgroups"). Thus, white collar workers in blue collar neighborhoods sometimes vote Democratic. Conflict also occurs between groups: white collar workers can be excluded, threatened, or repulsed by their blue collar neighbors. The tipping point concept suggests that individuals are assimilated by outgroups up to a critical outgroup density. Once that density is attained, individuals react adversely to increased outgroup concentrations, The politics of assimilation is replaced by a politics of conflict. [1]

Potential Patterns of Contextual Influence

Based upon this discussion, several potential patterns of variation in contextual influence can be identified. As parts A, B, and C of Figure 9.1 show, contextual influence has three possible directions: no influence, assimilation, and conflict. Each of these three examples assumes that the effects (or noneffects) are linear, that the gradient or magnitude of the influence is constant across context. A unit change in a contextual density has a uniform effect upon a political response independent from the location of that change on the social density continuum.

Parts D and E of Figure 9.1 display *nonlinear* patterns of influence

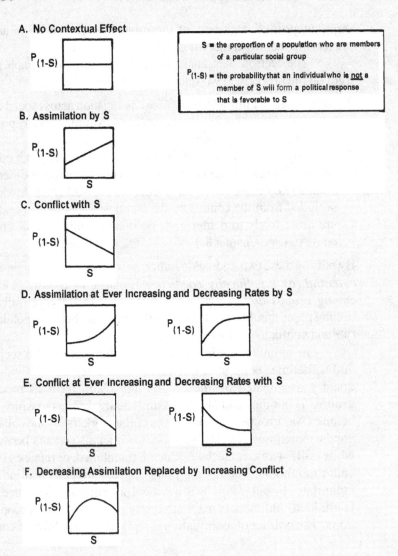

Figure 9.1. Potential patterns **of** contextual influence.

based upon assumptions of differential responsiveness to contextual stimuli across context. In each instance the magnitude of a contextual effect varies as a function of context with individual-level variables controlled. **As** the contextual outgroup density becomes more pronounced, individuals react (1) favorably at an ever increasing rate, (2) favorably at an ever decreasing rate, (3) conflictively at an ever increasing rate, and **(4)** conflictively at an ever decreasing rate. Finally, **Part** F of the figure presents the tipping point phenomenon. Individuals react favorably at a decreasing rate up to a point—the tipping point. After that point, individuals react conflictively at an ever increasing rate.

POLITICS AND TIPPING POINTS IN
BUFFALO NEIGHBORHOODS

The interdependence of conflict and assimilation, and the presence of tipping points, are empirical questions open to verification. The analysis turns to these questions, using the Buffalo data of Figure 4.1 (C) that are recreated in Figure **9.2** for the reader's convenience. The pattern of relationships exhibited in the figure is not adequately summarized on the basis of individual effects, contextual effects, and interactions between the two.

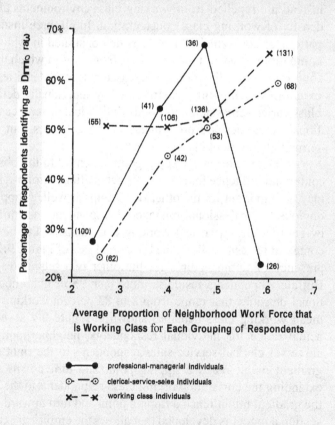

Figure 9.2. The percentage of white respondents identifying as Democrats by individual occupational class and the proportion of neighborhood residents who are working class. Cutting points on the horizontal axis for the proportion working class are chosen **as** quartile divisions for the entire white sample. The *N* sizes for each grouping of respondents are shown in parentheses. *Data source:* 1968 Buffalo survey.

The proportion of respondents identifying as Democrats varies **as** a nonlinear function of context *within* individual occupational categories. Further, these nonlinear patterns vary *across* the individual-level categories in substantively important ways.

First, reading from *right* to *left,* working class respondents are assimilated into nonworking class contexts at a generally decreasing rate. Second, reading from *left* to *right,* clerical-service-sales respondents are assimilated into working class contexts at a generally decreasing rate. Clerical-service-sales respondents are increasingly less receptive to working class contexts, and, conversely, working class individuals are increasingly less receptive to nonworking class contexts. Finally, reading from *left* to *right,* professional-managerial respondents cease being assimilated and instead are repelled from working class environments after some critical density of working class concentration. In all three instances a nonlinear pattern of contextual influence is demonstrated in which individuals become more resistant to assimilation by groups to which they do not belong (outgroups) as a function of increased outgroup densities. As a result, the extent to which politics is structured by individually defined occupational class varies across neighborhoods. Individual differences between occupational categories are pronounced at the extremes, but minimized at intermediate levels of class segregation.

The notion of a tipping point is central to the observed pattern of contextual influence for at least one occupational group in Figure 9.2, and it may be important for the other two groups as well. A tipping point is most obvious for professional-managerial respondents: assimilation is replaced by conflict after a critical working class density. Further, the aggregated contextual densities along the horizontal axis of Figure 9.2 might mask the presence of tipping points for the other two sets of respondents. These Buffalo respondents reside in more than 95 neighborhoods with occupational densities that range from 8 to 83 percent working class. Thus, the mean working class densities shown in Figure 9.2 severely truncate the actual range for individual respondents' neighborhoods. Extending the curve for clerical-service-sales respondents to the right suggests that the gradient might reach a tipping point and turn downward. Conversely, extending the curve for working class respondents to the left suggests that the gradient might reach a tipping point and turn upward. In the following section a model is developed that allows the empirical exploration of these possibilities.

A Model of the Political Response to Context

The concept of a tipping point can be incorporated into a mathematical model of the political response to context. Based on the work of Sprague (1976) and

Przeworski (1974), the effect of the neighborhood social context upon the extent to which a professional-managerial or clerical-service-sales individual politically sympathizes with the working class can be written as:

$$R = p_1 + p_2 S + p_3(1-S) \tag{9.1}$$

where

R = the individual's political response to context, conceived as the extent of political sympathy toward the working class

p_1 = the effect of individual occupational class upon the response

p_2 = the effect of interaction with the outgroup, in this case working class residents, upon the response

p_3 = the effect of interaction with the ingroup, in this case non-working class residents, upon the response

S = the probability of interacting with a working class resident measured as the proportion of residents in the neighborhood who are working class and assuming random social interaction (Coleman, 1964: chap. 17)

$(1-S)$ = the probability of interacting with a nonworking class resident measured as the proportion of residents in the neighborhood who are not working class and assuming random social interaction

This model acknowledges the possibility of individual-level effects, contextual effects, and, because the p_i are allowed to vary among individually defined groups, interdependencies between the two. The model does not allow for variations in contextual effects across context—the response to context is assumed to be linear. Social interaction with a particular group has an effect that is specified as being constant across context, and the result of interaction must therefore be *either* conflict *or* assimilation.

    Consider again the clerical-service-sales and professional-managerial respondents of Figure 9.2. This figure suggests that the effect of the outgroup, S, depends upon a tipping point that demarcates assimilation from conflict. Thus, the outgroup interaction term for these two individually defined groupings can be rewritten as:

$$p_2(T_w - S)S$$

where T_w is the critical tipping point density. **Working** class proportions less than this level produce a political response rooted in assimilation, and working class proportions greater than this level produce a response rooted in conflict.[2] Conversely, making use of the tipping point concept for workers results in the following outgroup interaction term:

$$p_2(T_n - (1-S))(1-S)$$

where T_n is the critical tipping point density: nonworking class proportions less than this level produce a political response rooted in assimilation, and nonworking class proportions greater than this level produce a response rooted in conflict. Thus, the substantive model for professional-managerial and clerical-service-sales respondents is

$$R = p_1 + p_2[(T_w - S)S] + p_3(1-S) \qquad (9.2)$$

And, the substantive model for working class respondents is

$$R = p_1 + p_2[(T_n - (1-S))(1-S)] + p_3 S \qquad (9.3)$$

Democratic Identification and the Political Response to Context

As it is conceived here, the political response to context cannot be directly observed; it can only be assessed as it affects various political behaviors. The observed variation in Democratic identification across context (see Figure 9.2) is a function of this political response in the same way that additional political behaviors might also be affected.

Other factors beside the political response to context are capable of affecting the probability of Democratic identification, however. A competing explanation for relationships between individual behaviors and contextual properties is that unconsidered individual-level factors are responsible (Hauser, 1974). According to **this** view, blue collar residents of blue collar neighborhoods are more apt to identify **as** Democrats than their counterparts in higher status neighborhoods because of lower income and educational levels. Thus, Democratic identification can be expressed **as** a function of the political response to context, **as** well **as** several other individual-level status factors:

$$D, = f(R, ED, INC) \qquad (9.4)$$

where D_x is the probability of Democratic identification by a member of group **x**, R is the political response to context (see equations 9.2 and 9.3), ED is individual education, and INC is individual income.

Logit for microdata provides an appropriate means for measuring the impact of these factors upon Democratic identification (Hanushek and Jackson, 1977). If **this** estimation technique is used, then the probability of Democratic identification among professional-managerial and clerical-service-sales respondents is expressed in the following, and by now familiar, nonlinear form:

$$D_x = 1/(1 + e^{-f}) \qquad (9.5)$$

where

$$f = p_1 + p_2[T_w - S)S] + p_3(1-S) + a_4 ED + a_5 INC \qquad (9.6)$$

The functional form, f, can be algebraically rearranged as follows:

$$f = a_1 + a_2S + a_3S^2 + a_4ED + a_5INC \qquad (9.7)$$

where

$$a_1 = p_1 + p_3$$
$$a_2 = p_2T_w - p_3$$
$$a3 = -p_2$$

The logistic estimation technique produces estimates for the a_i, but an inspection of equation **9.7** shows that the substantive parameters, T_w and the p_i, are underdetermined.

Fortunately, an additional constraint upon one of the parameters can be obtained based upon substantive criteria. The tipping point, $T_,$, represents a discontinuity in the response to an outgroup that changes from assimilation to conflict as a function of outgroup densities. It also represents that point at which favorable sympathies toward the outgroup should be at a maximum if more pronounced ingroup densities discourage such sympathies (as they should).

Thus, rules of differential calculus can be used to obtain an estimate for T_w. Setting the first order partial derivative of the functional form (equation **9.7**) with respect to S equal to zero and solving for S gives the tipping point:

$$T_w = -a_2/2a_3 \qquad (9.8)$$

This additional constraint upon a substantive parameter yields a determined system of equations.[3]

Taking account of the transposition of ingroup and outgroup results in the following determined system for the second substantive model (see equation 9.3):

$$a_1 = p_1 + p_2T_n - p_2$$
$$a2 = {}^2p_2 - p_2T_n - p_3$$
$$a3 = -p_2$$
$$1 - (-a_2/2a_3) = T_n$$

Statistical estimates for the a_i can be obtained for each of the three individually defined groupings through the estimation of a single equation (Wright, 1976b). This single equation uses dummy variables and contextual properties to measure the impact of context upon each individually defined occupational category.

Two different estimations of the logistic model, based on this procedure, are shown in Table **9.1**. The first estimation, shown in **part A**, includes the same contextual factors for each individual category. Using the t-values as guides, the effects of working class densities and the square of working class densities are established for everyone except the working class respon-

Table 9.1. Two Logistic Estimations of the Effects Due to Contextual- and Individual-Level Factors for Three Individually Defined Occupational Groups

$$D = 1/(1+e^{-f})$$

$$f = a_1 + a_2W + a_3CSS + a_4SB + a_5SB^2 + a_6SW + a_7SW^2$$

$$+ a_8SP + a_9SP^2 + a_{10}E + a_{11}I$$

		A. First *Specification* Coefficient	t-ratio	B. Second *Specification* Coefficient	t-ratio
Constant	(a_1)	−2.80	1.92	−2.79	1.92
W	(a_2)	3.12	1.90	3.31	2.31
CSS	(a_3)	.99	.57	.99	.57
SB	(a_4)	2.83	.80	2.05	2.50
SB^2	(a_4)	−.77	.23	(excluded)	
SW	(a_6)	10.54	2.40	10.54	2.40
sw^2	(a_7)	−8.17	1.97	−8.17	1.97
SP	(a_8)	21.48	2.73	21.48	2.73
SP^2	(a_9)	−26.58	2.51	−26.58	2.51
E	(a_{10})	−.13	4.05	−.13	4.05
I	(a_{11})	.02	.86	.02	.86
		$N = 783$		$N = 783$	

Computational Variables
S = the proportion of neighborhood residents who are working class
PM = 1 if respondent is professional-managerial; 0 otherwise

Variables in Equation
D = 1 if respondent identifies as Democrat; 0 otherwise
W = 1 if respondent is working class; 0 otherwise
CSS = 1 if respondent is clerical-service-sales; 0 otherwise
SB = WR(S)
SW = CSS(S)
SP = PM(S)
E = respondent's education calculated as the number of years of schooling (the highest category, 17, equals postgraduate)
I = respondent's family income in thousand dollar intervals (the three highest intervals are: $15,000–$19,999, $20,000–$24,999 $25,000 and over)

Data Source: 1968 Buffalo Survey.

Table **9.2.** Tipping Point Model Parameters for Professional-Managerial and for Clerical-Service-Sales Respondents

Parameter	*Professional-Managerial* Computation	Value
T_w	$-a_8/2a_9$	.40
p_1	a_1-p_3	8.06
p_2	$-a_9$	26.58
p_3	$p_2T_w-a_8$	−10.85

Parameter	*Clerical-Service-Sales* Computation	Value
T_w	$-a_6/2a_9$	.64
p_1 [a]	a_1-p_3	2.52
p_2	$-a_7$	8.17
p_3	$p_2T_w-a_6$	− 5.31

[a] The coefficient operating on the dummy variable for clerical-service-sales respondents, a_3, is left out of these calculations because its t-ratio falls **below** commonly accepted levels.

Source: Logit model of Table 10.1.

dents. The second specification of the model (in part B of the table) excludes the squared working class density for working class respondents (SB^2), thereby producing a statistically stable coefficient for the nonsquare working class density (SB). Substantively this means that no tipping point exists for working class respondents even though the relationship between working class densities and the political response to context appears to be nonlinear in Figure 9.2.4 Based upon the Table 9.1(B) coefficients, substantive parameters (the p_i) are obtained for professional-managerial respondents and for clerical-service-sales respondents. These parameters are shown in Table 9.2.

What Do the Parameters Mean?

First, the tipping points can be directly compared among individually defined status groupings. The tipping point for working class respondents that seems to be present in Figure 9.2 does not persist when the logistic model is estimated. Thus, the working class response may vary across context, but these working class individuals do not react in a conflictive manner to the presence of nonworking class residents—the response never "turns over" from assimilation to conflict.

Tipping points *are* present for the other two individually defined occupational groupings. The tipping point for professional-managerial respondents is 40 percent working class compared to a tipping point of *64* percent working class for clerical-service-sales respondents. In short, professional-managerial respondents turn from assimilation to conflict at a much lower working class density.

The other model parameters cannot be directly compared across individually defined social categories. As S and S^2 are highly correlated and have opposite effects upon the logit, their statistically estimated coefficients, the a_i, are interrelated. A second limitation upon the model parameters is that they do not directly predict the probability of Democratic identification. Rather, they predict the logit for the probability (see Appendix B). Because the logit is a nonlinear transformation of the probability, the magnitude of the parameters' effects upon the probability cannot be directly assessed or compared. Thus, for both reasons, the p_i are interdependent for a single grouping, and should not be compared across social categories.

The model parameters *can* be used to estimate the unobservable political response to the social context as it is expressed in equation 9.2. For both clerical-service-sales and professional-managerial respondents, the parameters show that ingroup interaction discourages a politically sympathetic response toward the working class. Outgroup interaction encourages such a response for respondents living in neighborhoods below the tipping point—.40 for professional-managerial and .64 for clerical-service-sales respondents—and discourages a sympathetic response for respondents living in neighborhoods with outgroup densities greater than the tipping point.

The parameters can also be used to decompose the contextual effect between outgroup and ingroup interaction. A total contextual effect can be conceived as the absolute value of the ingroup interaction term plus the absolute value of the outgroup interaction term. The percent of a contextual effect at a given density that is the result of outgroup or ingroup interaction can be determined by substituting in the appropriate density of workers, taking its absolute value, and dividing by the total contextual effect.

This procedure is employed in Figure 9.3. The figure displays, for both groups, *a predominant role for ingroup interaction.* The figure also shows that outgroup interaction is important as a factor encouraging conflict for both groups, but that this conflictive role is most pronounced for professional-managerial respondents. (These observations do not, of course, take into account the changing magnitudes of the total contextual effects, which also vary across context.)

Finally, these nonlinear patterns of susceptibility to contextual

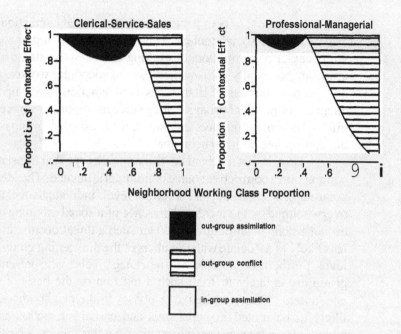

Figure 9.3. Proportion of total contextual effect attributable to outgroup assimilation, outgroup conflict, and ingroup assimilation at varying blue collar densities for clerical-service-sales and professional-managerial respondents. *Source:* The logit model of Table 9.1 (also see Table 9.2).

stimuli, which vary across individually defined groups, have important consequences for the structure of politics. Individual political loyalties are more highly structured by occupational class membership at the extremes of class segregation, and this structuring is minimized at intermediate levels of segregation (see Figure 9.2). In these intermediate neighborhoods the **mix** of ingroup and outgroup cues and responses results in a politics that minimizes individual-level political differences between occupational classes. Thus, the social context is not only important as a source of political influence on individual behavior, but also **as** a factor that alters the social structuring of politics.

Alternative Mechanisms for Contextual Influence

The tipping point **marks** a directional change in the political response to the social context, and it points toward two different sets of mechanisms that are responsible for translating the neighborhood social context into political influence. **In** a purely assimilation process (see Figure 2.2 and its discussion), the content of both personal and impersonal interaction is positively affected by the social context. Thus, individuals living in social contexts with heavier concentrations of working class individuals are more likely to associate personally with workers, and to encounter workers on an everyday, impersonal basis. Both types of interaction have important consequences for political behavior: they serve as important sources of political information and guidance, and they serve to establish group norms regarding appropriate political behavior.

How is this mechanism different from one that translates the social context into a conflictive source of political influence? The idea of a tipping point suggests that, beyond a certain level, individuals feel threatened or overwhelmed by the increased presence of a social grouping to which they do not belong—an outgroup. When such a threat occurs, individuals are less likely to associate with members of the threatening group at a personal level. Furthermore, people who react negatively to the presence of a social group are unlikely to form such a reaction on the basis of personalized encounters. Thus, conflictive responses to the neighborhood context are likely to be rooted in impersonal and casual interaction and its consequences for reference group formation, but this reference group function is far different from the norm setting function. Rather than setting norms, the reference group serves as a basis for comparison (Kelley, 1952). People compare another social grouping to their own, find the other group deficient or threatening or overwhelming, and react accordingly.

These mechanisms have been discussed in their ideal type form, but they clearly do not exist in isolation from each other. A process of assimilation appears to be overtaken by a process of conflict as a function of increased outgroup densities. Even when a tipping point is present, the resulting conflict is foreshadowed by decreased assimilation. Normative reference group functions and comparative reference group functions are interdependent parts of a larger whole: social and political loyalties and identities.

In short, different but interdependent mechanisms are likely to be responsible for responses to context rooted in conflict and assimilation. These mechanisms and responses have important implications for a commonly offered criticism of research on the social context. The self-selection criticism of research on context argues that individuals choose to live in socially reinforcing environments, thereby creating population distributions that give the artificial appearance of a contextual effect. As I have suggested before, this counterargument is at least plausible when an argument relating a behavior to context is based upon assimilation. Self-selection is much less persuasive when an argument centers upon conflict; people do not choose environments they do not like, or neighborhoods where they feel out of place. An explanation has been offered that accounts for the observed patterns of both assimilation and conflict; the self-selection alternative cannot do the same.

CONCLUSIONS

While the neighborhood social context is an important source of political influence, the effect of context is often complex. The magnitudes of the contextual effects considered here are not uniform either across occupational classes, or within occupational classes and across contexts. People form different responses to context as a function of varying individual-level characteristics, and people with the same individual-level characteristics form different responses as a function of different social mixes.

The central finding of this chapter can be stated as follows: these Buffalo respondents are, in general, less likely to demonstrate a politically congenial response to occupational groups other than their own when their own occupational group is less predominant in the population. The magnitude of the assimilation effect by an outgroup declines as a direct function of the ingroup population density. In some instances, when a tipping point is present, a numerically overwhelmed group even demonstrates a politically conflictive response to the numerically superior group.

CHAPTER 10

CONCLUSIONS AND CONSEQUENCES

This concluding chapter is aimed at accomplishing four tasks. First, answers are provided to the questions that motivate the study. Second, the consequences of the study for theories of urban social life and group-based politics are examined. Third, the study's conclusions are related to an important issue in urban areas: social segregation and exclusionary land use policies. Finally, attention is directed toward the consequences of this study for theories of democratic politics.

Some Answers to Questions

This investigation of neighborhoods and individual political behavior has been motivated by several questions that can be addressed on the basis of foregoing analyses.

First, does the neighborhood social context influence political behavior?

Yes. A range of behaviors and activities is shown to be subject to contextual influence: friendship selection, partisan loyalties, ethnic loyalties, residential satisfaction and white flight, and political participation. In each instance a set of behaviors is conditioned upon characteristics of people other than the actor. The actor's own characteristics do not fully determine his or her behavior.

Second, are some behaviors and some individuals more affected by the social context than others?

Once again, the answer is yes. In terms of partisan support, socially visible behaviors are generally affected more than less obvious behaviors. Thus, the opinions of discussants are affected more than the opinions of nondiscussants, and opinions more likely to be discussed are affected more than those that are less likely to be discussed. In terms of political participation, behaviors that involve social interaction are more affected than behaviors that do not. Not only are some individuals more affected by the social context than others, but also the direction of the contextual effect sometimes changes across individually defined social categories. Higher status contexts encourage participation among higher status individuals, but discourage it among lower status individuals. Members of the working class who associate exclusively with other workers are more likely to be Democrats if they live among the *middle class.*

Third, how does the influence of the social context compare to the influence of individual characteristics, and are the effects of these two sets of factors independent or interdependent?

The answer to the first part of this question varies across behaviors. For example, subjective identification as a Democrat is predicted on the basis of contextual social status at least as well as on the basis of individual social status. Some opinions toward political candidates, and subjective identifications with a particular ethnic group, are better predicted on the basis of individual characteristics, even though the behaviors are subject to contextual influence.

More important than the comparison of effects is the recognition of their interdependence. The effects of context vary across individuals, and the effects of individual characteristics vary across neighborhood contexts. Considering either set of factors in isolation produces misleading results and conclusions. Political behavior is a complex product of their interaction, and a fuller appreciation of politics requires an understanding of that interdependency.

Finally, how is the neighborhood social context translated into political influence?

The social context becomes politically influential by structuring social interaction at two levels: (1) personal, primary group interactions between friends, and (2) the casual, impersonal interactions that inescapably occur among an area's residents. Both are important to politics and political behavior, and both are subject to variations in the social context.

Social interaction at an interpersonal level is an important determinant of political behavior. People obtain much of their political information and many of their political cues through informal communication networks. As the choice of personal associates is often influenced and structured by residential proximity, the social context of an urban neighborhood influences the content of residents' personal interactions. Thus, the substance of the political information and cues that individuals informally receive often reflects a contextual bias.

Social identities, loyalties, and aspirations also have important consequences for politics. The social groups with which individuals identify serve as normative reference groups: people base political opinions and actions on perceived group norms. Attachments to a social group are subject to the influence of social interaction at both personal and impersonal levels. Not only intimate associates, but also people encountered in more casual, impersonal social situations affect these social anchors. As a result, the social context of an urban neighborhood influences political behavior by altering the loyalties and group norms upon which the behavior is based.

Impersonal social encounters sometimes lead to hostility and conflict as well as to assimilation. When white families leave a neighborhood because black families move in, or when low status individuals fail to engage in political participation because political activity is dominated by higher status people, a social group is serving a far different, comparative reference group function. Whites observe a black presence and act on the basis of racial differences; low status individuals identify political participation as an upper status activity and are intimidated by social differences.

Thus, the translation of the social context into political influence is rooted in processes of conflict and assimilation. Some social interactions result in politically sympathetic responses, but others produce hostility, intimidation, and exclusion. These two responses-—conflict and assimilation— constitute significant elements of politics, and they are rooted in the social context.

Social Contexts and Urban Social Life

This study supports the political importance of geographically based social relations. People who live together also encounter one another: opportunities for social interaction are circumscribed by the local social context. Even a choice as intimate as friendship selection appears to be constrained by local supply. More importantly, people who live together affect one another politically. Political choices are a function of individual characteristics, but they are also affected by social relations that are locationally specific.

Thus, the modern human condition is not adequately described in terms of atomized individuals who lack any significant social ties to their environments, or in terms of individuals who are cut adrift from the political guidance that comes with group membership. The social dependency of individual choice is a fundamental condition of human existence. Social relations are severely disrupted by urbanization, industrialization, ethnic emigrations, white flight, suburbanization, and so forth. But people do not construct significant political preferences in a social vacuum. When traditional social ties are severed, as they frequently are, new ones are established to take their place.

Wirth was correct when he identified the socially disintegrative effects of early twentieth century urbanism. A whole set of important social relationships was disrupted by the "size, density, and heterogeneity" of an

urban setting that was radically new and unfamiliar to many of the participants in the urbanization experience. Many institutions disappeared as a
result of this uprooting process. Old social structures and styles of life were
left in shambles, but new ones rapidly emerged to fill the void.

A new constellation of early twentieth century urban social institutions appeared in urban areas across the country: the ethnic parish, the union
hall, the political club, the neighborhood tavern. Many of these institutions,
as well as the systems of social relations they sustained, have in turn been
displaced by new disruptions in urban life. Midcentury suburbanization and
black migration from the rural south to urban centers across the nation
signalled a renewed process of social dislocation. The remnants of this
urban social system, with roots extending back to a period prior to Wirth's
time, are currently threatened by an economic shift from the frostbelt to the
sunbelt.

The important point is as follows: individuals do not live in social
isolation, and neither do they make political decisions in a socially isolated
fashion. People live in relationship to other people, and this fact of human
existence becomes even more important in an urban setting.

None of this is aimed at suggesting that the twentieth century
urbanization experience has been ineffectual in producing qualitative
changes in social relationships and social groups. Wirth may have been
correct in his assertion that urban dwellers tend to establish social relations
that are impersonal, superficial, transitory, and segmental. Still, this study
has shown that the social relations of urban dwellers are politically influential. In spite of large-scale social disruptions and a tentative social life,
political choices are nonetheless conditioned upon spatially based social
relations. Unfortunately, a major intellectual thrust following the ''passing
of community" tradition has been to treat political preferences in isolation,
when efforts should have been directed toward understanding the poltical
significance of transformed social relations for political life.

Some elements of urban society are certainly rootless and isolated.
Soaring crime rates and physically ravished urban landscapes point to huge
fissures in the urban social order. But analyses that focus too tightly on
these disjunctures fail to appreciate that urban social life, and social groups
in urban society, are often alive and well and firmly anchored in spatially
defined social contexts. That conclusion has important consequences for an
understanding of group-based politics in urban areas.

The Social Context of Group-Based Politics

Group-based politics is a central element in the conceptual apparatus of
political scientists, and even casual observers of American politics point

toward the importance of groups in politics. Labor votes Democratic, and the upper middle class votes Republican. The U.S. Chamber of Commerce is opposed to any extension of the welfare state, and wheat farmers are in favor of unrestricted trade and price supports. Against this backdrop of a common focus on the group and group-based politics, it is ironic that treatments of mass politics generally adopt a research methodology and theoretical perspective which ignore the group and focus upon artificially isolated individuals instead.

Part of this individualistic emphasis rests upon the assumption, either implicitly or explicitly stated, that group members adhere to the group on the basis of their own, individually perceived, political interests. Individual union members decide to vote Democratic because they individually recognize that Democratic candidates are more sympathetic to their own individual circumstances. Thus, the group is reduced to a summation of motives held by individual members, and group life has no independent meaning apart from the lives of individual members.

This study suggests that such an emphasis is misplaced. The group is truly more than an aggregation of individuals: it has a life of its own. According to Hamilton (1972: 308), "the prerequisite to any significant development of *class* consciousness (emphasis in original) would be the sharing of live experiences in that class milieu." A class consciousness — or a group consciousness — is unlikely to develop without the social support and stimuli provided to individuals by a well-integrated group. Individual concerns and interests must be reinforced by other individuals sharing the same set of interests and concerns.

Group members are more likely to act like group members if they reside among other group members, but group consciousness can also be reinforced by social interactions outside the group. Conflictive social interactions frequently serve to reinforce group boundaries — an important function of social conflict (Coser, 1956). In either event, conflict or assimilation, the integrity and self-awareness of the group cannot be understood by focusing solely upon individuals. The group must be conceived on the basis of social relations inside and outside the group.

None of this means that the individual is unimportant, or that individual circumstances are lacking in their ability to influence individual behavior. In Hamilton's words (1972: 61): "No amount of group influence is going to convince people that 'things are good' when indeed 'things are bad' (or vice versa)." People form responses to stimuli they receive through social interaction, and their responses are the complex products of their own circumstances, concerns, and viewpoints. The important point is that *they do respond.* Much political activity can be seen as a response to social experience, rather than as a psychological product of forces internal to the individual, or as the result of individual calculations regarding costs and benefits.

An excessively individualistic focus has produced some potentially misguided analyses of American politics. When confronted with a decline in group cohesiveness and class consciousness, many commentators point toward a classless society that is being produced as the result of occupational, social, or financial mobility within classes and groups. These declines in cohesiveness might just as well be the result of *residentid* mobility: the dispersal of working class neighborhoods, and the urban in-migration of farm populations. Hamilton (1972: 3 10-311) demonstrates that many current members of the working class are recent arrivals from rural areas whose social loyalties and political attitudes are rooted elsewhere. As time progresses the new arrivals may replace old loyalties with new ones, thereby reinvigorating a group which currently lacks cohesion.

Social Contexts as Policy Outputs

The composition of neighborhood social contexts is no accident, and neither is it the simple by-product of individual choice. The social composition of urban neighborhoods is, at least in part, the direct consequence of land use policies adopted at the local level by cities and suburbs throughout the nation (Danielson, 1976). Subdivision regulations and cautious builders insure that newly constructed, higher priced housing is not located adjacent to moderately or lower priced housing. Political pressure applied to public housing agencies results in low income public housing that is located in already low income areas, far away from middle class neighborhoods. Suburban zoning regulations that establish minimum lot sizes and square footage requirements create increased housing costs and produce economically differentiated populations across metropolitan areas. In summary, these locally adopted housing policies have the net effect of extending and accentuating economic segregation in metropolitan areas. Economically heterogeneous areas, like racially heterogeneous areas, have become rare occurrences.

Exclusionary housing policies have several points of relevance for this study. First, the policies structure individual choice as well as responding to it. Part of the motivation that lies behind the desire of builders and suburban politicians to provide economically differentiated residential areas is an anticipation of buyer preference, but the policies also limit individual choice. Few opportunities exist for individuals to live in economically integrated areas. Rather, the clear trend is toward increasing homogeneity in residential contexts (Judd, 1979).[1] This is especially important because the house itself is often the main motivation for residential relocation (Gans, 1967). Many people purchase the best house they can afford, and settle for the neighborhood that comes with it, an accessory that is frequently beyond their control. Thus, a self-selection argument which asserts that people choose a neighborhood on the basis of the neighborhood's political or social composition ignores the structured set of residential choices to which many people respond.

Second, policies that structure the social contexts of neighborhoods also structure politics by affecting residents' political behavior. Some social mixes produce conflict and other produce assimilation. Some contexts maximize group awareness and cohesiveness, and others minimize political differences between classes and groups. Thus, the creation of a socially segregated metropolis has consequences that extend beyond the creation of slums, middle class enclaves, and homogenized suburbs. It also affects the very structure and course of metropolitan politics.

Social Influence, Rationality, and Democratic Politics

More than 30 years ago, Berelson, Lazarsfeld, and McPhee (1954) suggested a revision of normative democratic theory in light of their empirical work on voting in Elmira. In particular they voiced concern over a theory of democracy that relied too heavily upon the civic capacities of individual citizens: "If the democratic system depended solely on the qualifications of the individual voter, then it seems remarkable that democracies have survived through the centuries" (p. 311). They attempted to reconcile the durability of many democratic systems with the civic incapacities of many individual citizens — their lack of knowledge, concern, and participation in politics, as well as their seeming lack of rationality in making political choices.* Traditional democratic theory, they concluded, is defective in its excessive focus upon individuals and individual capacities: "What are undervalued are certain collective properties that reside in the electorate as a whole and in the political and social system in which it functions" (**p. 3**12).

Berelson and his associates appear to have been on target in their concern regarding excessive individualism. *Perhaps* individuals ought to think for themselves and make up their own minds when they make political choices, but they most certainly do not. Political choices and activities are undertaken by individuals, but they are the end products of a systematic social process that exposes individuals to the influence of others. Any theory of democracy that prescribes otherwise sets up an inaccessible standard for citizen behavior.

At the same time, it is unnecessary to call into question the rationality of decisions made **as** the result of a social influence process. That is, an individual who decides to vote for a candidate on the basis of a friend's suggestion is no more irrational than an individual who decides to vote for a candidate on the basis of a newspaper's suggestion. Indeed, the first strategy may be *more* rational than the second. Anthony Downs **(1957)** explained that it is likely that rational individuals will reduce information costs by obtaining political information (guidance) from other people.

> Personal contacts with others who have already obtained data has the advantage of producing several other types of utility, such as pleasure in their company and ability to steer the discussion so as to gain more precise information. Also, it is usually easier to contact relatively well-informed persons than to locate free literature or broadcasts, which are scattered in many places. Finally, nonpersonal free data are often wholly subsidized by sources interested in promulgating their own viewpoint. Thus information issued by political parties, favor-buyers, representative groups, and other influencers is chosen strictly by their own selection principles, which are unlikely to coincide with those of any one citizen. In contrast, it is often relatively easy for a man to find someone he knows who has selection principles like his own. (p.229)

This seems to bring us full circle; individual rationality in politics presumes an ability on the part of individuals to take actions and make choices that are directed toward the achievement of conscious goals held by the individual (see Downs, **1957:4-11).** Politics is a complicated *affair,* however, so it is often difficult for individuals to decide which choices are appropriate, given their particular goals. (This ignores the equally difficult task of setting goals in the first place.) Thus, in their effort to minimize the truly significant costs of collecting information to make these choices, rational individuals turn to other individuals for help and assistance.

The conclusion is inescapable: social influence is a fully rational device in politics, both for the receiver and for the transmitter of political information. But this means that rational individuals are interdependent, and cannot be understood in isolation. The vision of democratic politics that emerges is not one of irrationality on the part of individuals, but rather one of interdependence.[3] The findings contained in these pages are fully compatible with theories of politics resting upon an assumption of individual rationality, but they call into question any theory of political behavior that ignores interdependence and social influence among citizens.

APPENDIX A: THE DATA BASE
FOR THIS STUDY

THE SURVEYS

The data base for this study employs two different surveys of individuals that have been combined with census tract data in an effort to link individual behavior to the social environment. Thus, the unit of analysis is the individual respondent, but measurement occurs at two levels: individual and contextual (at the tract level).

A two-wave survey of Buffalo and its immediately surrounding suburbs was conducted by four political science professors at the State University of New York at Buffalo: Everett F. Cataldo, Richard M. Johnson, Lyman A. Kellstedt, and Lester W. Milbrath. [1] The second wave of this survey, which was used for the present study, was conducted in the spring of 1968 and includes interviews with 1335 respondents. A modified cluster block sample design was used: blocks were randomly chosen on the basis of census tract data and clusters of households were chosen within blocks. At each selected dwelling unit a randomization procedure was used in choosing a household member to interview, but all respondents were at least 15 years of age. Some oversampling was done in black areas to insure an adequate black sample, and the race of the interviewer was matched to the race of the respondents. Efforts to compare the sample's population characteristics with aggregate population characteristics based upon census data show only minor deviations between the two (Kellstedt and Strand, 1973).

In addition to these Buffalo survey data, a survey of Detroit is employed as well. The Detroit data come from the 1966 Detroit Area Study conducted by Edward Laumann and his associates at the University of Michigan. The Detroit survey contains interviews with 985 adult white males, weighted to produce a sample of 1013. Complete documentation of the study design is contained in Laumann (1973).

In both studies great efforts were made by the collectors of the data to obtain randomly drawn, representative samples of the populations living in the two cities. However, the representativeness of the samples is not especially relevant to this study. There is no compelling need to produce a descriptive portrayal of Buffalo in 1968 or Detroit in 1966. It *is* important that the surveys contain no sampling biases that would compromise the results presented in this study, and there is no reason to believe that such a bias exists.

CENSUS TRACT DATA

After obtaining the Buffalo survey through the generosity of Professor Kellstedt, and the Detroit data through the generosity of the Interuniversity Consortium for Political and Social Research, this author matched and merged census tract data with the surveys. This was possible because respondents' 1960 census tract numbers were recorded in each survey. In the case of the Buffalo survey, tract data were collected for both 1960 and 1970.[2] The 1960 and 1970 tract boundaries for Buffalo do not coincide entirely, and thus some tracts were combined to achieve comparable boundaries between 1960 and 1970. The aggregation rule used in combining tracts was to arrive at the least inclusive boundaries that would achieve comparability between the two sets of tracts. These procedures establish three potential sets of data: 1960 data according to 1960 tracts, 1970 data according to the combined tracts, and interpolated estimates for 1968 based upon 1960 and 1970 data for the combined tracts. These interpolated estimates are used when appropriate, but in some instances interpolation is not possible, and either 1960 or 1970 data are used.

As in the case of Buffalo, census tract boundaries for Detroit do not entirely coincide between 1960 and 1970. For substantive reasons, only one census tract variable is used for the Detroit analyses—the working class proportion in the tract. The 1970 tract data are used to arrive at this measure for two reasons. First, they are nearer in time to the survey than the 1960 data. Second an interpolated measure was not feasible, because different population bases were used in constructing employment figures in the 1960 and 1970 censuses, thereby rendering the data noncomparable.

INDIVIDUAL-LEVEL MEASURES

Most individual-level variables are relatively straightforward and adequately explained in the text. Occupational status and objectively defined ethnicity are more complex, and they are explained in detail below.

Each respondent's occupational class is coded into one of three categories on the basis of the household head's occupation. The classifications are listed below:

I. Professional-Managerial
    1. professional, technical, and kindred workers
    2. managers, officials, and proprieters
II. Clerical-Service-Sales
    1. retail trade
    2. clerical and kindred occupations

   3. sales workers
   4. salesmen and sales clerks
   5. private household workers
   6. service workers
 111. Working Class
   1. craftsmen, foremen, and kindred workers
   2. operatives and kindred workers
   3. laborers

All other employment categories are designated as missing data.

A Buffalo respondent's ''general'' ethnicity, absent considerations of the particular ethnic group, is determined according to the parents' and grandparents' native status. If one or both of a respondent's parents were born in a foreign country, the respondent is coded as a first or second generation ethnic. Persons with one or more foreign born grandparents who are not first or second generation ethnics (no foreign born parents) are coded as third generation ethnics with the relevant number of foreign born grandparents. An individual who has no foreign born grandparents, and who is not black, **is** coded as a nonethnic white.

Determining objectively defined Polish and Italian ethnicity is a more complex undertaking. The procedure for defining Polish ethnicity among the white Buffalo respondents is outlined here, and a corresponding procedure is used for objectively defined Italian ethnicity:

I. A respondent is coded as a first or second generation Pole if the respondent's parent's status is Polish.

11. A respondent is coded as a third generation Pole if he or she is not coded as a first or second generation Pole and one of the following conditions hold.

  1. The respondent's parents' status is native born, but the respondent's paternal grandparents' status is Polish.

  2. The respondent's parents' status and paternal grandparents' status are native born, and the respondent's maternal grandparents' status is Polish.

  3. The respondent's parent's status is native born, and the respondent's maternal and paternal grandparents both have Polish status.

111. A respondent is coded as a nonethnic white if all the respondent's grandparents were born in the United States.

IV. A respondent is coded as "other ethnic" if he or she is not categorized in the above definitions and has at least one foreign born grandparent.

A respondent's parents and grandparents have their native born and Polish ethnic status determined according to the following scheme:

I. The set of parents or grandparents is coded as Polish if one of the following conditions hold.
    1. Both individuals were born in Poland.
    2. Only the male was born in Poland.
    3. The male was native born but the female was born in Poland.
II. The set of parents or grandparents is coded as native born if both individuals were born in the United States.

APPENDIX B: METHODOLOGICAL PITFALLS AND GOALS

Research efforts aimed at establishing the contextual dependency of individual behavior have not been free from criticism. By offering a carefully considered critique of contextual research, Hauser (1974) provides a research agenda for anyone attempting to establish the political importance of the social context. Hauser's five objections to assertions of contextual influence are outlined below. They offer goals for the study, and standards that the reader should employ in evaluating arguments and evidence.

First, Hauser suggests that merely observing a relationship between an individual behavior and a contextual property is insufficient. Explaining how the social context is translated into political influence is also important, and this study is deeply concerned with explicating the mechanisms that are responsible for this translation.

Second, how important are the contextual effects? Hauser suggests several standards for evaluating the magnitudes of effects; the procedure employed here generally compares contextual effects to individual effects.

Third, would the introduction of additional explanatory variables reduce or eliminate the observed contextual effect? Contextual relationships may be artifacts of other, often individual-level factors. In each of the analyses conducted here, various individual-level characteristics are entertained as alternative explanations for observed contextual effects.

Fourth, especially when an individual attribute and a contextual property affect a behavior in the same direction, individual-level measurement error can artificially increase the explanatory power of the contextual property. Reliable measurement is difficult both to achieve and to substantiate, but efforts are made here to consider simultaneously various individual attributes in order to alleviate this problem.

Finally, as Hauser points out, " . . . the membership of social organizations is typically subject to processes of social selection and attrition which partially determine the character of members" (1974: 374). In terms of the present effort, a contextual relationship might exist because people choose neighborhoods rather than because neighborhoods affect people. This self-selection criticism is the most difficult to answer conclusively: any cross-sectional research design rests upon a leap of faith in asserting causality. The issue is given extended treatment in this book, and efforts are made to offer logical and inferential evidence supporting the direction of asserted causal relationships.

APPENDIX C: THE MODEL OF FRIENDSHIP CHOICE

The model that is presented graphically in Figure 3.1 is readily translated into a mathematical statement that builds upon the work of James Coleman (**1964**: chap. 16). Coleman develops a model to consider the consequences of group size differences, relative to total population size, for the maintenance of norms or beliefs specific to a group (1964: **479**). A logically similar model is developed in Chapter 3 that relates the neighborhood social context to the construction of social networks and considers the implications of this relationship for the extent of discretion exercised by individuals in choosing intimate associates. The model is written as follows:

$$F_{ij}(k) = S_j(1) + (1-S_j(1))r_{ij}S_j(2) \\ + (1-S_j(1))r_{ij}(1-S_j(2))r_{ij}S_j(3) + \ldots \tag{C.1}$$

where

$F_{ij}(k) =$ the probability that a member of group i in context j will form a friendship with another member of group i after k opportunities for friendly association;

$S_j(n) =$ the social density of the ingroup, conceived as the proportion of the jth social context that is composed by fellow members of group i at the nth opportunity for friendly association; or the probability that such an opportunity for association will involve an encounter with a fellow member of group i, assuming random encounters (as opposed to nonrandom associations);

$1-S_j(n) =$ the social density of the *outgroup;* or the probability of an encounter with a member of the outgroup in the jth context at the nth opportunity for friendly association;

$r_{ij} =$ the probability that a member of the ith group in the jth context will reject association with a nonmember of i, having encountered one at an opportunity for friendly association.

Translating equation C.1 into English may be a useful exercise. Once again assume that group i denotes the middle class, and that all individuals belong to either the middle class or the working class. The probability that a middle class individual will form an association with another member of the middle class after one opportunity for forming a friendship is equal to the probability of encountering a middle class individual at the first opportunity. The probability that a middle class individual will form an association with another member of the middle class after two opportunities for forming associations is equal to (1) the probability of encountering a middle class individual at the first opportunity, plus (2) the probability of en-

162

countering a working class individual at the first opportunity, multiplied times the probability of rejection, multiplied times the probability of encountering a middle class individual at the *second* opportunity. This dynamically specified process proceeds indefinitely.

The development of the model in Chapter 3 implicitly assumes that the social density of a particular group is constant across associational opportunities, and the model may therefore be rewritten as:

$$F_{ij}(k) = S_j + (1-S_j)r_{ij}S_j + (1-S_j)^2 r_{ij}^2 S_j + \ldots \tag{C.2}$$
$$+ (1-S_j)^{k-1} r_{ij}^{k-1} S_j$$

or

$$F_{ij}(k) = \sum_{n=0}^{k-1} S_j (1-S_j)^n r_{ij}^n \tag{C.3}$$

The open form of equation C.2 is translated into a closed form as follows. First, multiply both sides of equation C.2 by $r_{ij}(1-S_j)$ to obtain:

$$F_{ij}(k)r_{ij}(1-S_j) = S_j r_{ij}(1-S_j) + S_j r_{ij}^2 (1-S_j)^2 \tag{C.4}$$
$$+ \ldots + S_j r_{ij}^k (1-S_j)^k$$

As a second step subtract equation C.4 from the respective sides of equation C.2, and rearrange the result in the following manner:

$$F_{ij}(k) - F_{ij}(k)r_{ij}(1-S_j) = S_j - S_j r_{ij}^k (1-S_j)^k \tag{C.5}$$
$$F_{ij}(k)[1 - r_{ij}(1-S_j)] = S_j - S_j r_{ij}^k (1-S_j)^k$$
$$F_{ij}(k) = \frac{S_j - S_j r_{ij}^k (1-S_j)^k}{1 - r_{ij}(1-S_j)}$$

As the person becomes settled into a social context and the number of opportunities for social interaction becomes very large, k also becomes very large. And because r_{ij} and $1-S_j$ are probabilities, they both lie between zero and one (ignoring the special cases when they equal zero or one), thereby reducing the quality $(S_j r_{ij}^k (1-S_j)^k)$ to zero. *So,* the model approaches:

$$F_{ij} = \frac{S_j}{1 - r_{ij}(1-S_j)} \tag{C.6}$$

as $k \rightarrow \infty$, that is, as "k" gets large. This is the form that is shown as equation *3.1*, and it is readily manipulated into the form of equation *3.3*.

APPENDIX D: THE LOGIT MODEL

The logit model for microdata provides a useful technique for estimating the effect of various factors upon the probability of an event. In this study the "event" is the report of some political or social behavior or attitude by a survey respondent. The technique resembles ordinary least squares regression in that each respondent is treated as an observation, and a coefficient is estimated for each independent variable, The coefficient predicts some change in a dependent variable as a function of a unit change in the independent variable. Logit for microdata has several advantages over ordinary least squares in this situation, however.

First, if a list of independent variables is regressed on a dichotomous dependent variable, the predicted dependent variable can be interpreted as a probability, but it will often result in predicted values less than zero and greater than one. Predicting impossible worlds is disadvantageous for empirically minded political scientists, and it is because of this that the logit model is preferable. [1] The logistic functions for the probability of an event's occurrence (P) and nonoccurrence $(1 - P)$ are expressed as:

$$P = 1/(1 + e^{-XB})$$
$$1 - P = 1/(1 + e^{XB})$$

where X is the matrix of independent variables including the constant, and B is the vector of coefficients that are to be estimated. Clearly, the coefficients do not provide a linear estimate of the probability. Rather they provide a linear estimate of the "logit," or the natural log of the odds ratio:

$$XB = L = \ln(P/(1-P))$$

The logit has several advantages. A unit change in the logit is related to a larger change in the probability when the probability is closer to .5, corresponding to the normal manner in which probabilities vary as a function of exogenous influences: a change from .8 to .9 is in some sense farther than a change from .5 to .6. Moreover, as the logit varies from negative infinity to positive infinity, the corresponding probability varies from zero to one, thereby eliminating the problem of predicting impossible worlds (see Figure D.1).

A second difference between the logit model and ordinary least squares is the technique used to estimate the coefficients. As its name implies, ordinary least squares provides an analytic solution which minimizes the sum of the squared residuals from the predicted regression line. The logit procedure makes use of a maximum likelihood technique aimed at maximizing a likelihood function rather than minimizing a residual variation function.

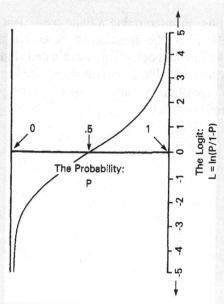

Figure D.1. The logit as a function of the probability.

Locating the actual maximum of the likelihood function requires that a system of nonlinear equations be solved for the coefficient values. Arriving at an analytic solution is impossible for all practical purposes, and thus an iterative procedure is used to arrive at a numeric solution for the coefficients.

A final difference between ordinary least squares regression and the logit model lies in the method for interpreting coefficients. The logit model is nonlinear, and thus readers should not attempt to interpret the magnitudes of coefficients directly. Rather, judgments regarding the magnitude of an explanatory variable's effect should be based upon variations in the predicted probabilities which result from changes in one explanatory variable while other explanatory variables are held constant. This method is used repeatedly in the text, and it is necessary because the model explicitly assumes that the effect of any single explanatory variable depends upon values of other explanatory variables and their coefficients.[2]

A t-ratio is reported along with each logit coefficient. Assuming a large sample, standardly accepted values for the t-ratio in evaluating the statistical veracity of a coefficient are 1.645 for a one-tail test at the .05 confidence level, and 1.960 for a two-tail test at the .05 confidence level. Along with Wonnacott and Wonnacott (1970: 24–27), the author is willing to argue that the one-tail test is appropriate whenever the direction of a coefficient is expected on substantive grounds. But this never becomes an important issue in the analyses conducted as part of this study.

Thus, in interpreting a logit coefficient, three steps are generally followed: First, the direction of the coefficient is ascertained. Second, the t-ratio for the coefficient is evaluated. Finally, the magnitude of the explanatory variable's effect is determined by predicting probabilities across the range of that variable while all other explanatory variables in the model are held constant.

NOTES
CHAPTER 1

1. The earlier cited works of Miller (1956) and Putnam (1966) offer exceptions to this rule, but even their work was unable to move beyond the county in identifying relevant social and political environments.
2. For an interesting article which does find urban-suburban life style differences see Tallman and Morgner (1970).
3. Wirth's vision is congruent with a tradition inside social theory that traces its origins to the work of Tonnies and Durkheim, and addresses the deterioration of traditional social institutions and traditional relationships in modem society. For Tonnies this concern is expressed as the eclipse of community by society (1957). For Durkheim, modem society is one in which organic solidarity has been replaced by mechanical solidarity (1933), a society in which functional ties have replaced ties of kinship and association. More recently, Nisbet (1953) and Komhauser (1959) have argued that modem society has disintegrated the intermediate social institutions that lie between the individual and the larger society, thereby making the individual susceptible to the appeals and control of a powerful political state.
4. This discussion is not intended to put the work of Wirth in direct competition with the work of Park and his associates. Indeed, Wirth wrote an extended and annotated bibliography for *The City* (1925: 161-228). Even a cursory reading of the two bodies of work, however, reveals a difference in emphasis. And these different emphases have produced important consequences for considerations of groups and group life in urban settings.
5. More complete documentation for the surveys is contained in Appendix A.
6. In both Buffalo and Detroit, census tract boundaries were modified between the 1960 and 1970 censuses. Most neighborhood measures employed in this study rely upon aggregated versions of the tracts that provide comparable boundaries between 1960 and 1970. The population averages cited in the text refer to these aggregated tracts. See Appendix **A** for a more complete description.

CHAPTER 2

1. In some instances other terms, such as "neighborhood effects," will be substituted for "contextual effects." This is done to avoid repetitious phrasing in situations where the meaning is unambiguous.
2. Any research effort aimed at identifying contextual effects must address a number of methodological challenges. Several of these methodological issues are outlined in Appendix B.
3. This reference group explanation is different from other reference group explanations that have been offered to account for contextual influence. Rather than asserting that the community serves as the point of reference (Elkin and Panning, 1975; Fitton, 1975; Putnam, 1966), the authors suggested that community-based social groups serve as the points of reference.

4. For mathematical treatments of various contextual influence mechanisms see: Sprague and Westefield (1979a, 1979b), Huckfeldt (1983c).

CHAPTER 3

1. Investigations of informant accuracy have called into question the quality of social network data: "People simply do not know, with any degree of accuracy, with whom they communicate" (Killworth and Bernard, 1976: 283). This criticism is probably overstated, at least as it relates to this study. Killworth and Bernard examined the accuracy with which informants remember the frequency and duration of communications, but the conception of network used here ("close friends") is based upon a personal intensity measure that is necessarily a subjective judgment.

2. The measure for social class used here is designed to separate individuals on the basis of working conditions, job security, prestige or social status, and monetary compensation. Perhaps the best justification for these categories is the respondents' own self-perceptions regarding class membership. Of those who identify with a social class, 78 percent of the professional-managerial respondents, 68 percent of the clerical-service-sales respondents, and 35 percent of the working class respondents identify as upper or middle class. This measure for objectively defined class membership suffers from some obvious shortcomings, however. Some foremen might be better classified as managers rather than workers, and some service employees might be better classified as workers. For this reason, it becomes essential that controls for other individual status characteristics be introduced in later contextual analyses. These controls help to guard against the danger of inferring a contextual relationship that is actually an artifact of unconsidered individual level factors (Hauser, 1974).

3. According to 1970 census figures, white professional-managerial men constitute approximately 27 percent of all white employed men in the Detroit Standard Metropolitan Statistical Area (SMSA) and 23 percent of all white employed men in the city of Detroit. White working class men constitute approximately 40 percent of white metropolitan area employed men, and approximately 52 percent of white employed men in the city. Our sample evidently overestimates professional-managerial presence in the population, and underestimates clerical-service-sales presence. Approximately 33 percent of white employed metropolitan area men, and approximately 25 percent of Detroit city white men, are clerical-service-sales.

4. The ten minute transportation definition of neighborhood is adequate for present purposes, roughly corresponding to the census tract definition employed here.

5. This analysis is not intended to give detailed consideration to the issue of localism, but it is important for later analyses to show that different occupational groups do not widely vary in degrees of localism, and that localism does not greatly vary within a single occupational group across working class contexts. For a more extended treatment using these data see Fischer, et al. (1977: chap. 7).

6. An algebraic development of the model can be found in Appendix C.

7. Equilibrium is a technical concept with useful substantive interpretations (Schelling, 1978: 25-27). In the present substantive context, it suggests an individual who has resided in an environment for a sufficient amount of time, and experienced sufficient social encounters, to establish a stable network of friendships.

8. An additional problem with the outgroup rejection parameter relates to the source of rejection. Members of a first group may infrequently associate with members of a second group because the second group will not accept them as associates. This problem is reduced (but not eliminated) through the use of an asymmetrical measure of association: a respondent's list of friends is not verified by examining whether the friendship object reciprocates the friendship. For a discussion of friendship reciprocity and these data see Laumann (1973).

9. The working class density is calculated on the basis of employed males in an effort at obtaining a single, dominant measure for each household in the neighborhood. Thus, a household with a working class male and a clerical female would be counted as working class.

10. Both the clerical-service-sales dummy variable and its interaction term fail to produce crisp t-values. Thus the middle class respondents are treated as a single group for the remainder of the analysis: the 89 clerical-service-sales respondents are combined with 196 professional-managerial respondents to obtain a larger sample. Such a procedure is substantively appropriate if the estimation of a main effect for the social context among the middle class as a whole can be justified. Analyzing these clerical-service-sales respondents separately produces a coefficient for S that lies in the appropriate direction, but a t-value that fails to achieve a satisfactory magnitude (.88). Thus, an alternative interpretation is that the neighborhood effect has not been demonstrated for clerical-service-sales respondents. Readers who adopt this latter interpretation should view the Table 3.3 and Figure 3.2 middle class results as being valid only for the 196 professional-managerial respondents. A crisp t-value persists for professional-managerial respondents even if they are analyzed separately (3.72).

11. Individual controls are introduced in an effort to satisfy one of Hauser's (1974) well-taken objections to assertions of contextual influence. These individual-level factors are likely to covary with both the social context and associational preference, and excluding them might artifically give weight to a contextual interpretation. Even these precautions do not wholly resolve the problem of working class individuals who choose middle class neighborhoods because they already have middle class friends.

12. Note that F_{ij} must be greater than S_j for r_{ij} to be a believable probability. This is merely a restatement of an earlier assumption: the probability of associating with an ingroup member must at least equal the probability of encountering an ingroup member, or, the probability of rejecting an ingroup member equals zero. Negative values for r_{ij}, produced by values of F_{ij} less than S_j, signify a breakdown in the model. Such a situation indicates that ingroups and out-

groups are improperly defined, at least for that particular context, or that friendship selection has become socially indiscriminate in these contexts. Projecting the values for r_{ij} beyond the observed range of working class densities in Figure 1(b) produces negative values.

CHAPTER 4

1. **As** Figure 4.1 shows, the effect of context sometimes varies within individual status categories as well. These variations have important implications for contextual conflict as well as assimilation and will be given more careful attention in Chapter 10.
2. For a general discussion of coefficients, t-values, and significance testing see Wonnacott and Wonnacott (1970:24–27). No claims are made here regarding the randomness of the Buffalo and Detroit surveys, and thus a strict probabilistic interpretation of the t-value is not warranted. Rather, it is reported as a well-known, general indicator of coefficient stability.
3. Interviewing took place during May and June, and the New York primary occurred in late June. Some respondents were interviewed after Robert Kennedy's death in early June. The opinions toward the candidates are measured on a five point scale: (1) oppose very much, (2) oppose somewhat, **(3)** neither favor nor oppose, (4) favor somewhat, *(5)* favor very much.
4. Using these same Buffalo data, the author finds insignificant contextual effects upon a range of social welfare opinions (Huckfeldt, 1977:chap. *5)*.
5. **A** simpler classification of individuals that merely separates those who discuss from those who do not fails to produce the same results.
6. The reader is again referred to the work of Foladare (1968): four days prior to a presidential election, contextual influence is more pronounced in relationship to vote choice than to party identification.
7. This finding regarding the susceptibility of discussants to contextual influence can be usefully contrasted to the work of Erbring, Goldenberger, and Miller (1980), which shows that people who talk about politics are less susceptible to the influence of the media. Discussants evidently tune out one source of information — the media — while they tune in another — social acquaintances.

CHAPTER 5

1. In determining the social density of ethnics in a neighborhood I **am** forced to base my calculation on the census category "foreign stock", which only includes first and second generation ethnics. The operating assumption is that neighborhoods with more first and second generation ethnics also have more third generation ethnics. Thus, no distinction is being made between the density of first and second generation ethnics versus the density of first, second, and third generation ethnics.
2. The lack of a statistically robust coefficient for the effect of first and second generation ethnicity upon Democratic loyalty does not mean that first and

second generation ethnics are anything less than good Democrats. They are counted as having four ethnic grandparents. Thus, being a first or second generation ethnic has no appreciable effect beyond being a third generation ethnic with four foreign-born grandparents.

3. Gabriel goes on to argue that the translation of ethnic consciousness is conditioned by individual social status.

4. See Appendix A.

5. Figure 5.2 shows a relationship between Polish identification and Polish neighborhoods among nonethnics, and to a lesser extent, among other ethnics. In terms of nonethnics, this is probably due to fourth generation Polish ethnics who identify as Poles, but are not included in the objective definition criteria. In terms of other (non-Polish) ethnics, it is probably a function of individuals with a mixed ethnic heritage, i.e., a Polish mother and a Hungarian father. The classification rule for determining objective ethnicity assumes, undoubtedly incorrectly, male dominance. Thus, in the example given the respondent would be classified as Hungarian in spite of a Polish mother.

6. The analysis of Table 5.2(A) is complicated due to the positive coefficient operating upon individual income. If educational attainment is interpreted as an indicator of social mobility and income as an indicator of material success, then these results are consistent with an individual social status explanation that suggests that individual mobility weakens ethnic bonds, even though material success strengthens these bonds when mobility is controlled.

7. The t-ratio for first or second generation status satisfied the .05 one-tail test, but narrowly fails the .05 two-tail test.

8. The differential effect of Polish neighborhoods upon Poles and non-Poles is substantively important because it helps answer a potential criticism of these results. If the effect was uniform across all groups, the conclusion offered here might be criticized on the grounds that Slominski's appeal is to a region of the city that happens to include many Polish ethnics, rather than to the Polish ethnic group that resides in a particular region. The weaker, but still relatively strong neighborhood effect upon non-Polish ethnics is particularly interesting, however. It suggests that Slominski's appeal is not wholly rooted in the Polish ethnic group. The social interaction process that encourages support for Slominski evidently occurs among different ethnic groups, but does not extend to individuals beyond these ethnic groups. Members of different ethnic groups may share common problems and a common outlook that supports ethnic politics in general terms, regardless of the particular ethnic group in question. Ms. Slominski, it appears, is able to take advantage of these commonalities. Thus, it makes good sense to think of ethnic politics as a phenomenon that is specific to the structure of a particular group, but also generalized across groups.

9. A more complete and formal presentation of this argument is contained in Huckfeldt and Kohfeld with Stabrowski (1983).

CHAPTER 6

1. These probabilities are calculated from Table 6.3 by assuming mean values for social distance, black densities, low income densities, individual income, and individual education.

2. Most whites are committed to racial equality at an abstract, impersonal, legalistic level. At other levels they experience a form of racial anxiety rooted in feelings of racial disapproval and traditional moral values—' 'symbolic racism," and fears of potential racial threats (Sears and McConahy, 1973: 138-141). These forms of racial disapproval are pervasive and have been shown to be excellent predictors of political behavior relevant to issues of race (Sears and Kinder, 1971). The two attitudinal variables used here are aimed at tapping these more subtle manifestations of racial hostility. Symbolic racism is measured by the opinion toward King, which taps white attitudes toward a quest for social justice. (King was assassinated shortly before the interviewing began.) Feelings of potential racial threats are measured by the opinion toward neighborhood integration, which moves from the abstract to more personal and immediate issues of living space. Neither of these conceptualizations of racial hostility is definitive, however. A broader definition for racism might incorporate feelings of insecurity as racist responses in and of themselves.

3. Schelling (1972) showed that, even if black concentrations are the only impetus for white flight, relatively low levels of hostility can produce extremely high levels of segregation due to the interdependence of individual behavior.

CHAPTER 7

1. Respondents less than 21 years of age were excluded because that was the legal voting age in 1968, and because political participation, more than the other political behaviors and activities considered in this study, is primarily an adult activity. The resulting sample consists of 877 adult whites.

2. Different respondents were undoubtedly referring to different activities when they responded that they had worked to get people registered. Some people were probably involved in well-organized voter registration drives, while others had only encouraged a friend to register. The crucial unifying characteristic of these activities is that they require social interaction.

3. Contextual social status and the interaction between contextual social status and individual social status are highly correlated ($R^2 = .81$). Strong evidence exists, however, to suggest that multicollinearity is not a problem: (1) the t-values for the coefficients are robust, and (2) the coefficients lie in the substantively expected opposite directions.

4. The range of the index of socially based participation is from 0 to 21 with a standard deviation of 4.7. The range for the index of individually based participation is from 0 to 12 with a standard deviation of 2.4.

5. The data are also compatible with an interpretation asserting that normally high levels of participation among higher status individuals are discouraged in lower status neighborhoods. This counterargument suggests that a status discrepancy phenomenon is operating at all individual status levels—any individual is less

likely to participate where other status groupings predominate. An interpretation such as this is especially attractive from the standpoint that it effectively counters any self-selection objection, but it probably overstates the hesitancy of higher status individuals, especially higher status individuals in the American political environment, to assert themselves in lower status contexts. Finally, the argument offered here rests upon a significant body of literature that suggests that participation is a learned behavior encouraged by higher status norms and other active participants.

CHAPTER 8

1. For several dynamic treatments of contextual influence, see Brown (1981) and Huckfeldt and Sprague (1983).
2. This additional control is included because subjective class identification is at least weakly related to the neighborhood context, and people who identify with a class might be more likely to seek out fellow class members as friends. Thus, the control is part of a conservative attempt to avoid producing a contextual relationship that is actually an artifact of excluded individual level variables (Hauser, 1974).
3. This divergent contextual effect is not an artifact of several respondents who lie near the extremes of the working class densities. Among working class respondents who exclusively associate with working class friends, 38 live in neighborhoods below the median working class density of 56 percent, and 126 live in neighborhoods above that median density. Eighty percent of the 38 respondents below the median, and 61 percent of the 126 respondents above the median, identify as Democrats.

CHAPTER 9

1. For an alternative formulation of the tipping point related to a different contextual issue, see Schelling (1972).
2. The tipping point is a useful conceptual device, but it should not be overextended or misconstrued. For example, the tipping point is not conceived as a single value applicable to all individuals within an occupational category; it is better thought of as a mean value for a group as a whole. Further, the tipping point is not being stated in dynamic terms, even though it has interesting dynamic implications. This cross-sectional view of the tipping point sees it as a critical outgroup density that demarcates basically different relationships between social groupings. Individuals imbedded in contexts with lower outgroup densities are part of a social relationship rooted in assimilation, while individuals imbedded in contexts with higher outgroup densities are part of a social relationship rooted in conflict.
3. The second derivative $2a$, determines whether the calculated tipping point represents a reaction to the S or $1-S$ population. If the second derivative is negative, the tipping point is a maximum and must be a reaction to the S population. If the second derivative is positive, the tipping point is a minimum and must be a reaction to the $1-S$ population.

4. Not only does the coefficient for SB^2 fail to satisfy most null hypothesis rejection criteria, but it is also negative resulting in a negative second derivative, Thus, the calculated tipping point represents a maximum, i.e., a reaction to the S population. Substantively, we would be forced to argue that workers react hostilely to workers once the tipping point density is attained. (See note 3.)

Taking account of the missing tipping point for working class respondents, the revised model for these individuals becomes:
$$R = p_1 + p_2 (1-SB) + p_3 SB$$
This model results in the following underdetermined system:
$$p_1 = a_1 + a2 - P2$$
$$p_2 = P3 + a_4$$
$$p_3 = a_4 + p_2$$
This model, and the exclusion of SB^2 in Part B of Table 9.2 assumes that the underlying relationship is linear. If we drop that assumption and exclude SB instead, a positive coefficient results for SB^2 that satisfies the statistical criterion established in Table 9.2. However, keeping SB^2 and excluding "SB" does not change the conclusion that no meaningful tipping point exists for the workers. The minimum of the resulting function is: $SB = 0$, but that is a trivial result that does not qualify as a tipping point. Workers can have no effect when there are no workers, and the direction of the effect never changes. In order to have a meaningful tipping point, it is necessary that statistically satisfactory coefficients exist for both SB and SB^2. Thus the workers' response to context may be nonlinear, but it does not involve a tipping point.

CHAPTER 10

1. At the same time that the residential sorting process in metropolitan areas tended to produce social and economic homogeneity in residential contexts, it may have also produced more heterogeneity in terms of occupational class composition. Two events in post-World War II America stand out: (1) suburbanization and (2) a rising standard of living among unionized workers. The coupling of these two factors made it possible for many workers to move into more expensive housing, and thereby expose themselves to a variegated social context. Indeed, Stephens (1981) makes a similar argument to explain the decline of class politics in Sweden following the war.
2. According to Berelson and his associates, " . . .the usual analogy between the voting 'decision' and the more or less carefully calculated decisions of consumers or businessmen or courts, incidentally, may be quite incorrect. For many voters political preferences may better be considered analogous to cultural tastes. . . .Both have their origin in ethnic, sectional, class, and family traditions. Both exhibit stability and resistance to change for individuals but flexibility and adjustment over generations for the society as a whole. Both seem to be matters of sentiment and disposition rather than 'reasoned preferences.' . . .both are characterized more by faith than by conviction and by

wishful expectation rather than careful prediction of consequences" (p. 310-311). My own perspective is that this overstates the case, and underestimates the abilities of individual voters.

3. John Sprague first suggested to me the value of contrasting interdependence and rationality. For a fascinating demonstration of the complex interdependencies that complicate the lives of rational actors see Schelling (1978).

APPENDIX A

1. Support for their research came primarily from the Office of Economic Opportunity and also from the State University of New York.

2. Census tract data were taken from the Detroit and Buffalo volumes of U.S. Bureau of the Census, *Census of Population and Housing: 1960, Census Tracts, Final Report* (Washington: U.S. Government Printing Office, 1962); and U.S. Bureau of the Census, *Census of Population and Housing: 1970, Census Tracts, Final Report* (Washington: U.S. Government Printing Office, 1972.)

APPENDIX D

1. Using ordinary least squares with a dichotomous dependent variable is also problematic because the resulting error structure is heteroskedastic.

2. The logit model is explained in numerous places. For an especially readable account, see Hanushek and Jackson (1977).

REFERENCES

Alford, Robert R., and Harry M. Scoble (1968). "Sources of Local Political Involvement," *American Political Science Review* 62(December): 1192–1206.

Alwin, Duane F. (1976). "Assessing School Effects: Some Identities," *Sociology of Education* 49(October): 294–303.

Axelrod, Moms (1956). "Urban Structure and Social Participation," *American Sociological Review* 21(February): 13–18.

Bell, Wendell (1957). "Anomie, Social Isolation, and the Class Structure," *Sociometry* 20(June): 105-116.

Bell, Wendell, and Marion D. Boat (1957). "Urban Neighborhoods and Informal Social Relations," *American Journal of Sociology* 62(January): 391–398.

Bell, Wendell, and Maryanne T. Force (1956). "Urban Neighborhood Types and Participation in Formal Associations," *American Sociological Review,* 21(February): 25–34.

Benton, J. Edwin, and Gerald C. Wright (1979). "Comparison of Contextual Effects in Partisan and Non-Partisan Elections." Paper delivered at the annual meeting of the Southern Political Science Association, Gatlinburg, Tennessee, November.

Berelson, Bernard R., Paul F. Lazarsfeld, and William N. McPhee (1954). *Voting: A Study of Opinion Formation in a Presidential Election.* Chicago: University of Chicago Press.

Berger, Bennett M. (1960). *Working-class Suburb: A Study of Auto Workers in Suburbia.* Berkeley: University of California Press.

Besag, Frank, and Philip Cook (1970). *Anatomy of a Riot: Buffalo, 1967.* Buffalo: University Press at Buffalo.

Blalock, H.M., Jr. (1969). "Status Inconsistency, Social Mobility, Status Integration and Structural Effects," *American Sociological Review,* 32(October): 790–801.

Blau, Peter M. (1957). "Formal Organizations: Dimensions of Analysis," *American Journal of Sociology* 63(July): 58–69.

——— (1956). "Social Mobility and Interpersonal Relations," *American Sociological Review* 21(June): 290–295.

——— (1960) "Structural Effects." *American Sociological Review* 25(April): 178-193.

——— (1960). "A Theory of Social Integration." *American Journal of Sociology* 65(May): 545–556.

Boyd, Lawrence H., Jr. and Gudmund Iversen (1979). *Contextual Analysis: Concepts and Statistical Techniques.* Belmont, Calif.: Wadsworth.

Breton, Raymond (1964). "Institutional Completeness of Ethnic Communities and the Personal Relations of Immigrants," *American Journal of Sociology* 70(September): 193–205.

Brown, Courtney (1981). "Group Membership and the Social Environment: Multiple Influences on Political Attitudes and Behaviors." Ph.D. dissertation, Washington University, St. Louis.

Brown, Thad A. (1981). "On Contextual Change and Partisan Attitudes." *British Journal of Political Science* 11(October): 427–448.

Burgess, Ernest W. (1925). "The Growth of the City: An Introduction to a Research Project." In Park et al., *The City,* chap. 2.

——— ed. (1926). *The Urban Community.* Chicago: University of Chicago Press.

Butler, David, and Donald Stokes (1974). *Political Change in Britain: The Evolution of Electoral Choice.* New York: St. Martin's.

Campbell, Angus, Philip E. Converse, Warren E. Miller, and Donald E. Stokes (1960). *The American Voter.* New York: Wiley.

177

Campbell, Angus, Gerald Gurin, and Warren E. Miller (1954). *The Voter Decides.* Evanston, Ill.: Row, Peterson.

Campbell, Angus, Philip E. Converse, Willard L. Rodgers and Robert Marans (1976). "The Residential Environment." In Angus Campbell, Philip E. Converse, and Willard L. Rodgers (eds.) *The Quality of American Life: Perceptions, Evaluations and Satisfaction,* chap. 7. New York: Russell Sage.

Cataldo, Everett F., Richard M. Johnson, Lyman A. Kellstedt, and Lester W. Milbrath (1970). "Card Sorting as a Technique for Survey Interviewing," *Public Opinion Quarterly* 34(Summer): 202–215.

Coleman, James S. (1964). *Introduction to Mathematical Sociology.* New York: Free Press.

Converse, Philip E. (1962). "Information Flow and the Stability of Partisan Attitudes." *Public Opinion Quarterly* 26 (Winter): 578–599.

Coser, Lewis A. (1956). *The Functions of Social Conflict.* Glencoe, Ill.: Free Press.

Cox, Kevin R. (1970). "Geography, Social Contexts, and Voting Behavior in Wales, 1861–1951." In Erik Allardt and Stein Rokkan (eds.), *Mass Politics,* pp. 117–159. New York: Free Press.

———— (1970). "Residential Relocation and Political Behavior: Conceptual Model and Empirical Tests." *Acta Sociologica* 13:40–53.

———— (1974). "The Spatial Structuring of Information Flow and Partisan Attitudes." In Doggan and Rokkan, *Social Ecology,* pp. 157–186.

———— (1969). "The Voting Decision in a Spatial Context." In Christopher Board, Richard J. Charley, and Peter Haggett (eds), *Progress in Geography: International Reviews of Current Research,* pp. 81–117. New York: St. Martin's.

Dahl, Robert A. (1961). *Who Governs? Democracy and Power in an American City.* New Haven: Yale University Press.

Danielson, Michael N. (1976). *The Politics of Exclusion.* New York: Columbia University Press.

Davis, James A. (1966). "The Campus as a Frog Pond: An Application of the Theory of Relative Deprivation to Career Decisions of College Men." *American Journal of Sociology* 72(July): 17–31.

———— (1961). "Compositional Effects, Role Systems, and the Survival of Small Discussion Groups. " *Public Opinion Quarterly* 25(Winter): 574-584.

Davis, James A., Joe L. Spaeth, and Carolyn Huson (1961). "Analyzing Effects of Group Composition," *American Sociological Review* 26(April): 215–225.

Dawson, Richard E., Kenneth Prewitt, and Karen S. Dawson (1977). *Political Socialization,* 2nd ed. Boston: Little, Brown.

Dogan, Mattei, and Stein Rokkan, eds. (1974). *Social Ecology.* Cambridge, Mass.: M.I.T. Press. (First published as *Quantitative Ecological Analysis in the Social Sciences* in 1969.)

Durkheim, Emile (1933). *The Division of Labor in Society,* transl. George Simpson. Glencoe, Ill.: Free Press. (Originally published in 1893.)

———— (1951). *Suicide,* transl. John A. Spaulding and George Simpson. New York: Free Press. (Originally published in 1897.)

Elkin, Stephen L., and William H. Panning (1975). "Structural Effects and Individual Attitudes: Racial Prejudice in English Cities." *Public Opinion Quarterly* 39(Summer): 159–177.

Ennis, Philip H. (1962). "The Contextual Dimenson in Voting." In William McPhee and William A. Glaser (eds.), *Public Opinion and Congressional Elections,* pp. 180–211. New York: Free Press.

Erbring, Lutz, Edie N. Goldenberg, and Arthur H. Miller (1980). "Front-Page News and Real-World Cues: A New Look at Agenda Setting by the Media," *American Journal of Political Science,* 24(February): 16-49.

Erbring, Lutz and Alice A. Young (1979). "Individuals and Social Structure: Contextual Effects as Endogenous Feedback," *Sociological Methods and Research* 7(May): 396–430.

Eulau, Heinz (1976). "Social Networks, Contextual Analysis, and Electoral Behavior." Stanford University, mimeographed.

Farkas, George (1974). "Specification, Residuals, and Contextual Effects." *Sociological Methods and Research* 2(February): 333–363.

Finifter, Ada W. (1974). "The Friendship Group as a Protective Environment for Political Deviants." *American Political Science Review,* 68(June): 607–625.

Fischer, Claude S. (1975). "The Metropolitan Experience." In Hawley and Rock, *Metropolitan America in Contemporary Perspective,* pp. 201–234.

———— (1976). *The Urban Experience.* New York: Harcourt, Brace, Javonovich.

Fischer, Claude S., et al. (1977). *Networks and Places: Social Relations in the Urban Setting.* New York: Free Press.

Fitton, Martin (1973). "Neighborhood and Voting: A Sociometric Examination," *British Journal of Political Science* 3(October): 445–472.

Foladare, Irving S. (1968). "The Effect of Neighborhood on Voting Behavior." *Political Science Quarterly* 83(December): 516–529.

Fuchs, Lawrence H. (1955). "American Jews and the Presidential Vote," *American Political Science Review* 49(June): 385–401.

Gabriel, Richard A. (1972). "A New Theory of Ethnic Voting." *Polity* 4 (Summer): 405–428.

Gans, Herbert J. (1967). *The Levittowners: Ways of Life and Politics in a New Suburban Community.* New York: Pantheon.

———— (1962). *The Urban Villagers: Group and Class in the Life of Italian-Americans.* New York: Free Press.

Gatlin, Douglas S., Michael Giles, and Everett F. Cataldo (1978). "Policy Support Within a Target Group: The Case of School Desegregation." *American Political Science Review* 72(September): 985–995.

Giles, Michael W., and Marilyn K. Dantico (1982). "Political Participation and Neighborhood Social Context Revisited." *American Journal of Political Science* 26(February): 144–150.

Giles, Michael W., and Gerald C. Wright (1979). "Social Status and Political Behavior: The Impact of Residential Context." Paper delivered at the annual meeting of the Midwest Political Science Association, Chicago, April 19–21.

Goldthorpe, John H., et al. (1968). *The Affluent Worker: Political Attitudes and Behavior.* Cambridge: Cambridge University Press.

Green, Bryan S.R. (1971). "Structural Effects and Social Area Analysis," *Sociology* 5(January): 1–19.

Greenberg, Stanley B. (1974). *Politics and Poverty: Modernization and Response in Five Poor Neighborhoods.* New York: Wiley.

Greer, Scott (1956). "Urbanism Reconsidered: A Comparative Study of Local Affairs in a Metropolis," *American Sociological Review,* 21(February): 19–25.

Guest, Avery M., and James A. Weed (1976). "Ethnic Residential Segregation: Patterns of Change," *American Journal of Sociology* 81(March): 1088–1111.

Hamilton, Richard (1972). *Class and Politics in the United States.* New York: Wiley.

———— (1975). *Restraining Myths: Critical Studies of U.S. Social Structure and Politics.* New York: Halsted Press (Wiley).

Hanushek, Eric A., and John E. Jackson (1977). *Statistical Methods for Social Scientists.* New York: Academic Press.

Hauser, Robert M. (1974). "Contextual Analysis Revisited," *Sociological Methods and Research* 2(February): 365–375.

Hawkins, Brett W., and Robert A. Lorinskas, eds. (1970). *The Ethnic Factor in American Politics.* Columbus, Ohio: Charles E. Merrill.

Hawley, Amos H., and Vincent P. Rock, eds. (1975). *Metropolitan America in Contemporary Perspective.* New York: Halsted Press (Wiley).

Hawley, Amos H., and Basil G. Zimmer (1970). *The Metropolitan Community: Its People and Government.* Beverly Hills, Calif.: Sage.

Hirschman, Albert O. (1970). *Exit, Voice and Loyalty.* Cambridge, Mass.: Harvard University Press.

Huckfeldt, R. Robert (1977). "Political Behavior and the Social Contexts of Urban Neighborhoods." Ph.D. dissertation, Washington University, St. Louis.

———— (1979). "Political Participation and the Neighborhood Social Context," *American Journal of Political Science,* 23(August): 579–592.

———— (1980). "Variable Responses to Neighborhood Social Contexts: Assimilation, Conflict, and Tipping Points," *Political Behavior* 2(3): 231–257.

———— (1983a). "The Social Contexts of Ethnic Politics: Ethnic Loyalties, Political Loyalties, and Social Support." *American Politics Quarterly,* 99(January): 91–123.

———— (1983b). "Social Contexts, Social Networks, and Urban Neighborhoods: Environmental Constraints on Friendship Choice." *American Journal of Sociology,* 89(November): 651–669.

———— (1983c). "The Social Context of Political Change: Durability, Volatility, and Social Influence," *American Political Science Review,* 77(December): 929–944.

———— (1983d) "Social Contexts, Political Environments, and the Dynamics of Voter Preference." Paper delivered at the annual meeting of the American Political Science Association, Chicago.

———— (1984). "Political Loyalties and Social Class Ties: The Mechanisms of Contextual Influence," *American Journal of Political Science,* 28(May): 399–417.

Huckfeldt, R. Robert, C.W. Kohfeld, and T.W. Likens (1982). *Dynamic Modeling: An Introduction.* Sage University Paper Series on Quantitative Applications in the Social Sciences, series no. 07-027. Beverly Hills: Sage.

Hunter, Albert (1974). *Symbolic Communities: The Persistence and Change of Chicago's Local Communities.* Chicago: University of Chicago Press.

Hyman, Herbert H. (1969). *Political Socialization: A Study in the Psychology of Political Behavior.* New York: Free Press.

Jackman, Mary R., and Robert W. Jackman (1983). *Class Awareness in the United States.* Berkeley: University of California Press.

Judd, Dennis R. (1979). *The Politics of American Cities: Private Power and Public Policy.* Boston: Little, Brown.

Kantowicz, Edward R. (1975). *Polish-American Politics in Chicago. 1888–1940.* Chicago: University of Chicago Press.

Kantrowitz, Nathan (1973). *Ethnic and Racial Segregation in the New York Metropolis: Residential Patterns Among White Ethnic Groups, Blacks and Puerto Ricans.* New York: Praeger.

Kasarda, John D., and Morris Janowitz (1974). "Community Attachment in Mass Society,"

American Sociological Review, 39(June): 328–339.

Katz, Daniel, and Samuel J. Eldersveld (1961). "The Impact of Party Activity Upon the Electorate," *Public Opinion Quarterly*, 25(Spring): 1–24.

Katz, Elihu (1957). "The Two-step Flow of Communication: An Up-to Date Report on a Hypothesis," *Public Opinion Quarterly*, 21(Spring): 67–78.

Katz, Elihu, and Paul F. Lazarsfeld (1955). *Personal Influence: The Part Played by People in the Flow of Mass Communication.* Glencoe, Ill.: Free Press.

Keller, Suzanne (1968). *The Urban Neighborhood: A Sociological Perspective.* New York: Random House.

Kelley, Harold H. (1952). "Two Functions of Reference Groups." In Guy E. Swanson, Theodore M. Newcomb, and Eugene L. Hartley (eds.), *Readings in Social Psychology*, pp. 410–414. New York Henry Holt.

Kelley, Harold H., and Edmund Volkart (1952). "The Resistance to Change of Group Anchored Attitudes." *American Sociological Review* 17(August): 453–465.

Kellstedt, Lyman A. and Paul J. Strand (1973). "Political Trust and Political Participation: Some Implications for Urban Politics." Prepared for delivery at the annual meeting of the Southwestern Political Science Association, Dallas, March 22–24.

Key, V.O., Jr., with the assistance of Alexander Heard (1949). *Southern Politics; In State and Nation.* New York: Knopf.

Knoke, David, and James H. Kuklinski (1982). *Network Analysis.* Sage University Paper Series on Quantitative Applications in the Social Sciences, series no. 07-028. Beverly Hills: Sage.

Kornblum, William (1974). *Blue Collar Community.* Chicago: University of Chicago Press.

Kornhauser, Arthur, Harold L. Sheppard, and Albert J. Mayer (1956). *When Labor Votes: A Study of Auto Workers.* New York: University Books.

Kornhauser, William (1959). *The Politics of Mass Society.* New York: Free Press.

Langton, Kenneth P. (1969). *Political Socialization.* New York: Oxford University Press.

Langton, Kenneth P., and Ronald Rapoport (1975). "Social Structure, Social Context, and Partisan Mobilization: Urban Workers in Chile." *Comparative Political Studies* 8(October): 318–344.

LaPonce, J.A. (1974). "Ethnicity, Religion, and Politics in Canada: A Comparative Analysis of Survey and Census Data." In Dogan and Rokkan, *Social Ecology*, pp. 187–216.

Laumann, Edward O. (1973). *Bonds of Pluralism: The Form and Substance of Urban Social Networks.* New York: Wiley.

Lazarsfeld, Paul F., Bernard Berelson, and Hazel Gaudet (1968). *The People's Choice*, third ed. New York: Columbia University Press.

Lenski, Gerhard E. (1966). *Power and Privilege: A Theory of Social Stratification.* New York: McGraw-Hill.

Lieberson, Stanley (1963). *Ethnic Patterns in American Cities.* New York: Free Press.

Lipset, Seymour Martin (1963). *Political Man: The Social Bases of Politics.* Garden City, NY: Anchor Books.

Lorinskas, Robert A., Brett W. Hawkins, and Stephen D. Edwards (1969). "The Persistence of Ethnic Voting in Urban and Rural Areas: Results from the Controlled Election Method." *Social Science Quarterly*, 49(March): 891-899.

Marans, Richard W., and Willard Rodgers (1975). "Toward an Understanding of Community Satisfaction. In Hawley and Rock, *Metropolitan America in Contemporary Perspective*, pp. 201–234.

Mayhew, Bruce H., and Roger L. Levinger (1976). "Size and the Density of Interaction in Human Aggregates." *American Journal of Sociology* 82(July): 86–110.

McClosky, Herbert, and Harold E. Dahlgren (1959). "Primary Group Influence on Party Loyalty," *American Political Science Review* 53(September): 757–776.

McKenzie, R.D. (1933). *The Metropolitan Community*. New York: McGraw-Hill.

McPhee, William N., with Robert B. Smith and Jack Ferguson (1963). "A Theory of Informal Social Influence." In William N. McPhee, *Formal Theories of Mass Behavior*, chap. 2, New York: Free Press.

Michelson, William (1970). *Man and His Urban Environment: A Sociological Approach*. Reading, Mass.: Addison-Wesley.

Milbrath, Lester W., and M. L. Goel (1977). *Political Participation: How and Why Do People Get Involved in Politics?* Chicago: Rand McNally.

Miller, Warren E. (1956). "One-Party Politics and the Voter," *American Political Science Review* 50(September): 707–725.

Miller, W.L. (1978). "Social Class and Party Choice in England: A New Analysis," *British Journal of Political Science*, 8(July): 257–284.

Nelli, Humbert S. (1979). *Italians in Chicago. 1880-1930*. New York: Oxford University Press.

Newcomb, Theodore M. (1957). *Personality and Social Change: Attitude Formation in a Student Community*. New York: Dryden. (Originally published in 1943.)

Nisbet, Robert A. (1953). *The Quest for Community: A Study of the Ethics of Order and Freedom*. New York: Oxford University Press.

Orbell, John M. (1970). "The Impact of Metropolitan Residence on Political and Social Orientations," *Social Science Quarterly* 51(December): 634–648.

——— (1970). "An Information-Flow Theory of Community Influence." *Journal of Politics* 32(May): 322–338.

Orbell, John M., with Kenneth S. Sherrill, (1969). "Racial Attitudes and the Metropolitan Context: A Structural Analysis," *Public Opinion Quarterly*, 33(Spring): 46–54.

Parenti, Michael (1967). "Ethnic Politics and the Persistence of Ethnic Identification." *American Political Science Review*, 61(September): 717–726.

Park, Robert E. (1925). "The City: Suggestions for the Investigations of Human Behavior in the Urban Environment." In Park et al., *The City*, chap. 1.

——— (1952). "The City as a Social Laboratory." In Robert Ezra Park, *Human Communities: The City and Human Ecology, Volume II. The Collected Papers of Robert Ezra Park*, edited by Everett Cherrington Hughes et al., chap. 4. Glencoe, Ill.: Free Press.

Park, Robert E., Ernest W. Burgess, and Roderick D. McKenzie (1925). *The City*. Chicago: University of Chicago Press.

Pettigrew, Thomas F. (1959). "Regional Differences in Anti-Negro Prejudice." *Journal of Abnormal and Social Psychology* 59(July): 28–36.

Pomper, Gerald (1966). "Ethnic and Group Voting in Nonpartisan Municipal Elections," *Public Opinion Quarterly*, 30(Spring): 79–97.

Prysby, Charles L. (1975). "Neighborhood Class Composition and Individual Partisan Choice: A Test with Chilean Data," *Social Science Quarterly*, 56(September): 225–238.

Przeworski, Adam (1974). "Contextual Models of Political Behavior." *Political Methodology* 1(Winter): 27–61.

Przeworski, Adam, and Glaucio A.D. Soares (1971). "Theories in Search of a Curve: A Contextual Interpretaton of Left Vote," *American Political Science Review* 65(March): 51–68.

Putnam, Robert D. (1966). "Political Attitudes and the Local Community." *American Political Science Review* 60(September): 640–654.

Riesman, David, in Collaboration With Reuel Denny and Nathan Glazer (1950). *TheLonely Crowd: A Study of the Changing American Character.* New Haven: Yale University Press.

Schelling, Thomas C. (1972). "The Process of Residential Segregation: Neighborhood Tipping," In Anthony H. Pascal (ed.), *Racial Discrimination in Economic Life,* pp. 157–184. Lexington, Mass.: Lexington Books (D.C. Heath).

——— (1978). *Micromotives and Macrobehavior.* New York: Norton.

Schnore, Leo F. (1972). *Class and Race in Cities and Suburbs.* Chicago: Markham.

Sears, David O., and Donald R. Kinder (1970). "The Good Life, 'White Racism,' and the Crowd: A Study of the Changing American Character. New Haven: Yale University Los Angeles Voter." Paper delivered at the annual meeting of the Western Psychological Association, Los Angeles.

——— (1971). "Racial Tensions and Voting in Los Angeles," In Werner Z. Hirsch (ed.), *Los Angeles: Viability and Prospects for Metropolitan Leadership.* New York: Praeger.

Sears, David O., and John B. McConahy (1973). *The Politics of Violence: The New Urban Blacks and the Watts Riot.* Boston: Houghton-Mifflin.

Segal, David R., and David Knoke (1970). "Political Partisanship: Its Social and Economic Bases in the United States." *The American Journal of Economics and Sociology,* 29(July): 252–262.

Segal, David R., and Marshall W. Meyer (1974). "The Social Context of Political Partisanship." In Dogan and Rokkan, *Social Ecology,* pp. 217–232.

Segal, David R., and Stephen H. Wildstrom (1970). "Community Effects on Political Attitudes: Partisanship and Efficacy." *Sociological Quarterly* 11(Winter): 67–86.

Sheingold, Carl A. (1973). "Social Networks and Voting: The Agenda." *American Sociological Review* 38(December): 712–720.

Shevky, Eshref, and Wendell Bell (1955). *Social Area Analysis; Theory, Illustrative Application and Computational Procedures.* Stanford, Calif.: Stanford University Press.

Shevky, Eshref, and Marilyn Williams (1949). *The Social Areas of Los Angeles: Analysis and Typology.* Berkeley: University of California Press.

Sprague, John (1976). "Estimating a Boudon Type Contextual Model: Some Practical and Theoretical Problems of Measurement," *Political Methodology* 3: 333–353.

——— (1982). "Is There a Micro Theory Consistent with Contextual Analysis?" In E. Ostrom (ed.), *Strategies of Political Inquiry,* pp. 99–121. Beverly Hills: Sage.

Sprague, John, and Louis P. Westefield (1977). "Collaborative Research on Politics in Context." Washington University, St. Louis, unpublished paper.

——— (1979a). "Contextual Effects from Behavioral Contagion." Washington University, St. Louis, Political Science Paper No. 22.

——— (1979b). "An Interpretive Reconstruction of Some Aggregate Models of Contextual Effects." Washington University, St. Louis, Political Science Paper No. 41.

Stabrowski, Br. Donald (1984). "A Political Machine, An Ethnic Community, and South Bend's West Side: 1900–1980." Ph.D. dissertation, University of Notre Dame.

Stephens, John D. (1981). "The Changing Swedish Electorate: Class Voting, Contextual Effects, and Voter Volatility," *Comparative Political Studies* 14(July): 163–204.

Stouffer, Samuel A., et al. (1949). *The American Soldier: Vol. I. Adjustment During Army Life.* Princeton: Princeton University Press.

Suttles, Gerald D. (1968). *The Social Order of the Slum: Ethnicity and Territory in the Inner*

City. Chicago: University of Chicago Press.

———— (1972). *The Social Construction of Communities.* Chicago: University of Chicago Press.

Taeuber, Karl E., and Alma F. Taeuber (1965). *Negroes in Cities: Residential Segregation and Neighborhood Change.* Chicago: Aldine.

Tallman, Irving, and Romona Morgner (1970). "Life Style Differences among Urban and Suburban Blue-collar Families." *Social Forces* 48(March): 334–348.

Tannebaum, Arnold S., and Jerald G. Bachman (1964). "Structural Versus *American Journal of Sociology* 69(May): 585–595.

Tate, C. Neal (1974). "Individual and Contextual Variables in British Voting Behavior: An Exploratory Note." *American Political Science Review,* 68(December): 1656–1662.

Theil, Henri (1970). "On the Estimation of Relationships Involving Qualitative Variables," *American Journal of Sociology* 75(May): 585–595.

Tingsten, Herbert (1963). *Political Behavior: Studies in Election Statistics,* transl. Vilgot Hammarling. Totowa, N.J.: Bedminster. (Originally published in 1937.)

Tonnies, Ferdinand (1957). *Community and Society,* transl. and edited by Charles P. Loomis. Lansing: Michgan State University Press. (Originally published in 1887.)

Truman, David B. (1964). *The Governmental Process: Political Interests and Public Opinion.* New York: Knopf.

Valkonen, Tapani (1969). "Community Context and Politicization of Individuals," *Acta Sociologica,* 12: 144–155.

———— (1974). "Individual and Structural Effects in Ecological Research." In Dogan and Rokkan, *Social Ecology,* pp. 53–68.

Verba, Sidney, and Norman H. Nie (1972). *Participation in America: Political Democracy and Social Equality.* New York: Harper & Row.

Weatherford, M. Stephen (1980). "The Politics of School Busing: Contextual Effects and Community Polarization," *Journal of Politics,* 42(August): 747–765.

———— (1982). "Interpersonal Networks and Political Behavior," *American Journal of Political Science,* 26(February): 117–143.

White, Harrison C., Scott A. Boorman, and Ronald L. Breiger (1976). "Social Structures from Multiple Networks. I. Blockmodels of Roles and Positions." *American Journal of Sociology* 81(January): 730–780.

Whyte, William Foote (1955). *Street Corner Society: The Social Structure of an Italian Slum.* Chicago: University of Chicago Press.

Whyte, William H., Jr. (1956). *The Organization Man.* New York: Simon and Schuster.

Wilson, Robert A. (1971). "Anomie in the Ghetto: A Study of Neighborhood Type, People, and Anomie.": *American Journal of Sociology* 77(July): 66–68.

Wirt, Frederick M., Benjamin Walter, Francine F. Rabinovitz, and Deborah R. Hensler (1972). *On the City's Rim: Politics and Policy in Suburbia.* Lexington, Mass.: Lexington Books (D.C. Heath).

Wirth, Louis (1938). "Urbanism as a Way of Life," *Americana Journal of Sociology,* 44(July): 1–24.

Wolfinger, Raymond E. (1963). "The Influence of Precinct Work on Voting Behavior." *Public Opinion Quarterly* 27(Fall): 387–389.

———— (1965). "The Development and Persistence of Ethnic Voting," *American Political Science Review* 59(December): 896–908.

Wonnacott, Ronald J., and Thomas H. Wonnacott (1970). *Econometrics.* New York: Wiley.

Wood, Robert C. (1959). *Suburbia: Its People and Their Politics.* Boston: Houghton Mifflin.

Wright, Gerald C. (1976a). "Community Structure and Voting in the South." *Public*

Opinion Quarterly, 40(Summer): 200–2 15.

———— (1976b). "Linear Models for Evaluating Conditional Relationships," *American Journal of Political Science* 20(May): 349–373.

———— (1977). "Contextual Models of Electoral Behavior: The Southern Wallace Vote." *American Political Science Review,* 71(June): 497–508.

Zehner, Robert B., and F. Stuart Chapin, Jr. (1974). *Across the City Line: A White Community in Transition.* Lexington, Mass.: Lexington Books (D.C. Heath).

INDEX

To Jo Burgess, who is the embodiment of our family motto: Live well, laugh often and love much.

CONTENTS

FIGURES

TABLES

PREFACE

When I was first learning economics, the world was in the middle of the Cold War. The choice was very clear. Either you embraced the market-oriented economic approach of Western capitalism or you favored the state-owned and operated system of Soviet-style socialism.

Prevailing views on the environment were equally stark. Either you viewed economic growth as the source of prosperity and well-being or you disdained growth as the main cause of Earth's environmental destruction.

Today, too often our policy debates concerning both the economy and the environment are still colored by these old arguments. The purpose of this book is to put these archaic views to one side and rethink how economics should grapple with our greatest challenge today: Planet Earth is being destroyed, and we are the cause of its demise.

This challenge is both immense and urgent. Scientists believe that the world has entered a new geological epoch, called the "Anthropocene." Since the mid-twentieth century, human activity has become the dominant influence on the global environment. We are altering basic Earth system processes through climate and land use change, pollution, freshwater use and many other impacts.

If current trends continue, in the coming decades we are likely to face global warming of 2–4°C or more, massive biodiversity losses and species extinction, chronic freshwater scarcity and other unknown environmental disruptions. If we are too slow to act, or do too little too late, the Earth will be irrevocably damaged, and future generations will be much worse off than today.

The recent COVID-19 pandemic has not lessened the urgency of this challenge. In many ways it has reinforced the need for action. After all, the risk of disease outbreaks is connected to other environmental threats, such as global land use change and biodiversity and habitat loss. Moreover, as the world economy recovers, so will its unrelenting exploitation of our remaining global environmental resources and sinks.

In short, Planet Earth is now extremely fragile, and it is no longer a problem that we can leave future generations to fix. Global environmental change is already affecting the lives and livelihoods of billions today, and we are exacerbating this problem by delaying actions to deal with it. The longer we wait, the more the costs of inaction rise. Now is the time for humankind to respond to these growing risks.

There is no longer a choice between economic growth and the environment. Protecting and restoring the natural world is essential for human welfare and well-being.

The aim of this book is to identify what steps we need to take to avert the growing environmental risks to our planet. The world urgently needs more innovative thinking on policies and economics for an increasingly "fragile" Earth, and this book offers one vision of the way forward.

Ultimately, this is a book about hope. As people around the world face global environmental crises and suffer their dire consequences, they are demanding new policies. By rethinking markets, institutions and governance, we can formulate a strategy for better stewardship of the global environment. What is more, such a strategy can be workable and affordable, but it will require commitment from all stakeholders in our economy: governments, businesses and consumers.

Overall this entails a commitment of our economies to sustainability and an understanding that policies associated with "greening" economic activity promote better stewardship of the Earth. We need to move beyond the growth versus the environment debate and instead develop new ways of sustaining well-being for all while minimizing environmental risks. Above all, we need to "decouple" wealth creation and economic prosperity from environmental degradation, so that economic development and growing populations no longer threaten the very processes that sustain Earth systems and our economies. This is necessary to protect our fragile Earth while ensuring that future generations have at least the same economic opportunities as our current one. We must also do this in a way that reduces wealth and income inequality, alleviates poverty and ensures that economic development is more inclusive.

These issues need to be addressed urgently, yet they are still largely ignored in current economic thinking. The purpose of this book is to start the process of identifying new economic and policy ideas for an increasingly "fragile" planet. The book explores how improving markets, institutions and governance can correct the underpricing of nature and, ultimately, enhance the ability of economies to meet the environmental challenges of the Anthropocene. It illustrates how this can be done with four critical human threats to the global environment: climate change, land use and biodiversity loss, freshwater scarcity and deteriorating marine and coastal habitats. And it explains what public policies are needed to jump-start the transition, and the additional actions required for greening business and finance.

Ensuring a "safe" Anthropocene is the major sustainability challenge facing humankind today. Meeting this challenge places a significant responsibility on economics to lead the way in designing new policies and strategies. The aim of this book is to explain what "economics for a fragile planet" might look like. In a post-COVID world, it is more necessary than ever.

ACKNOWLEDGMENTS

This book would not be possible without the encouragement, support and input of Jo Burgess. For over thirty years, we have worked closely on many of the topics covered in this book. I have lost count of the number of times that Jo has inspired me in applying economics to tackle complex environmental problems. Our many discussions as I was writing this book were instrumental to several of the ideas expressed here. And of course, the comments Jo has provided on early drafts of chapters have improved the manuscript and my writing considerably.

I would like to thank Chris Harrison and Phil Good of Cambridge University Press for encouraging me in this project, and for waiting patiently for me to complete it. Chris has always been keen to publish my work in economics, and he has been supporting my publishing endeavors at Cambridge University Press for nearly two decades. Phil was enthusiastic about this book proposal from the moment I pitched it to him, and he has enthusiastically advocated for and supported its publication throughout.

I am also grateful to Colorado State University (CSU), and especially my colleagues in the Department of Economics, the School of Global Environmental Sustainability and the College of Liberal Arts. Academic freedom is a precious commodity, and I am lucky to be at an institution where it is highly valued. Without the support of CSU and my colleagues for my work and ideas, I am not sure it would have been possible to write this book.

Because the book in many ways is a reflection of my views gained over a lifetime's career in environmental economics, I owe a debt of gratitude to a long list of teachers, mentors, coauthors, collaborators and institutions who have helped me to develop my ideas throughout the years. Thank you for your support, for your inspiration and, above all, for helping me think and learn.

1 INTRODUCTION

Humankind must accept stewardship of Planet Earth and urgently act on it.

It used to be that only climate activists, environmentalists and street protestors talked about "saving the Earth." Today, this sentiment is expressed by nearly everyone – from citizens to academics to government officials and boardroom executives.

At the 2020 World Economic Forum in Davos, Peter Brabeck-Letmathe, former chairman and CEO of Nestlé, announced:

> Planet Earth is sick ... so we have to heal it.[1]

And, as Partha Dasgupta explained in his landmark review of *The Economics of Biodiversity*:

> The solution starts with understanding and accepting a simple truth: our economies are embedded within Nature, not external to it.[2]

This shift in sentiment, although welcome, has been a long time coming.

In the 1960s, the economist Kenneth Boulding argued that humankind's future depends on transforming the current "cowboy economy," which treats Earth's resources and sinks as essentially limitless, to a "spaceman economy" that respects the finite biosphere of "Spaceship Earth." Boulding contrasted these two economies in this way:

> I am tempted to call the open economy the "cowboy economy," the cowboy being symbolic of the illimitable plains and also associated with reckless, exploitative, romantic, and violent

behavior, which is characteristic of open societies. The closed economy of the future might similarly be called the "spaceman" economy, in which the earth has become a single spaceship, without unlimited reservoirs of anything, either for extraction or for pollution, and in which, therefore, man must find his place in a cyclical ecological system which is capable of continuous reproduction of material form even though it cannot escape having inputs of energy.[3]

In the 1970s, the historian Arnold Toynbee noted that humankind has always exploited nature with little regard of the environmental impact. Whereas previously we only "devastated patches of the biosphere," this changed with the Industrial Revolution. It gave us the "power to damage and despoil the biosphere irremediably":

> Before the Industrial Revolution, Man had devastated patches of the biosphere ... But, before he had harnessed the physical energy of inanimate nature in machines on the grand scale, Man had not had it in his power to damage and despoil the biosphere irremediably. Till then, the air and the ocean had been virtually infinite, and the supply of timber and metals had far exceeded Man's capacity to use them up. When he had exhausted one mine and had felled one forest, there had always been other virgin mines and virgin forests till waiting to be exploited. By making the Industrial Revolution, Man exposed the biosphere, including Man himself, to a threat that had no precedent.[4]

Ten years later, the scientist James Lovelock elaborated on the possible dire – and irreversible – consequences if we fail to curtail global environmental degradation:

> Anything that makes the world uncomfortable to live in tends to induce the evolution of those species that can achieve a new and more comfortable environment. It follows that, if the world is made unfit by what we do, there is the probability of a change in regime to one that will be better for life but not necessarily better for us ... The things we do to the planet are not offensive nor do they pose a geophysiological threat, unless we do them on a large enough scale ... When all this is taken into account we are indeed in danger of changing the Earth away from the comfortable state it was once in.[5]

Several decades on, the world may be beginning to heed the warnings of Boulding, Toynbee and Lovelock, but we have yet to halt the "danger of changing the Earth away from the comfortable state it was once in."

According to the Intergovernmental Panel on Climate Change (IPCC), by failing to reduce global greenhouse gas emissions, we are destined to live in "a world of worsening food shortages and wildfires, and a mass die-off of coral reefs as soon as 2040 — a period well within the lifetime of much of the global population."[6] Mammals and other species may also be on the verge of "biological annihilation" as forests and other natural habitat continue to be converted and degraded.[7] Currently, at least one-third of fish stocks are overfished; one-third to half of vulnerable marine habitats have been lost; and a substantial fraction of the coastal ocean suffers from pollution, eutrophication, oxygen depletion and is stressed by ocean warming.[8] Rising freshwater scarcity is a present-day danger for the 1.6–2.4 billion people currently living within watersheds with inadequate supplies and exposed to climate change.[9]

Unless we control these alarming trends, they could endanger the health and livelihoods of millions and the sustainability of our economies. Even in a world recovering from the worst health pandemic in more than 100 years and the deepest economic recession since the Great Depression of the 1930s, humankind's devastating impacts on the biosphere remain our biggest global challenge.

So, it is not surprising that, in its first global survey since the COVID-19 outbreak, the World Economic Forum found that four environmental risks – plus the threat of infectious disease outbreaks – are the top five global threats to humankind.[10] These four risks are: extreme weather, climate action failure, human environmental damage and biodiversity loss.

All of these trends and concerns suggest that humankind's relationship with the biosphere is at a critical juncture. Planet Earth could be on the cusp of destabilization, and we may not have many years left to change this path.

The Anthropocene

Human impacts on Earth are now so significant that we have created an entirely new geological epoch – the *Anthropocene*.[11] This era began with the late twentieth-century "Great Acceleration" of population growth, industrialization and mineral and energy use, and has continued unabated since.[12] Human activity has become the dominant influence on the global environment. We are altering basic Earth system processes at an increasing rate through climate and land use change, pollution, freshwater use and many other impacts. As a result, the Earth system could be approaching a "tipping point" that could change it irrevocably, with potentially disastrous impacts for humanity.[13]

We do not really know what will happen once this Earth system threshold is crossed (see Figure 1.1). The system may well be out of human control or influence, and will be driven by its own internal dynamics. But if the Great Acceleration continues, one possible outcome is a "catastrophic" Anthropocene, with global warming of 2–4°C or

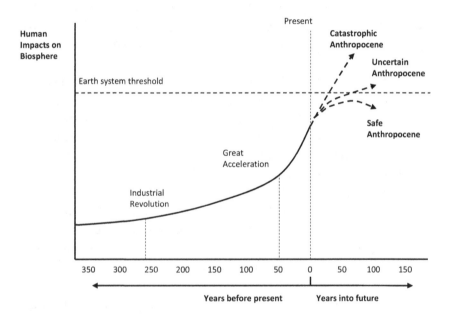

Figure 1.1 Human impacts on Planet Earth
Notes: Since 1970, rapid industrialization, population growth, resource use and pollution have caused a "Great Acceleration" in human impacts on the biosphere. If these impacts continue, in a few decades we could produce a "catastrophic" Anthropocene that would threaten humanity. Even if human impacts are moderated somewhat, crossing the Earth system's threshold would lead to an "uncertain" Anthropocene with unpredictable consequences for the planet. Only by reducing human impacts significantly over the next few decades are we likely to avoid exceeding the Earth system threshold, or "tipping point," and create a relatively "safe" Anthropocene.

more, massive biodiversity losses and species extinction, chronic fresh-water scarcity and other unknown environmental disruptions.[14] If we exceed the Earth system threshold, we could end up in an "uncertain" Anthropocene, where the environmental consequences are difficult to predict and would likely cause serious, and possibly irreversible, damages to ecosystems, society and economies. Only if we act now, and with sufficient efforts to "decouple" human impacts on the planet from economic activity and continued population growth, are we likely to be able to maintain a "safe" Anthropocene that evades Earth's "tipping point."

Some scientists advocate that, to prevent an uncertain or cata-strophic Anthropocene, human impacts on the global environment must be kept within the "planetary boundaries" that protect key Earth system processes. They suggest that there are "nine such processes for which we believe it is necessary to define planetary boundaries: climate change; rate of biodiversity loss (terrestrial and marine); interference with the nitrogen and phosphorus cycles; stratospheric ozone depletion; ocean acidification; global freshwater use; change in land use; chemical pollution; and atmospheric aerosol loading."[15]

Although there are disagreements over this "planetary bound-ary" perspective, there is growing scientific consensus that Planet Earth is increasingly fragile, and it is no longer a problem that we can leave future generations to fix. Global environmental change is occurring now, already affecting the lives and livelihoods of billions today, and only getting worse as we delay actions to deal with it. The longer we wait, the more the costs of inaction rise and the risk of potentially catastrophic change occurs. As the scientists Timothy Lenton and Hywell Williams conclude, "regardless of whether it is approaching a global tipping point, we can all agree that the biosphere is in trouble."[16]

We cannot afford to wait any longer. It is now time for human-kind to accept stewardship of Planet Earth and to act on it.

This is the contribution of the following book. It begins with acknowledging the "simple truth" – as the quote by Partha Dasgupta so eloquently states – that "our economies are embedded within Nature, not external to it." This modest yet powerful change in our economic view of the world can help guide how we rethink our markets, insti-tutions and governance. And, from these changes, flow a plethora of new incentives, innovations and investments that can transform our economies to become more sustainable and inclusive.

The purpose of this book is to start this process of more innovative thinking on economics and policies for an increasingly "fragile" planet. It requires addressing three crucial questions:

- How do we reduce human impacts on the biosphere to ensure a safe Anthropocene, and if so, what are the implications for our markets, institutions and governance?
- As environmental risks continue to mount, how do we design and run our economies to avoid and mitigate these risks in an inclusive and sustainable manner?
- What policies are required to "decouple" wealth creation and economic prosperity from environmental degradation, to sustain per capita welfare and simultaneously limit environmental risks?

These questions need to be addressed urgently. They represent the major sustainability challenge facing the world today. Yet current economic and policy thinking has largely ignored them.

Throughout this book, we will explore why this has to change and how to do it. The first step is to approach the relationship between nature and economy differently than we have in the past. Tackling the sustainability crisis requires new ways of viewing the world around us, and that in turn, requires some principles to guide economic and policy thinking.

This book proposes five such principles:

- Ending the underpricing of nature
- Fostering collective action
- Accepting absolute limits
- Attaining sustainability
- Promoting inclusivity

These principles underlie the approach to economics and policy taken in this book.

Underpricing Nature

Ending the *underpricing of nature* is listed as the first principle, as it lies at the heart of the sustainability crisis.

The failure to take the true value of the environment into account is pervasive in all economies. Poor institutions and governance further exacerbate this disincentive, thus fostering even more environmental mismanagement.

This book explores how improving markets, institutions and governance can correct the underpricing of nature, and ultimately, enhance the ability of economies to meet the environmental challenges of the Anthropocene.

Economists have always maintained that the key measure of an economy's progress is its ability to create wealth. Today, it is widely recognized that the "real wealth" of a nation comprises three distinct capital assets: manufactured *physical capital*, such as roads, buildings, machinery and factories; *human capital*, such as skills, education and health embodied in the workforce; and *natural capital*, including land, forests, fossil fuels and minerals. In addition, natural capital also comprises those ecosystems that through their natural functioning and habitats provide important goods and services to the economy, or *ecological capital*. But the world economy today is squandering, rather than accumulating, key sources of wealth.

Despite rising natural resource scarcity and increasing environmental and ecological damage, the growth and structure of production in modern economies continues to use more resources and energy. We are not facing up to the rising economic and social costs of increasing natural resource use, pollution and ecological scarcity. We hide these costs by underpricing natural capital in our market, policy and investment decisions.[17] As a consequence, we are using up natural resources as fast as ever, increasingly polluting the environment and rapidly running down our endowment of ecological capital.

This raises two important questions:

- If natural and ecological capital are valuable sources of economic wealth, why are we squandering these assets?
- If ecological scarcity and natural capital loss are on the rise, why are we are we doing so little to address these problems?

The key to this paradox is the underpricing of nature in our economies: The increasing costs associated with many environmental problems – climate change, freshwater scarcity, declining ecosystem services and increasing energy insecurity – are not routinely reflected in markets. Nor have we developed adequate policies and institutions to provide other ways for the true costs of environmental degradation to be taken into account. This means that decision makers do not receive the correct price signals or incentives to adjust production and consumption activities. All too often, policy distortions and failures compound ecological scarcity, pollution and resource overexploitation by further encouraging wasteful use of natural resources and environmental degradation.

As David Pearce and I argued some years ago, this process has become a *vicious cycle* in today's economies:

> Important environmental values are generally not reflected in markets, and despite much rhetoric to the contrary, are routinely ignored in policy decisions. Institutional failures, such as the lack of property rights, inefficient and corrupt governance, political instability and the absence of public authority or institutions, also compound this problem. The result is economic development that produces excessive environmental degradation and increasing ecological scarcity. As we have demonstrated, the economic and social costs associated with these impacts can be significant.[18]

This vicious cycle can also be depicted visually, as shown in Figure 1.2. Markets and policy decisions currently do not reflect the rising economic costs associated with exploiting the environment. The result is that economic development today produces much more environmental damage and ecosystem harm than it needs to. Such development leads to even more resource depletion, pollution, degradation of ecosystems and, ultimately, rising ecological scarcity. But the rising economic and social costs associated with these impacts and scarcity continue to be "underpriced" by markets and ignored by policies. The vicious cycle is perpetuated, and the current pattern of economic development persists.

Inadequate institutions and governance exacerbate this vicious cycle. Corruption, poor laws, lack of enforcement, inept public administration, insufficient regulation and political instability plague environmental management in many areas of the world; so does lobbying by powerful interest groups that gain considerably from the status quo. But perhaps the biggest challenge facing the world today is the lack of effective collective governance and agreements among nations as to how best to address the growing number of challenges and environmental risks that are occurring on a global scale – climate change, biodiversity loss, freshwater scarcity and the decline of oceans and seas.[19]

Rising environmental risks are one dimension of the problem. Another dimension is the increased societal risks. The vicious cycle also creates a structural imbalance in the economy, where the lack of green innovation and investments prevent the transition from a fossil

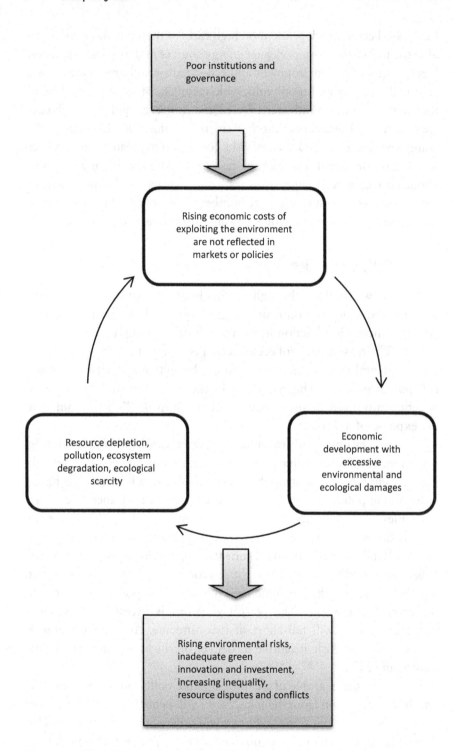

Figure 1.2 The vicious cycle of underpricing nature

fuel-based economy dependent on high rates of material and nonrenewable use to one that fosters cleaner energy sources and uses less resources. Degradation of the environment and ecosystems also impacts inequality, as it is the poorer and more vulnerable members of society that depend the most on nature and are affected the worst by pollution, climate change, natural disasters and other environmental risks. Ultimately, the rising environmental and societal risks could lead to greater conflicts over scarce environmental and natural resources. Already, there is concern about how climate change, disasters, water scarcity and other environmental threats are displacing large numbers of people, leading to enforced migration and exacerbating tensions and disputes among nations.

Collective Action

As we shall see throughout this book, one of the key mechanisms for reducing environmental degradation and threats is *collective action*, which is joint action in the pursuit of a common goal.

The reason why collective action is required for reducing many environmental risks is that the resulting benefits are what economists call *public goods*.[20] The reduction in the environmental "bad" may benefit many individuals at once, and no individual's gain comes at the expense of another.

For example, improvement in water quality through limiting pollution, removing sediment or controlling temperature extremes can have the characteristics of a public good. If I live by a lake that has had a reduction in pollution, any benefits I receive from the cleaner lake water do not lessen the benefits of others also living by the lake. All of us gain from a cleaner lake, and we enjoy these benefits simultaneously.

Realizing such an environmental improvement usually requires collective action. The members of a group who benefit need to act together to secure the outcome that has the most potential to benefit the group as a whole. The reason why this is necessary is because individual action will fall short of this outcome. Any single member who benefits has little incentive to deliver on the action that yields the most gain to all.

Take the example of cleaning up lake pollution. If I pay for the removal of pollution from the lake, then I will benefit from the resulting improvement in water quality. But so will others living by the lake. The difference is that they have no incentive to pay for the pollution removal, because I have already done so. I may decide that it might be worthwhile making such an investment anyway. But more often than not, because removing pollution from water is likely to be expensive, and I know that I cannot charge others for this benefit, I would probably not act on my own to curb lake pollution. As other individuals using the lake would reach the same conclusion, the pollution cleanup will not occur.[21]

As we shall see in this book, collective action is increasingly required to deal with a variety of environmental threats – from pollution to resource depletion to ecosystem and biodiversity loss to global environmental risks. Moreover, such action is required by groups of individuals, communities, businesses, regional and local governments and nations. It will certainly be necessary for addressing the top five global threats to humankind identified by the World Economic Forum: extreme weather, climate action failure, human environmental damage, infectious diseases and biodiversity loss.

Absolute Limits

As noted previously, some scientists advocate that, to prevent an uncertain or catastrophic Anthropocene, human impacts on the global environment must be kept within the "planetary boundaries" that protect key Earth system processes. Such boundaries impose *absolute limits* on human exploitation of critical global biophysical sinks or resources. For example, advocates of this approach have proposed boundaries to restrict depletion of terrestrial net primary production, freshwater, species richness, assimilative capacity for various pollutants, forest land area and the global carbon budget for 1.5°C or 2.0°C warming.[22]

Whether one agrees or not with the need for such absolute limits to safeguard the health of Earth's life-support systems, this viewpoint has been shaping approaches to sustainability for some time.[23] As pointed out by Robert Kates and colleagues, "Meeting fundamental human needs while preserving the life-support systems of planet Earth is the essence of sustainable development."[24]

In the next two chapters we will explore the scientific arguments for and against this perspective, as well as its implications for an "economics for a fragile planet." Regardless of the differing views on the planetary boundary debate, an important consensus is emerging that global environmental risks are mounting, and some control of the human sources of these threats is necessary to ensure a safe, as opposed to an uncertain or catastrophic, Anthropocene.

Accepting absolute limits on our cumulative environmental impacts on the biosphere has implications for both economics and policy.

Such a perspective challenges economists to reconsider whether there is an absolute limit on human exploitation of critical global biophysical sinks or resources. Over the years, some economists have advanced this view on sustainability. As we saw with the quote earlier in this chapter, it began with the economist Kenneth Boulding in the 1960s, who argued that the Earth is ultimately finite, and thus transition to a "spaceship economy" that respects such limits is unavoidable. However, this perspective was largely rejected by Boulding's fellow economists.[25]

But with the mounting scientific evidence on rising global environmental risks, and the possible need to safeguard essential Earth system life-support processes, economic views on absolute limits are beginning to change. Economic approaches to sustainability are increasingly recognizing the need to curb human activities threatening critical Earth system processes, resources and sinks.[26]

As we shall see in this book, the recognition that our planet is not a limitless source of exploitation for humankind is a simple – but ultimately profound – insight. Acknowledging that certain Earth system processes and vital resources cannot be endlessly polluted, depleted and degraded is an important starting point for thinking how best to ensure a safe Anthropocene in an efficient and sustainable manner.

It also has important policy implications. Accepting that the economy is embedded within nature and that the economy, in turn, must safeguard the health of Earth's life-support systems is essential for developing the correct policies to manage such an economy. And, we need the right policies to foster the institutions, incentives and innovations necessary to limit the rising global environmental risks posed by climate change, biodiversity loss, water scarcity and other major human impacts on the biosphere.

However, recognizing limits on humankind's endless exploitation of the Earth is not enough. As leading scholars in natural and social sciences have concluded: "Keeping within planetary boundaries requires that we make better and more cost-effective use of the finite resources and sinks available to us."[27] Such efficient use is essential, but it must also be sustainable as well as inclusive.

Sustainable and Inclusive Development

By ending the underpricing of nature and invoking collective action, we can go a long way toward realizing outcomes that have the greatest potential benefits at the least possible costs. This is an important efficiency goal of choosing the right policies among the options available to us.

However, in a world of rising global environmental risks, efficiency does not necessarily guarantee sustainability. As we have seen, one important rationale for minimizing these risks is to ensure a safe Anthropocene with healthy Earth life-support systems, well-functioning ecosystems and sufficient resources and sinks not just for ourselves but for our children and their offspring as well. In other words, we should ensure that future generations have at least the same level of economic opportunities and well-being that we presently enjoy. This concern about *intergenerational equity* is at the heart of the concept of sustainability.

For example, most interpretations of sustainability today are based on the consensus reached by the mid-1980s World Commission on Environment and Development (WCED), which defined sustainable development as "development that meets the needs of the present without compromising the ability of future generations to meet their own needs."[28] But as we have noted previously, meeting this objective may require accepting absolute limits on the global economy's accelerating pollution, depletion and degradation of key ecosystems, resources and sinks.

In other words, as David Griggs and coauthors point out, attaining sustainability requires "safeguarding Earth's life-support system, on which the welfare of current and future generations depends." Consequently, they suggest modifying the WCED definition of sustainability to "development that meets the needs of the present while safeguarding Earth's life-support system, on which the welfare of current and future generations depends."[29]

As we shall explore in this book, such a sustainable path for our economies will require additional policies and collective action to counter rising global environmental risks and safeguard key Earth system processes. The protection of essential environments that may be subject to irreversible conversion could require the implementation of a whole suite of bold and innovative policy approaches to invest in global public environmental goods.[30]

However, ensuring that development is sustainable does not necessarily guarantee that it is also inclusive. For one, imposing any limits on human exploitation of critical global sinks and resources raises important issues of *intragenerational equity*.[31] If current access to these sinks and resources is unequally distributed and dominated by wealthy nations, regions and individuals, then additional policies may be necessary either to improve access by the poor or to ensure that they are adequately reimbursed for any additional burdens imposed by reduced access.

Related to this concern is the growing income and wealth inequality over the past several decades. Since 1980, there has been rising inequality in most of the world's regions, as the top 10 percent increased their share of income. A major factor has been the unequal distribution of the growth in global income over past decades between the rich and poor. While the poorest half of the global population has seen its income grow significantly, especially in China, India and other Asian countries, since 1980 the top 1 percent richest individuals in the world captured twice as much growth as the bottom 50 percent.[32]

In addition, wealth inequality has worsened during the COVID-19 pandemic. The world's richest have become wealthier and poverty reduction has suffered a major setback. Worldwide, the wealth of billionaires increased by $3.9 trillion during the pandemic in 2020, whereas the total number of people living in extreme poverty may have increased from 70 million to 200–500 million, the first rise in over two decades.[33]

These worsening inequality trends pose a challenge to any sustainable development strategy. Ensuring that such a strategy is inclusive is even more of a priority in the coming decades, given the skyrocketing unemployment and likely disproportionate impacts on low-income households and countries caused by the pandemic. As we will discuss in later chapters, there a number of policies that economies could adopt that could both "green" a post-pandemic recovery and ensure more equitable and just distributions of benefits. Tackling the trend of growing wealth inequality may also require additional collective actions to make economic development and the world economy more inclusive in the coming decades.

Economics for a Fragile Planet

To summarize, ensuring a "safe" Anthropocene is the major sustainability challenge facing humankind today. Meeting this challenge places a significant responsibility on economics to lead the way in designing new policies and strategies. The aim of this book is to explain what this "economics for a fragile planet" might look like. The five principles outlined in this introductory chapter are the building blocks for this new economic thinking and can help guide our policy approaches.

Chapter 2 reviews the mounting scientific evidence of the growing "fragility" of the Earth system and its implications for the planet. It traces the long history of how humans have exploited nature to create wealth, starting with the Agricultural Transition 10,000 years ago up to the Fossil Fuel Age and its global consequences. The chapter then focuses on the four threats created by current human impacts on the biosphere: climate change, land use and biodiversity loss, freshwater scarcity and deteriorating marine and coastal habitats. Each of these global challenges will be examined in more detail in later chapters (see Chapters 4–7).

The need to curb human activities threatening critical Earth system processes, resources and sinks is an important starting point for thinking how best to manage our planet in an efficient, sustainable and inclusive manner. Chapter 3 explains how this can form the basis for an "economics for a fragile planet." This perspective began with Kenneth Boulding in the 1960s, who argued that the Earth is ultimately finite, and thus, transition to a "spaceship economy" that respects such limits is unavoidable. The implications are that the exploitation of Earth's sources of natural resources and sinks for pollution is not limitless, and that it is essential to end the *underpricing of nature* that currently ignores the rising costs associated with ecological scarcity and environmental degradation. This requires in turn rethinking the markets, institutions and governance needed for a green and inclusive economic transformation. The overall objective should be to manage an economy's overall stock of physical, human and natural capital to sustain per capita human welfare while limiting global environmental risks.

Chapter 4 focuses on how this new thinking is critical to addressing climate change. International action is failing to deliver on slowing greenhouse gas emissions to keep the planet from warming dangerously, yet considerable progress is occurring by some countries, companies, states or provinces, and even cities. Chapter 4 argues that ending the underpricing of fossil fuels is essential to a low-carbon transition. Major economies must lead by removing fossil fuel subsidies and employing carbon taxes and other policies to further reduce the social cost of fossil fuel use, and allocate any resulting revenue to public support for green innovation and key infrastructure investments. Ending the underpricing of fossil fuels in low- and middle-income countries must occur through policies that are compatible with achieving immediate development objectives, such as ending poverty and especially the widespread "energy poverty" in rural areas. Climate policies need also to expand beyond actions by national governments and instead focus on a "bottom-up" strategy that supports and expands initiatives by corporations, local governments and other "sub-national" entities that are pushing and innovating low-carbon strategies.

Land use change by humans has transformed ecosystem patterns and processes across most of the terrestrial biosphere, a global change that could be potentially catastrophic for both humankind and the environment. Chapter 5 explores how this threat is related to the underpricing of natural landscape in all economies, and how addressing this critical problem is essential to creating the incentives, institutions and innovations needed to change humankind's relationship with nature. The underpricing of natural landscape also perpetuates rural poverty, and the impacts of land use change are borne increasingly by the poor. Decoupling development from excessive land use change leading to ecosystem decline is necessary to make our economies both more sustainable and inclusive. Global biodiversity conservation is also plagued by underfunding, as the international community struggles to compensate developing countries for protecting valuable terrestrial habitats. Collective action will require commitments not only by rich countries to assist poorer ones in protection and restoration efforts, but also by the private sector to invest in nature to reduce the risks from biodiversity and ecosystem loss.

Rising freshwater scarcity is a present-day danger that is likely to worsen as supplies become increasingly scarce. Chapter 6 takes the view that the current overuse of freshwater supplies worldwide is as much a failure of water management as it is a result of scarcity. Outdated governance structures and institutions, combined with continual underpricing, have perpetuated the overuse and undervaluation of water, requiring reforms to markets and policies to ensure that they adequately capture the rising economic costs of exploiting water resources to foster more conservation, control of pollution and ecosystem protection. The result will be more efficient allocation of water among its competing agricultural; industrial and urban uses; fostering of water-saving innovations and further mitigation of water scarcity and its costs.

Chapter 7 argues that, if we are to halt humankind's unrelenting exploitation of marine sources and sinks, we need to change our economic approach to oceans and coasts. It begins with addressing the underpricing of marine capital and their services and the underfunding of ocean and coastal conservation. Addressing these challenges must be the focus of global collective action. The savings and revenues generated can also be allocated to support global funds and investments in marine capital and protection. However, more comprehensive cooperation between the international community, national governments and the private sector is required to develop global policies to protect vulnerable coastal populations and disappearing marine habitats, such as coral reefs and mangroves, and the deep sea.

Chapter 8 elaborates further on the public policies needed for "greening" economic activity and promoting better stewardship of the environment. The focus is primarily on strategies that governments might adopt to achieve economy-wide green transformation for more efficient, sustainable and inclusive development. The chapter explores what these short- and long-term policy efforts will look like, providing examples from both major economies and low- and middle-income countries. At the center is ending the underpricing of nature to unleash the economic potential of green developments for generating economy-wide innovation and prosperity, and more equitable income and wealth distribution.

Public polices alone cannot build a green economy for a safe Anthropocene. In any economy, the catalyst for change comes from private investment, financing and innovation. Chapter 9 examines the evidence of growing adoption and initiatives by corporations, businesses and the financial system to incorporate actions to mitigate environmental risks and improve the global environment, and looks in particular at the possibility of private sector action to move toward better environmental stewardship. Firms increasingly find that improved environmental performance reduces their overall cost of capital and their attractiveness to potential investors. However, better environmental scarcity and risk management by firms requires a range of complementary policies for green financing and investment, ending the underpricing of nature and taxing major biosphere exploiters. Corporations that are willing to become biosphere stewards should also collaborate with governments in collective action to address global environmental risks.

The concluding chapter brings together the main themes and messages of the book. Chapter 10 argues that the economics for a "fragile planet" is about ensuring that our economies can attain a "safe," as opposed to "catastrophic" or "uncertain" Anthropocene (see Figure 1.1). To be successful, such a transition must transform our markets, institutions and governance to reduce human impacts on the biosphere; mitigate environmental risks in an inclusive and sustainable manner; and decouple wealth creation and economic prosperity from environmental degradation. Above all, we must end the underpricing of nature so that our institutions, incentives and innovations reflect the growing ecological and natural resource scarcity that our current economic use of the environment has created. Taking this first step is essential to developing an economics for an increasingly fragile planet.

Notes

1 As quoted by Johnny Wood, "Q and A: This Is How Stakeholder Capitalism Can Help Heal the Planet." World Economic Forum, January 20, 2020. www.weforum.org/agenda/2020/01/stakeholder-capitalism-environment-planet.
2 Quoted from p. 2 of *The Economics of Biodiversity: The Dasgupta Review – Headline Messages.* https://assets.publishing.service.gov.uk/government/uploads/system/uploads/attachment_data/file/957629/Dasgupta_Review_-_Headline_Messages.pdf For Professor Sir Partha Dasgupta's full report, see Dasgupta (2021).
3 Boulding (1966), pp. 7–8.
4 Toynbee (1978), pp. 17 and 566. See also Barbier (2011) for an in-depth exploration of how exploitation of natural resource and land frontiers, from the Agricultural Transition 10,000 years ago to the present day, has influenced economic development and progress.
5 Lovelock (1988), pp. 178–179.
6 From www.nytimes.com/2018/10/07/climate/ipcc-climate-report-2040.html.
7 Ceballos et al. (2017) used the term "biological annihilation" to describe the current species extinction crisis. Other global assessments that illustrate how land use change is leading to unprecedented loss of biodiversity and ecosystem services include Bar-On et al. (2018); Elhacham et al. (2020); IPBES (2019); and Newbold et al. (2016).
8 See Duarte et al. (2020) for further details on these trends.
9 Gosling and Arnell (2016). For other global water scarcity trends and issues, see Barbier (2019b).
10 WEF (2021). The World Economic Forum bases its assessment of the likelihood and impact of various risks on a global survey of businesses, governments and individuals.

11 Scientists believe that the Anthropocene started as a distinct geological epoch in the mid-twentieth century. See Waters et al. (2016). The biologist Eugene Stoermer and the Nobel Prize–winning atmospheric chemist Paul Crutzen are credited with coining the term "Anthropocene." See Crutzen (2002), Crutzen and Stoermer (2000); and Steffen et al. (2011).

12 According to Steffen et al. (2015a), p. 2: "The term 'Great Acceleration' was first used in a working group of a 2005 Dahlem Conference on the history of the human–environment relationship (Hibbard et al. 2006)." It was also used by Steffen et al. (2007) to describe the "second phase" of the Anthropocene (from 1945 to ca. 2015). See also McNeill and Egelke (2016) for an "environmental history" of the Great Acceleration. What has been widely known as the "Great Acceleration" graphs of global socioeconomic and Earth system long-run trends were originally designed and constructed as part of the synthesis project of the International Geosphere-Biosphere Programme (IGBP), and which show how human impacts on the planet have accelerated since 1950–2000 compared to the long-run trends from 1750 onward (Steffen et al. 2004 and 2007). These graphs and trends have been updated to 2010 by the IGBP and are available at their website www.igbp.net/globalchange/greatacceleration.4.1b8ae20512db692f2a680001630.html and also presented in Steffen et al. (2015a).

13 Lenton et al. (2008) first postulated the possibility of tipping points or "elements" in the Earth's climate systems. A special issue edited by Schellnhuber (2009) then extended the concept to other Earth system processes. Rockström et al. (2009) used the possibility of such human-induced stresses on the Earth system to develop the "planetary boundaries" concept.

14 One such "catastrophic" Anthropocene outcome is the "Hothouse Earth" state described by Steffen et al. (2018).

15 Rockström et al. (2009), p. 472. See also Steffen et al. (2015b) and Lade et al. (2020).

16 Lenton and Williams (2013), p. 382.

17 For our purposes, *ecological scarcity* can be defined as the loss of the myriad contributions that ecosystems make to human well-being as these natural systems are exploited for human use and economic activity. These contributions include not only loss of recreation opportunities, harvests of wild resources and genetic material but also many vital benefits, such as natural hazard protection, nutrient uptake, erosion control, water purification and carbon sequestration. All these valuable goods and services provided by ecosystems are now called *ecosystem services* for short, or as the Millennium Ecosystem Assessment defines them, "ecosystem services are the benefits people obtain from ecosystems" (MA 2005). For the original definition of *ecological scarcity* see Barbier (1989), pp. 96–97: "The fundamental scarcity problem ... is that as the environment is increasingly being exploited for one set of uses (e.g., to provide sources of raw material and energy, and to assimilate additional waste), the quality of the environment may deteriorate. The consequence is an increasing *relative scarcity* of essential natural services and ecological functions ... In other words, if 'the environment is regarded as a scarce resource', then the 'deterioration of the environment is also an economic problem.'"

18 Pearce and Barbier (2000), p. 157.

19 This governance challenge for individual nations to agree collectively to "saving the biosphere" was noted by Toynbee (1978), pp. 592–593: "Since the dawn of civilization, Man's master institution has been states – in the plural, not in the singular; for, to date, there has never been one single state embracing the whole living generation of mankind all round the globe ... The present-day global set of local sovereign states is not capable of keeping the peace, and it is also not capable of saving the biosphere

from man-made pollution or of conserving the biosphere's non-replaceable natural resources … In the age in which mankind has acquired the command over nuclear power, political unification can be accomplished only voluntarily, and, since it is evidently going to be accepted only reluctantly, it seems probable that it will be delayed until mankind has brought upon itself further disasters of a magnitude that will induce it to acquiesce at last in global political union."

20 Economists usually distinguish *public* from *private goods* based on two properties: rivalry and excludability in use or consumption. When a good is *rival*, then one person's use of the good reduces the amount available for everybody else. When a good is *exclusive*, then one user can exclude others from consuming the good at the same time.

21 This example of improving water quality of a lake is excerpted from Barbier (2019b, chapter 1).

22 See, for example, Dinerstein et al. (2017); Gerten et al. (2013); Lade et al. (2020); Mace et al. (2014); Newbold et al. (2016); Rockström et al. (2009); Running (2012); and Steffen et al. (2015).

23 For further discussion, see Barbier (2021); Clark and Harley (2020); Griggs et al. (2013); and Kates et al. (2001).

24 Kates et al. (2001), p. 641.

25 See Barbier (2021) for an overview of the evolution of economic views on natural resource scarcity, and how these views have changed in recent years due to the mounting scientific evidence on ecosystem and biodiversity loss, rising global environmental risks and the need to safeguard essential Earth system life-support processes.

26 This changing respective is reflected, most recently, in the review of the economics of biodiversity by Dasgupta (2021).

27 Sterner et al. (2019), p. 19.

28 WCED (1987), p. 43.

29 Griggs et al. (2013), p. 306.

30 See, for example, Barbier et al. (2018); Dasgupta (2021); and Sterner et al. (2019).

31 See, for example, the review of critiques of the planetary boundary framework by Biermann and Kim (2020), who note the many equity and development concerns raised about the "global limits" concept underlying this framework.

32 These trends in inequality since 1980 are from Alvaredo et al. (2017).

33 See Oxfam (2021); UN (2020); and World Bank (2020).

2 HUMANKIND AND THE PLANET

According to scientists, Earth is a single, integrated system at the planetary level. It has existed for about 4.6 billion years and has coevolved with life for the vast majority of that time. Over this long existence, the Earth system has been through all kinds of shocks – internal and external – and embarked on numerous transitions and evolutionary pathways.

Our species *Homo sapiens* arrived relatively recently in the Earth system. Scientists believe that modern humans emerged in Africa sometime between 100,000 and 150,000 years ago and quickly spread around the globe.

However, humans have only really flourished in the last 12,000 years, during the relatively stable environmental and climatic period called the *Holocene*. This geological era began with the last major glacial epoch, or Ice Age. Since then, there have been smaller climatic shifts – notably the "Little Ice Age" between about 1200 and 1700 AD. But generally, the Holocene has been relatively warm and environmentally benign. It has enabled major terrestrial, freshwater and marine ecosystems to evolve and stabilize. Most notably, it has allowed humans to multiply, prosper and become the dominant species on our planet.

As we noted in Chapter 1, human activity is now on the verge of altering irrevocably the functioning of the Earth system. Since the mid-twentieth-century "Great Acceleration" of population growth, industrialization and mineral and energy use, we have impacted the biosphere so significantly that scientists believe that humans have created a new geological age – the *Anthropocene*.[1]

The fundamental challenge of the Anthropocene is how much humans can continue to modify the structure and functioning of the Earth system and still keep it sufficiently stable to support human life as we know it. As the global environmental risks caused by our activities mount, there is a real danger of inflicting significant and long-lasting changes to the entire Earth system. Crossing this "tipping point" is likely to be very harmful for humans, ecosystems and life itself. The Earth system will survive, but the favorable conditions of the Holocene may not. There will be rapid and substantial changes to the global climate and environment that will make it hostile to human habitation. It is in this sense that our planet has become "fragile." We risk transforming an Earth system with favorable climatic and environmental conditions into an unknown and alien world in which humans may struggle to exist.

However, the Earth did not become stressed and less resilient overnight. The increased "fragility" of the Holocene state of the Earth system and the rise in four critical threats to the global environment – climate change, land use and biodiversity loss, freshwater scarcity and deteriorating marine and coastal habitats – is the culmination of a long process of human impacts on the Earth system over the past 10,000 years. The purpose of this chapter is to briefly overview this process, highlighting the key historical eras when our relationship with nature changed irrevocably. I focus on five eras: the rise of agriculture 10,000 years ago and up to around 1000 AD; the emergence of global trade and the world economy (1000–1500 AD); the period of Global Frontiers (1500–1750); the fossil fuel age (1750–1970); and the Great Acceleration (1970–present). We conclude by reviewing the mounting scientific evidence that the last era has led to growing environmental risks and the existential threat of transcending planetary boundaries.

Early Human Impacts on the Earth System

Much of the current predicament of our planet has arisen through the long history of how humans have exploited *nature* to create *wealth*.[2]

This process has evolved and accelerated dramatically in recent eras, yet for most of our existence, humans have had little impact on the surrounding environment. Until 10,000 years ago or so, all humans lived as hunter-gatherers and had little interest in accumulating material possessions, land or natural resources. In these societies, mobility and adaptability to nature were the key social traits that guaranteed economic survival of individuals and their communities. Material wealth as we know it today was a meaningless concept for early humans. Humans were few in number and scarce. In contrast, natural wealth was everywhere and plentiful. Finding new hunting and foraging grounds was relatively easy, and the raw materials for clothing and other essential items for survival were readily available in the wild. There was no need to hoard, possess or protect natural assets.[3]

The first major change in humans' relationship with nature was the rise of agriculture. Around 10,000 years ago, farmers and herders supplanted hunter-gatherers, and *wealth creation* began in earnest. Sedentary agricultural activities tied humans to specific locations, fertile land, forests for timber; mines and other natural resources became valuable sources of production; food and other commodities were produced in surplus and traded; and human settlements grew and expanded into nations and empires. For a few thousand years this process began tentatively, with experimentation in crop planting by sedentary hunter-gatherers in different parts of the world. By 5000 BC much of the global population lived by farming, and by 3000 BC the first agricultural-based "empire states" emerged.[4]

Once agriculture became the dominant economic activity, humans associated affluence with the accumulation of fertile land and key natural resources, such as wood, water, building stone, precious stones and gems and metals. Labor was important but less so than livestock for food, transport, work and even warfare. In other words, basic natural resource assets – or *natural capital* – were the main sources of economic wealth for both individuals and human societies. One consequence was that human societies also became less egalitarian, as sharing and cooperation gave way to accumulation of individual wealth and affluence. Creation of such surpluses led to dominance by elites, social status and stratification.[5]

Amassing this natural wealth fostered the evolution of permanent agricultural settlements of large villages and towns into more complex and populated urban centers and political states – the emergence of cities and empires. This occurred in a number of regions across the world from 3000 BC to 1000 AD. Although dependent on surrounding agricultural land for food surpluses, the urban centers that controlled these great empires and early civilizations also required a variety of natural resources to sustain their economic wealth and power, and to provide security in times of drought, plague, war and other calamities. Imperial expansion and urban growth required securing new supplies of fertile land, natural resources and raw materials.

As early civilizations grew and their populations and empires expanded, their drive to obtain and exploit more natural wealth placed increasing stress on the surrounding environment. It also caused social conflicts and warfare between states. Many major city-states and empires suffered from serious problems of natural resource depletion and environmental degradation (see Table 2.1). The resulting ecological catastrophe may have been a factor in the civilization's eventual collapse.[6]

Although significant human-induced environmental degradation at the local and regional levels did occur through expansion of early civilizations and empire, the global impact was negligible. This continued throughout early history as human populations and their economic activity expanded still further.

The second major shift in humankind's relationship with the biosphere took place between 1000 and 1500 AD with the emergence of global trade. Trade was always important to agricultural-based societies as they sought more natural wealth to exploit and consume. Just as the emerging city-states and civilizations of 3000 BC–1000 AD could not exist without an agricultural base producing large food surpluses for their urban-based populations, they also became dependent on securing raw materials from trade with nearby resource-abundant regions.

So successful was trade in helping nations accumulate wealth that the expansion of local and regional trade networks continued across the globe. Trade sometimes supplanted, and other times aided, the appropriation of fertile land and other natural resources through conflict, conquest and colonization. The result was that regional trade networks continued to grow and merge. These networks coalesced into a nascent "world economy" by 1000 AD, and from 1000 to 1500, the upsurge in trade between countries and regions ushered in an unprecedented era of global population and economic growth. By 1500, an international economy was firmly established. Over this 500-year period, world population nearly doubled, and the value of global production per person increased from $436 to $566.[7]

Trade fostered wealth creation. That is, trade facilitated access to the most important sources of "wealth" across the world. Economies

Table 2.1. Civilizations and environmental degradation, 3000 BC–1000 AD

Civilization	Period	Human-Induced Environmental Degradation
Sumer, Southern Mesopotamia	2200–1700 BC	Soil salinity; land degradation; deforestation; river and canal silting
Egypt, Nile Valley[a]	2200–1700 BC	Deforestation; land degradation; soil salinity; wildlife extinction
Harappa, Indus Valley	1800–1500 BC	Land degradation; overgrazing; salinity; deforestation; flooding
Crete	ca. 1500 BC	Deforestation; soil erosion
Mycenaean Greece	1200–1000 BC	Deforestation; soil erosion; overgrazing
Assyrian Empire[b]	1000–600 BC	Deforestation
Greek city-states	ca. 500–200 BC	Deforestation; soil erosion; river silting; flooding; pollution
Chin and Han dynasties, China[c]	221 BC–220 AD	Deforestation; flooding; erosion; river silting; wildlife extinction
Roman Empire	200–500 AD	Land degradation; deforestation; soil erosion; river siltation; air and water pollution; lead poisoning; wildlife extinction
Satingpra Empire, Thailand[d]	500–850 AD	Deforestation; land degradation
Various dynasties, China[e]	600–1000 AD	Deforestation; flooding; erosion; river silting
Various empires, Japan	600–850 AD	Deforestation; flooding; erosion; river silting
Maya, Central America[f]	830–930 AD	Land degradation; erosion; deforestation; river silting; weed incursion;
Srivijaya, Sumatra	ca. 1000 AD	Deforestation

Notes: Period refers to either the approximate period of decline of the civilization and/or when evidence of extensive human-induced environmental damage is cited.
[a] From Chew (2006); Hughes (2001); and Issar and Zohar (2004).
[b] From Parker (2002).
[c] See also Elvin (1993) and Hughes (2001).
[d] From Stargart (1998).
[e] See also Elvin (1993) and McNeill (1998).
[f] From Culbert (1988), Hughes (2001); and Johnson (2003).
Source: From Chew (2001) unless otherwise indicated.

were still overwhelmingly agrarian. This meant that the main sources of wealth had not changed since the emergence of agricultural-based empires starting around 3000 BC. Economic wealth was still principally defined by the three most important assets of agricultural societies: fertile land, natural resources and raw materials. Precious gems and metals were status symbols of wealth but were growing in importance as "stores" of value and as "mediums of exchange" to pay for items of trade. The most important forms of reproducible capital were dwellings, basic tools and utensils, livestock and labor, especially in the form of slaves.

Figure 2.1 characterizes the major regions involved in the emerging world trade system around 1200–1300. This figure indicates how differences in natural resource endowments and ecological conditions influenced the specialization and trade in different natural resource-based products by region. This was not yet a truly global economy, as it excluded the American and Australian continents, as well as large parts of sub-Saharan Africa and much of the Pacific. However, the largest economies in the world, which contained most of the world's population, were connected by this extensive trading network.

The long-distance trade networks in raw materials, precious metals, spices and other commodities represented in Figure 2.1 may not have caused significant global ecological impacts. Yet the nascent world economy laid the foundation for such impacts to begin emerging from 1500 onward. First, the growth in trade fostered not only the exchange of goods but also the rapid transmission of people, ideas, technologies, religions and, unfortunately, pathogens.[8] Second, trade encouraged people to find new sources of natural resources to exploit. This meant that economies became even more dependent on "opening up" new frontiers of land and natural resources to such exploitation. Third, wealth accumulation through trade also created both the means and the opportunities for more powerful states and empires to appropriate land and natural resources through conquest and colonization of neighboring and distant territories. Finally, trade encouraged a new type of economy to emerge – market- and commercially oriented and based on long-distance trade – essentially the hallmark of Western European economies.

For several centuries, the wealth and power of Western European states grew as a result of long-distance trade and exploitation of new frontiers of land and natural resources within Europe and neighboring regions. It was a logical extension of this strategy to expand

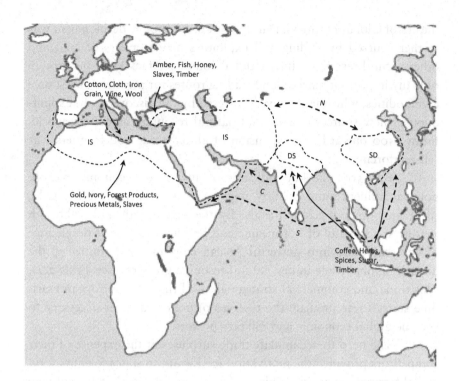

Figure 2.1 The emerging world economy, ca. 1200–1300 AD
Notes: IS = Islamic states of North Africa, Middle East and West Asia
(e.g., Abbasids, Almohads, Arabs, Ayyubids, Ghurids, Kwaresmians, Ortoquids,
Salgharids, Seljuks and Zengids, ca. 1200).
DS = Delhi Sultanates (Mamluk Dynasty, 1206–1290).
SD = Sung Dynasty (during Southern Sung, 1127–1279).
N = Northern east–west trade route.
C = Central east–west trade route.
S = Southern east–west trade route.
Source: Barbier (2011), figure 4.1.

their dominance of trade and natural resources to the global level. By
the twelfth and thirteenth centuries, Western Europe specialized in select
natural resource products, including some processed products, and key
services such as commerce and maritime transport. It was no longer
"underdeveloped" but more of a "semi-developed" or "middle-
income" region. By 1500, Western Europe had the highest per capita
GDP levels in the world, and the largest share of global GDP after China
and India.[9]

The period from 1500 to 1750 represented another important
shift in humankind's exploitation of the Earth, and it became known as

the era of Global Frontiers. During this age, economic development was further spurred by finding and exploiting new frontiers of land and other natural resources. International commerce facilitated the growth of many important markets and trading routes for a variety of resource commodities, which in turn were fostered by the discovery and exploitation of new sources of land and natural resources across the world. From 1500 onward, the expansion of global trade and frontiers was self-reinforcing.

By 1500, the key indicator of any state's economic wealth, political influence and military might was its ability to accrue gold, silver and other precious metals. By the seventeenth and eighteenth centuries, a handful of European states had leveraged their dominance of key sea routes into powerful "ocean empires" that controlled the lucrative global trade in key natural resource products (see Table 2.2). This trade and commercial strategy allowed the small European maritime states to accumulate the reserves of gold and silver necessary to become global economic and military powers.

The need to accumulate trade surpluses at the expense of their competitors provided the motivation for European states to embark on global frontier expansion. This in turn spurred the exploitation of new sources of natural resources and provided the justification for the promotion of trade and mercantilist policies. Through its unrelenting exploitation of the Global Frontiers from 1500 onward, Western Europe obtained a vast array of natural wealth, land frontiers for settlement, as well as fishing, plantation, mining and other resource frontiers. These frontiers not only provided an outlet for poor populations emigrating from Europe and other regions in search of better economic opportunities but also created large resource windfalls to the benefit of European economies.

For the first time in human history, exploitation of the environment occurred on a global scale for economic development and enhancing human welfare. As the economic historian Eric Jones notes, Europe had four main "Extra-European resources" that "were vast, varied, and cheap": ocean fisheries, including for whale and seal; the boreal woods of Northern Europe; land in the tropics and subtropics for growing sugar, tobacco, cotton, indigo and rice; and land in temperate North and South America, South Africa, Australia and the steppes of southern Russia for growing grain.[10] European states controlled these global land and resource frontiers first through trade, discovery and exploration,

Table 2.2. Ocean empires and natural resource trade, seventeenth and eighteenth centuries

Regions	Main Products	European States
East Indies (Malaysian peninsula; Indonesian archipelago)	Spices, pepper, medicinal herbs, dyestuffs, woods, sugar	Portugal, the Netherlands, France, England
India (Cambay, Malabar and Coromandel coasts; Bengal; Ceylon)	Textiles, metalwork, silk, pepper, spices, indigo, saltpeter	Portugal, the Netherlands, France, England, Denmark
China	porcelain, silk, tea	Portugal, the Netherlands, France, England
Guinea (west coast of Africa from Cape Verde to Cape Lopez)	Slaves, gold, ivory, feathers	Portugal, the Netherlands, France, England, Denmark, Sweden, Spain, Brandenburg States
West Indies (Caribbean islands)	Sugar, tobacco, cotton, rice, dyestuffs	Spain, the Netherlands, France, England, Denmark, Sweden
South America (e.g. Mexico, Guyana and Brazil)	Sugar, silver, tobacco, cotton, rice, dyestuffs	Spain, the Netherlands, Portugal
North America (e.g. Canada and thirteen American colonies)	fish, fur, timber, cotton, tobacco, rice	England, France, Spain, the Netherlands, Russia, Denmark, Sweden

Source: Barbier (2011), table 5.3.

followed by conquest and colonization of territory. As the historian Alfred Crosby suggests, this "biological expansion" of Western European states across the globe can be characterized as a process of "ecological imperialism," in which new lands, natural resources and peoples were conquered, subjugated and exploited.[11]

Global migration changed significantly after 1500. Before the sixteenth century, when people migrated to settle new lands or exploit abundant natural resources, they were restricted to moving to nearby uninhabited areas, such as previously untouched forests, wetlands, grassland and hills, or to adjacent territories and borderlands.

As shipping technologies and long-distance sea transport improved and became less costly, from the sixteenth century onward migration became more global. For the first time in world history, transoceanic settlement and exploitation of new lands occurred. For example, between 1500 and 1760, nearly 6 million people immigrated to the "New World" colonies of North and South America. Notably, of these more than 60 percent were Africans shipped involuntarily as slaves. As a result, over this period the ratio of slave to European immigrants to the American colonies was 2 to 1.[12]

The colonization strategy for Global Frontiers was driven by the desire to seek and accumulate wealth from "unclaimed" regions, and to do this before others could acquire and appropriate them. The manner in which land and natural resources were exploited was influenced by geography, climate, disease and other environmental factors that determined "whether European colonists could safely settle in a particular location."[13] In environments that were less conducive to settlement and caused high mortality among settlers (e.g. tropical diseases such as malaria and yellow fever), the formation of extractive states and the use of slavery to exploit natural resources was more likely. "In fact, the main purpose of the extractive state was to transfer as much of the resources of the colony to the colonizer."[14] These extractive states tended to prevail in the tropical regions of Latin America and the Caribbean, Asia and sub-Saharan Africa. However, in environments more favorable to settlement, such as Canada, the United States, Australia, New Zealand and temperate South America, the creation of "neo-Europes" occurred.[15] In these temperate regions, Europeans settled in large numbers and the colonial settlers tried to replicate European institutions with strong emphasis on private property and market incentives to spur commercial activities and checks against government power.

The global exploitation of land and natural resources from 1500 to 1750 was not just a European phenomenon. It occurred on an extensive scale across the world, especially in the agricultural-based empires of China, India, Russia and the Middle East.[16] For example, the Mughal Empire (1526–1707) in India depended on aggressive expansion of its agricultural land base.[17] By 1690, the Mughal Empire's territory comprised 3.2 million km² and around 100 million people – nearly the entire Indian subcontinent except for its southern tip. The Mughal Empire promoted frontier settlement and cultivation of new lands, starting with the rest of the River Ganges plain in the mid-sixteenth century and then across the Bengal Delta (now modern-day Bangladesh). This was accomplished in three steps. First, through conquest and pacification in the eastern delta. Second, forest clearing, conversion of wetlands to rice paddies and pioneer settlement that greatly increased agricultural production. Finally, urbanization and industrialization in the form of export-oriented silk and cotton textiles. Such frontier expansion and development continued under British conquest and colonial rule well into the nineteenth and twentieth centuries.

In sum, by 1750 humankind's impact on Planet Earth had reached a global scale. No longer was human-induced environmental degradation, resource exploitation and land conversion confined to local or regional impacts. Global domination of nature and surrounding environments had become the norm for early modern economies, and was synonymous with continued economic progress, wealth creation and social power. Although humankind had yet developed the technical means or sources of energy that could inflict irreversible damage on major biomes or the entire biosphere, the trend of exploiting the environment for sources of raw materials, new land and energy, or as a sink for waste and pollution, had been set for all economies. This soon paved the way for exponentially growing economic pressures on the natural environment during the nineteenth and twentieth centuries, which has continued up to the present day. In other words, by 1750, the world economy was poised to inflict massive destruction of nature on a global scale – it only lacked the means to do so. The environmental consequences of this economic exploitation of "unending frontiers" has been summarized succinctly by the environmental historian John Richards:

> The early modern near-doubling of human numbers generated new pressures on the natural world ... shared long-term historical processes – settlement frontiers, biological invasions, and the world hunt – imposed shattering changes on regional ecosystems around the world. During the early modern period, there was an irresistible, and seemingly irreversible trend towards more intensive human control and use of the land and the natural environment. As this occurred, those intricate local assemblages of vegetation and fauna that had long flourished with far less human intervention lost complexity, lost diversity, lost numerous species, and sometimes were even

eradicated completely ... These processes once underway, have continued with little restraint or diversion in the nineteenth and twentieth centuries.[18]

The Fossil Fuel Age

From 1750 onward, with the onset of the Industrial Revolution, the global balance between humankind and nature changed dramatically. As the historian Arnold Toynbee noted, "By making the Industrial Revolution, Man exposed the biosphere, including Man himself, to a threat that had no precedent."[19]

Much has been written about the causes and consequences of the Industrial Revolution. Here, we focus on its most important consequence for humankind's relationship with the planet: *the rise of the global fossil fuel age.*

Up until the mid-eighteenth century, the economic wealth of Western Europe and the other great economic powers in Asia and the Near East was roughly equal. This wealth was largely associated with accumulation of agricultural land, livestock, gold, silver and other precious metals and gems, and in many places, the "ownership" of human labor (slaves, serfs or indentured servants). The Industrial Revolution, which started in Western Europe and quickly spread across the globe, irrevocably altered both the process of creating wealth and its composition. It did so through a massive shift in the innovation, productivity and structure of economies. Industrialization in Europe transformed an "advanced organic economy" dependent on land and traditional energy sources, such as water, wind, biomass, animal and human power, to a mineral-based economy, capable of achieving unparalleled levels of sustained growth in manufactures and agriculture through exploiting the new and relatively abundant fossil fuel energy resources.[20]

However, these changes did not happen all at once in the mid-eighteenth century, but took centuries to unfold. They centered on key innovations, which were in turn the culmination of decades of scientific and knowledge advances in Western economies. These advances were, in turn, directly related to the vast accumulation of wealth created through global domination of nature and surrounding environments. This wealth allowed Western states to invest in the creation of new

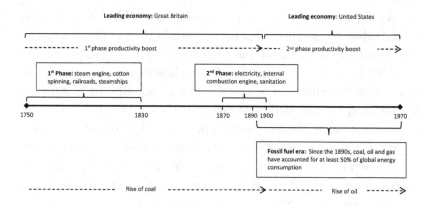

Figure 2.2 Key timelines of the Industrial Revolution, 1750–1970
Notes: The first phase of key innovations of the Industrial Revolution occurred between 1750 and 1830, and centered on steam power and coal. They led to the global economic dominance of Great Britain and boosted the productivity of all industrializing nations that followed Britain's example until 1900. The second phase of innovations of the Industrial Revolution were between 1870 and 1900, and were based largely on electricity and the internal combustion engine – made possible by the new hydrocarbons oil and gas. These innovations led to the economic rise of the United States, which became the model for twentieth-century industrialization and boosted global productivity until 1970.
Source: Barbier (2015), figure 2.2

scientific ideas, processes and applications that unleashed the energy potential of a new and abundant resource – fossil fuels – that ultimately transformed their economies and societies.

As Figure 2.2 indicates, this process comprised two distinct "phases" of key innovations and fossil fuel use starting in 1750, which caused significant impacts on global economic development and productivity for many decades after the initial inventions were introduced. Figure 2.2 depicts the timelines associated with the key innovations linked to these two distinct phases of the Industrial Revolution.[21]

The first phase of the Industrial Revolution occurred between 1750 and 1830. This centered on key inventions, such as the steam engine, cotton spinning, railroads and steamships (see Figure 2.2). These innovations helped propel Great Britain to global economic and political dominance, and they had lasting impacts on all industrializing economies up until 1900. The second phase of the Industrial Revolution centered on key innovations between 1870 and 1900, such as electricity, the internal combustion engine, water and sanitation systems, refrigerated transport and oil and gas refining. These innovations spurred considerable industrial, transport and urban developments that boosted productivity until 1970, and led to the economic rise and worldwide dominance of the United States.

As indicated in Figure 2.2, by the late nineteenth century, the spread of industrialization across the globe had ushered in fully the fossil fuel age. As suggested by the scientist Vaclav Smil, this era started as "sometime during the 1890s when of crude oil, and a small amount of natural gas began supplying more than half of the world's total primary energy needs."[22] This new era of fossil fuel energy quickly led to two important global trends. First, world energy consumption began growing exponentially. Second, the composition of energy consumption changed dramatically throughout the two phases of the Industrial Revolution.

By 1900, global energy consumption had doubled from what it was in 1800. By 1970, consumption was five times greater still. In 1800, biomass energy sources – fuelwood, charcoal and crop residues – comprised 80 percent of world energy consumption. However, the nineteenth-century industrialization of major economies led to the rapid spread of coal consumption and the replacement of charcoal for indoor heating and metal production by coal, coke and gas. By 1900, fossil fuels had surpassed biomass in global energy consumption. In the early twentieth century, gas and oil use, for heating, electricity generation and transportation, began their meteoric rise, with oil supplanting coal as the dominant fuel by the early 1960s. By the 1970s, more than 90 percent of global energy consumption consisted of fossil fuels.[23]

The dawn of the fossil fuel age also meant that this resource displaced fertile land as the dominant source of natural wealth required by economies. Innovations ensured that fossil fuels were cheaper to discover, extract and develop, and improvements in transportation reduced the costs of shipping these bulky resources within and between countries. Fossil fuel use became associated with wealth accumulation of all economies, but the expansion of trade and transport networks reduced the costs of exploiting new and abundant sources and shipping them to any economy in the world. As the fossil fuel age progressed, fossil fuels became a global commodity traded on international markets, and economies could industrialize and grow richer without necessarily having their own domestic sources of cheap and accessible fossil fuels.

Inexpensive and abundant supplies of fossil fuels profoundly changed the structure of economies, transforming agriculture and transportation while creating new industries and modes of production. Fossil fuel consumption, industrialization and economic development was instrumental for the vast improvement in material living standards, life expectancy and quality of life for humans during this era. In 1700, around 500 million people lived on the planet; by 1970 the global population had reached 4 billion. Over this period, real gross domestic product (GDP) per person more than quadrupled. In 1700, average real GDP per capita in the world was around $1,400, and by 1970 it was over $6,200.[24]

The fossil fuel era and the industrialization of economies brought other critical transformations as well. There was a dramatic change not only in our use of energy, but also land, water and raw materials. The expansion in energy and raw material use also created more land, air and water pollution and inorganic and toxic wastes.

In agriculture, cheap fossil fuel energy made other inputs, notably fertilizer, machines and even irrigation water, inexpensive substitutes for traditional productive assets such as land, draught animals and labor. Agricultural productivity, in terms of both output per land and labor used, increased significantly. Falling transportation costs and the expanding road and rail networks facilitated the rapid transport of farming inputs and outputs across countries. Dramatic improvements in shipping, and then air transport, spurred falling international costs of transporting agricultural commodities, raw materials, minerals and fossil fuels. The globalization of commodity markets and trade enabled all economies to have better and cheaper access to a wider type and quantity of natural resources compared to their own sovereign endowments. As a result of global trade, all economies, and especially high-income countries such as the United States, Western Europe, Japan and others, could sustain their economic expansion through consuming energy, mineral and raw material products well in excess of their natural endowments of these commodities.

By the twentieth century, rapid industrialization was facilitated by the exponential growth in fossil fuel energy use, largely attributable to three "prime movers" that radically altered productive capacities and industrial energy efficiency in the economy: electricity generation, the internal combustion engine and the development of the petroleum-based chemical industry. The lead economy in this global development was the United States (see Figure 2.2). As other countries have continued to follow this "US model" of development ever since, it is highly instructive to explore how this structural transformation first occurred in the United States during the twentieth century.

For example, the first three decades of the twentieth century saw a remarkable transition in the United States from firm-generated steam power to electrical energy purchased from central power stations. Centralization of electricity generation and expansion of the grid network led, in turn, to an exponential growth in energy use by US firms and households in less than three decades. In 1910, 25 percent of factories used electric power, but by 1930, 75 percent of factories used electricity; similarly, the use of electric lighting by urban households increased from 33 percent in 1909 to 96 percent by 1939.[25]

The abundant US supplies of petroleum fostered the development of the internal combustion engine, the automobile and the use of roads. As with electrification, the automobile and a national road network helped transform the entire US economy.[26] The emergence of the petroleum industry in the United States in the 1920s and 1930s also led to the rise of the economically important petro-chemical industry. The latter industry and its products, including plastics, oils and resins, chemical fertilizers and synthetic rubber, would in turn have important linkages to the development of other sectors of the economy, including as we have seen, the automobile and aircraft industries and the transformation of US agriculture.[27]

As the US economy became more energy-intensive during the twentieth century, it also increased its use of raw materials, such as industrial minerals, metals, agricultural and wood products, nonrenewable organics and crushed stone, sand and gravel. In a modern economy, material and energy use is inexorably linked. For example, the construction and maintenance of paved roads for automobiles and other motorized transport requires more crushed stone, sand and gravel, and the demand for these road-building materials requires additional freight transport. Increased electrification allows improvement in mining and extractive technologies, and the processing of the resulting minerals and ores, as well as the creation of improved alloys, entail more energy use.[28] As a consequence, nonfuel material use in the US economy also increased exponentially throughout the twentieth century. But the composition of US material use also changed, from renewables to nonrenewables. In 1900, about 41 percent of total material use came from renewable resources, such as agricultural, fishery, forestry and wildlife products. But by 1950, the share of renewable resources had declined to just 10 percent of overall material use. By 2000, materials from renewable resources accounted for just 5 percent of material consumption in the US economy, and nonrenewables 95 percent.[29]

The Industrial Revolution changed the structural dependence of a modern economy on its natural resource base, but the global frontier expansion and exploitation continued unabated. During the fossil fuel age, innovation and enhanced productivity have typically enabled more prosperity and economic growth, and more, not less, natural resource use. For example, although modern economies became increasingly less dependent on agriculture, throughout the Industrial Revolution considerable global land use change continued to occur. From 1750 to 1970, global forest and woodland area declined by over 6 million km², and savannah and grassland by 4.5 million km², as cropland area expanded dramatically.[30] In 1750, global cropland area occupied around 5.5 million km², and it tripled to 17.5 million km² by 1970. Despite the growth in productivity from new techniques, mechanization, high-yielding varieties and modern inputs; increasing human and livestock populations, changing diets and rising demand for food, fiber and fodder meant that more and more cropland needed to be found for "feeding the world."[31]

The fossil fuel age has also led to more, rather than less, exploitation of global freshwater resources. The hallmark of the modern era has been to try to meet every new demand for water – whether it is for agricultural or municipal and industrial use, for domestic food production or expanding exports to other countries – by finding and harnessing new supplies of freshwater. This has been the "hydraulic mission" of the modern era, and it was made possible by the considerable technological advances, economic wealth and energy resources generated by the Industrial Revolution. The global spread of industrialization further cemented the association between economic progress and increased water appropriation, control and use. As a consequence, in modern economies, water use management, and its accompanying innovations, institutions and incentives, is dominated by this "hydraulic mission" of finding and exploiting more freshwater resources.[32]

Water has always been critical for agriculture. In fact, water is still predominantly used for growing crops and raising livestock, which today accounts for 70 percent of water withdrawals globally, and 81 percent in low-income countries.[33] So as agriculture expanded worldwide from 1750 onward, so did global water use. Water has typically been treated as a plentiful and "free input" to agricultural production, much like other natural resources such as soils and energy from the sun. Because of this, there was little development of water markets for trade, and no incentive to treat water as a scarce capital asset to be managed and conserved.

Industrialization also brought rapid expansion of cities and urban populations, leading to additional demands for increased water use and sanitation. During the eighteenth and nineteenth centuries, spreading urbanization and rising population densities caused major water pollution problems and threats of deadly water-borne diseases, such as cholera and typhoid. As cities in Europe, North America and the rest of the industrializing world grew, they struggled to provide adequate clean water and sanitation on a large scale for their numerous residents.

To cope with these growing demands, cities developed extensive public infrastructure and water supply systems, often drawing on multiple freshwater sources across vast distances. Thus, the development of modern publicly funded urban water systems was both a consequence of and necessary for the growth of large cities, increasing urban populations and industrial expansion. More importantly, it solidified the modern mindset that solving the problem of large-scale water use and waste disposal is largely an engineering problem. The bigger the city and its population, the more clean drinking and other water supplies must be found, and the quicker and more efficiently the resulting volumes of waste water must be channeled away and disposed of away from urban areas. As industrialization has spread, and cities and populations expanded, so has this vast water supply and processing system. Today, the global water infrastructure supporting large cities supplies 668 million liters of water daily, and although these cities occupy only 1 percent of the Earth's land surface, their total sources of water cover 41 percent of that surface.[34]

The expansion of fossil fuel use, industrialization and cities also created a new environmental problem – local and regional air pollution. The energy economist Roger Fouquet has documented the rise of British coal consumption and air pollution from 1820 through the twentieth century.[35] Rapid coal use caused large environmental damages during the First Phase of the Industrialization, when coal was the dominant fossil fuel and Britain the leading industrial power (see Figure 2.2).

Coal consumption rose from 20 million metric tons in 1820 to 160 million in 1900. Air pollution also grew significantly over this period. In London, the concentration of total suspended particulates in the air increased from just under 400 micrograms per cubic meter (μg/m^3) in 1800 to 600 μg/m^3 in 1890.[36] This expanding coal use caused numerous deaths through lung disease and accidents to miners and air pollution in cities. Fouquet estimates that the value of lives lost amounted to 4 percent of Britain's GDP in 1820; climbed to 9 percent by 1850; and then peaked at 20 percent of GDP between 1870 and 1890.

Marine fishing and its surrounding coastal and marine environment were also transformed by industrialization and increased fossil fuel use.[37] Industrialization in the eighteenth and nineteenth centuries, along with the development of railways, steam-driven trawlers and ice storage, led to the global expansion of commercial marine fisheries. From the 1930s onward, diesel-powered trawlers and mechanization of fishing gear dominated the global industry. In just twenty years, marine fish catch more than tripled, from 14 million metric tons in 1950 to 53 million metric tons in 1970.[38] Overfishing inevitably ensued, with consequent destruction and degradation of marine, estuarine and coastal habitats and food webs. For example, the marine scientist Heike Lotze and colleagues have estimated that, in 12 once diverse and productive estuaries and coastal seas worldwide, fishing and other human impacts have depleted more than 99 percent of formerly important species; destroyed more than 65 percent of seagrass beds and wetland habitat; degraded water quality; and accelerated species invasions during the past 150–300 years.[39]

To summarize, during the fossil fuel age from 1750 to 1970, industrialization, mechanization and fossil fuel consumption led to extraordinary leaps in economic development, population levels, material living standards, life expectancy and quality of life for humans worldwide. But these same factors also caused massive environmental impacts, not just locally and regionally but increasingly on a planetary scale. In the twentieth century, despite two world wars and a global economic depression, the magnitudes of global environmental change of both the human drivers and their impacts were significant (see Table 2.3). However, it has really been since 1970, that both these drivers and their environmental impacts accelerated, during the current era of the "Great Acceleration."

Table 2.3. Magnitudes of global environmental change, 1890s to 1990s

Indicator	Coefficient of increase, 1890s to 1990s
Drivers	
Human population	4
Urban proportion of human population	3
Total urban population	14
World economy	14
Industrial output	40
Energy use	13–14
Coal production	7
Freshwater use	9
Irrigated area	5
Cropland area	2
Pasture area	1.8
Pig population	9
Goat population	5
Cattle population	4
Marine fish catch	35
Impacts	
Forest area	0.8 (20% decrease)
Bird and mammal species	0.99 (1% decrease)
Fin whale population	0.03 (97% decrease)
Air pollution	2–10
Carbon dioxide (CO_2) emissions	17
Sulfur dioxide (SO_2) emissions	13
Lead emissions	8

Sources: Adapted from McNeill (2000, pp. 360–361) and McNeill (2005, tables 1 and 2).

The Great Acceleration

This current era, which began in the late twentieth century, is the "Great Acceleration" of population growth, industrialization and mineral and energy use.

The term "Great Acceleration" was first coined by the working group of a 2005 conference on the history of the human–environment relationship.[40] However, it was really inspired by the long-term trends of human drivers and their global environmental impacts compiled by the International Geosphere-Biosphere Programme (IGBP) – the so-called Great Acceleration graphs – that illustrate how human impacts on the planet have accelerated in the second half of the twentieth century compared to the long-run trends since 1750.[41]

The most significant aspect of this era is the "acceleration" of four critical human threats to the global environment – climate change, land use and biodiversity loss, freshwater scarcity and deteriorating marine and coastal habitats. Figure 2.3 depicts some of the key trends that have defined the Great Acceleration of human activity and its impacts on the biosphere.

Since 1970, trends in agricultural production, fish harvest, freshwater use, bioenergy production and harvest of materials have increased, in response to population growth, rising demand and technological development. Over this period, the global human population has more than doubled (from 3.7 to 7.6 billion), rising unevenly across countries and regions; and per capita gross domestic product is four times higher – with ever-more distant consumers shifting the environmental burden of consumption and production across regions.[42]

As shown in Figure 2.3, from 1970 to the present, the expansion of energy use, carbon dioxide and fisheries production has been even greater than the doubling of global population. Freshwater use has largely kept pace with population growth. Global agricultural land use has expanded more modestly, by 30 percent. However, in low- and middle-income countries the expansion in crop and pasture land has been more significant, over 45 percent since 1970.

Land use change, habitat destruction and biodiversity loss in the tropics are primarily driven by the ongoing demand for agricultural production, mining and timber in these regions. As a consequence, tropical natural forests have declined by 11 percent since 1990.[43]

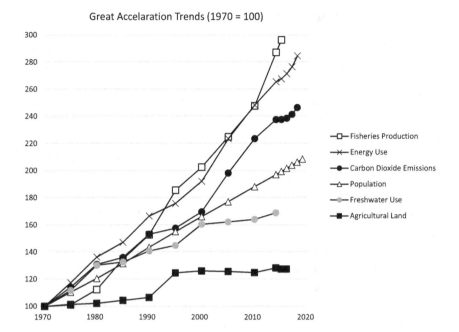

Figure 2.3 Key Great Acceleration trends since 1970
Source: Fisheries production (volume of aquatic species caught for all commercial, industrial, recreational and subsistence purposes); population (total global population); and agricultural land (land area that is arable, under permanent crops and under permanent pastures) are from World Bank, World Development Indicators https://databank.worldbank.org/reports.aspx?source=world. Energy use (primary energy consumption) is from BP Statistical Review of World Energy www.bp.com/en/global/corporate/energy-economics/statistical-review-of-world-energy.html. Carbon dioxide emissions (CO_2 emissions from fossil fuels and cement) is from Le Quéré et al. (2018). Global Carbon Project; Carbon Dioxide Information Analysis Centre (CDIAC) www.globalcarbonatlas.org/en/CO2-emissions; Freshwater use (global freshwater withdrawals, cubic meter per year) is from Hannah Ritchie and Max Roser (2017) – "Water Use and Stress." Published online at OurWorldInData.org: https://ourworldindata.org/water-use-stress

At the same time, since 1970, we have experienced a 60 percent decline in the populations of mammals, birds, fish, reptiles and amphibians.[44]

The nearly threefold rise in fisheries production over the past several decades is one reason why marine life is on the brink of a precipice. At least one-third of fish stocks are now overfished; one-third to half of vulnerable marine habitats have been lost; and a substantial fraction of the coastal ocean suffers from pollution, eutrophication, oxygen depletion and is stressed by ocean warming.[45] An additional disturbing trend in recent decades has been the exponential growth in marine plastic pollution. In 1970, there was an estimated 30,200 tonnes of plastics floating in global oceans. By 2020, this amount had risen to nearly 1.2 million tonnes.[46]

Because of this mounting toll on the global environment, some scientists are warning that humans are now on the verge of altering the Earth system irrevocably. Unless the Great Acceleration of human impacts on the global environment is slowed down, and possibly halted, we are becoming perilously close to inflicting significant and long-lasting changes to the entire Earth system. The Great Acceleration, which is the hallmark of the Anthropocene Age, has led to increased prosperity for most, but at the expense of growing environmental risks and even the threat of transcending *planetary boundaries*.

Planetary Boundaries

Humans have flourished on Earth for the last 12,000 years, thanks to the relatively stable and supportive environmental and climatic conditions of the Holocene era. This favorable global environment has enabled agriculture to evolve and expand; industrialization and complex human societies to emerge; and economies and trading networks to develop and multiply. This has also led to wealth and prosperity for many, but not all. At the same time, such economic gains have been achieved through unsustainable extraction of our natural resources; pollution of our lands, water and air beyond their ability to assimilate it; and the conversion and alteration of ecological functions and systems at the local, regional and global level.

Because humans now dominate the Earth system, we have entered a new era – the Anthropocene. Our actions are altering the global environment and we control its fate. As the previous section has documented, this Great Acceleration of human activity and impacts shows little signs of abating. This has several implications. We could be on the verge of altering the Earth system irrevocably and disrupting its stable Holocene-like state. We could be entering an "uncertain" Anthropocene, with unpredictable environmental consequences and possibly irreversible, damages to ecosystems, society and economies. We could end up in a "catastrophic" Anthropocene, with global warming of 2–4°C or more, massive biodiversity losses and species extinction, chronic freshwater scarcity and other unknown environmental disruptions.[47] Under these conditions, our planet may no longer be a hospitable and supportive environment for human habitation and well-being.

Avoiding these outcomes and producing a relatively "safe" Anthropocene is the greatest challenge facing humankind today. Some scientists suggest that, to protect key Earth system elements and processes, major human impacts on the global environment should be kept within *planetary boundaries*. Establishing such boundaries is the only way to avoid exceeding "tipping points" or "thresholds" that could lead to irrevocable changes in the entire Earth system, with potentially catastrophic impacts for humanity.[48]

Proponents of this view identify nine impacts resulting from human activity that should be subject to planetary boundaries:

- Climate change
- Loss of biosphere integrity (e.g. marine and terrestrial biodiversity loss)
- Land system change (e.g. land use change, such as deforestation and land degradation)
- Freshwater use
- Biochemical flows (e.g. effluents that interfere with nitrogen and phosphorous cycles)
- Ocean acidification
- Atmospheric aerosol loading
- Stratospheric ozone depletion
- Novel entities (e.g. new substances and modified organisms that have undesirable environmental impacts, such as toxic chemicals and plastics)[49]

If unchecked, each of these impacts on the global environment could place human population growth and economic activity on an unsustainable trajectory that crosses critical thresholds and destabilizes the entire Earth system. This could endanger its capacity to support and sustain humanity. According to the scientist Will Steffen and colleagues, establishing planetary boundaries for these nine impacts "aims to help guide human societies away from such a trajectory by defining a 'safe operating space' in which we can continue to develop and thrive."[50] It is also important that the boundary defining the safe operating space for human activities should include a "buffer" that both accounts for "uncertainty in the precise position of the threshold" and "also allows society time to react to early warning signs that it may be approaching a threshold and consequent abrupt or risky change."[51]

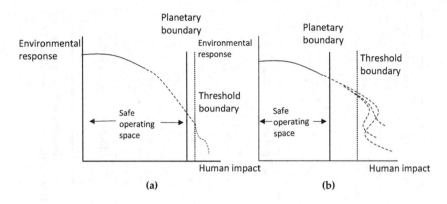

Figure 2.4 Establishing a planetary boundary
Notes: Past environmental responses (solid line curve) to a human-induced impact are
unlikely to provide a good indication of future responses (dotted line curves), and
uncertainty over irreversible threshold effects makes it difficult to predict the
threshold boundary (vertical dotted line). To avoid unknown "tipping points" that
lead irreversibly to these undesirable effects, scientists recommend establishing a
planetary boundary (vertical solid line) well before any unpredictable threshold
effects in environmental response could start occurring. Thus, a planetary boundary
defines a finite safe operating space for human activity and its environmental impacts.
Panel (a) illustrates the case when there is less uncertainty associated with predicting
future threshold effects, so that the planetary boundary can be established relatively
close to the predicted threshold boundary. Panel (b) illustrates the alternative case
where there is considerable uncertainty over threshold effects, and so the planetary
boundary should be set well before any possible threshold boundary.

Figure 2.4 illustrates how setting a planetary boundary to limit
a key human impact on the global environment should take into
account the uncertainty over possible future threshold effects.

The planetary boundary framework clearly aims to put a break
on the environmental degradation associated with the Great
Acceleration. Specifying a planetary boundary to demarcate a "safe
operating space" for each of the nine human impacts listed will place
an absolute limit on human exploitation of critical global biophysical
sinks or resources. For example, various advocates of this approach
have proposed boundaries to restrict depletion of terrestrial net primary
production, freshwater, species richness, assimilative capacity for various pollutants, forest land area and the global carbon budget for 1.5°C
or 2.0°C warming.[52]

However, as Table 2.4 indicates, some scientists may believe
that we may be already perilously close to – and may even have

Table 2.4. Suggested planetary boundaries and current human impacts

Planetary Boundary	Indicator of Human Impact	Pre-industrial Value	Current Value	Boundary Value[a]	Zone of Uncertainty[b]
Climate change	Atmospheric CO_2 concentration	280 ppm	398.5 ppm	350 ppm	450 ppm
Terrestrial biodiversity	Biodiversity intactness index	100%	84.6%	90%	30%
Land system change	Area of forested land remaining	100%	62%	75%	54%
Phosphorous (P) cycle loading	P flows from fertilizers, eroded soils	0 Tg P yr^{-1}	14 Tg P yr^{-1}	6.2 Tg P yr^{-1}	11.2 Tg P yr^{-1}
Nitrogen (N) cycle loading	Industrial and intentional biological fixation of N	0 Tg N yr^{-1}	150 Tg N yr^{-1}	62 Tg N yr^{-1}	82 Tg P yr^{-1}
Ocean acidification	Carbonite ion concentration aragonite saturation compared to pre-industrial	100%	84%	80%	70%
Freshwater use	Consumptive blue water use	~0 km^3 yr^{-1}	2,600 km^3 yr^{-1}	4,000 km^3 yr^{-1}	6,000 km^3 yr^{-1}
Aerosol loading	Aerosol optical depth	0.17	0.30	0.25	0.50
Stratospheric ozone depletion	Total column ozone at mid-latitudes	290 DU	2.2% reduction	5% reduction	10% reduction

Notes: [a]Planetary boundary defining a safe operating space for human activity and its environmental impacts (i.e. the vertical solid line in Figure 2.4); [b]Upper bound of a "zone of uncertainty," a range of increasing risk beyond the boundary value (i.e. the vertical dotted line in Figure 2.4); ppm = parts per million; DU = Dobson unit, a unit of measurement of the amount of a trace gas in a vertical column through the Earth's atmosphere.

Sources: Lade et al. (2020) and Steffen et al. (2015)

exceeded – the planetary boundaries for some human impacts. For example, for carbon dioxide emissions, remaining forest area and aerosol loading, we may have transcended the safe operating space for human activity and may have entered the "buffer zone" where unpredictable threshold effects could occur. Worse still, we may have already overloaded the global nitrogen and phosphorous cycles.

In addition, interactions among these various impacts may amplify their effects on the Earth system. For example, global forest loss can lead to greater carbon dioxide and other greenhouse gas emissions, increasing carbon dioxide–equivalent emissions in the atmosphere, and thus exacerbating climate change. Equally, a changing climate disrupts precipitation and causes temperature rises, which can reduce the amount of freshwater available for human use. As Steven Lade and colleagues found, this can lead to important trade-offs between the safe operating space available for some human impacts. For example, if carbon dioxide (CO_2) emissions are low, then high levels of agricultural activity are safe and vice versa. But high levels of both CO_2 emissions and agricultural activity cannot be safely maintained.[53]

However, some scientists are critical of the planetary boundary framework. One argument is that, although there is convincing evidence that human drivers can cause regime shifts at local and regional scales, the evidence for planetary tipping points in the terrestrial biosphere remains unconfirmed.[54] With the exception of climate change, which is inherently a global phenomenon caused by greenhouse gases emitted worldwide, most environmental change occurs locally and has mainly regional impacts. What is more, key environmental sources and sinks – from ecosystems and biodiversity to freshwater to nitrogen and phosphorous – are not distributed equally across the world. Thus, it does not make sense to have globally prescribed limits for most of the human impacts on the biosphere. Instead, policies and incentives should be targeted at limiting those impacts that are leading to excessive and destructive loss of the environment and growing risks. Or, as the ecologists José Montoya, Ian Donohue and Stuart Pimm maintain, to control most environmental impacts, "the focus must be on appropriate scales and variables that we can measure operationally," whereas in contrast, "the boundaries framework lacks clear definitions, or it has too many conflicting definitions, does not specify units, and fails to define terms operationally, thus prohibiting application by those who set policy or manage natural resources."[55] In practice, local, regional and global management is not necessarily mutually exclusive, and management at one level can reinforce it at another.

To be clear, none of the scientists who debate the relevance of planetary boundaries are questioning whether the Great Acceleration in human impacts on the biosphere is causing massive harm to the Earth's climate, oceans and lands.[56] For example, a critic of the planetary boundary framework, Stuart Pimm, was one of the first to demonstrate that the rate of extinction of species due to the exploitation of the planet by people is 100–1,000 times higher than prehuman extinction.[57] And, along with his fellow critics Montoya and Donohue, Pimm goes on to argue that "mounting evidence demonstrates the patterns and mechanisms by which biodiversity loss alters the provision of functions and the stability of ecosystems. We can now assess and monitor how losses in biodiversity affect different ecosystems. This in turn allows the effectiveness of a given environmental policy to be determined."[58] Equally, in reviewing the scientific evidence for and against tipping points in the terrestrial biosphere, Timothy Lenton and Hywell Williams conclude that "regardless of whether it is approaching a global tipping point, we can all agree that the biosphere is in trouble."[59]

In addition, as noted in the Chapter 1, there are also many equity and development concerns about imposing any limits on human exploitation of critical global sinks and resources inherently.[60] If current access to these sinks and resources is unequally distributed and dominated by wealthy nations, regions and individuals, then additional policies may be necessary either to improve access by the poor or to ensure that they are adequately reimbursed for any additional burdens imposed by reduced access.

Finally, some may believe that the COVID-19 pandemic and the resulting downturn in the world economy have mitigated human impacts on the biosphere. But evidence suggests that any respite has either been short-lived, or for some impacts, even worse during the outbreak. There was a temporary fall in global greenhouse gas emissions in 2020, when the world economy stagnated, but emissions are returning to previous levels as the past pattern of global economic development and energy use resumes.[61] On the other hand, land clearing for mining, agriculture, forestry and other commercial activities – often illegal – increased significantly during the pandemic, as governments diverted resources to COVID-19 or failed to protect remote regions. In 2020, the world lost more than 4.2 million hectares in tropical primary forest, which is a 12 percent increase over the area cleared in 2019.[62] The pandemic has also caused rising debt levels and budget cuts in low- and middle-income countries, which has affected their management, protection and restoration of natural areas and ecosystems.

As global environmental risks continue to multiply, we urgently need policies and actions to save the biosphere. Science shows us that the Earth system provides natural resources, pollution sinks, ecosystem services and essential life-support functions. This natural capital plays an essential role in human survival and well-being. Due to misuse and overexploitation, global natural capital is becoming increasingly scarce and fragile, and the Earth system itself may be in danger of destabilization. Institutions and incentives for investment, innovation and improved management of Earth's valuable natural capital is critical. This is where economics can contribute, and the five principles outlined in Chapter 1 can help guide our policies and actions. The rest of the book explains what should be done to ensure a safer and more prosperous Anthropocene.

Notes

1 See Crutzen (2002); Crutzen and Stoermer (2000); McNeil and Engelke (2016); Steffen et al. (2011); and Waters et al. (2016).

2 Further discussion of key eras of how human economies developed through natural resource exploitation, and the impact on the global environment, can be found in Barbier (2011). For more details, please see the many references cited in this work.

3 See Smith et al. (2010). This article is one of a series of papers appearing in a special section of *Current Anthropology* from a detailed and comprehensive study of the transmission of wealth and inequality in prehistoric societies, including hunter-gatherer and early agricultural societies.

4 The classic treatise on the domestication of animal and plant species and the impact on early human society is Diamond (1997). See also Barbier (2011), chapter 2 and Bellwood (2005).

5 For an excellent summary of recent research on this process, see Deborah Rogers. "Inequality: Why egalitarian societies died out." *NewScientist* July 25, 2012. Available at www.newscientist.com/article/dn22071-inequality-why-egalitarian-soci eties-died-out.

6 The idea that environmental degradation was a proximate cause of the collapse of many empires and civilizations is controversial, yet is gaining prominence. Yoffee (1988) credits the environmental writer, Rice Odell, for first postulating in the mid-1970s the thesis that "environmental degradation" was "among the most important and best attested of the proximate causes of collapse" of states and civilizations. More recently, Diamond (2005) has popularized the notion that ecological degradation and collapse were responsible for the eventual demise of many ancient civilizations. However, this "environmental collapse" thesis has been criticized as

oversimplifying societal decline, which is complex and rarely attributable to a single cause; see Butzer (2012) and Haldon et al. (2018).

7 Based on Maddison (2003), tables 8a and 8b.

8 This was, after all, the age of the Black Death and numerous other plagues that were spread via trade and the corresponding movement of people, goods and animals. For example, the bubonic plague – the Black Death – appears to have been brought by overland routes from Central Asia to China, where it caused successive cycles of epidemics until as late as 1393, while at the same time moving westward to the Middle East and Western Europe via the old Silk Roads as well as the new spice trade sea routes. The Black Death spread quickly in the Western Hemisphere. It reached Crimea by 1345, and Constantinople, Alexandria, Cairo, Cyprus and Sicily in 1347; from there it spread to the great ports of Pisa and Genoa and the rest of Europe via southern France. By 1351, the plague had largely died out in the Western Hemisphere.

9 From Maddison (2003), table 8.b. Maddison's estimates for 1500 indicate that China's share of world gross domestic product (GDP) was 24.9 percent; India's share was 24.4 percent; and Western Europe's share was 17.8 percent. GDP per capita was $600 in China; $550 in India; and $771 in Western Europe, of which the main economies were France, Germany, Italy, the Netherlands, Spain and the United Kingdom.

10 Jones (1987), pp. 80–82.

11 Crosby (1986).

12 Engerman and Sokoloff (1997). Slavery was critical to the new "Atlantic economy" that emerged between 1500 and 1860. As described by Findlay (1993, p. 322), "the pattern of trade across the Atlantic that prevailed from shortly after the time of the discoveries down to as late as the outbreak of the American Civil War came to be known as the 'triangular trade', because it involved the export of slaves from Africa to the New World, where they produced sugar, cotton, and other commodities that were exported to Western Europe to be consumed or embodied in manufactures, and these in turn were partly exported to Africa to pay for slaves." This "triangular trade" corresponded to its own unique pattern of European exploitation of the abundant land and natural resource frontiers of the New World (for more details, see Barbier 2011, chapter 6). For example, Inikori (1992, p. 152) argues that "the growth of Atlantic commerce during the period was a function of commodity production in the Americas," and virtually all the key export commodities of the region were produced by slave labor – gold, silver, sugar, coffee, cotton, tobacco and rice. Moreover, Inikori (1992, p. 155) adds: "The importance of African slavery to Atlantic commerce went beyond the production of the American commodities that were traded. The forced migration of millions of Africans to the extremely low-density territories of the Americas, where they were forced to produce export commodities, provoked an Atlantic-wide division of labor that was the very foundation of Atlantic commerce." This division of labor had two consequences. First, it created an "extractive" frontier of export-oriented commodities in tropical Latin America and the southern US, which contrasted with the emerging and largely subsistence "settlement" frontiers of North America. Second, "the violent production of captives for export to the Americas became virtually the only function performed by western Africa in the Atlantic system."

13 Acemoglu et al. (2001), p. 1373.

14 Acemoglu et al. (2001), p. 1370. A point ignored by Acemoglu et al. (2001) but emphasized by others, notably Crosby (1986), Diamond (1999) and Livi-Bacci (1997), is that disease and environmental conditions also played an important role

in the success of European colonization. That is, by bringing in imported diseases from Europe, such as smallpox, tuberculosis and measles, European colonists effectively decimated many indigenous populations who had no genetic resistance to such diseases. This further enhanced the ability of Europeans to establish successful colonies, regardless of whether they were in temperate regions with permanent settlements by Europeans or "extractive states" with minimal settlement in tropical climates.

15 Crosby (1986, pp. 3–7) coined the term "neo-Europes," which he identifies as lands that "are all completely or at least two-thirds in the temperate zones" and in which people of European descent "compose the great majority" of the present-day population. Note that Crosby's definition also poses some problems for identifying which countries and regions in temperate South America are truly "neo-Europes." For example, Argentina, Uruguay and southern Brazil (Paraná, Santa Catarina and Rio Grande du Sul) fit both his criteria and are included. However, Chile does not and appears to be excluded: "In contrast, Chile's people are only about one-third European; almost all the rest are *mestizo*" (Crosby 1986, p. 3). Curiously, Crosby simply ignores Paraguay, even though at least half of its territory lies below the Tropic of Capricorn, and like southern Brazil, the majority of the population in the region is mainly of European descent. Despite these difficulties in identifying which of the present-day countries of South America quality as "neo-Europes," Crosby (p. 3) concludes: "But if we consider the vast wedge of the continent poleward of the Tropic of Capricorn, we see that the great majority are European."

16 See, for example, Barbier (2011), chapter 5; Chew (2001); Elvin (1993); Hughes (2001); McNeill (1998); and Richards (2003).

17 Richards (2003), pp. 26–38.

18 Richards (2003), pp. 617–618.

19 Toynbee (1978), p. 566.

20 See Thomas (1985) and Wrigley (1988).

21 In depicting the Industrial Revolution as two distinct phases (see also Figure 2.2), I am following the pioneering long-run analysis by Gordon (2017). In addition, Gordon contends that there was a third phase of the Industrial Revolution with the computer and internet revolution that began around 1960 and reached its climax in the dot.com era of the late 1990s, but its main impact on productivity was short-lived, lasting until the 2010s. However, none of these phases of the Industrial Revolution has allowed any economy to transition from the fossil fuel age.

22 Smil (2005), p. 28. See also Etemad et al. (1991); Fouquet (2008); and Smil (2010).

23 From Smil (1994) and (2010), except for the estimates for the 1970s, which is from BP (2019).

24 These historical statistics for global population and GDP per capita are from the Maddison Project Database, version 2018 (Bolt et al. 2018). Real GDP per capita is in US$ 2011.

25 Nelson and Wright (1992), p. 1945.

26 As noted by Nelson and Wright (1992), pp. 1944–1945, "The automobile industry was the most spectacular American success story of the interwar period, a striking blend of mass production methods, cheap materials, and fuels. Despite barriers to trade and weak world demand, U.S. cars dominated world trade during the 1920s, and motor vehicles dominated American manufacturing exports."

27 Nelson and Wright (1992), p. 1946. From the 1920s onward, the parallel development of the aircraft industry and air transport across the United States spurred further economic integration by increasing the mobility of people, cargo and even the mail. By 1950, total air traffic in the United States reached one billion miles,

which for the first time equaled total railroad mileage in the country. See Meinig (2004), pp. 87–96.

28 Both trends are noted by Smil (2006), p. 7 and pp. 87–88: "Intensifying traffic necessitated large-scale construction of paved roads, and this was the main reason for hugely increased extraction of sand, rock, and limestone whose mass now dominates the world's mineral production and accounts for a large share of freight transport ... Rapid growth of aggregate material consumption would not have been possible without abundant available energy in general, and without cheaper electricity in particular. In turn, affordable materials of higher quality opened up new opportunities for energy industries thanks to advances ranging from fully mechanized coal-mining machines and massive offshore oil drilling rigs to improved efficiencies of energy converters. These gains were made possible not only by better alloys but also by new plastics, ceramics, and composite materials."

29 Wagner (2002), pp. 6–7 and figure 5. Wagner defines "nonrenewable organic materials" as all products derived from feedstocks of petroleum and natural gas and coal for nonfuel applications, including resins used in the production of plastics, synthetic fibers and synthetic rubber; feedstocks used in the production of solvents and other petro-chemicals; lubricants and waxes; and asphalt and road oil.

30 Ramankutty and Foley (1999), who reconstruct historical croplands, forest and woodlands, savannah and grasslands and abandoned cropland from 1700 to 1992. Their data was downloaded from the Global Land Use Database, Center for Sustainability and the Global Environment (SAGE), Nelson Institute for Environmental Studies, University of Wisconsin, www.sage.wisc.edu. In 1750, global forest and woodland area was 60 million km² and less than 47 million km² in 1970. Savannah and grassland was almost 32 million km² in 1750, and 27 million km² in 1970.

31 Federico (2005).

32 This evolving water resource management ethos that emerged from the Industrial Revolution is described succinctly by Saveniji et al. (2014), pp. 320–321: "The increased exploitation of freshwater and the related development of societies has been made possible by increasing knowledge of water engineering, large-scale water supply, flood mitigation and irrigation ... Equipped with new technological powers, a new generation of engineers emerged that had a new hydraulic, mission: that of 'taming' nature and making it orderly ... During the last decades of the 19th century and the first decades of the 20th century, the water landscape was transformed in various places, including but not limited to India, Sudan, Mali, Egypt, the USA, Brazil, Spain and the Netherlands. These developments, associated with large and powerful water bureaucracies ... allowed for unprecedented growth in the production of agricultural commodities and energy and confirmed the belief that man could fully control water and be the master of nature" (pp. 320–321). As explained in Barbier (2019b), the continued pursuit of this "hydraulic mission" has had implications for the growing crisis in global water management today.

33 FAO (2012).

34 McDonald et al. (2014). This study focused on water use of a sample of urban agglomerations greater than 750,000.

35 Fouquet (2011).

36 As Fouquet (2011), p. 2383 notes: "For comparison, TSP concentrations for Delhi in the 1990s, one of the most polluted cities in the world, were around 370 μg/m³."

37 See, for example, Jackson et al. (2001) and (2011); Lotze and Milewski (2004); Lotze et al. (2006); Pitcher and Lam (2015); and Roberts (2007).

38 From the "Great Acceleration" graphs of the International Geosphere-Biosphere Programme (IGBP), available at www.igbp.net/globalchange/greatacceleration.4

.1b8ae20512db692f2a680001630.html and also presented in Steffen et al. (2015a). Note that global marine fish catch reached its peak of 72–73 million metric tons between 1994 and 1997, and has since declined. By 2010, it had fallen to 64 million metric tons.

39 Lotze et al. (2006).

40 Hibbard et al. (2006). See also McNeil and Egelke (2016) and Steffen et al. (2007) and (2015a).

41 The original graphs can be found in Steffen et al. (2004) and (2007). These graphs and trends have been updated to 2010 by the IGBP and are available at their website www.igbp.net/globalchange/greatacceleration.4.1b8ae20512db692f2a680001630 .html and also presented in Steffen et al. (2015a).

42 From IPBES (2019). However, Ellis et al. (2013) point out that, although human populations and land use have increased, agricultural intensification and the adoption of technologies enabling dramatic increases in food production from a given area of agricultural land have also risen in the modern era as populations have grown and become wealthier. They argue that agricultural intensification processes may be even more important to understanding the future of land use change as a force transforming the Earth system. This is an argument that we will be taking up again in Chapter 5.

43 Based on the Food and Agriculture Organization of the United Nations (FAO) Forest Resources Assessment (FRA) 2015 data, www.fao.org/forest-resources-assessment/ explore-data/en.

44 WWF (2018).

45 Duarte et al. (2020).

46 Based on Hannah Ritchie (2019) "Where Does Our Plastic Accumulate in the Ocean and What Does That Mean for the Future?" Published online at OurWorldInData. org https://ourworldindata.org/where-does-plastic-accumulate. The original source of the data is Lebreton et al. (2019).

47 One such "catastrophic" Anthropocene outcome is the "Hothouse Earth" state described by Steffen et al. (2018).

48 Lenton et al. (2008) first postulated the possibility of tipping points or "elements" in the Earth's climate systems. A special issue edited by Schellnhuber (2009) then extended the concept to other Earth system processes. Rockström et al. (2009) used the possibility of such human-induced stresses on the Earth system to develop the "planetary boundaries" concept.

49 See, for example, Lade et al. (2020); Rockström et al. (2009); Steffen et al. (2015).

50 Steffen et al. (2015), p. 737.

51 Steffen et al. (2015), pp. 737–738.

52 See, for example, Dinerstein et al. (2017); Gerton et al. (2013); Lade et al. (2020); Mace et al. (2014); Newbold et al. (2016); Rockström et al. (2009); Running (2012); and Steffen et al. (2015).

53 Lade et al. (2020).

54 See, for example, Brook et al. (2013) and Montoya et al. (2018).

55 Montoya et al. (2018), p. 73 and p. 71. A similar criticism is made by the economist Alan Randall (2021, pp. 10–11), "The intuition for PBs can be defended most convincingly for global public goods. Several of the PBs [planetary boundaries] are of this kind: genetic diversity, with a PB that already has been violated; carbon and climate, in the amber zone; ocean acidification and atmospheric ozone depletion, with some SOS [safe operating spaces] intact; and atmospheric aerosol loading, with uncertain status. In all of these cases, the problem shed is global and a PB at global scale makes sense. The remaining PBs—freshwater use, land systems, ecosystem

integrity, and biochemical flows—are not, or at least not entirely, planetary in that the problem sheds tend to be more localized and most of the rewards for management at the problem-shed level are enjoyed at that level. Many problems concerning freshwater and biogeochemical flows are manifested and best managed at the watershed level. Land systems to feed the world may be a global issue, but urban greenspace is much more a local concern. It can be argued that for problems that are manifested mostly at the problem-shed level, there is ample scope and motivation for variation across problem sheds in place-based objectives, approaches, and solutions."

56 For a fascinating insight into the various arguments of this scientific debate, see Bob Lalasz. "Debate: What Good Are Planetary Boundaries?" Cool Green Science, March 25, 2013, available at https://blog.nature.org/science/2013/03/25/debate-what-good-are-planetary-boundaries.

57 Pimm et al. (1995).

58 Montoya et al. (2018), p. 73.

59 Lenton and Williams (2013), p. 382.

60 See, for example, Biermann and Kim (2020).

61 Andrijevic et al. (2020); Le Quéré et al. (2020); and Tollefson (2021).

62 See Mikaela Weisse and Liz Goldman. "Primary Rain Forest Destruction Increased 12% from 2019 to 2020." Global Forest Watch. March 31, 2021 www .globalforestwatch.org/blog/data-and-research/global-tree-cover-loss-data-2020.

3 ECONOMICS FOR A FRAGILE PLANET

Chapter 1 argued that at the heart of the global crisis in sustainability is the *underpricing of nature*. The rising costs associated with many environmental problems – climate change, freshwater scarcity, declining ecosystem services and increasing energy insecurity – are not routinely reflected in markets. Nor have we developed adequate policies and institutions to provide other ways for the true costs of environmental degradation to be taken into account. As a consequence, ecological scarcity, pollution and resource overexploitation are pervasive; wasteful use of natural resources and environmental degradation persists; and global environmental risks – including the threat of new pandemics – continue to mount.

Chapter 2 noted that this process has accelerated so significantly since the mid-twentieth century that we are in danger of pushing the Earth system beyond critical "tipping points" for healthy functioning. This "Great Acceleration" of population growth, industrialization and mineral and energy use has created a new human-dominated era on Earth. The fundamental challenge of the Anthropocene is how to manage and limit the global environmental risks caused by our overexploitation of nature so that the entire Earth system is not permanently destabilized. Ensuring a "safe" Anthropocene is the major sustainability challenge facing humankind today.

To meet this challenge, we need to rethink our economic approach to nature and the planet. As we suggested in Chapter 1, it begins with some basic principles that can guide us to thinking about the economics for an increasingly "fragile" planet. The first principle, as we have already noted, is ending the underpricing of nature. The other important principles are fostering collective action, accepting absolute limits and encouraging development that is not only efficient but also sustainable and inclusive. These principles underlie the approach to economics and policy taken in this book. This chapter further outlines and explores the foundation for this approach.

We begin with a very simple – but ultimately profound – insight. If we accept the view that "our economies are embedded within Nature, not external to it,"[1] then this should lead to the recognition that our planet is not a limitless source of exploitation for humankind. Acknowledging that certain Earth system processes and vital resources cannot be endlessly polluted, depleted and degraded is an important starting point for thinking how best to manage our planet in an efficient, sustainable and inclusive manner.

Spaceship Earth

The need to curb human activities threatening critical Earth system processes, resources and sinks aligns with economic approaches to sustainability that recognize global limits on natural capital exploitation by economies. This perspective on sustainability began with the economist Kenneth Boulding in the 1960s, who argued that the Earth is ultimately finite, and thus transition to a "spaceship economy" that respects such limits is unavoidable.[2]

In "The Economics of the Coming Spaceship Earth," Boulding suggests that there are essentially two types of economies. The first is the prevailing economic system, which he calls the *cowboy economy*. According to Boulding, "the cowboy" is an appropriate metaphor for the modern economy, as it is "symbolic of the illimitable plains and also associated with reckless, exploitative, romantic, and violent behavior."[3]

The key feature of the cowboy economy is its dependence on exploiting *unending frontiers*. As we saw in Chapter 2, this process is not new in human history. Since the Agricultural Transition 12,000 years ago, economies have developed and flourished by finding and exploiting new sources of land, raw materials, water and energy.[4]

Boulding maintains that the cowboy economy's reliance on the environment as an unending frontier is deeply rooted in "one of the oldest images of mankind":

Primitive men, and to a large extent also men of the early civilizations, imagined themselves to be living on a virtually illimitable plane. There was almost always somewhere beyond the known limits of human habitation, and over a very large part of the time that man has been on earth, there has been something like a frontier. That is, there was always some place else to go when things got too difficult, either by reason of the deterioration of the natural environment or a deterioration of the social structure in places where people happened to live. The image of the frontier is probably one of the oldest images of mankind, and it is not surprising that we find it hard to get rid of.[5]

Figure 3.1 illustrates how the cowboy economy treats the environment as an "illimitable plane." The economic system produces goods and services for consumption, which increases human welfare. These economic activities depend on the surrounding environment as a source of raw material and energy inputs, water and land and also as a sink for pollution and waste. However, if the economic system views the environment as an "illimitable plane," then as production and consumption expand, they will draw on more and more of the environment's sources and sinks.

When these uses of the environment are considered unlimited, then our economy will develop as if there is little or no cost associated with increasing resource depletion or pollution. And there is little to stop it developing in this way. The economic system will go on treating the environment as if it is essentially a "free" source of new resources and a sink for waste, and ignores any costs associated with rising environmental degradation. Rising ecological and natural resource scarcity are dismissed as economic problems, because our institutions, incentives and innovations are geared toward treating the environment, its resources and sinks as being perpetually abundant rather than limited and scarce. In short, our economy was structured and built for an *era of abundance* rather than for one of rising natural resource and ecological scarcity, and any resulting global environmental risks.

But there is an alternative. Boulding called it the "spaceman" or *spaceship economy*. This type of economy recognizes that it is part of a larger "closed" system, "in which the earth has become a single spaceship, without unlimited reservoirs of anything, either for extraction or for pollution, and in which, therefore, man must find his place in a

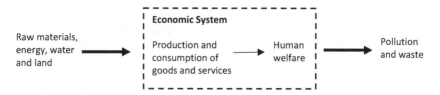

Figure 3.1 The "illimitable plane" of the cowboy economy
Notes: In the cowboy economy, the economic system treats the environment as an "illimitable plane," which it can draw on for more and more resources and pollute with little or no cost.

cyclical ecological system which is capable of continuous reproduction of material form even though it cannot escape having inputs of energy."[6] Consequently, Boulding believed that transition to a spaceship economy was inevitable – not because we would run out of fossil fuels, minerals, forests and other key natural resources to exploit – but because "spaceship Earth" will eventually constrain how much we can keep utilizing its various sources and sinks "for extraction or for pollution."[7]

Boulding's view that the Earth system imposes limits on the economy is not new; classical economists from the late eighteenth and nineteenth centuries, such as Thomas Malthus, "found resource scarcity inherent in the finiteness of the globe."[8] However, given that he was writing in the 1960s, Boulding was prescient in anticipating concerns decades later over the state of the world's ecosystems and Earth system processes, and their ability to sustain growing human populations and economies. As we saw in Chapter 2, these concerns now suggest that essential Earth system processes – and the rising global environmental risks from disrupting them – place limits on the expansion of global human activity.

Figure 3.2 depicts how the spaceship economy is embedded within the "closed" Earth system. Production and consumption activities still draw on sources of resources and sinks for pollution, but now this process is constrained by the "planetary boundaries" that protect key Earth system processes from climate change, biodiversity loss, land use change, freshwater scarcity and other impacts causing global environmental risks. Recall from Chapter 2, that the rationale for establishing planetary boundaries on human exploitation of key sinks and resources is to avoid "tipping points" or "thresholds" that could lead to irrevocable changes in the Earth system, with potentially catastrophic

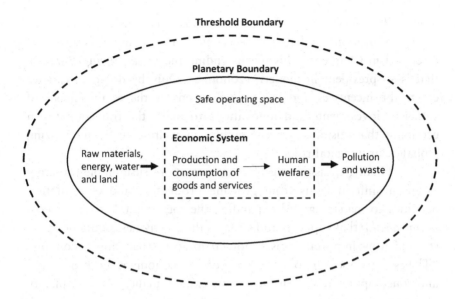

Figure 3.2 The spaceship economy
Notes: Although the spaceship economy still depends on exploiting the environment as a source of resources and a sink for pollution, this process is constrained by the safe operating space defined by planetary boundaries. The purpose of such boundaries is to prevent the human activities and populations that use the environment from permanently disrupting key Earth system processes and resources, which could lead to potentially catastrophic consequences for humanity.

impacts for humanity. Consequently, a spaceship economy will stay within the limits demarcated by safe operating spaces for using critical sources of resources and sinks for pollution so as to limit the rising global environmental risks posed by climate change, biodiversity loss, water scarcity and other major human impacts on the biosphere.

There are three implications of the spaceship economy.

First, exploitation of Earth's sources of natural resources and sinks for pollution is not limitless. Demarcating safe operating spaces to reduce the global environmental risks arising from human uses of critical global sinks and resources requires managing them efficiently and sustainably. This in turn implies that the economic system must take into account the increasing *scarcity* of the ecosystems, resources and pollution reservoirs as these vital components of the global environment are used up or degraded.

As a result, the rising costs associated with natural resource scarcity and increasing environmental and ecological damage can no longer be ignored, and instead must be reflected in the market allocations and policy decisions of the economic system. As discussed in Chapter 1, this means ending the *underpricing of nature* that is so prevalent in modern economies. Only by doing so can we create the incentives and institutions to ensure the establishment of sufficient investments and innovations to make the transition to an economy that sustains per capita human welfare while minimizing global environmental risks.

Finally, transitioning to a greener, more sustainable economy means a shift in focus from growing production and consumption activities to managing and expanding the total capital stock, or *economic wealth* that supports and sustains these activities. Boulding again stressed how important this is for creating a "spaceship" economy: "The essential measure of the success of the economy is not production and consumption at all, but the nature, extent, quality, and complexity of the total capital stock."[9]

As Chapter 1 suggested, there are three key components of this "total capital stock":

- manufactured or reproducible *physical capital*, such as roads, buildings, machinery and factories
- *human capital*, such as skills, education and health embodied in the workforce
- *natural capital*, including land, forests, water resources, fossil fuels and minerals

In addition, natural capital also comprises those ecosystems that through their natural functioning and habitats provide important goods and services to the economy, or *ecological capital*.

It is worth exploring further why managing and increasing this portfolio of economic wealth is critical to the sustainability of an economy.

Total Capital Stock

As we saw in Chapter 2, avoiding unknown tipping points in the Earth system is essential if we want to ensure a "safe" as opposed to an "uncertain" – or even "catastrophic" – Anthropocene for humankind. Thus, one critical objective of managing the *total capital stock* of the economy – which comprises physical, human and natural capital – is to *limit global environmental risks*.

This certainly requires managing natural capital so as to limit climate change, biodiversity loss, land use conversion, freshwater scarcity and other impacts of human activity causing global environmental risks. However, managing natural capital to reduce environmental degradation and risks does not occur in isolation; it also involves changes in physical and human capital.

For example, transitioning to clean energy for electricity to help control global warming means reducing use of fossil fuels and replacing them with solar, wind, tidal and other clean energy sources. To do so will entail changes to infrastructure and other physical capital investments and hiring more workers with the skills necessary for this purpose. Utilizing more renewables for electricity generation will require different types of power plants; developing smart grids and transmission systems; and improving battery capacity and storage. It will also mean more workers that have the skills and knowledge for developing, manufacturing, assembling and installing clean energy electricity generation and transmission. Consequently, changes in the entire stock of natural, physical and human capital is necessary to boost clean energy for electricity and reduce the threat of global warming.

However, the total capital stock also serves another important purpose. For any economy, physical, human and natural capital are essential for supporting, maintaining and enhancing production and consumption, which in turn increase human welfare. The total capital stock is essentially the *economic wealth* that sustains welfare. As human populations are increasing, then this means that an economy's overall wealth also must be managed to ensure, at the very least, that per capita human welfare does not decline over time.

Consequently, the second objective for managing the *total capital stock* of the economy is to *sustain per capita human welfare.*[10]

Figure 3.3 summarizes these two objectives for managing the total capital stock of the economy. If we want to both sustain human welfare and limit global environmental risks, then our economies must accumulate a portfolio of economic wealth that can achieve both goals. This is an important change in our overall approach to our economies and the environment. In the past, we have always treated the environment as an unending frontier of available natural capital to exploit (see Figure 3.1) However, if we are to ensure a safe Anthropocene, we must recognize that there are limits on the economy's exploitation of nature's critical sources and sinks so as to limit global environmental risks

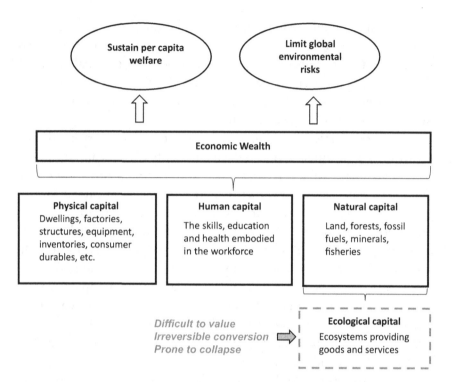

Figure 3.3 Managing economic wealth
Notes: Economic wealth, or the total capital stock, comprises physical, human and natural capital. It should be managed to sustain per capita human welfare and to limit global environmental risks. One challenge is that an important type of natural capital – ecosystems providing goods and services – is difficult to value, subject to irreversible conversion and prone to collapse.

(see Figure 3.2). There are trade-offs between, on the one hand, exploiting more natural capital to increase production and consumption and, on the other, rising climate change, biodiversity loss, land use conversion, freshwater scarcity and other risks. Managing physical, human and natural capital to sustain human welfare is still critical, but equally important is managing this wealth to bring environmental threats under control. Both objectives are therefore essential to an economics for a "fragile" planet.

As Figure 3.3 indicates, the portfolio of assets comprising economic wealth is not just human and physical capital, but also an economy's endowment of natural resources and ecosystems. But there are some unique challenges for managing some forms of natural capital, especially ecosystems proving goods and services, which are difficult to value or restore and are prone to collapse if severely disturbed or degraded.

Natural Capital

It is relatively straightforward to view some valuable renewable and exhaustible natural resource stocks found in the environment, such as mineral ores, energy reserves, fisheries and forests, as stores of wealth.[11] Because such natural resource are a valuable source of marketed material and energy inputs for economies, they are similar to a "natural" savings account. If exploited, reserves of these resources in the environment are supplied and sold in markets for material and energy inputs to yield a current and future flow of income. This is akin to withdrawing money from a savings account, or owning company shares or other investments that pay out income dividends. Consequently, as they can yield a stream of benefits over time, in this case income through depletion, then just like any other asset or investment in the economy, natural resource stocks exploited for marketed material and energy inputs can be viewed as a special type of capital asset – a form of "natural wealth."

However, the environment also provides other important benefits, or "services," that support an economy and boost the welfare of people. They can be wide-ranging – from absorbing pollution and waste to the enjoyment of nature from recreation or tourism, to protecting and supporting production activities through controlling floods, storms and droughts. Such services provided by the surrounding environment are valuable to our economy, regardless of whether or not there exists a market for them. In principle, then, the concept of "natural capital" should also include all environmental assets that provide important and valuable benefits to humankind.

For instance, in the early 1970s, the economists Rick Freeman, Robert Haveman and Allen Kneese proposed that the environment should be considered a "capital good" for the wide and diverse range of "services" that it generates, beyond marketed material and energy inputs:

> [We] view the environment as an asset or a kind of nonreproducible capital good that produces a stream of various services for man. Services are tangible (such as flows of water or minerals), or functional (such as the removal, dispersion, storage, and degradation of wastes or residuals), or intangible (such as a scenic view).[12]

Note that two of these services provided by nature – absorbing pollution and scenic views – cannot be purchased in markets, yet as Freemen and colleagues argue, these are important benefits provided to human-kind that should make us view the environment as an "asset."

Increasingly we have come to realize that many of the "functional" or "intangible" services of the environment can be attributed to a very specific type of "natural capital" – *ecosystems*. These unique systems in nature also produce many beneficial goods and services over time, and thus also comprise part of the total capital stock of an economy:

> Natural capital consists not only of specific natural resources, from energy and minerals to fish and trees, but also of interacting ecosystems. Ecosystems comprise the abiotic (nonliving) environment and the biotic (living) groupings of plant and animal species called communities. As with all forms of capital, when these two components of ecosystems interact, they provide a flow of services. Examples of such ecosystem services include water supply and its regulation, climate maintenance, nutrient cycling, and enhanced biological productivity.[13]

Consequently, because they produce goods and services that support economic activity and enhance human welfare, ecosystems are also important economic assets – or *ecological capital*.

Ecosystems should be viewed as highly valuable capital assets, because they produce a very wide range of beneficial ecosystem goods and services – often called *ecosystem services* for short. This can be seen in Table 3.1 with the example of wetland ecosystems and their services.

The Ramsar Convention on Wetlands of International Importance defines wetlands as "areas of marsh, fen, peatland, or water, whether natural or artificial, permanent or temporary, with water that is static or flowing, fresh, brackish or salt, including areas of marine water, the depth of which at low tide does not exceed six metres."[14] This broad definition encompasses a wide range of wetland ecosystems, including coastal wetlands, freshwater swamps and marshes, floodplains and peatlands.

Table 3.1 provides some examples of how specific wetland goods and services are linked to the underlying ecological structure and functioning that are unique to these ecosystems. This structure and functioning is shaped, in turn, by key hydrological processes. As emphasized by wetland ecologists, these processes are critical to the functioning and structure of wetland ecosystems: "The hydrology of the landscape influences and changes the physiochemical environment,

Table 3.1. Examples of wetland ecosystem services

Ecosystem Structure and Function	Ecosystem Goods and Services
Attenuates and/or dissipates waves, buffers wind	Coastal protection
Provides sediment stabilization and soil retention	Erosion control
Water flow regulation and control	Flood protection
Groundwater recharge/discharge	Water supply
Provides nutrient and pollution uptake, as well as retention, particle deposition	Water purification
Generates biogeochemical activity, sedimentation, biological productivity	Carbon sequestration
Climate regulation and stabilization	Maintenance of temperature, precipitation
Generates biological productivity and diversity	Raw materials and food
Provides suitable reproductive habitat and nursery grounds, sheltered living space	Maintains fishing, hunting and foraging activities
Provides unique and aesthetic landscape, suitable habitat for diverse fauna and flora	Tourism, recreation, education, and research
Provides unique and aesthetic landscape of cultural, historic or spiritual meaning	Culture, spiritual and religious benefits, bequest values

which in turn, along with hydrology, determines the biotic communities that are found in the wetland."[15] The consequence is that the ecosystem services provided by wetlands are driven by hydrology, and understanding how changes in hydrological processes affect the delivery of these services is crucial to determining the impact on human welfare.

As is clear from Table 3.1, a wide range of valuable goods and services to humans arise in myriad ways via the unique structure, hydrology and other key functions of wetlands. For example, the plants and animals found in these ecosystems might be harvested or hunted for food, collected for raw materials or simply valued because they are aesthetically pleasing. Some of the ecosystem functions of coastal wetlands, such as nutrient and water cycling, can also benefit humans through purifying water, controlling floods, protecting against coastal storms, reducing pollution, sequestering carbon or simply by providing more pleasing environments for recreation. Finally, because they are unique habitats often with important cultural significance, wetlands are often cherished in their own right simply for existing, and this is a value that we would like to see future generations, including our children, enjoy.

The example of wetland ecosystems also illustrates two other important points about the benefits associated with ecological capital.

First, we do not create ecosystems. They freely produce a wide array of goods and services that are not accounted for by the economic system, yet we benefit from them.

Second, although ecosystem goods and services provide very valuable benefits, most ecosystem goods and services are available for free. We do not have to pay for them, as healthy ecosystems provide their valuable benefits to us through their natural structure and functioning – as Table 3.1 illustrates for wetland ecosystems.

Consequently, ecosystems are very unusual but a valuable form of wealth to our economy, and should be considered an important form of natural capital in our total capital stock.

Nevertheless, as the economist Partha Dasgupta (2008, p. 3) maintains, compared to, say, human-made reproducible capital, ecosystems are a very unique form of wealth:

> Ecosystems are capital assets. Like reproducible capital assets (roads, buildings, and machinery), ecosystems depreciate if they are misused or are overused. But they differ from reproducible capital assets in three ways: (1) depreciation of natural capital is frequently irreversible (or at best the systems take a long time to recover), (2) except in a very limited sense, it isn't possible to replace a depleted or degraded ecosystem by a new one, and (3) ecosystems can collapse abruptly, without much prior warning.[16]

This quote stresses three important aspects of ecological capital. First, the benefits, or valuable goods and services, which are generated by ecosystems are wide-ranging. Second, although like other assets in the economy an ecosystem can be increased by investment, such as through restoration activities, ecosystems are frequently depleted or degraded, for example, through habitat destruction, land conversion, pollution impacts and so forth. Finally, if ecosystems are irrevocably degraded or depleted, or equivalently, their restoration is prohibitively expensive, such irreversible conversion can increase the risk of ecological collapse. That is, large shocks or sustained disturbances to ecosystems can set in motion a series of interactions that can breach ecological thresholds that cause the systems to "flip" from one functioning state to another. Although it is possible under certain conditions for the system to recover to its original state, under other conditions the change might be permanent.

These three characteristics of ecosystems – irreversibly depleted, irreplaceable and prone to collapse – also explains why ecological capital is so vital to one of the key objectives for our economy, which is to *limit global environmental risks*. As we saw in Chapter 2, such risks have accelerated in recent decades because of large-scale degradation and destruction of many important ecosystems. Consequently, as we shall see in the next several chapters, the result is increasing problems with climate change, marine and terrestrial biodiversity loss, land use change and freshwater scarcity. Even newer risks, such as the possibility of a disease outbreak caused by transmission from animals to humans, can be traced to ecosystem loss and overexploitation, namely from the trade in wildlife and the destruction of their habitats.

Natural Resource and Ecological Scarcity

There is one principal reason why modern economies are squandering valuable natural and ecological capital and failing to act on rising global environmental risks. The increasing costs associated with many environmental problems – climate change, freshwater scarcity, declining ecosystem services and increasing energy insecurity, and the risks of disease outbreaks – are not routinely reflected in markets. Nor have we developed adequate policies and institutions to correct this market failure or to provide other incentives for production and consumption activities to take into account the rising costs of increasing environmental impacts. Frequently, policy distortions and failures compound ecological scarcity, pollution and resource overexploitation by further encouraging wasteful use of natural resources and environmental degradation.

This underpricing of nature is especially problematic for ecological capital, which is largely ignored by the economic system and whose many valuable services are not routinely exchanged in markets. In contrast, some forms of natural capital, such as land, forests, fossil fuels and ores and minerals, are marketed, and their increasing scarcity can be reflected in market prices. Even for these resources, however, many of their ecological impacts, pollution damages and other environmental effects are not included in markets. So once again, we are back to the problem of the *underpricing of nature* that we discussed in Chapter 1 and captured in Figure 1.2.

There is an even bigger ecological scarcity challenge. As we saw in Chapter 2, a growing scientific literature argues that there are *planetary boundaries* that must be respected in order to protect the Earth system from abrupt, and possibly catastrophic, changes. Specifying a planetary boundary establishes a *safe operating space*, which in turn places an absolute limit on human exploitation of critical global biophysical sinks or resources (see Figure 3.2). Depending on the type of planetary boundary, the finite limit could be in terms of terrestrial net primary production, available freshwater for consumption, species richness, assimilative capacity for various pollutants, forest land area or the global carbon budget.[17]

Accepting limits on global human impacts does not mean that the problem of natural resource and ecological scarcity is no longer relevant. On the contrary, managing finite safe operating spaces entails taking into account increasing scarcity and generating the necessary values, incentives and investments to alleviate it. As argued by Thomas Sterner and colleagues, "Keeping within planetary boundaries requires that we make better and more cost-effective use of the finite resources and sinks available to us."[18]

Consequently, the paramount challenge for developing an economics for an increasingly fragile planet is to end the underpricing of nature so that our institutions, incentives and innovations reflect the growing ecological and natural resource scarcity that our current economic use of the environment has created. In the next few chapters, we will examine what it means to tackle specific natural resource scarcity problems in this way. We will look at climate change (Chapter 4); land use change and biodiversity (Chapter 5); freshwater (Chapter 6); and oceans and coasts (Chapter 7). For each of these major problems, we will use the basic principles developed in this chapter to explain how economics can tackle the problem of sustaining human welfare while limiting global environmental risks. Moreover, we will explain how ending the underpricing of nature is the key to overcoming rising ecological and natural resource scarcity, which is at the heart of managing environmental issues that are critical for our sustainable future.

As a final point, so far in this book, we have focused on the problem of avoiding global environmental risks, which is essential if we want to ensure a "safe" Anthropocene for humankind in the coming decades. As we shall see in the next four chapters, this may require limiting depletion of the global carbon budget to keep Earth's warming to 1.5°C or possibly 2°C; slowing or halting tropical deforestation and other terrestrial habitat losses; mitigating growing freshwater scarcity; and controlling pollution, overfishing and destruction of our oceans and coasts. But it must also be recognized that reducing human exploitation of critical global environmental sinks and resources raises important issues of fairness and equity. These concerns over the distribution of wealth and the impacts on disadvantaged and vulnerable populations as we overcome natural resource and ecological scarcity are vitally important. The next four chapters explore how we should meet this challenge as well for managing climate change, freshwater, land use change and biodiversity and oceans and coasts.

Ending the Underpricing of Nature

To conclude, this chapter has argued that we must change the relationship between the economy and nature.

Until now, humankind has viewed our planet as a limitless source of exploitation, to be endlessly polluted, depleted and degraded to meet the needs of our expanding economic activity and growing population. As illustrated in Figure 3.1, treating the environment as an "illimitable plane" means that, as production and consumption proceed, they will draw on more of the environment's sources of natural resources and sinks for pollution. Until this process changes, economic progress will always be linked with greater appropriation, control and use of the environment, and in turn, increased utilization of nature means greater prosperity and human welfare.

As we saw in Chapter 2, our perception of nature as abundant, freely available and easily accessible goes back to the Agricultural Transition more than 10,000 years ago. It has continued throughout human history, carried on during the Industrial Revolution and afterward and has persisted until the present day. As a consequence, in today's economies, our institutions, incentives and innovations, are dominated by the paradigm of finding and exploiting more natural resources and pollution sinks as if they are perpetually abundant.

But what works in an era of abundance is detrimental in an age of increasing natural resource and ecological scarcity. That is why, as argued in this chapter, the rising global environmental risks we face today are predominantly the result of institutions, incentives and innovations that are incapable of mitigating scarcity. They work instead to underprice nature, thus accelerating our overuse of it.

Chapter 1 outlined how our current economic incentives, institutions and innovations have perpetuated this vicious cycle of underpricing nature (see Figure 1.2). Markets and policy decisions currently do not reflect the rising economic costs associated with exploiting the environment. The result is that economic development today produces much more environmental damage and ecosystem harm than it needs to. Such development leads to even more resource depletion, pollution, degradation of ecosystems and, ultimately, rising ecological scarcity. But the rising economic and social costs associated with these impacts and scarcity continue to be "underpriced" by markets and ignored by policies. The vicious cycle continues on, and the current pattern of economic development persists.

However, if we correct this pattern of underpricing of nature, we could instead create a "virtuous cycle" of managing increasing natural resource and ecological scarcity and global environmental risks. And when value is fully accounted for, natural capital can provide an engine for economic development that sustains and enhances human welfare. This virtuous cycle is depicted in Figure 3.4.

It starts with governance regimes and institutions that are suitable for managing the rapidly changing conditions of resource availability and scarcity, including the threat posed by climate change and other global environmental risks. If need be, there may be a call for creating safe operating spaces and other constraints on human impacts on the environment. Ending the underpricing of nature also requires reforms to markets and policies to ensure that they adequately capture the rising economic costs of exploiting scarce resources and ecosystems. These costs include not only the full costs of exploiting natural resources and pollution sinks but also environmental damages from degrading ecosystems and any social impacts of inequitable distribution. The costs associated with rising global environmental risks will also needed to be reflected in our markets and policies. Incorporating these costs will ensure that economic development will minimize environmental and ecological damages, which in turn will lead to more resource

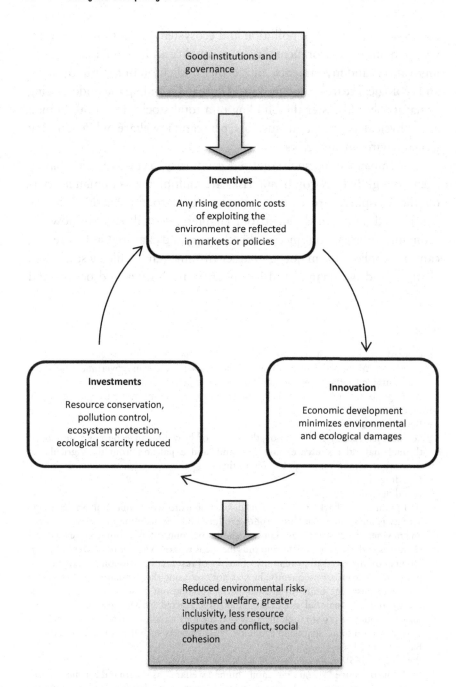

Figure 3.4 Ending the underpricing of nature: a virtuous cycle

conservation, control of pollution and ecosystem protection. The result will be reduced environmental risks, inequality and conflict; more green innovations and investments; and further mitigation of natural resource and ecological scarcity and its costs. Ultimately, ending the underpricing of nature should foster the building of a total stock of natural, human and physical capital that sustains per capita welfare while limiting global environmental risks.

Implementing such solutions is not easy. Yet it is essential in an age where global environmental risks are multiplying as human impacts on the biosphere are causing massive harm to the Earth's climate, oceans and lands. In the next four chapters, we will explore how the economic approach outlined in this chapter, and captured in Figure 3.4, can be applied to major global environmental challenges: climate change, land use change and biodiversity, freshwater and oceans and coasts.

Notes

1 Quoted from p. 2 of *The Economics of Biodiversity: The Dasgupta Review – Headline Messages.* https://assets.publishing.service.gov.uk/government/uploads/system/uploads/attachment_data/file/957629/Dasgupta_Review_-_Headline_Messages.pdf. For Professor Sir Partha Dasgupta's full report, see Dasgupta (2021).
2 Boulding (1966).
3 Boulding (1966), p. 7.
4 See Barbier (2011) for an in-depth review of how human economies developed through natural resource exploitation and land expansion from the Agricultural Transition 12,000 years ago to present times.
5 Boulding (1966), p. 1.
6 Boulding (1966), pp. 7–8.
7 As I point out in Barbier (2021), this distinction as to what limits human economic activity is important. Boulding (1966) produced his "Spaceship Earth" essay during an era when the concern was mainly with the environment as a source of key natural resources and a sink for waste, and thus the focus was on whether there were physical "limits" on the physical availability of stocks of resources as economies expand and populations grow. Consequently, he was not espousing the popular concerns at that time over possible "limits to growth" from running out of strategically important energy and raw material stocks, as famously predicted by Meadows et al. (1972). Instead, Boulding (1966) took the view that the Earth itself was ultimately finite, and thus transition to a "spaceship economy" that respects such limits is unavoidable.
8 Barnett and Morse (1963), p. 58.
9 Boulding (1966), p. 8.
10 I call this objective "sustain per capita human welfare" as shorthand for the sustainability goal that economic development today must ensure that future generations are left no worse off than present generations. Or, as some economists have succinctly put it, *per capita* welfare should not be declining over time (Arrow et al. 2012 and Pezzey 1989). As explained in Barbier (2019c), this economic interpretation of

sustainability is directly related to the definition proposed by WCED (1987, p. 43): "Sustainable development is development that meets the needs of the present without compromising the ability of future generations to meet their own needs."

11 In fact, for some time, economists have treated this type of natural resource as an asset or capital stock that provides a present value stream of "income," and that resource depletion is linked to the depreciation of this capital value. For example, more than 100 years ago, Lewis Cecil Gray argued that, "It is easy to determine how much the capital value of a coal mine is reduced by the process of this use. But this capital value is nothing more than the present value of the surplus income from the mine during a period of time, – that is, the present value of the total rent which it will yield" (Gray 1914, p. 468). This capital approach was developed formally by Hotelling (1931), who demonstrated that the rate of return from holding onto exhaustible resources as an asset must grow at a rate equal to the interest rate, which represents the returns on all other capital in an economy. Ever since Hotelling, treating natural resources, such as land, forests, fossil fuels, ores and minerals, as a form of capital has become a standard approach in economics. For further discussion of the economic concept of natural capital, see Barbier (2019c).

12 Freeman et al. (1973), p. 20.

13 Barbier and Heal (2006), p. 1.

14 From "An Introduction to the Convention on Wetlands (Previously the Ramsar Convention Manual)." Ramsar Convention Secretariat, Gland, Switzerland. Available at www.ramsar.org/sites/default/files/documents/library/handbook1_5ed_introductiontoconvention_e.pdf.

15 Mitsch et al. (2009), p. 2.

16 Dasgupta (2008), p. 3.

17 Steffen et al. (2015). See also Chapter 2 for further discussion.

18 Sterner et al. (2019), p. 19.

4 CLIMATE CHANGE

Climate change clearly illustrates the need to implement the principles underlying the economics of a fragile planet.

The good news is that there is scientific consensus on what our absolute limit should be. According to the Intergovernmental Panel on Climate Change, we need to contain global warming to 2°C compared to preindustrial levels, and if possible, to 1.5°C.

The bad news is that a lot of action is urgently needed to reduce greenhouse gas emissions.

Global temperatures have already reached 1°C above preindustrial levels, and we are increasingly experiencing more extreme weather, rising sea levels, diminishing Arctic sea ice and other environmental impacts. To keep global warming to 1.5°C means reducing human-caused emissions of carbon dioxide (CO_2) significantly so that the world can reach "net zero" emissions by 2050.[1] This requires balancing all global emissions produced by humans with an equivalent amount of CO_2 removed from the atmosphere.

According to the Energy & Climate Intelligence Unit, only two countries – Bhutan and Suriname – have achieved net zero emissions so far. Just eleven other countries plus the European Union have either legally adopted the target or have proposed legislation to do so.[2] Still, there was some respite due to the COVID-19 pandemic. After rising steadily each decade, global CO_2 emissions fell by 6.4 percent, or 2.3 billion tonnes, in 2020 – equivalent to double Japan's annual emissions.[3]

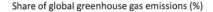

Share of global greenhouse gas emissions (%)

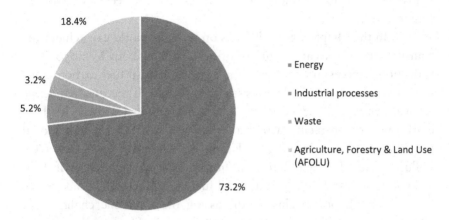

Figure 4.1 Global greenhouse gas emissions by sector, 2016
Notes: In 2016, global greenhouse gas emissions from all sectors was 49.4 billion
tonnes of carbon dioxide-equivalent ($GtCO_2e$). Emissions from energy include from
industry (24.2 percent); buildings (heat and electricity, 17.5 percent); transport
(16.2 percent); and other sources (15.3 percent).
Source: Hannah Ritchie. "Sector by Sector: Where Do Global Greenhouse Gas
Emissions Come From?" OurWorldinData.org September 18, 2020. Based on data
from Climate Watch, World Resources Institute, Washington, DC. Available at
https://ourworldindata.org/ghg-emissions-by-sector

But it is unlikely that the economic slowdown induced by the
pandemic will help much in achieving net zero emissions by 2050. The
2020 fall in global CO_2 emissions may be temporary, as the world
economy continues to rebound.[4] Unless the pattern of economic development and energy use changes, the world will soon return to recent
trends. Emissions rose by 1 percent annually over the past decade as
growth in energy use from fossil fuels outpaced the rise of low-carbon
sources and activities, especially in low- and middle-income countries.[5]
The world would need to cut carbon emissions from fossil fuels by at
least 6 percent each year for the next decade to limit global warming
to 1.5°C.[6]

Achieving this goal requires a rapid transition away from fossil
fuels to low-carbon sources of energy. As shown in Figure 4.1, energy
accounts for over 73 percent of global greenhouse gas (GHG) emissions,
mainly from transport, buildings and industry. The next largest source

(18.4 percent) is from agriculture, forestry and other land use, whose contribution to global GHG emissions has been increasing in recent years.[7]

In this chapter, we will focus on how the world can achieve the transition to a low-carbon future of net zero emissions by 2050. This transition is necessary to "bend the curve" in fossil fuel carbon emissions over the next two decades (see Figure 4.2). If the post-pandemic recovery in the world economy leads to continued growth in these emissions of 1 percent each year, then we will fail to limit global warming to 1.5°C. Instead, as Figure 4.2 confirms, fossil fuel CO_2 pollution must fall by 6 percent annually. This can only occur if there is a substantial shift away from fossil fuel use in the next decade or so.

The chapter begins by discussing the economic challenge of climate change, and why ending the underpricing of fossil fuels is critical to meeting this challenge. Equally important is the role of collective

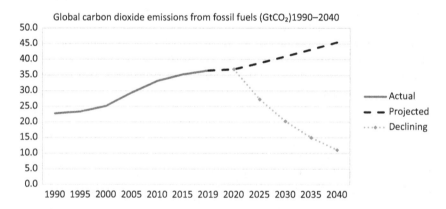

Figure 4.2 Bending the fossil fuel carbon dioxide emissions curve
Notes: Carbon dioxide (CO_2) emissions from the use of coal, oil and gas (combustion and industrial processes), the process of gas flaring and the manufacture of cement. From 1990 to 2019, global CO_2 emissions from fossil fuels rose from 23.3 gigatonnes (Gt) to 36.8 Gt (solid black line). Over 2010 to 2019, emissions rose at approximately 1 percent annually. If they continue to rise at this rate from 2020 onward, projected fossil fuel carbon emissions will reach 45.5 Gt in 2040 (dashed black line). In contrast, the UN estimates that fossil fuel carbon emissions must decline by 6 percent annually to contain global warming to less than 1.5°C (see https://news.un.org/en/story/2020/12/1078612). This suggests a substantial bend in the emissions curve (dotted gray line).
Source: 1990–2019 data are from Friedlingstein et al. (2020), available at www .globalcarbonatlas.org/en/CO2-emissions

action, not only at the global and national level but also to mobilize initiatives by corporations, local governments and other "sub-national" entities that are pushing and innovating low-carbon strategies. Both the impacts of climate change, and possibly the burden of the energy transition, are likely to be unevenly felt. Designing policies that are inclusive and address inequality are essential to achieving the low-carbon economy of the future.

Economics for a Fragile Climate

As Nicholas Stern and colleagues emphasized in their landmark review of the economics of climate change, one of the major tasks in motivating climate action is to demonstrate that the costs of reducing greenhouse gas (GHG) emissions today are more than offset by the benefits of reduced climate damages in the future.[8]

One way in which economists assess this trade-off is by estimating the *social cost of carbon*. This is a measure of all future damages associated with a tonne (t) of GHG emissions, translated into today's money.[9] Such an estimate is important for determining how much we should "pay" for carbon today, or equivalently, how much it should cost to cut emissions. If the social cost of carbon tells us that emitting one tonne translates into $50 of damages in today's money, then it signals that we should keep reducing emissions up to the point where abating the last ton of carbon costs us $50. This also tells us what the "price" of greenhouse gas emissions in our economy should be. If we were to tax emissions, the tax should be set at $50 per ton of carbon emitted. Once this tax is imposed, GHG polluters will have an incentive to reduce all emissions up to that cost of abatement, and pay a tax on any emissions that cost more than $50 per ton to mitigate.[10] In addition to reducing emission today, pricing carbon would create incentives for investments and innovations to lower carbon emissions in the future.

In practice, determining the social cost of carbon requires considerable information on the physical, ecological, and economic impacts of climate change. As these impacts will continue to unfold over years and decades, and are therefore uncertain and hard to predict, it has proven difficult to estimate future damages. Determining how best to translate these future estimates into today's money has also been controversial.[11]

However, many regions are already experiencing the effects of drought, flooding, wildfires, sea level rise and other environmental impacts. This means that the damages from climate change are increasingly felt today – and not in the distant future. It also implies that the social cost of carbon is certainly not zero. In fact, as the risks of climate change increase and become more evident, estimates of the social cost of carbon are rising. In 2010 in the United States, it was thought to be $20 per tonne at most. Now, the social cost of carbon is estimated to be at least $50 per tonne of carbon emitted, if not well over $100.[12]

Another way of thinking about the economics of climate change is to determine how much it would cost to reduce GHG emissions to keep within the absolute warming limits of 1.5°C or 2°C.[13] Unfortunately, there is a cost of "doing nothing." The longer we wait to take policy actions to reduce emissions, the costs of staying within these global warming limits will rise. Even with the drop in emissions caused by the pandemic, we are still on a path to increase global temperatures by 3–5°C by the end of the century. To avoid this outcome, and reach the overall goal of net zero emissions in carbon by 2050 for every country, will require a substantial drop in emissions, especially from fossil fuels. The UN estimates that, between 2020 and 2030, global fossil fuel use is expected to increase by 2 percent each year, whereas if the world is to keep within the 1.5°C limit, fossil fuel use must decline by around 6 percent per year.[14] And, of course, if we delay reducing our consumption of fossil fuels today, we will need to make more dramatic and costly cuts in our fossil fuel use in future years.

Although all countries should aim to achieve the zero net emissions goal, there is one set of economies that should take the lead. The largest and most populous economies of the world comprise the Group of 20 (G20). The members of the G20 include Argentina, Australia, Brazil, Canada, China, France, Germany, India, Indonesia, Italy, Japan, Mexico, Russia, Saudi Arabia, South Africa, South Korea, Turkey, the United Kingdom, the United States and the European Union. In the coming years, these major economies will have a large say in how the world economy recovers from the coronavirus pandemic, and whether it can achieve the energy transition away from fossil fuels.

For one, the sheer scale of the G20 economies and their population means that they drive human economic activity and its impacts on climate. They comprise nearly two thirds of the world's population and land area; 82 percent of GDP; and 80 percent of CO_2 emissions.[15] If the global pattern of energy consumption is to change, it is the G20 that will provide many of the innovations for this transformation. These economies dominate the "green race" for competitiveness and innovation in key global industries affecting energy use, such as machinery, motor vehicles, engines and turbines, steam generators, iron and steel, batteries, electricity generation and distribution and domestic appliances.[16] Consequently, the policies that the G20 adopt in the next decade or so will have important implications not just domestically but also for whether or not the world economy transitions away from fossil fuel dependency.

However, such an energy transition cannot occur unless we end the underpricing of fossil fuels and foster timely collective action.

Underpricing of Fossil Fuels

Policy discussions of possible solutions to climate change invariably focus on the urgent need for our economies to switch from fossil fuels to renewables and other low-carbon sources. This will certainly require developing new technologies, such as the deployment of solar, wind and other clean energy sources for electricity generation and industrial use, and promoting low-emission and electric vehicles for transport. In recent years, there have been important technological breakthroughs in a number of these green innovations, and as a result, clean energy technologies are becoming increasingly affordable.

But the reality is that we have yet to see signs of a major energy transition away from dependency on fossil fuels in our economies. The main reason, as pointed out by the economist Dieter Helm, is the *underpricing of fossil fuels*:

> The reason for this relative lack of basic technical progress are many and varied. Yet there is one overwhelmingly powerful factor: cheap fossil fuels have blunted the need for change ... If the world is to address climate change, this continued relative price advantage for fossil fuels will have to be addressed by influencing the price through taxing or permitting carbon.[17]

The underpricing of fossil fuels occurs in two ways. First, the market prices we currently pay for fossil fuels do not include the social cost of carbon – the climate change damages associated with greenhouse gas emissions from burning these fuels. Other costs of burning fossil fuels, most notably air pollution that causes illness and deaths, are also not included in market prices. Second, in many countries, exploration, production and consumption subsidies artificially lower the price of the fossil fuels in energy markets.

The upshot is that current markets for coal, oil and natural gas, as well as for their key products – electricity generation, diesel and gasoline – not only exclude climate change damages and other environmental impacts, but the prices in these markets are frequently subsidized. Such underpricing means that there is not a level playing field between fossil fuel and clean energy investments, as fossil fuels do not face the full social and economic costs of their development and use. This substantially distorts the attractiveness of investing in and using these sources of energy compared to clean energy alternatives.

The cost of renewable energy, especially solar and wind, has declined considerably in recent years, and reached levels of market competitiveness with fossil fuels, most notably in electricity generation.[18] But by underpricing fossil fuels, the cost advantage of renewables for electricity generation and other energy uses disappears. As long as economies persist with subsidizing the exploration, production and consumption of fossil fuels, as well as fail to effectively price carbon and pollution, the transition to a clean energy economy is postponed. As a consequence, global fossil fuel use and its greenhouse gas emissions will continue to rise.

Researchers at the International Monetary Fund, led by David Coady and Ian Parry, estimate that the underpricing of fossil fuels costs the world economy \$5.2 trillion each year, which is 6.5 percent of global gross domestic product (GDP).[19] If instead fossil fuels were properly priced, then annual global CO_2 emissions would have been 28 percent lower; fossil fuel air pollution–related deaths 46 percent lower; and fiscal revenues \$2.8 trillion higher (3.8 percent of global GDP).

These direct gains from curtailing subsidies and taxing carbon emissions from fossil fuels are substantial. But there are other benefits, too, from ending underpricing. It requires adopting the right policies, which might be different for the major G20 economies as opposed to the rest of the world.

Major Economies

The world's twenty largest and most populous countries – the G20 – must lead the way on ending the underpricing of fossil fuels. They account for the vast bulk of the world economy as well as its greenhouse gas emissions – and they are the leading economies driving the global "green race" in environmental innovation and industries.

The persistent underpricing of fossil fuels in the G20 is therefore a major deterrent to an energy transition in the world economy and the achievement of the 2050 net zero emission target for greenhouse gas emissions. This transition is also hindered by market failures that inhibit more widespread clean energy and other green innovations in G20 economies, and the lack of sufficient infrastructure, such as smart electricity grids, vehicle charging networks, mass transit systems and other support for widespread adoption of low-carbon energy for electricity, transport and industry.

To lead the global energy transition toward the net zero emission goal, G20 economies need to adopt a policy strategy that ends the underpricing of fossil fuels and fosters clean energy innovation and infrastructure investments. Such a strategy will involve two steps: first, removing fossil fuel subsidies and employing carbon taxes and other policies to further reduce the social cost of fossil fuel use; second, allocating any revenue that is gained or saved from these pricing policies to public support for green innovation and key infrastructure investments.[20]

As indicated in Figure 4.3, much of the global underpricing of fossil fuels occurs in the G20. Subsidies and the failure to include the carbon, environmental and health damages of fossil fuels cost sixteen G20 economies around $3.2 trillion annually, which is around 70 percent of the global underpricing of fossil fuels (see Figure 4.3). In China, underpricing amounted to over $1.4 trillion each year; in the United

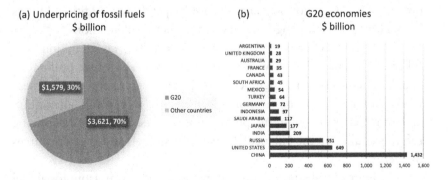

Figure 4.3 The underpricing of fossil fuels
Source: Coady et al. (2019)

States nearly $650 billion; in Russia over $550 billion; in India almost $210 billion; and in Japan over $175 billion (see Figure 4.3).

The underpricing of fossil fuels by G20 economies has certainly contributed to rising carbon emissions globally and to the ongoing threat of global warming and the associated costs. But much of the environmental and economic costs caused by such underpricing are borne locally within countries through air pollution deaths, morbidity and congestion costs, excessive fiscal spending and consumption and supply inefficiencies.

By continuing to underprice fossil fuels, major economies are also setting a bad precedent for other countries to follow. Already, a number of economies are emulating the G20 example. Underpricing is significant in Iran ($111 billion annually); Ukraine ($61 billion); Thailand ($40 billion); Kazakhstan ($29 billion); and United Arab Emirates ($22 billion).[21]

Basing an economy on the underpricing of fossil fuels means that its energy use and GHG emissions go hand in hand. Rather than eliminating the dependence on fossil fuels, their continuing development and use are encouraged. Although coal-fired power plants are the single largest contributor to the growth in global CO_2 emissions, annual support for coal by G20 governments includes $27.6 billion in public finance; $15.4 billion in fiscal support; and $20.9 billion in state–owned enterprise investments. In addition, there are significant annual subsidies for the exploration and exploitation of new reserves of fossil fuels.[22]

Ending the underpricing of fossil fuels in G20 economies would not only remove a major market disincentive to the energy transition in the world economy but also raise substantial revenue for these economies.[23] How G20 governments choose to spend these additional funds is also critical to spurring the transition to net zero emissions.

Pricing reforms that remove exploration, consumption and other public subsidies, as well as taxing carbon and other pollutants, could nonetheless raise significant revenues over many years. These funds could be used to support clean energy R&D and innovation and other critical long-term public investments. Even partial pricing reforms could "tip the balance" between fossil fuels and cleaner sources of energy.

For example, just a 10–30 percent subsidy swap from fossil fuel consumption to investments in energy efficiency and renewable energy electricity generation could substantially improve the transition to a low-carbon economy. Already, some progress along these lines has been made in two emerging market G20 economies, India and Indonesia. A study of twenty-six countries – ten of which are in the G20 – found that the removal of fossil fuel subsidies on its own reduces greenhouse gas emissions by 6 percent on average for each country from 2018 until 2025.[24]

Despite the overwhelming evidence of the harm from underpricing fossil fuels, G20 governments are generally resistant to end subsidies and adopt carbon pricing. One of the obstacles is the widespread perception among some policymakers that doing so is "bad" for the economy. Yet, increasingly studies show that this view is largely unfounded – the gains from ending underpricing, including from taxing or permitting carbon, outweigh any losses.[25]

Nonetheless, utmost care is needed to ensure that any fossil fuel pricing reforms are complemented by other policy measures that mitigate potential short-term negative effects on poorer and more vulnerable households, and displaced workers, who might be adversely affected by the subsidy removal. Countries that remove fossil fuel subsidies and adopt carbon pricing need to pay close attention to the design, sequencing and communication of such a policy to ensure long-term success and avoid the significant political challenges involved.

Any distributional effects can also be offset by additional policy measures. For example, the Canadian province of British Colombia designed its carbon tax to be revenue-neutral, using any funds raised to reduce corporate and personal income taxes and the burden on low-income households.[26] Other possible options are to recycle revenues to lessen payroll taxes, pay annual dividends to households, raise the minimum wage, provide payments or retraining for displaced workers and reduce burdens for vulnerable households affected by the green transition.

One of the more important uses of the revenues saved or raised through ending the underpricing of fossil fuels in G20 economies is to address the lack of sufficient public sector support for green research and development (R&D) leading to innovation. These include R&D subsidies, public investments, protecting intellectual property and other initiatives to spur more widespread clean energy innovation by businesses.

Long-term public support for clean energy R&D is necessary, because without it, the private sector will "underinvest" in such activities.

For example, long-term public support is required to provide an important impetus for rapid economy-wide innovation through "technology spillovers." These occur when the inventions, designs and technologies resulting from the R&D activities by one firm or industry spread relatively cheaply and quickly to other firms and industries. These include cross-firm externalities, industry-wide learning, skill development or agglomeration effects. However, spillovers also undermine the incentives for a private firm or industry to invest in R&D activities. A private investor bears the full costs of financing R&D and may improve its own technologies and products as a result, but the investor receives little or no returns from the subsequent spread of these innovations throughout the economy. The consequence is that private firms and industries routinely underinvest in R&D, and the result is less economy-wide innovation overall.

As pointed out by the economist Dani Rodrik, such market disincentives for investing in innovation "exist in general for all kinds of new technologies, whether they are of the green or dirty kind. However, their novelty, their highly experimental nature, and the substantial risks involved for pioneer entrepreneurs suggest green technologies may be particularly prone to these failures."[27] Such market disincentives have proven to be a significant deterrent to clean energy innovation and development in both G20 and other economies. Even among the major economies involved in the "green race" to become competitive leaders globally, economy-wide green innovation falls well short of the level necessary to generate a transition from fossil fuel dependency.[28]

The underinvestment in clean energy and other green innovations in G20 economies is occurring just at a time when new technology developments are needed to drive the energy transition of the world economy. Figure 4.4 indicates how environmental innovations per capita have been declining in recent years in the G20 and six major economies, with the possible exception of South Korea. This decline is important, as just four of these economies account for nearly two thirds of the green technologies worldwide – the United States (24 percent), Japan (19 percent), Germany (11 percent) and South Korea (11 percent).[29]

Two economies that have actively pursued policies to support green innovation through expanded government support have been China and South Korea. From 2010 to 2016, China doubled its share of environmentally related inventions worldwide, and South Korea increased its share of government R&D devoted to environmental technologies by 28 percent. As a result, over this period South Korea's share of global green innovation has increased from 8.7 percent to

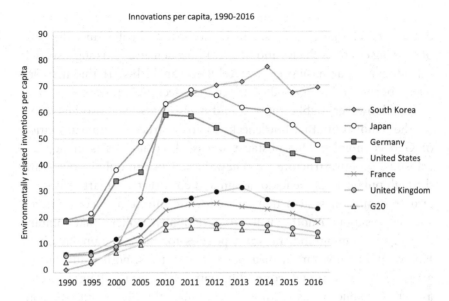

Figure 4.4 Environmental innovations per capita, 1990–2016
Source: OECD "Green Growth Indicators," OECD Environment Statistics https://doi.org/10.1787/data-00665-en

11.0 percent, and it is now producing nearly seventy environmentally related inventions per person. Among the public programs that support green R&D in Korea are tax credits and allowances, tax reductions for the wages of R&D workers and accelerated depreciation of capital used for R&D. Together, these public programs amount to 0.3 percent of GDP, which is one of the highest levels of support among major economies.[30]

More public investment to support clean energy and other environmental innovations will require additional funding by all G20 governments. But there is good news, too, on the costs of promoting clean energy and other environmentally related technologies. The high costs today of reducing carbon emissions through some low-carbon technologies could fall quickly if the right policies are adopted.[31]

Expenditures targeted at clean energy R&D will lead to lower costs and wider adoption, as the technology becomes more familiar, innovation spreads and production scales up. One example is the rapid fall in solar panel costs that has occurred worldwide. There is also a network, or "chicken and egg," effect where increasing demand for a clean-energy technology or product fosters related innovations that lower cost. For example, purchases of electric vehicles will stimulate demand for charging stations, which once installed will reduce the costs of running electric vehicles and further boost demand. This suggests that subsidies for purchasing electric vehicles can kick-start this network effect, but should be phased out once the effect takes hold.

However, public support and investments may also be critical for the removal of other bottlenecks to green structural transformation of G20 economies. One obstacle across all economies is inadequate transmission infrastructure for renewables. This can only be overcome through public investments to design and construct a "smart" electrical grid transmission system that can integrate diffuse and conventional sources of supply. Another is urban development policies that combine municipal planning and transport policies for more sustainable cities. Finally, public investment in mass transit systems, both within urban areas and major routes connecting cities has been a long-neglected aspect of public infrastructure development throughout many economies. These and other areas of possible long-term investments for a green recovery are important areas for future research.

To summarize, the lack of public sector support for private green R&D and insufficient public investments to overcome other obstacles to low-carbon development in G20 economies are serious impediments that need to be addressed. However, in a world recovering from the pandemic, it may be difficult to find the additional funds for these public investments. Estimates suggest that the governments of major economies may have spent up to $30 trillion by 2023 just to deal with the health and economic crises caused by the pandemic.[32] This is where the additional revenues and funds saved through the combination of fossil fuel subsidy removal and carbon and other environmental taxes could be useful.

These pricing reforms will correct market disincentives that deter decarbonization, but they can also provide much-need financing of public support for clean energy innovations and key infrastructure investments in G20 economies. This combination of policies in the G20 could have a powerful impact on whether or not the world economy achieves zero net greenhouse gas emissions by 2050. As we shall see in other chapters, the three-pronged policy approach of removing existing distortionary subsidies, establishing taxes to correct externalities and then using the revenue that is freed-up or generated to invest in protecting or regenerating environmental assets, can be applied to other economic sectors and environmental issues.

Low- and Middle-Income Economies

As major economies take the lead on ending the underpricing of fossil fuels, other economies should follow. However, it is important to recognize that low- and middle-income countries may face unique challenges, especially in the aftermath of the COVID-19 pandemic.

COVID-19 has been especially difficult for developing economies. The additional financial burdens on governments have led to rising debt, and for the first time in years, poverty in these countries is likely to rise. It is estimated that the pandemic will have caused an additional 150 million people (1.4% of the world's population) to fall into extreme poverty.[33]

Even before the pandemic, we were still a long way from achieving key sustainability and development objectives for the most vulnerable people in low- and middle-income countries. In 2019, an estimated 736 million people lived in extreme poverty; 821 million were undernourished; 785 million people lacked basic drinking water services; and 673 million were without sanitation. About 3 billion people did not have clean cooking fuels and technology, and of the 840 million people without electricity, 87 percent lived in rural areas.[34]

This suggests that ending the underpricing of fossil fuels in low- and middle-income countries must occur through policies that are compatible with achieving immediate development objectives, such as ending poverty and especially the widespread "energy poverty" in rural areas.

Like the G20 economies, low- and middle-income countries could implement a "subsidy swap" for fossil fuels, whereby the savings from subsidy reform for coal, oil and natural gas consumption are allocated to fund clean energy investments. In 2018, fossil fuel consumption subsidies reached $427 billion annually, of which nearly $360 billion were in developing countries.[35] As discussed previously, a 10–30 percent subsidy swap from fossil fuel consumption to investments in energy efficiency and renewable energy electricity generation could "tip the balance" between fossil fuels and cleaner sources of energy. Partial reforms in India, Indonesia, Morocco and Zambia have already shown some progress. IISD (2019b) show that removal of fossil fuel subsidies on its own in twenty-six countries – twenty-two of which are low and middle income – would reduce greenhouse gas emissions by 6 percent on average for each country.[36]

However, there is an additional important use of the savings from subsidy removal in low- and middle-income countries. In poorer economies, a fossil fuel subsidy swap should also be used to facilitate greater dissemination and adoption of renewable energy and improved energy efficiency technologies in rural areas. It could also be used to support the adoption of clean cooking and heating technologies. This is critical for reducing energy poverty across developing countries. Morocco, Kenya and South Africa illustrate how different public policy approaches can facilitate the adoption and deployment of renewable energy and improved energy efficiency technologies in rural areas.[37]

A fossil fuel subsidy swap to support energy efficiency and renewable energy in rural areas would also have important equity gains. In low- and middle-income economies, it is mainly wealthier, urban households that benefit from fossil fuel consumptions subsidies, whereas it is rural households that increasingly comprise the extreme poor. Across twenty developing countries, the poorest fifth of the population received on average just 7 percent of the overall benefit of fossil fuel subsidies, whereas the richest fifth gained almost 43 percent.[38]

Low- and middle-income countries also need assistance in developing carbon pricing schemes. A key international program is the World Bank's Partnership for Market Readiness (PMR), which since 2011 has supported emerging economies and developing countries design and deploy carbon pricing to facilitate the reduction of emissions. The PMR has currently provided funding and technical assistance to twenty-three countries, accounting for 46 percent of the global GHG emissions. In early 2021, the PMR will be succeeded by the Partnership Marketing Implementation (PMI) scheme. The PMI aims to support additional low- and middle-income countries in the development and implementation of carbon pricing over the ten next years but needs an initial capitalization of $250 million to do so.[39]

The international community should support and expand the PMI to ensure not only its initial capitalization but also that the scheme can provide assistance to many more low- and middle-income countries to adopt carbon pricing. In addition, the PMI should also help countries set up mechanisms and investments for key development priorities, whether it is to alleviate poverty, expand renewables and energy efficiency or to provide direct payments to businesses and households. As we shall discuss further in Chapter 6, one possible use of some revenues is to invest in *natural climate solutions* aimed at mitigating carbon emissions and conserving, restoring and improving land management to protect biodiversity and ecosystem services.

Wider adoption of carbon pricing by low- and middle-income countries can also be tied to debt relief. Because of the global economic slowdown, many of these countries have incurred higher debt and borrowing during the COVID-19 pandemic. The World Bank, the International Monetary Fund and the G20 established a Debt Service Suspension Initiative (DSSI), which offered temporary suspension of debt-service payment until mid-2021 for the world's poorest counties. The DSSI has provided some financial relief and enabled low-income countries to concentrate their resources on social, health and economic spending in response to the pandemic.[40]

However, this is only a temporary suspension, rather than a comprehensive debt relief program, for the world's poorest countries. As pointed out by Ulrich Volz and colleagues, there is potentially a "vicious cycle" between climate vulnerability, debt and financial risk:

> There is a danger that vulnerable developing countries will enter a vicious circle in which greater climate vulnerability raises the cost of debt and diminishes the fiscal space for investment in climate resilience. As financial markets increasingly price climate risks, and global warming accelerates, the risk premia of these countries, which are already high, are likely to increase further. The impact of Covid-19 on public finances risks reinforcing this vicious circle.[41]

To break this vicious circle, Volz and colleagues propose a comprehensive private and public debt relief program, conditional on indebted countries undertaking additional actions or investments in climate adaptation and mitigation. This could potentially be a win-win strategy for addressing the climate and debt crises, provided that the additional climate actions should include a commitment by participating low- and middle-income countries to ending the underpricing of fossil fuels in their economies. If financial markets are increasingly pricing climate risks, then by removing subsidies and pricing carbon, countries are signaling to these markets that their economic decisions and investments are also incorporating these risks. By undertaking subsidy reforms and carbon pricing in exchange for debt relief, these countries will be reestablishing their credit worthiness with financial investors and markets.

Finally, low- and middle-income countries also need other forms of assistance to help their economies manage a transition to a low-carbon economy as well as the impacts of climate change that are occurring already. At the very minimum, richer countries must keep their promises made in the Paris Agreement to provide $100 billion dollars a year for mitigation, adaptation and resilience in developing countries.

Collective Action

One of the key mechanisms for reducing global climate risks is collective action. Reducing these risks will benefit the whole world, but unless enough countries take action, we may not achieve the goal of containing these risks by limiting global warming to less than 1.5°C.

Even though we have known about the consequences of global warming for decades, countries have been slow to mobilize collective action to address this problem.

Perhaps the most important breakthrough in recent years was the 2015 Paris Climate Change Accord. Countries that are signatories to this agreement initially committed to limit global temperature rise to 2°C, and now to 1.5°C. This target requires substantial reductions in greenhouse gas (GHG) emissions by 2050. The accord did not require signatories to agree on how to implement these objectives. Instead, it allowed individual countries to set their own national targets, abatement policies and timelines for emission reductions, all subject to five-year review.

Although the Paris Accord is a significant milestone in obtaining a global agreement to slow climate change, unless countries step up their commitments to reduce GHG emissions, it is unlikely that the current national pledges under the agreement will achieve the 1.5°C goal, much less the more ambitious target recommended by the scientific community. To meet this target, countries need to triple their current emission reduction efforts, and increase their efforts fivefold.[42]

While nations are lagging behind in achieving GHG reductions, carbon mitigation by subnational jurisdictions within countries, such as states, provinces, cities and local governments, appears to be on the rise globally. Subnational agencies and nonstate actors may play an important role in initiating critical change required to meet the long-term goals of the Paris Agreement. Many subnational jurisdictions in Brazil, China, India, Indonesia, Japan, Mexico, Russia, South Africa, the United States and the European Union have announced voluntary pledges and low-carbon strategies designed to advance the goals of the Paris Agreement.[43] Of the sixty-four carbon pricing initiatives currently implemented or scheduled for implementation across the globe, which cover 12 billion tonnes of carbon (i.e. 22 percent of global GHG emissions), thirty-five are by subnational jurisdictions.[44]

Across the globe, 823 cities and 101 regions have adopted net-zero carbon targets. These local governments represent more than 846 million people, or 11 percent of the world population, and emit more than 6.5 billion tonnes of GHGs annually, which is more than US emissions in 2018. But as with national governments, implementation still lags behind announced targets. Only 227 cities or regions (24 percent) have incorporated their net-zero targets into formal policies and legislations, and 339 cities or regions (43 percent) have released action plans to achieve their stated targets.[45]

As more local governments adopt net zero carbon targets, they are increasingly cooperating to form regional and international agreements to coordinate emission mitigation strategies and boost abatement, which can provide important spillover effects and prevent leakage. There needs to be more support for and coordination of such agreements by the international community as well as national governments. This is especially important if "bottom-up" initiatives involve scaling up carbon markets and pricing at the local level to have more of an impact nationally or even globally.[46]

But it is also important to view subnational agreements as complements to, rather than replacements for, national pledges and global collective action to mitigate climate change. To date, there has been a sizeable gap between policy commitments and actual carbon abatement implementation at both the national and subnational levels. It is imperative that the focus of both subnational and national approaches to reducing GHG emissions focus on closing this gap. If the emission reductions pledged under the Paris Climate Change Agreement were fully implemented, the gap between current policies and the Paris goals would be reduced by as much as a third.[47] Support for subnational approaches, renewed commitments by national governments and global agreements must all work toward ensuring the goal of limiting global warming to 1.5°C.

Collective action in mitigating climate change should also involve the private sector. Across the globe, more and more businesses are also embracing the net zero carbon target. Over 1,500 companies have pledged to meet this goal. They have a combined annual revenue of $11.4 trillion, which is more than half of the US yearly GDP, and account for 3.5 billion tonnes of GHG emissions, which is equivalent to the annual releases of India.[48]

There are several reasons why an increasing number of businesses are setting net zero targets and acting on it (see Chapter 9 for further discussion). Firms increasingly find that improved climate risk management reduces their overall cost of capital and improves their attractiveness to potential investors. In turn, more investors and financial institutions require assurance that firms are managing climate risks; mitigating the damages that arise from global warming; and incorporating these assessments into their long-term business strategies and investment decisions. As a result, firms, investors and financial institutions are increasingly seeking formal and verifiable confirmation that businesses are managing climate risks and curtailing emissions. Greater transparency on firms' climate actions also signals to investors and banks that they can provide long-term financing knowing that these actions are reducing the vulnerability of businesses to climate risks.

An important tool that is increasingly used to convey whether or not new investments are taking on climate risks is *internal carbon pricing*. It places a monetary value on greenhouse gas emissions, which firms can then factor into investment decisions and management operations. Internal carbon pricing gives businesses an incentive to shift investments to low-carbon alternatives, and helps them achieve their greenhouse gas targets, such as the net zero carbon goal. This can also be attractive to address shareholder concerns and to demonstrate corporate leadership in climate action.

Financial institutions are also interested in using internal carbon pricing to evaluate the relative climate risks of various investments and loans. For investors, such pricing can assist screening and evaluation of equities and other assets for their relative climate risks and opportunities. For banks, internal carbon pricing can highlight potential loans or credit lines with high risks or opportunities for emission mitigation, which can factor into assessing the overall credit worthiness of borrowers and in establishing lending criteria. As more financial institutions adopt internal carbon pricing, it provides further incentive for businesses to follow suit. If a company realizes that banks and investors are tracking and monitoring its assets and credit worthiness based on climate risks, then it will incorporate these risks and pricing in business investments, supply chains and operations.

Although financial institutions recognize the potential of using internal carbon pricing to measure climate risks and opportunities in their investments and lending, there are currently no clear guidelines or methodology across global institutions for setting an internal carbon price so as to evaluate various private sector investments.[49] Without such guidance, adopting an internal price for carbon may do little to change a firm's long-term investment decisions or commitment to take climate damage into account. As long as guidelines are lacking and the methodology remains unclear, it is also difficult for banks and investors worldwide to evaluate carbon risks and opportunities and incorporate them into financial decision-making.

An urgent priority for the global financial sector is to establish criteria and methods for incorporating climate risks and opportunities in their lending and investment decisions. Such guidelines should specify how to apply internal carbon pricing to investment and lending processes; how to determine the appropriate price for carbon to use; and to help banks and investors determine how much of their portfolio should be subject to pricing. There also needs to be an international accrediting body to certify best practices globally and to assist in the monitoring of business performance in terms of internalizing climate risks and pricing.

In sum, a common misperception is that collective action to combat climate change is solely the prerogative of national governments. There is clearly much more work that countries need to do to meet the net zero GHG emissions goal. But the uptake of collective action by local governments and regions and by businesses and financial institutions around the world is also critical to success in curbing global warming. Mitigating the worst effects of climate change will take a high level of coordination within and across all these different actors. Post-Paris negotiations and actions must focus on all these possible efforts to control global warming, and must design effective institutions and means to build on and coordinate them.

Inclusive Climate Action

Climate action at all levels – local, regional, national and global – must also be inclusive. Transitioning to a low-carbon economy will create winners and losers in every economy.

Ideally, such a transition that revitalizes innovation and investment will put the world economy on a more inclusive development path, including generating net gains in employment, improving income and wealth distribution, and targeting gains toward vulnerable populations and poor countries. Ensuring that any low-carbon development path is also inclusive is even more of a priority in the coming decades, given the skyrocketing unemployment and likely disproportionate impacts on low-income households and countries caused by the pandemic.

As this chapter has emphasized, for low- and middle-income countries, any such strategy must be compatible with achieving immediate development objectives, such as ending poverty and especially the widespread energy poverty in rural areas. Policies such as a "subsidy swap" from support of fossil fuels to improving rural renewable energy use and efficiency meet this objective. In addition, wider adoption of carbon pricing and other low-carbon policies by poorer countries can also be tied to debt relief.

But it is less clear what an overall transition to a low-carbon economy might entail for employment, the distribution of wealth and income and poverty.

There is often a presumption that, although there will be some job losses, the net gain in employment is likely to be positive. For example, one estimate suggests that a low-carbon transition will cause low-carbon employment to rise by 65 million people by 2030, more than offsetting employment losses in declining sectors, leading to a net gain of 37 million jobs.[50] Another study estimates that, limiting climate change to 2°C, would create approximately 24 million jobs at the loss of approximately 6 million jobs, producing a net increase in employment of 18 million by 2030.[51]

Some climate-friendly recovery plans for the coronavirus pandemic are also optimistic that there will be net job gains. The International Energy Agency (IEA) proposes one such three–year investment and pricing strategy. It projects that the pandemic could cost three million jobs globally, and a low-carbon recovery could result in another 3 million lost in fossil fuel–related sectors, such as vehicles, construction and industry. However, the recovery could save or create roughly 9 million jobs, mainly through energy efficiency, improving the electricity grids and renewables. In addition, if investments in developing countries are targeted at reducing energy poverty, around 420 million people would obtain clean-cooking technologies and nearly 270 million would gain access to electricity.[52]

But the OECD is more cautious about climate friendly jobs: "Robust empirical evidence of the overall employment effects of ambitious green policies is still lacking. Major transformations of the economy towards green growth are very scarce, and this complicates econometric analysis."[53]

Too often, the comparison is made between the employment and distribution implications of a green transformation compared to the current economy today. Instead, the comparison should be with the employment, distribution and poverty implications of a future economic scenario of global warming of greater than 2°C. There are, after all, the two future scenarios that the world is facing.

In sum, assessing the distributional impacts of climate action is extremely important. Unfortunately, we currently know little about the possible income and wealth implications of a low-carbon transition compared to a future economic scenario with significant global warming. Structural transformation and technological change toward less fossil fuel use and more clean energy are bound to have significant income and wealth impacts – but so will a world with extreme climate events, sea level rise and disruptions to agriculture, forestry and other economic sectors. As some studies have indicated, there may be a net employment gain overall from a low-carbon transition, but there are some important sectors and workers in the economy that may lose out. All of these effects are likely to have distributional consequences, and we must be prepared to address them as the low-carbon transition takes hold.

To some extent, the distribution effects can be offset by additional policy measures. Earlier it was noted that a range of policies could be considered in major economies, such as reducing payroll taxes, paying annual dividends to households, raising the minimum wage and providing payments or retraining for displaced workers. In low- and middle-income countries, additional investments could be targeted to reduce poverty and inequality, including increasing rural renewable energy use and energy efficiency; expansion of health and education services; improvements in sanitation and drinking water supply; protection of ecosystem services that support rural livelihoods; and targeting agricultural research and extension to poor smallholders on less favorable agricultural land.

However, implementing such policies and investment during a low-carbon transition will require substantial additional funding. This is again where recycling the revenues from removal of fossil fuel subsidies and imposing taxes on carbon and other environmental damages can help. If sufficiently large, the revenues gained from ending the underpricing of fossil fuels could fund both an ambitious strategy of public investments for the low-carbon transition as well as a range of policies and programs to offset the distributional consequences of the transition.

As Table 4.1 indicates, there is plenty of scope to expand carbon pricing worldwide. Currently, twenty-five economies have

Table 4.1. National carbon pricing initiatives, 2020

	Carbon Price (US$/ tCO$_2$e)	Year Implemented	GHG Emissions Covered (MtCO$_2$e)	Share of Country's GHG Emissions Covered	Annual Revenues (US$ mn)
Carbon Taxes					
Argentina	5.94	2018	88.1	20%	179
Canada	22.63	2019	155.3	19%	1,371
Chile	5.00	2017	57.6	39%	166
Colombia	4.45	2017	45.7	24%	111
Denmark	27.70	1992	25.3	40%	520
Estonia	2.33	2000	0.9	3%	3
Finland	72.24	1990	40.7	36%	1,420
France	6.98	2014	171.7	35%	8,968
Iceland	30.01	2010	1.4	29%	41
Ireland	30.30	2010	32.4	49%	481
Japan	2.76	2012	909.1	68%	2,438
Latvia	10.49	2004	2.6	15%	9
Liechtenstein	105.69	2008	0.1	26%	4
Mexico	2.79	2014	380.7	46%	210
Norway	57.14	1991	46.5	62%	1,374
Poland	0.08	1990	16.1	4%	1
Portugal	27.52	2015	23.3	29%	281
Singapore	3.66	2019	44.8	80%	N/A
Slovenia	20.16	1996	5.0	24%	81
Spain	16.85	2014	9.2	3%	120
South Africa	7.38	2019	512.2	80%	N/A
Sweden	133.26	1991	44.2	40%	2,314
Switzerland	104.65	2008	18.2	33%	1,235

Table 4.1. cont'd

	Carbon Price (US$/tCO₂e)	Year Implemented	GHG Emissions Covered (MtCO₂e)	Share of Country's GHG Emissions Covered	Annual Revenues (US$ mn)
United Kingdom	23.23	2013	135.8	23%	1,098
Ukraine	0.35	2011	221.2	71%	48
Emission Trading Schemes (ETS)					
Australia	11.09	2016	344.2	50%	0
Canada	N/A	2019	70.9	9%	0
European Union	30.14	2005	2,249.1	45%	16,011
Kazakhstan	1.16	2013	182.0	50%	0
New Zealand	22.45	2008	45.3	51%	251
South Korea	18.80	2015	489.0	70%	179
Switzerland	19.79	2008	6.0	11%	9

Notes: tCO₂e = tonnes of carbon dioxide equivalent. MtCO₂e = megatonnes of carbon dioxide equivalent. European Union ETS also includes Norway, Lichtenstein and Iceland
Source: World Bank, Carbon Pricing Dashboard https://carbonpricingdashboard.worldbank.org/map_data. Data last updated November 1, 2020.

adopted carbon taxes, and seven have emission trading schemes (ETS). But for most of these schemes, the price placed on carbon is too low. The World Bank recommends that carbon pricing should be at a minimum \$40–\$80 per tonne of carbon dioxide-equivalent (tCO₂e) for a country to attain the Paris Agreement temperature target.[54] Only five countries – Finland, Liechtenstein, Norway, Sweden and Switzerland – impose carbon taxes within this range or higher. For most countries, the share of a country's GHG emissions covered is low, well below 50 percent in most cases. A few countries have ETS or tax schemes that account for 70 percent or more of their emissions, but the carbon price in these economies is set very low.

Other economies should join those depicted in Table 4.1 and set up carbon pricing. In addition, the economies that already have such schemes have plenty of scope to raise their prices, increase the amount of GHG emissions subject to carbon pricing or do both. Consequently, there is considerable scope for all economies to employ or expand carbon pricing to assist them achieving their commitments to the Paris Agreement and raise significant revenues to fund the low-carbon transition as well as make it more inclusive.

The extra revenues gained from carbon pricing could allow many economies to experiment with innovative policies to reduce inequality.

One such policy initiative that has been quietly gaining momentum during the COVID-19 pandemic is the universal basic income (UBI). Such a scheme involves a guaranteed income for adults, usually in the form of a monthly cash payment of $500–$1,000. It is considered "basic," because a UBI provides money to pay rents or mortgages; to buy groceries, clothing and other necessities; and to cover medical or childcare expenses. Above all, a guaranteed monthly income would provide economic security for the poor and unemployed, facilitate part-time work, ensure money for education or job training and increase saving.[55]

As the economic and health crises of the pandemic have surged around the world, so have calls to adopt UBI schemes or to expand existing pilot and local programs.[56] COVID-19 has caused massive unemployment and economic hardship, and chronic poverty has worsened significantly. It has also constrained efforts to improve human capital accumulation through educational attainment, health and training, and undermined progress toward establishing a more highly skilled workforce. It could take years, if not decades, to address the consequences for many households and individuals.

Advocates of UBI argue that it is a long-term replacement for short-term fiscal stimulus and emergency relief for post-COVID economies that have already poured massive amounts into unemployment insurance and other social safety nets during the pandemic. It could also mitigate any adverse income and employment impacts on households that were caused by a low-carbon transition. As funding UBI is expensive, recycling funds from reducing fossil fuel subsidies and pricing carbon would be one way to fund such schemes on a permanent and secure basis. Canada and Switzerland are already experimenting with such a carbon price-and-dividend scheme, which rebates revenue back to households. If the dividend is distributed on an equal per capita basis, then lower income households and the unemployed would not only receive a guaranteed payment but also benefit most from the increase in their monthly income.[57]

There may also be a need for innovative policies targeted at displaced workers, especially from the fossil fuel industry. One approach would be to pay workers to plug abandoned and orphaned oil and gas wells, which would also reduce GHG emissions. During the pandemic, Canada carried out a $1.7 billion scheme to do this as part of its stimulus response. In the United States, there are 2.1 million abandoned wells emitting around 280,000 tonnes of methane each year. A national program to plug these wells could employ 120,000 fossil fuel workers, who might otherwise be laid off during a low-carbon transition.[58]

Conclusion

With climate change we have a clear objective. We must limit global warming to 1.5°C, and to do that, we need to achieve net zero carbon emissions by 2050.

It is imperative that all actors in the global economy embrace this goal – rich and poor countries, businesses, consumers and governments and local as well as national jurisdictions.

There are signs of progress. The 2015 Paris Climate Change Agreement established a benchmark for global climate action by countries. More and more nations, firms and local governments are embracing climate action, and there is a surge in the use of carbon pricing to curb emissions.

Despite this global uptake, the transition to a low-carbon economy remains a challenge. Underpricing of fossil fuels is still widespread, and carbon prices are too low to generate the necessary incentives and innovation for such a transition. Banks and investors will discount climate risks, businesses will be slow to decarbonize their operations and supply chains and consumers will resist switching to more low-carbon goods and services.

Ending the underpricing of fossil fuels is the key to achieving the zero net carbon emissions goal. The G20 and other major economies must take the lead, by adopting a two-part strategy: first, removing fossil fuel subsidies and employing carbon taxes and other policies to further reduce the social cost of fossil fuel use; second, allocating any resulting revenue to public support for green innovation and key infrastructure investments. The revenues from taxing or permitting carbon could also be directed to lessen payroll taxes, pay annual dividends to households, raise the minimum wage and provide payments or retraining for displaced workers.

The international community should also provide assistance to low- and middle-income countries to help them end the underpricing of fossil fuels in their economies. Wider adoption of carbon pricing and other low-carbon policies by poorer countries can also be tied to debt relief. Above all, ending the underpricing of fossil fuels in low- and middle-income countries must occur through policies that are compatible with achieving immediate development objectives, such as ending poverty and especially the widespread "energy poverty" in rural areas. The revenues generated or saved could generate investments that increase rural renewable energy use and energy efficiency; expand health and education services; improve sanitation and drinking water supply; protect ecosystem services that support rural livelihoods; and target agricultural research and extension to poor smallholders on less-favorable agricultural land.

Such a strategy is essential to achieve a transition to a low-carbon economy that is sustainable and inclusive.

Implementing such a strategy clearly requires collective action to combat the pressing global problem of climate change. International efforts so far are failing to deliver on slowing greenhouse gas emissions to keep the planet from warming dangerously. Yet considerable progress is occurring by some countries, companies, states or provinces, and even cities.

Consequently, our policies need to expand beyond actions by national governments and also build on a "bottom-up" strategy that supports and expands initiatives by corporations, local governments and other "subnational" entities that are pushing and innovating low-carbon strategies. Mitigating the worst effects of climate change will take a high level of coordination within and across all these different actors – or to quote Jessica Green and colleagues, create "a balance of bottom-up and top-down in linking climate policies."[59]

In the coming years, delayed efforts to combat climate change may result in a "forceful, abrupt, and disorderly" response by governments.[60] This will incur high costs, an unequal sharing of the burden of transition and the possible failure to safeguard humanity within an increasingly inhospitable planet. The alternative is developing the international architecture, institutions and incentives to spur collective action that would limit global warming and ensure the well-being of individuals across the planet now and in years to come.

Notes

1 These projections and targets are from IPCC (2018). Although the difference between a 1.5°C and 2°C target may seem small, it can have profound consequences for the planet and humankind. As explained by Priyardarshi Shukla, cochair of IPCC Working Group III, "Limiting global warming to 1.5°C compared with 2°C would reduce challenging impacts on ecosystems, human health and well-being, making it easier to achieve the United Nations Sustainable Development Goals." www.ipcc.ch/2018/10/08/summary-for-policymakers-of-ipcc-special-report-on-global-warming-of-1-5c-approved-by-governments/#:~:text=%E2%80%9CLimiting%20global%20warming%20to%201.5,of%20IPCC%20Working%20Group%20III.

2 https://eciu.net/netzerotracker, accessed on March 1, 2021. The eleven countries are Sweden, the United Kingdom, France, Denmark, New Zealand, Hungary, Canada, South Korea, Spain, Chile and Fiji.

3 Tollefson (2021).

4 Andrijevic et al. (2020); Le Quéré et al. (2020); and Tollefson (2021).

5 Jackson et al. (2019) and Peters et al. (2020).

6 UNEP (2019) suggests that emissions from all sources must decline by 7.6 percent from 2020 onward, and the UN indicates the world will need to decrease fossil fuel production by roughly 6 percent per year between 2020 and 2030 to keep global warming under 1.5°C. See "The Race to Zero Emissions and Why the World Depends on It." *UN News* 2 December 2020. https://news.un.org/en/story/2020/12/1078612.

7 For example, IPCC (2020) estimates that agriculture, forestry and other land use may have contributed as much as 23 percent of human-caused emissions between 2007 and 2016. The most important reason for this increase may be land conversion. Friedlingstein et al. (2020) estimate that between 2010 and 2019, 86 percent of total carbon emissions were from fossil fuel CO_2 emissions and 14 percent were from land use change.

8 Stern et al. (2006).

9 By "today's money," I mean the standard economic approach of translating the costs of future damages into the equivalent amount of dollars today. This is known as the *present value* of future dollars, which in this case is obtained by discounting the cost of future damages from climate change.

10 The alternative market-based mechanism used to impose a price on carbon is the "cap and trade" system. This approach imposes an overall limit on the amount of greenhouse gas emissions that are allowed by all polluters, divides this quota up among the polluters, but then allows them to buy and sell permits to establish a market and price for them. If the social cost of carbon is $50 per tCO_2e, then the overall cap should be set and the trades regulated so that the price of emission permits equals this cost.

11 For example, the report by Stern et al. (2006) launched an important debate among economists as to how future damages from climate change should be translated into

today's money, and how this calculation should handle uncertainty over these damages. See Arrow et al. (2013); Nordhaus (2007); and Weitzman (2007). There have been calls (e.g. Revesz et al. 2014) for future IPCC assessments to improve economic models of climate change so as to refine estimates of the social cost of carbon as a guide for policy. For excellent overviews of the economics of climate change, see Helm (2015) and Nordhaus (2015).

12 Gernot Wagner. "It's Too Late for Big Oil's Pivot to a Carbon Tax." *Bloomberg Green* March 4, 2011. https://gwagner.com/risky-climate-api.

13 As shown by Barbier and Burgess (2017), one method is the *user cost approach* to assess the economic costs of different policy options for "using up" the world's remaining "carbon budget." This budget is the cumulative amount of anthropogenic CO_2 emissions limiting global warming below 1.5° or 2°C. The user cost approach treats the global carbon budget as a nonrenewable asset that is depleted by annual greenhouse gas (GHG) emissions. For each emission scenario, it is then possible to estimate the remaining lifetime of the carbon budget and the economic losses associated with this depletion. Different policy options to abate emissions can then be evaluated in terms of how much it reduces these losses by extending the lifetime of the remaining carbon budget.

14 "The Race to Zero Emissions and Why the World Depends on It." *UN News* 2 December 2020. https://news.un.org/en/story/2020/12/1078612.

15 From the World Bank's World Development Indicators https://databank.worldbank.org/source/world-development-indicators.

16 Fankhauser et al. (2013).

17 Helm (2015), p. 218.

18 See, for example, *Lazard's Levelized Cost of Energy Analysis – Version 13.0.* November 7, 2019. ww.lazard.com/perspective/lcoe2019.

19 Coady et al. (2019). Their method of estimating the underpricing of fossil fuels is based on calculating differences between actual consumer fuel prices and how much consumers would pay if prices fully reflected supply costs plus the taxes needed to address environment damages, such as the costs of climate change, local pollution, traffic congestion, accidents and road damage and revenue requirements.

20 For example, Bertram et al. (2015) find that a combination of three polices – (1) carbon pricing; (2) support for low-carbon energy technologies and (3) a moratorium on new coal-fired power plants – is best at reducing efficiency losses to economies and lowers distributional impacts in achieving global warming targets." Thus, the authors maintain that this combination of policies may be the most efficient and inclusive way of attaining climate action goals. Other policies may also help. In their review of climate change mitigation policies implemented in five major economies, China, the European Union, India, Japan and the United States, Fekete et al. (2021) identify a number of consistently successful policies for renewable energy, fuel efficiency, electrification of passenger vehicles and forestry.

21 Fekete et al. (2021).

22 Bast et al. (2014) and Gençsü et al. (2019).

23 Based on the estimates by Coady et al. (2019) of the revenues generated globally from ending this underpricing, the G20 could raise $1.94 trillion annually, or around 3.7 percent of their aggregate real GDP (Barbier 2020a).

24 IISD (2019a) and (2019b). The ten G20 economies are Brazil, China, Germany, India, Indonesia, Mexico, Russia, Saudi Arabia, South Africa and the United States.

25 For example, analysis of the macroeconomic implications of imposing carbon taxes in major economies find no adverse, and possibly even positive, impacts on GDP and overall employment (Metcalf 2019; Metcalf and Stock 2020).

26 Metcalf (2019) and Yamazaki (2017).

27 Rodrik (2014), p. 470.

28 See, for example, Barbier 2016a; Fankhauser et al. 2013; Harrison et al. 2017; and Rodrik 2014.

29 Based on the indicator "development of environmentally related technologies, % of inventions worldwide, 2016" from OECD. Green Growth Indicators. OECD Environment Statistics. https://doi.org/10.1787/data-00665-en.

30 These data are from OECD. Green Growth Indicators. OECD Environment Statistics. https://doi.org/10.1787/data-00665-en. For more discussion of the Korean government's strategy, see Barbier (2020a).

31 Gillingham and Stock (2018).

32 Assi et al. (2020).

33 From UN (2020) and World Bank (2020). For an overview of the many sustainability and development challenges faced by low- and middle-income countries due to the pandemic, see Barbier and Burgess (2020).

34 UN (2019).

35 From www.iea.org/topics/energy-subsidies. Accessed on May 8, 2020.

36 IISD (2019a) and (2019b).

37 For more discussion of the different policy approaches adopted in these countries, see Barbier (2020b) and Pahle et al. (2016).

38 Arze del Granado et al. (2012).

39 See www.worldbank.org/en/topic/climatechange/brief/partnership-for-market-implementation.

40 World Bank (2021).

41 Volz (2020), p. 21.

42 UNEP (2019).

43 Hsu et al. (2018).

44 From https://carbonpricingdashboard.worldbank.org. Accessed on March 1, 2021.

45 See Data-Driven EnviroLab and NewClimate Institute (2020).

46 Green et al. (2014); Hsu and Rauber (2021); Iverson et al. (2020); and Jordon et al. (2015).

47 Roelfsema et al. (2020).

48 Data-Driven EnviroLab and NewClimate Institute (2020).

49 Navigant, The Generation Foundation and CDP. (2019). See also S&P Global. "The Big Picture on Climate Risk." www.spglobal.com/en/research-insights/featured/the-big-picture-on-climate-risk, which indicates the average carbon price risk premium over time (2030–2050) across the globe (for investors) going from $15 to $200 per ton carbon by 2050.

50 NCE (2018).

51 ILO (2018).

52 IEA (2020).

53 OECD (2017a), p. 11.

54 World Bank (2019).

55 Standing (2017).

56 See, for example, www.visualcapitalist.com/map-basic-income-experiments-world/#:~:text=UBI%20operates%20by%20giving%20people,searching%20for%20better%20employment%20options and www.cnbc.com/2020/04/16/coronavirus-crisis-could-pave-the-way-to-a-universal-basic-income.html.

57 https://en.unesco.org/inclusivepolicylab/analytics/greening-basic-income. See also Bailey and Bertelsen (2018) and James K. Joyce. "Let's Pay Every American to Reduce Emissions." *Politico* July 23, 2019. www.politico.com/agenda/story/2019/

o for further details on how a carbon price-and-dividend scheme works and its benefits.

58 Raimi et al. (2020).

59 Green et al. (2014).

60 See Carbon Pulse, "'Forceful, Abrupt' International Climate Action Response to Birth US Carbon Price by 2025 – Experts." March 21, 2021. https://carbon-pulse.com/124274.

5 LAND USE CHANGE AND BIODIVERSITY

As we saw in Chapter 2, the main cause of terrestrial ecosystem and biodiversity loss is conversion and degradation of natural habitats, such as forests, wetlands and grasslands. The principal threats are from agriculture, forestry, infrastructure, human settlements and other economic activities.

Land use change by humans has transformed ecosystems across the terrestrial biosphere. This could be potentially catastrophic for both humankind and the environment. The dramatic decline in plant and animal species has been so swift that scientists warn that we may be facing "biological annihilation" in coming decades.[1]

The scale and speed of this loss and its impacts have been immense. Terrestrial ecological communities worldwide have lost more than 20 percent of their original biodiversity.[2] Natural ecosystems have declined by almost half during the past fifty years, and approximately one quarter of all terrestrial species are threatened with extinction.[3] Land use pressures have reduced local biodiversity intactness – the average proportion of natural biodiversity remaining in local ecosystems – beyond safe limits across the majority of the world's land surface.[4] Land use change could be contributing around 15 percent of total global carbon emissions.[5] Even protected areas are not safe. As much as one third of global protected land is under intense human pressure.[6]

Scientists have proposed a number of planetary boundaries that demarcate essential aspects of the ecosystem that we need to preserve, in order to halt destruction of the remaining natural landscape.

These include measures based on indices of biodiversity intactness; species abundance or richness; net primary productivity; and no net loss of natural ecosystems.[7] However, setting even modest global limits to protect some of the world's remaining natural areas has so far failed. The Convention on Biological Diversity, signed by 196 countries in 1992, made a pledge to conserve 17 percent of the world's terrestrial areas by 2020. But current rates of land use change and ecological decline suggest that this target has not been met (see Chapter 2).

Because of the concern over accelerating losses of ecosystems and biodiversity, some scientists are advocating even more ambitious goals for conserving the Earth's remaining natural areas. One suggestion is to protect 30 percent of the planet's surface for nature and to designate an additional 20 percent as climate stabilization areas to keep global warming below 1.5 °C.[8]

But adopting such a limit could come with a high cost. If half of Earth is preserved for nature, the vast majority of current land use expansion would have to stop. The result could be 15–31 percent less global cropland area; 10–45 percent less pastureland; and 23–25 percent less land for feed, biofuel and other nonfood crops.[9] Such potential trade-offs will continue to fuel debates over whether or not to impose limits on human destruction of the terrestrial biosphere – or even if a planetary boundary approach is the most effective way of controlling current threats to natural habitats.

Nonetheless, there is consensus among scientists that we need urgently to "bend the curve" of biodiversity loss and ecosystem destruction. As explained by the biologist Georgina Mace and colleagues:

> The degradation of nature is among the most serious issues that the world faces, but current targets and consequent actions amount, at best, to a managed decline. Required now are bold and well-defined goals and a credible set of actions to restore the abundance of nature to levels that enable both people and nature to thrive.[10]

One indicator used to track "the degradation of nature" is the Living Planet Index (LPI), which covers thousands of populations of mammals, birds, reptiles, amphibians and fish from around the world.[11] The LPI declined by more than two-thirds from 1970 to 2016 (see Figure 5.1). If current trends continue, the index will fall to around 15 percent of its 1970 level by 2050. At a minimum, we must reverse this decline so that

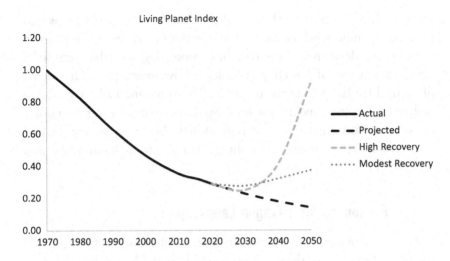

Figure 5.1 Bending the biodiversity loss curve
Notes: The global Living Planet Index (LPI) represents 20,811 populations of 4,392 species of mammals, birds, amphibians, reptiles and fish. The base year for the LPI is 1970 (LPI = 1.00). Actual shows the LPI trend from 1970 to 2016 (solid black line), based on LPI data from WWF (2020), available at WWF/ZSL https:// livingplanetindex.org/data_portal. Projected indicates the LPI projections from 2016 onward based on the 2000–2016 annual decline rate (dashed black line). High Recovery shows the LPI projections based on 92 percent recovery of 1970 levels by 2050 (Mace et al. 2018). Modest Recovery indicates the LPI projections based on 90 percent recovery of 2010 levels by 2050 (Leclère et al. 2020).

global populations and species are able to make a modest recovery to nearly their 2010 LPI level by 2050. An even more ambitious goal is to ensure almost full recovery to the 1970 level.

Halting degradation of the terrestrial biosphere will require a major transformation in how economies use land and nature. This chapter will explore different policy initiatives, both globally and within countries, to address this critical problem. First, we explain how addressing the underpricing of nature is essential to creating the incentives, institutions and innovations needed to change humankind's conversion and use of natural landscape. Second, we look at how underpricing also perpetuates rural poverty in many countries. The impacts of land use change are not evenly distributed but borne increasingly by the most vulnerable and poorest human populations. Decoupling development from excessive land use change leading to ecosystem decline is necessary to make our economies both more sustainable and inclusive. Third, global biodiversity conservation is also plagued by underfunding, as the international community struggles to compensate developing countries for protecting valuable terrestrial habitats. The rest of this chapter looks at how to end the underpricing of natural landscape and the underfunding of nature. Collective action will require commitments not only by rich countries to assist poorer ones in protection and restoration efforts, but also by the private sector to invest in nature to reduce the risks from biodiversity and ecosystem loss.

Economics for a Fragile Landscape

In Chapter 3, we explained that ecosystems are an important source of "wealth" as they support economies and boost the welfare of people. In addition, many individuals value nature for its own intrinsic worth. The traditions, culture and way of life of many local communities and indigenous people are intimately connected with their surrounding environment. Consequently, ecosystems should be viewed as highly valuable capital assets to humankind, because they produce a very wide range of beneficial ecosystem goods and services – often called *ecosystem services* for short.

These ecological values and benefits may be irreversibly lost when we degrade or convert nature. The fact that we ignore the rising cost of ecosystem loss signals that there is something fundamentally wrong in the economics of managing our increasingly fragile terrestrial landscape.

The main flaw, as we saw in Chapter 3, is the *underpricing of nature* – or more specifically in the case of terrestrial ecosystem and biodiversity decline, the *underpricing of natural landscape*. Modern economies are squandering valuable natural and ecological capital and failing to act on rising global environmental risks. This is because the ecosystem services provided by natural habitats are not routinely reflected in markets. Most of their ecosystem goods and services are available for free. We do not have to pay for them, as healthy ecosystems provide their valuable benefits to us through their natural structure and functioning. This is certainly the problem for much of the world's remaining natural landscape, which is largely ignored by the economic system and whose many valuable services are not routinely exchanged in markets.

But the problem is even worse. Not only do we not pay for the ecological degradation caused by land use change, but often we subsidize the economic activities that lead to this destruction. As the economist Partha Dasgupta points out, we are not just pricing ecosystems and their services too cheaply, we are actually giving them a "negative price," which is tantamount to paying some economic activities to destroy nature:

> The current structure of market prices works against our common future; the biosphere is precious but priced cheaply, if it is priced at all. Worse, owing to a wide range of government subsidies, some services come with a negative price.[12]

Consequently, the paramount challenge for decoupling our economies from ecologically destructive land use change is to end the underpricing of natural landscape. Only then will our institutions, incentives and innovations reflect the growing ecological and natural resource scarcity that is caused by continuing land use change. Unless we remove environmentally harmful subsidies that encourage destructive land use practices and correct the cheap cost of converting natural habitats, we cannot begin to address the problem of excessive loss and degradation of our terrestrial ecological capital.

Taking the scarcity of ecosystems and biodiversity into account will induce changes in our use of valuable natural landscapes, and encourage less conversion and more conservation and restoration. Ending underpricing will also encourage the sustainable intensification of existing land uses and the reduction in food and agricultural waste.

Since the dawn of agriculture over 10,000 years ago, land use intensification has been pivotal in influencing the ecological impacts of humankind. As Erle Ellis and colleagues argue:

> The single most important lesson from assessing changes in land use across the Holocene is that changes in the productivity of land-use systems, and especially productivity per area of land, has likely been the main long-term driver of change in human impact on the terrestrial biosphere. The pace of agricultural intensification is, therefore, also likely to remain a major determinant of future land change and our ability to meet societal demands for food, feed, housing, and energy.[13]

Intensification of agriculture, forestry and other land uses, reducing waste and adopting sustainability practices will be essential to "bending the curve" of global ecological decline and biodiversity loss.[14]

Boosting the productivity and sustainability of land use systems in low- and middle-income countries is especially a priority, if we want to reduce conversion of the world's remaining forests, wetlands and other natural habitat. David Tilman and coauthors estimate that, if current trends of agricultural intensification in wealthier nations and the pattern of land clearing in poorer nations were to continue, one billion additional hectares (ha) of land would be cleared globally for crops by 2050. On the other hand, greater agricultural intensification in all countries would mean only 250,000 million more hectares of land cleared.[15]

Addressing this problem is especially urgent in tropical developing countries, where agricultural land expansion continues to occur at the expense of natural forest (see Figure 5.2). Tropical forests are one of the most biologically rich and ecologically important biomes on Earth. Nearly all the world's tropical natural forest is located in low- and middle-income countries. Since 1990, these countries have lost 15 percent of these forests. Over the same period, land for agricultural production in tropical developing economies has expanded by 13 percent, and land just for cereal production has increased by 27 percent. Additional causes of rapid land use change in developing countries are the expansion of forestry, mining and other extractive activities.[16]

The fact that agricultural and other primary production activities are prevalent in low- and middle-income economies should not be surprising. Most developing economies, and the majority of the populations living within them, depend directly on land and natural resources. For many of these economies, primary product exports account for the vast majority of their export earnings, and one or two primary commodities often make up the bulk of exports.[17] In low-income countries, agricultural value added accounts for an average of 30 percent of GDP, and nearly 70 percent of employment is in natural resource-based sectors, such as agriculture, forestry, fishing or hunting.[18]

But simply because many low- and middle-income economies are highly dependent on their land and natural resources does not mean that they should underprice their economically and ecologically valuable natural landscape. Rather than help their economies develop and end poverty, such underpricing actually works against sustainable and inclusive development.

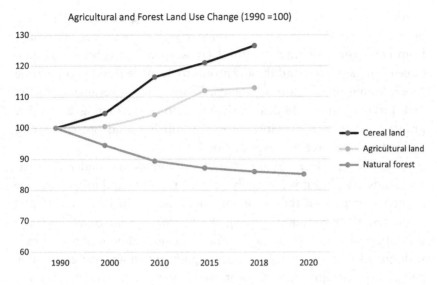

Figure 5.2 Land use in tropical low- and middle-income countries, 1990–2020
Notes: Cereal land refers to a cultivated area of wheat, rice, maize, barley, oats, rye, millet, sorghum, buckwheat and mixed grains. Agricultural land refers to the share of land area that is arable; under permanent crops; and under permanent pastures. Natural forest is naturally regenerating forest, which is predominantly composed of trees established through natural regeneration. Cereal and agricultural land data are from World Development Indicators, available at https://databank.worldbank.org/source/world-development-indicators. Natural forest data are from the Food and Agriculture Organization of the United Nations (FAO) Global Forest Resources Assessment (FRA) 2020, available at https://fra-data.fao.org/WO/fra2020/home. Low- and middle-income countries are economies with 2019 per capita gross national income (GNI) of US$12,535 or less. Countries are defined as tropical following FAO FRA 2015 domain classification. In 2020, natural forest in tropical low- and middle-income countries comprised 1,710 million hectares (ha), which is 99 percent of all tropical natural forest worldwide and 46 percent of all global natural forest.

Underpricing and Rent Seeking

Underpricing of land and natural resources constrains sustainable economic development in several ways. First, it is inefficient, and may encourage what economists call *rent seeking*. If an economy has abundant resources to exploit, but the natural landscape containing these resources is valued only as a potential reserve to be tapped for valuable agricultural, mineral and other primary products, then the costs of exploitation are considered negligible but the gains in terms of commercial profits could be substantial. As long as this is the case, primary product activities will continue to seek more profits – or rents – from converting additional natural landscape. This process will continue until there are no additional profits to be made through converting or exploiting more natural habitats. Worse still, government policies that promote and subsidize agriculture, forestry, mining and other primary production activities encourage further land use conversion and natural resource overexploitation.

This problem may occur in all economies that underprice natural landscape, but it is especially prevalent in low- and middle-income countries because of their economic dependence on land and natural resources. Moreover, underpricing also reinforces poor governance and institutions. If rent-seeking exploitation of land and natural resources is widespread in an economy, then the significant short-term gains often perpetuate inadequate government oversight, poor environmental regulations and management, corruption, land grabbing and other illegal practices. Lack of property rights or their enforcement and other institutional failures also encourage more rent-seeking exploitation of land and natural resources. In turn, weak governance and institutions that fail to control rent-seeking provide further incentives to continue with wasteful and unsustainable management of land and natural resources.

The economists Halvor Mehlum, Karl Moene and Ragnar Torvik explore this potential interaction between resource rent-seeking, institutional quality and long-run economic performance.[19] They argue that, if an economy has good-quality institutions, with low corruption, effective rule of law, well-defined property rights and so on, then resource rent-seeking behavior will be modest. If a "resource bonanza" occurs, such as a rise in commodity prices or a discovery of new land or resources to exploit, the effect of the bonanza will be to raise the profits from productive entrepreneurship in the economy, including from investment to increase productivity from existing land and resource use. Overall economic performance will therefore improve. But if an economy has poor institutions, then resource rent-seeking is encouraged rather than deterred. Any bonanza will expand "resource grabbing" at the expensive of productive entrepreneurship in the economy, and the result is not only overexploitation of land and resources but also less economic development. Mehlum and colleagues found evidence across eighty-seven countries to support this outcome. Institutional quality appears to determine the economic performance of resource-dependent economies. Those with better institutions had higher economic growth than those economies with poorer institutions.

Given the incentives created by the underpricing of natural landscape, poor institutions and rent seeking, increasingly it is commercially oriented agricultural and extractive activities that are responsible for much of the land use change occurring in developing countries.[20] These activities include plantation agriculture, ranching, forestry, fossil fuels and mining activities. The result is often export-oriented extractive enclaves with little or no forward and backward linkages to the rest of the economy.[21] This means that the gains from extractive activities have few spillover benefits, and do not boost development in other sectors of the economy. In addition, developing countries have been actively promoting these commercial activities as a means to expanding the primary products sector, especially in the land-abundant regions of Asia, Latin America and Africa.[22]

What is more, the gains and losses from underpricing and rent seeking worsen inequality. The benefits from commercial primary production activities derived from land use change and natural landscape decline are often concentrated in the hands of a few wealthy owners. In contrast, the costs of land use change and natural landscape decline are often borne by poor rural households and communities.

Underpricing, Poverty and Inequity

Rural poverty is still pervasive in most low- and middle-income countries. Despite increasing urbanization, the rural population in developing regions is expected to stay above 3.1 billion for the next thirty years, placing continuing pressure on available land and natural resources.[23] In addition, current global poverty trends suggest that the poor are increasingly rural, dependent on agriculture and predominantly young.[24]

As long as the chronic underpricing of natural resources persists, aided and abetted by resource rent-seeking and poor institutions and governance, then rural poverty will remain an ongoing problem. The prospect of quick and easy profits from natural resource exploitation attracts wealthy investors away from manufacturing and other dynamic sectors of the economy. The latter sectors do not develop, and may even decline, thus reinforcing the continued and overwhelming dependence of the economy on land use change and natural resource exploitation for the majority of its exports and for overall development. In addition, weak political and legal institutions not only encourage rent-seeking by wealthy investors in the resource-based sectors of the economy, but also allow the most valuable natural resources of the economy to be "transferred" to rich and powerful individuals.

There are many ways that this may occur, but the outcome is usually always the same: Poor rural households are unable to compete in existing land and resource markets or to influence policy decisions that determine the allocation of more valuable natural resources, and thus the rural poor continue to be confined to marginal land and resource areas to exploit for their economic livelihoods. Moreover, since these regions are relatively poor, very little public or private investments flow to these locations. Thus the concentration of the rural poor in marginal land and resource areas is perpetuated.

Inequality in access to valuable land and natural resources is therefore an important outcome of many rural areas of poor countries. Wealthier individuals and interests use their social and economic power to secure greater access to valuable environmental resources, including land, minerals, energy, gems, water and even fuelwood. Such problems are exacerbated by government policies that favor wealthier households in markets for these key natural resources, and especially land. As explained by Hans Binswanger and Klaus Deininger, "rural elites" in developing countries are often "able to steer policies and programs meant to increase rural productivity into capital-intensive investment programs for large farms, thus perpetuating inequality and inefficiency."[25]

In addition, poor rural households are affected the most by loss of surrounding natural landscape and ecosystems. In many rural areas, poor households rely on natural resources both as a supplement to consumption needs and income and as part of overall insurance and coping strategies for avoiding the income and subsistence losses associated with natural disasters and other shocks.[26] Ecosystem services such as drinking-water supply, wild foods, fuelwood and other benefits contribute from 20 to 30 percent of the income of the rural poor, and even a larger share for the poorest households.[27]

Indigenous people, too, are under threat from land use change. At least a quarter of the worlds' land surface is managed by 370 million indigenous people, who have created and maintained mosaics of crops, forest and pasture for millennia. These traditional land uses overlap with about 40 percent of all terrestrial protected areas and ecologically intact landscapes, such as boreal and tropical primary forests, savannas and marshes. Because their livelihoods, society and culture are interconnected with the natural landscape, the land inhabited by indigenous people is better managed and conserved compared to other areas. Yet despite the importance of indigenous lands to global conservation, they are the most vulnerable to and threatened by appropriation for resource exploitation by commercial primary production priorities.[28]

Underfunding of Nature

Ending the underpricing of natural landscape in all countries, including low- and middle-income countries, is vital to reducing global loss of terrestrial ecological capital and biodiversity. The other imperative is to end the *underfunding of nature* worldwide.

Table 5.1 summarizes the extent of the current underfunding problem.

Global financing for nature conservation and protection amounts to around $78–$91 billion each year (see Table 5.1). It includes domestic spending by eighty-one countries ($68 billion) and private expenditure ($6.6–$13.6 billion). The latter comprises biodiversity offsets, sustainable commodities, forest carbon finance, payments for ecosystem services, water quality trading and offsets, philanthropic spending, private contributions to conservation nongovernmental organizations (NGOs) and private finance leveraged by bilateral and multilateral public development finance. International public finance for nature, in the form of bilateral and multilateral assistance to low- and middle-income countries, is $3.9–$9.3 billion each year.

Just under $100 billion a year to fund nature sounds like a lot. But it isn't.[29]

For one, governments spend considerably more on damaging nature (see Table 5.1). Public subsidies to agriculture and fossil fuels that are environmentally harmful amount to almost $500 billion per year. That is more than five times the amount spent globally by the public and private sector on nature conservation and protection. Governments also provide environmentally beneficial subsidies to nature, but they currently average less than $1 billion per year.

In comparison, the economic benefits provided by nature are substantial (see Table 5.1). The World Economic Forum analyzed 163 industry sectors and their supply chains, and found that $44 trillion

Table 5.1. Global underfunding of nature

Category	Amount per Year	Description and Source
Funding from all sources	**$78.3–$90.7 billion**	OECD (2020a).
Public domestic finance	$67.8 billion	Average annual spending between 2015 and 2017 by eighty-one countries (OECD 2020a).
Public international finance	$3.9–$9.3 billion	Bilateral and multilateral official development assistance and concessional flows (OECD 2020a).
Private sector finance	$6.6–$13.6 billion	Average annual spending between 2015 and 2017 on biodiversity offsets, sustainable commodities, forest carbon finance, payments for ecosystem services, water quality trading and offsets, philanthropic spending, private contributions to conservation NGOs and private finance leveraged by bilateral and multilateral public development finance ($41–$155 million annually).
Subsidies		
Environmentally harmful public subsidies	$482 billion	Fossil fuel subsidies ($370 billion, OECD 2019a) and support to potentially environmentally harmful agricultural production ($112 billion, OECD 2020b).
Environmentally beneficial public subsidies	$0.89 billion	2012–2016 average (OECD 2019a).
Benefits from nature		
Economic production	$44 trillion	Global value added of 163 industry sectors and their supply chains that are moderately or highly dependent on nature and its services (WEF 2020).

Table 5.1. cont'd

Category	Amount per Year	Description and Source
Funding needs		
Costs of tropical natural climate solutions (NCS)	$618 billion	Author's estimates based on thirty-five tropical countries with cost-effective NCS and median NCS cost of 5.5 percent of GDP (Griscom et al. 2020).
Costs of restoring degraded landscape	$350 billion	Costs of restoring 350 million hectares of degraded forest and agricultural land (Ding et al. 2019).
Costs of reducing pandemic risk	$9.6 billion	Direct forest protection payments to reduce tropical deforestation in areas at highest risk of wildlife–human disease spillover (Dobson et al. 2020).

of global value added is moderately or highly dependent on nature and its services. This amounts to over half of the world's GDP. Even if these benefits are overestimated by a magnitude of ten or even one hundred, they suggest that nature is grossly underpriced and underfunded worldwide.

There are also three additional funding needs for global nature conservation: reducing the greenhouse gas emissions contributed by land use change; restoring degraded landscapes; and reducing the risks of future disease outbreaks caused by wildlife habitat loss.

As we saw in Chapter 4, land use change may contribute close to 15 percent of global greenhouse gas emissions, and it may be even a larger share in poorer economies.[30] As the economists Alex Bowen and Sam Fankhauser (2011, p. 157) note, "the most important source of greenhouse gas emissions in low-income countries remains, by some distance, *land-use change and forestry*. Together it accounts for 50% of low-income country emissions."[31] Greenhouse gas emissions from land use change in tropical developing economies can be reduced significantly through natural climate solutions (NCS), which conserve, restore and improve land management to protect biodiversity and ecosystem services. As indicated in Table 5.1, the additional funding needed to implement cost-effective NCS in thirty-five tropical low- and middle-income countries that show potential for such approaches could be well over $600 billion per year.

The costs of restoring globally 350 million hectares of degraded forest and agricultural land amounts to around $350 billion annually (see Table 5.1). However, public funding for such activities is only $41 billion per year, and private investment about $10 billion. The annual shortfall in global funding of landscape restoration is therefore about $300 billion. Yet, for every dollar invested in restoring degraded forest, anywhere from $7 to $30 in economic benefits are generated.[32]

Nearly two-thirds of emerging infectious diseases spread from animals to humans, and three quarters of them originate in wildlife.[33] An important cause of this spread is the reduction in natural habitat, which increases the likelihood of disease spillovers between infected animals.[34] If we want to prevent future pandemics from wildlife-borne diseases, such as COVID-19, we must also reduce exploitation and protect our natural habitat. The estimated price tag for reducing defor-estation of tropical habitats with highest risk of virus spillover from wildlife to humans is just under $10 billion per year (see Table 5.1).

What is clear from all these estimates of the underfunding of nature is that the largest financing gap occurs in the protection and conservation efforts in low- and middle-income countries.

Most of the world's remaining terrestrial biodiversity and nat-ural landscape is in developing economies. Over three-quarters of species are found in the tropics, which is mainly occupied by low- and middle-income countries.[35] Yet, as noted, the international community spends at most around $9 billion each year to aid these countries in their effort to protect and conserve nature. There may be an additional $500 million contributed through private finance mobilized by international aid agencies (see Table 5.1). Current global funding to support conser-vation efforts in developing countries, who host the vast majority of biodiversity, is woefully inadequate to prevent habitat loss and over-exploitation. This underinvestment is a major reason why the world is not preserving sufficient natural landscape biodiversity.

Figure 5.3 illustrates the economic implications of this under-funding. As the figure shows, the global benefits of nature conservation (gray line) are much greater than the benefits accruing to developing countries (black line). Left on their own to finance protected areas, the latter countries will conserve insufficient natural landscape (Point A). Existing international funding has boosted conservation efforts in

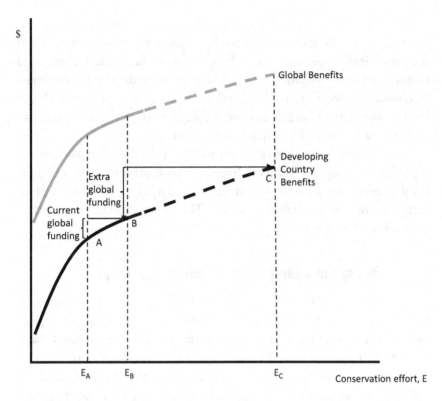

Figure 5.3 Conserving global natural landscape

Notes: Most of the world's remaining terrestrial natural landscape is in developing countries. Its global benefits (gray line) exceed the benefits to developing countries (black line). If this remaining natural landscape is not conserved and protected at high levels, it will disappear due to continued habitat loss and overexploitation (dotted gray and black lines). As it is costly for developing countries to fund nature conservation on their own, they are willing to pay for only so much conservation (Point A). Current international funding boosts conservation efforts in developing countries so some additional natural landscape is saved (Point B). Extra funding is still required to reach safe levels of nature conservation (Point C). Unless this additional funding is forthcoming, the remaining global natural landscape and its benefits are in danger from inadequate conservation and protection and irreversible, and potentially catastrophic, loss (i.e. dotted gray and black lines may eventually disappear).

low- and middle-income economies so some additional nature is saved (Point B), but current global conservation efforts still fall far short of what is need to attain safe levels of nature conservation worldwide (Point C). Unless this additional funding is forthcoming, the remaining global natural landscape and its benefits could eventually disappear.

If terrestrial ecosystems and global biodiversity are to be saved, we need to rethink the international framework for cooperation, and at the same time, foster investment by those with the greatest ability and incentive to conserve biodiversity. And, if we want developing countries to conserve more terrestrial natural landscape, ecological capital and biodiversity that yields global benefits, we have to devise more creative and innovative ways for helping them do so.

To summarize, the only way to "bend the curve" of the current rapid loss of ecosystems and biodiversity is to address the two economic ills that are behind this loss: ending the *underpricing of natural landscape* and *the underfunding of nature*. The rest of this chapter explains how this can be done.

Ending the Underpricing of Natural Landscape

A key step in ending the underpricing of natural landscape is to remove environmentally harmful subsidies. In Chapter 4, we argued that the transition to a clean energy economy requires removing subsidies to fossil fuels to curtail their underpricing. To control inefficient and unsustainable land use, we must also curtail environmentally harmful subsidies in agriculture, mining and other activities converting and degrading natural landscape.

As indicated in Table 5.1, such subsidies for agriculture alone amount to more than $100 billion per year. That exceeds global spending on nature conservation from public and private sources. In other words, if we removed all environmentally harmful subsidies in agriculture, and devoted the released funds to natural landscape protection instead, we would double the financing for nature worldwide.

There are concerns that, for low- and middle-income countries, fertilizer and other agricultural input subsidies are necessary to spur intensification of land use, ensure food security and promote exports. This is especially the case in sub-Saharan Africa, where low fertilizer and input use are viewed as constraints on higher agricultural yields and intensification. This in turn contributes to deforestation, shortened fallows and unsustainable land use. Subsidizing inputs has been the primary policy approach for addressing these problems in Africa. Fertilizer subsidies in ten countries containing half of Africa's population are around $1 billion per year and represent as much as a quarter of public expenditure on agriculture in these countries.[36]

Reviews of input subsidy programs in sub-Saharan Africa indicate that they have largely failed to achieve the objectives of widespread agricultural intensification and more sustainable land use.[37] Universal subsidy programs have benefited mainly large farmers who grow fertilizer-intensive crops, and not poor smallholders. The effect on improving agricultural intensification and land use expansion has been limited. Targeted subsidies to smallholder farmers have had more success, but there is also evidence that fertilizer subsidies have undermined other sustainable management strategies to improve yields. The subsidies have tended to benefit wealthier smallholders, who are more likely to be able to purchase fertilizer at commercial prices. These problems are often compounded by poor design and implementation of targeted subsidy programs. As Stein Holden has pointed out, "The fundamental reason for this is that they have been captured by elites who are able to reap the lion's share of the benefits and at the same time gain political support from the rural masses that hope to benefit from the subsidies."[38]

A better approach to increase agricultural intensification and reduce deforestation in Africa and other developing regions is to remove agricultural input subsidies and invest the savings in targeted investments to enhance sustainable land use among poor rural smallholders. Smallholder agriculture in most remote and marginal agricultural areas of Africa, Asia and Latin America is still a low development priority. Yet, targeting policies and investments to improve smallholder agriculture, land distribution and livelihoods in marginal environments could be a significant catalyst for green transformation in many low- and middle-income economies. In these countries, about 70–80 percent of farms are smaller than 2 ha, and they occupy about 30–40 percent of available agricultural land.[39] Investments and policies that support sustainable smallholder land use and livelihood diversification not only reduce poverty but also encourage environmental protection and land regeneration, especially in remote land-abundant areas.[40]

For example, as Susanna Hecht notes for rural Latin America, "cheap food policies, poverty alleviation programs of conditional cash transfers, and migration coupled to the transformations in tenurial regimes that legalized traditional holdings (and not just of natives) were substantive as drivers of forest maintenance and forest recovery than specifically environmental policies simply because the number of households affected by migration, remittances, cash transfers and tenure changes was so significant."[41] Similarly, Michael Knudson and Niels Fold find that state regulation of the cocoa sector in Ghana, along with regulation of informal land tenure arrangement and labor contracts, have spurred increased efficiency among private cocoa purchasing companies; reduced the marginalization of farmers with small landholdings; and limited unnecessary land expansion. The overall effect of the policy has been to improve the livelihoods of cocoa-growing smallholders by preserving their access to a vital source of income and facilitating their market integration, which has led in turn to their investing in their existing land and reducing excessive conversion. As Knudson and Fold conclude, "there are strong poverty reduction arguments behind sustaining a landholding structure in which small-scale farmers are able to maintain both their land and a relatively stable income without seriously reducing production and land productivity."[42]

Investments and policies that improve and diversify the livelihoods of smallholders can also have the additional side benefits when smallholders see additional value from protecting and restoring natural areas and from afforestation on their own lands. For example, as pointed out by Hecht, much of the decline in deforestation trends in Latin America can also be attributable to the "woodland green revolution," which has arisen through the cultivation of non-timber forest products, timber and tree-based crops by smallholders and their protection of the surrounding natural landscape.[43]

Removing agricultural subsidies would also help in reducing the enormous waste in the global agricultural system, especially in the production and consumption of food. Any savings from greater efficiency could also be deployed to protect ecosystems and natural landscape, and to invest in climate-resilient farming systems and methods.

Eliminating subsidies and reducing waste will not on their own end the underpricing of natural landscape. It may also be necessary to tax pesticides, fertilizers, forest products and timber harvests that place an additional cost on the use of land and natural resources or on environmentally damaging pollution. Such taxes can help ensure that agriculture, forestry and other land uses are not excessively degrading the environment, overexploiting natural resources and unnecessarily converting ecosystems. In addition, the revenues raised from these taxes can be channeled into the conservation, restoration and sustainable use of natural landscape and ecosystems.

Since 1980, such *biodiversity-relevant taxes* have been rising steadily in fifty-nine countries. However, these taxes are still too small to have a significant impact on the underpricing of nature. They generate only about $7.5 billion a year in revenue, equivalent to around 1 percent of the total revenue from all environmentally relevant taxes.[44] In comparison, environmentally harmful agricultural subsidies are fifteen times greater (see Table 5.1).

Increasing use of biodiversity-relevant taxes to deter excessive loss of ecological capital is clearly a priority. But more innovative policies are also required.

The Group of 20 (G20) countries with substantial tropical areas, such as Australia, Brazil, India, Indonesia and Mexico, should impose a *tropical carbon tax*.[45] This is a levy on fossil fuels that is invested in natural climate solutions (NCS) aimed at conserving, restoring and improving land management to protect biodiversity and ecosystem services. NCS are a relatively inexpensive way of reducing tropical land use change, which is not only a major cause of global biodiversity loss but an important source of greenhouse gas emissions. For example, cost-effective tropical NCS can mitigate 6,560 10^6 tonnes of CO_2e in the coming decades at less than $100 per 10^3 tonnes of CO_2e, which is about one quarter of emissions from all tropical countries.[46]

Costa Rica and Colombia have already adopted a tropical carbon tax strategy. If a policy similar to Colombia's was put in place by India, it could raise $916 million each year to invest in natural habitats that benefit the climate; similarly, Brazil could fund $217 million annually; Mexico $197 million; and Indonesia $190 million.[47] A more ambitious policy of taxation and revenue allocation could yield nearly $6.4 billion each year for natural climate solutions in India; $1.5 billion for Brazil; $1.4 billion for Mexico; and $1.3 billion for Indonesia.

Natural climate solutions, such as reversing deforestation, reforestation, increasing soil carbon levels and enhancing wetlands, are increasingly considered cost-effective investments for mitigating greenhouse gas emissions from land use for temperate G20 economies as well.[48] NCS can provide over one third of the cost-effective climate mitigation needed by 2030 to stabilize warming to below 2°C, with one third of this mitigation costing $10 per 10^3 tonnes of carbon dioxide-equivalent (CO_2e) emissions or less.[49] At this cost, the United States could abate 299 million tonnes CO_2e of greenhouse gas emissions annually through NCS, which would also provide other benefits, such as air and water filtration, flood control, soil conservation and wildlife habitats.[50] Most importantly, investing in NCS places a value on nature and its services, and sends a market signal that ecological capital is a valuable economic asset that is worth holding onto rather than converting to other land uses.

Developing countries other than G20 members should also consider adopting a tropical carbon tax. As noted, two low- and middle-income economies, Costa Rica and Colombia, have already adopted such a strategy. If twelve other megadiverse countries roll out a policy similar to Colombia's, they could raise $1.8 billion each year between them to invest in natural habitats that benefit the climate.[51] A more ambitious policy of taxation and revenue allocation could yield nearly $13 billion each year for natural climate solutions.

Moreover, such a strategy can be "pro-poor." As noted previously, poor rural households and indigenous people are affected the most by loss of natural landscape and ecosystems. Ecosystem services such as drinking-water supply, wild foods, fuelwood and other benefits contribute from 20 to 30 percent of the income of the rural poor, and even a larger share for the poorest households. The benefits to indigenous people are possibly greater, as their livelihoods, society and culture are so closely intertwined with surrounding natural areas.

Increasing the value of natural landscape in policy and market decisions is also critical to two other strategies for low- and middle-income economies: improving the efficiency and sustainability of primary production and decoupling land use change from rural development.

Case study evidence from both successful agricultural and mineral development suggests that improving the efficiency and sustainability of primary production for economy-wide gains will require resource-enhancing technological change in primary production activities; strong forward and backward linkages between the resource-based primary production sector and the rest of the economy; and substantial knowledge spillovers in primary production and across resource-based activities.[52] If guided effectively by public policy, research and extension, country-specific knowledge and technical applications in primary production can effectively expand what appears to be a "fixed" resource endowment of a country, whether it is mineral resources or agricultural land. As noted by William Maloney, even in Latin America, which has largely underperformed in terms of resource-based innovation and growth, there have been some "success stories" following this model: "Monterrey in Mexico, Medellín in Colombia, and São Paolo in Brazil all grew to become dynamic industrial centers based on mining and, in the latter two cases, coffee."[53]

Resource-enhancing technological change, knowledge spill-overs and strong forward and backward linkages are also critical to structural transformation of agriculture in developing economies, including Africa, which has struggled to emulate the rapid agricultural growth of Asia and other regions.[54] The priority should be to achieve productivity growth through sustainable intensification of agriculture and food systems to increase incomes while strengthening resilience and reducing environmental impact. Productivity growth should also boost expansion of the rural non-farm economy through income and demand effects, and as many households diversify their earnings between the farm and non-farm sectors, gains from the non-farm economy are often reinvested in further agricultural intensification. Many poor economies, especially in Africa, will need agricultural innovations that are more suitable to diverse cropping systems, marginal environments and vari-able agro-ecological conditions. This will require development and dissemination of drought-tolerant and pest-resistant crop varieties, inte-grated agro-forestry systems and improved varieties of sorghum, millet, cassava and other secondary crops.

Ending the underpricing of natural landscape is critical to both improving the efficiency and sustainability of primary production and to sustainable intensification of agriculture. As long as natural land-scape is underpriced, then there is little economic incentive to invest in increasing the economic returns to existing agricultural land and natural resource exploitation.

Pricing natural landscape appropriately may also be important for decoupling agricultural and rural development from continued land expansion and deforestation. But instead, most countries have attempted to control land use change through more direct policies, such as imposing environmental regulations and limiting forest conversion, with mixed results.[55]

Even though there are signs that environmental restrictions can limit excessive agricultural land expansion, their effectiveness remains limited as long as forests and other natural landscape are undervalued compared to agricultural uses. For example, in the Brazilian Amazon, appreciation of land values due to soy expansion has contributed to significant deforestation and conversion of other natural habitat, because these areas are treated as if they have no other value. Cattle ranching is still pervasive, and although it is a relatively low-value land use with limited land productivity, rangeland expansion continues to generate substantial deforestation because natural forest is considered worth even less.[56]

In an attempt to control tropical deforestation from primary product industries, in 2011 Indonesia implemented a moratorium on new concessions for oil palm plantations, timber plantations and logging activity on primary forests and peatlands. Jonah Busch and colleagues found that, in the first few years after its implementation, the moratorium has had a significant impact on reducing deforestation, although the effect would be substantially larger if the moratorium was extended to limit forest loss on existing oil palm and timber concessions or deforestation on lands where no concessions officially exist. In addition, the authors conclude that decoupling agricultural and timber developments from deforestation would be even more effective if moratorium controls were combined with price-based instruments, such as carbon payments, payments for ecosystem services, taxes on deforestations or certified environmentally sustainable products, "all of which attempt to raise the private value of maintaining land as forest relative to converting land to agriculture."[57]

Ending the underpricing of nature in market and policy decisions is also vital for any effort to impose global limits, such as *no net loss of ecosystems*, on humankind's destruction of the biosphere.

No Net Loss

As noted in the Introduction, various planetary boundaries for controlling the decline of ecological capital have been proposed. These include measures based on indices of biodiversity intactness, species abundance or richness, net primary productivity and no net loss of natural ecosystems.

Chapter 2 discussed a number of concerns raised about establishing planetary boundaries for biodiversity and other Earth system processes. Some question the relevance of establishing global boundaries to control land use change and biodiversity loss, as most of the drivers are at the local, regional or country level. Instead, they argue that policies and incentives should be developed nationally, and then most effectively implemented at the local or regional level to limit excessive and destructive impacts on the environment.[58]

A further problem is the difficulty of establishing planetary boundaries based on scientific measures of biodiversity, ecosystem integrity and other key ecological characteristics of natural landscape. As explained by the economists Giannis Vardas and Anastasios Xepapadeas, this challenge is exacerbated by "the complexity of ecosystems and by important and interrelated uncertainties, a number of which include sources such as major gaps in global and national monitoring systems; the lack of a complete inventory of species and their actual distributions; limited modelling capacity and lack of theories to anticipate thresholds; emergence of surprises and unexpected consequences."[59]

Because of these complications, some have argued that specifying global limits to land use change and biodiversity decline should focus on simpler criteria, such as *no net loss of ecosystems*. Sandra Díaz and colleagues argue including this objective in the post-2020 globally biodiversity framework of the Convention on Biological Diversity (CBD). The authors suggest as possible goals no net loss of natural ecosystem area and integrity by 2030 relative to 2020, and by 2050, a net gain of 20 percent of area and integrity of natural ecosystems and a 20 percent gain of integrity of managed ecosystems. There should also be no loss of "critical" ecosystems that are rare, vulnerable, or essential for planetary function, or which cannot be restored.[60]

However, the CBD appears to be moving toward an even more straightforward goal for its post-2020 global biodiversity framework: the "30 by 2030" target. This proposal calls for protection of 30 percent of the planet's land and water surface by 2030, nearly doubling the existing conservation and protected areas globally.[61]

In addition to such "no net loss" and "30 by 2030" targets, planetary boundaries have been proposed for some of the world's critical ecosystems and biomes. One such habitat critical for global biodiversity are natural forests, which are declining especially in tropical regions (see Figure 5.2). These forests are predominantly composed of trees established through natural regeneration, and thus their ecological integrity is compromised if they are converted to agriculture or if they are replaced by plantation forests with a handful of tree species or less.

Two possible planetary boundaries for natural forests have been proposed. Will Steffen and colleagues advocate preserving 75 percent of the original global natural forests and 85 percent of boreal and tropical natural forests. Eric Dinerstein and coauthors recommend protecting half of the terrestrial realm, which includes all natural forest globally.[62] Such conditions suggest that agriculture, forestry, mining and other primary production activities are limited to using or converting only part of the remaining natural forest area. For example, in the case of tropical natural forests, Steffen and colleagues suggest that this "safe operating space" for primary production is only 15 percent of the forest area, whereas for Dinerstein and colleagues these activities may safely operate in 50 percent of the remaining area.

However, establishing a no net ecosystem loss rule, designating how much natural landscape should be protected or designating a planetary boundary for natural forest and other critical global habitats is not the end of the story. As in the case of Indonesia's moratorium on deforestation discussed in the previous section, setting such an absolute limit on destructive land use change is much less effective – and perhaps impossible to achieve – if the underpricing of natural landscape persists.

It all comes down to economic incentives. As we have seen, underpricing natural landscape sends a signal that natural areas are worth less compared to converting them to agriculture, timber forestry, mining and other commercially valuable land uses. The result is that too much natural area will be converted and degraded.

But suppose there is a limit placed on how much a particular ecosystem, such as natural forest, can be converted to agriculture and other commercial uses. This limit means that there is now less remaining natural forest available for these primary production activities to convert. It has become increasingly scare and thus even more valuable. The danger now is that, unless the underpricing of natural landscape is halted, the gap between the value of keeping natural landscape intact and the value of converting it to another land use will grow.

This creates several problems. First, if producers and consumers do not receive signals through market prices that forest land and its resources are valuable and becoming scarce, then they will fail to switch to alternative uses in a timely manner. Constraints in the availability of essential inputs into productions will undermine production of valuable goods and services, and could slow economic growth and development. Furthermore, the failure to receive market signals of scarcity will lead to the underinvestment in diversification to reduce dependency on key natural resource and environmental benefits. This could make the economy vulnerable to exports shocks and stresses. In addition, in the absence of proper pricing, any remaining natural forest that is safe to convert to agriculture and other land uses will be deforested too quickly. Once that happens, owners of primary production activities will have a strong incentive to ignore the limit on deforestation and to convert illegally natural forest that is supposed to be preserved.

To overcome these perverse incentives, there should be a tax imposed on deforesting the remaining forest area that is safe to convert. This tax should reflect the value of all the benefits that this forest area provides to everyone in the region or country containing this area. But in addition, the tax should rise over time to reflect the remaining forest's increasing scarcity value as it is depleted. By eliminating the gap between the value of keeping the natural forest intact and converting it to another land use, the tax would now provide an incentive to slow down the rate of deforestation of the remaining natural forest that is allowed to be converted. If necessary, the tax rate could rise over time to extend the lifetime of this forest area indefinitely.

To illustrate how such pricing of natural landscape can support an absolute limit on natural landscape conversion, Joanne Burgess and I explore the two proposals for planetary boundaries on tropical natural forests just discussed.[63] As Will Steffen and colleagues suggest that 85 percent of these forests should be preserved, then the remaining "safe operating space" for possible conversion by agriculture, forestry, mining and other primary production is only 15 percent of the forest area. In comparison, because Dinerstein and colleagues propose that half of tropical natural forests should be protected, primary production may safely operate in 50 percent of the remaining area.

We find that the size of the forest area that is allowed to be deforested – 15 percent versus 50 percent – impacts significantly the lifetime of this remaining area before it is completely depleted. However, irrespective of the initial size of this safe operating space, its lifetime can be significantly extended by imposing a tax on forest conversion that captures all the benefits of the remaining forest, and also rises over time as the forest is depleted. If the safe operating forest is extremely valuable for its ecosystem services, then a very high tax should be imposed to extend the lifetime of the remaining forest indefinitely. Such a tax will signal that the value of conserving the safe operating space of forest is significantly high, and thus over time much more of the forest will be conserved rather than converted to an alternative use.

For example, in the most stringent case, if the remaining safe operating space is 15 percent of the original tropical natural forest area in 1990, then complete deforestation could occur in 11–21 years from 2015 onward if no tax is imposed to control deforestation. In comparison, imposing a tax that includes the foregone ecosystem benefits and the rising scarcity value from deforestation extends the lifetime of this safe operating space for tropical natural forests to sixty-five years. If the value of ecosystem benefits lost to deforestation is extremely large, then the tax should be even higher, in which case deforestation of the safe operating space may be delayed hundreds of years, or not deforested at all.

The lesson to be learned from this exercise is that simply imposing a limit or boundary on how much natural landscape can be used or converted is important for determining *ecologically* how much of nature we should preserve. But it is not a substitute for ending the underpricing of natural landscape. As we have seen in this chapter, only by ending such underpricing can we determine *economically* how to manage efficiently and sustainably our remaining natural landscape.

Or, as Thomas Sterner and colleagues put it, "keeping within planetary boundaries requires that we make better and more cost-effective use of the finite resources and sinks available to us."[64]

Collective Action

As we discussed previously, if global land use change and biodiversity loss are to be halted, then we must also end the underfunding of nature.

Most of the world's remaining terrestrial ecosystems and biodiversity are found in low- and middle-income countries, yet current global funding to support conservation efforts by these countries is woefully inadequate to prevent habitat loss and overexploitation. Simply put, if we want to "bend the biodiversity curve" we need to find creative and innovative ways to fund more conservation by developing countries.

The global value attributed to remaining natural landscape is significant. As we saw previously, its contribution to the value added of industries and their supply chains could amount to as much as half of the world's GDP (see Table 5.1). According to the 2020 Global Risks Report, biodiversity loss is one of the five greatest risks faced by humankind, and it is also intertwined with other significant risks, such as climate change.[65]

The consumption pattern and habits of rich countries also bear some responsibility for the rapid decline in terrestrial ecosystems and biodiversity in developing countries. Florence Pendrill and colleagues found that 29–39 percent of deforestation–related greenhouse gas emissions is caused by international trade, mainly in beef and oilseeds. As a result, one sixth of the carbon footprint of the average diet in the European Union is due to tropical deforestation.[66]

However, if the rest of the world does substantially increase its funding of conservation investments in poorer countries, it could have a major impact on saving ecosystems and biodiversity. Even relatively small increases in funding could make a major difference.

For example, fifty-nine tropical developing countries spend nearly $370 million annually on conservation, yet are still experiencing biodiversity decline of 1.9% on average per year (see Table 5.2). If $1 million in additional annual funding was available for these countries, there would be an 18.5% reduction in biodiversity decline. If funding increased by $5 million per year, the rate of biodiversity decline would be reduced by almost 61%. The gains from $5 million extra spending each for some megadiverse countries would also be substantial, such as Peru (54%), Brazil (42%) and Papua New Guinea (33%). With $5 million a year of extra funding, Madagascar would be able to transition from a declining to an improving biodiversity trend.

Given the urgency of "bending" the biodiversity loss curve (see Figure 5.1), the key question is what collective action is needed globally to end the underfunding of nature worldwide.

One avenue is for wealthier countries not only to increase the amount of their own domestic spending on nature conservation but also to devote substantially more bilateral and multilateral assistance to poorer countries (see Table 5.1).

Increasing domestic conservation investments can provide much needed economic benefits, including jobs, which should be an important consideration as major economies recover from the COVID-19 pandemic. For example, ecosystem restoration in the United States provides direct employment for 126,000 workers and generates

Table 5.2. Increasing global conservation funding to developing countries

Country	Average Annual Biodiversity Decline	Average Annual Conservation Spending $ Million	Reduction in Biodiversity Decline from a $1 Million Spending Increase	Reduction in Biodiversity Decline from a $5 Million Spending Increase
Brazil	0.4%	20.85	9.03%	42.18%
Colombia	1.0%	14.83	5.57%	26.96%
Democratic Republic of Congo	0.6%	2.12	6.38%	31.22%
Ecuador	1.3%	3.91	4.81%	23.44%
Indonesia	3.7%	18.69	7.66%	33.85%
Madagascar	0.0%	13.93	30.77%	Recovery
Malaysia	6.7%	9.21	1.64%	8.07%
Papua New Guinea	2.8%	8.83	7.09%	32.84%
Peru	0.3%	16.28	11.25%	54.31%
Philippines	1.5%	6.11	5.02%	24.27%
10 megadiverse countries	1.8%	114.76	8.9%	30.8%
59 tropical countries	1.9%	369.05	18.5%	60.8%

Notes: Based on Waldron et al. (2017). All countries are low- and middle-income economies, with 2019 per capita gross national income (GNI) of US$12,535 or less. Megadiverse countries identified by Mittermeier et al. (1997). This classification is used to set conservation priorities internationally, see www.worldatlas.com/articles/ecologically-megadiverse-countries-of-the-world.html. Recovery indicates transition to an improving biodiversity trend.

$9.5 billion in economic output annually, while creating a further 95,000 indirect jobs and $15 billion in household spending.[67]

The returns to increased conservation investment in developing countries could be even greater. Based on data from sixteen low- and middle-income countries, Nicoletta Batini and colleagues find that, for every dollar spent in conservation, almost seven dollars more are generated in the economy after five years. The authors attribute these high returns to three factors. First, conversation spending sponsored by donors supplement domestic resources in developing countries rather than crowd them out. Second, conservation actions in these countries are highly labor-intensive and create jobs. Finally, as discussed earlier in this chapter, conservation of natural landscape protects ecosystem services that support the economic livelihoods of the rural poor, including water, food, fodder, resource harvests and protection from extreme events.[68]

One way that richer countries could fund more conservation in poorer economies is to step up their investments in biodiversity offsets and payments for ecosystem services.

Biodiversity offsets are conservation actions, such as protecting threatened forests or restoring wetlands, which are intended to compensate for unavoidable losses to natural habitats caused by other investments in the economy. The objective is to ensure at least a no net loss of biodiversity and, where possible, a net gain. Globally, about $5 billion is spent annually on biodiversity offsets.[69] However, much of these offsets occur domestically within wealthier economies. Richer countries and multilateral agencies need to increase their assistance to low- and middle-income countries for funding biodiversity offsets.

Payments for ecosystem services are market transactions, usually direct cash or credit payments, made by those who benefit from ecosystem services to landowners who have agreed to provide these services through specific actions, such as habitat conservation or restoration. The type of ecosystem services generated include watershed protection, carbon sequestration, water quality benefits, biodiversity conservation and wildlife habitat benefits. Ten large, publicly funded payments for ecosystem services programs account for around $10 billion of global funding annually. In addition, private schemes that pay for watershed protection services provide financing of around $15 million each year.[70]

There is plenty of scope to expand public and private payments for ecosystem services, and especially to fund more projects in developing countries. Such schemes should focus on tropical countries where natural climate solutions are most cost-effective and to reduce tropical deforestation in areas at highest risk of wildlife–human disease spillover (see Table 5.1). Tropical countries that benefit most from the extra spending on biodiversity conservation should also be a priority (see Table 5.2).

The pandemic has also caused rising debt levels and budget cuts in low- and middle-income countries. As we have discussed in Chapter 4, there is an opportunity to employ a comprehensive private and public debt relief program, conditional on indebted countries undertaking additional actions or investments in climate adaptation and mitigation. This could potentially be a win-win strategy for addressing the climate and debt crises, provided that the additional climate actions should include a commitment by participating low- and middle-income countries to ending the underpricing of fossil fuels in their economies.

In a similar way, lender countries could offer lower interest rates and principal repayments in return for increasing biodiversity and natural area protection in borrowing countries, in exchange for the latter delivering on additional conservation actions and investments. The basic idea of such *debt-for-nature swaps* involves restructuring or canceling some of a nation's foreign debt in exchange for investment in greater conservation of natural areas. Such deals have existed since the late 1980s. Since 1990, debt-for-nature swaps by the United States canceled approximately $1.8 billion owed by twenty-one low- and middle-income countries. The swaps generated $400 million for conservation. Debt-for-nature swaps carried out by all other high-income countries totaled $1 billion of debt canceled and generated about $500 million for conservation. Evidence suggests that the US bilateral debt-for-nature deals have been associated with lower rates of forest loss in borrowing countries.[71]

If debt-for-nature swaps are to be effective in closing the funding gap for global nature conservation, clearly more deals need to be made and key shortcomings addressed. One option is to expand the range of conservation actions to include a commitment by participating low- and middle-income countries to ending the underpricing of natural landscape. By undertaking subsidy reforms and pricing land conversion in exchange for debt relief, these countries will be reestablishing their credit worthiness with financial investors and markets. This could potentially be a win-win strategy for addressing both the debt crisis and underfunding of nature faced by many developing countries.

Another way to close the funding gap is to expand the use of *green bonds* for biodiversity and sustainable land use investments. These are debt instruments where the proceeds are used exclusively to finance or refinance projects with environmental benefits. First issued in by the European Investment Bank in 2007 and the World Bank in 2008, green bonds reached a market value of $258 billion in 2019. The Luxembourg Stock Exchange established the first dedicated Green Exchange (LGX) that includes trading in green bonds in 2016.[72] The issuers of green bonds are typically local and national governments, corporations and multilateral development agencies and banks.

While the global market for green bonds is growing, their focus is mainly on renewable energy, energy efficiency, green transport and other climate change mitigation investments. Green bonds are rarely used to finance biodiversity conservation and sustainable land use. Climate change, energy and transport have accounted for around 80 percent of green bonds; land use projects only 3 percent.[73]

The main issuer of green bonds for investments in low- and middle-income economies is the World Bank. Since 2008, the bank has issued green bonds to raise $17 billion for eligible projects worldwide. Of these commitments, nearly $12 billion in green bond proceeds have been disbursed to support 106 projects in thirty-one developing countries. But 66 percent of the projects funded have been for renewable energy, energy efficiency and clean transportation. Only 17 percent have been allocated to agriculture, land use, forests and ecological resources, with a total allocation of just over $1.3 billion.[74]

If greens bonds are to catalyze more biodiversity and sustainable land use investments, especially in developing countries, several limitations need to be overcome. Two key challenges are the relatively small scale of many conservation projects compared to clean energy and transport investments, and as a result, the perceived relative low returns and significant risk of investing in biodiversity and sustainable land use. The average value of issued green bonds is $150 million, but individual conservation projects in low- and middle-income countries are unlikely to reach such a scale, unless they are bundled into larger investment opportunities.[75]

There are creative ways of doing this. The first is that developing country governments, working with aid agencies issuing green bonds such as the World Bank, local governments and NGOS could identify and combine individual natural landscape projects from various localities and regions into a single nationwide investment portfolio. A green bond could then be issued for the entire portfolio of projects, and then disbursed to individual regional and local investments.

Green bonds could also be issued to support other scalable conservation actions, such as a countrywide program of payments for ecosystem services, biodiversity offsets, ecological restoration or for expanding protected areas, their policing and monitoring. A good example is Mexico's recently completed $350 million Forests and Climate Change program, which was partially funded by the issuance of a World Bank green bond. The project supported rural communities' sustainable management of forests, generated additional income for these communities from forest products and services and significantly reduced greenhouse gas emissions from deforestation and forest degradation.[76]

But if we really want to end the underfunding of global biodiversity, the corporate world needs to step up.

As noted previously in this chapter, $44 trillion of global value added across 163 global industrial sectors and their supply is moderately or highly dependent on nature and its services. This is more than half of the world's GDP (see Table 5.1). The dependence on terrestrial natural landscape is possibly even higher for key sectors, such as forestry and agricultural industries.

Along with Joanne Burgess and Thomas Dean, I examined the benefits from greater participation and investments in global biodiversity conservation by these two sectors.[77] By spending $15–$30 billion annually to protect natural forests worldwide, the forest products industry would attain its own industry sustainable forest management goals. Agriculture also has an incentive to protect habitats of wild pollinators, who along with managed populations enhance global crop production by $235–$577 billion each year.

We go on to argue that, to capitalize on these incentives for business to conserve nature, the world needs a new type of global biodiversity agreement that goes beyond simply establishing targets designating how much of the planet to protect but finds new ways to end the global funding gap. One way is for such an agreement to allow formal participation by leading corporations in forestry, agricultural and other sectors that benefit from conservation. In exchange for committing to the agreement, the corporations would have to commit funding to conserve natural areas and sustainable land use globally. We estimate that the resulting increase in industry revenues and profits could provide $25–$50 billion annually for global conservation, which would help close the funding gap.

In sum, we have to scale up and align finance for biodiversity and natural landscape conservation from all sources, public and private. For example, it is estimated that we need at least three if not four times the amount of current annual spending on natural-based solutions, if the world is to meet its climate change, biodiversity and land degradation targets.[78] Actions by individual governments and businesses are important, but this must be a collective effort. As many businesses worldwide are the main beneficiaries from nature and its services, it is time that they step up to do their part. In Chapters 8 and 9, we will explore further the main ways in which both business and the government can contribute to the economics of a fragile planet.

Conclusion

There are two principle causes of the current rapid loss of global terrestrial ecosystems and biodiversity: the *underpricing of natural landscape* and *the underfunding of nature*.

If natural areas are priced too cheaply, then we will find it cheaper to convert them to agriculture, forestry and other land uses than to protect or preserve them. By underfunding nature, we provide little incentives for conserving or restoring ecosystems and habitats.

Decoupling development from excessive land use change and ecosystem loss is necessary to make our economies both more sustainable and inclusive. This outcome is crucial if we want to generate the incentives, innovations and governance necessary to transition to sustainable intensification of agriculture, forestry and other land uses; reduce food and waste; and ultimately, "bend the curve" of ecological and biodiversity decline.

Such a transition is also more inclusive than the current pattern of development that undervalues ecological benefits. As long as the chronic underpricing of natural landscapes persists, aided and abetted by resource rent-seeking and poor institutions and governance, then rural poverty will remain a chronic problem in much of the developing world. In addition, poor rural households and indigenous people benefit the most from nature and its services, and have the most to lose from declining ecosystems and biodiversity.

Most of the world's remaining terrestrial biodiversity and natural landscape is in low- and middle-income countries. Yet current global funding to support conservation efforts in these countries is woefully inadequate to prevent habitat loss and overexploitation. This underinvestment is another reason why the world is not preserving sufficient natural areas.

If catastrophic global biodiversity decline is to be avoided, we need to rethink the international framework for cooperation, and at the same time, foster investment by those with the greatest ability and incentive to conserve biodiversity. And, if we want developing countries to conserve more natural areas, ecological capital and biodiversity that yield global benefits, then we have to devise more creative and innovative ways for helping them do so.

The good news is that we have at our disposal a growing number of financial instruments and mechanisms to spur collective action by rich countries to assist poorer ones in protection and restoration efforts, and by the private sector to invest in nature to reduce the risks posed by biodiversity and ecosystem loss. These include biodiversity offsets, payments for ecosystem services, debt-for-nature swaps, green bonds and international environmental agreements. There are creative ways of to scale up and align finance for biodiversity and natural landscape conservation from all sources, public and private. Moreover, these mechanism should be used in conjunction with demonstrable policy reforms that end the underpricing of natural landscape.

In a nutshell, we can establish all the global targets we want – protecting 30 percent of the Earth's surface by 2030, no net loss of natural ecosystems or planetary boundaries on ecological loss – but until we tackle the perverse incentives caused by the underpricing of natural landscape and the underfunding of nature, we will continue to fall short of any global goals to halt ecosystem decline and biodiversity loss. Corporate leaders, policy experts and even some world leaders are increasingly acknowledging that declining ecological capital is one of the greatest risks faced by humankind. It is time we recognize that managing our remaining fragile natural landscape is just as much an economic challenge as an ecological one.

Notes

1 See Ceballos et al. (2017). Other global assessments that illustrate how land use change is leading to unprecedented loss of biodiversity and ecosystem services include Bar-On et al. (2018); Díaz et al. (2019); Dinerstein et al. (2017); Elhacham et al. (2020); IPBES (2019); Leclère et al. (2020); Mace et al. (2018); and Newbold et al. (2016).
2 Díaz et al. (2019).
3 IPBES (2019).
4 From Newbold et al. (2016), who estimate that natural biodiversity remaining in local ecosystems exceeds safe limits across 58.1 percent of the world's land surface.

5 Friedlingstein et al. (2020) estimate that between 2010 and 2019, 86 percent of total carbon emissions were from fossil fuel CO_2 emissions and 14 percent were from land use change.

6 Jones et al. (2018).

7 See, for example, Díaz et al. (2020); Lade et al. (2020); Mace et al. (2014); Newbold et al. (2016); Running (2012); and Steffen et al. (2015).

8 Dinerstein et al. (2019). The main proponent of this global conservation goal of preserving half of the Earth is the biologist Edward O. Wilson. See Wilson (2016) and also Dinerstein et al. (2017).

9 Mehrabi et al. (2018).

10 Mace et al. (2018), p. 448.

11 Species richness and relative abundance are often the two factors that are considered when measuring species diversity, which is the most common interpretation of biological diversity. Species richness refers to the number of species in an area, community or ecosystem, and relative species abundance measures how common a species is relative to the other species found in an area, community or ecosystem. The Living Planet Index (LPI) is a measure of the state of the world's biological diversity based on population trends of vertebrate species from terrestrial, freshwater and marine habitats. The current LPI comprises 4,801 species and 27,580 populations. All indices are weighted by species richness, giving species-rich taxonomic groups in terrestrial, marine and freshwater systems more weight than groups with fewer species. For more details, see WWF (2020) and WWF/ZSL. https:// livingplanetindex.org/data_portal.

12 Dasgupta (2021), p. 234.

13 Ellis et al. (2013), p. 7985

14 Allott et al. (2020); Leclère et al. (2020); Mehrabi et al. (2018); Springmann et al. (2018); and Tilman et al. (2011).

15 Tilman et al. (2011).

16 Barbier (2019a) and (2020b); Busch and Ferretti-Gallon (2017); Carrasco et al. (2017); Gibbs et al. (2014); Hosonuma et al. (2012); Laurence et al. (2014); Leblois et al. (2018); Meyfroidt et al. (2014); and UNCCD (2017).

17 Barbier (2019a) and Venables (2016).

18 From the World Development Indicators, available at https://databank.worldbank .org/source/world-development-indicators.

19 Mehlum et al. (2006). Since this study, there has been a growing economics literature examining this interaction; for example, for reviews, see Badeeb et al. (2017); Barbier (2019a); Havranek et al. (2016); Kolstad (2009); Papyrikis (2017); and van der Ploeg (2011).

20 See, for example, Barbier (2019a) and (2020b); Busch and Ferretti-Gallon (2017); Carrasco et al. (2017); Chomitz et al. (2007); DeFries et al. (2010); Deininger and Byerlee (2012); Gibbs et al. (2010); Hosonuma et al. (2012); Lambin and Meyfroidt (2011); Laurence et al. (2014); Leblois et al. (2018); and Meyfroidt et al. (2014).

21 Barbier (2019a); van der Ploeg (2011); and Venables (2016).

22 Barbier (2019a); Chomitz et al. (2007); Deininger and Byerlee (2012); Hosonuma et al. (2012); and Meyfroidt et al. (2014).

23 United Nations (2014).

24 Castañeda et al. (2018).

25 Binswanger and Deininger (1997), p. 1996.

26 Angelsen and Dokken (2018); Angelsen et al. (2014); Barbier (2019a); Barbier and Hochard (2018); Debela et al. (2012); Delacote (2009); Díaz et al. (2019); Garnett et al. (2018); Hallegatte et al. (2015); López-Feldman (2014); McSweeney (2005);

Narain et al. (2008); Narloch and Bangalore (2018); Noack et al. (2019); Robinson (2016); Takasaki et al. (2004); Vedeld et al. (2007); and Wunder et al. (2014).

27 Angelsen et al. (2014) and Vedeld et al. (2007).

28 Díaz et al. (2019) and Garnett et al. (2018).

29 As a comparison, UNEP (2021) finds that approximately $133 billion per year is invested in *nature-based solutions*, which are broadly defined as actions to protect, sustainably manage and restore natural or modified ecosystems, while also addressing societal challenges, such as food security, climate change, water security, human health, disaster risk and social and economic development. UNEP (2021) assesses that 86 percent ($115 billion) of the annual funding for nature-based solutions is from public sources, and 14 percent ($18 billion) from private sources. The report excludes investments in the marine environment but does include mangroves. UNEP (2021) maintains that, if the world is to meet its climate change and biodiversity targets, annual funding for nature-based solutions needs to increase threefold by 2030 and fourfold by 2050, or around $536 billion per year.

30 Friedlingstein et al. (2020) estimate that between 2010 and 2019, 86 percent of total carbon emissions were from fossil fuel CO_2 emissions and 14 percent were from land use change.

31 Bowen and Sam Fankhauser (2011), p. 157.

32 Ding et al. (2019) and Verdone and Seidl (2017).

33 Cunningham et al. (2017) and Jones et al. (2008).

34 Cunningham et al. (2017); Faust et al. (2018); Gibb et al. (2020); Johnson et al. (2020); and Shah et al. (2019).

35 Barlow et al. (2018).

36 Jayne et al. (2018).

37 Holden (2019) and Jayne et al. (2018).

38 Holden (2019), p. 516.

39 Lowder et al. (2016).

40 See, for example, the many case studies and examples from low- and middle-income countries cited in Bachewe et al. (2018); Barbier (2019a) and (2020b); Barbier and Hochard (2018) and (2019); Barrett et al. (2017); Fan and Chan-Kang (2004); Hecht (2014); Holden (2019); Huang (2018); Larson et al. (2016); and Pingali (2012).

41 Hecht (2014), p. 899.

42 Knudson and Fold (2011), p. 386.

43 Hecht (2014).

44 OECD (2020c).

45 Barbier et al. (2020).

46 Griscom et al. (2020).

47 Barbier et al. (2020).

48 EASAC (2019); Fargione et al. (2018); and Griscom et al. (2017).

49 Griscom et al. (2017).

50 Fargione et al. (2018).

51 Barbier et al. (2020).

52 For reviews of this evidence, see Barbier (2019a) and (2020b); Maloney (2002); Nülle and Davis (2018); and Wright and Czelusta (2004).

53 Maloney (2002), p. 112.

54 Bachewe et al. (2018); Barrett et al. (2017); and Pingali (2012).

55 From 2000 to 2015, there were encouraging signs that the combination of improved environmental regulations to control deforestation and regional economic development policies in the Brazilian Amazon may have had some success in decoupling agricultural development from land expansion (Barbier 2019b; Cardoso da Silva

et al. 2017; Caviglia-Harris et al. 2016; Fekete et al. 2021, Macedo et al. 2012; Tritsch and Arvor 2016). Thus, over this period, increasing commercial production activities, wider socioeconomic gains and reduced land expansion and deforestation may have occurred in some locations. This was largely attributed to land use policies that promoted efficient use of already cleared land through intensification while restricting deforestation, combined with regional policies that encouraged agglomeration economies that spurred innovation, supply chain diversification and reduced market access for commercial primary producers in existing agricultural areas. Similar policy strategies may have also been effective in decoupling commercial crop expansion and deforestation in other tropical regions (Busch et al. 2015; Carrasco et al. 2017; Knudsen and Fold 2011; Meyfroidt et al. 2014; Newton et al. 2013). Unfortunately, policy changes in Brazil after 2015 loosened environmental regulations on deforestation and failed to control land clearing, which have set back the overall strategy of decoupling development and widespread land use change, especially in Amazonia.

56 Cardoso da Silva et al. (2017); Holland et al. (2016); Richards (2015); Richards et al. (2014); and Walker et al. (2009).

57 Busch et al. (2015), p. 1331.

58 See Brook et al. (2013); Montoya et al. (2018); and Randall (2021).

59 Vardas and Xepapadeas (2010), p. 380.

60 Díaz et al. (2020). The authors also propose specific goals for species, genetic diversity and nature's contribution to people.

61 See www.cbd.int/doc/c/3064/749a/0f65ac7f9def86707f4eaefa/post2020-prep-02-01-en.pdf. The suggestion of this target is based on the "Global Deal for Nature" proposed by Dinerstein et al. (2019), who suggest increasing global conservation and protected areas to 30 percent of the world's surface by 2030.

62 Dinerstein et al. (2017) and Steffen et al. (2015).

63 Barbier and Burgess (2019).

64 Sterner et al. (2019), p. 19.

65 WEF (2020).

66 Pendrill et al. (2019).

67 BenDor et al. (2015) and OECD (2020c).

68 Batini et al. (2021). The sixteen countries are Burkina Faso, Burundi, Cambodia, Cameroon, Central African Republic, Chad, Ghana, Guatemala, Madagascar, Malawi, Mozambique, Niger, Senegal, Sierra Leone, Tanzania and Uganda.

69 OECD (2020c).

70 OECD (2020a) and (2020c).

71 Sommer et al. (2019). However, Cassimon et al. (2011) find that debt-for-nature swaps have also typically displayed a number of shortcomings: They often fail to deliver additional resources to the debtor country or to the government budget; often fail to deliver more resources for conservation purposes; often have a negligible effect on overall debt burdens; and are often in conflict with principles of alignment with government policy and institutions. As the authors find, some of these shortcomings are present in the specific case of a debt-for-nature swap between the United States and Indonesia.

72 Chahine and Liagre (2020) and World Bank (2019a). Note that, as traded assets, the market valuation of green bonds does not necessarily reflect the amount of money raised by issuers of green bonds to finance environmental projects. As Chahine and Liagre (2020, p. 1) comment about the rapid expansion in the market value of green bonds in recent years: "A lot of this growth has been captured by different stock exchanges where Green Bonds are listed."

73 Chahine and Liagre (2020).
74 World Bank (2019a).
75 Chahine and Liagre (2020).
76 World Bank (2019a).
77 Barbier et al. (2018).
78 UNEP (2021).

6 FRESHWATER

When the history of the early twenty-first century is written, scholars will be perplexed by a puzzling paradox. With overwhelming scientific evidence pointing to growing overuse and scarcity of freshwater, why did the world not mobilize it vast wealth, ingenuity and institutions to avert this crisis?

Freshwater is the most beneficial of Earth's resources, as it has no substitute in supporting life. Yet, humankind continues to exploit water as if it will always be freely available. We treat water as though it has little value, even as freshwater supplies dwindle in the face of rising demand. The result is that water scarcity is on the rise around the world, and it is magnified by climate change, rainfall variability, rising temperatures, drought and land use change.

Since 2012, the World Economic Forum has listed water crises as one of the most perilous global risks in terms of economic impact.[1] Every year, water shortages impact the lives of one third of the world's population, and this number could double over the next few decades because of climate change.[2] By 2030, 700 million people could be displaced by intense water scarcity, mostly in the poorest regions of the world.[3] By 2040, at least sixty-five countries could face high or extreme water stress.[4] Many of them are low- and middle-income countries, which are expanding water use because of their growing populations and economies.

The global demand for water is projected to continue growing. Global agriculture and food security depend on water. Irrigation, which accounts for 40 percent of agricultural production globally, currently consumes 70 percent of the world's freshwater supplies. And irrigation keeps expanding with growing populations and demand for food. Total harvested irrigated area is expected to increase from 421 million hectares (ha) in 2000 to 473 million ha by 2050.[5]

As a result, numerous regions face future water risks to agriculture, especially northeast China, southwest United States and northwest India, which could have consequences for global production and food security.[6] Already, agriculture worldwide is being impacted by more frequent and severe droughts. From 1983 to 2009, approximately three fourths of the global harvested area of maize, rice, soy and wheat experienced drought-induced yield losses. This amounted to 454 million hectares affected and a cumulative production loss of $166 billion.[7]

But people will need water for other uses too; these include drinking supplies, sanitation, cities and industries, and for new agricultural activity, such as biofuel production. There is also the unfilled water needs of the world's poor. An estimated 785 million people – more than 1 in 10 – lack access to safe water, and nearly 2 billion people – over 1 in 4 – do not have access to basic sanitation.[8] These growing demands for water plus the vagaries of global climate change will place increasing pressure on using scarce water resources for agriculture and may threaten food security, poverty alleviation and economic development.

This chapter takes the view that the current overuse of freshwater supplies worldwide is as much a failure of water management as it is a result of scarcity. Outdated governance structures and institutions, combined with continual underpricing, have perpetuated the overuse and undervaluation of water, requiring reforms to markets and policies to ensure that they adequately capture the rising economic costs of exploiting water resources to foster more conservation, control of pollution and ecosystem protection. The result will be efficient allocation of water among its competing agricultural, industrial and urban uses; fostering of water-saving innovations; and further mitigation of water scarcity and its costs.

In short, the impending global water crisis can be avoided, provided that we recognize that the chronic underpricing of water lies at the heart of the problem. Overcoming the institutional, governance and incentive failures that have perpetuated such underpricing is the only way to move from a "vicious cycle" of mismanagement of water and its rising scarcity to a "virtuous cycle" of managing water to alleviate this scarcity. Moreover, addressing this challenge can be accomplished in a way that leads to more inclusive as well as sustainable use of our freshwater supplies to meeting growing global demands. This is the economic challenge of managing water in the twenty-first century.

Freshwater Boundaries

Growing global water demands and increasing scarcity suggest that the risk of water crises is one of the greatest challenges for ensuring a "safe" Anthropocene in the coming decades. Of all the potential "planetary boundaries" discussed in Chapter 2, managing the critical threats of rising human consumption of water and destruction of freshwater ecosystems to the Earth's available supplies may prove to be the most urgent task in protecting an increasingly "fragile" planet.[9]

For one, global freshwater supplies are limited. Only around 3 percent of the world's water is fit for human consumption, and 99 percent of this supply is either frozen in glaciers and pack ice or found underground in aquifers. Freshwater ecosystems, such as ponds, lakes, streams, rivers and wetlands, account for the remaining 1 percent of the world's freshwater sources. Lakes and rivers, which are the main sources for human consumption of freshwater, contain just 0.3 percent of total global reserves.[10]

But freshwater ecosystems are increasingly threatened by both human impacts and environmental change. The main human threats to these ecosystems arise from management and extraction of more water: modification of river systems, inland waters and wetlands and water withdrawals for flood control, agriculture or water supply. Pollution and eutrophication by agricultural, industrial and urban waste; over-harvesting of inland fisheries; and the introduction of invasive alien species are further degrading freshwater ecosystems and biodiversity. Climate change, nitrogen deposition, shifts in precipitation and runoff and other global environmental changes interact with human threats to magnify the dangers to freshwater ecosystems in many parts of the world.

Ultimately, the physical and ecological limits on our use of freshwater supplies will start to bind, with increasingly severe economic and social implications. More frequent and severe water crises worldwide will become the norm. Rising water shortages and scarcity will raise the costs of exploiting additional water resources; constrain economic growth and development; worsen inequality; and increase the likelihood of civil unrest and conflicts. Many regions and countries will be unable to escape the rising economic costs of harnessing more water resources for their growing economies and populations. As existing freshwater supplies dwindle, it will become increasingly expensive to develop alternative sources of supply, and to deliver water to where it is needed most. New technologies for augmenting freshwater supplies, such as removing salt from seawater through desalination, are still not cost-effective on a large scale for many parts of the world. Instead, as available water from freshwater ecosystems and surface supplies fail to keep up with demand, the only cheap alternative is to extract "groundwater," the water found underground in aquifers. But available groundwater supplies are rapidly disappearing too, and the remaining supplies are harder to find and more costly to extract.

Simply put, in the near future, regions facing greater water stress and declining per capita availability of supplies should expect the economic and social costs of exploiting more water resources to rise. Certainly, it is helpful to know how much regional and national supplies of water will be available to sustain future human consumption. But as scientists estimating the freshwater planetary boundaries – or "PB-Water" for short – have warned:

> Ultimately, quantifying planetary or local water boundaries is not enough. Equally important is an associated assessment and evaluation of local and global demand for water and other natural resources, together with a systematic exploration of opportunities to stay below the PB-Water.[11]

This is the perspective adopted by this chapter. Global freshwater supplies are physically limited in availability, and human demands continue to grow. Water scarcity is already rising in many regions, and the problems associated with this scarcity will only worsen unless we meet the economic challenge of managing this crisis.

The Economic Challenge of the Water Crisis

Averting the threats and consequences of future water crises, chronic shortages and rising scarcities is an especially daunting challenge. It is made worse because a basic principle – the rising economic and social costs of exploiting more water resources – is ignored in our current market and policy decisions for managing and using water.

Why we continue to disregard these important signals of the impending threat of a global water crisis – despite water being the most essential resource for human existence and survival – is the great *water paradox* facing humankind today.[12] In short, the current overuse of freshwater supplies worldwide is as much a failure of water management as it is a result of scarcity.

At the heart of the crisis in global water management is the persistent *underpricing of water.* The increasing environmental and social costs associated with freshwater scarcity are not routinely reflected in markets. Nor have we developed adequate policies and institutions to handle these costs. This means that economies do not have the correct price signals or incentives to adjust production and consumption activities to balance water use with supply; protect freshwater ecosystems; and support necessary technological innovations. All too often, policy distortions and institutional and governance failures compound water scarcity by encouraging wasteful use of water and ecosystem degradation.

This process has become a vicious cycle (see Figure 6.1). Markets and policy decisions currently do not reflect the rising costs associated with exploiting more freshwater resources. This in turn leads to freshwater infrastructure and investments that are accompanied by higher environmental and social damages. These damages are reflected in increased depletion of water resources, pollution, degradation of freshwater ecosystems and, ultimately, rising water scarcity. But because the economic costs of this scarcity continue to be ignored in decision-making, the consequences for current and future well-being are underestimated. The end result is the chronic underpricing of water, which poor institutions and inadequate governance structures perpetuate.

Unraveling this vicious circle and making it virtuous is one of the biggest challenges facing humankind. As depicted in Figure 6.2, it starts with designing water governance regimes and institutions that are suitable for managing the rapidly changing conditions of water availability and competing demands, including the threat posed by climate change.

Ending the underpricing of water also requires reforms to markets and policies to ensure that they adequately capture the rising economic costs of exploiting water resources. These costs include not only the full cost recovery of water infrastructure supply but also environmental damages from degrading ecosystems and any social

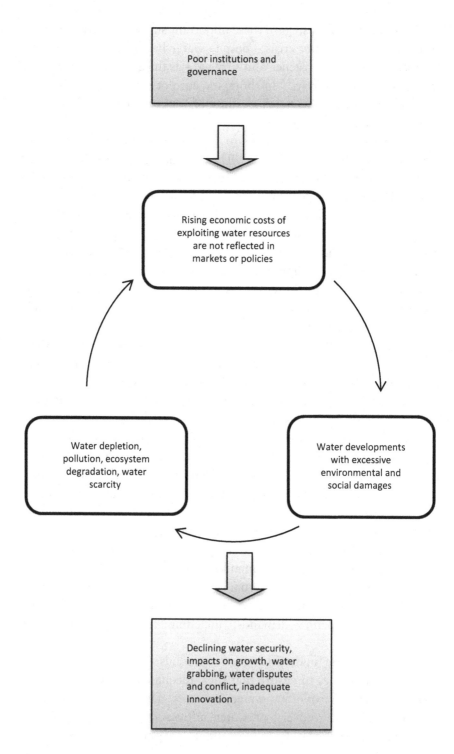

Figure 6.1 The vicious cycle of mismanaging water use and scarcity
Source: Based on Barbier (2019b), figure 1.1

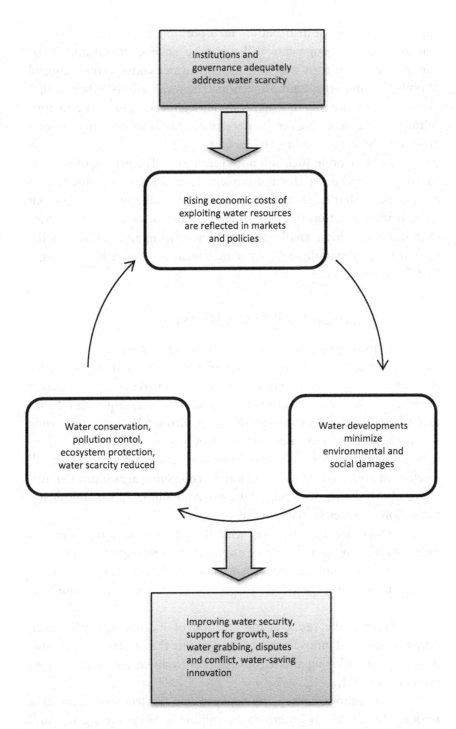

Figure 6.2 The virtuous cycle of managing water use and scarcity
Source: Based on Barbier (2019b), figure 1.2

impacts of inequitable distribution. Incorporating these costs will ensure that all water developments will minimize environmental and social impacts, which in turn will lead to more water conservation, control of pollution and ecosystem protection. The result will be efficient allocation of water among its competing agricultural, industrial and agricultural uses; fostering of water-saving innovations; and further mitigation of water scarcity and its costs.

Implementing such solutions is not easy. The pricing of water is contentious, and designing and implementing a marketing mechanism for a resource that has long been underpriced are major challenges. But rising scarcity and the growing threat of water crises mean that it is time to grapple with these challenges and view pricing and markets as the basis for a new paradigm in water management as part of ensuring a "safe" Anthropocene.

Transforming the Hydraulic Mission

Transforming our management of water from a vicious to a virtual cycle is the key to averting a global crisis. Outdated governance structures and institutions, combined with continual underpricing, have perpetuated the overuse and undervaluation of water, requiring reforms to markets and policies to ensure that they adequately capture the rising economic costs of exploiting water resources to foster more conservation, control of pollution and ecosystem protection. The result will be efficient allocation of water among its competing agricultural, industrial and urban uses; fostering of water-saving innovations; and further mitigation of water scarcity and its costs.

There are two reasons why this transformation requires a rethinking of our basic economic approaches to managing water.

First, our policies, governance and institutions that guide water management today were developed when water was abundant, not scarce.

Second, the result is the creation of incentives, investments, infrastructure and innovations that perpetuate the outdated "hydraulic mission" of developing and harnessing new freshwater supplies to meet growing demands.

Throughout history, humankind has treated freshwater as a resource that is always there to be exploited. Since the Agricultural Transition 10,000 years ago, our perception of water is that it is abundant, freely available and easily accessible. Our approach to water has been straightforward; by developing better and cheaper ways of tapping, transporting and using water, we can sustain our growing human populations and economies. As a result, economic progress has always been linked with increased water appropriation, control and use, and in turn, increased utilization of water meant greater prosperity and human welfare.

The Industrial Revolution dramatically changed our ability to harness water resources, as it generated considerable technological, economic and energy resources to capture, exploit and convey water in substantially large quantities. These resources have allowed us to design and build massive and sophisticated engineering structures – dams, dykes, pipelines and reservoirs – to move water from where it is abundant, and sometimes unwanted, to cities, farms and populations that have growing demands. We treat, recycle and redistribute waste water to prevent contamination of natural sources of freshwater and to extend its consumption. These water developments, in turn, have fostered significant expansion of agriculture, industries and cities; helped cement the relationship between increased economic prosperity and water use; and improved the health and well-being of billions of people through advances in safe drinking water and sanitation.

This paradigm of water development has become the "hydraulic mission" of the modern era.[13] Its aim is to meet every new demand for water – whether it is for agricultural or municipal and industrial use, for domestic food production or expanding exports to other countries – by obtaining and utilizing new supplies of freshwater. As a consequence, in today's economies, water use management, and its accompanying institutions, incentives and innovations, is dominated by the "hydraulic mission" of finding and exploiting more freshwater resources.

But what works in an era of freshwater abundance is detrimental in an age of increasing water scarcity. That is why the global water crisis today is predominantly a crisis of inadequate and poor water management. Institutions, incentives and innovations that are geared toward providing more freshwater supplies to meet growing demands are incapable of mitigating water scarcity.

One outcome is that water is not allocated to its highest valued use, and there is much wasteful water consumption. For example, water use in agriculture is often inefficient, which has led to the overexploitation of groundwater resources as well as the depletion of the natural flow of major rivers. Policy distortions and mismanagement increasingly promote the export of water-intensive commodities from water-scarce regions and countries, including further depletion of groundwater sources. Worse still, such policies encourage *water grabbing*, which is the practice of rich countries and large companies acquiring fertile land and water resources in other countries and regions to grow and export crops. Too often, the water "grabbed" is excessive, and as a result, increases food insecurity, malnourishment and even conflicts in the targeted areas.[14]

Africa appears to be a frequent target of global water grabbing. Since 2000, more than 22 million hectares have been contracted to large-scale land acquisitions across the region. Most acquisitions are planted with water-intensive commercial crops, such as sugarcane, jatropha and eucalyptus. The result has been increasing local pressures, competition and conflicts over freshwater resources.[15] Globally, as much as 41 million hectares and about 490 km^3 of freshwater resources in low- and middle-income countries may have been targeted by water grabbing, affecting rural livelihoods and local environments in all regions.[16]

Perhaps the most extreme manifestation of the global hydraulic mission has been the development of water "megaprojects" in semi-arid and arid environments worldwide.[17] These schemes are large-scale and costly infrastructure investments, usually involving dams, diversions, canals and pipelines, for water-transfer schemes that aim to attract large numbers of people to desert areas through encouraging agricultural, industrial and urban development. Although such projects have been magnificent engineering achievements, and often succeeded in their objectives of transforming deserts with cities, people and economic activity, too often they have been huge economic and financial failures.

A classic example is the Central Arizona Project (CAP), which was the largest and most expensive water transfer project in US history.[18] Completed in 1992, the CAP invested over $5 billion to divert water from the Colorado River and transport it by canals to support irrigated agriculture in Phoenix, Tucson and surrounding areas of the southwestern state of Arizona in the United States. Although farmers received the water, irrigation fees were unable to cover the investment. Several agricultural water districts went bankrupt; the substantial loan burden was shifted to urban residents and taxpayers; and the remaining debt will not be paid off until 2046.

Developing similar megaprojects for economic development and population expansion in water-scarce areas of the world still remain a dominant paradigm. Twenty extremely large cities, containing about 300 million people, face chronic water stress.[19] Six of these cities are in China, five in India and several others are in developing countries. In addition, five of the major water-stressed cities rely heavily on cross-basin transfers, which is the transportation of water from one river basin to another. These five cities – Tokyo, Karachi, Los Angeles, Tianjin and Chennai – currently transfer nearly 17 billion liters of water daily across river basins to supply their populations. In addition to Los Angeles, five other large cities facing water stress – New Delhi, Mexico City, Karachi, Beijing and Lima – are located in desert environments.

Transforming how freshwater resources and ecosystems are used is necessary to ensure a virtuous rather than a vicious cycle of water management in the Anthropocene Age. The key to this transformation are four important steps: reforming water institutions and governance; ending the underpricing of water; supporting new innovations that encourage saving rather than overusing water; and managing global water resources and potential conflicts.

Reforming Governance and Institutions

Currently, there is a mismatch between water governance and management. Because they were created during periods of relative water abundance, today's governance regimes and institutions are inadequate for addressing rising water scarcity and the threats posed by climate change. Of particular concern is the lack of sufficient regulations or institutions in most countries governing use of groundwater resources. Treating freshwater as an unpriced resource that governments should provide "freely" to all users is another pervasive problem. A further challenge is that governance regimes are often based on arbitrary political and administrative boundaries, whereas effective and efficient management of water resources, especially in response to environmental and human impacts, require governance across geographical boundaries, such as river basins and watersheds.

Managing river basins and watershed catchments is important to resolving the growing water crisis. For the past several decades, there have been calls for *integrated water resource management*, with its focus on the management of river and other bodies of surface water as the appropriate governance unit in deciding how the water should be allocated to various competing uses.

Historically, governance of river basins has followed political and administrative, rather than hydrological, boundaries. Rivers and watersheds typically meander across different provinces, states, districts and countries, and contain many different cities and municipalities.

To overcome these complications, river basin management and planning is often instigated "top down" from the national level. Such efforts have proven difficult to implement and coordinate. Irrigation, industrial and municipal uses of water are typically administered through separate government agencies and bureaucracies. Jurisdiction over environmental uses of water may also be spread across different administrative units. For example, in the United States, water pollution is regulated by the Environmental Protection Agency, water-based recreation and tourism by the Department of Interior and inland freshwater fisheries by the Wildlife Service. These sectoral and administrative divisions over water use and sectors further complicate institutional arrangements for integrated river basin management and basin-wide planning.

Yet some progress is being made and important lessons are being learned. For example, Canada has attempted over several decades to implement integrated river basin management. Table 6.1 outlines the key lessons learned from this shared experience in Canada. The fundamental features and major challenges listed in the table are important starting points for all countries developing institutional arrangements for river basin management and planning to manage increasing water scarcity and competing demands. However, it is equally important to recognize that there is no single best practice in formulating such institutional arrangements; instead, as the Canadians have learned, "All the provinces and territories in Canada have developed unique approaches or governance models."[20]

Flexibility in governance is also important for improving river basin management and planning in countries and regions that are facing more pressing water problems, including the threats posed by climate. Table 6.2 summarizes the key findings of an assessment of the strengths and weaknesses of governance efforts to address water scarcity and improvement integrated in four critical and large river basins: the Colorado in the United States and Mexico, the Yellow (Huang He) in China, the Murray-Darling in Australia and the Orange-Senqu in southern Africa (Botswana, Lesotho, Namibia and South Africa).

Table 6.1. Integrated river basin management: key features and challenges

Key features[1]

The catchment or river basin rather than an administrative or political unit is the management unit.

Attention is directed to upstream–downstream, surface–groundwater and water quantity–quality interactions.

Interconnections of water with other natural resources and the environment are considered.

Environmental, economic and social aspects receive attention.

Stakeholders are actively engaged in planning, management and implementation to achieve an explicit vision, objectives and outcomes.

Key challenges[2]

Determining the appropriate boundary for the catchment or river basin unit.

Ensuring the accountability of catchment-scale or basin-scale decisions and decision-making bodies.

Appropriate "scaling up" from local administrative or political units (municipalities, districts, counties, etc.) and "scaling down" from national-level units (e.g. nations, states and provinces).

Accounting and controlling for all of the physical, social or economic factors outside of the catchment or river basin unit that may impact upon the area within its borders, and vice versa.

Accounting and controlling for all of the policy decisions outside of the catchment or river basin unit that may impact upon the area within its borders, and vice versa.

Notes: [1]From Shrubsole et al. (2017).
[2] From Cohen and Davidson (2011).

Although governance across the four river basins varies considerably, there are five important insights on river basin governance and management that could be useful to all countries:

- Crises can provide a catalyst for reform.[21]
- The need for economic valuation of freshwater ecosystem services to evaluate the trade-offs between consumptive and instream uses.
- Water management plans should take into account the inherent variability of rivers and streams shared between water users and instream uses for environmental benefits.

Table 6.2. Comparison of governance of four major river basins

River Basin	River Length (km)	Basin Area ('ooo km²)	Catalyst for Reform	Key Governance Features
Colorado, United States and Mexico	2,100	622	Environmental concerns	Multiple jurisdictions that coordinate actions across the basin; limited use of water markets to allocate water between and within states.
Yellow (Huang He), China	5,464	752	Severe drought	Single basin authorities plan and manage water across jurisdictions; top-down water allocations by central government.
Murray-Darling, Australia	2,589	1,061	Severe drought	Single basin authorities plan and manage water across jurisdictions; decentralized administration and extensive use of water markets to allocate flows.
Orange-Senqu, Botswana, Lesotho, Namibia, South Africa	2,300	973	End of Apartheid in South Africa	Multiple jurisdictions that coordinate actions across the basin; limited use of water markets to allocate flows.

Source: Grafton et al. (2013).

- The use of water markets and trades to help reduce the costs of reallocating water to environmental benefits, especially during times of low in-stream flows.
- The contribution of centralized and nested water governance structures within basin-wide management institutions to revise water allocations as environmental conditions, scientific knowledge and societal values change.

An important institutional challenge is the reform of groundwater governance worldwide. Given that this freshwater resource is found well below the surface – often very deep underground and requiring extensive drilling to reach – it is not easy to determine how much of the resource is available, how fast we are using it up or how quickly the water is naturally recharged. Equally, it is unclear what we are dumping or leaking into the resource to pollute it.

Groundwater governance in most countries developed from the customary principle of *rule of capture*. According to this principle, the owner of the land under which groundwater is found has an exclusive right to abstract and use it for whatever purpose the water is needed. As long as wells were dug by hand or by limited mechanical methods, there was little need to change private ownership and user rights to groundwater. However, the "hydrological mission" of the modern era, and especially the improvements in drilling technology, tubewells and pumping, has severed the link between land ownership and the right to abstract groundwater. As development needs require more water use and employ more advanced drilling and pumping methods, individual and community control and use of groundwater become obsolete. For example, in developing countries, customary "rule of capture" is still widespread in rural areas for domestic use, small-scale agriculture and livestock rearing, but it does not apply when public infrastructure projects tap groundwater for large-scale municipal, industrial or agricultural use.

Establishing effective groundwater ownership regimes – whether public or private – is necessary for improved management, but it is only the start (see Table 6.3). Monitoring the quality and quantity of groundwater levels – from major deep aquifers to frequently used, shallow and small underground freshwater – is an important task for determining the state of the resource. In addition, legal frameworks for groundwater can differ widely in recognizing the hydrologic connection between surface water and groundwater and the protection of water quality. Finally, there needs to be coordination of groundwater planning and management between the national and local levels, and with other sectors of the economy, such as agriculture, energy and industry.

Designing governance regimes and institutions to overcome these challenges requires well-funded, transparent monitoring and information systems combined with broad, multilevel participatory processes that support learning. Institutional arrangements should be strong enough to establish clear lines of authority and rules, yet allow sufficient flexibility to adapt as environmental, economic and social conditions change. There also needs to be sufficient resources for

Table 6.3. Groundwater governance: key features and challenges

Key features[1]
Requires monitoring and assessment of the state of the resource and its use.
Requires establishing clear ownership and user rights over abstraction and protection, whether private or public.
Should not be managed in isolation but conjunctively with other water sources.
Both the quantity and quality of groundwater should be comanaged, and thus be harmonized with uses of the surrounding landscape and watershed.
Requires coordination of groundwater planning and management between the national and local levels.
Groundwater planning and management should be in conjunction with other sectors, such as agriculture, energy, health, urban and industrial development and the environment.

Key challenges[2]
The extent of the resource and rate of recharge are often unknown, and monitoring and assessment costs are high.
Water quality is affected by diffuse sources of pollution, for example, agricultural runoff, storm water from urban areas, saltwater intrusion, waste dumps, underground storage of toxic substances.
Use and ownership rights are often poorly defined
Lack of an effective regulatory and legal framework for controlling groundwater use or quality.
Lack of coordination across sectors on policies toward groundwater use; for example, agricultural versus environmental policies, crop production versus groundwater protection, industrial uses and toxic waste disposal, etc.

Notes: [1] From de Chaisemartin et al. (2017).
[2] From FAO (2016).

integrated planning and allocation of responsibilities across jurisdictions and sectors.

Ending the Underpricing of Water

Water markets have long been promoted as one of the most efficient ways of reallocating water, especially under growing scarcity and rising demands. As water scarcity worsens worldwide, there is growing interest in finding ways to reduce water consumption and to allocate the saved water to higher valued uses. Well-functioning water markets and trades can facilitate water conservation and reallocation. Other pricing reforms are also required to improve water management, control excessive use and conserve resources. These include more efficient pricing of water and sanitation services; increasing cost-effective delivery of clean water and sanitation in developing countries; using economic instruments to manage water quality and pollution; and reducing or eliminating irrigation and other agricultural subsidies that lead to overuse and pollution of water.

In many parts of the world, historical water rights usually mean that farmers have first claim on water for irrigation. The main costs to farmers are the pumping, conveying and energy expenses of irrigating their fields. They typically do not pay for how much water they use. Thus, the cost of irrigation to farmers is often much lower than the cost of water used for industrial and municipal purposes in a nearby city. Supplying water to the city requires expensive investments in piping and distribution networks, and there are also the costs of hooking up and supplying varying amounts of water to each residence, business or firm. This cost difference between irrigation versus municipal and industrial use is the basis for trade. Farmers can sell some of their excess water to urban areas, which is much cheaper for the city to buy. Municipal and industrial users gain from purchasing the water, because they are able to pay lower prices and can increase consumption. Farmers receive revenues for selling their excess water, and they will most likely be more efficient in the use of irrigation water, as it now has a higher opportunity cost – any water wasted could instead be sold at higher prices to the city.

If creating markets to sell water from low-value users (e.g. irrigation) to high-value users (e.g. municipalities and industry) is such a "win-win" for both parties, why do we not see such markets popping up everywhere?

Many economists and water policy experts have been asking this question for decades. The general consensus is that there are widespread problems of institutional, market and policy failures that inhibit the creation of such water markets. Tackling these failures is critical both to promoting water markets, and ultimately, to ending the underpricing of water.

One major obstacle is that, in many parts of the world, water rights are tied to land ownership. This is done directly through riparian rights, whereby all landowners whose property adjoins a river, lake or other bodies of water or lies above a groundwater resource, have the right to make "reasonable" use of it. Consequently, selling all or some of this "right to water" cannot occur without the owner selling the land as well. Facilitating more water markets and correcting the artificially low prices for some uses depends crucially on ensuring that water rights are fully separated from land ownership and land use decisions.

However, even where water rights and land ownership are separated, there are still considerable barriers to establishing water markets and trading. Three barriers are especially prohibitive:

- the search costs of identifying and matching willing buyers and sellers
- the investments in physical infrastructure necessary for transporting water from sellers to buyers
- the legal costs of creating and enforcing contracts and obtaining regulatory permission[22]

Despite these difficulties in establishing successful water markets, in a number of countries and regions the development of water markets has shown the potential to help mitigate problems of overuse and scarcity. One of the largest and most ambitious efforts is occurring in the Murray-Darling River Basin in Australia – which covers an area of approximately one million square kilometers (km^2) – and has been transitioning over several decades from a traditional regulatory and administrative water-abstraction regime to a more bottom-up and market-driven process, overseen by a basin-wide management authority. A major aim of the governance reforms has been to foster water markets, through separating water abstraction entitlements from land titles and lowering other transaction costs that inhibit trading.[23]

The buying and selling of permanent and temporary water entitlements has now been in place for over thirty years. The principal buyers and sellers of water rights in the Murray-Darling River Basin are irrigators, who account for 90 percent of the freshwater diverted in the basin. Overall, these water markets have been considered a success in ensuring that water is allocated to its highest value use; in assisting farmers in overcoming prolonged drought and other hydrological risks; and in delivering improved environmental outcomes and other social objectives. Trading has also encouraged greater on-farm water conservation and innovations to reduce use. Most farmers that depend on irrigation in the Murray-Darling River Basin now actively engage in water trading, and many believe that the markets are beneficial to their businesses, reduce risks and promote water conservation.

However, less trade in water has occurred between famers with water entitlements and nonagricultural users, such as mining, manufacturing, electricity production or cities. Almost all trading has been between farmers. There have been substantial purchases of water entitlements held for irrigation by the federal government, mainly to preserve instream flows for environmental protection as well as to limit overall abstraction in the river basin. This has proved critical for reducing basin-wide water extractions, and also appears to have mitigated successfully the worst environmental impacts of the recent severe drought in the region. Thus, the Murray-Darling River Basin schemes may be an important example of using markets to alleviate scarcity and encourage conservation within irrigation, but has yet to demonstrate success in famers selling water to nonagricultural users.

In comparison, in the western United States there is increasing realization that the only way to meet the growing municipal, industrial, recreational and environmental water demands will be through reallocating water out of agriculture. There are some encouraging signs that water markets are starting to play a role in this reallocation of water.[24] A number of different states and regions are experimenting with a wide-range of transaction mechanisms, which include both direct and indirect transfers of ownership. Direct transfers involve buying the actual water right, whereas indirect transfers occur when a water user buys shares of an irrigation district or its network to gain water resources, and the district retains the overall right. Sellers also lease rights to other users, but still retain the right for future use. This is often done through water supply agreements, single or multiple-year leases and water banks.

Water banking is an especially encouraging method of trading water between agricultural and nonagricultural users. Two of the more promising uses of water banks are by the city of Santa Fe, New Mexico and the state of Arizona.[25]

In 2005, the Santa Fe City Council required developers to tender sufficient water rights to cover the amount of water required by any development project in the metropolitan area for commercial, residential, industrial or other purpose. Developers began purchasing rights from farmers, and depositing them in a city-operated water bank. When the developer initiated construction of the project, then sufficient water rights would have to be withdrawn to cover the water use associated with the project. The costs of acquiring the water needed for additional urban development would therefore be absorbed into the cost of new projects. If the project was stalled or canceled, the banked water rights could be sold to another developer or water user. Santa Fe also enacted an aggressive water conservation program and adopted tiered water rates that rise on a per unit basis as city residents consume additional water. The combination of the water banks, conservation program and tiered water rates has reduced water use per person in Santa Fe by 42 percent since 1995.

The western state of Arizona has also been experimenting with water banks, especially to control groundwater use. Arizona allows municipal, industrial and other water users to store water in exchange for credits that they can transfer to other users. A unique feature of the Arizona approach is that it counts water stored underground naturally in aquifers as part of this credit scheme. This approach is facilitated by Arizona laws that restrict the use of groundwater in several of the state's most important aquifers, which combined with additional statutory and regulatory provisions, allows for the creation and recovery of credits for trade in stored groundwater. Arizona's water banking of groundwater credits and control of use also facilitates trading of surface water, as water users no longer can resort to "free" groundwater as an alternative to buying and selling water. As a result, numerous transactions of surface water and groundwater have occurred between various municipal interests, water providers and private parties.

Water markets are also spreading in other regions and countries throughout the world, including in low- and middle-income countries. For example, two contrasting approaches have been taken by India and China, with India developing a more "bottom-up" approach to creating water markets and China a more "top-down" method.[26]

In India, water markets are emerging spontaneously from local trading. Informal water markets have existed within irrigation districts for decades, sometimes illegally. The most common form of trading is between larger and wealthier farmers, with access to groundwater through tubewells and pumps or surface water through lift irrigation systems, who extract and sell water to poorer and smaller farmers without such equipment. Payment can be made in cash, labor or shares of crops. Although most water sales are for irrigation, sales for non-agricultural uses, such as brick making and urban domestic use, also occur. These informal water markets are highly localized and vary across regions. With poor regulations for water use, monitoring and enforcement, the markets can lead to problems with ove-abstraction and sustainability, as well as concerns over monopoly and excessive pricing. Consequently, India needs urgently to develop the necessary institutional and regulatory framework to support the functioning and development of many existing local water markets. If India is able to make the institutional and regulatory changes needed to make informal water markets an efficient and more equitable option for water management, it could provide important lessons for many other developing countries where such markets are emerging spontaneously and growing rapidly.

At the opposite end of the spectrum, China is experimenting with the development of water markets within a governance and political legacy of centralized administrative control and decision-making over the allocation of water resources. Similar to India, groundwater markets are emerging in which owners of tubewells are selling extracted water, mostly to fellow villagers and in some cases to farmers elsewhere. However, in recent years, the Chinese government has also began promoting the legal framework for formal establishment of a tradable water rights system, in which usage rights are initially allocated to both regions and enterprises that could then sell any excess water saved from these allocations. Several water-trading projects funded by the state have also been developed.

Despite the emergence of these informal and formal water markets, water resource allocation in China is still subject to strong administrative control. Clearly, what is needed in China is a more flexible policy and institutional environment that encourages decentralized trading in water rights and uses among individuals and enterprises to flourish. This will require more inter-agency cooperation as well as coordinated efforts between national, provincial and local governments. In addition, China needs to take similar steps as outlined for India to foster and encourage the informal groundwater markets that are emerging in many rural areas.

One of the urgent areas for water pricing reform in all countries is for water and sanitation.[27] Much of the water and sanitation services supplied to municipalities, industries and large-scale irrigation developments is through large-scale and expensive publicly funded infrastructure projects and utilities. Although prices and tariffs may be charged for these services, they are largely administrative and rarely cover the full costs of operating and managing the water supply and sanitation infrastructure – let alone the construction costs and possible environmental impacts of the investment. For example, a survey of more than 1,500 utilities worldwide finds that only 14 percent generate enough revenue to cover the total economic costs of service provision, whereas only 35 percent of the utilities are able to cover the operation and maintenance costs of service provision.[28]

Even in wealthy countries, governments typically pay a large share of the investment costs, and also often subsidize the operating costs, for water and sanitation services delivered to municipal and industrial users. Only in France and Japan do consumers cover fully the operating costs of these services. However, in Japan the government pays for the entire investment costs for water development infrastructure, whereas the French government funds half these costs.[29]

Overall, governments around the world pay about $320 billion annually in subsidies for water and sanitation services. Only $30 billion of these subsidies are in richer countries; they are mainly spent by governments in low- and middle-income countries. The majority of the subsidies go to water, urban and networked services provided by utilities, and not for measures to make water supply and sanitation affordable for those in need. As a consequence, these subsidies are largely inequitable. An average of 56 percent of water and sanitation subsidies are captured by the wealthiest 20 percent of the population, while only 6 percent are captured by the poorest 20 percent.[30]

There is clearly greater scope in many countries to end the chronic underpricing of water and sanitation services to improve cost recovery and lead to greater water conservation by users. If designed correctly, the pricing scheme could reduce the burden of higher prices on low-income families paying for water and sanitation services.

A water pricing scheme can achieve these three objectives if it includes:

- a *fixed service charge* per month for any residence or business connected to the water and sanitation service system, to cover the costs of operating and maintaining the water system
- a *two-* or *multi-tier block rate charge* per unit of water used per month, which means that the costs borne by any residence or business would vary with the amount of water and sanitation services delivered and used each month

The purpose of the flat rate charge would be to cover the fixed costs of operating and maintaining the water and sanitation system. Any residence or business that is connected to the system would pay the fixed service charge, regardless of how much water is used. The amount of the charge should be to ensure that consumers pay a greater share for the operation of the entire system, and where appropriate, a larger contribution of the investment costs of improving or extending the system. The variable block rate charge would provide an incentive for residences and businesses to conserve water, and the two- or multi-tier block rate would address the concern about the impacts of water pricing on low-income families. For example, the first-tier price would be set low to cover the amount of water that low-income households typically consume each month through water and sanitation services. However, a higher charge would be placed on monthly use that is above the limit, ensuring that all households have an incentive to conserve their water use.[31]

However, in low- and middle-income countries, care must be taken in applying increasing block tariffs. In many countries, such tariffs are used to subsidize water use by poorer households, but unfortunately poor design and implementation often means that such tariffs fail in that objective. First, block tariffs apply only to households who are already connected to networked water supplies. In both rural and urban areas within developing countries, many of the poorest households are not connected to the piped network and therefore do not benefit from the subsidized water. In addition, often the correlation between piped water use and income is low, which means that even among connected users the subsidies delivered through the lower blocks are poorly targeted. As a consequence, block pricing only appears to work reasonably well for middle-income households, while it may not benefit significantly poorer households and may not induce much conservation by high-income households.[32]

If water pricing schemes generate sufficient revenues for local utilities and governments, then some of these funds could be used for complementary investment programs and subsidies for the adoption of selected water-saving technologies by consumers, such as low-flow toilets, drip irrigation and more water-efficient appliances (e.g. dishwaters, washing machines and bathrooms). The subsidy program could also be targeted specifically to low-income households, who would otherwise find it difficult to pay for water-saving appliances and innovations.

Such an approach can work even in low- and middle-income countries. Balancing the objectives of cost recovery, conservation and equity has also been an issue for Columbia, which has attempted to implement water pricing reforms for urban water and sanitation services.[33] Beginning in the mid-1990s, a series of reforms were enacted to revise the pricing structure to recover the costs associated with investment, operation and delivery of water and sewage services. Implementation of the reforms began in 2006, and after several years, they appeared to improve cost recovery significantly and restore the financial viability of utilities. The reforms include a subsidy program for basic water consumption to cushion the financial impact on poorer urban households. Although this may improve the equity of the new tariff structure, the subsidies may reduce the effectiveness of water pricing for conservation. There is also concern of the long-term financing of the subsidy program. Thus, the next step for Columbia is to balance phasing out the subsidies with better incentives for conservation.

A major and urgent challenge of developing countries is extending water and sanitation services to the millions of people in these countries who currently do not have any access. As noted at the beginning of this chapter, 785 million people – more than 1 in 10 – lack access to safe water, and nearly 2 billion people – over 1 in 4 – do not have access to basic sanitation.

In many developing countries, expecting that the government will invest in, maintain and operate a large-scale supply infrastructure and network to deliver clean water and sanitation to every resident for free or with little payment is no longer an option. Nor can the international community have sufficient financial resources or the will to aid every developing country government in achieving such a goal. Instead, the strategy for targeting and sequencing water-related services in developing countries should prioritize the needs and income levels of the intended beneficiaries; their ability to pay for improved clean water and sanitation; and the overall costs of providing clean water and sanitation services.

First, the main reason why a large number of households in developing countries lacks access to clean water and basic sanitation is because they are poor. Extending water services to poor households through expensive, large-scale infrastructure and supply networks will mean that these households are rarely able to afford to pay for these services, despite the benefits. The result is that this financial burden will be borne solely by governments and public utilities, and as we saw in the aforementioned case of Columbia, this can quickly result in a financial disaster for utilities and poor cost recovery.

Thus, the first step would be to find methods of improving access to clean water and sanitation for poor households that are sufficiently cost-effective and cheap that the households can afford to pay for them. Three small-scale interventions that do not involve large-scale infrastructure and supply networks for delivering clean water and sanitation include rural water supply programs that provide communities with deep boreholes and public hand pumps, community-led total sanitation campaigns (CLTS) and biosand filters for household water treatment. These interventions are not only affordable by extremely poor households and communities but also generate essential health and economic benefits. Both boreholes and biosand filters can be scalable to large number of communities in developing countries, and the filters can be used by households in both rural and low-density urban areas. The resulting cost reductions make such interventions affordable and facilitate user payments even in the poorest regions, such as rural Africa.[34]

In cities with rapidly growing economies, the high costs of investing in and operating conventional water and sanitation network infrastructure may be worthwhile, but only if the financial challenge of constructing and extending such networks can be met through pricing schemes that are affordable to the residents and industries that benefit from these services. It is essential that pricing mechanisms be designed to achieve greater cost recovery, equity and conservation. This will mean that poor households will have to be protected and possibly even subsidized to avoid unfair financial burdens, but as economic growth proceeds and incomes grow, more households should be expected to contribute to cost recovery and conserve water use. This is for several reasons. First, there is a strong association between household income and the provision of both piped water and sewer services from a modern and large-scale supply network, especially among urban households in developing countries. As the income of households rise, they not only want these modern services but also can afford to pay toward the operating costs and investments of the supply networks providing such services.

Pricing and other economic instruments can also help to reduce the growing impact of pollution on the quality of rivers, aquifers, lakes and other freshwater sources. As long as the environmental damages to water quality remain "unpriced," too much pollution will occur, and the use of freshwater as a sink for pollutants will be excessive.

There are two principal ways to improve the pricing of pollution impacts on water quality.

The first approach is through charging households and industries for their wastewater and sewage discharges. This can be either in the form of a flat-rate fee or a tax that rises with the amount of pollution discharge.

The second approach is tradable permits for water pollution. The first step is to set a cap or limit on the total allowable amount of effluent, such as nitrates, phosphates, raw sewage or chemicals, which can be discharged into the water source over a given period of time. Once the cap is established, permits can be issued and then allocated or sold to those discharging the pollutants, such as firms in an industry or farmers who have pollution runoff from irrigating their crops. The total number of permits issued must be equal to the maximum amount of pollution allowed under the cap. However, if it is too expensive to reduce pollution levels, a firm or farmer may choose instead to buy more permits from another firm or farmer, who finds it cheaper to abate pollution and thus has excess permits to sell. Thus, the market for trading permits determines a price for pollution permits, which is essentially equivalent to the cost of discharge.

If properly implemented, water pollution taxes will motivate those responsible for the discharges to reduce wastewater and sewage, reuse or recycle water and switch to cleaner production process. Although some charges have been successful in reducing pollution, most instruments are not set high enough to cover the additional damages from discharges, which limit their effectiveness in controlling pollution and improving water quality. Too often wastewater fees for industries and households are included in water bills, appear as fixed charges per dwelling or are included in property taxes. Such charging mechanisms dilute the effectiveness of the fees as a tax on water pollution, and thus provide less incentives for reducing effluents. Sewage and pollution charges are increasingly imposed on industries, but often these fees are included in the overall cost of water and sanitation services to firms, and frequently as a flat fee. As the costs of these services apportioned to sewage have little to do with environmental damages and are not related to the amount of sewage released, such fees are less effective in controlling pollution.

One of the difficulties in establishing successful water quality tradable permit schemes has been accounting for the mix of water

Table 6.4. Promising water quality trading schemes

Program	Pollutant	Sources
Hunter River Salinity Trading Scheme, Australia	Salinity	Coal mines, power plants
South Nation River Total Phosphorus Management Program, Canada	Phosphorus	Industries, municipalities, agriculture
Lake Taupo, New Zealand	Nutrients	Grazing-based agriculture
California Grasslands Area, United States	Selenium	Agriculture
Tar-Pamlico River Basin, United States	Nutrients	Agriculture
Connecticut Nitrogen Credit Exchange, United States	Nitrogen	Wastewater treatment plants
Greater Miami Watershed Trading Pilot, United States	Nutrients	Industries, municipalities, agriculture
Pennsylvania Nutrient Credit Exchange, United States	Nutrients	Industries, municipalities, agriculture

Sources: Horan and Shortle (2011); Olmstead (2010); and Shortle (2013).

pollutants that come from a variety of different sources. A particularly difficult problem has been reducing nutrient pollution water, which is usually the result of runoff from farmland. Consequently, successful trading schemes have generally been for single pollutants from one type of source, although as Table 6.4 shows, several water quality trading programs and pilot projects around the world are showing progress for controlling a variety of water pollutants.

One of the most successful applications of tradable permits to control nutrient pollution is in the Tar-Pamlico River Basin of North Carolina in the United States.[35] Municipalities and other single sources purchase agricultural nutrient reduction credits for nitrogen and phosphorous from the Tar-Pamlico Basin Association, which acts as an intermediary between the farmers who were issued the credits and the municipalities and other sources. Since the purchase price of the credits were lower than the costs for abating pollution faced by the municipalities and other sources, they were willing to buy the credits. The farmers, in turn, found it cheaper to reduce their nitrogen and phosphorous effluent and sell excess credits. The result has been significant reduction in nitrogen and phosphorous concentrations in the basin.

As discussed previously, farmers worldwide generally pay too little for the water they use for irrigation, as they often do not have to contribute to the capital, operation and maintenance costs of the irrigation infrastructure that delivers water to the farm. In addition, many governments heavily subsidize agricultural production, either directly or by supporting the incomes of farmers. Total subsidy support to agriculture in fifty-four countries around the world amounts to around $619 billion per year, of which around $446 billion (72 percent) are provided as support for producers. This amounts to around 12.5 percent of gross farm receipts.[36] This means that, for every dollar earned in revenues by farms, 12.5 cents came from some kind of agricultural subsidy. Such subsidies lead to more production than necessary, and thus contribute to further overuse of agricultural inputs, including irrigation water.

Although removal of irrigation and agricultural subsidies is politically difficult, there is increasing evidence that such subsidies are perpetuating problems of agricultural overuse of water that is worsening problems of water allocation and scarcity. Water pricing reforms in agriculture must therefore begin with ending the underpricing of irrigation and of agricultural subsidies that lead to overproduction and excessive water use by farmers. At the very least, we should aim to remove the $112 billion annual support to potentially environmentally harmful agricultural production worldwide, much of which leads to overuse or pollution of water through farming (see Table 5.1).

Increasing the price of water may actually benefit farmers, as it may encourage them to adopt more efficient irrigation technologies that raise water productivity. By comparing water pricing, subsidizing efficient irrigation technology and water rationing, a simulation study of farmers in the Tulare River Basin of California's Central Valley found that charging more for water was the most effective method of increasing agricultural water productivity. Water pricing encouraged investment in more efficient irrigation technology and reduced water consumption from reduction in percolation to groundwater or return flow. Thus, a 20 percent increase in water price raises agricultural water productivity by 43 percent.[37]

Ideally, pricing for irrigation should be similar to the efficient pricing for water and sanitation services discussed previously.

An irrigation pricing scheme that improves cost recovery, encourages water conservation and reduces the burden of higher prices on poor farming smallholders would have the following elements:

- a *fixed service charge* per irrigation season that contributes to the costs of capital, operation and maintenance costs of the irrigation infrastructure that delivers water to the farm
- a *volumetric charge* that varies with the amount of water used on the farm per irrigation season
- a *lower initial-tier block rate* for the volumetric charge that would set a reduced price for irrigation up to an upper limit that corresponds to how much water poor smallholders typically use during an irrigation season

The need to use irrigation pricing to improve cost recovery, conserve water and reduce inequity is especially important in developing countries, where agricultural area is still expanding through the investment and development of large–scale irrigation supply projects.

In India, government subsidies account for 14 percent of the country's gross domestic product, and a significant share is allocated to irrigation.[38] One of the leading states in India for irrigated agriculture is Andhra Pradesh, which is still expanding infrastructure development. For example, current plans are to create another 4.5 million hectares (ha) of irrigated land at a cost of around $37 billion. However, irrigation is heavily subsidized in Andhra Pradesh, which is becoming an increasing financial burden as the supply infrastructure and network expands. The level of irrigation subsidies increased from just under $10 million in 1980–1981 to $188 million in 1999–2000. Current estimates suggest that the subsidies of the three newest major water irrigation projects in Andhra Pradesh amount to $282 million. These subsidies and the failure to recover costs, especially for operation and maintenance of irrigation networks, have contributed to problems in the state and across India with underutilization of the irrigation potential, inequity in irrigation, indifferent quality of irrigation, wastage of irrigation water, waterlogging, soil salinity and alkalinity, unsustainability of irrigated farming and substantial financial losses due to low pricing of water. Even where water charges exist, they are extremely low and many farmers fail to pay them.

To assist in cost recovery of irrigation investments and networks, China imposes an agricultural water supply tariff to contribute to capital costs as well as operation and maintenance expenditures.[39] Since 2014, tariffs were imposed on large and medium-sized irrigation projects, with the aim of covering at least the operational and management expenditures associated with the project, and if possible, capital costs and any environmental impacts. Smaller irrigation projects have tariffs on the extension of canal systems, which aim to contribute to operation and maintenance costs. Additionally, a fee is imposed on agricultural users of groundwater who exceed quota limits. This fee is also higher for regions with groundwater depletion problems.

But in most low- and middle-income countries, government subsidies for irrigation persist. The subsidies contribute to overuse of water, inefficiencies and inequality, as irrigation is often allocated by land holding area and thus any subsidies disproportionately benefit larger and wealthier farmers.[40] Two types of subsidies are frequently employed in developing countries. Irrigation water is often priced below its cost of supply, and may not even cover the operation and maintenance costs of irrigation systems. A conservative estimate of such subsidies in developing countries is $30 billion per year (Kjellingbro and Skotte 2005). Irrigation also benefits from cross-subsidies from power generation, whereby buyers of hydroelectricity pay for the dam and other infrastructure and the stored water is allocated to irrigation with little cost recovery. Although the amount of such cross-subsidies is unknown, they are used frequently in low- and middle-income countries (Brelle and Dressayre 2014; Ward 2010). Removal of such subsidies would improve the efficiency of agricultural production, boost the competitiveness of smaller producers and poor economies, reduce environmental degradation and, most importantly, reduce significantly water use by global agriculture.

In sum, ending the underpricing of water would have a significant impact on the efficiency, sustainability and equity of water supply and sanitation services and water use in agriculture. The first step in this process is the removal of the $112 billion annual support to potentially environmentally harmful agricultural production worldwide, and the rationalization of the $320 billion annually in subsidies for water and sanitation services. Some of the latter funds in low- and middle-income countries could be redirected to provide a better balance between rural and urban water and treatment subsidies and to fund measures to make water supply and sanitation affordable for those in need. In rural areas, developing countries should also consider implementing a "subsidy swap" from irrigation to support investments in clean water and improved sanitation.[41]

Phasing out these subsidies could have another important benefit. It would provide many governments with the funds to finance public support, policies and investments to spur private research and development (R&D) that is necessary for the "new wave" of water saving and efficient technologies that are critical to meeting future water demands and rising scarcity.

Water-Saving Innovations

Reforming institutions and ending the underpricing of water are essential to averting the global water crisis. Equally important is the role of innovation.

Recent technical advances, such as desalinization of salt water, geographical information systems (GIS) and remote sensing have the potential for managing and increasing freshwater supplies. There is also new generation of urban water supply systems that can improve efficiency and sustainable use. Water use in agriculture, too, can benefit from a range of innovations in irrigation technologies and delivery systems.[42]

To some extent, better governance and institutions for managing water; more efficient water pricing; and well-functioning markets to allocate water among competing and growing demands will spur the development of new water-saving technologies and distribution systems. If our decisions concerning how water is allocated and used begin to reflect the actual economic, social and environmental costs of these decisions, then there will be increasing incentives to research, develop and adopt new technologies that increase the productivity of water, reduce inefficient and wasteful use and improve the additional value gained from consuming water.

But even if we overcome the problems of underpricing of water and the lack of good governance and appropriate institutions, fostering the new wave of water technologies will require additional policies to support and spread these innovations. That is, a comprehensive strategy for promoting and disseminating water-saving innovations requires a combination of *technology-push policies* that induce greater private R&D and learning-by-doing; *pricing and market-based policies* that increase the returns to investments in water-efficient technologies; and *policies targeting barriers to adoption* of these technologies. Not only are these policies complementary in achieving greater water conservation and management of demand but also the revenues gained or saved from the pricing and market-based policies can be allocated to financing technology-push policies and any programs aimed at removing the barriers to water efficiency.

Figure 6.3 illustrates the comprehensive strategy for water-saving innovation. Subsidy removal and cost recovery along with water pricing and markets will generate additional revenue and cost savings. These financial savings and revenues could be used to fund the specific technology-push policies necessary to spur water-saving technological innovation, such as subsidies for private and public R&D necessary for this innovation; fostering decentralized water-saving systems; and so forth. There should also be funding for policy actions that target specific market, information and technological barriers to adoption of water-saving technologies.

For example, as noted, environmentally harmful agricultural subsidies among major global producing countries amount to approximately $112 billion annually, and support for water and sanitation services costs another $320 billion each year. Phasing out some or all of these subsidies would not only reduce significantly water use and lead

Subsidy Removal and Cost Recovery
Removing irrigation and environmentally
harmful agricultural subsidies
Rationalization of subsidies and improved
cost recovery of water supply and sanitation

Water Pricing and Markets
Efficient water pricing
Creating water markets
Water quality trading and prices, permit
auctions, effluent taxes

Technology-Push and Adoption Policies
Public support for private R&D in water-saving technologies
Fostering decentralized water-saving systems
Dissemination of information on water-saving technologies
Strengthened patent rules, government-financed technology competitions
Investments and policies for overcoming market, information and
technological barriers to adoption

Figure 6.3 A comprehensive water-saving innovation strategy

farmers, municipal and industrial water users and utilities to invest in more water-saving technologies; the savings also would provide countries with additional funds to invest in the technology-push and adoption policies indicated in Figure 6.3.

For some countries, irrigation subsidies themselves are extremely high, and should be rationalized. For example, earlier we discussed the case of the state of Andhra Pradesh in India, where irrigation subsidies associated with three major water projects were estimated to be just over $282 million. If these subsidies were phased out through improved recovery of capital, operation and maintenance costs, then the savings could be redirected to expanding some of the integrated water management programs and pilot projects in India aimed at removing barriers to the adoption of water-saving irrigation systems by farmers. Similarly, subsidies for urban water supply in developing countries could be redirected to improve water-saving innovations to expand network services in fast-growing cities and improve delivery through repairing leaks, limiting service interruptions, maintaining sufficient water pressure – especially in peripheral areas – and improving safe water reuse.[43]

As countries move to more efficient water pricing; create markets and trading schemes for reallocating water among competing uses; and develop auctions, effluent taxes and trading systems to reduce water pollution and improve quality, additional revenues will be raised. The first priority of these funds should be to ensure the long-run sustainability and functioning of these market and trading systems, especially as they expand in coverage. However, any additional funds generated could also be used to support technology-push and adoption policies outlined in Figure 6.3 that would induce greater economy-wide innovation and implementation of water-saving technologies.

Collective Action

Two pressing global issues that should be a priority for collective action are potential conflicts over trans-boundary water resources and "water grabbing." Both are manifestation of the growing worldwide water crisis. As water becomes increasingly scare and valuable, and countries fail to manage competing uses, they are increasingly looking outside their borders to obtain additional supplies.

A major complication in global water management is that many countries share their sources of water, as river basins, large lakes, aquifers and other freshwater bodies often cross national boundaries. Such trans-boundary water sources are an important, and growing, source of water for many people, countries and regions. Although there are currently more than 300 international freshwater agreements, many shared water resources still lack any type of joint management structure, and some existing international agreements need to be updated or improved.[44] Cooperation to resolve disputes over water is becoming increasingly problematic, and compounding these difficulties is the number of countries that share multiple water resources. Modification of freshwater ecosystems and watersheds and global environmental threats such as climate change will also make management of trans-boundary water resources increasingly difficult.

As discussed earlier in this chapter, many countries with scarce water resources, large populations and sufficient wealth are meeting their current and future food security needs through "water grabbing" – investing in other countries to acquire fertile land and water resources. Water grabbing could have adverse impacts on food production and even malnourishment in targeted countries, many of which are developing economies. If future land and water acquisitions continue to occur mainly in poor economies, they could generate disputes and conflict over the legality of the expropriation; the basis of compensation; meeting the needs of local people for water; protecting the environmental integrity of ecosystems; and ensuring food security in targeted countries.

There are two major trans-boundary management issues that need to be addressed urgently.

First, many international river basins and other shared water resources still lack any type of joint management structure, and some existing international agreements need to be updated or improved. This problem is especially critical in shared river basins in which countries are planning major infrastructure projects to meet future water needs, yet there are no formal agreements with neighbors on management.

Second, even where water-sharing agreements exist, they may not account adequately for possible future disruptions caused by water scarcity and climate change. For example, when multiple countries share a river or other water body, the competition over available water resources will intensify if climate is more variable and causes periodic water shortages. Under such conditions, satisfying rising freshwater demand while at the same time adhering to past agreements could be a major challenge for policy makers.

For trans-boundary water bodies that lack an agreement, an important first step is to determine which shared water resources should be a priority for negotiating agreements and for assistance from the international community. There should be two criteria for making this selection:

- *Low-hanging fruit*: These are the rivers and other trans-boundary water resources that are most likely to yield a successful international agreement relatively quickly and through only a modest amount of assistance from the international community.
- *High risk of conflict*: These are the rivers and other trans-boundary water resources that have high risk of future conflict, yet because countries sharing these waters are unlikely on their own to reach agreement without international assistance, they have the most need of such assistance and thus the potential greatest returns.[45]

Basins with high risk of conflict are of most concern. The vulnerable basins are largely in developing countries – several in Southeast Asia, South Asia, Central America, the northern part of South America, the southern Balkans and across Africa. These basins are already in areas of considerable political tension, and in some cases, sites of past conflicts. Thus, directing international assistance to these countries to negotiate treaties should be a priority.

An additional challenge is to determine to what extent water scarcity and climate change are likely to hinder successful negotiation of trans-boundary water treaties, or renegotiation of additional treaties. There should be concern about the impacts of climate change on trans-boundary resources in regions that are already displaying very high water variability, periodic shortages and frequent drought. Especially vulnerable are the Nile, Niger, Okavango and Zambezi river basins and Lake Chad, and the Euphrates-Tigris, Kura-Araks, Colorado and Rio Grande river basins. The Kura-Araks river basin should especially be a priority for an agreement, given its high risk of conflict. Existing agreements for managing trans-boundary water resources will need to take into account and develop mechanisms for addressing the likely impact of climate change on water availability.

Rising water scarcity may be an important motivator for countries to reach agreement over water sharing – especially before scarcity becomes too extreme. Shlomi Dinar and colleagues have found that increasing water scarcity is not always detrimental to cooperation over shared water resources. Instead, trans-boundary water-sharing is most likely to occur when scarcity is moderate rather than very low or high. With moderate scarcity, countries have the incentive and motivation to cooperate on water sharing, and thus the likelihood of an agreement is high. Cooperation is also enhanced by good governance, diplomatic relations and trade, and whether wealthier states can provide incentives to poor countries to participate in an agreement.[46] This suggests that timely collective action to spur international water-sharing is important.

Meanwhile, water grabbing is on the rise globally. In addition, almost all the targeted countries are low- and middle-income economies, and the majority of countries responsible for water grabbing are high-income economies.[47] This has raised concerns about problems of governance, conflict, adequate compensation, local water needs, environmental protection and food security in targeted countries.

Effective trans-boundary agreements on sharing water could reduce the incentive for powerful countries to target weaker neighbors for water grabbing. For example, China joining the Mekong River Basin Agreement would deter it from meeting its water and agricultural needs by expanding land and water acquisitions in the lower basin countries (Thailand, Laos, Cambodia and Vietnam).

However, acquiring water and land resources overseas still needs international regulation and monitoring, especially for targeted low- and middle-income economies. One way to do this is for countries that are currently responsible for much of the water grabbing worldwide to collaborate with the main targeted countries to form an international body for overseeing large-scale global water and land acquisitions. Such an international committee for monitoring and regulating these acquisitions could comprise the major developing and developed countries that are responsible for much of the water grabbing worldwide.

The main purpose of the international body would be to formulate a set of principles governing large-scale acquisitions of water and land globally. These principles should embody the conditions under which such acquisitions would lead to a fair and efficient outcome for both parties – sellers and buyers. In addition, the body should monitor and evaluate acquisitions occurring in developing countries to ensure that any concerns about governance, conflict, adequate compensation, local water needs, environmental protection and food security in targeted countries are adequately addressed.

Overall, the purpose of such international regulation and monitoring is to minimize any potential negative impacts of acquiring land and water resources overseas by water-scarce countries, which is essential to a strategy of managing global water resources efficiently and equitably.

Conclusion

Managing increasing global water scarcity and the risk of more frequent water crises may be one of the most important challenges of the Anthropocene Age.

There are two possible paths for managing water, which will determine whether we end up in a "safe" Anthropocene that avoids the growing risks from our mismanagement of water or if we come perilously close to a "tipping point" for global freshwater.

If we continue to persist with institutions, incentives and innovation that chronically underprice water, then as water scarcity afflicts more and more of the world's population we will see a future of declining water security, freshwater ecosystem degradation and increasing disputes and conflicts over remaining water resources. At some point over the coming decades, the resulting rise in economic, social and environmental costs will force drastic changes in our approach to managing global water. But the social and economic costs of such a transformation will be abrupt, expensive and highly disruptive. Human societies and economies may be totally unprepared for such unanticipated and chaotic changes.

Even if we are able to handle crises, the problem of addressing rising economic, social and environmental costs remain. Under the current management paradigm, we will probably rely mainly on regulation and restrictions on water use, and possibly even rationing, to control these costs. This may do the trick in terms of controlling competing uses and rising costs, but such regulatory solutions are themselves inefficient and thus costly in the long run.

The alternative path to managing water is the one offered by this chapter.

If in anticipation of the coming decades of increasing water scarcity we are able to develop appropriate governance and institutions for water management, instigate market and policy reforms and address global management issues, then improved innovation and investments in new water technologies and better protection of freshwater ecosystems should secure sufficient beneficial water use for a growing world population. Although the solutions outlined in this chapter are difficult to implement, they offer a way to "decouple" human impacts on the planet's limited freshwater resources from economic activity and continued population growth, and ensuring that we end up in a "safe" Anthropocene that is not threatened by rising water scarcity and widespread crises.

Notes

1 WEF (2021).
2 Gosling and Arnell (2016).
3 UN (2019).
4 Tianyi Luo, R. Young and Paul Reig. 2015. "Aqueduct projected water stress rankings." Technical note. Washington, DC: World Resources Institute, August 2015. Available at www.wri.org/publication/aqueduct-projected-water-stress-country-rankings.
5 Rosegrant et al. (2009).
6 OECD (2017).
7 Kim et al. (2019).
8 UN (2019).
9 See, for example, Bunsen et al. (2021); Gerten et al. (2016); and Kummu et al. (2016).
10 Shiklomanov (1993).
11 Gerten et al. (2016), p. 556.
12 Barbier (2019b).
13 Savenije et al. (2014).
14 Dell'Angelo et al. (2018) and Rulli et al. (2013).
15 Johansson et al. (2016).
16 Chiarelli et al. (2016).
17 Sternberg (2016).
18 Avery (2018); Glennon (2018); Hanemann (2002); and Sternberg (2016).
19 McDonald et al. (2014).
20 Shrubsole et al. (2017).
21 For example, Gruère et al. (2018) found that water-related events, such as droughts, floods or water impacts from pollution, were a catalyst not just in terms of implementing integrated river basin management but also for reforms of water policies in agriculture. Similarly, Berbel and Esteban (2019) discuss how droughts were instrumental for instigating water policy reforms in Spain, the Murry-Darling river basin in Australia and California.
22 For more discussion, see Barbier (2019b) and Olmstead (2010). See also Easter and Huang (2014); Grafton et al. (2020); Hanemann and Young (2020); and Wheeler and Garrick (2020).
23 For more on the Murray-Darling river basin water market and management reforms, see Barbier (2019b); Berbel and Esteban (2019); Grafton and Horne (2014); Grafton et al. (2013) and (2016); Gruère et al.(2018); Hanemann and Young (2020); Wheeler and Garrick (2020); Wheeler et al. (2014); and Young (2014).

24 For more on water markets in the western United States, see Barbier (2019b); Brewer et al. (2008); Broadbent et al. (2017); Brookshire et al. (2004); Culp et al. (2014); Garrick and Aylward (2012); Goemens and Pritchett (2014); Griffin (2012); Hanemann and Young (2020); Leonard et al. (2019); and Libecap (2011).

25 The following two examples of water banking in Santa Fe, New Mexico and Arizona are from Avery (2018); Broadbent et al. (2017); Culp et al. (2014); Glennon (2018); and Podgorski (2019). Montilla-López et al. (2016) note that the use of water banks are well-established in other western states, notably California, and in Australia. Water banks have also been more recently introduced in Chile and Spain.

26 The following two examples of contrasting approaches to water markets in China and India are from Acharyya et al. (2018); Barbier (2019b); Easter and Huang (2014); Lewis and Zheng (2019); Moore (2015); Pawariya et al. (2017); Saleth (2014); and Svensson et al. (2019).

27 Andres et al. (2019); Barbier (2019b); Convery (2013); Dinar et al. (2015); Easter (2009); Garrick et al. (2020); Grafton (2017); Grigg (2019); Hope et al. (2020); Kocchar et al. (2015); Nauges and Whittington (2017); OECD (2012); and Whittington et al. (2008).

28 Andres et al. (2019).

29 OECD (2012).

30 Andres et al. (2019). The authors' estimates of global water supply and sanitation services exclude China and India, and so the subsidies ae likely to be significantly more than $320 billion annually. See also Kocchar et al. (2015).

31 As explained by Garrick et al. (2020), p. 11, "A simple increasing block-rate structure can make it possible to ensure that the overall amount of revenue raised is proportional to costs while still providing an economic incentive to change behavior at the margin if the location of the point at which price changes from one block to the other is chosen carefully. In effect, the switch point sends a *quantity* signal to water users: you can use more water if you like but, if you use more than this amount, you will be paying *more*."

32 Andres et al. (2019); Kocchar et al. (2015); Nauges and Whittington (2017); and Zapana-Churata et al. (2021).

33 Fernández (2015). Similar issues are confronting other Latin American countries with fast-growing urban populations with lack of access to water and sanitation services and unreliable supplies. See Zapana-Churata et al. (2021).

34 Barbier (2019b); Grigg (2019); Hope et al. (2020); Whittington et al. (2008); and (2020).

35 This example is from Olmstead (2010).

36 OECD (2020b).

37 Medellí-Azuara et al. (2012).

38 This example of India is based on Palanisami et al. (2011) and (2015).

39 Shen and Wu (2017).

40 Barbier (2019b); Brelle and Dressayre (2014); Gany et al. (2019); Kjellingbro and Skotte (2005); Toan (2016); and Ward (2010).

41 Such an irrigation "subsidy swap" is part of a post-COVID sustainability and development strategy put forward by Barbier and Burgess (2020).

42 See Barbier (2019b), chapter 7, for further discussion of these potential water-saving technological advances.

43 Zapana-Churata et al. (2021).

44 See the International Freshwater Treaties Database, available at https://transboundarywaters.science.oregonstate.edu/content/international-freshwater-treaties-database.

45 Based on the criteria outlined in Song and Whittington (2004). The following classification of critical international river basins in need of trans-boundary agreements is from Barbier (2019b), chapter 8, which is based on combining the criteria from Song and Whittington (2004) with the classification of river basins at risk of future conflict from de Stefano et al. (2017).

46 Dinar (2009) and Dinar et al. (2011).

47 Barbier (2019b); Chiarelli et al. (2016); Dell'Angelo et al. (2018); Johansson et al. (2016); and Rulli et al. (2013).

7 OCEANS AND COASTS

If you stand on a beach or a cliff overlooking the sea, the ocean before you seems limitless, stretching to the horizon and beyond.

But this image of an unending blue frontier is an illusion. Our oceans and coasts are becoming overcrowded, marine biodiversity overexploited and the seas increasingly polluted.

Nearly 2.4 billion people, around 40 percent of the global population, live within 100 kilometers of the ocean. More than 600 million people inhabit low-lying coastal areas that are less than 10 meters above sea level, and almost two-thirds of the world's cities with populations of more than 5 million are located in these vulnerable coastal zones. Such areas are increasingly exposed to sea level rise, flooding and extreme storm events. These threats are on the rise. Population expansion, economic development and urbanization continue to degrade estuarine and coastal ecosystems that protect against storm surge, saline intrusion and erosion.[1]

Since 1970 there has been a nearly threefold increase in fisheries production, but this is being harvested from a dwindling stock of fish. At least one third of fish stocks are overfished; one third to half of vulnerable marine habitats have been lost; and a substantial fraction of our coastal waters suffers from pollution, eutrophication, oxygen depletion and higher temperatures. In addition, illegal, unreported and unregulated catch affects about one fifth of global fishing, costing up to $50 billion in lost income and $4 billion in foregone tax revenues each year.[2] Because of these threats, much of our seafood-producing marine fisheries could collapse by 2050 if not sooner.[3]

Almost 80 percent of all pollution in seas and oceans comes from land-based activities, and as much as 80 percent of marine litter consists of plastic. Marine plastic pollution has been rising exponentially. In 1970, there was 30,200 tonnes of plastics floating in global oceans. By 2020, this amount had mushroomed to nearly 1.2 million tonnes.[4] Our exploitation and pollution of the marine environment has now reached the deep sea, which is on the verge of "industrialization," through expansion of oil, gas and mineral extraction and trawling of deeper and deeper waters.[5]

These rising risks stem from the *underpricing of marine capital*. We are happy to exploit our oceans as a source of fish, minerals, energy, transport and other commercially valuable products, and use it as a vast dump for our litter, plastics and waste. But we are not prepared to pay for the marine ecosystems that are degraded or destroyed by these activities. Even worse, we provide substantial subsidies to encourage environmentally harmful fishing practices, mineral and energy extraction and coastal habitat conversion.

We also poorly manage our marine environment. Most nearshore waters and sea beds are carved up into territorial seas and exclusive economic zones (EEZs). Individual countries exert exclusive rights over how their coastal waters and EEZs and seas are managed. But that still leaves much of the world's high seas and ocean floor as *global commons*, which are beyond national jurisdiction. In the past few decades, the number of marine treaties for managing the fisheries, minerals, pollution and mammal species of the ocean commons has increased dramatically. However, the speed and scale of human impacts on the marine environment, and the poor regulation and enforcement of many treaties, have undermined efforts to collectively manage the global ocean commons.[6]

One pressing need is to recognize the value of our ocean and coasts as carbon sinks. Over the past two centuries, the marine environment has absorbed as much as half of all greenhouse gases emitted through human activity.[7] *Blue carbon* habitats, such as marshes, mangroves, sea grass beds and other vegetated coastal and marine ecosystems, are among the most prolific carbon sinks on Earth. Yet, these blue carbon habitats are disappearing, along with marine life generally, as we plunder oceans for resources and pollute them with our litter and waste.

Our current exploitation of oceans and costs may also be inequitable. There is growing alarm over *ocean and coastal grabbing*.

These are actions and policies that deprive small-scale fishers access to fishing grounds, dispossess local communities of coastal resources or undermine traditional rights to marine environments and habitats.[8] Such practices may have a devastating impact on the livelihoods of coastal communities, especially in low- and middle-income countries. Around 97 percent of the world's fishers live in developing countries, and fishing is often the major source of their food and income. Small-scale fisheries supply almost half of the world's seafood, often for local consumption and markets.[9]

Yet current governance and exploitation of our oceans often come at the expense of local coastal communities, indigenous people and small-scale fishers. Marine resources are increasingly controlled by large-scale commercial interests. The ten largest companies in eight major ocean industries generate, on average, 45 percent of each industry's total revenues. Across all eight industries, the 100 largest corporations account for 60 percent of total revenues.[10]

This chapter will explore how our economic approach to managing oceans and coasts must change to address these growing threats and concerns. This will require a major transformation of how the ocean economy uses the marine environment. It can only occur if we end the underpricing of marine capital and fund adequately its global conservation. But we must also act collectively to manage and regulate use of our oceans, and to do so in a sustainable and inclusive manner.

Economics for a Fragile Ocean

In popular documentaries and writings, the ocean is often portrayed as *Earth's last frontier*. Around 70 percent of our planet's surface is covered by water, yet at most 10 percent of it has been fully explored.

Unfortunately, characterizing the marine environment as a "frontier" can be misleading – and creates perverse incentives.

As explained in Chapter 3, if we view the surrounding environment as a "limitless" frontier, then we will go on treating nature recklessly, as if it is essentially a "free" source of new resources and sink for absorbing waste, and ignore any costs associated with rising environmental degradation. This is essentially how our current *ocean economy* treats the marine environment.

This economy comprises a wide range of industries – fishing, offshore energy, mineral extraction, shipping and coastal tourism.

It generates between 3.5 and 7 percent of world gross domestic product and around 31 million jobs, and may double in size by 2030.[11] These ocean-based industries are supported and sustained by a diverse array of *marine capital* comprising estuarine and coastal ecosystems, marine resources, species and habitats that stretch from shorelines to the deep sea. But because we continually exploit the ocean as if it is a limitless frontier, we are running down our marine capital at an unprecedented rate. As this capital depreciates, it undermines the sustainability of the ocean economy and the people dependent on it. Yet we continue to ignore these losses as we deplete and pollute our oceans.

In addition to supporting the ocean economy, the marine environment provides other important benefits to humankind. Oceans and coasts are a source of food and water, protect against natural hazards and help mitigate climate change. In addition, the oceans are vital to informal employment, subsistence and livelihoods for coastal communities in low- and middle-income countries. Although there is growing recognition that expansion of the ocean economy is occurring at the expense of these other benefits, we often ignore these trade-offs in our economic decisions.

One consequence is that coastlines are becoming more crowded with people, cities and economic activity. But this development has resulted in the loss of many important estuarine and coastal ecosystems – mangroves, salt marsh, seagrass beds, kelp forests, coral and oyster reefs and sand dunes. As these habitats disappear, we do not value or appreciate the important benefits that are lost.

Since the 1970s, most of the waters surrounding our coastlines have been designated as exclusive economic zones (EEZs) that are regulated and controlled by the nations with territorial rights over these zones. It may be that national sovereignty of EEZs has led to some control over how these waters are exploited, but they are still treated as if they are unending sources of fish, minerals, energy and other resources, and perpetual sinks for pollution and litter. Even further out from shore, the poorly regulated and managed high seas and deep seabed beyond national jurisdiction are simply inviting unrelenting expansion of oil, gas and mineral extraction and trawling into deeper and deeper waters.[12]

In essence, we still run and manage our ocean economy today as we have done for millennia. The difference is that today we must finally face up to the consequences of the unprecedented speed and scale of marine environmental degradation.

Humankind has always exploited marine resources. The dispersal of early humans out of Africa into Southeast Asia and Oceania largely occurred through crossing oceans and seas to settle successive coastlines and islands. Coastal resource depletion, through harvesting shellfish and other aquatic resources in intertidal zones, may have been the first significant ecological impacts by humankind. Exploitation of marine resources and coastal settlement also occurred in the Americas, shortly after humans arrived. As a result, "dense human populations and cultural complexity arose in many coastal regions when or where agriculture was not practiced but a wealth of marine resources were available."[13]

Once permanent human settlement occurred 10,000 years ago, exploitation of marine resources and coastal habitat conversion began in earnest. As noted by the ecologist Heike Lotze and colleagues, "Estuarine and coastal transformation is as old as civilization yet has dramatically accelerated over the past 150 to 300 years."[14] Their research shows that human impacts have depleted more than 90 percent of formerly important marine species, destroyed at least 65 percent of seagrass and wetland habitat, degraded water quality and accelerated species invasions.

In recent centuries, the scale and range of human impacts on oceans and coasts have increased significantly. Between 1500 and modern times, at least twenty marine species have gone extinct. Today, an increasing number of marine species are threatened, with 830 currently classified as critically endangered, endangered or vulnerable. Causes of extinction include overexploitation and habitat loss, pollution, ocean warming and acidification, and anoxia (low dissolved oxygen).[15] These human impacts are now interacting to damage the marine environment. In 45 percent of the cases of species loss and 42 percent of extinctions, multiple human impacts were involved, often with exploitation and habitat loss acting as the main catalysts.[16]

The economic challenge we face is how to manage the benefits we receive from our ocean economy while minimizing the risks arising from our overexploitation, pollution and degradation of marine environments. We need to stop treating the ocean as an "endless frontier" and decouple ocean and coastal economic development from the ongoing destruction of marine life.

If we are to halt humankind's unrelenting exploitation of marine sources and sinks, we need to change our economic approach to oceans and coasts. It begins with addressing the underpricing of marine capital and its services and the underfunding of ocean and coastal conservation.

Underpricing of Marine Capital

A key step in ending the underpricing of marine capital is the removal of environmental harmful subsidies, such as those supporting unsustainable fishing.

Global marine fisheries receive about $35 billion each year in subsidies, of which $22 billion is for capacity-enhancing purposes. The latter subsidies prop up fishery operations that would otherwise be uneconomic and drive exploitation of fisheries beyond sustainable levels.[17] Fishing subsidies also encourage dumping of fish bycatch that has no commercial value, cause excessive trawling of ecologically sensitive sea beds and lead to additional releases of carbon stored in the ocean floor.

This environmental impact, just in terms of carbon releases, is significant. For example, around 4.9 million km², or 1.3 percent of the global ocean, is trawled each year. The resulting disturbance to the seafloor results in an estimated 1.47 billion tonnes of CO_2 emitted per year. This is equivalent to how much carbon is released annually by the global aviation industry.[18]

Marine fishing subsidies are also highly inequitable. They benefit mainly large industrial-scale industrial fleets, often at the expense of small-scale fishers. Almost 90 percent of capacity-enhancing subsidies go to industrialized fleets, thus increasing the unfair competitive advantage that these large-scale fishing operations already have.[19] Industrial fleets are, in turn, behind increasing conflicts with small-scale fishers and contribute to the growing problem of illegal, unreported and unregulated fishing in some regions.[20] For example, conflicts over fisheries in the coastal waters of Africa have mostly been the result of competition between industrial and small-scale fishers. Almost half of fish catches in Africa are illegal, and much of this activity is attributed to industrial fleets. By engaging in illegal fishing, these fleets can hinder access to fishing resources by small-scale and local fishers, and drive up their costs through overexploitation and ecological damages.[21]

The expansion of subsidized industrial fleets at the expense of small-scale fishers impacts global livelihoods and poverty. Between

85 and 98 percent of the world's 3.2 million active marine fishing vessels are small scale. They support around 22 million fishers, who make up about 44 percent of all fishers globally. Additionally, another 100 million people may be involved in the post-harvest activities of small-scale fishing.[22] Just in Africa alone, small-scale fisheries and post-harvesting sustain 35 million people.[23]

The ecological, equity and economic implications of global fishery subsidies highlight the overall poor governance and management of many marine fisheries. This is another aspect of the underpricing problem, as poor management practices encourage a *race to fish*. This incentive further exacerbates overfishing and excessive depletion of fisheries. As explained by the economist Rob Stavins, "Because no one holds title to fish stocks in the open ocean, for example, everyone races to catch as much as possible. Each fisherman receives the full benefit of aggressive fishing—a larger catch—but none pays the full cost, an imperiled fishery for everyone."[24]

According to Anna Birkenbach, David Kaczan and Marty Smith, the race to fish leads to a number of ecological and economic impacts in addition to the depletion of fishing capital:

> In fisheries, the competitive race to fish compresses fishing seasons, with detrimental ecological and economic effects and increased occupational risks ... Racing threatens fish stocks; contributes to bycatch, discarding, and habitat disruption; increases the cost of fishing; decreases revenues by creating market gluts and steering product towards lower value uses; and heightens safety risks because vessels are less able to avoid hazardous weather.[25]

To get an idea of how costly some of these impacts are, Chris Costello and colleagues investigate what would happen if sound management reforms were implemented to control the race to fish. They find that in nearly every country, the management reforms would lead to recovery of marine fish stocks (as measured by fish biomass), higher catch levels and thus more seafood supply, and additional profits for fishers. If the reforms were applied to only fisheries currently suffering from severe depletion, annual catch would increase by 2 million tonnes; profits would rise by $31 billion; and biomass would expand by 388 million tonnes. When all fisheries are managed effectively, catch rises over current levels by 16 million tonnes; profits by $53 billion; and biomass by 619 million tonnes.[26]

But of course our coasts and oceans provide other important benefits too. Unfortunately, many of these valuable services of marine capital are "underpriced" in our decisions that impact our oceans and costs. As a result, we allow this capital to depreciate and degrade, thus imperiling its benefits to current and future generations.

To illustrate this problem, we will look more closely at one type of marine capital – estuarine and coastal ecosystems – and the consequences for two vital services they provide – protection against storms and sequestration of carbon.

There is no doubt that estuarine and coastal habitats, such as marsh, mangroves, seagrass beds, tidal flats, kelp forests and near-shore reefs, are suffering considerable loss from the impacts of the expansion of the ocean economy. The main threats are from (i) land reclamation and conversion to agriculture, aquaculture, ports and urban areas; (ii) construction of dams, dykes, polders, drainage channels, dredging that modify the natural hydrology, connectivity and sedimentology; (iii) overfishing and overexploitation of other aquatic resources; and (iv) the effects of climate change, sea level rise, warming oceans, pollution and other human-induced environmental changes.[27]

As much as one third of estuarine and coastal habitats may have been lost in the past 100 years or so, although some estimates suggest that well over half of these habitats have disappeared.[28] Since the 1970s, estuarine and coastal ecosystems have continued to decline, with annual rates of loss of 0.82–1.21 percent per year.[29] Between 1996 and 2016, there was a net decline of 5,807 km^2 of mangrove area, equivalent to 4.0 percent of the 1996 area. From 1984 to 2016, 16 percent of tidal flats were lost, with 3.1 percent disappearing from 1999 to 2016.[30]

The rapid disappearance of estuarine and coastal ecosystems has raised concerns over their role in protecting coastal communities from storms that damage property, cause deaths and inflict injuries. This benefit has been largely ignored in the decisions that have led to such habit decline. Yet, a number of studies indicate that the value of storm protection provided by estuarine and coastal ecosystems is substantial.

For example, Michael Beck and colleagues estimate that the absence of the protective benefit of coral reefs would double the annual expected damages from flooding globally and triple the costs from frequent storms. Improved reef management would especially benefit Indonesia, Philippines, Malaysia, Mexico and Cuba, with each country reducing annual flood damages by at least $400 million.[31]

Jacob Hochard, Stuart Hamilton and I analyze the impact of mangrove extent in protecting economic activity in coastal regions from cyclones between 2000 and 2012 for nearly 2,000 tropical and subtropical communities globally. The results show that more mangroves between the shoreline and inland areas provide increased protection. For a community with an average cover of 6.3m of mangroves extending inland from the seaward edge, direct cyclone exposure can reduce economic activity permanently by 5.4–6.7 months, whereas for a community with 25.6m of mangroves extending inland from the shoreline, the loss in activity is 2.6–5.5 months.[32]

Pelayo Menéndez and coauthors value the global flood protection benefits of mangroves at over $65 billion per year, and estimate that the loss of all mangroves would mean that 15 million more people worldwide would be susceptible to annual flooding. The countries benefiting the most include the United States, China, India, Mexico, Vietnam and Bangladesh.[33]

The protection provided by estuarine and coastal habitats against storms, sea level rise and coastal flooding may be especially important to poorer rural populations in low- and middle-income countries. Around 267 million people live in the rural low-elevation coastal zones of developing countries, just under half of the total population of these countries living in such zones. Approximately a third of the population (85 million) in rural low-elevation coastal zones are poor, and nearly all of them are found in low-income (47 million) or lower- middle-income countries (37 million). For such poor rural populations, the "natural" barriers of mangroves, seagrass beds, coral reefs and other surrounding habitats are the only protection of their homes, livelihoods and lives.[34]

Another important global benefit of estuarine and coastal habitats is their sequestration of carbon. As mentioned previously, *blue carbon* habitats, such as marshes, mangroves, sea grass beds and other vegetated coastal and marine ecosystems, are among the most prolific carbon sinks on Earth. Various studies suggest that protecting and restoring mangroves, salt marshes, seagrasses and wild seaweed belts could potentially mitigate around 0.50 and 1.38 billion tonnes of carbon annually by 2050.[35] Yiwen Zeng and colleagues find that as much as one fifth of all mangrove areas can be conserved through carbon finance and that roughly half of this is cost-effective and financially sustainable. If such financing is forthcoming, then it would mitigate nearly 30 million tonnes of carbon annually.[36]

Conservation of mangroves, salt marshes and seagrasses can also achieve many additional environmental benefits, including increasing biodiversity, coastal resilience and climate change. These benefits can significantly increase the value attributed to marine capital, beyond their use for storm protection or carbon storage. For example, Daniel Petrolia, Matthew Interis and Joonghyun Hwang found that households on average are willing to pay $149 for increased storm surge protection through coastal wetland restoration in southeast Louisiana, but are willing to pay $973 for restoration when the additional ecosystem benefits of supporting wildlife habitat and commercial fisheries are also included.[37]

The various goods and services provided by estuarine and coastal systems are especially significant for sustaining the livelihoods of people living in the coastal areas of low- and middle-income countries. Resources harvested and collected directly from these habitats and the small-scale fisheries supported by them are important for food security, subsistence and cash income. For example, local coastal communities in Thailand accumulated gains in income from collecting mangrove products worth $484–$584 per hectare (ha), and an additional $708–$987 per ha from coastal fisheries that are supported by mangroves serving as breeding and nursery habitat for the fish. Such benefits are considerable when compared to the average annual income of coastal households in Thailand, which ranges from $2,606 to $6,623, and where typically the poorest households have annual incomes of $180 or lower.[38]

Coastal communities around the world also have a strong cultural connection with their marine environment. A survey of households in coastal areas of Papua New Guinea found that people ascribed most importance to the benefits of estuarine and coastal ecosystems that contributed to their livelihoods, especially for food, income and shelter through activities such as fishing, collecting forest and reef materials. But respondents also stressed the importance of marine habitats for local traditions, environmental knowledge, the heritage for future generations and stewardship of the environment.[39]

In sum, we are losing our marine capital because it is grossly underpriced. Many important values provided by the marine environment are ignored or discounted in our decisions to exploit, convert and pollute our coastlines and seas. The ocean economy is expanding rapidly, and because marine ecosystems are undervalued, this expansion is occurring at the expense of rapid habit depletion and degradation. In some cases, such as the example of fishing subsidies indicates, over-exploitation of the underlying capital is actually encouraged, with harmful economic, environmental and distributional consequences. Ending such underpricing is therefore essential for decoupling the ocean economy from the destruction of marine environment.

Protecting Marine Life

Because of the mounting concern over the rapid decline in marine capital, there are growing calls to protect more ocean and coastal habitats. In effect, such proposals suggest placing global limits on the use of the marine environment as a source for resources and sinks for waste. The most frequent management tool advocated for enforcing such limits is expanding the world's network of *marine protected areas.*

Marine protected areas that restrict use are often called *no-take marine reserves.* They are highly protected zones of the oceans and coasts where extractive and destructive activities are banned, such as fishing, mining, dumping and pollution. Currently, only 7 percent of the global marine environment has been designated or proposed for protection, and only 2.7 percent is implemented as fully or highly protected.[40] Consequently, there is a growing consensus that we need urgently to safeguard a lot more of our ocean, if we are to save marine life and the valuable benefits it provides.[41]

As we noted in Chapter 5, oceans have been included as part of the "30 by 30" goal that is the centerpiece of the Convention on Biological Diversity's post-2020 global biodiversity framework. This proposal calls for protecting 30 percent of the planet's land and water surface by 2030. In line with this target, many scientists, nongovernmental organizations and government leaders have also called for extending highly protected zones to at least 30 percent of the ocean by 2030.[42]

However, designating how much of the global ocean should be protected is not the end of the story. There are three additional challenges. The first challenge is to determine which human threats to oceans and coasts can be best controlled by establishing marine protected areas. The second is to recognize that the protection goals of marine reserves are more difficult to achieve as long the underpricing of marine capital persists. And finally, the potential distributional impacts of marine reserves need to be addressed.

Marine protected areas are most effective in reducing threats to oceans and coasts that are associated with overfishing, mining and habitat destruction. They are less effective in addressing nutrient pollution, ocean warming and acidification. But even if marine protected areas are aimed at limiting overexploitation and habitat loss, they often fail to achieve their full potential due to illegal harvesting, mining and conversion, poor monitoring and enforcement and inadequate reserve size. In addition, marine reserves are most likely to generate the greatest conservation gains if they are situated in overfished or damaged habitats, yet this is not always considered a priority in determining which areas to protect.[43]

For example, strategically expanding the existing global marine reserve network to protect an additional 5 percent of the ocean containing depleted fisheries could increase future catch by at least 20 percent and generate an additional 9–12 million tonnes of seafood annually.[44] However, focusing just on the fishing benefits of marine reserves may come at the expense of other benefits, such as biodiversity and ecosystem benefits or carbon storage. As Enric Sala and his colleagues have shown, prioritizing different combinations of these benefits will determine how much of the ocean needs to be protected; how the reserves should be distributed between Excusive Economic Zones and the high seas; and what trade-offs among the various benefits might occur.[45]

However, expanding marine reserves to conserve oceans and coasts will be less effective as long as the underpricing of marine capital persists. This sends a signal that the remaining unprotected marine environment is worth less intact compared to using it as a source for fishing, mining or other extractive activities or as a sink for pollution and waste. The result is that these unprotected areas will be depleted and degraded too much and too quickly.

Figure 7.1 illustrates why this outcome might occur, with the example of establishing a no-take marine reserve in an area that is subject to extensive fishing by an industrial trawling fleet. Assume that the marine habitat of the fishery extends across an area A_o. Figure 7.1 indicates what might happen if there is ongoing underpricing of fishing capital, which comprises the marine habitat and the fish stock it contains.

As we discussed previously, three types of underpricing of fishing capital commonly occur. Fisheries are often poorly managed, so that each vessel in a fishing fleet has an incentive to race to fish until no vessel can make more money. In addition, industrial fleets are often

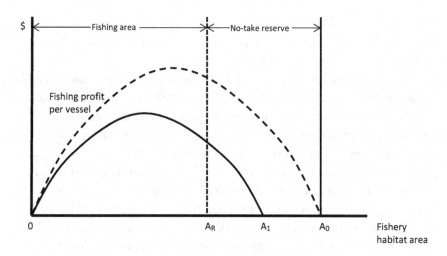

Figure 7.1 Marine reserve creation with underpricing of fishing capital

Notes: The entire fishing habitat area is A_o. If the fishery is poorly managed, each vessel has an incentive to race to fish up to area A_1, until it makes no more profit. Subsidies increase the profit per vessel (dotted line) so that the entire habitat area A_o is fished. A no-take marine reserve is established to protect area A_o-A_R. But if underpricing persists, then each vessel still has an incentive to deplete the remaining fishing area A_R as fast as possible to make more profits, and also to increase profits even further by fishing illegally in the reserve area A_o-A_R.

subsidized, so that they have higher profits and thus a further incentive to overfish. Finally, fishing fleets do not take into account any additional ecological damages that they inflict, which include dumping of fish bycatch that has no commercial value; excessive damages to the seabed from bottom trawling; and additional releases of carbon stored in the ocean floor.

Figure 7.1 shows the case where such underpricing prevails. If the fishery is poorly managed so that each vessel has an incentive to race to fish to make more profit, then the entire fleet will expand the area fished until no vessel can make any more money. This means that the fleet will fish up to area A_1. However, subsidies to the fishing fleet boost the profit of each vessel further and encourage even more fishing. In Figure 7.1, this is represented by the dotted line showing a higher profit per vessel. The result is that the fleet will now fish the entire habitat area A_o.

Because the fishery is severely depleted and the marine habitat is suffering significant ecological damages from trawling, a no-take marine reserve of area A_o-A_R is created. The hope is that the reserve will eventually allow the fishery and its habitat to recover, and eventually boost the catch and thus profits of the fleet from fishing in the remaining area where it is allowed to happen.

Unfortunately, this is unlikely to happen. For one, subsidies and poor governance mean that each vessel has a strong incentive to "race to fish." As this term implies, the fleet will deplete as quickly as possible the remaining unprotected fishing area A_R indicated in Figure 7.1 In addition, each vessel also knows that it can increase its profit by illegally fishing in the reserve area A_o-A_R. This incentive to illegally trawl the reserve will increase as more of the legal fishing zone is overfished. As the fishery is poorly managed and monitored, it is likely that increased trawling in the reserve will be illegal, unreported and unregulated. The end result is that both the fishing area and the no-take reserve will become overfished and ecologically damaged, and the reserve will fail to achieve its conservation benefits.

This outcome is all too common across the globe.[46] The effectiveness of no-take reserves is undermined by poor management inside the reserve and in surrounding fishing areas, illegal fishing and failures to control ecological damages caused by fishing. In some instances, these factors combine to spur preemptive overfishing in anticipation of the creation of a marine protected area. For example, Grant McDermott and colleagues estimate that, if the policy of placing 30 percent of all marine waters in no-take marine reserves by 2030 is announced, it could catalyze the race to fish incentive, so that the percentage of fisheries experiencing overfishing would increase from 65 to 72 percent.[47]

In comparison, halting the underpricing of fishing capital can help the no-take reserve achieve its conservation goals. This is illustrated in Figure 7.2.

Suppose sound management reforms are implemented to control the race to fish. Each vessel now has an incentive to maximize its profits rather than fish more area until its profit is driven to zero. In addition, the fleet no longer receives any subsidies. As shown in Figure 7.2, the fleet will fish area A^*. If no-take marine reserve is established to protect area A_o-A_R, it does not affect this outcome. In addition, a tax on harvest or license fee payment on area fished will ensure that all vessels take into account costs of bycatch dumping, trawler damage or any other impacts of fishing on the marine habitat. Each vessel still maximizes profit, but the area fished is reduced further to A^{**}. Because fishing vessels cannot increase their profits further, and

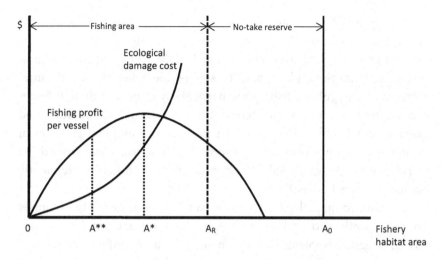

Figure 7.2 Marine reserve creation with no underpricing of fishing capital
Notes: The entire fishing habitat area is A_o. If the fishery is properly managed and there are no subsidies, each vessel has an incentive to maximize profits and thus fish up to area A^*. If the fleet also pays for any ecological damage, then it will fish up to area A^{**}. If a no-take marine reserve is established to protect area A_o-A_R, the fleet has no incentive to increase profits even further through overfishing or by fishing illegally in the reserve area.

there is no incentive to overfish, the marine reserve can successfully achieve its conservation goals without threat of illegal fishing. Although not shown in the figure, once fish stocks in the reserve start to recover, and migrate to the fishing area, catch and profits of the fishery will also start to rise.

There is some evidence of better fishing regulation reinforcing marine protected areas. Timothy White and colleagues find that the creation of the five largest marine protected areas (MPAs) since 2013 in exclusive economic zones (EEZs) of the Pacific Ocean since 2013 have not encouraged overfishing by industrial fleets. But this may have happened because the regions in which these MPAs are located experienced little fishing pressure beforehand. In addition, four of the five EEZs had in place significant restrictions and management on industrial fishing before the MPAs were created. As the authors conclude, "Taken together, these regulations and patterns of fishing suggest that waters of these nations received a form of partial protection prior to their implementation as no-take MPAs."[48]

Although the examples focus on the importance of ending the underpricing of fishing capital for ensuring the effectiveness of marine reserves in controlling overexploitation and illegal fishing by industrial fleets, the same principle applies to small-scale fisheries. Illegal, unreported and unregulated fishing are particularly critical in these fisheries because they are widely scattered and are difficult to monitor, and management practices that allow for the recovery and conservation of exploited stocks are difficult to enforce for these fisheries. Around the world, the target for illegal fishing by small-scale fishers is frequently marine protected areas.[49]

Controlling illegal fishing by small-scale fishers also requires avoiding conflicts over how marine protected areas have been conceived, designed, implemented and managed. These conflicts often occur because the conservation of biodiversity is prioritized over the needs of local coastal communities, which as we noted previously, are highly dependent on small-scale fishers. If the establishment of marine reserves impose significant costs on local people, and have distributional consequences that favor the wealthy over the poor, it usually exacerbates tensions and can encourage illegal fishing in reserves. Once again, the outcome can undermine the effectiveness of marine protected areas and the attainment of their conservation goals.[50]

Expanding marine protected areas is an important conservation objective, but on its own, it will not save our oceans and coasts. Ending the underpricing of marine capital and addressing the distributional and equity concerns of local coastal communities are essential to this task. But achieving any ambitious goals for marine conservation will be a moot point, unless we also address the current and widening funding gap between the investments needed and the financing available for conservation.

Underfunding of Oceans and Coasts

As we saw in Chapter 5, current global spending to support conservation of terrestrial ecosystems and habitats is woefully inadequate compared to the need. This underinvestment is a major reason why the world is not preserving sufficient natural landscape and biodiversity.

The same is true for financing marine conservation. There is a large gap between the investments required to protect and conserve

Table 7.1. Returns to marine conservation investments

Action	Benefit-Cost Ratio	Description and Source
Conservation of mangroves	88:1	Conservation of 15,000–30,000 hectares per year based on halting annual mangrove loss (Konar and Ding 2020)
Restoration of mangroves	2:1	184,000–290,000 hectares per year (Konar and Ding 2020)
Decarbonize international shipping	2:1–5:1	Konar and Ding (2020)
Increase production of sustainably sourced ocean-based food in diets	10:1	Konar and Ding (2020)
Marine protected area expansion	1.4:1–2.7:1	Based on six different scenarios for protection and expansion (Brander et al. (2020).

oceans and coasts and current funding levels for marine capital. This *underfunding of oceans and coasts* is yet another reason why our marine environment is in peril.

On the face of it, the underfunding of marine conservation is a puzzle. As Table 7.1 shows, there are significant returns to investment to a number of actions that would protect, restore or use more sustainably marine capital.

Restoration of mangroves and marine protected area expansion show the lowest returns, but even for these actions the benefits are almost double the costs (see Table 7.1). The benefits from decarbonizing international shipping could be up to five times more than the costs, and sustainably increasing seafood production is ten times greater. The largest returns are to conservation of mangroves, which have a benefit-cost ratio of 88:1.

Yet, despite these large returns, global marine conservation is woefully inadequate. There is a wide gap between current funding and investment needs.

Table 7.2 illustrates the *marine underfunding* problem.

Global funding for sustainable use, protection and conservation of oceans and coasts amounts to just $1.3 billion each year (see Table 7.2).

Table 7.2. Global underfunding of oceans and coasts

Category	Amount per Year	Description and Source
Funding from all sources	$1.3 billion	Based on $13 billion from all sources over the past ten years (de Vos and Hart 2020).
Public international finance	$0.5 billion	Based on $5 billion in official development assistance over the past ten years (de Vos and Hart 2020).
Private sector finance	$0.8 billion	Based on $8.3 billion in philanthropic spending and private contributions to conservation NGOs over the past ten years (de Vos and Hart 2020).
Subsidies		
Marine fisheries	$35 billion	$22 billion are potentially environmentally harmful (Sumaila et al. 2019).
Benefits from nature		
Economic production	$1.5 trillion	Global value added of ocean industries (fishing, shipping, offshore wind, maritime and coastal tourism and marine biotechnology), which is expected to increase to $3 trillion by 2030 (OECD 2016).
Funding needs		
Costs of mangrove conservation	$28.8–$57.5 billion	Costs of halting global mangrove loss (Konar and Ding 2020).
Costs of mangrove restoration	$3.5–$5.5 billion	Costs of restoring all degraded mangroves globally from 2020 and 2050 (Konar and Ding 2020).
Costs of decarbonizing international shipping	$76.7 billion	Based on $12.3 trillion operating and capital costs over thirty years for decarbonizing shipping (Konar and Ding 2020).

Table 7.2. cont'd

Category	Amount per Year	Description and Source
Costs of sustainable management of marine fisheries	$5–$7 billion	Additional costs of management reform ($13–$15 billion) compared to current management costs ($8 billion) for marine fisheries (Mangin et al. 2018).
Costs of increasing fully protected marine areas	$7.7 billion	Costs of increasing fully protected marine areas from 2.7 to 10 percent of the ocean (Sumaila et al. 2020b).

In comparison, annual fishing subsidies alone are $35 billion, of which $22 billion are known to be environmentally harmful. In other words, the world is prepared to spend $20 billion more on supporting ecologically damaging fishing operations than we are willing to devote to conserving marine capital.

Yet, the benefits of that capital are substantial (see Table 7.1). Currently, ocean industries generate $1.5 trillion in global value added, which is expected to double by 2030.

As Table 7.1 indicates, there are also four beneficial marine conservation investments that urgently need funding: mangrove conservation and restoration, decarbonizing international shipping, sustainable seafood production and expansion of marine protected area. Table 7.2 provides estimates of the likely annual costs of each of these marine conservation priorities.

Halting global mangrove deforestation completely could cost at least $29 billion annually, and possibly even double that amount (see Table 7.2). Restoring degraded mangrove areas could cost another $3–$6 billion annually over thirty years. The bill is likely to be even higher if conserving and restoring other ecologically and economically important estuarine and coastal ecosystem, such as marsh, seagrass beds, tidal flats, kelp forests and near-shore reefs, are also included.[51]

The annual costs of decarbonizing international shipping could amount to $77 billion over the next thirty years (see Table 7.2). This action could have a considerable impact on global greenhouse emissions. Currently, shipping is responsible for around 1 billion tonnes of carbon emission each year, which is 3 percent of global emissions from human activity. The emissions from international shipping are expected to double by 2050.[52]

Implementing management reforms to end the "race to fish" in global fisheries will require around $5–$7 billion annually (see Table 7.2). Such reforms are essential to end the underpricing of fishing capital that is perpetuating unsustainable overfishing around the world. It is also vital to ensuring that seafood production can sustainably meet growing global demand.

However, sustainably producing food from our oceans will also require improved management of species farmed in the ocean, or *mariculture*. Chris Costello and colleagues maintain that, although the production of wild fisheries is approaching its ecological limits, current mariculture production is not. It therefore could be sustainably increased through policy reforms and technological advancements. If such reforms and innovations are forthcoming, the mariculture's current share of 16 percent of seafood production could rise to 44 percent by 2050.[53]

As noted previously in this chapter, although 7 percent of the global marine environment has been designated or proposed for protection, only 2.7 percent is currently fully or highly protected. Expanding the coverage of these marine protected areas to 10 percent of the ocean and coasts would cost nearly $8 billion per year (see Table 7.2). This is the minimum required for marine capital conservation. If we aim to apply the "30 by 30" protection target to oceans, then the bill for expanding fully protected areas to 30 percent of the marine environment would be a much higher price tag. However, the benefits to society of meeting this target vastly outweigh the costs of funding this goal.

In sum, closing the funding gap between what is needed for marine conservation and what is currently being spent is an urgent priority. Moreover, the failure to invest in key marine actions, such as estuarine and coastal habitat conservation and restoration, decarbonizing international shipping, sustainable seafood production and expansion of marine protected area, is a missed economic opportunity. Addressing the underfunding of ocean and coasts and ending the underpricing of marine capital must be the main focus of global collective action.

Collective Action

An important transition in ocean governance occurred with the United Nations Convention on the Law of the Sea (UNCLOS) in 1982.

The treaty successfully organized the ocean space into three areas: sovereign territory; areas under national jurisdiction; and areas beyond national jurisdiction.[54]

UNCLOS created the current legal framework where coastal states have sovereign rights over the marine resources and habitats in a 200-nautical-mile exclusive economic zone (EEZ) and on the continental shelf also beyond 200 nautical miles. The mineral resources on the deep seabed beyond national jurisdiction are the common heritage of mankind, and the International Seabed Authority is tasked with their management. The high seas, also beyond national jurisdiction, are governed by a wide range and increasing number of treaties to govern freedom of transport, species management, pollution and climate change. For example, all nations that are signatories to UNCLOS have the right to fish the high seas, but are expected to cooperate on the conservation and development of living marine resources in the ocean space beyond national jurisdiction.[55]

As we have discussed in this chapter, there are increasing calls for ocean governance and management to undergo another transformation. With the rise in global threats – from overfishing and illegal fishing to deteriorating and loss of marine species and habitats, to rising pollution and waste dumping to climate change, sea level rise and ocean acidification – a wide range of proposals and demands for change have emerged. These include applying the "30 by 30" objective to expand marine protected areas; controlling plastic pollution; managing oceans and blue carbon sinks to control climate change; reducing overfishing and illegal fishing; "integrated" ocean management across sovereign territory; EEZs and the high seas and deep sea bed.[56]

These are all laudable objectives for ocean governance and management reforms. But as we have also stressed throughout this chapter, attaining these objectives will require collective action to address the two critical failures in the economics of oceans and coasts: the underpricing of marine capital and the underfunding of marine conservation.

In effect, what is urgently needed is a new global agreement on oceans and coasts that addresses these two economic failures. There should be three aims of such an agreement:

- Phasing out subsidies for fishing, extractive activities and other industries in the ocean economy

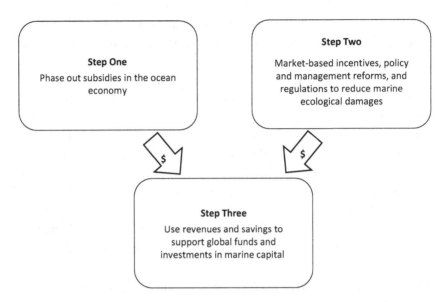

Figure 7.3 Global collective action for oceans and coasts

- Implementing market-based incentives, management reforms, regulations and other incentives to reduce ecological damages from ocean economy industries
- Using any financial savings and revenues generated to support global funds and investments for conserving, restoring and protecting marine capital in an inclusive manner

We can also envision these aims as three distinct steps in the process of fostering global collective action on oceans and coasts (see Figure 7.3).

An immediate aim is for all coastal nation-states to agree on removing subsidies for fishing, extractive activities and other sectors of the ocean economy operating in their territorial waters, EEZs and areas beyond national jurisdiction. As we have seen, fishing subsidies alone cost $35 billion a year, benefiting mainly industrial fishing fleets; contribute to overfishing and ecological damages; exacerbate illegal fishing; and worsen inequality and poverty. Subsidies may also be driving increased exploration and industrial exploitation of the vast and fragile deep sea, not only by fisheries but for energy and minerals. For example, as we noted in Chapter 4, there are significant annual subsidies for the exploration and exploitation of new reserves of fossil fuels.[57]

Countries should also agree to adopt policy reforms and regulations to promote more sustainable management of marine capital, and to adopt taxes, license fees, tradable quotas and other market-based incentives to deter marine ecological damages incurred by various ocean industries. Coastal states adopt such reforms for industries in their own territorial waters and EEZs, and push for them as well for industries operating in the marine environment beyond national jurisdiction.

As we have seen, especially using the example of ocean fisheries, management reforms, improved regulations and market-based incentives to limit environmental impacts are critical to more sustainable and inclusive uses of marine capital. In the case of fisheries, they are important to control the race to fish, reduce illegal fishing and support marine protected areas. Similar reforms, regulations and incentives should be applied to other sectors of the marine economy, from energy and mineral activities to ocean transport to marine tourism.

The revenues and finances saved from ending the underpricing of marine capital could be directed to the investments and conservation actions identified in Tables 7.1 and 7.2. Global funds could assist low- and middle-income countries in conserving and restoring estuarine and coastal habitats; sustainably producing food from capture fisheries and mariculture; decarbonizing international shipping; and expanding marine protected areas.

Developing countries may also need global assistance to control illegal fishing and reduce plastic pollution.

Illegal, unreported and unregulated fishing in poorer countries can involve illegal encroachment by foreign industrial fleets in EEZs and territorial waters; incursion of fleets in waters reserved for small-scale fishers; and poaching in marine reserves. Reducing these activities requires improving monitoring, control and surveillance, especially in many low- and middle-income countries. It may also require the development of catch documentation systems as well as third-party certification of fisheries. These are costly investments, often with little immediate economic returns. When a country is plagued by high levels of illegal fishing by foreign fleets, addressing this encroachment can lead to recovery of fisheries and increases in local catch and profit. But if local fleets and small-scale fishers are behind illegal fishing, then there can be significant initial losses incurred if this practice is curtailed, which can be especially significant for small-scale fishers. Consequently, control of illegal fishing may also require additional expenditures on compensating for any negative impacts on the poor and most vulnerable fishers.[58]

One use of the money raised or saved from ending the under-pricing of marine capital is to establish a global fund for assisting low- and middle-income countries in reducing illegal fishing. The first step could be to aid countries to adopt a policy similar to that of Indonesia, which curtails illegal encroachment of foreign fleets in its EEZ and where international assistance of Indonesia's monitoring, control and surveillance efforts has been key.[59] The second step is to expand policies to include catch documentation systems, third-party certification, control of artisanal illegal fishing and compensation schemes to reduce any burdens on poorer coastal households.

Developing countries may need global assistance for control of marine plastic pollution. Although plastic production occurs mainly in richer countries, most marine debris comes from low- and middle-income countries, with more than 50 percent originating from China, Indonesia, the Philippines, Vietnam and Sri Lanka. Plastic pollution is also a transboundary challenge, especially when it comes to removal of plastic debris from areas beyond national jurisdiction. Significant reductions in plastic pollution can nevertheless be achieved through the adoption of pricing policies and regulations, such as bans or charges on plastic use and landfilling, disposal fees and deposit-refund systems, which encourage a shift from producing, using and disposing of plastics to increased substitution, recycling and reuse.[60]

Critical to reducing plastic pollution in oceans could be the establishment of a global fund to assist developing countries in stemming their outflow of plastic waste. The main aim of the fund would be to enhance adoption of preventative measures, focusing on improving collection services; closing leakage points in collection facilities; improved disposal technologies; and recycling. The fund could also assist developing countries in devising economic incentive schemes that reduce plastic use and products that cannot be easily recovered, reused or recycled. Examples include taxes and bans on the landfilling of plastic waste, and government procurement policies and tax incentives for manufacturers that incorporate recycled content in products.[61]

A global fund may also be needed for ecosystem monitoring of the deep sea. Such monitoring is essential for expanding our capacity to protect and restore deep-sea ecosystems and their resources. Estimates suggest that it would cost $2–$3 billion for implementing and deploying twenty strategically placed monitoring networks, with additional maintenance costs of $200–$300 million per year.[62]

However, global collective action to save oceans and coasts should not just come from governments. The private sector must also contribute, both through investment and financing.

We have already noted that ocean industries generate $1.5 billion in global value added, which is expected to double by 2030. Ten companies dominate each of the eight main ocean industries, and these large companies together account for 45 percent of all revenues (see Table 7.3). If these companies and industries set aside some of their revenues to protecting marine capital, it could make a significant difference in bridging the current gap in conservation funding versus needs.

If the top ten companies in every ocean industry set aside 10 percent of their revenues, this could raise an additional $83 billion each year for marine conservation investment (see Table 7.3). If all companies participated, the amount raised would be $186 billion.

An extra $86–$183 billion would go a long way to meeting some of the key funding needs for marine conservation (see Table 7.2). Moreover, companies in specific industries should be contributing to some of these investments anyway. For example, the shipping industry comprising container shipping, shipbuilding and repair, port activities and marine equipment and construction, should be contributing to the $77 billion required each year to decarbonize maritime shipping. Offshore oil and gas should offset its own greenhouse gas emissions by investing in mangrove conservation and restoration and other blue carbon actions. Cruise tourism could devote its 10 percent of revenues to helping expand marine protected areas and conservation and restoration of coral reefs and other estuarine and coastal habitats.

Recent conservation efforts in the seafood sector offer some promise that the private sector may be moving toward such cooperation. For example, ten of the thirteen seafood companies that control up to 16 percent of the global marine catch and 40 percent of the largest and most valuable stocks have committed to the Seafood Business for Ocean Stewardship initiative for more sustainable management of seafood resources and the oceans.[63] They now need to back up such commitments with actual investments to improve management and conservation of fishing capital. As Table 7.3 indicates, the seafood industry could contribute anywhere from $4 to $28 billion each year for such objectives. Such an investment makes perfectly good financial sense for seafood companies. The seafood industry should view this investment as a down payment on the $58 billion in additional profits

Table 7.3. Annual revenues and potential marine conservation investments of ocean industries

Industry	Industry Annual Revenues ($ Billion)	Revenue Share of Top Ten Companies	Top Ten Annual Revenues ($ Billion)	Potential Top Ten Annual Conservation Investment ($ Billion)	Potential Industry Annual Conservation Investment ($ Billion)
Offshore oil and gas	830	51%	423	42	83
Offshore wind	37	48%	18	2	4
Seafood	276	15%	41	4	28
Container shipping	156	85%	133	13	16
Shipbuilding and repair	118	67%	79	8	12
Port Activities	38	82%	31	3	4
Marine equipment and construction	354	18%	64	6	35
Cruise tourism	47	93%	44	4	5
All industries	1,856		833	83	186

Notes: Potential conservation investment based on 10 percent of annual revenues. Top ten companies in each industry together account for 45 percent of revenues from all industries.
Source: Virdin et al. (2021).

that it would receive each year from more sustainably managed fisheries.[64]

An alternative to voluntary contributions of the ocean industries is to impose a tax on their revenues and profits. For example, the High-Level Panel for a Sustainable Ocean Economy has called for implementing a global tax on the profits of ocean industries to generate revenue for marine capital investments, such as conservation and restoration, sustainable management and capacity-building in poorer countries. A 0.1 percent tax levied on the 100 largest ocean corporations could yield $1.1 billion each year for such actions.[65]

In sum, more comprehensive cooperation between the international community, national governments and the private sector is required to develop global policies to protect vulnerable coastal populations and the deep sea, and especially to bridge the funding gap for marine conservation.[66] It is clear that ocean industries have the most to gain from such conservation, and consequently, the focus should be on their contributing more to preserving and protecting marine capital that is vital to their businesses.

There are also a number of financial mechanisms that the private sector could use to fund marine conservation.[67] In Chapter 5, we discussed how the rapidly growing green bond market could be used to support protection and restoration of natural landscape, especially in developing countries. Such debt instruments could also be tapped for financing more marine conservation.

Although the green bond market is now worth over $250 billion and has its own dedicated Green Exchange as part of the Luxembourg Stock Exchange, only a small amount of these financing instruments are used to fund nature conservation.[68] Even less are devoted to investments in oceans and coasts.

However, there are signs that this is changing. World Bank–issued green bonds have been used to finance coral reef rehabilitation in Indonesia, which is expected to reduce destructive fishing, benefit fishing communities and protect 1.4 million hectares of marine habitat. Green bonds in the Seychelles are funding improved management of marine areas and fisheries, which could create 5 million hectares of sustainable-use marine protected areas, rebuild fisheries and increase landed bycatch sold in local markets. This could expand significantly value chains, employment and revenues in domestic fisheries.[69]

The Seychelles is proving to be a market innovator in financing large-scale marine capital investments through bonds. In 2018, the government launched the world's first sovereign "blue bond" to finance sustainable fishing practices and marine protection. The program is supported by loans, guarantees and credit support by a range of multi-lateral donors, nongovernmental organizations and financial institutional investors. The Seychelles blue bond has raised $15 million to finance sustainable management of small-scale fisheries; the rebuilding of fish stocks; management plans for the country's EEZ; and marine protected areas.[70]

The insurance industry also has a financial interest in investing in coastal and estuarine habitats because of their mitigation of costly and deadly storm events. For example, protecting coastal wetlands could save the insurance industry $52 billion annually through reducing flood damage losses. Based on this savings, the insurance industry could easily invest $5–$10 billion each year in conserving and restoring these habitats.[71]

An innovative reef insurance program has been implemented in the state of Quintana Roo, Mexico. A partnership between local stakeholders, The Nature Conservancy and the global reinsurance company Swiss Re has created a Coastal Zone Management Trust (CZMT). Payments from the tourism industry will finance efforts by the CZMT to build the resilience of coral reefs to storm damage and to purchase insurance from Swiss Re that guaranteeing a payout of $25–$70 million to restore the reefs in the case of an extreme storm occurring. The scheme covers a forty-mile section of the coral reef.[72]

Inclusive Ocean and Coastal Development

Throughout this chapter, we have emphasized how sustainable use and protection of oceans and coasts are vital to the livelihoods of coastal communities, especially for the poorer households in low- and middle-income countries. Ending the underpricing and underfunding of marine capital would therefore benefit considerably the coastal poor.

But there are also other important ways to ensure that the ocean economy is not only more sustainable but also inclusive.

The various collective actions explored in this chapter must also emphasize more inclusive governance. We need to transition from a top-down to a bottom-up approach to managing our oceans and coasts. As we move to an era in which collective action – especially to address underfunding of marine capital and the underpricing of the global ocean commons – becomes paramount, we must broaden the participation of stakeholders in solving these issues.

One encouraging sign has been the formation of the High Level Panel for a Sustainable Ocean Economy in 2018. This initiative has brought together heads of state and world leaders in business, nongovernmental organizations, multilateral agencies and private foundations to think creatively about how to address many of these important collective action and governance challenges.[73]

Local coastal communities and indigenous people also need to be included in ocean governance. Collective actions must increasingly find ways to involve and protect the interests of indigenous people and local communities on coasts and islands. This includes not only management of inshore seas and waters but also governance of the global ocean commons.[74]

Another important stakeholder group is small-scale fishers. As we have seen, nearly all fishing vessels in the world can be classified as small scale, and small-scale fisheries supply almost half of the world's seafood, often for local consumption and markets. Their economic significance is especially important in low- and middle-income countries. Small-scale fishing is vital to the livelihoods of the coastal poor.

It is clear that some of the more difficult challenges in managing the ocean economy, such as control of illegal, unreported and unregulated fishing, cannot take place without the cooperation of small-scale fishers. They are often the victims of incursion of fleets in waters reserved for small-scale fishing, but also the perpetrators of some illegal activities, such as poaching in marine reserves and illegal selling of bycatch. If we are to make rapid and lasting gains in controlling illegal fishing, then we must take into account how national and collective actions for addressing this problem might impact the economic livelihoods of small-scale fishers and involve them as important partners in these actions.

In addition, we should also consider direct actions to support small-scale fishers. One possibility is a *subsidy swap* from large-scale fishing fleets to investing in the protection, management and investment in small-scale fisheries. As we have noted, the $35 billion in annual fishing subsidies mainly benefit large-scale industrial fleets, encourage overfishing and damage to the marine environment, and often place small-scale fishers at a competitive disadvantage. If all or some of the fishing subsidies are phased out, they could instead be redirected to financing improved management and regulation of small-scale fisheries; rebuilding fish stocks and habitats that support these fisheries; and to provide technical and marketing assistance to the post-harvest activities dependent on small-scale fisheries.

Giving greater voice to indigenous people, coastal communities and small-scale fishers in policies and decisions shaping a more sustainable ocean economy is critical for overcoming the growing concern over ocean and coastal grabbing. These are actions and policies that deprive small-scale fishers access to fishing grounds; dispossess local communities of coastal resources; or undermine traditional rights to marine environments and habitats. As we expand marine protected areas, blue carbon projects, habitat restoration and other actions that limit or restrict the ocean economy, we must make sure that such policies do not become another form of ocean and coastal grabbing.[75] Ensuring that greater conservation and restoration of marine capital leads to an ocean economy that is both sustainable and inclusive is vital for avoiding this pitfall.

Conclusion

Our marine environment is no longer an endless frontier. As our ocean economy expands, and we exploit our marine assets as if they are an unending source of fish, minerals, energy, transport and other commercially valuable products, as well as a vast dump for our litter, plastics and waste, we are in danger of losing the ocean capital that is vital to sustaining it. This means accepting limits on the overexploitation of marine species and habitats, coastal ecosystem loss and pollution of our seas.

Critical to building a more sustainable and inclusive ocean economy is reducing these threats to our oceans and coasts. The overall aim must be to decouple the ocean economy from continued depreciation and loss of marine capital. The economics of increasing fragile oceans and rising costs must be based on the principle that ignoring the decline in marine capital is neither efficient nor sustainable. This means tackling the two most important economic failures that are preventing the decoupling of the ocean economy from marine environmental degradation: the underpricing of marine capital and the underfunding of conservation and restoration of habitats.

A transition to a more sustainable ocean economy is bound to be more inclusive than the current pattern of development that undervalues marine ecosystems and the benefits they provide. Local communities, indigenous people and small-scale fishers depend on these benefits for their livelihoods and to escape poverty. The current pattern of ocean economic development ignores this relationship, and through a vast network of subsidies, policies and management regimes, perpetuates the gains to major ocean industries, companies and wealthy stakeholders at the expense of the poor and less advantaged.

National and local governments have the jurisdiction to undertake the necessary actions for promoting a more sustainable ocean economy for their coasts, nearby seas and exclusive economic zones. But collective action is needed for tackling the vast global ocean commons beyond national jurisdiction. Both local, national and collective action must involve a wide group of stakeholders, governments, multilateral agencies, ocean industries, nongovernmental organizations and foundations and coastal communities, indigenous people and small-scale fishers.

The good news is that there is growing recognition that building a sustainable and inclusive ocean economy is essential in the coming years. This will require collective action to address the underpricing of marine capital and to bridge the funding gap for conservation. We cannot just declare global targets – such as protecting 30 percent of the ocean surface by 2030. True progress will require tackling the underpricing and underfunding challenges for our oceans and coasts. And, this will require a commitment by all stakeholders in a more sustainable and inclusive ocean economy.

Notes

1 "Factsheet: Peoples and Oceans," The Ocean Conference, United Nations, New York, June 5–9, 2017. www.un.org/sustainabledevelopment/wp-content/uploads/2017/05/Ocean-fact-sheet-package.pdf and Barbier (2014).
2 Cabral et al. (2020); Long et al. (2020); and Sumaila et al. (2020a).
3 "Factsheet: Peoples and Oceans," The Ocean Conference, United Nations, New York, June 5–9, 2017. www.un.org/sustainabledevelopment/wp-content/uploads/2017/05/Ocean-fact-sheet-package.pdf; Costella et al. (2016); Duarte et al. (2020); Newton et al. (2020); Worm (2016); Worm and Branch (2012); and Worm et al. (2006).
4 Based on Hannah Ritchie (2019) "Where Does Our Plastic Accumulate in the Ocean and What Does That Mean for the Future?" Published online at OurWorldInData.

org. https://ourworldindata.org/where-does-plastic-accumulate. The original source of the data is Lebreton et al. (2019). See also Abbott and Sumaila (2019); Almroth and Eggert (2019); Jambeck et al. (2015); Raubenheimer and McIlgorm (2018); and Vince and Hardesty (2018).

5 Barbier et al. (2014); Da Ros et al. (2019); Danovaro et al. (2017); and Van Dover et al. (2014).

6 Al-Abdulrazzak et al. (2017); Barbier et al. (2014); Danovaro et al. (2017); Schrijver (2016); Spalding and de Ycaza (2020); and Winther et al. (2020).

7 "Factsheet: Peoples and Oceans," The Ocean Conference, United Nations, New York, June 5–9, 2017. www.un.org/sustainabledevelopment/wp-content/uploads/2017/05/Ocean-fact-sheet-package.pdf.

8 Bavinck et al. (2017); Bennett et al. (2015) and (2021); Beymar-Farris and Bassett (2012); Foley and Mather (2019); and Vierros et al. (2020).

9 "Factsheet: Peoples and Oceans," The Ocean Conference, United Nations, New York, June 5–9, 2017. www.un.org/sustainabledevelopment/wp-content/uploads/2017/05/Ocean-fact-sheet-package.pdf. See also Schuhbauer and Sumaila (2016).

10 Virdin et al. (2021). The eight marine industries are: offshore oil and gas, marine equipment and construction, seafood, container shipping, shipbuilding and repair, cruise tourism, port activities and offshore wind. For more on the growing inequity of ocean exploitation, see Österblom et al. (2020).

11 Duarte et al. (2020); OECD (2016); and Sumaila et al. (2020b).

12 Barbier et al. (2014); Da Ros et al. (2019); Danovaro et al. (2017); and Van Dover et al. (2014).

13 Erlandson and Fitzpatrick (2008), p. 7. See also Fitzpatrick (2020); Friess et al. (2019); Harnik et al. (2012); and Mannino and Thomas (2002).

14 Lotze et al. (2006), p. 1806. See also Friess et al. (2019) and Harnik et al. (2012).

15 Harnik et al. (2012).

16 Lotze et al. (2006).

17 Sumaila et al. (2019).

18 Sala et al. (2021) and Nicola Jones. "Why the Market for 'Blue Carbon' May Be Poised to Take Off." Yale Environment 360 April 13, 2021. https://e360.yale.edu/features/why-the-market-for-blue-carbon-credits-may-be-poised-to-take-off.

19 Schuhbauer et al. (2017).

20 Belhabib et al. (2019); Long et al. (2020); Spijkers et al. (2019); Victorero et al. (2018); and Widjaja et al. (2020).

21 Belhabib et al. (2019).

22 Schuhbauer et al. (2017).

23 Belhabib et al. (2019).

24 Stavins (2011), p. 87. As a consequence of this race to fish, "two externalities may be said to be present. One is a contemporaneous externality (as with any public good) in which there is over-commitment of resources: too many boats, too many fishermen, and too much effort as everyone rushes to harvest before others. The other is an intertemporal externality in which overfishing reduces the stock and hence lowers future profits from fishing ... Ruin is not the outcome of the commons, but rather excessive employment of capital and labor, small profits for participants, and an excessively depleted resource stock" (Stavins 2011, pp. 88–89).

25 Birkenbach et al. (2017).

26 Costello et al. (2016). Similarly, Birkenbach et al. (2007) examine what would happen in thirty-nine US fisheries if they were managed through the imposition of catch shares. This market-based regulation allocates individual fishers a portion of the yearly total allowable catch (TAC). Securing each agent's share of the catch is

hypothesized to end any incentive to "race to fish" by allowing fishers to harvest flexibly over time, maximize profits and avoid hazards at sea. The authors find that catch shares lengthen the season and reduce the pressure to overfish, thus creating incentives to reduce costs; improve product quality; time the catch to market demand; and avoid safety risks.

27 Friess et al. (2019); Goldberg et al. (2020); Madin and Madin (2015); Murray et al. (2019); Newton et al. (2020); Waycott et al. (2009); and Wear (2016).

28 Davidson (2014) and Hu et al. (2017).

29 Davidson et al. (2018). See Davidson and Finlayson (2018) and (2019) for reviews of the global status and trends in estuarine and coastal habitats.

30 Murray et al. (2019) and Richards et al. (2020). For a comparison of recent mangrove loss trends with past trends, see Friess et al. (2019).

31 Beck et al. (2018).

32 Hochard et al. (2019).

33 Menéndez et al. (2020).

34 Barbier and Hochard (2018).

35 Gattuso et al. (2018) and Hoegh-Guldberg et al. (2019).

36 Zeng et al. (2021).

37 Petrolia et al. (2014).

38 Barbier (2007).

39 Lau et al. (2019).

40 Sala et al. (2021). Based on the Marine Protected Area Atlas. https://mpatlas.org.

41 Costello and Ballantine (2015); Duarte et al. (2020); Horta e Costa et al. (2016); Lester et al. (2009); Sala et al. (2021); and Worm et al. (2006).

42 See www.pewtrusts.org/en/research-and-analysis/articles/2021/01/27/the-drive-to-protect-30-percent-of-the-ocean-by-2030. The origin of the "30 by 30" target is the "Global Deal for Nature" proposed by Dinerstein et al. (2019), which suggests increasing global conservation and protected areas to 30 percent of the world's surface by 2030.

43 Cabral et al. (2020); Costello and Ballantine (2015); Duarte et al. (2020); Edgar et al. (2014); and Sala et al. (2021).

44 Cabral et al. (2020).

45 Sala et al. (2021).

46 Belhabib et al. (2019); Costello and Ballantine (2015); Donlan et al. (2020); McDermott et al. (2019); Nahuelhual et al. (2018); Victorero et al. (2018); Widjaja et al. (2020); and Yamazaki et al. (2015).

47 McDermott et al. (2019). Note also that a key assumption underlying Figure 7.1 is that the marine habitat is already under severe pressure from industrial fishing, and the purpose of the no-take marine reserve is to assist the recovery of the fishery and habitat. However, Kuempel et al. (2019) find that less than 2 percent of marine protected areas globally have been created in places under high pressure of overexploitation. Relatively low-threat ecoregions had 6.3 times more strict protection than high-threat ecoregions.

48 White et al. (2020), p. 1577.

49 Andreu-Cazenave et al. (2017); Battista et al. (2018); Belhabib et al. (2019); Donlan et al. (2020); Nahuelhual et al. (2018); and Widjaja et al. (2020).

50 Bennett and Deardon (2014); Burbano and Meredith (2020); Chaigneau and Brown (2016); and Cinner et al. (2014).

51 In a review of the cost and feasibility of global marine restoration, Bayraktarov et al. (2016) find that mangroves were the least expensive ecosystem to restore, whereas corals were the most expensive. The other ecosystems with mid-range restoration costs are seagrass beds, salt marshes and oyster reefs.

52 Konor and Ding (2020).

53 Costello et al. (2020). The two main types of ocean farming are finfish and bivalve mariculture. Common farmed marine finfish include snapper, red drum, salmon, halibut, tuna and cod. Typical bivalve species farmed are oyster, clam, scallop and mussel.

54 Spalding and de Ycaza (2020).

55 Al-Abdulrazzak et al. (2017); Spalding and de Ycaza (2020); and Winther et al. (2020).

56 See, for example, Barbier et al. (2014); Danovaro et al. (2017); Dinerstein et al. (2019); Gattuso et al. (2018); Hoegh-Guldberg et al. (2019); Long et al. (2020); Raubenheimer and McIlgorm (2018); Sala et al. (2021); Spalding and de Ycaza (2020); Sumaila et al. (2020a); Vince and Hardesty (2018); and Winther et al. (2020).

57 Bast et al. (2014) and Gençsü et al. (2019).

58 Cabral et al. (2020); Sumaila (2019); and Sumaila et al. (2020a).

59 Indonesia's approach is to sink illegal vessels, ban foreign fishing vessels and ban transfers of fish at sea. As Cabral et al. (2020) show, these actions have reduced fishing effort and thus overexploitation, mainly caused by illegal foreign fleet operations, to a level where limited expansion in domestic legal fishing effort can occur without undermining the overall sustainability of fisheries. The result is a decrease in total (legal and illegal) fishing effort by 25 percent, but the potential to increase sustainably local fishing catch by 14 percent and profits by 12 percent.

60 Abbott and Sumaila (2019); Almroth and Eggert (2019); Jambeck et al. (2015); Raubenheimer and McIlgorm (2018); and Vince and Hardesty (2018).

61 See Raubenheimer and McIlgorm (2018) for further details on such a global fund.

62 Danovaro et al. (2017).

63 Osterblöm et al. (2017). See Osterblöm et al. (2020) and Virdin et al. (2021) for other voluntary marine conservation initiatives undertaken by ocean industries and companies.

64 For example, Barbier et al. (2018) suggest that, based on the $53 billion in additional annual profits it would receive from more sustainable management of global fisheries as estimated by Costello et al. (2016), the seafood industry could afford to contribute $5–$10 billion annually on investments and management reforms that lead to more conservation of marine biomass stocks.

65 Osterblöm et al. (2020) and Virdin et al. (2021).

66 Barbier et al. (2018); Duarte et al. (2020); Iyer et al. (2018); Osterblöm et al. (2020); Sumaila et al. (2020b); and Virdin et al. (2021).

67 Iyer et al. (2018) provide an overview and comparison of many of these mechanisms, as well as case studies of their applications, to coral reefs and other marine habitats.

68 Chahine and Liagre (2020) and World Bank (2019a).

69 World Bank (2019a).

70 Iyer et al. (2018).

71 Barbier et al. (2018) and Colgan et al. (2017).

72 Iyer et al. (2018) and Sumaila et al. (2020b).

73 For more on the High Level Panel for a Sustainable Ocean Economy, see https://oceanpanel.org.

74 Bavinck et al. (2017); Bennett et al. (2021); Foley and Mather (2019); Osterblöm et al. (2020); Spalding and de Ycaza (2020); and Vierros et al. (2020).

75 Bavinck et al. (2017); Bennett et al. (2015) and (2021); Beymar-Farris and Bassett (2012); Foley and Mather (2019); and Vierros et al. (2020).

8 PUBLIC POLICIES

A simple message runs throughout this book. Our primary policy challenge in the coming decades is to design and run our economies to limit ecological scarcities and global environmental risks in a sustainable and inclusive manner. Tackling this challenge requires five principles to guide our economic actions and policies:

- Ending the underpricing of nature
- Fostering collective action
- Accepting absolute limits
- Attaining sustainability
- Promoting inclusivity

The previous chapters show how these principles can be put to work to overcome climate change, natural landscape and biodiversity loss, freshwater scarcity and deteriorating oceans and coasts. Such policies and actions are part of the process of building a *green economy*. This requires transforming and managing our economies so that they can sustain human welfare, improve social equity and, at the same time, limit global environmental risks and ecological scarcities.

This chapter elaborates further on the public policies that individual countries could adopt to "green" their economic activities and promote better stewardship of the environment. As the focus is mainly on actions adopted at the national level, the chapter will discuss strategies that governments might implement to achieve economy-wide green transformation.

How to do this is not a mystery. For several decades, economists have identified the policies needed to start this *green transition*. In a nutshell, "making economies more sustainable requires urgent progress in three key policy areas: valuing the environment, accounting for the environment, and creating incentives for environmental improvement."[1]

The first two policy initiatives are essential to ensuring that the wider social benefits associated with valuable ecosystems, habitats and biodiversity are properly valued and accounted for in economic decision-making.[2] These ecological values need to be increasingly incorporated into our measures of economic wealth, so that we can more accurately account for the depreciation in valuable natural systems, resources and sinks. Without this valuation and accounting, we are in danger of ignoring the "simple truth" that "our economies are embedded within Nature, not external to it."[3] By failing to accept this "simple truth," we end up instead perpetuating the economic myth that our planet provides a limitless source of exploitation for humankind.

The previous four chapters provide many examples of how valuing and accounting for nature's various benefits are crucial to overcoming ecological scarcities and global environmental risks. This chapter explores in more detail the third set of policies aimed at creating the incentives for environmental improvement to build a greener economy. As discussed in Chapter 1, correctly aligned incentives are essential to such a transition. Many of our environmental goods and service are allocated through markets, but important values associated with nature and ecological capital often are not. In addition, market and policy failures often lead to the misuse and overexploitation of the environment.

The good news is that more and more local, regional and national governments are adopting market-based initiatives for controlling pollution and resource exploitation. For example, currently forty-six national and thirty-five subnational jurisdictions around the world are pricing carbon.[4] In addition, nineteen low- and middle-income countries have developed a national action plan for designing and piloting market-based instruments for greenhouse gas mitigation.[5] There are now a wide-range of market-based incentives in use across the globe, especially energy and carbon taxes, petroleum product taxes, waste disposal, water abstraction charges, taxes on fertilizers and pesticides and air pollution charges.[6]

The bad news is that the underpricing of nature is still rife in all economies. As we have seen in previous chapters, it is the underlying cause of the ecological scarcities and global environmental risks we face:

climate change, natural landscape and biodiversity loss, water scarcity and deteriorating marine habitats. Moreover, underpricing of nature is not equitable. It favors the rich at the expense of the poor.

Clearly, we have a lot to do to build greener economies. This chapter explains what needs to be done and how public policies can make it happen.

The Green Economy in a Post-pandemic World

Some might argue that greening the economy may be a luxury given the global health and economic crises caused by the coronavirus pandemic.

However, greening the world economy is even more urgent in a post-pandemic world.

First, the pandemic has not reversed the accelerating environmental risks that the world is facing.

As Chapter 4 noted, it is unlikely that the economic slowdown induced by the pandemic will help much in achieving net zero emissions by 2050. Evidence suggests that the 2020 fall in global CO_2 emissions may be temporary, and as the world economy continues to rebound, the world is likely to see rising emissions.[7]

Other environmental threats may have worsened during the pandemic. The crisis has led to a weakening of environmental regulations and their enforcement worldwide, with consequences for environmental quality, pollution, land use change and resource overexploitation.[8] Land use change in the tropics appears to have increased, rather than declined. Land clearing for mining, agriculture, forestry and other commercial activities – often illegal – rose significantly, as governments diverted resources to COVID-19 or failed to protect remote regions. In 2020, during the pandemic, the world lost more than 4.2 million hectares in tropical primary forest, which is a 12 percent increase over the loss that occurred in 2019.[9]

At the beginning of the coronavirus outbreak, there was great hope that stimulus spending to revive economies would also involve substantial investments in clean energy, natural climate solutions and other environmental actions. However, that has not been the case. Of the nearly $15 trillion in announced spending across the world's largest fifty countries in 2020, only about $341 billion, or 2.5 percent, went to long-term green investments.[10]

Well before the pandemic, global inequality was on the rise. In recent decades, economic growth has become less inclusive. Since

1980 the top 1 percent richest individuals in the world captured twice as much growth as the bottom 50 percent.[11] Less inclusive growth is a major cause of increasing wealth inequality. Simply put, the rich are getting richer, and acquiring a greater share of global wealth.

Figure 8.1 depicts global wealth distribution at the end of 2019 – just as the COVID-19 outbreak occurred.

At the end of 2019, the least wealthy – those with net worth of $10,000 or less – comprise 54 percent of the world's adult population, but accounted for less than 1.5 percent of global wealth (see Figure 8.1). In comparison, people who are millionaires or richer make up 1 percent of the world's population yet they own more than 43 percent of global assets. What is more, the aggregate wealth of the rich has grown nearly fourfold since 2000, so that their share of global wealth increased by 5 percent.[12]

Wealth is also unevenly distributed across the world. North America and Europe comprise only 17 percent of the adult population worldwide but account for 55 percent of global wealth. In contrast, the population share was three times the wealth share in Latin America;

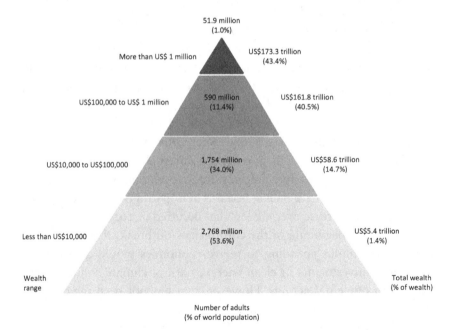

Figure 8.1 The global wealth pyramid, 2019
Source: Shorrocks et al. (2020)

four times the wealth share in India; and nearly ten times the wealth share in Africa.[13]

The pandemic has exacerbated global inequality. Since the outbreak, the world's richest have become wealthier and poverty reduction has suffered a major setback. Worldwide, the wealth of billionaires increased by $3.9 trillion during the pandemic in 2020, whereas the total number of people living in poverty may have expanded by 200–500 million. Around 70–100 million could fall into extreme poverty, the first rise in over two decades. Shared prosperity – the relative increase in the incomes of the bottom 40 percent of the population compared to that of the entire population – was projected to drop sharply in nearly all economies between 2020 and 2021, and will decline even more if the pandemic's economic impacts continue to fall disproportionately on poor people.[14]

These impacts of the COVID-19 outbreak on extreme poverty and shared prosperity could be especially devastating for the inclusivity of global development. Even before the pandemic, we were still a long way from achieving key sustainability and development objectives for the most vulnerable people and countries. In 2019, an estimated 736 million people lived in extreme poverty; 821 million were undernourished; 785 million people lacked basic drinking water services; and 673 million were without sanitation. About 3 billion people did not have clean cooking fuels and technology, and of the 840 million people without electricity, 87 percent lived in rural areas. As many as twenty-eight poor countries are projected to fall short of attaining SDGs 1–4, 6 and 7 by 2030.[15]

In sum, the pandemic has failed to halt – and may have even exacerbated – the global trends of rising environmental impacts and increasing inequality. This means that it is even more urgent that the post-pandemic world economy embarks on an inclusive and green transition.

As the Organization for Economic Cooperation and Development (OECD) argued at the height of the outbreak:

> For the economic recovery from the COVID-19 crisis to be durable and resilient, a return to "business as usual" and environmentally destructive investment patterns and activities must be avoided. Unchecked, global environmental emergencies such as climate change and biodiversity loss could cause social and economic damages far larger than those caused by COVID-19.

To avoid this, economic recovery packages should be designed to "build back better". This means doing more than getting economies and livelihoods quickly back on their feet. Recovery policies also need to trigger investment and behavioural changes that will reduce the likelihood of future shocks and increase society's resilience to them when they do occur.[16]

The rest of this chapter explores the public policies needed to build a more inclusive and green economy.

Building the Green Economy

Building a greener economy is the key to ensuring a safe and prosperous Anthropocene for humankind.

But what should this economic transition look like? The following description in a United Nations report is most apt:

> A *green economy* results in "improved human wellbeing and social equity, while significantly reducing environmental risks and ecological scarcities," and thus "in a green economy, growth in income and employment should be driven by public and private investments that reduce carbon emissions and pollution, enhance energy and resource efficiency, and prevent the loss of biodiversity and ecosystem services. These investments need to be catalysed and supported by targeted public expenditure, policy reforms and regulation changes."[17]

Such a green economy is clearly very different from present-day "brown" economies. Transitioning from a fundamentally brown economy to a greener one is a considerable challenge. Meeting this challenge is vital, and needs to be accomplished sooner rather than later as global environmental risks mount.

The recognition that this goal is critical and urgent has led to calls for increased government spending on greening the economy to meet stated targets, such as the UN objective that all nations achieve zero net carbon emissions by 2050, or the promise by some politicians to achieve a 100 percent clean energy economy in ten or twenty years, or the conservation goal of protecting 30 percent of the planet's land and water surface by 2030.

Setting ambitious green targets is important. It is also essential that we design a workable and cost-effective economic strategy to achieve these outcomes. What is more, such a strategy cannot rely just on governments to fund more green investments and expenditures to jump start the transition. Such massive packages of public spending – or "Green New Deals" – have a role to play, if designed effectively. But these investments have to be affordable, and revenues must be generated to pay for them.

More fundamentally, rethinking markets, institutions and governance to end the underpricing of nature and create appropriate incentives is the key to any successful strategy for greening economies today. As we discussed in Chapter 1, the lack of green investment and innovation is a *symptom* of the structural imbalance and disincentives created by the underpricing of nature, not the *cause* of this imbalance. As every physician knows, treating symptoms does not address the underlying cause. At best, the treatment will be ineffective; at worst it will be counterproductive and do more harm than good. Similarly, ending the vicious cycle of underpricing nature is necessary to achieve the structural change required for greening economies.

Designing the right policy and investment strategy to build a green economy may be the most important task of governments in the Anthropocene Age, along with other socioeconomic objectives such as maintaining the rule of law, providing national security, fostering democratic institutions and ensuring social welfare.[18] But government policies must enable the incentives, investments and innovations needed to make this green transition possible, and must accomplish this in an inclusive manner.

Rethinking markets, institutions and governance to end the underpricing of nature should not be a license for wholesale replacement of private with public ownership; swamping the economy with public spending and regulations that deter private investment, innovation and entrepreneurship; the creation of barriers to entry and bolstering of dominant companies; and saddling taxpayers and future generations with unsustainable levels of debt.

Instead, any successful strategy for building a green economy will require two important elements:

- An initial push to jump-start the transition in the short term
- Policies to sustain the momentum toward green structural transformation in the longer term

Moreover, as we have discussed in previous chapters, the suite of policies should be different for the largest, richest and most populous economies of the world as opposed to the more numerous, smaller and poorer economies.

Choosing the right set of policies to jump-start the green transition and sustain the momentum to transform economies is especially important in the aftermath of the COVID-19 pandemic, which has been devastating to all economies and social welfare.

Major Economies

The largest and most populous economies comprise the Group of 20 (G20). The members of the G20 include Argentina, Australia, Brazil, Canada, China, France, Germany, India, Indonesia, Italy, Japan, Mexico, Russia, Saudi Arabia, South Africa, South Korea, Turkey, the United Kingdom, the United States and the European Union. In the coming years, these major economies will have a large say in how the world economy recovers from the coronavirus pandemic, and how it achieves a more sustainable and inclusive development path.

For one, the sheer scale of the G20 economies and their population means that they drive global economic activity and its impacts on the environment. They comprise nearly two-thirds of the world's population and land area; 82 percent of GDP; and 80 percent of global CO_2 emissions.[19]

In addition, if the pattern of global development is to change, it is the G20 that will provide many of the innovations for this transition. Eight of the G20 economies – China, France, Germany, Italy, Japan, South Korea, the United Kingdom and the United States – dominate the "green race" for environmental competitiveness and innovation in key global industries, such as machinery, motor vehicles, engines and turbines, steam generators, iron and steel, batteries, electricity generation and distribution and domestic appliances.[20] Consequently, the policies that these economies adopt for their post-pandemic recovery and beyond will have important implications not just domestically but also for the future greening of the world economy, the distribution of global wealth and the mitigation of the growing environmental risks of the Anthropocene.

One encouraging sign in recent years has been the growing recognition that the urgency of the planetary climate and environmental crisis requires a sustained and concerted commitment by governments of major economies to jump-start their green transition. These public policy and investment commitments are now commonly referred to as *Green New Deals* – after Roosevelt's New Deal of the 1930s to revive the US economy during the Great Depression.

Calls for Green New Deals emerged around the time of the 2008–2009 Great Recession. Such plans aimed to create jobs and boost the economy, while simultaneously greening the recovery through supporting clean energy, promoting energy efficiency and reducing pollution and waste.[21]

Once the Great Recession ended, however, so did enthusiasm for Green New Deals; that is, until more recently, when the concept was revived just before the COVID-19 outbreak.[22] As noted, however, very little spending on green recovery actually occurred during the pandemic. Only about 2.5 percent of worldwide expenditure to combat health and economic crises could legitimately be considered long-term green investments. Nonetheless, there are notable exceptions.

In December 2019, the European Union (EU) launched its Green Deal, and has continued to push forward with this plan despite the COVID-19 outbreak. The central objective of the EU Green Deal is to achieve net zero greenhouse gas emissions for Europe by 2050, largely by targeting investments in low-carbon energy and energy efficiency. It also contains ambitious green goals for other sectors, including construction, biodiversity, energy, transport and food.

The main pillar of this strategy is EU Green Deal Investment Plan.[23] This calls for mobilizing $1.2 trillion over ten years, half of which will come from the EU budget and the rest from leveraging private and public sources, including from the European Investment Bank. Much of the money will be for energy-related investments, buildings and low-emission vehicles. Other investments are expected for greening agriculture, controlling biodiversity loss and pollution and the protection of natural capital. At least $120 billion will be for the Just Transition Mechanism, which provides targeted support to help vulnerable regions, communities and workers disadvantaged by the transition away from fossil fuels.

The EU is also exploring additional carbon pricing measures, beyond the current European Emissions Trading Scheme. These include the possibility of revising current EU rules to allow European-wide carbon taxation and introducing a carbon adjustment border mechanism (CABM).[24] The latter is essentially a tax on high-carbon imports, which is essentially a deterrent to EU businesses transferring production to other countries with laxer emission constraints and then importing goods and services back to Europe.

The continuing interest worldwide in triggering a green transition – even in the wake of the economically devastating COVID-19 pandemic – is encouraging. As noted, such actions are an important first step in "building back better" for all major economies. But to be successful, and to ensure a safe and prosperous Anthropocene, we need to proceed to the second step of developing a policy strategy that sustains momentum toward a green structural transformation.

Such a long-term strategy for promoting the necessary incentives and investments should have three components:

- Phasing out environmentally harmful subsidies
- Implementing market-based incentives to reduce environmental damages
- Using any resulting financial savings and revenues to support green innovation, investment and conservation

We can also think of these three components as three distinct steps in the process of green structural transformation (see Figure 8.2).

The first two steps are, of course, also important to ending the *underpricing of nature*, which prevents our economies from limiting global environmental risks in a sustainable and inclusive manner.

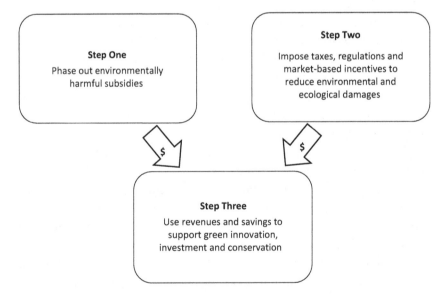

Figure 8.2 A strategy for green structural transformation in major economies

The previous chapters discussed examples of how these steps are necessary if we are to tackle some of the most pressing environmental problems – global warming, land use change, water scarcity and declining marine environments.

But we have also seen how removing environmentally harmful subsidies and pricing environmental "bads" can not only provide incentives to correct resource exploitation, pollution and environmental risks but also help overcome the *underfunding of nature*. It is especially important that major economies take the lead on such a strategy.

For example, Chapter 4 argued that one of the more important uses of the revenues saved or raised through removing fossil fuel subsidies and pricing carbon in G20 economies is to address the lack of sufficient public sector support for research and development (R&D) leading to low-carbon innovations. These include R&D subsidies, public investments, protecting intellectual property and other initiatives to spur more widespread clean energy innovation by businesses. Other forms of public investments may also be critical for green structural transformation of G20 economies, such as a "smart" transmission infrastructure for renewables; more reliable and faster charging networks for electric vehicles; building more "sustainable" cities and urban transport systems; and natural climate solutions.

Other chapters have identified other parts of the economy where underpricing needs to be corrected. This includes removing environmental harmful subsidies in agriculture and other land-using sectors and imposing taxes and other market-based incentives to deter excessive loss of ecological capital (see Chapter 5). We also need reforms to markets and policies to ensure that they adequately capture the rising economic costs of exploiting water resources (see Chapter 6). And finally, conservation of oceans and coasts requires the removal of environmental harmful subsidies, such as those supporting unsustainable fishing, and that our markets and policies reflect the many benefits provided by the marine environment (see Chapter 7). Widespread adoption by such market-based incentives and pricing reforms for managing land use, water and oceans and coasts in the marine environment will generate or save substantial revenue that major economies could invest instead in protecting and restoring their natural landscape, freshwater ecosystems and marine environment.

Some might argue that such a strategy for green structural transformation is not necessary. After all, in recent decades, there have been signs of nascent green sectors emerging in almost all major economies. There are five such sectors that have been growing rapidly in recent years:

- energy from renewable resources
- energy efficiency
- pollution abatement and materials recycling
- natural resources conservation and ecological restoration
- environmental compliance, education, training and public awareness[25]

However, these sectors still remain "green niches" within fundamentally brown economies that are still dependent on overuse of fossil fuels and other natural resources and are causing too much environmental and ecological damage. In order to end the underpricing of nature and to unleash the economic potential of green developments for generating economy-wide innovation and prosperity, then the scale of structural transformation needed is well beyond simply expanding the five green sectors.

As the economist Sam Fankhauser and his colleagues have pointed out, if we "interpret green growth as an economy-wide transformation, rather than the expansion of the environmental goods and services sectors," then there are several strategic sectors whose transformation is central to the creation of a green economy.[26] These areas include industrial processes, which need to become cleaner and more resource efficient (e.g. iron and steel); sectors that are important for energy efficiency on the supply side (electricity distribution systems) and the demand side (domestic appliances); the energy supply chain for electricity generation and other industrial processes (steam generators, engines and turbines, electric motors and transformers); and car manufacturing (low-emission and electric vehicles) and key components (accumulators, primary cells and batteries).

Fostering such economy-wide change requires the type of concerted, three-step strategy outlined in Figure 8.2. As Fankhauser and coauthors argue, for an economy to embark on green transformation and innovation, "public policy is important. A key challenge for the green economy is to overcome persistent market failures (e.g. on innovation) and externalities (e.g. pricing the environment), which requires well-designed and consistent public policy intervention. Business decisions on investment and R&D in particular respond to such policy signals."[27]

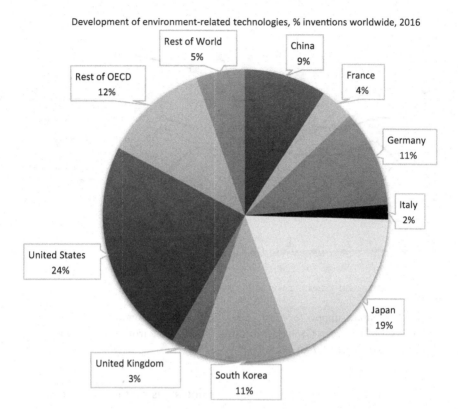

Development of environment-related technologies, % inventions worldwide, 2016

Figure 8.3 Major economies and global green innovation
Notes: The Organization for Economic Cooperation and Development (OECD) is
an intergovernmental economic organization with thirty-seven member countries.
For a list of countries see www.oecd.org/about/members-and-partners. Between
2010 and 2016, South Korea's share of global green innovation rose from 8.7% to
11%. During the same period, China's share increased from 4.6% to 9.3%, and the
United States' from 23.4% to 24.1%. Japan's share declined from 22.6% to 19.0%;
Germany's from 13.3% to 10.8%; Italy's from 1.7% to 1.6%; the United
Kingdom's from 3.2% to 3.1%; and France's from 4.1% to 3.8%.
Source: OECD "Green Growth Indicators," OECD Environment Statistics
https://doi.org/10.1787/data-00665-en

The eight economies that dominate the global "green race" for
environmental competitiveness and innovation account for around
83 percent of green R&D worldwide (see Figure 8.3). The United
States alone is responsible for about a quarter of global innovation.
For the foreseeable future, these eight countries will continue to be the
source of the R&D that will be essential for any global green
structural innovation.

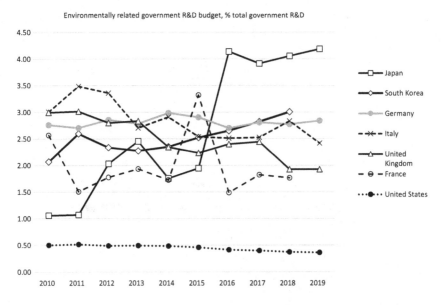

Figure 8.4 Public support for green innovation in major economies
Source: OECD "Green Growth Indicators," OECD Environment Statistics
https://doi.org/10.1787/data-00665-en

However, there have been warning signs that green innovation has been waning in key economies.

For one, as we noted in Chapter 4, environmental innovations per capita have been declining in all major economies in recent years. The one possible exception is South Korea, which has producing nearly seventy environmentally related inventions per person since 2010 – the highest per capita green innovation in the world (see Figure 4.4).

In addition, many economies are devoting a smaller – not a bigger – share of government R&D to environmental innovation. Since 2010, the share of public R&D budgets spent on environmental technologies has been shrinking in France, Germany, Italy, the United Kingdom and the United States (see Figure 8.4). As these five countries account for 43 percent of the world's innovation, this trend could have a detrimental impact on global green structural transformation. Yet, as Figure 8.4 shows, these five economies devote less than 3 percent of public R&D support to green technologies, and in the United States, it is less than 0.4 percent.

In comparison, Japan and South Korea have expanded government support to enhance green innovation. Since 2010, both countries have increased significantly the share of government R&D devoted to environmental technologies (see Figure 8.4). Japan now allocates well over 4 percent of its government budget for this purpose. Although there are no data available on how its public support for environmental technologies has grown in recent years, China is also promoting green innovation through government R&D policies.

For China and South Korea, their increasing public support for environmentally related R&D may be paying off in terms of the "green race." South Korea's contribution to global green innovation rose from 8.7 percent to 11.0 percent between 2010 and 2016. China also doubled its share of green inventions worldwide, from 4.6 percent to 9.3 percent (see Figure 8.3).

South Korea has viewed public support for environmentally related technologies as part of its long-term efforts to green its industrial strategy. After the 2008–2009 Great Recession, its government established a US$72 million renewable energy fund to attract private investment in solar, wind and hydroelectric power projects. In recent years, South Korea has also emerged with a competitive advantage and significant green innovation in basic chemical industries (excluding fertilizer) and special purpose machinery. As part of its long-term strategy, South Korea is developing green technologies to manufacture fuel cells, heat pumps and high-efficiency lighting. Other government programs that support green R&D include tax credits and allowances, tax reductions for the wages of R&D workers and accelerated depreciation of capital used for R&D, which at 0.3 percent of GDP has created one of the highest levels of support among major economies.[28]

In sum, the three-part strategy outlined in Figure 8.2 is critical for green structural transformation in major economies. Not only is it important for ensuring a safe and prosperous Anthropocene, but in the coming decades, such a strategy could also determine who are the winners and losers in the green race for global environmental competitiveness and innovation.

Low- and Middle-Income Economies

Green transformation is also possible – and necessary – for low- and middle-income countries, but the process must take into account their specific needs and constraints. These economies often face considerable challenges in implementing green transformation, including a large informal economy; high levels of poverty and inequality; weak capacity and resources for innovation and investment; and inadequate governance and institutions.[29] Nonetheless, the overall objective should be the same: encouraging development that is efficient, sustainable and inclusive.

If a greener development path is to be a catalyst for economy-wide transformation and poverty alleviation in developing countries, then it must be reconciled with the key structural patterns and conditions of natural resource use and poverty. For many developing countries, primary product exports account for the vast majority of their export earnings. In addition, the poor in these economies are increasingly rural, dependent on agriculture and predominantly young. Many economies also have a substantial share of their rural population located on less favored agricultural land and in remote areas, thus encouraging "geographic" poverty traps. Finally, both economic development and greenhouse gas (GHG) emissions continue to be coupled to considerable land use change in developing countries, especially for the poorer economies.[30]

Successful transformation in these economies will be through policies targeted in four key areas:

- improving the efficiency and sustainability of primary production
- decoupling rural development from land use expansion
- investments in smallholders in marginal agricultural regions
- expanding renewable energy and green technology adoption in rural areas[31]

We have outlined many of these policies in previous chapters. For example, Chapter 5 discusses how the ending the underpricing of natural landscape is essential to improving the efficiency and sustainability of primary production activities in many low- and middle-income countries, including providing the incentives for more innovation and investment to decouple such activities from landscape conversion. In addition, controlling land use expansion by commercial primary product activities requires a combination of environmental regulations to control deforestation; regional policies that encourage agglomeration economies; and market-based incentives to reduce forest loss and degradation. Targeting research, extension, marketing services and land tenure arrangements to improve the livelihoods of the rural poor in remote land-abundant regions also show promise. And finally, as outlined in

Chapter 4, facilitating greater dissemination and adoption of renewable energy and improved energy efficiency technologies in rural areas also depends on overcoming key obstacles, such as the lack of long-term financing schemes; poor private sector participation; inadequate institutional structure; lack of coordination between local and national governments; and the weak purchasing power of rural communities.

Similarly, Chapter 6 argued the need for developing countries to decouple agricultural and economic development from increasing freshwater scarcity, especially as new demands for water arise through urbanization and industrial growth. Such a strategy will require investments to protect freshwater ecosystems and to enhance water-saving innovations that increase the productivity of water; reduce inefficient and wasteful use; and improve the additional value gained from consuming water.

Chapter 7 also found that all countries – rich and poor – need to adopt policy reforms and regulations to promote more sustainable management of marine capital, and to adopt taxes, license fees, tradable quotas and other market-based incentives to deter marine ecological damages incurred by various ocean industries. Low- and middle-income countries urgently require investments in conserving and restoring estuarine and coastal habitats; sustainably producing food from capture fisheries and mariculture; decarbonizing international shipping; and expanding marine protected areas.

These additional policies and investments may be a tall order, as many low- and middle-income countries will take a long time to recover from the economic devastation caused by the COVID-19 pandemic. As noted previously, the outbreak has been especially difficult for developing countries. It has slowed growth and development, thrown millions back into poverty and forced governments to spend billions on emergency health measures through skyrocketing public debt.

But in the wake of the pandemic, the international community may not be much help either. During the outbreak, global debt rose by $24 trillion in 2020, and reached 335 percent of global GDP.[32] Many wealthy countries may need to start paying off their debt rather than provide additional financial and technical support for green transformation in low- and middle-income countries. Emergency measures established during the pandemic, such as the Debt Service Suspension Initiative, did provide poorer countries a temporary respite from debt payments, but there is yet to be any sign of a comprehensive debt relief program for the world's poorest countries.[33]

In sum, low- and middle-income countries should still aim for the type of green transformation strategy outlined in Figure 8.2, but it should be tailored to their development needs and priorities. In addition, to finance the necessary programs and investments, developing countries may need to rely on their own resources – even though they are also strapped for finances.

The first two steps, which involve ending the underpricing of nature, must still be a priority. Environmentally harmful subsidies for fossil fuels, agriculture, fisheries, water and other economic activities are rising globally, and increasingly so in low- and middle-income countries.[34] In these economies as well, increased use of environmental taxation and other market-based incentives not only has the potential to improve pricing of externalities and discourage environmentally damaging behavior but also raise additional revenues.[35]

But in a post-pandemic world, developing countries may also have to choose wisely as to which pricing reforms and policies should be adopted that best reconcile sustainability and long-term development goals, such as alleviating poverty, reducing hunger, improving access to basic services and improving equity. This requires identifying policies that can:

- Yield immediate progress toward key development goals.
- Align economic incentives for sustainability and green transformation.
- Have potential for funding any additional investments.

The previous chapters have identified a range of innovative policies and pricing reforms that meet these criteria. Here, we summarize two types of policies that could be implemented immediately and are effective: *subsidy swaps* applied to fossil fuels, irrigation and marine fisheries and a *tropical carbon tax*.

As proposed in Chapter 4, low- and middle-income countries could implement a subsidy swap for fossil fuels, whereby the savings from subsidy reform for coal, oil and natural gas consumption are allocated to fund clean energy investments. In 2018, fossil fuel consumption subsidies reached $427 billion annually, of which nearly $360 billion were in developing countries.[36] In many developing countries, a 10–30 percent subsidy swap from fossil fuel consumption to investments in energy efficiency and renewable energy electricity generation could "tip the balance" between fossil fuels and cleaner sources of energy. Partial reforms in India, Indonesia, Morocco and Zambia have already shown some progress in that direction. A study by the International Institute for Sustainable Development shows that removal of fossil fuel subsidies on its own in twenty-six countries – twenty-two of which are low- and middle income – would reduce greenhouse gas emissions by 6 percent on average for each country.[37]

In addition, a fossil fuel subsidy swap should be used to facilitate greater dissemination and adoption of renewable energy and improved energy efficiency technologies in rural areas. It could also fund programs to support the adoption of clean cooking and heating technologies. As discussed in Chapter 4, this is critical for reducing energy poverty across developing countries. Morocco, Kenya and South Africa illustrate how different public policy approaches can facilitate the adoption and deployment of renewable energy and improved energy efficiency technologies in rural areas.

Such a fossil fuel subsidy swap would also be more equitable. In low- and middle-income economies, it is mainly wealthier, urban households that benefit from fossil fuel consumptions subsidies, whereas it is rural households that increasingly comprise the extreme poor. Across twenty developing countries, the poorest fifth of the population received on average just 7 percent of the overall benefit of fossil fuel subsidies, whereas the richest fifth gained almost 43 percent.[38]

As explained in Chapter 6, developing countries could also implement a subsidy swap for irrigation to support investments in clean water and improved sanitation. Irrigation subsidies lead to overuse of water, inefficiencies and inequality, as irrigation is often allocated by land holding area and thus any subsidies disproportionately benefit larger and wealthier farmers. Irrigation water is often priced below its cost of supply, and may not even cover the operation and maintenance costs of irrigation systems. Irrigation also benefits from cross-subsidies from power generation. Buyers of hydroelectricity pay for the dam and other infrastructure and the stored water is allocated to irrigation with little cost recovery.

Reallocating irrigation subsidies to improve water supply, sanitation and wastewater infrastructure is an urgent need in all developing countries. The strategy for targeting and sequencing water-related services in developing countries should prioritize the needs of poorer households; their ability to pay for improved clean water and sanitation; and the overall costs of providing such services. For example, three interventions that do not involve large-scale infrastructure and supply networks for delivering clean water and sanitation include rural water supply programs that provide communities with deep boreholes and public hand pumps; community-led total sanitation campaigns; and biosand filters for household water treatment. These interventions are not only affordable by poor households and communities but also generate essential health and economic benefits post-pandemic, and protect women and children, who are worst affected by a lack of clean water and sanitation.

Chapter 7 suggests that developing countries should also adopt a subsidy swap from large-scale fishing fleets to invest in the protection, management and investment in small-scale fisheries. Annual fishing subsidies mainly benefit large-scale industrial fleets; encourage overfishing and damage to the marine environment; and often place small-scale fishers at a competitive disadvantage. If all or some of the fishing subsidies are phased out, the savings could instead be redirected to financing improved management and regulation of small-scale fisheries; rebuilding fish stocks and habitats that support these fisheries; and providing technical and marketing assistance to the post-harvest activities dependent on small-scale fisheries.

Finally, developing countries could also consider adopting a tropical carbon tax as discussed in Chapter 5. This is a levy on fossil fuels that is invested in natural climate solutions (NCS) aimed at mitigating carbon emissions and conserving, restoring and improving land management to protect biodiversity and ecosystem services. NCS are a relatively inexpensive way of reducing tropical land use change, which is a major source of greenhouse gas emissions.

Costa Rica and Colombia have already imposed a tax on carbon from fossil fuels to fund NCS. If twelve other megadiverse countries roll out a policy similar to Colombia's, they could raise $1.8 billion each year between them to invest in natural habitats that benefit the climate. A more ambitious policy of taxation and revenue allocation could yield nearly $13 billion each year for natural climate solutions.[39]

Moreover, such a strategy can be "pro-poor." Ecosystem services such as drinking-water supply, food provision and cultural services contribute almost 30 percent of the income of households who live in forests, and even a larger share for the poor.[40] Such services can make an important contribution to ending extreme poverty, reducing hunger, improving health and meeting many of the other basic needs of households in forested areas of developing countries.

Some low- and middle-income economies will also benefit from the third stage of green transformation, through supporting green industrial development and innovation (see Figure 8.2). For these economies, the right combination of industrial policies can sustain a shift to cleaner and more energy-efficient production processes. But as in the case of transforming rural sectors, the approach to greening industrial development must be realistic.

With the exception of large emerging market economies, such as China and India, it is unlikely that many low- and middle-income economies could win a global "green race" to become major exporters of green industrial manufactures, such as vehicles, solar panels, wind turbines, storage batteries, energy-saving appliances and similar products.[41] Instead, governments in developing countries should focus more on adapting and phasing in existing green technologies for economy-wide benefits rather than expecting to develop and nurture infant green industries to substitute for imports, leapfrog to a clean-energy economy or compete on world markets.

That is, for most low- and middle-income economies, green industrial policies should "look at sectors with a fairly established set of technologies available on the global market that can be adapted to local requirements."[42] Such an industrial strategy is also compatible with green structural transformation in these economies, provided that the overall aims are to improve livelihoods, reduce environmental degradation and alleviate widespread poverty, especially in rural areas.

Policies for a More Inclusive Economy

Earlier in this chapter, we noted how the worsening inequality trends in the decades that led up to the COVID-19 pandemic pose a challenge to any strategy for greening economies. Ensuring that development is both sustainable and inclusive is even more of a priority, given that the pandemic has most likely deepened inequality further in all economies.

Tackling the trend of growing wealth inequality may require additional public policies targeted and ensuring that economic development is more inclusive in the coming decades. Here are a few initiatives worth considering.

One possibility is for governments to tax "social bads."[43] Taxing harmful products and activities, from alcohol to gambling, is a long-established practice. It makes sense to extend the taxation of "societal ills" to activities that have enabled a select few to become disproportionately rich and then utilizing the proceeds to fund protection of the environment or public services and income support for the poor. One example is the "tropical carbon tax" discussed previously, which places a levy on greenhouse gas emissions that raises funds for investing in natural climate solutions that protect natural habitats and ecosystems that benefit largely the poor.

Another possibility is a financial transaction tax (FTT). A small FTT collected on the sale of financial assets, such as stock, bonds or futures, would have a negligible effect on trade, but could raise substantial funds. For example, a tax of 0.1 percent on equities and 0.02 percent on bonds could bring in about $48 billion from G20 member states.[44]

A variant of the FTT is a currency transaction tax, or Tobin tax, named after James Tobin, the economist who proposed it in the 1970s. Foreign exchange transactions total around $800 trillion annually, which means that a Tobin tax of only 0.05 percent could raise as much as $400 billion a year.[45]

Another variant is a financial activities tax (FAT) on the profits and wages of financial institutions, to raise revenue from the financial sector's activities more generally. In effect, such a FAT would be a levy on the value added by a financial institution, and thus if the institution was earning excessive profits or overpaying its employees and providing them with unwarranted bonuses, then such a tax would discourage these practices.[46] Estimates suggest that a 5 percent FAT levied on twenty-one major economies could yield almost $100 billion per year.[47]

Other taxes are also promising. A 10 percent tax on global arms exports, for example, could raise up to $5 billion annually. Additional tobacco-sales taxes in G20 and other European Union (EU) countries could generate an extra $10.8 billion; global aviation-fuel taxes $27 billion; and shipping-fuel taxes $37 billion.[48]

One concern with these taxes is that national governments will face intense lobbying pressures from the industries affected by these taxes, and it is difficult for a number of nations to agree on collective action to impose such taxes if there are significant holdouts. For example, this is what happened in the aftermath of the Great Recession of 2008–2009, when the European Union proposed an FTT at the G20 summit in Cannes, France, in November 2011 as a way to raise development funding for poorer countries.[49] Although favorably received by many G20 countries, the proposal failed to secure full backing because of opposition from the United States, the United Kingdom and Canada, all of which worried about the FTT's added financial burden to their banks.

However, the prolonged economic crisis caused by the COVID-19 pandemic has revived interest in various financial taxation mechanisms. For example, the European Union has agreed "in principle" to adopt a Tobin tax among its twenty-seven member states.[50] One of the rationales for the plan is to raise funds to redress rising inequality, which as we have noted, is becoming a priority post-pandemic.

At the heart of this wealth imbalance is the financial sector. Not only is financial wealth growing more concentrated among the wealthiest in economies, but the driving force behind wealth inequality is the increasing earnings gap between high- and low-skilled individuals.[51]

The main cause of this growing wage disparity in an economy is the "race" between education and technology.[52] Technological innovation increases the demand for more highly skilled workers. Although investments in the education, training and health of workers may boost the supply of such workers, the increase in recent decades has failed to keep pace with the rising demand. The result is that there is a growing scarcity of highly skilled workers. This scarcity of human capital not only leads to redundancy and underemployment for labor with the wrong set or little skills, but also allows those with the right set of skills, education and training to capture a bigger share of the wealth created in an economy. The consequence is a widening wealth gap between rich and poor.

There is now evidence of a growing income and wealth gap between high- and low-skilled workers for a wide range of economies. For example, the OECD (2011, page 31), found that "the evolution of earnings inequality across OECD countries over the past few decades could be viewed mainly as the difference between the demand for and supply of skills ... the outcome of a 'race between education and technology.'"[53] Similarly, as developing and emerging market economies increasingly adopt the skill-biased technologies of advance economies and the demand for skilled labor rises globally, there is also increasing pressure of the relative wages of skilled workers and inequality worldwide. Thus, the rising demand for highly skilled labor, and the subsequent inequality in income earnings and wealth, appears to be a global phenomenon.[54]

One way to address the problem of insufficient human capital accumulation, and thus end the growing wage disparity in economies, is to implement a two-part strategy. First, adopt levies on the activities of financial institutions to raise revenue and reduce financial market risk, and second, invest the revenue in improving the education, health and training of more potential workers. This would ensure the supply of highly skilled workers to better match the pace of skill-biased technological change.[55]

A second approach is to use any funds raised by financial sector taxes – as well as levies on other social "bads" such as arms sales, tobacco, aviation and shipping fuel or carbon – to directly support the poor. One such policy initiative that has been quietly gaining momentum during the pandemic is the universal basic income (UBI).

UBI is a guaranteed income for adults, usually in the form of a monthly cash payment of $500–$1,000. It is considered "basic," because a UBI provides money to pay rents or mortgages; buy groceries, clothing and other necessities; and to cover medical or child care expenses. Above all, a guaranteed monthly income would provide economic security for the poor and unemployed; facilitate part-time work; ensure money for education or job training; and increase saving.[56]

As the economic and health crises of the pandemic have surged around the world, so have calls to adopt UBI schemes or to expand existing pilot and local programs.[57] COVID-19 has caused massive unemployment and economic hardship, and chronic poverty has worsened significantly. It has also constrained efforts to improve human capital accumulation through educational attainment; health and training; and has undermined progress toward establishing a more highly skilled workforce. It could take years, if not decades, to address the consequences for many households and individuals. Advocates of UBI argue that it could eventually replace increasingly costly programs that economies have been forced to expand during the COVID-19 pandemic, such as unemployment insurance and other social safety nets. As funding UBI is also expensive, using the funds from financial sector taxes and increased charges on other "social ills" would be one way to fund such schemes on a permanent and secure basis.

Conclusion

Public policies are important for enabling a sustainable and inclusive transformation of all economies. Formulating the right strategy is especially crucial in a world recovering from the health and economic crises caused by the global pandemic.

As outlined in this chapter, the policies chosen must be creative, forward-looking and just. At the center of the strategy should be reforms to get the incentives right: removing environmentally harmful subsidies; ensuring that environmental damages are properly priced; and properly funding environmental benefits. Ending the underpricing of nature provides an opportunity to create opportunities from crises, and to enable the economic potential of green developments to generate economy-wide innovations and prosperity.

Ending the underpricing of nature is essential to ensure that the rising economic costs of exploiting scarce resources and ecosystems are adequately reflected in our market incentives, governance and institutions. The result will be reduced environmental risks, inequality and conflict; more green innovations and investments; and further mitigation of natural resource and ecological scarcity and its costs. Ultimately, this leads to the building of a greener economy that sustains per capita welfare while limiting global environmental risks.

But a complete strategy also requires public policies and investments aimed at developing complementary infrastructure and innovations for a green structural transformation. Each economy should also use the revenues earned and saved from such pricing reforms to invest in necessary infrastructure and investments. This is increasingly important in a post-pandemic world, where global debt is at an all-time high and many governments have little fiscal space for massive outlays on long-term investment plans.

Moreover, the selection of policy actions must be appropriate. They should be different for the largest, richest and most populous economies of the world as opposed to the more numerous, smaller and poorer economies. If designed correctly, any strategy of investment and pricing reforms will also put economies on a more inclusive path, including generating net gains in employment; improving income and wealth distribution; and targeting gains toward vulnerable populations and poor countries.

Although this chapter has emphasized that public policies are
pivotal in nurturing the incentives, investments and innovations needed
for an inclusive green transition, the goal should not be an economy that
is controlled and dominated by government. To the contrary, as we
shall see in the next chapter, investors and businesses are vital to
ensuring that a green structural transformation takes place, and indeed,
may be pivotal to determining whether it occurs at all.

Notes

1 Barbier and Markandya (2012), p. 1. See also Pearce et al. (1989), which put forward
 the first "blueprint" of economic policies for greening economies.
2 See Barbier (2011) and Dasgupta (2021).
3 Quoted from p. 2 of *The Economics of Biodiversity: The Dasgupta Review –
 Headline Messages*. https://assets.publishing.service.gov.uk/government/uploads/
 system/uploads/attachment_data/file/957629/Dasgupta_Review_-_Headline_
 Messages.pdf. For the full report, see Dasgupta (2021).
4 See https://carbonpricingdashboard.worldbank.org, accessed May 17, 2021.
5 Partnership for Market Readiness. Implementing Country Participants. www.thepmr
 .org/content/participants, accessed on May 17, 2021.
6 See OECD. www.oecd.org/env/tools-evaluation/environmentaltaxation.htm.
7 Andrijevic et al. (2020); Le Quéré et al. (2020); Tollefson (2021).
8 Barbier (2020a) and Helm (2020).
9 See Mikaela Weisse and Liz Goldman. "Primary Rain Forest Destruction Increased
 12% from 2019 to 2020." Global Forest Watch. March 31, 2021. www
 .globalforestwatch.org/blog/data-and-research/global-tree-cover-loss-data-2020.
10 O'Callahan and Murdock (2021).
11 Alvaredo et al. (2017).
12 Shorrocks et al. (2019).
13 Shorrocks et al. (2020). As the authors note, the wealth distribution within countries
 is also typically skewed. The top 1% wealthiest individuals in a country typically
 own 25–40% of all wealth, and the top 10% own 55–75%.
14 Oxfam (2021); UN (2020); and World Bank (2020).
15 Moyer and Hedden (2020) and UN (2019).
16 OECD (2020d).
17 UNEP (2011), p. 16.
18 As Toynbee (1978), p. 585 points out, some of these "principle functions of governments" have a long history, whereas others have evolved more recently: "Before the
 Industrial Revolution, the two principal functions of governments had been to
 maintain domestic law and order and to make war on the governments and peoples
 of foreign states. The inhuman conditions of work and life that the Industrial
 Revolution imposed on a new social class, the workers in mechanized factories,
 compelled governments to undertake a third function: the provision for social
 welfare." To this, I would add that the lessons of the twentieth century – especially
 its two world wars and the decades-long Cold War – suggest that establishing and
 then protecting democratic institutions, voice and accountability have become
 another essential government function. Now, as we enter deeper into the
 Anthropocene as the twenty-first century progresses, building the green economy
 must be another principle function.

19 From the World Bank's World Development Indicators. https://databank.worldbank.org/source/world-development-indicators.

20 Fankhauser et al. (2013).

21 The journalist Tom Friedman is often credited with coming up with the idea of the Green New Deal in a 2007 opinion editorial, and certainly he popularized the concept. See Thomas L. Friedman. "A Warning from the Garden." *The New York Times* January 19, 2007. www.nytimes.com/2007/01/19/opinion/19friedman.html. However, it is now believed that the idea first emerged through the Green New Deal Task Force, first formulated by a coalition of Green Parties from Europe and around the world. See Andrew Stewart. "Sorry Democrats, the Green Party Came Up With the Green New Deal!" *Counterpunch* November 29, 2018. www.counterpunch.org/2018/11/29/sorry-democrats-the-green-party-came-up-with-the-green-new-deal. In July 2008, the United Kingdom's Global Green New Deal Group published "A Green New Deal" of "joined-up policies to solve the triple crunch of the credit crisis, climate change and high oil prices ... Focusing first on the specific needs of the UK." See https://neweconomics.org/2008/07/green-new-deal. During the 2008–2009 Great Recession, I was asked by the UN Environment Programme to construct a Global Green New Deal, a plan to rethink the world economic recovery. The plan was eventually published as Barbier (2010). For the "lessons learned" from the Great Recession for more recent strategies for a post-pandemic green recovery, see Barbier (2020a and 2020b).

22 After she was elected to the US Congress in November 2018, Representative Alexandria Ocasio-Cortez promised to introduce a Green New Deal as part of her legislative agenda. In February 2019, Representative Ocasio-Cortez and Senator Ed Markey proposed a Green New Deal for the United States. It called for massive government spending over ten years to shift the United States to 100 percent reliance on renewable energy. Details of their plan can be found at https://ocasio-cortez.house.gov/sites/ocasio-cortez.house.gov/files/Resolution%20on%20a%20Green%20New%20Deal.pdf. Similar Green New Deal plans were soon put forward for other economies, such as the European Union, the United Kingdom and Australia.

23 See European Commission, Sustainable Europe Investment Plan: European Green Deal Investment Plan, COM (2020) 21, January 14, 2020. https://eur-lex.europa.eu/legal-content/EN/TXT/?uri=CELEX:52020DC0021.

24 See https://ec.europa.eu/taxation_customs/commission-priorities-2019-24/european-green-deal-what-role-can-taxation-play_en. For more on how CABMs work, see Cosbey et al. (2019). As explained in Chapter 5, emissions trading schemes are an alternative to carbon taxation in providing a market-based incentive for reducing greenhouse gas emissions. For example, the EU Emission Trading Scheme works on the "cap and trade" principle. A cap is set on the total amount of certain greenhouse gases that can be emitted by the industries and their companies covered by the system. Within the cap, companies receive or buy emission allowances that they can trade with one another as needed. Companies that can more cheaply abate will sell part of their allowances to companies that find it more expensive to do so. As a result, the cap should always be met, and the price of allowances is effectively the price on carbon-equivalent emissions. However, as discussed in Chapter 5, in practice there have been some problems in the effectiveness of the EU scheme as carbon pricing mechanism.

25 These sectors are based on the US Bureau of Labor Statistics' designation of "green goods and services." See www.bls.gov/ggs/ggsoverview.htm#definition. Barbier (2015), chapter 8 provides further evidence and discussion of recent expansion of these sectors in some major economies.

26 Fankhauser et al. (2013), p. 903.
27 Fankhauser et al. (2013), p. 911. Similarly, the Asian Development Bank (ADB 2013, pp. 18–19), identifies "low-carbon green growth" in Asia as "a process of structural change," which envisions patterns of industrial development, specialization and innovation, "thereby defining low-carbon development as the capacity of an economy to generate new dynamic activities." Thus, a major component of this strategy is to ensure the dissemination of low-carbon and energy-saving technologies; the adaption and dissemination of these technologies throughout the economy; support for infant green firms; government procurement policies to achieve mainstream emission reduction targets; and public sector investments to support these industrial developments. In other words, the approach advocated is to enhance economy-wide "green" structural transformation through a combination of "public investment and industrial as well as trade policies, aiming at encouraging in both cases a strong private sector response."
28 For further discussion, see Barbier (2020a); Fankhauser et al. (2013); Hwang et al. (2014); Jones and Yoo (2012); and Mathews (2012).
29 For more discussion, see Anderson et al. (2016); Barbier (2016b) and (2020c); Dercon (2014); and Resnick et al. (2012).
30 For further discussion and evidence of these trends, see previous chapters, especially Chapter 5, and Barbier (2019a).
31 The full results of this review and analysis can be found in Barbier (2020c).
32 Emre Tiftik and Khadija Mahmood. "COVID Drives Debt Surge – Stabilization Ahead?" Global Debt Monitor. Institute of International Finance. February 17, 2021. www.iif.com/Portals/0/Files/content/Global%20Debt%20Monitor_Feb2021_vf.pdf.
33 For further discussion of post-pandemic debt relief, see Volz et al. (2020).
34 As discussed in Chapters 4–7, a number of studies document the scale of environmentally harmful subsidies globally, including their increasing use in low- and middle-income countries. For example, the Organization for Economic Cooperation and Development (OECD) and the International Energy Agency (IEA) estimate that subsidies and government support for fossil fuel production and use amount to around $340 billion per year globally (OECD/IEA 2019). According to the OECD, in 2016–2018, fifty-three countries provided $705 billion in support to the agricultural sector – a figure that is likely to continue increasing in the future as more developing countries adopt such subsidies. Around 75 percent of this amount was transferred directly to farmers (OECD 2019a). Although some of this support may have beneficial effects by paying farmers to adopt conservation practices or investment in ecosystems and their services, the vast majority of these subsidies especially for increased production are environmentally harmful (Bellmann 2019). Researchers at the International Monetary Fund (IMF) estimate that water subsidies provided through public utilities are estimated at about $456 billion globally, encouraging wasteful use and exacerbating scarcity (Kolchar et al. 2015). Global fishery subsidies amounted to $35.4 billion in 2018, of which $22.2 billion are environmentally damaging (Sumaila et al. 2019).
35 OECD (2019b), figure 3.3, p. 70 estimates that environmental taxes account for 2% of total revenue in Brazil; 3.6% in China; 4% in Argentina; 5% in Colombia; 5.4% in South Africa; 6% in Chile; 9.5% in Mexico; 10% in Costa Rica; 12.7% in India; and 13% in Turkey.
36 From www.iea.org/topics/energy-subsidies. Accessed on May 8, 2020. Consumption subsidies artificially lower the market price of fossil fuel products so that it is cheaper for consumers of these products to buy and use them.

37 IISD (2019b).

38 Arze del Granado et al. (2012).

39 Barbier et al. (2020).

40 Angelsen et al. (2014).

41 For further discussion, see Barbier (2016b) and Fankhauser et al. (2013).

42 Kemp and Never (2017), p. 67.

43 Barbier (2012) and (2015).

44 Barbier (2012).

45 Barbier (2012).

46 For further discussion, see Barbier (2015); Claessens et al. (2010); Matheson (2012); and Grahl and Lysandorij (2014).

47 Barbier (2015).

48 Barbier (2012).

49 Barbier (2012).

50 See www.bloomberg.com/opinion/articles/2020-07-27/the-eu-s-financial-transac tion-tax-is-resurrected.

51 See Alvaredo et al. (2017); Barbier (2015); Piketty (2014); and Piketty and Zucman (2014).

52 For further discussion, see Goldin and Katz (2008).

53 OECD (2011), p. 31. The Organization for Economic Cooperation and Development (OECD) member countries that were the focus of the study include: Australia, Austria, Belgium, Canada, Chile, Czech Republic, Denmark, Finland, France, Germany, Greece, Hungary, Ireland, Israel, Italy, Japan, Luxembourg, Mexico, the Netherlands, New Zealand, Norway, Portugal, Spain, Sweden, Turkey, the United Kingdom and the United States.

54 See, for example, Barbier (2015); Jaumotte et al. (2013); Lee and Vivarelli (2006); and Meschi and Vivarelli (2009). In the aftermath of the Great Recession of 2008–2009, some even warned that growing wealth inequality in the world economy was also increasing stability and risk of repeated global crises within the financial system (Claessens et al. 2010; Stierli et al. 2014). This argument is summarized in Credit Suisse's 2014 *Global Wealth Report*: "Some commentators have claimed that rising equity prices are a consequence – as well as a cause – of rising inequality. It is suggested that rising income inequality in the United States from the 1970s onwards raised the disposable income of the top groups, who typically save a higher proportion of their income ... this led to an increase in funds seeking investment opportunities, driving down interest rates and raising stock prices, which in turn created further capital gains for the top income groups, propelling income inequality to even higher levels. In addition, the fall in interest rates encouraged the housing bubble that developed in the United States in the early 2000s and fuelled the unsustainable growth of debt, which triggered the financial crisis of 2007–2008. If this account is even partially true, it raises concerns about the implications of the widespread rise in wealth inequality since 2008, and about the implications for equity markets once low interest rates are no longer regarded as a priority by central banks" (Stierli et al. 2014, p. 34).

55 See Barbier (2015) and Claessens et al. (2010) for further details on how this strategy could be implemented.

56 Standing (2017).

57 See, for example, www.visualcapitalist.com/map-basic-income-experiments-world/#: ~:text=UBI%20operates%20by%20giving%20people,searching%20for%20better %20employment%20options and www.cnbc.com/2020/04/16/coronavirus-crisis-could-pave-the-way-to-a-universal-basic-income.html.

9 BUSINESS

The term *business* refers to any organization that seek profits by producing and distributing goods and services to satisfy market demands. Businesses are fundamental to any market economy. Modern economies do not exist without businesses, and they are, in turn, the engine powering all economies. The environment is often critical to business: It is the source of materials and the sink for waste products. The environment can act as a constraint on business but can also provide unique opportunities.

The previous chapter explored how public policies can be the main instigators of green and inclusive economic transformation. Government laws, investments, taxes, subsidies and regulations, and the institutions and governance to manage them, are central to jump-starting the green transition of any economy. The overall aim of public policies is to transform an economy that treats nature as a source of unending stocks of natural resources to exploit and environmental sinks to pollute, to one that respects limits; minimizes global environmental risks; and strives for sustainable and inclusive development.

But in a market economy, the agents of change are businesses. Public policies and other actions are simply enabling conditions that facilitate transformation. If we want to transition to a more sustainable and inclusive economy, it is business that will make it happen. Or not.

The purpose of the following chapter is to focus on the role of business in transforming our economies to ensure a safer Anthropocene. Like the economy itself, businesses are at a critical turning point. Some businesses are recognizing and embracing the responsibility and benefits of environmental protection and sustainable management. There is also evidence that businesses could become an important catalyst for green economic transformation. Firms increasingly find that improved climate and environmental risk management reduces their overall cost of capital and their attractiveness to potential investors.[1] In turn, investors are requiring better quantitative assessments of how firms are managing these risks, mitigating the potential damages and incorporating these assessments in their long-term investment decisions. In this chapter, we will examine some of the evidence of growing adoption and initiatives by corporations and businesses to incorporate actions to mitigate environmental risks and improve the global environment.

However, businesses may not necessarily be benign agents of change. In fact, some firms, especially large corporations, may have a vested interest in resisting a green transition. They prefer policies that enable a brown rather than a green economy, as they benefit from the underpricing of nature, including subsidies for fossil fuels and other raw materials; unpriced pollution and ecological damages; and lack of accountability for environmental threats. What is more, some large corporations use political lobbying and their market dominance to ensure that institutions, governance and incentives favorable to perpetuating the brown economy remain in place.

If we want better environmental scarcity and risk management by firms then we need to consider what additional policies are required to facilitate this change. The rules governing the financial system should also support investment decision-making that takes into account environmental sources of risk and opportunity. Central banks can advance this objective by establishing environmental risk management and reporting requirements and adjusting capital provisioning to account for underpriced environmental threats. There is also a need to develop international guidelines and common policy and legal frameworks to support and streamline such initiatives.

Finally, we need also to consider giving corporations and business a "seat at the table" for collective action to address global environmental risks. As previous chapters have pointed out, collective action by governments is certainly needed to address such risks, whether they stem from climate change, land use and biodiversity loss, freshwater scarcity or deteriorating marine environments. But corporations may also have a stake in averting such risks, and more importantly, may have the means and market power to address these challenges. Perhaps it is time to reconsider international environmental agreements to allow businesses a greater role in collective action.

Business in the Anthropocene

Much has been written about the potential role of businesses in a greener, more sustainable economy. Often, the focus is on the need for businesses to become agents of social and environmental responsibility, and the incentives for them to develop a "green" business strategy. This is a necessary and essential goal.

But it also important to be realistic. Businesses are not going to become "green" overnight simply because we would like them to. As previously discussed, many might have strong incentives to resist such change and actively lobby against it.

In particular, there are several features of modern businesses that will influence their potential role in a green economy.

In all economies, the dominant business structure is the *corporation*. Although businesses can take many forms, such as sole proprietorship, partnerships, cooperatives and so on, the corporation is the most prevalent in market economies. Corporations are legal entities that are separate from their owners. They can be either government or privately owned, and can either be a profit-making or a nonprofit organization. However, we normally consider a corporate business to be a privately owned and for-profit limited liability company. It is owned by its shareholders, who elect a board of directors to guide the corporation and hire its managerial staff.

All businesses, and certainly corporations, have an incentive to grow by expanding their market share. As the entrepreneur Pavan Sukhdev has pointed out, the "key drivers" of success for a corporation are "demand creation and expansion, product innovation, and low-cost production." The result is that corporations have four defining characteristics:

> First, determined pursuit of *size and scale* in order to achieve market dominance. Second, aggressive *lobbying* for regulatory and competitive advantages. Third, the extensive use of *advertising*, largely unhindered by ethical considerations, in order to influence consumer demand and, often, to create entirely new demand by playing on human insecurities and "turning wants

into needs" which can only be satisfied with new products. And finally, aggressive use of borrowed funds to "leverage" the investment that shareholders have made in their corporations.[2]

Given these features, many corporations strive to become global entities – and a large number achieve this goal. A multinational (or "transnational") corporation contains operations and subsidiaries in more than one country, and its organization, production and sales strategy are globally oriented. There are currently about 60,000 multinational corporations that control more than 500,000 subsidiaries worldwide and account for half of international trade.[3]

This quest for global market dominance by large corporations will have a direct bearing on how we manage environmental threats during the Anthropocene. Table 9.1 identifies twelve major economic sectors exploiting global environmental resources and sinks that are dominated by a small number of companies. As transnational corporations (TNCs), these firms have considerable leeway in controlling their markets. Consequently, as Carl Folke and colleagues point out, "a handful of TNCs have a major direct or indirect influence on the world's ocean, the global atmosphere and terrestrial biomes, system components that serve critical functions in Earth's dynamics." In other words, whether or not we end up with a safe, uncertain or catastrophic Anthropocene may depend on these TNCs engaging in "stewardship of the biosphere."[4]

In some key sectors, the economic activities of market-dominating TNCs have already endangered critical Earth System processes, such as climate stability. A substantial amount of the global carbon budget necessary to prevent warming in excess of $1.5°$ or $2°C$ has been depleted since the Industrial Revolution, mainly by major producers of fossil fuel and cement. For example, cumulative emissions by twenty major companies in these markets accounted for nearly 30 percent of industrial carbon emissions worldwide from 1751 to 2010, and ninety major emitters contributed 63 percent of total emissions.[5]

Large corporations control the fate of many other important global environmental resources and sinks (see Table 9.1). For example, as discussed in Chapter 7, the alarming rise in plastic marine pollution is due to single-use waste. Yet, over half of this waste is produced by just twenty large companies, and 90 percent by 100 polymer producers. Single-use plastics are also an important industrial source of greenhouse

Table 9.1. Market concentration and global environmental exploitation

Sector	Global Market Concentration
Agricultural commodities	Five companies account for 90% of palm oil trade; three companies control 60% of cocoa grindings; eight companies control 54% of soybean exports or processing; three companies account for 42% of banana exports; and ten companies process 42% of coffee.
Agrochemicals	Four companies control 84% of the pesticides market and ten companies account for 56% of the fertilizers market.
Animal pharmaceuticals	Ten firms account for 83% of the market.
Commercial seeds	Three companies control 60% of the market.
Mining	Five companies produce 91% of platinum; 88% of palladium; and 62% of cobalt. Ten companies produce 64% of nickel; 52% of iron; 50% of copper; 45% of zinc; 34% of silver; and 30% of gold.
Fossil fuels	Ten companies control 72% of proved oil reserves and 51% of proved natural gas reserves.
Cement	Ten companies produce over 30% of the world's cement.
Forestry	Ten companies produce 25% of paper and board.
Seafood	Thirteen companies catch 11–16% of marine harvest and 19–40% of commercially valuable marine stocks. Five companies are responsible for 48% of farmed Atlantic salmon.
Container shipping[a]	Ten companies account for 85% of industry annual revenues of $118 billion.
Offshore oil and gas[a]	Ten companies account for 51% of industry annual revenues of $830 billion.
Plastics[b]	Twenty polymer producers account for 55% of single-use plastic waste, and 100 companies account for 90% of single-use waste.

Notes: [a] From Virdin et al. (2021). See also Table 7.3 for other ocean economy sectors with significant market concentration.
[b] From Charles et al. (2021).
Source: Adapted from Folke et al. (2019), tables 1 and 2, unless otherwise noted.

gas emissions, as 98 percent of these plastics are produced from fossil fuel feedstock. If current trends continue, by 2050 greenhouse gas emissions from single-use plastics will triple and account for 10 percent of all emissions.[6]

Clearly, large corporations that dominate key markets need to be involved in the transition to sustainability if we are to protect critical Earth systems and the future for humanity. But large firms with market power face a trade-off of incentives that could lead them to be either *exploiters of the biosphere* versus *stewards of the biosphere*.[7]

On the one hand, dominant firms with considerable market power globally have a strong incentive to be *exploiters of the biosphere*. By virtue of their market power and political clout, TNCs can maintain the "business as usual" status quo, which guarantees large profits through continued exploitation of global environmental resources and sinks. Through their sheer size and scale, many large corporations can also protect their market dominance by creating price-based barriers to entry for new, smaller and possibly "greener," firms wishing to enter the industry. In this way, dominant firms can perpetuate their growing market concentration and monopoly power in the key economic sectors exploiting the global environment, and there is little incentive to change this business strategy.

A number of factors reinforces such an outcome.[8] For one, because of their global reach, many transnational corporations that exploit environmental resources and sinks operate in countries and regions that do not have strong political institutions. Such places are often rife with corruption, political instability, human rights violations, weak rules of law and even armed conflict. Additionally, many TNCs wield considerable political and lobbying power, which enables them to evade regulation of their environmental activities. Finally, many large corporations take advantage of political differences to push for their economic agenda, even while seeming to act in line with public policies and regulations. That is why, for example, "many car manufacturers are developing low-carbon vehicles while at the same time lobbying for less-stringent emissions standards, making them both 'good' and 'bad' at the same time."[9]

Nonetheless, some large corporations may have an incentive to become *stewards of the biosphere*. They may view their long-term business strategy and survival aligning with less exploitation, and possibly even conservation, of key environmental resources and sinks.

Shareholder demand for greater environmental responsibility and the threat of court action can reinforce this incentive.[10] Furthermore, domination by a handful of large firms may make it easier to coordinate and reach an agreement on conservation and sustainable management objectives across an industry. In such cases, market dominance may actually assist the conservation motive rather than thwart it. Because it has a secure market share, a corporation can cooperate with other large firms in joint stewardship of the environment. To secure its long-term profits and market-based activities, a TNC may value more sustainable management of the global environmental resources and sinks on which it depends. Moreover, such a strategy can impact the entire industry. As argued by Folke and colleagues, "should dominant TNCs impose effective sustainability standards throughout their supply chain, this could influence both upstream and downstream market actors, including small and medium enterprises."[11]

In Chapter 7, we cite one possible example of this occurring. Recent conservation efforts in the global seafood sector offer some promise that large TNCs might have an incentive to cooperate on better stewardship of a key resource stock. For example, ten of the thirteen seafood companies that control up to 16 percent of the global marine catch and 40 percent of the largest and most valuable stocks have committed to the Seafood Business for Ocean Stewardship initiative for more sustainable management of seafood resources and the oceans.[12] As a result, the world's largest seafood retailer has stated its commitment to only harvesting seafood that is certified as sustainable. Such market leadership has encouraged other retailers to follow their example, and this has led to a rapid increase in global seafood certification.[13]

The seafood industry now needs to back up such commitments with actual investments to improve management and conservation of fishing capital. This would make commercial sense for the industry. As we showed in Chapter 7, the seafood industry could contribute anywhere from $4 to $28 billion each year for such objectives (see Table 7.3). Such an investment could yield as much as $58 billion in additional annual profits for seafood companies from more sustainably managed fisheries.

Clearly, if we want to ensure a safer Anthropocene through a transition to greener economies, we need more corporations and businesses generally becoming biosphere stewards rather than exploiters. There are three ways that this may occur:

- Environmental risks increasingly translate into increased overall risks for businesses and their operations, and so they have a direct incentive to mitigate them.
- Investors and shareholders increasingly require that companies better manage environmental risk; mitigate their potential damages; and incorporate these assessments into their long-term investment decisions.
- Policies that facilitate businesses and investors to take into account environmental risks and performance in their financing and investment decisions.

The next sections examine each of these key mechanisms in turn.

Business and Environmental Risks

Every year, the World Economic Forum provides an assessment of the likelihood and impact of various global risks based on a survey of businesses, governments and individuals. In its first global survey since the COVID-19 outbreak, the World Economic Forum found that four environmental risks – extreme weather, climate action failure, human environmental damage and biodiversity loss and ecosystem collapse – are among the top five global threats to humankind.[14]

Awareness of environmental risks is on the rise in the business world. Increasingly, evidence suggests that global environmental change and its nature-related risks are costly to business investments and operations. The World Economic Forum analyzed 163 industry sectors and their supply chains, and found that $44 trillion of global value added is moderately or highly dependent on nature and its services. This amounts to over half of the world's GDP.[15] Even if these benefits are overestimated, they suggest that a lot of businesses worldwide are highly vulnerable to rising environmental risks. As previous chapters have documented, this is clearly the case for the major environmental threats that the world is facing today: global warming, land use change and biodiversity loss, freshwater scarcity and deteriorating oceans and coasts.

Individual businesses and even large corporations are taking note of the potential costs of these environmental risks. Even though individual firms have little control over how or when the impact from any external environmental risk might occur, firms are increasingly aware that they will likely incur some additional costs to their investments and operations if exposed to the risk. Thus, firms are starting to see the direct financial benefits of undertaking *environmental risk management*. This involves a firm undertaking preventive or remedial actions to avoid or reduce its exposure to such threats, whether they are due to climate change, increasing natural resource scarcity, water shortages, ecological damages, regional air pollution or some other hazardous environmental event. Such actions could involve investments to protect or adapt to sea level rise, contingency plans for increased water shortfalls or chronic scarcity, setting aside emergency funds for unexpected waste or pollution cleanup, improved health and safety measures to protect employees and so forth.

As we have noted in previous chapters, environmental risk management by some industries may also involve direct investment in nature conservation.

One example is the direct financial interest to the global insurance industry in investing in coastal and estuarine habitats (see Chapter 7). Because these habitats are "natural barriers" to costly and deadly storm events, protecting coastal wetlands could save the insurance industry $52 billion annually through reducing flood damage losses. Based on this savings, the insurance industry could easily invest $5–$10 billion each year in conserving and restoring these habitats.[16] The reef insurance program in the state of Quintana Roo, Mexico is an example of this investment principle. In addition to using tourism revenue to restore and maintain reefs, the program purchases insurance from Swiss Re that guarantees a payout of $25–$70 million to restore a forty-mile section of coral reef in the case of an extreme storm occurring.[17]

Environmental risk management by a firm can also involve reducing or preventing its own environmentally damaging activities. This can be achieved in two ways.[18]

First, environmental laws and regulations often entail threatening a firm with penalties, litigation and stricter environmental controls if it fails to comply with such measures. Consequently, conforming to environmental laws and regulations governing pollution, waste disposal, natural resource use and even greenhouse gas emissions may be one form of environmental risk management.

In addition, a firm may choose to reduce the occurrence and impacts of environmental damages from its own operations, such as investing in pollution prevention, reducing water use, switching to alternatives to fossil fuels, improving landfill disposal, limiting hazardous wastes, internal pricing to reduce greenhouse gas emissions and so forth. Managing these regulation and operational environmental threats can be significant to a firm. Evidence for eighty-eight firms indicates that environmental risk from failing to comply with regulations is most frequently associated with large probability and major detrimental impacts, while environmental risk associated with a firm's operations has a low probability but often catastrophic impacts.[19]

Related to regulatory risk is *policy risk*. Policy action can significantly impact a firm, whether it is removal of fossil fuel and other environmentally harmful subsidies, pricing of carbon, water or ecological damages and taxes or bans on single-use plastics and other environmentally harmful products. Companies that fail to anticipate such major changes in policies, and to adjust their business practices and investment choices accordingly, may find themselves losing substantial market share, business opportunities and profits.

For example, in Chapter 4 we discussed the growing use of *internal carbon pricing* by many companies. It places a monetary value on greenhouse gas emissions, which firms can then factor into investment decisions and management operations. Internal carbon pricing gives businesses an incentive to shift investments to low-carbon alternatives, and helps them achieve their greenhouse gas targets, such as the net zero carbon goal. This can also be attractive to address shareholder concerns and to demonstrate corporate leadership in climate action.

A 2020 survey by the CDP of over 5,900 companies worldwide reveals not only the growing use of internal carbon pricing but also how its use is closely tied to whether or not firms are likely to face more stringent climate policies and regulations. The survey found an 80 percent increase in the number of companies planning or using an internal carbon price since 2014. Nearly half (226) of the world's 500 biggest companies are either putting a price on carbon or planning to do so within the next two years, more than double the number from CDP's last survey in 2017. In addition, companies that expect carbon pricing regulation are five times more likely to use an internal price on carbon than companies that do not. In comparison, of the 3,000 or more companies that do not anticipate carbon pricing policies to be imposed on them in the next three years, only 14 percent use or plan to implement internal carbon pricing.[20]

But there are also business opportunities from managing environmental risks, too.

One estimate suggests that successful green transition in three socioeconomic systems – food, land and ocean use, infrastructure and the built environment and energy and extractives – would require up to $2.7 trillion of annual investment by businesses worldwide. But such investments would also deliver $10.1 trillion of annual business opportunities and 395 million jobs by 2030.[21] For transforming global food and land use systems alone, there is a possible annual business opportunity of $4.5 trillion.[22]

Although the magnitude of such investments and returns can be debated, the key point is that green transformation is not always a cost to business. Controlling environmental and other nature-related risks should not be viewed simply as a damage-limitation exercise. There are new business opportunities and significant financial gains to be made by companies that are at the forefront of green transitions. "Ultimately the role of business in these transitions will vary by sector and region," but to realize potential gains, every business has an incentive to "identify the transitions that are relevant to them and the role they can play in leading or supporting them."[23]

Green Finance

As noted previously, one of the hallmarks of modern businesses is that they make "aggressive use of borrowed funds to 'leverage' the investment that shareholders have made in their corporations."[24] But this reliance on borrowing by corporations and other businesses means that they must respond to the growing concerns of financial institutions, investors and regulators about business exposure to global environmental risks.

Increasingly, investors are requiring better quantitative assessments of how firms are managing these risks, mitigating the potential damages and incorporating these assessments into their long-term investment decisions. Central banks, regulators and financial institutions are also worried about the business risks associated with climate change, ecological scarcity, resource exploitation, natural hazards, pollution and other environmental threats.

These concerns by financial investors, institutions and regulators over environmental risks are leading to a surge in *green finance*. As explained by the World Bank:

Firstly, investors are looking for investment opportunities arising from the conservation, restoration, and sustainable use of nature—to use the language of climate finance, to "finance green". Secondly, investors are trying to direct financial flows away from projects with negative impacts on biodiversity and ecosystem services, and towards projects that mitigate negative impact or pursue positive environmental impacts as a co-benefit.[25]

Both parties – firms and investors – are seeing the potential financial gains from such investment opportunities to reduce environmental risks.

Improved environmental risk management by firms affects their overall cost of capital and their attractiveness to potential investors. Consequently, better environmental performance provides a signal to financial investors that firms can sustain higher debt capacity, require less expensive debt and warrant lower equity risk premiums.[26]

This suggests that businesses that actively manage their environmental risk or improve nature-friendly performance will therefore increase the willingness of investors to provide long-term financing of such firms, as well as increase the rate of return on such investments. In other words, the financial and environmental performance of businesses is becoming more intertwined. There is increasing evidence of this trend. Out of 132 published studies, 78 percent find a positive relationship between corporate sustainability and financial performance.[27]

Consequently, improved environmental risk management and performance may provide self-reinforcing gains to both firms and investors. Firms with superior environmental performance and risk management are more likely to disclose publicly such information, and the more firms that provide such assessments are likely to improve the credibility of such reporting information. Investors will increasingly use such assessments to evaluate the overall credit worthiness and riskiness of firms, and reward firms that appear to be less risky investments with additional credit, less expensive debt and lower risk premiums. The result is that better environmental risk management will benefit firms by overcoming capital constraints on their operations and provide the incentives to reduce further any environmentally damaging activities that may contribute to climate change, natural resource scarcity and pollution. Improved management may also foster corporate governance and management practices that encourage more reliable environmental assessments and reporting and better overall environmental performance.

Already, this interest in green finance has prompted a boom in environmentally friendly stocks worldwide. For example, *The Economist* tracked the performance of more than 180 firms, ranging from renewable-power producers and electrical vehicle-makers to energy-efficiency outfits and recyclers. Since the start of 2020, this portfolio of companies has more than doubled in value. The greenest 25 percent of firms saw their share prices rise by 110 percent. To some extent, this boom in green stocks is attributable to the expansion of funds specializing in environmental and social investing. But mainstream investment funds are also increasingly growing green, reflecting the general growth in demand by all financial investors in green stocks.[28]

As previous chapters have noted, another indication of the recent interest in green financing is the rapid growth in the market for *green bonds*. These are debt instruments where the proceeds are used exclusively to finance or refinance projects with environmental benefits. The issuers of green bonds are typically local and national governments and multilateral development agencies and banks, but corporations and other businesses are also using these instruments. Although the first green bonds were issued in 2007–2008, by 2019 they reached a market value of $258 billion and there is now a dedicated Green Exchange (LGX) in the Luxembourg Stock Exchange that trades in green bonds.[29]

New green financial instruments are also being developed. One promising investment tool are *sustainability linked loans*, which ties interest rates and other costs of capital borrowing to key sustainability performance indicators. The way such loans work is that both the lender and the borrower agree on sustainability targets, and if they are met, the borrower benefits from a reduction in the interest rate on the loan. In 2019, such loans increased by 168 percent and reached a total volume of $122 billion. In early 2020, the Finnish forest–based company UPM tied the interest on its $900 million credit facility to meeting its goal of having a net positive impact on biodiversity in the company's forests in Finland, as well as a separate carbon reduction target. A similar credit arrangement has been made by Bunge, one of the world's largest agricultural producers, which links interest payments to increasing traceability for its main agricultural commodities and the adoption of sustainable practices across its wider soybean and palm supply chain.[30]

The growth in green stocks, bonds and instruments is an encouraging sign of the growing investor interest in greening financial markets. However, as previous chapters have noted, green financing as a catalyst for transforming business operations worldwide still faces considerable challenges.

For one, not all nature-related sectors are benefiting from the boom in green financing. The green stocks that are surging in value are mainly clean energy companies. Similarly, green bonds are rarely used to finance biodiversity conservation, sustainable land use and marine environmental protection. Climate change, energy and transport have accounted for around 80 percent of green bonds; land use projects only 3 percent. Even fewer are devoted to investments in oceans and coasts.[31]

Moreover, the growth in green financing is occurring mainly in wealthier countries, and it has yet to impact significantly biodiversity conservation and other nature-related private investments in low- and middle-income countries. Hopefully, as green financing makes an impact on the sustainability of supply chains of multinational corporations, this will have an impact on corporate operations and subsidiaries operating in emerging markets and developing countries.

We should also be cautious in attributing all the recent booms in the value of green stocks and bonds to a surge in green financing. As traded assets, the market valuation of green stocks and bonds do not necessarily reflect the amount of money raised by investors to finance environmental projects. In both markets, there may be more of a "green bubble" effect driving the recent surge in stocks and bonds than a sustained push in favor of greening financial markets.[32]

Ultimately, if green financing is to become a catalyst for more corporate and business investment in improved environmental risk management and performance worldwide, then green stocks, bonds and instruments need to increase significantly in *scope* and *scale*. Green financial instruments need to be scaled up, replicated to a wider range of economic sectors and countries and influence the entire supply chains of major corporate industries.

Nonetheless, the potential for greening financial markets is real. Even as it expresses concern about the current "green bubble" in clean energy stocks, *The Economist* concludes that investor interest and demand for greener assets are not an illusion, and may be the beginning of a long-run trend toward greening stock markets worldwide:

> Still, many investors are optimistic. Few think that the energy transition will go into reverse. They argue that the prospects for the sector as a whole are promising, even if some firms end up being duds. Comparisons to the tech industry at the turn of the century abound. Like the internet, decarbonisation will lead to structural change in the global economy. Capital will have to flow towards cleaner technologies. The process will create winners and losers ... But it is worth remembering that, two decades after the dotcom bust, tech firms make up 38% of the market capitalisation of the S&P 500.[33]

Although such an optimistic view is encouraging, much work needs to be done to ensure that financial markets work to enable capital "to flow towards cleaner technologies" and to other environmentally friendly capital investments worldwide. Enabling these conditions will require, in turn, policies that facilitate businesses and investors to take into account environmental risks and performance in their financing and investment decisions.

Policies for Greening Business

Better environmental risk management and performance could potentially benefit both investors and firms, as well as lead to less overall environmental damages from pollution, natural resource scarcity and climate change. The potential economic and environmental gains to investors, firms and society suggest that there is an important role for policies that support improved environmental risk management in investment decisions. The result should be closer convergence between the environmental and financial performance of firms, thus fostering more environmentally friendly investments; more sustainable growth and development; and increased incentives for innovation and technological change.

To encourage more widespread and consistent implementation of environmental risk management, assessments and reporting will require three key policies:

- Financial regulations that support investment decision-making that takes into account improved environmental performance

- Establishing better environmental risk management and reporting requirements
- Developing international guidelines and common policy and legal frameworks to support better environmental risk management, assessments and reporting globally[34]

As prudential authorities and regulators of the financial system, central banks should ensure that the rules governing the financial system support investment decision-making that takes into account improved environmental performance; establish mandatory, enforceable and transparent environmental risk management and reporting requirements; and adjust capital provisioning to account for underpriced environmental risks, including those from climate change, natural disasters and natural resource scarcity.

Financial authorities need to implement such policies and regulations, because without them, firms are likely to underinvest in environmental risk management. As argued by Li Cai and colleagues, although initiatives to reduce corporate environmental risk (CER) and improve environmental performance are generally associated with lower levels of systematic risk and capital constraints for firms, such initiatives "typically require initial investments that do not have a short-term payoff and are likely to have no positive pay-off even in the long-run." Consequently, "managers do not invest in CER initiatives unless legally required to do so."[35]

Mandated and enforced environmental risk and performance reporting can be seen as a complementary regulatory instrument to data provided by public registers in assessing environmental performance. If such mandated disclosures are fully transparent, they can induce firms to reduce and manage environmental risk in order to mitigate interventions by investors, environmental stakeholders and regulatory authorities. In addition, financial authorities could assist with best practice and guidance on standardized environmental risk and performance reporting, which would assist firms in developing positive linkages between improved environmental performance, systemic risk management and financial success.

Finally, as firm managers increasingly take environmental and sustainability reporting seriously, they are looking for better guidance and regulations from policymakers on such measures. In fact, the lack of direction from financial authorities has been cited as a key barrier to improved corporate environmental management and more widespread adoption of reporting and public policy.[36] For example, Howard Covington and coauthors argue that there needs to be "more and better quantitative assessments of systemic climate risk and, in particular, the risk to investment portfolios, to help to clarify the relevant obligations" of investors, lenders and firms.[37] In addition, financial authorities and central banks need to work with credit rating agencies, investment analysts and regulators of equity markets to develop greater transparency in how they include environmental factors in their analysis of firms and to develop common reporting standards. The UN Environment Programme's Finance Initiative has identified weaknesses in the current approach, which is "a patchwork of overlapping requirements and gaps in the coverage of issues, such as the impact of natural disasters and the potential for asset stranding in high carbon sectors."[38]

Financial authorities and central banks must also ensure that any mandatory environmental risk management and reporting requirements are effective in improving the overall environmental and financial performance of firms. In developing improved reporting, it is important to distinguish between three different environmentally based activities undertaken by firms:

- *Environmental management measures*, which include the development of a corporate environmental strategy; integration of environmental issues into strategic planning processes; environmental practices; process-driven initiatives; product-driven management systems; environmental certification; environmental management system adoption; and participation in voluntary environmental improvement programs.
- *Environmental performance assessments*, which evaluate environmental impacts through use of specific indicators, such as carbon dioxide emissions, physical waste, water consumption, toxic release, chemical spills, raw material input use or materials recycling.
- *Environmental disclosures*, which describe the various environmental impacts of a firm's activities, and may involve information on toxic releases, environmental accidents and crises, as well as announcements of specific environmental investments.[39]

The positive link between a firm's financial and environmental performance appears to be most enhanced by environmental management measures as opposed to performance assessments or disclosures, which tend to be ad hoc, vary in quality and sporadic.[40] There seems to be several reasons for this outcome.

Compared to performance assessments and disclosures, environmental management measures are less subject to *green washing*, that is, aiming to improve a firm's external image with respect to environmental performance regardless of whether or not an actual improvement takes place. In addition, the adoption of environmental management measures often signals that managers have adopted a proactive and positive approach to improving a firm's environmental performance, and have begun integrating such an approach into the overall operational objectives and strategy of the firm. There also appears to be a positive linkage between greater adoption of environmental management measures and "integrated reporting," which is an assessment of a firm's financial, governance, environmental and social performance. Finally, firms that adopt environmental management measures, especially as part of integrated reporting, usually seek outside assurance or verification of the legitimacy and quality of such initiatives and reports.

Consequently, ensuring that mandatory environmental risk management and reporting requirements are effective can improve the overall environmental and financial performance of firms, and encourage more sustainable growth and development. This has three policy implications.

First, the overall aim should be to encourage and assist firms in developing a corporate environmental strategy that integrates environmental risk and performance management into strategic planning processes. That is, the adoption of environmental improvement measures as a strategic goal by a firm's managers appears to be the most effective approach to environmental risk management.

Second, as far as possible, any mandatory environmental reporting requirements and measures should also encourage firms to adopt such assessments through integrated reporting of their financial, governance, environmental and social performance. However, to facilitate more widespread adoption of integrated or sustainability reporting, public authorities must develop more reliable and comprehensive guidelines, which should improve business performance by highlighting key priorities; providing benchmarks and targets; and assisting comparisons across business sectors. In addition, any mandatory environmental or sustainability reporting measures will need external monitoring, assurance and verification of their legitimacy and quality. Some corporate organizations are also considering the adoption and implementation of sanctions on members who do not meet agreed benchmarks and targets to enforce progress toward sustainability.

Third, additional public policies could encourage more voluntary strategic environmental actions by firms. As summarized by David Ervin and colleagues, "policies that enable firms to differentiate themselves based on their environmental performance and increase their competitiveness, that provide technical assistance and lower costs of adoption and that raise the significance of environmental issues for firms can induce more voluntary initiatives." Specifically, "actions to assure competitive markets, improve credible information about facility environmental management and performance for investors and consumers and provide technical assistance to lower development costs and educational programs to enhance public environmental consciousness and increase firms' expertise could accelerate voluntary business environmental activity."[41]

Evaluating environmental impacts and improving reporting procedures across countries requires development of international guidelines and common policy and legal frameworks with standardized data and risk measures. There is also a need for global cooperation on coordinating and developing common practical frameworks, methodologies and tools to provide a systematic approach to monitor and integrate environmental factors into credit and investment risk assessments.

Two related initiatives show promise for developing such common international frameworks and reporting procedures. These are the Task Force for Climate-Related Financial Disclosures (TCFD) and the Taskforce for Nature-Related Financial Disclosures (TNFD), as well as their counterpart within the financial system, the Network for Greening the Financial System (NGFS) of central banks and supervisors.

The G20-initiated Task Force on Climate-Related Financial Disclosures (TCFD) was created in 2015 to develop consistent climate-related financial risk disclosures for use by companies, banks and investors in providing information to stakeholders. It is hoped that improved reporting and information will induce companies to incorporate climate-related risks and opportunities into their risk management and strategic planning processes. Many large businesses have voluntarily adopted the framework proposed by the TCFD for identifying, measuring and managing climate risks. More than 1,500 organizations – including over 1,340 companies with a combined market capitalization of $12.6 trillion and financial institutions responsible for assets of nearly $150 trillion – have signed up to support the TCFD's recommendations. Over 110 regulators and governmental jurisdictions worldwide support the TCFD, including the governments of Belgium, Canada, Chile, France, Japan, New Zealand, Sweden and the United Kingdom.[42]

The Task Force on Nature-Related Financial Disclosures (TNFD) is a new global initiative, which aims to help financial institutions and companies to develop consistent reporting on all types of environmental risks. The TNFD aims to build upon the success of the Task Force on Climate-Related Financial Disclosures. The TNFD is currently developing its framework, which will aid organizations to understand, disclose and manage the financial risks and opportunities associated with the deteriorating state of nature and a transition to an economy consistent with meeting future nature-related international agreements such as the UN Convention on Biological Diversity (CBD) and the ambitions set out in its forthcoming Post-2020 Global Biodiversity Agenda. The TNFD framework will be tested and refined in 2022 before its launch and dissemination in 2023.[43]

Both the TCFD and TNFD have support within the global financial system through the Network for Greening the Financial System (NGFS). Launched in 2017, the NGFS is a voluntary group of central banks and supervisors worldwide who have agreed to share best practices in the development of climate and environmental risk management in the financial sector and to mobilize finance for support of the transition to more sustainable economies. As of the end of 2020, the NGFS has eighty-three members, covering all the major global banks and two-thirds of insurers. Its main contribution is a series of nonbinding recommendations for central banks, supervisors, policymakers and financial institutions to enhance their role in the greening of the financial system, including the need to achieve robust and internationally consistent climate and environment-related disclosure.[44]

These initiatives indicate that the global financial system is taking climate and environment risks seriously, and that there is an urgent need to develop international guidelines, common policy and legal frameworks, and assessment and reporting criteria to manage these risks. However, actual implementation of the various recommendations is voluntary, and it is too early to assess how widespread or effective they have been in "greening" the global financial system. In addition, the emphasis has been largely on promoting disclosure and assessment of environmental risks rather than specific adoption of management measures and strategies to reduce such risks. Hopefully, as the global financial system further develops common international frameworks and reporting procedures for assessing climate and environmental risks, they will evolve to the next stage of recommending best practices for incorporating such risks in business management and strategies and identifying the policies necessary to encourage such practices.

Toward Green Transformation of Business

Policies that encourage the greening of business and finance are vitally important for ensuring that the world economy transitions to a more sustainable path. But they are not on their own sufficient for such a green transformation.

Ultimately, finance will flow to where there are major investment opportunities, and businesses will respond to market incentives to capitalize on these opportunities to capture profits and market share. As long as underpricing of nature remains pervasive throughout all economies, these investment opportunities and market incentives will reinforce finance and business to capitalize and profit from inherently "brown" rather than "green" sectors, industries and products. That is, the lack of green investment and innovation by businesses in all economies is a *symptom* of the structural imbalance and disincentives created by the underpricing of nature, not the *cause* of this imbalance.

This reinforces the main message of this book. Rethinking markets, institutions and governance to end the underpricing of nature is the key to any successful strategy for greening economies today. As business and finance are the main engine underlying all economies, it follows that ending the vicious cycle of underpricing nature is an essential step in the green transformation of this engine.

This key policy message was emphasized by the World Bank, in its landmark report *Mobilizing Private Finance for Nature*:

> Although awareness of the importance of biodiversity and nature conservation is growing, market failures and policy failures mean that it is proving difficult to translate this awareness into action. Awareness of the importance of biodiversity and nature, and the material risks to the real and financial sectors which degradation poses is increasing—not least due

to the 2020 COVID-19 pandemic. Failure to account for the social and environmental externalities associated with biodiversity loss has resulted in the underpricing of biodiversity risk and poorly-informed investment and policy decisions ... Simply put, nature has value, but not a price.[45]

But there is another policy issue that was raised at the beginning of this chapter. Many economic sectors exploiting global environmental resources and sinks are dominated by a small number of companies (see Table 9.1), and these large firms with market power face a trade-off of incentives that could lead them to be either *exploiters of the biosphere* or *stewards of the biosphere.*

As we have explored in this chapter, some dominant firms increasingly recognize that their corporate interests might align with biodiversity stewardship. Others are being reluctantly nudged into this realization by their investors or a changing policy environment. Yet other corporations and industries are resisting change, actively attempting to thwart it and often hedging their bets in anticipation of future policy directions.

A good example of the latter is what is occurring in the US fossil fuel industry. Writing in *Forbes*, the economist Theresa Ghilarcucci notes that while "major fossil fuel companies including Exxon Mobil and BP have thrown their support behind the carbon tax, perhaps seeing a way to avoid for costly regulations of their businesses. But that does not mean they won't continue to fight for their own privileges." Consequently, the US fossil fuel industry spends billions each year to protect the underpricing of fossil fuels, including maintaining federal tax breaks and subsidies. "It is economically rational for fossil fuel companies to hire expensive lobbyists, provide campaign contributions, and work to capture regulatory agencies. Between 2000 and 2016, the fossil fuel industry spent an estimated $370 million just in federal lobbying. Companies spend so much on lobbying because they see ways to 'buy' regulatory advantages."[46]

The US fossil fuel industry is unlikely to be alone. A number of major corporations and industries worldwide have similar incentives to use their market dominance of key economic sectors exploiting global environmental resources and sinks to continue as *exploiters of the biosphere* for as long as possible. Moreover, they will also use their economic clout to "'buy' regulatory advantages" and thwart public policies that will alter this status quo.

Governments need to overcome such political pressure and tax the excess corporate profits of such biodiversity exploiters.[47] The revenues raised could also address the many *underfunding of nature* challenges identified in previous chapters. These include investing in natural climate solutions that are cost-effective in both storing carbon and protecting biodiversity; conserving more critical terrestrial, freshwater and marine ecosystems; cleaning up pollution from plastics, waste and chemicals; and similar nature-related investments.

The revenues could also be allocated to public research and development (R&D) support for the many economy-wide green innovations discussed in Chapter 8. Or, the funds could be targeted to specific green R&D needs of the industries and sectors taxed. They could finance public support for technological innovations that can further lengthen the lifetime of the affected environmental stocks or sinks or lead to improved efficiencies in products and processes that decouple them from environmental harm. For example, taxes on the profits of single-use plastic producers could be directed to support of innovations to remove existing macro- and micro-plastic pollution in oceans; reduce the content of fossil fuel use in plastics; and improve the substitution of multiuse and recyclable plastics in end-use products.

In sum, three major policies are likely required for encouraging the successful green transformation of businesses:

• Ending the underpricing of nature
• Policies for greening finance and business
• Taxing major biosphere exploiters

These three policy pillars are essential to greening businesses and the economy. As summarized in Figure 9.1, with these policies in place, it is possible to envision a "virtuous cycle" in which businesses, including large corporations with global market dominance, take into account environmental risks in their business and investment decisions; enact strategies to limit these risks in their management and operations; and actions to conserve and restore critical environmental sinks and stocks.

Collective Business Action

As emphasized throughout this book, one of the key mechanisms for reducing global environmental risks is collective action. Certainly, collective action by businesses can lead to greater scaling of their biosphere stewardship and make it more effective.

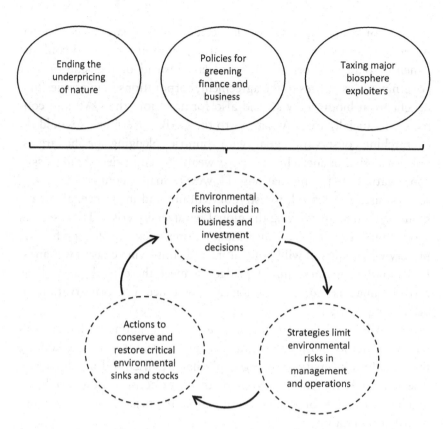

Figure 9.1 A strategy for green transformation of business
Notes: The three policy pillars of ending the underpricing of nature; policies to green finance and business; and taxing biosphere exploiters can engender a virtuous cycle of green business transformation.

One way this can occur is through businesses and industries organizing their own collective action. In this chapter and in Chapter 7, we have cited the case of ten major seafood companies coming together to establish the Seafood Business for Ocean Stewardship initiative (SEABOS). SEABOS commits its members to more sustainable management of marine resources and the oceans.[48] Across many different sectors, at least 300 leading companies have invested in the sustainable management of their natural resource and environmental assets over the past two decades, and several thousand other companies have incorporated sustainability considerations into their business strategies.[49]

But as major corporations and other industries demonstrate their willingness to act as stewards of their biosphere, there should also be ways to offer them a "seat at the table" of international efforts to reduce global environmental risks.

For example, if the world decides to negotiate a new Global Agreement on Biodiversity (GAB), participation in the accord could be widened to include private stakeholders. Instead of focusing on just governments as parties to the agreement, corporations in industries that benefit from biodiversity should also formally join the GAB and contribute financially to it. As parties to the GAB, governments would set overarching conservation goals with countries pledging specific targets, policies and timelines. In addition, wealthier countries should assist conservation in poorer nations. However, major companies in key sectors, such as seafood, forestry, agriculture and insurance, also have a financial stake in averting the global biodiversity crisis. These sectors should agree on targets for increasing marine stocks, protecting forests, preserving habitats of wild pollinators and conserving coastal wetlands. Individual companies should pledge to meet these goals as well as provide financial and technological assistance for conservation in developing countries.

Allowing participation of major corporations and industries willing to act as biosphere stewards could be one way of overcoming the global biodiversity "funding gap" that we discussed in Chapter 5. The industries that benefit from biodiversity conservation should be willing to contribute some of this financial gain to more global conservation.

For example, in a recent study, Jo Burgess, Tom Dean and I have estimated that the resulting increase in revenues and profits in the seafood, forestry and insurance industries alone could provide $25–$50 billion annually for global conservation. For example, the seafood industry stands to gain $53 billion annually from a $5 billion to $10 billion investment each year in a global agreement on biodiversity, while the insurance industry could see an additional $52 billion with a similar investment. By spending $15–$30 billion annually, the forest products industry would attain its sustainable forest management goals. Agriculture also has an incentive to protect habitats of wild pollinators, who along with managed populations enhance global crop production by $235–$577 billion annually.[50]

Such a GAB would represent a "new wave" of international agreements that would engage government and industry, and hopefully other non-state actors, in a manner unparalleled in the history of global environmental conservation. This approach could be applied to other global environmental risks and threats (see Table 9.1).

In effect, such a "new wave" of global collective action could encourage major corporations to become better "biosphere stewards." Industries and corporations could see that participating as partners with governments in managing key global environmental resources and sinks not only is an important long-run business strategy but also translates into an improved bottom line with shareholders.

Conclusion

If green transformation is to take hold in our economies, business will be the fulcrum leading to this transition. There are clear signs that the global business community, and the financial system supporting it, is starting to take environmental risks seriously. Green stocks and bonds are on the rise; financial investors are increasingly asking businesses to assess climate and other environmental risks; and the financial system is formulating international guidelines for environmental performance disclosures.

There is also an important role and responsibility for consumers. By demanding more sustainably produced goods and services through markets, consumer behavior can provide feedback to producers and instigate change. Just as shareholders and investors can vote with their dollars in boardrooms, consumers have a powerful vote through patterns of spending in markets for goods and services.

But we are not yet at the "tipping point" where global business and finance will turn green.

The main obstacle remains the widespread *underpricing of nature*. As we noted at the beginning of this chapter, quoting Pavan Sukhdev, "key drivers" determining success for modern business continues to be "demand creation and expansion, product innovation, and low-cost production."[51] As long as the policy climate continues to enable business to ignore climate and environmental risks; subsidizes environmentally harmful production and consumption; and natural capital is given zero value in investment decisions, then "business as usual" means more – not less – destruction of nature.

Consequently, this chapter reinforces the main message of this book. Rethinking markets, institutions and governance to end the underpricing of nature is the key to any successful strategy for greening economies today. And that strategy must begin with ensuring that business and finance have the incentives to become greener.

However, to be successful, there must be two additional pillars to such a strategy aimed at business: policies targeted to greening finance, and business and taxation of major biosphere exploiters.

There are a number of specific policies that could encourage more widespread and consistent implementation of environmental risks by business and the financial system worldwide. These include the widespread adoption of financial regulations that support investment decision-making that takes into account improved environmental performance; establishing better environmental risk management and reporting requirements; and developing international guidelines and common policy and legal frameworks to support better environmental risk management, assessments and reporting globally.

But even if green business and finance are on the rise, there may still be strong incentives of major corporations that benefit from exploitation of global environmental stocks and sinks to resist change. Taxing the excess corporate profits of such biodiversity exploiters may be the only solution to alter such recalcitrance. In addition, the revenues raised could help address the many underfunding of nature challenges identified in previous chapters.

Taxing major biodiversity exploiters could be an important "stick" to help initiate change. An equally important "carrot" might be to offer those major corporations that are willing to become biosphere stewards a "seat at the table" for collective action to address global environmental risks. As major corporations increasingly have a stake in averting such risks, and more importantly, may have the means and market power to address these challenges, they may become ideal partners with governments in managing vital environmental sinks and stocks. Perhaps it is time to reconsider international environmental agreements to allow businesses a greater role in such collective action.

With these policies in place, it is possible to envision a "virtuous cycle" in which businesses, including large corporations with global market dominance, take into account environmental risks in their business and investment decisions; enact strategies to limit these risks in their management and operations; and actions to conserve and restore critical environmental sinks and stocks (see Figure 9.1). Creating such a virtuous cycle may be the only way of fostering a green transition of the world economy to ensure a safer Anthropocene.

Notes

1 For further discussion and examples, see Barbier and Burgess (2018).
2 Sukhdev (2012), pp. 6–7.
3 From https://espace-mondial-atlas.sciencespo.fr/en/topic-strategies-of-transnational-actors/article-3A11-EN-multinational-corporations.html.
4 Folke et al. (2019), p. 1397. As Folke et al. (2019), p. 1396 also point out, "We recognize that small and medium-sized enterprises also play a key role, but many such enterprises are either part of TNCs' global supply chains or serve a domestic market only."
5 Heede (2014).
6 Charles et al. (2021).
7 See Barbier and Burgess (2021) for a formal analysis and discussion of these trade-offs.
8 Barbier and Burgess (2021); Etzion (2020); and Schneider et al. (2020).
9 Etzion (2020), p. 493.
10 See, for example, "ExxonMobil Loses a Proxy Fight with Green Investors." *The Economist* May 29, 2021. www.economist.com/business/2021/05/23/what-a-proxy-fight-at-exxonmobil-says-about-big-oil-and-climate-change.
11 Folke et al. (2019), p. 1398.
12 Osterblöm et al. (2017). See Osterblöm et al. (2020) and Virdin et al. (2021) for other voluntary marine conservation initiatives undertaken by ocean industries and companies.
13 Lubchenco et al. (2017).
14 WEF (2021). Not surprisingly, the fifth risk is the threat for infectious disease outbreak.
15 WEF (2020).
16 Barbier et al. (2018) and Colgan et al. (2017).
17 Iyer et al. (2018) and Sumaila et al. (2020b).
18 Barbier and Burgess (2018); Dobler et al. (2014); and Sharfman and Fernando (2008).
19 Dobler et al. (2014).
20 CDP (2021).
21 WEF (2020).
22 FOLU (2019).
23 WEF (2020), p. 14.
24 Sukhdev (2012), p. 7.
25 World Bank (2020a), p. 39.
26 Aktas et al. (2011); Albertini (2013); Alshehhi et al. (2018); Barbier and Burgess (2018); Busch and Friede (2018); Cai et al. (2015); Chava (2014); Cheng et al. (2014); Endrikat et al. (2014); Hange et al. (2019); Sharfman and Fernando (2008); and World Bank (2020a).
27 Alshehhi et al. (2018). See also Busch and Friede (2018); Endrikat et al. (2014); and Hang et al. (2019).
28 "The Green Meme. A Green Bubble? We Dissect the Investment Boom." *The Economist* May 22, 2021. www.economist.com/finance-and-economics/2021/05/17/green-assets-are-on-a-wild-ride.
29 Chahine and Liagre (2020) and World Bank (2020a).
30 World Bank (2020a).

31 Chahine and Liagre (2020); Dixon et al. (2021); and World Bank (2020a).

32 For example, in their own analysis of the recent boom in green stocks, *The Economist* finds evidence that much of the recent demand is creating at least a "green froth" for some stocks, if not an overall "bubble" for all green stocks. See "The Green Meme. A Green Bubble? We Dissect the Investment Boom." *The Economist* May 22, 2021. www.economist.com/finance-and-economics/2021/05/17/green-assets-are-on-a-wild-ride. Similar trends are noted for green bonds. As Chahine and Liagre (2020, p. 1) comment about the recent expansion in the market value of green bonds: "A lot of this growth has been captured by different stock exchanges where Green Bonds are listed."

33 From "The Green Meme. A Green Bubble? We Dissect the Investment Boom." *The Economist* May 22, 2021. www.economist.com/finance-and-economics/2021/05/17/green-assets-are-on-a-wild-ride.

34 For further details and discussion of these three recommendations, see Barbier and Burgess (2018); Barker et al. (2020); Beare et al. (2014); Cai et al. (2015); Covington et al. (2016); Dixon et al. (2020); Dobler et al. (2014); Ervin et al. (2013); UNEP FI (2015), (2020) and (2021); and World Bank (2020a). The following summarizes the key aspects of each of these recommendations.

35 Cai et al. (2015), p. 25.

36 Barbier and Burgess (2018); Barker et al. (2020); Beare et al. (2014); Covington et al. (2016); Dixon et al. (2020); Ervin et al. (2013); UNEP (2015), (2020) and (2021); and World Bank (2020a).

37 Covington et al. (2016), p. 156.

38 UNEP FI (2015), p. 46.

39 This categorization is based on Albertini (2013).

40 Albertini (2013); Alshehhi et al. (2018); Barbier and Burgess (2018); Beare et al. (2014); Busch and Friede (2018); Ervin et al. (2013); Lai et al. (2016); Pérez-López et al. (2015); and Sierra-García et al. (2015).

41 Ervin et al. (2013), p. 405.

42 TCFD (2020). The TCFD was created by the Financial Stability Board (FSB), which is an international body that monitors and makes recommendations about the global financial system. The FSB was established after the G20 London summit in April 2009 as a successor to the Financial Stability Forum.

43 TNFD (2021). See also discussion of the potential aims and scope of the TNFD in Dixon et al. (2020) and World Bank (2020a).

44 NGFS (2021). Dixon et al. (2021) note that the NGFS is already expanding the range of environmental risks to include broader nature-based solutions. For example, the NGFS has launched a Study Group on Biodiversity and Financial Stability. In addition, there have been a number of initiatives by individual banks and insurers who are NGFS members to explore the links between nature-related risks and financial investments.

45 World Bank (2020a), p. 94. As a footnote to this passage, the World Bank report acknowledges a quote from me, "When people talk about natural capital not being assigned a value, it's not true. We have put a price on nature. And that price is zero," which is drawn from my interview with Helen Avery, "Part 1: Conservation Finance: Can Banks Embrace Natural Capital?" Biodiversity Finance Initiative, United Nations Development Programme (BIOFIN-UNDP). October 8, 2019. www.biodiversityfinance.net/news-and-media/conservation-finance-can-banks-embrace-natural-capital-part-1.

46 Theresa Ghilarducci. "Why Big Business Might Welcome a Carbon Tax." *Forbes* May 11, 2019. www.forbes.com/sites/teresaghilarducci/2019/03/11/why-big-business-might-welcome-a-carbon-tax/?sh=352fe4c52b5d.

47 As we show in Barbier and Burgess (2021), a tax on the excess profits of a monopoly exploiting a finite environmental resource stock or sink has other advantages. The tax reduces the excess profits of the producer but does not affect the equilibrium price or quantity produced in the monopoly market. This means that the monopolist still has an incentive to conserve the stock or sinks, thus extending its lifetime. In comparison, other types of taxes, such as a tax levied on the output of a monopoly, may increase the marginal costs of the producer and lead to a further reduction in the rate of resource exploitation. However, unlike a tax on excess profits, part of the burden of an output tax may be shifted to the consumers in the form of higher prices.

48 For more discussion, see Österblom et al. (2017) and Chapter 7.

49 Folke et al. (2019).

50 Barbier et al. (2018).

51 Sukhdev (2012), p. 6.

10 CONCLUSION

Our economy and our environment are at a crossroads.

We can continue, as we have been doing, and view nature as something outside of the economic system. An unlimited source of bounty that is there for our exploitation and use.

Or we can accept that our economy is part of nature, and not external to it. And that our accelerating use of Earth's remaining resources and pollution sinks is leading to irrevocable ecological damage and rising economic costs, which must ultimately have a limit.

Scientists are increasingly warning us that there are constraints on our unrelenting exploitation of the biosphere. Human impacts on Earth are now so significant that we have created an entirely new geological epoch – the *Anthropocene*. This era began with the late twentieth–century "Great Acceleration" of population growth, industrialization and mineral and energy use, and has continued unabated since. The considerable scale of these impacts is altering basic Earth system processes at an alarming rate through climate and land use change, pollution, freshwater use and many other disruptions. As a result, we may be at the edge of a "tipping point" or "threshold" that could change irrevocably the Earth system, with potentially disastrous impacts for humanity.

Taking the wrong turn at this crossroads could lead to an economic and environmental crisis of unprecedented proportions.

The main aim of this book is to take this scientific perspective seriously, and to explore how our economies and polices need to change in order to avoid an "uncertain" – or possibly even "catastrophic" – Anthropocene. To be successful such a transition must accomplish three aims:

- Transforming our markets, institutions and governance to reduce human impacts on the biosphere
- Mitigating environmental risks in an inclusive and sustainable manner
- Decoupling wealth creation and economic prosperity from environmental degradation

Meeting these objectives goes beyond simply reducing natural resource use and pollution. It requires rethinking how we view the relationship between our economies and nature. This is what is meant by an *economics for a fragile planet*. If we want to ensure a "safe" Anthropocene, we need to put our economic system within nature, and thus create a more environmentally sustainable and inclusive economy.

This is a tall order. And it needs to be done quickly, because of the increasing threats facing us. Global environmental change is occurring now, already affecting the lives and livelihoods of billions today, and only getting worse as we delay actions to deal with it. The longer we wait, the more the costs of inaction rise, and the more likely we will experience potentially catastrophic change.

Some may argue that the global COVID-19 pandemic should take precedence. Surely the priority should be overcoming the economic and health crises caused by the worldwide outbreak, and not worrying about environmental issues? Others believe that the pandemic may have bought us some time, as the global downturn has mitigated human impacts on the biosphere. Still others are more concerned about the next disease outbreak, and its possible devastating consequences, and maintain that addressing problems in nature is less urgent.

But any respite caused by the pandemic will be short-lived. And, unfortunately, the belief that we can postpone addressing global environmental risks is misplaced.

Even as the pandemic was spreading rapidly, human impacts on the biosphere remained a threat. There was a temporary fall in global greenhouse gas emissions in 2020, when the world economy stagnated, but emissions have risen again as the past pattern of global economic development and energy use resumed.[1] Land clearing for mining, agriculture, forestry and other commercial activities – often illegal – actually rose during the pandemic, as governments diverted resources to

COVID-19 or failed to protect remote regions. In 2020, the world lost more than 4.2 million hectares in tropical primary forest, which is a 12 percent increase over the area cleared in 2019.[2] The pandemic has also caused rising debt levels and budget cuts in low- and middle-income countries, which have affected their management, protection and restoration of natural areas and ecosystems. The economic benefits accrued during the pandemic have largely boosted the wealth of the rich, while job losses and environmental deterioration have overwhelming impacted those less well-off in society.

Disease outbreaks are not isolated events but tied to other environmental threats, such as loss of natural habitats. Nearly two-thirds of emerging infectious diseases spread from animals to humans, and three-quarters of them originate in wildlife.[3] An important cause of this spread is the reduction in natural habitat, which increases the likelihood of disease spillovers between infected animals and humans.[4] Simply put, if we want to prevent future pandemics, such as COVID-19, we must also reduce exploitation and protect our natural habitat.

It appears, then, that the World Economic Forum is correct in its evaluation of future risks. In its first *Global Risk Report* since the COVID-19 outbreak, the WEF found that the top five global threats to humankind are four environmental risks – extreme weather, climate action failure, human environmental damage and biodiversity loss. The fifth is the threat of infectious disease outbreaks.[5]

Ensuring that over the coming decades our economies navigate a trajectory toward a "safe" Anthropocene remains the greatest challenge facing the world.

To meet this challenge, this book has proposed five basic principles to guide the economics we need for an increasingly "fragile" planet:

- Ending the underpricing of nature
- Fostering collective action
- Accepting absolute limits
- Attaining sustainability
- Promoting inclusivity

This book has demonstrated how these principles are the foundation for addressing the main environmental threats facing the world economy: climate change (Chapter 4); loss of natural habitat and biodiversity (Chapter 5); freshwater scarcity (Chapter 6); and deteriorating oceans and coasts (Chapter 7). In addition, we require public actions to ensure a green and inclusive structural transformation (Chapter 8) and approaches for greening business and finance (Chapter 9).

This strategy needs to be comprehensive, and carefully designed and implemented, because the task is enormous and urgent. It is time to rethink our markets, institutions and governance structures and put them to work to ensure a "safer" Anthropocene in the next few decades.

Although all five principles are key to the success of this strategy, this book has especially emphasized the first one – *ending the underpricing of nature*.

Taking this first step is essential to developing an economics for an increasingly fragile planet. We need to end the underpricing of nature so that our institutions, incentives and innovations reflect the growing ecological and natural resource scarcity that our current economic use of the environment has created. Without this change, we will not transform our economies so that they are capable of sustaining per capita welfare while simultaneously limiting environmental risks.

As explained throughout this book, the underpricing of nature represents a fundamental misbalance in wealth creation in our economies today. Despite rising natural resource scarcity and increasing environmental and ecological damage, the growth and structure of production in modern economies continues to use more resources and energy. We are not facing up to the rising economic and social costs of increasing natural resource use, pollution and ecological scarcity. We hide these costs by underpricing natural capital in our market, policy and investment decisions. As a consequence, we are using up natural resources as fast as ever; increasingly polluting the environment; and rapidly running down our endowment of natural capital, including irreplaceable ecosystems.

In short, of the three sources of capital that underpin wealth in our economy – physical, human and natural capital – we seem to value only two of them – manufactured *physical capital*, such as roads, buildings, machinery and factories, and *human capital*, such as skills, education and health embodied in the workforce. Our natural endowment of land, ecosystems, natural habitats, environmental resources and sinks are undervalued and squandered. This occurs in a myriad of ways. The increasing costs associated with many environmental problems – climate change, freshwater scarcity, declining ecosystem services and increasing energy insecurity – are not routinely reflected in markets. Nor have we developed adequate policies and institutions to provide other ways for the true costs of environmental degradation to be taken into account. This means that decision makers do not receive the correct price signals or incentives to adjust production and consumption activities. All too often, policy distortions and failures compound ecological scarcity, pollution and resource overexploitation by further encouraging wasteful use of natural resources and environmental degradation. Given that the benefits of environmental exploitation generally accrue to the wealthy and the costs burden the poor, this pattern of development has also exacerbated inequalities.

This fundamental distortion in our economies needs to end if we are to achieve more environmentally sustainable development and a safer Anthropocene. In short, how we treat natural capital is an outcome of how our economic system prices it:

> When people talk about natural capital not being assigned a value, it's not true. We have put a price on nature. And that price is zero.[6]

It is time we end this travesty and ensure that nature has a price in our economic system that is commensurate with the value it provides our livelihoods and well-being. If we want to change the relationship between economy and nature, pricing nature is where we need to start.

We know which road to take, and we need to do it now.

Notes

1 Andrijevic et al. (2020); Le Quéré et al. (2020); and Tollefson (2021).

2 See Mikaela Weisse and Liz Goldman. "Primary Rain Forest Destruction Increased 12% from 2019 to 2020." Global Forest Watch. March 31, 2021. www .globalforestwatch.org/blog/data-and-research/global-tree-cover-loss-data-2020.

3 Cunningham et al. (2017) and Jones et al. (2008).

4 Cunningham et al. (2017); Faust et al. (2018); Gibb et al. (2020); Johnson et al. (2020); and Shah et al. (2019).

5 WEF (2021). The World Economic Forum bases its assessment of the likelihood and impact of various risks on a global survey of businesses, governments and individuals.

6 As quoted in Helen Avery, "Part 1: Conservation Finance: Can Banks Embrace Natural Capital?" Biodiversity Finance Initiative, United Nations Development Programme (BIOFIN-UNDP). October 8, 2019. www.biodiversityfinance.net/news-and-media/conservation-finance-can-banks-embrace-natural-capital-part-1. In fact, as the economist Partha Dasgupta points out, we are not just pricing ecosystems and their services too cheaply, we are actually giving them a "negative price," which is tantamount to paying some economic activities to destroy nature: "The current structure of market prices works against our common future; the biosphere is precious but priced cheaply, if it is priced at all. Worse, owing to a wide range of government subsidies, some services come with a negative price" (Dasgupta 2021, p. 234).

REFERENCES

Abbott, Joshua K. and U. Rashid Sumaila. 2019. "Reducing Marine Plastic Pollution: Insights from Economics." *Review of Environmental Economics and Policy* 13(2):327–336.

Acemoglu, Daron, Simon Johnson and James A. Robinson. 2001. "The Colonial Origins of Comparative Development: An Empirical Investigation." *American Economic Review* 91(5):1369–1401.

Acharyya, Achiransu, Madhusudan Ghosh and Rabindra N. Bhattacharya. 2018. "Groundwater Market in West Bengal, India: Does It Display Monopoly Power?" *Studies in Microeconomics* 6:105–129.

Aktas, Nihat, Eric De Bodt and Jean-Gabriel Cousin. 2011. "Do Financial Markets Care about SRI? Evidence from Mergers and Acquisitions." *Journal of Banking & Finance* 35(7):1753–1761.

Al-Abdulrazzak, Dalal, Grantly R. Galland, Loren McClenachan and John Hocevar. 2017. "Opportunities for Improving Global Marine Conservation through Multilateral Treaties." *Marine Policy* 86:247–252.

Albertini, Elisabeth. 2013. "Does Environmental Management Improve Financial Performance? A Meta-Analytical Review." *Organization & Environment* 26:431–457.

Allott, Joseph, Adrano Canela, Glen O'Kelly and Samuel Pendergraph. 2020. "Data: The Next Wave in Forestry Productivity." McKinsey & Company.

Almroth, Bethanie Carney and Håkan Eggert. 2019. "Marine Plastic Pollution: Sources, Impacts, and Policy Issues." *Review of Environmental Economics and Policy* 13(12):317–326.

Alshehhi, Ali, Haitham Nobanee and Nilesh Khare. 2018. "The Impact of Sustainability Practices on Corporate Financial Performance: Literature Trends and Future Research Potential." *Sustainability* 10(2):494. www.mdpi.com/2071-1050/10/2/494.

Alvaredo, Facundo, Lucas Chancel, Thomas Piketty, Emmanuel Saez and Gabriel Zucman. 2017. *World Inequality Report 2018*, World Inequality Lab. https://wir2018.wid.world.

Anderson, Zachary R., Koen Kusters, John McCarthy and Krystof Obidzinski. 2016. "Green Growth Rhetoric versus Reality: Insights from Indonesia." *Global Environmental Change* 38:30–40.

Andres, Luis A., Michael Thibert, Camilo Lombana Cordoba, Alexander V. Danilenko, George Joseph and Christian Borja-Vega. 2019. "Doing More with Less: Smarter Subsidies for Water Supply and Sanitation." World Bank, Washington, DC.

Andreu-Cazenave, Miguel, Maria Dulce Subida and Miriam Fernandez. 2017. "Exploitation Rates of Two Benthic Resources across Management Regimes in Central Chile: Evidence of Illegal Fishing in Artisanal Fisheries Operating in Open Access Areas." *Plos One* 12(6):e0180012.

Andrijevic, M., C. F. Schleussner, M. J. Gidden, D. L. McCollum and J. Rogelj. 2020. "COVID-19 Recovery Funds Dwarf Clean Energy Investment Needs." *Science* 370(6514):298–300.

Angelsen, Arild and Therese Dokken. 2018. "Climate Exposure, Vulnerability and Environmental Reliance: A Cross-Section Analysis of Structural and Stochastic Poverty." *Environment and Development Economics* 23:257–278.

Angelsen, Arild, Pamela Jagger, Ronnie Babigumira et al. 2014. "Environmental Income and Rural Livelihoods: A Global-Comparative Analysis." *World Development* 64:S12–S26.

Arrow, K. J., Cropper, M., Gollier, C., Groom et al. 2013. "Determining Benefits and Costs for Future Generations." *Science* 341:349–350.

Arrow, Kenneth J., Partha Dasgupta, Lawrence H. Goulder, Kevin J. Mumford and Kirstin Oleson. 2012. "Sustainability and the Measurement of Wealth." *Environment and Development Economics* 17(3):317–353.

Arze del Granado, F., D. Coady and R. Gillingham. 2012. "The Unequal Benefits of Fuel Subsidies: A Review of Evidence from Developing Countries." *World Development* 40:2234–2248.

Asian Development Bank (ADB) and Asian Development Bank Institute (ADBI). 2013. *Low-Carbon Green Growth in Asia: Policies and Practices*. ADB and ADBI, Manila.

Avery, Christopher E. 2018. "New Flexibility on the Central Arizona Project Canal: The Tucson/Phoenix Exchange and the System Use Agreement." *Arizona Journal of Environmental Law and Policy* 8(3):89–100.

Bachewe, Fantu N., Guush Berhane, Bart Minten and Alemayehu S. Taffesse. 2018. "Agricultural Transformation in Africa? Assessing the Evidence in Ethiopia." *World Development* 105:286–298.

Badeeb, Ramez Abubakr, Hooi Hooi Lean and Jeremy Clark. 2017. "The Evolution of the Natural Resource Curse Thesis: A Critical Literature Survey." *Resources Policy* 51:123–134.

Bailey, David and Greg Bertelsen. 2018. *A Winning Trade. Policy Analysis.* Climate Leadership Council, Washington, DC. https://clcouncil.org/media/A-Winning-Trade-1.pdf.

Bar-On, Yinon M., Rob Phillips and Ron Milo. 2018. "The Biomass Distribution on Earth." *Proceedings of the National Academy of Sciences* 115:6506–6511.

Barbier, Edward B. 1989. *Economics, Natural Resource Scarcity and Development: Conventional and Alternative Views.* Earthscan Publications, London.

Barbier, Edward B. 2007. "Valuing Ecosystem Services as Productive Inputs." *Economic Policy* 22(49):178–229.

Barbier, Edward B. 2010. *A Global Green New Deal: Rethinking the Economic Recovery.* Cambridge University Press, New York.

Barbier, Edward B. 2011. *Scarcity and Frontiers: How Economies Have Developed through Natural Resource Exploitation.* Cambridge University Press, New York.

Barbier, Edward B. 2012. "Tax 'Societal Ills' to Save the Planet." *Nature* 483:30.

Barbier, Edward B. 2014. "A Global Strategy for Protecting Vulnerable Coastal Populations." *Science* 345:1250–1251.

Barbier, Edward B. 2015. *Nature and Wealth: Overcoming Environmental Scarcity and Inequality.* Palgrave Macmillan, London.

Barbier, Edward B. 2016a. "Building the Green Economy." *Canadian Public Policy* 42:S1–S9.

Barbier, Edward B. 2016b. "Is Green Growth Relevant for Developing Countries?" *Resource and Energy Economics* 45:178–191.

Barbier, Edward B. 2019a. *Natural Resources and Economic Development*, 2nd ed. Cambridge University Press, New York.

Barbier, Edward B. 2019b. *The Water Paradox: Overcoming the Global Crisis in Water Management.* Yale University Press, London.

Barbier, Edward B. 2019c. "The Concept of Natural Capital." *Oxford Review of Economic Policy* 35(1):14–36.

Barbier, Edward B. 2020a. "Building a Greener Recovery: Lessons from the Great Recession." *Covid-19 Green Recovery Working Paper Series.* United Nations Environment Programme (UNEP), Geneva. www.greengrowthknowledge.org/guidance/building-greener-recovery-lessons-great-recession.

Barbier, Edward B. 2020b. "Greening the Post-pandemic Recovery in the G20." *Environmental and Resource Economics* 76:685–703.

Barbier, Edward B. 2020c. "Is Green Rural Transformation Possible in Developing Countries?" *World Development* 131:104955.

Barbier, Edward B. 2021. "The Evolution of Economic Views on Natural Resource Scarcity." *Review of Environmental Economics and Policy* 15 (1):24–44.

Barbier, Edward B. and Geoffrey M. Heal. 2006. "Valuing Ecosystem Services." *The Economists' Voice* 3: No. 3, Article 2. www.bepress.com/ev/vol3/iss3/art2.

Barbier, Edward B. and Jacob P. Hochard. 2018. "The Impacts of Climate Change on the Poor in Disadvantaged Regions" *Review of Environmental Economics and Policy* 12:26–47.

Barbier, Edward B. and Jacob P. Hochard. 2019. "Poverty-Environment Traps." *Environmental and Resource Economics* 74(3):1239–1271.

Barbier, Edward B. and Joanne C. Burgess. 2017. "Depletion of the Global Carbon Budget: A User Cost Approach." *Environment and Development Economics* 1–16.

Barbier, Edward B. and Joanne C. Burgess. 2018. "Policies to Support Environmental Risk Management in Investment Decisions." *International Journal of Global Environmental Issues* 17(2/3):117–129.

Barbier, Edward B. and Joanne C. Burgess. 2019. "Scarcity and Safe Operating Spaces: The Example of Natural Forests." *Environmental and Resource Economics* 74(3):1077–1099.

Barbier, Edward B. and Joanne C. Burgess. 2020. "Sustainability and Development after COVID-19." *World Development* 135:105082

Barbier, Edward B., and Joanne C. Burgess. 2021. "Sustainable Use of the Environment, Planetary Boundaries and Market Power." *Sustainability* 13 (2):949. https://doi.org/10.3390/su13020949.

Barbier, Edward B., David Moreno-Mateos, Alex D. Rogers et al. 2014. "Protect the Deep Sea." *Nature* 505:475–477.

Barbier, Edward B., Joanne C. Burgess and Thomas J. Dean. 2018. "How to Pay for Saving Biodiversity." *Science* 360(6388): 486–488.

Barbier, Edward B., Ricardo Lozano, Carlos Manuel Rodriguez and Sebastian Troëng. 2020. "Adopt a Carbon Tax to Protect Tropical Countries" *Nature* 578:213–216.

Barker, Sarah, Ellie Mulholland and Temitope Onifade. 2020. *The Emergence of Foreseeable Biodiversity-Related Liability Risks for Financial Institutions. A Gathering Storm?* Commonwealth Climate and Law Institute, Oxford. https://ccli.ouce.ox.ac.uk/wp-content/uploads/2020/09/CCLI-Biodiversity-liability-risks-report-vFINAL.pdf.

Barlow, Jos, Filipe França, Toby A. Gardner et al. 2018. "The Future of Hyperdiverse Tropical Ecosystems." *Nature* 559:517–526.

Barnett, Harold J. and Chandler Morse. 1963. *Scarcity and Economic Growth: The Economics of Natural Resource Availability*. Johns Hopkins University Press, Baltimore.

Barrett, Christopher B., Luc Christiaensen, Megan Sheahan and Abebe Shimeles, 2017. "On the Structural Transformation of Rural Africa." *Journal of African Economies* 26:111–135.

Batini, Nicoletta, Mario Di Serio, Matteo Fragetta, Giovanni Melina and Anthony Waldron. 2021. "Building Back Better: How Big Are Green Multipliers?" *IMF Working Paper WP/21/87*. International Monetary Fund, Washington, DC.

Battista, Willow, Rainer Romero-Canyas, Sarah Lindley Smith et al. 2018. "Behavior Change Interventions to Reduce Illegal Fishing." *Frontiers in Marine Science* 5:403.

Bavinck, Maarten, Fikret Berkes, Anthony Charles et al. 2017. "The Impact of Coastal Grabbing on Community Conservation–A Global Reconnaissance." *Maritime Studies* 16(1):1–17.

Bayraktarov, Elisa, Megan I. Saunders, Sabah Abdullah et al. 2016. "The Cost and Feasibility of Marine Coastal Restoration." *Ecological Applications* 26 (4):1055–1074.

Beare, Dan, Ruvena Buslovich and Cory Searcy. 2014. "Linkages between Corporate Sustainability Reporting and Public Policy." *Corporate Social Responsibility and Environmental Management* 21:336–350.

Beck, Michael W., Iñigo J. Losada, Pelayo Menéndez, Borja G. Reguero, Pedro Díaz-Simal and Felipe Fernández. 2018. "The Global Flood Protection Savings Provided by Coral Reefs." *Nature Communications* 9(1):1–9.

Belhabib, Dyhia, U. Rashid Sumaila and Philippe Le Billon. 2019. "The Fisheries of Africa: Exploitation, Policy, and Maritime Security Trends." *Marine Policy* 101:80–92.

Bellmann, Christophe. 2019. *Subsidies and Sustainable Agriculture: Mapping the Policy Landscape*. Hoffmann Centre for Sustainable Resource Economy, Royal Institute of International Affairs, Chatham House, London.

Bellwood, Peter. 2005. *First Farmers: The Origins of Agricultural Societies*. Blackwell Publishing, Oxford.

BenDor Todd, T. William Lester, Avery Livengood, Adam Davis and Logan Yonavjak. 2015. "Estimating the Size and Impact of the Ecological Restoration Economy." *PLoS ONE* 10(6):e0128339.

Bennett, Nathan James and Philip Dearden. 2014. "Why Local People Do Not Support Conservation: Community Perceptions of Marine Protected Area Livelihood Impacts, Governance and Management in Thailand." *Marine Policy* 44:107–116.

Bennett, Nathan James, Hugh Govan and Terre Satterfield. 2015. "Ocean Grabbing." *Marine Policy* 57:61–68.

Bennett, Nathan James, Jessica Blythe, Carole Sandrine White and Cecilia Campero. 2021. "Blue Growth and Blue Justice: Ten Risks and Solutions for the Ocean Community." *Marine Policy* 125:104387.

Berbel, Julio and Encarna Esteban. 2019. "Droughts as a Catalyst for Water Policy Change. Analysis of Spain, Australia (MDB), and California." *Global Environmental Change* 58:101969.

Bertram, Christoph, Gunnar Luderer, Robert C. Pietzcker, Eva Schmid, Elmar Kriegler and Ottmar Edenhofer. 2015. "Complementing Carbon Prices with Technology Policies to Keep Climate Targets within Reach." *Nature Climate Change* 5:235–239.

Beymer-Farris, Betsy A. and Thomas J. Bassett. 2012. "The REDD Menace: Resurgent Protectionism in Tanzania's Mangrove Forests." *Global Environmental Change* 22(2):332–341.

Biermann, Frank and Rakhyun E. Kim. 2020. "The Boundaries of the Planetary Boundary Framework: A Critical Appraisal of Approaches to Define a 'Safe Operating Space' for Humanity." *Annual Review of Environment and Resources* 45:497–521.

Binswanger, Hans P. and Klaus Deininger. 1997. "Explaining Agricultural and Agrarian Policies in Developing Countries." *Journal of Economic Literature* 35:1958–2005.

Birkenbach, Anna M., David J. Kaczan and Martin D. Smith. 2017. "Catch Shares Slow the Race to Fish." *Nature* 544(7649):223–226.

Bolt, Jutta, Robert Inklaar, Herman de Jong and Jan Luiten van Zanden. 2018. "Rebasing 'Maddison': New Income Comparisons and the Shape of Long-Run Economic Development" Maddison Project Working Paper, nr. 10, available for download at www.ggdc.net/maddison.

Boulding, Kenneth E. 1966. "The Economics of the Coming Spaceship Earth." In H. Jarrett, ed. *Environmental Quality in a Growing Economy*, Johns Hopkins University Press, Baltimore, pp. 3–14.

BP. 2019. *BP Statistical Review of World Energy 2019*, www.bp.com/statisticalreview.

Brander, Luke M., Pieter Van Beukering, Lynn Nijsten et al. 2020. "The Global Costs and Benefits of Expanding Marine Protected Areas." *Marine Policy* 116:103953.

Brelle, F. and E. Dressayre. 2014. "Financing Irrigation." *Irrigation and Drainage* 63:199–211.

Brewer, Jedidiah, Robert Glennon, Alan Ker and Gary Libecap. 2008. "Water Markets in the West: Prices, Trading, and Contractural Forms." *Economic Inquiry* 46(2):91–112.

Broadbent, Craig D., David S. Brookshire, Don Coursey and Vince Tisdell. 2017. "Futures Contracts in Water Leasing: An Experimental Analysis Using Basin Characteristics of the Rio Grande, NM." *Environmental and Resource Economics* 68:569–594.

Brook, Barry W., Erle C. Ellis, Michael P. Perring, Anson W. Mackay and Linus Blomqvist. "Does the Terrestrial Biosphere Have Planetary Tipping Points?" 2013. *Trends in Ecology & Evolution* 28(7):396–401.

Brookshire, David S., Bonnie Colby, Mary Ewers and Philip T. Ganderton. 2004. "Market Prices for Water in the Semiarid West of the United States." *Water Resources Research* 40(9):W09S04

Bunsen, Jonas, Markus Berger and Matthias Finkbeiner. 2021. "Planetary Boundaries for Water–A Review." *Ecological Indicators* 121:107022.

Burbano, Diana V. and Thomas C. Meredith. 2020. "Conservation Strategies through the Lens of Small-Scale Fishers in the Galapagos Islands, Ecuador: Perceptions Underlying Local Resistance to Marine Planning." *Society & Natural Resources* 33(10):1194–1212.

Busch, Jonah and Jens Engelmann. 2018. "Cost-Effectiveness of Reducing Emissions from Tropical Deforestation, 2016–2050." *Environmental Research Letters* 13:015001

Busch, Jonah and Kalifi Ferretti-Gallon. 2017. "What Drives Deforestation and What Stops It? A Meta-*Analysis.*" *Review of Environmental Economics and Policy* 11(1):3–23.

Busch, Jonah, Kalifi Ferretti-Gallon, Jens Engelmann et al. 2015. "Reductions in Emissions from Deforestation from Indonesia's Moratorium on New Oil Palm, Timber, and Logging Concessions." *Proceedings of the National Academy of Sciences* 112:1328–1333.

Busch, Timo and Gunnar Friede. 2018. "The Robustness of the Corporate Social and Financial Performance Relation: A Second-Order Meta-Analysis." *Corporate Social Responsibility and Environmental Management* 25(4):583–608.

Butzer, Karl W. 2012. "Collapse, Environment and Society." *Proceedings of the National Academy of Sciences* 109(10):3632–3639.

Cabral, Reniel B., Darcy Bradley, Juan Mayorga et al. 2020. "A Global Network of Marine Protected Areas for Food." *Proceedings of the National Academy of Sciences* 117(45):28134–28139.

Cahine, Paul and Ludwig Liagre. 2020. *How Can Green Bonds Catalyse Investments in Biodiversity and Sustainable Land-Use Projects.* Global Landscapes Forum and Luxembourg Green Exchange. www .globallandscapesforum.org/wp-content/uploads/2020/10/How-can-Green-Bonds-catalyse-investments-in-biodiversity-and-sustainable-land-use-projects-v12_Final.pdf.

Cai, Li, Jinhua Cui and Hoje Jo. 2015. "Corporate Environmental Responsibility and Firm Risk." *Journal of Business Ethics* 1–32.

Cardoso da Silva, Jose Maria, Shivangi Prasad and José A. Felizola Diniz-Filho. 2017. "The Impact of Deforestation, Urbanization, Public Investment, and Agriculture on Human Welfare in the Brazilian Amazon." *Land Use Policy* 65:135–142.

Carrasco, L. R., T. P. L. Nghiem, Z. Chen and E. B. Barbier. 2017. "Unsustainable Development Pathways Caused by Tropical Deforestation." *Science Advances* 3(7):e1602602.

Cassimon, Danny, Martin Prowse and Dennis Essers. 2011. "The Pitfalls and Potential of Debt-for-Nature Swaps: A US-Indonesia Case Study." *Global Environmental Change* 21:93–102.

Castañeda, A., D. Doan, D. Newhouse et al. 2018. "A New Profile of the Global Poor." *World Development* 101:250–267.

Caviglia-Harris, Jill L., Erin O. Sills, Andrew Bell, Daniel Harris, Katrina Mullan and Dar Roberts. 2016. "Busting the Boom-Bust Pattern of Development in the Brazilian Amazon." *World Development* 79:82–96.

CDP. 2021. *Putting a Price on Carbon: The State of Internal Carbon Pricing by Corporates Globally.* April 2021. CDP Worldwide. www.cdp.net/en/research/global-reports/putting-a-price-on-carbon.

Ceballos, Gerardo, Paul R. Ehrlich and Rodolfo Dirzo. 2017. "Biological Annihilation via the Ongoing Sixth Mass Extinction Signaled by Vertebrate Population Losses and Declines." *Proceedings of the National Academy of Sciences* 114(30):E6089–E6096.

Chaigneau, Tomas and Katrina Brown. 2016. "Challenging the Win-Win Discourse on Conservation and Development: Analyzing Support for Marine Protected Areas." *Ecology and Society* 21(1):36.

Charles, Dominic, Laurent Kimman and Nakul Saran. 2021. *The Plastics Waste Maker Index.* Minderoo Foundation, Perth. https://cdn.minderoo.org/content/uploads/2021/05/18065501/20210518-Plastic-Waste-Makers-Index.pdf.

Chava, Sudheer. 2014. "Environmental Externalities and Cost of Capital." *Management Science* 60:2223–2247.

Cheng, Beiting, Ioannis Ioannou and George Serafeim. 2014. "Corporate Social Responsibility and Access to Finance." *Strategic Management Journal* 35:1–23.

Chew, Sing C. 2001. *World Ecological Degradation: Accumulation, Urbanization, and Deforestation 3000 B.C.–A.D. 2000.* Altamira Press, New York.

Chew, Sing C. 2006. "Dark Ages: Ecological Crisis Phases and System Transition." In Barry K. Gillis and William R. Thompson, eds. *Globalization and Global History.* Routledge, London, pp. 163202.

Chiarelli, Davide Danilo, Kyle Frankel Davis, Maria Cristina Rulli and Paolo D'Odorico. 2016. "Climate Change and Large-Scale land Acquisitions in Africa: Quantifying the Future Impact on Acquired Water Resources." *Advances in Water Resources* 94:231–237.

Chomitz, K. M., P. Buys, G. De Luca, T. S. Thomas and S. Wertz-Kanounnikoff. 2007. *At Loggerheads? Agricultural Expansion, Poverty Reduction, and Environment in the Tropical Forests.* The World Bank, Washington, DC.

Cinner, Joshua E., Tim Daw, Cindy Huchery et al. 2014. "Winners and Losers in Marine Conservation: Fishers' Displacement and Livelihood Benefits from Marine Reserves." *Society & Natural Resources* 27(9):994–1005.

Claessens, S., M. Keen and C. Pazarbasioglu. 2010. *Financial Sector Taxation: The IMF's Report to the G-20 and Background Material*. September, 2010. International Monetary Fund, Washington, DC. www.taxpolicycenter.org/sites/default/files/imf-studies.pdf.

Clark, William C. and Alicia G. Harley. 2020. "Sustainability Science: Toward a Synthesis." *Annual Review of Environment and Resources* 45:331–386.

Coady, David, Ian Parry, Nghia-Piotr Le and Baoping Shang. 2019. "Global Fossil Fuel Subsidies Remain Large: An Update Based on Country-Level Estimates." *IMF Working Paper WP/19/89*, International Monetary Fund, Washington, DC.

Cohen, Alice and Seanna Davidson. 2011. "An Examination of the Watershed Approach: Challenges, Antecedents, and the Transition from Technical Tool to Governance Unit." *Water Alternatives* 4(1):1–14.

Colgan, Charles S., Michael W. Beck and Siddharth Narayan. 2017. "*Financing Natural Infrastructure for Coastal Flood Damage Reduction*." Lloyd's Tercentenary Research Foundation, London. https://digitalcommons.usm.maine.edu/cgi/viewcontent.cgi?article=1010&context=climatechange.

Convery, Frank J. 2013. "Reflections – Shaping Water Policy: What Does Economics Have to Offer?" *Review of Environmental Economics and Policy* 7 (1):156–174.

Cosbey, Aaron, Susanne Droege, Carolyn Fischer and Clayton Munnings. 2019. "Developing Guidance for Implementing Border Carbon Adjustments: Lessons, Cautions, and Research Needs from the Literature." *Review of Environmental Economics and Policy* 13(1):3–22.

Costello, Christopher, Daniel Ovando, Tyler Clavelle et al. 2016. "Global Fishery Prospects under Contrasting Management Regimes." *Proceedings of the National Academy of Sciences* 113(18):5125–5129.

Costello, Christopher, Ling Cao, Stefan Gelcich et al. 2020. "The Future of Food from the Sea." *Nature* 588(7836):95–100.

Costello, Mark J. and Bill Ballantine.2015. "Biodiversity Conservation Should Focus on No-Take Marine Reserves: 94% of Marine Protected Areas Allow Fishing." *Trends in Ecology & Evolution* 30(9):507–509.

Covington, Howard, James Thornton and Cameron Hepburn 2016. "Shareholders Must Vote for Climate Change Mitigation." *Nature* 530:156.

Crosby, Alfred. 1986. *Ecological Imperialism: The Biological Expansion of Europe 900–1900*. Cambridge University Press, New York.

Crutzen, Paul J. 2002. "Geology of Mankind." *Nature* 415:23.

Crutzen, Paul J. and Eugene F. Stoermer. 2000. "The 'Anthropocene'." *Global Change Newsletter No. 41* (May):17–18.

Culbert, T. Patrick. 1988. "The Collapse of Classic Maya Civilization." In Norman Yoffee and George L. Cowgill, eds. 1988. *The Collapse of Ancient States and Civilizations*. University of Arizona Press, Tucson, pp. 69–101.

Culp, Peter W., Robert Glennon and Gary Libecap. 2014. *Shopping for Water: How the Market Can Mitigate Water Scarcity in the American West*. The Hamilton Project, Washington, DC.

Cunningham, Andrew A., Peter Daszak and James L. N. Wood. 2017. "One Health, Emerging Infectious Diseases and Wildlife: Two Decades of Progress?" *Philosophical Transactions of the Royal Society B* 372:20160167.

Da Ros, Zaira, Antonio Dell'Anno, Telmo Morato et al. 2019. "The Deep Sea: The New Frontier for Ecological Restoration." *Marine Policy* 108:103642.

Danovaro, Roberto, Jacopo Aguzzi, E. Fanelli et al. 2017. "An Ecosystem-Based Deep-Ocean Strategy." *Science* 355(6324):452–454.

Dasgupta, Partha. 2008. "Nature in Economics." *Environmental and Resource Economics* 39:1–7.

Dasgupta, Partha. 2021. *The Economics of Biodiversity: The Dasgupta Review*. HM Treasury, London. https://assets.publishing.service.gov.uk/government/uploads/system/uploads/attachment_data/file/962785/The_Economics_of_Biodiversity_The_Dasgupta_Review_Full_Report.pdf.

Data-Driven EnviroLab & NewClimate Institute. 2020. *Accelerating Net Zero: Exploring Cities, Regions, and Companies' Pledges to Decarbonise*. Research report prepared by the team of: Angel Hsu, Zhi Yi Yeo, Amy Weinfurter et al. (NewClimate Institute). https://newclimate.org/wp-content/uploads/2020/09/NewClimate_Accelerating_Net_Zero_Sept2020.pdf.

Davidson, Nick C. 2014. "How Much Wetland Has the World Lost? Long-Term and Recent Trends in Global Wetland Area." *Marine and Freshwater Research* 65(10):934–941.

Davidson, Nick C. and C. Max Finlayson. 2018. "Extent, Regional Distribution and Changes in Area of Different Classes of Wetland." *Marine and Freshwater Research* 69(10):1525–1533.

Davidson, Nick C. and C. Max Finlayson. 2019. "Updating Global Coastal Wetland Areas Presented in Davidson and Finlayson (2018)." *Marine and Freshwater Research* 70:1195–1200.

Davidson, Nick C., Etienne Fluet-Chouinard and C. Max Finlayson. 2018. "Global Extent and Distribution of Wetlands: Trends and Issues." *Marine and Freshwater Research* 69(4):620–627.

Davis, Katrina J., Gabriel M. S. Vianna, Jessica J. Meeuwig, Mark G. Meekan and David J. Pannell. 2019. "Estimating the Economic Benefits and Costs of Highly-Protected Marine Protected Areas." *Ecosphere* 10(10):e02879.

de Chaisemartin, Marguerite, Robert G. Varady, Sharon B. Megdal et al. 2017. "Addressing the Groundwater Governance Challenge." In E. Karar, ed. *Freshwater Governance for the 21st Century, Global Issues in Water Policy 6*, Springer, Dordrecht.

De Stefano, L., Jacob D. Petersen-Perlman, Eric A. Sproles, Jim Eynard and Aaron T. Wolf. 2017. "Assessment of Transboundary River Basins for

Potential Hydro-Political Tensions." *Global Environmental Change* 45:35–46.

de Vos, Klaas and Ben Hart. 2020. *The Ocean Finance Handbook: Increasing Finance for a Healthy Ocean*. Friends of Ocean Action, Geneva. www3 .weforum.org/docs/WEF_FOA_The_Ocean_Finance_Handbook_April_2020 .pdf.

Debela, Bethleham, Gerald Shively, Arild Angelsen and Mette Wik. 2012. Economic Shocks, Diversification, and Forest Use in Uganda. *Land Economics* 88:139–154.

DeFries R., T. Rudel, M. Uriarte and M. Hansen 2010. "Deforestation Driven by Urban Population Growth and Agricultural Trade in the Twenty-First Century." *Nature Geoscience* 3:178–801.

Deininger, K. and D. Byerlee. 2012. "The Rise of Large Farms in Land Abundant Countries: Do They Have a Future?" *World Development* 40:701–714.

Delacote, Philippe. 2009. "Commons as Insurance: Safety Nets or Poverty Traps?" *Environment and Development Economics* 14:305–322.

Dell'Angelo, Jampel, Maria Cristina Rulli and Paolo D'Odorico. 2018. "The Global Water Grabbing Syndrome." *Ecological Economics* 143: 276–285.

Dercon, Stefan. 2014. "Is Green Growth Good for the Poor?" *The World Bank Research Observer* 29:163–185.

Diamond, Jared. 1997. *Guns, Germs, and Steel: The Fates of Human Societies*. W. W. Norton & Co., New York.

Diamond, Jared. 2005. *Collapse: How Societies Choose to Fail or Succeed*. Allen Lane, London.

Díaz, Sandra, Josef Settele, Eduardo S. Brondizio et al., eds. 2019. "Pervasive Human-Driven Decline of Life on Earth Points to the Need for Transformative Change." *Science* 366(6471):eaax3100. https://science.sciencemag.org/ content/366/6471/eaax3100/tab-pdf.

Díaz, Sandra, Noelia Zofra-Calvo, Andy Purvis et al. 2020. "Set Ambitious Goals for Biodiversity and Sustainability." *Science* 370(6515):411–413.

Dinar, Ariel, Victor Pochat and José Albiac-Murillo, eds. 2015. *Water Pricing Experiences and Innovations*. Global Issues in Water Policy 9, Springer, Dorcrecht.

Dinar, Shlomi. 2009. "Scarcity and Cooperation along International Rivers." *Global Environmental Politics* 9(1):108–135.

Dinar, Shlomi, Ariel Dinar and Pradeep Kurukulasuriya. 2011. "Scarcity and Cooperation along International Rivers: An Empirical Assessment of Bilateral Treaties." *International Studies Quarterly* 55(3):809–833.

Dinerstein, Eric, Carly Vynne, Enric Sala et al. 2019. "A Global Deal for Nature: Guiding Principles, Milestones, and Targets." *Science Advances* 5(4): eaaw2869.

Dinerstein, Eric, David Olson, Anup Joshi et al. 2017. "An Ecoregion-Based Approach to Protecting Half the Terrestrial Realm." *BioScience* 67 (6):534–545.

Ding, Helen, Sofia Faruqi, Andrew Wu et al. 2019. *Roots of Prosperity: The Economics and Finance of Restoring Land.* World Resources Institute, Washington, DC.

Dixon, Charlie, Bryan Vadheim, Ciaran Burks, Deven Azevedo and Jason Eis. 2021. *The Climate-Nature Nexus: Implications for the Finance Sector.* Finance for Biodiversity Initiative, London. www.f4b-initiative.net/post/the-climate-nature-nexus-implications-for-the-financial-sector.

Dobler, Michael, Kaouther Lajili and Daniel Zéghal. 2014. "Environmental Performance, Environmental Risk Management and Risk Management." *Business Strategy and the Environment* 23:1–17.

Dobson, Andrew P., Stuart L. Pimm, Hannah Lee et al. 2020. "Ecology and Economics for Pandemic Prevention." *Science* 369(6502):379–381.

Donlan, C. Josh, Chris Wilcox, Gloria M. Luque and Stefan Gelcich. 2020. "Estimating Illegal Fishing from Enforcement Officers." *Scientific Reports* 10 (1):1–9.

Duarte, Carlos M., Susana Agusti, Edward B. Barbier et al. 2020. "Rebuilding Marine Life. *Nature* 580:39–51.

Easter, K. William. 2009. "Demand Management, Privatization, Water Markets, and Efficient Water Allocation in Our Cities." In L. A. Baker, ed. *The Water Environment of Cities.* Springer, Dordrecht, pp. 259–274.

Easter, K. William and Qiuqiong Huang, eds. 2014. *Water Markets for the 21st Century: What Have We Learned? Global Issues in Water Policy 11.* Springer, Dordrecht.

Edgar, Graham J., Rick D. Stuart-Smith, Trevor J. Willis et al. 2014. "Global Conservation Outcomes Depend on Marine Protected Areas with Five Key Features." *Nature* 506(7487):216–220.

Elhacham, Emily, Liad Ben-Uri, Jonathon Grozovski, Yinon M. Bar-On and Ron Milo. 2020. "Global Human-Made Mass Exceeds All Living Biomass." *Nature* 588:442–444.

Ellis, Erle C., Jed O. Kaplan, Doran Q. Fuller, Steve Vavrus, Kees Klein Goldewijk and Peter H. Verburg. 2013. "Used Planet: A Global History." *Proceedings of the National Academy of Science* 110(20):7978–7985.

Elvin, Mark. 1993. "Three Thousand Years of Unsustainable Growth: China's Environment from Archaic Time to the Present." *East Asian History* 6:7–46.

Endrikat, Jan, Edeltraud Guenther and Holger Hoppe. 2014. "Making Sense of Conflicting Empirical Findings: A Meta-Analysis of the Relationship between Corporate Environmental and Financial Performance." *European Management Journal* 32:735–751.

Engerman, Stanley L. and Kenneth L. Sokoloff. 1997. "Factor Endowments, Institutions, and Differential Paths of Growth among New World Economies." In Stephen Haber, ed. *How Latin America Fell Behind: Essays on the Economic Histories of Brazil and Mexico*. Stanford University Press, Stanford, pp. 260–304.

Erlandson, Jon M. and Scott M. Fitzpatrick. 2006. "Oceans, Islands, and Coasts: Current Perspectives on the Role of the Sea in Human Prehistory." *Journal of Island & Coastal Archaeology* 1(1):5–32.

Ervin, David, Junjie Wu, Madhu Khanna, Cody Jones and Teresa Wirkkala. 2013. "Motivations and Barriers to Corporate Environmental Management." *Business Strategy and the Environment* 22:390–409.

Etemad, Bouda, Jean Lucini, Paul Bairoch and Jean-Claude Toutain. 1991. *World Energy Production 1800–1995*. Centre National de la Recherche Scientifique and Centre D'Histoire Economique Internationale, Geneva.

Etzion, Dror. 2020. "Corporate Engagement with the Natural Environment." *Nature Ecology & Evolution* 4(4):493–493.

European Academies Science Advisory Council (EASAC) (2019) Forest Bioenergy, Carbon Capture and Storage, and Carbon Dioxide Removal: An Update. EASAC, Brussels https://easac.eu/publications/details/forest-bioenergy-carbon-capture-and-storage-and-carbon-dioxide-removal-an-update.

Fan, Shenggen and Connie Chan-Kang. 2004. "Returns to Investment in Less-Favoured Areas in Developing Countries: A Synthesis of Evidence and Implications for Africa." *Food Policy* 29:431–444.

Fankhauser, Sam, Alex Bowen, Raphael Calel, Antoine Dechezleprêtre, James Rydge and Misato Sato. 2013. "Who Will Win the Green Race? In Search of Environmental Competitiveness and Innovation." *Global Environmental Change* 23:902–913.

Fargione, Joseph E., Steven Bassett, Timothy Boucher et al. 2018. "Natural Climate Solutions for the United States." *Science Advances* 4:eaat1869.

Faust, Christina L., Hamish I. McCallum, Laura S. P. et al. 2018. "Pathogen Spillover during Land Conversion." *Ecology letters* 21(4):471–483.

Federico, Giovanni. 2005. *Feeding the World: An Economic History of Agriculture, 1800–2000*. Princeton University Press, Princeton, NJ.

Fekete, Hanna, Takeshi Kuramochi, Mark Roelfsema et al. 2021. "A Review of Successful Climate Change Mitigation Policies in Major Emitting Economies and the Potential of Global Replication." *Renewable and Sustainable Energy Reviews* 137:11062.

Fernández, Diego. 2015. "Water Pricing in Colombia: From Bankruptcy to Full Cost Recovery." In A. Dinar, V. Pochat and J. Albiac-Murillo, eds. *Water Pricing Experiences and Innovations*. Global Issues in Water Policy 9, Springer, pp. 117–138.

Findlay, Ronald. 1993. "The 'Triangular Trade' and the Atlantic Economy of the Eighteenth Century: A Simple General-Equilibrium Model." In R. Findlay, ed.

Trade, Development and Political Economy: Essays of Ronald Findlay. Edward Elgar, London, pp. 321–351.

Fitzpatrick, Scott M. 2020. "Ancient Aquaculture and the Rise of Social Complexity." *Proceedings of the National Academy of Sciences* 117 (17):9151–9153.

Foley, Paul and Charles Mather. 2019. "Ocean Grabbing, Terraqueous Territoriality and Social Development." *Territory, Politics, Governance* 7 (3):297–315.

Folke, Carl, Henrik Österblom, Jean-Baptiste Jouffray et al. 2019. "Transnational Corporations and the Challenge of Biosphere Stewardship." *Nature Ecology & Evolution* 3(10):1396–1403.

Food and Agriculture Organization of the United Nations (FAO). 2012. *Coping with Water Scarcity: An Action Framework for Agriculture and Food Security.* FAO Water Report 38. FAO, Rome.

Food and Agriculture Organization of the United Nations (FAO). 2016. *Global Diagnostic on Groundwater Governance.* FAO, Rome.

Food and Land Use (FOLU) Coalition. 2019. *Growing Better: Ten Critical Transitions to Transform Food and Land Use.* September 2019. FOLU. www.foodandlandusecoalition.org/global-report.

Fouquet, Roger. 2008. *Heat, Power and Light: Revolutions in Energy Services.* Edward Elgar, Cheltenham.

Fouquet, Roger. 2011. "Long Run Trends in Energy-Related External Costs." *Ecological Economics* 70:2380–2389.

Freeman, A. Myrick III, Robert H. Haveman and Allen V. Kneese. 1973. *The Economics of Environmental Policy.* John Wiley, New York.

Friedlingstein, Pierre, Michael O'Sullivan, Matthew W. Jones et al. 2020. "Global Carbon Budget 2020." *Earth System Science Data* 12:3269–3340.

Friess, Daniel A., Kerrylee Rogers, Catherine E. Lovelock et al. 2019. "The State of the World's Mangrove Forests: Past, Present, and Future." *Annual Review of Environment and Resources* 44:89–115.

Gany, A. Hafield A., Prachi Sharma and Sahdev Singh. 2019. "Global Review of Institutional Reforms in the Irrigation Sector for Sustainable Agricultural Water Management, including Water Users' Associations." *Irrigation and Drainage* 68:84–97.

Garnett, Stephen T., Neil D. Burgess, John E. Fa et al. 2018. "A Spatial Overview of the Global Importance of Indigenous Lands for Conservation." *Nature Sustainability* 1:369–374.

Garrick, Dustin and Bruce Aylward. 2012. "Transaction Costs and Institutional Performance in Market-Based Environmental Water Allocation." *Land Economics* 88(3):536–560.

Garrick, Dustin, W. Michael Haneman and Cameron Hepburn. 2020. "Rethinking the Economics of Water: An Assessment." *Oxford Review of Economic Policy* 36(1):1–23.

Gattuso, Jean-Pierre, Alexandre K. Magnan, Laurent Bopp et al. 2018. "Ocean Solutions to Address Climate Change and Its Effects on Marine Ecosystems." *Frontiers in Marine Science* 5:337.

Gerten, Dieter, Holger Hoff, Johan Rockström, Jonas Jägermeyr, Matti Kummu, and Amandine V. Pastor. 2013. "Towards a Revised Planetary Boundary for Consumptive Freshwater Use: Role of Environmental Flow Requirements." *Current Opinion in Environmental Sustainability* 5(6):551–558.

Gibb, Rory, David W. Redding, Kai Qing Chin et al. 2020b. "Zoonotic Host Diversity Increases in Human-Dominated Ecosystems." *Nature* 584:398–402.

Gibbs, H. K., A. S. Ruesch, F. Achard et al. 2010. "Tropical Forests Were the Primary Sources of New Agricultural Lands in the 1980s and 1990s." *Proceedings of the National Academy of Sciences* 107:16732–16737.

Glennon, Robert. 2018. "Water Exchanges: Arizona's Most Recent Innovation in Water Law and Policy." *Arizona Journal of Environmental Law and Policy* 8 (3):1–21.

Goemans, Christopher and James Pritchett. 2014. "Western Water Markets: Effectiveness and Efficiency." In K. W. Easter and Q. Huang, eds. *Water Markets for the 21st Century: What Have We Learned?* Global Issues in Water Policy 11, Springer, Dordrecht, pp. 305–330.

Goldberg, Liza, David Lagomasino, Nathan Thomas, and Temilola Fatoyinbo. 2020. "Global Declines in Human-Driven Mangrove Loss." *Global Change Biology* 26(10):5844–5855.

Goldin, Claudia and Lawrence F. Katz. 2008. *The Race between Education and Technology*. Harvard University Press, Cambridge, MA.

Gordon, Robert J. 2017. *The Rise and Fall of American Growth: The US Standard of Living since the Civil War*. Princeton University Press, Princeton, NJ.

Gosling, Simon N. and Nigel W. Arnell. 2016. "A Global Assessment of the Impact of Climate Change on Water Scarcity." *Climatic Change* 134:371–385.

Grafton, R. Quentin. 2017. "Responding to the 'Wicked Problem' of Water Insecurity." *Water Resources Management* 31:3023–3041.

Grafton, R. Quentin and James Horne. 2014. "Water Markets in the Murray-Darling Basin." *Agricultural Water Management* 145:61–71.

Grafton, R. Quentin, James Horne and Sarah Ann Wheeler. 2016. "On the Marketisation of Water: Evidence from the Murray-Darling Basin, Australia." *Water Resources Management* 30:913–926.

Grafton, R. Quentin, Jamie Pittock, Richard Davis, John Williams, Guobin Fu et al. 2013. "Global Insights into Water Resources, Climate Change and Governance." *Nature Climate Change* 3:315–321.

Grafton, R. Quentin, Long Chu and Paul Wyrwoll. 2020. "The Paradox of Water Pricing: Dichotomies, Dilemmas, and Decisions." *Oxford Review of Economic Policy* 36(1):86–107.

Grahl, John, and Photis Lysandrou. 2014. "The European Commission's Proposal for a Financial Transactions Tax: A Critical Assessment." *JCMS: Journal of Common Market Studies* 52(2):234–249.

Gray, L. C. 1914. "Rent under the Assumption of Exhaustibility." *Quarterly Journal of Economics* 28:466–489.

Green, Jessica F., Thomas Sterner and Gernot Wagner. 2014. "A Balance of Bottom-Up and Top-Down Climate Policies." *Nature Climate Change* 4:1064–1067.

Griffin, Ronald C. 2012. "The Origins and Ideals of Water Resource Economics in the United States." *Annual Reviews of Resource Economics* 4:353–377.

Grigg, Neil S. 2019. "Global Water Infrastructure: State of the Art Review." *International Journal of Water Resources Development* 35:181–205.

Griggs, David, Mark Stafford-Smith, Owen Gaffney et al. 2013. "Sustainable Development Goals for People and Planet." *Nature* 495:305–307.

Griscom, Bronson W., Jonah Busch, Susan C. Cook-Patton et al. 2020. "National Mitigation Potential from Natural Climate Solutions in the Tropics." *Philosophical Transactions of the Royal Society B: Biological Sciences* 375 (1794):20190126.

Griscom, Bronson W., Justin Adams, Peter W. Ellis et al. 2017. "Natural Climate Solutions." *Proceedings of the National Academy of Sciences* 114 (44):11645–11650.

Gruère, Guillaume, Collette Ashley and Jean-Joseph Cadilhon. 2018. "Reforming Water Policies in Agriculture: Lessons from Past Reforms." *OECD Food, Agriculture and Fisheries Papers* No. 113. OECD, Paris.

Haldon, John, Lee Mordechai, Timothy P. Newfield et al. 2018. "History Meets Palaeosceince: Consilience and Collaboration in Studying Past Societal Responses to Environmental Changes." *Proceedings of the National Academy of Sciences* 115(13):3210–3218.

Hallegatte, Stephane, Mook Bangalore, Laura Bonanigo et al. 2015. *Shock Waves: Managing the Impacts of Climate Change on Poverty.* The World Bank, Washington, DC.

Hanemann, W. Michael. 2002. "The Central Arizona Project." Working Paper 937, Giannini Foundation of Agricultural Economics, University of California, Berkeley.

Hanemann, W. Michael and Michael Young. 2020. "Water Rights Reform and Water Marketing: Australia vs the US West." *Oxford Review of Economic Policy* 36(1):108–131.

Hang, Markus, Jerome Geyer-Klingeberg and Andreas W. Rathgeber. 2019. "It Is Merely a Matter of Time: A Meta-Analysis of the Causality between Environmental Performance and Financial Performance." *Business Strategy and the Environment* 28(2):257–273.

Harnik, Paul G., Heike K. Lotze, Sean C. Anderson et al. 2012. "Extinctions in Ancient and Modern Seas." *Trends in Ecology & Evolution* 27(11):608–617.

Harrison, A., L. Martin and S. Nataraj. 2017. "Green Industrial Policy in Emerging Markets." *Annual Review of Resource Economics* 9:253–274.

Havranek, Tomas, Roman Hovrath and Ayaz Zeynalov. 2016. "Natural Resources and Economic Growth: A Meta-Analysis." *World Development* 88:134–151.

Hecht, Susanna B. 2014. "Forests Lost and Found in Tropical Latin America: The Woodland 'Green Revolution.'" *Journal of Peasant Studies* 41:877–909.

Heede, Richard. 2014. "Tracing Anthropogenic Carbon Dioxide and Methane Emissions to Fossil Fuel and Cement Producers, 1854–2010." *Climatic Change* 122(1):229–241.

Helm, Dieter. 2015. *The Climate Crunch: Revised and Updated*, 2nd ed. Yale University Press, London.

Helm, Dieter. 2020. "The Environmental Impacts of the Coronavirus." *Environmental and Resource Economics* 76:21–38.

Hibbard, Kathy A., Paul J. Crutzen, Eric F. Lambin et al. 2006. "Group Report: Decadal-Scale Interactions of Humans and the Environment." In Robert Costanza, ed. *Sustainability or Collapse? An Integrated History and Future of People on Earth*. MIT Press, Cambridge, MA, pp. 341–378.

Hochard, Jacob P., Stuart Hamilton and Edward B. Barbier. 2019. "Mangroves Shelter Coastal Economic Activity from Cyclones." *Proceedings of the National Academy of Sciences* 116(25):12232–12237.

Hoegh-Guldberg, Ove, Ken Caldeira, Thierry Chopin et al. 2019. "The Ocean as a Solution to Climate Change: Five Opportunities for Action." World Resources Institute, Washington, DC. www.oceanpanel.org/climate.

Holden, Stein. 2019. "Economics of Farm Input Subsidies in Africa." *Annual Reviews of Resource Economics* 11:501–522.

Holland, Tim G., Oliver T. Coomes and Brian E. Robinson. 2016. "Evolving Frontier Land Markets and the Opportunity Cost of Sparing Forests in Western Amazonia." *Land Use Policy* 58:456–471.

Hope, Rob, Patrick Thomson, Johanna Koehler and Tim Foster. 2020. "Rethinking the Economics of Rural Water in Africa." *Oxford Review of Economic Policy* 36:171–190.

Horan, Richard D. and James S. Shortle. 2011. "Economic and Ecological Rules for Water Quality Trading." *Journal of the American Water Resources Association* 47(1):59–69.

Horta e Costa, Bárbara, Joachim Claudet, Gustavo Franco, Karim Erzini, Anthony Caro and Emanuel J. Gonçalves. 2016. "A Regulation-Based Classification System for Marine Protected Areas (MPAs)." *Marine Policy* 72:192–198.

Hosonuma, N., M. Herold, V. De Sy et al. 2012. "An Assessment of Deforestation and Forest Degradation Drivers in Developing Countries." *Environmental Research Letters* 7:044009.

Hotelling, H. 1931. "The Economics of Exhaustible Resources." *Journal of Political Economy* 39:137–175.

Hsu, Angel and Ross Rauber. 2021. "Diverse Climate Actors Show Limited Coordination in a Large-Scale Text Analysis of Strategy Documents." *Communications Earth & Environment* 2:30. www.nature.com/articles/s43247-021-00098-7.

Hsu, A., A. Weinfurter, A. Feierman et al. 2018. "Global Climate Action of Regions, States and Businesses Research Report," published by Data Driven Yale, New Climate Institute, PBL Netherlands Environmental Assessment Agency, The Hague. https://datadrivenlab.org/wp-content/uploads/2018/08/YALE-NCI-PBL_Global_climate_action.pdf.

Huang, Jikun. 2018. "Facilitating Inclusive Rural Transformation in the Asian Developing Countries." *World Food Policy* 4(2):31–55.

Hughes, J. Donald. 2001. *An Environmental History of the World: Humankind's Changing Role in the Community of Life.* Routledge, London.

Hwang, Won-Sik, Inha Oh and Jeong-Dong Lee. 2014. "The Impact of Korea's Green Growth Policies on the National Economy and Environment." *The BE Journal of Economic Analysis & Policy* 4(4):1585–1614.

Inikori, Joseph E. 1992. "Slavery and Atlantic Commerce." *American Economic Review* 82(2):151–157.

Intergovernmental Panel on Climate Change (IPCC). 2018. *Summary for Policymakers.* In *Global Warming of 1.5°C.* An IPCC Special Report on the impacts of global warming of 1.5°C above preindustrial levels and related global greenhouse gas emission pathways, in the context of strengthening the global response to the threat of climate change, sustainable development, and efforts to eradicate poverty [V. Masson-Delmotte, P. Zhai, H.-O. Pörtner et al. (eds.)]. World Meteorological Organization, Geneva. www.ipcc.ch/site/assets/uploads/2018/10/SR15_SPM_version_stand_alone_LR.pdf.

Intergovernmental Panel on Climate Change (IPCC). 2020. *Summary for Policymakers.* In: *Climate Change and Land.* An IPCC Special Report on climate change, desertification, land degradation, sustainable land management, food security, and greenhouse gas fluxes in terrestrial ecosystems

[P. R. Shukla, J. Skea, E. Calvo Buendia et al. (eds.)]. IPCC, Geneva. www.ipcc
.ch/site/assets/uploads/sites/4/2020/02/SPM_Updated-Jan20.pdf.

Intergovernmental Science-Policy Platform on Global Biodiversity and Ecosystem
Services (IPBES). 2019. *Global Assessment Report on Biodiversity and
Ecosystem Services*. E. S. Brondizio, J. Settele, S. Díaz and H. T. Ngo, eds.
IPBES secretariat, Bonn. https://ipbes.net/global-assessment-report-
biodiversity-ecosystem-services.

International Energy Agency (IEA). 2020. *Sustainable Recovery*. IEA, Paris. www
.iea.org/reports/sustainable-recovery.

International Institute for Sustainable Development (IISD). (2019a) *Fossil Fuel to
Clean Energy Subsidy Swaps: How to Pay for an Energy Revolution*. IISD,
Winnipeg.

International Institute for Sustainable Development (IISD). (2019b) *Raising
Ambition through Fossil Fuel Subsidy Reform: Greenhouse Gas Emissions
Modelling Results from 26 Countries*. IISD, Winnipeg.

International Labor Organization (ILO). 2018. *Greening with Jobs: World
Employment Social Outlook 2018*. ILO, Geneva. www.ilo.org/wcmsp5/
groups/public/—dgreports/—dcomm/—publ/documents/publication/wcms_
628654.pdf.

Issar, Arie S. and Marranyah Zohar. 2004. *Climate Change – Environment and
Civilization in the Middle East*. Springer-Verlag, Berlin.

Iverson, Terence W., Joanne C. Burgess and Edward B. Barbier. 2020. "Are Subnational Agreements for Carbon Abatement Effective?" *Energies* 13:3675.
https://doi.org/10.3390/en13143675.

Iyer, Venkat, Katy Mathias, David Meyers, Ray Victurine and Melissa Walsh.
2018. *Finance Tools for Coral Reef Conservation: A Guide*. Wildlife
Conservation Society, New York and Conservation Finance Alliance,
Washington, DC. www.conservationfinancealliance.org/news/2019/2/28/cfa-
publication-finance-tools-for-coral-reef-conservation-a-guide.

Jackson, Jeremy B. C., Karen E. Alexander and Enric Sala, eds. 2011. *Shifting
Baselines: The Past and Future of Ocean Fisheries*. Island Press, Washington, DC.

Jackson, Jeremy B. C., Michael X. Kirby, Wolfgang H. Berger et al. 2001.
"Historical Overfishing and the Recent Collapse of Coastal Ecosystems."
Science 293:629–637.

Jackson R., P. Friedlingstein, R. Andrew, J. Canadell, C. Le Quéré and G. Peters.
2019. "Persistent Fossil Fuel Growth Threatens the Paris Agreement and
Planetary Health." *Environmental Research Letters* 14:121001.

Jambeck, Jenna R., Roland Geyer, Chris Wilcox et al. 2015. "Plastic Waste
Inputs from Land into the Ocean." *Science* 347(6223):768–771.

Jaumotte, Florence, Subir Lall and Chris Papageorgiou. 2013. "Rising Income
Inequality: Technology, or Trade and Financial Globalization?" *IMF
Economic Review* 61(2):271–309.

Jayne, Thomas S., Nicole M. Mason, William J. Burke and Joshua Ariga. 2018. "Review: Taking Stock of Africa's Second-Generation Agricultural Subsidy Program." *Food Policy* 75:1–14.

Johansson, Emma Li, Marianela Fader, Jonathan W. Seaquist and Kimberly A. Nicholas. 2016. "Green and Blue Water Demand from Large-Scale Land Acquisitions in Africa." *Proceedings of the National Academy of Sciences* 113 (41):11471–11476.

Johnson, Christine K., Peta L. Hitchens, Pranav S. Pandit et al. 2020. "Global Shifts in Mammalian Population Trends Reveal Key Predictors of Virus Spillover Risk." *Proceedings of the Royal Society B* 287(1924):20192736.

Johnson, Kevin J. 2003. "The Intensification of Pre-industrial Cereal Agriculture in the Tropics: Boserup, Cultivation Lengthening, and the Classic Maya." *Journal of Anthropological Archaeology* 22:126–161.

Jones, Eric L. 1987. *The European Miracle: Environments, Economics and Geopolitics in the History of Europe and Asia*, 2nd ed. Cambridge University Press, Cambridge.

Jones, Kate E., Nikkita G. Patel, Marc A. Levy et al. 2008. "Global Trends in Emerging Infectious Diseases." *Nature* 451(7181): 990–993.

Jones, Kendall R., Osctar Venter, Richard A. Fuller et al. 2018. "One-Third of Global Protected Land Is under Intense Human Pressure." *Science* 360 (6390):788–791.

Jones, Randall and Byungseo Yoo. 2012. Achieving the "Low Carbon Green Growth" Vision in Korea, OECD Economics Department Working Papers No. 964, OECD, Paris.

Jordan, Andrew J., Dave Huitema, Mikael Hildén et al. 2015. "Emergence of Polycentric Climate Governances and Its Future Prospects." *Nature Climate Change* 5:977–982.

Kates, R. W., W. C. Clark, R. Corell et al. 2001. "Sustainability Science." *Science* 292(5517):641–642.

Kemp, R. and B. Never. 2017. "Green Transition, Industrial Policy, and Economic Development." *Oxford Review of Economic Policy* 33:66–84.

Kim, Wonsik, Toshichika Iizumi and Mototki Nishimori. 2019. "Global Patterns of Crop Production Losses Associated with Droughts from 1983 to 2009." *Journal of Applied Meteorology and Climatology* 58(6):1233–1244.

Kjellingbro, Peter M. and Maria Skotte. 2005. *Environmentally Harmful Subsidies: Linkages between Subsides, the Environment and the Economy.* Environmental Assessment Institute, Copenhagen.

Knudsen, Michael H. and Niels Fold. 2017. "Land Distribution and Acquisition Practices in Ghana's Cocoa Frontier: The Impact of a State-Regulated Marketing System." *Land Use Policy* 28(2):378–387.

Kochhar, Kalpana, Catherine Pattillo, Yan Sun et al. 2015. *Is the Glass Half Empty or Half Full? Issues in Managing Water Challenges and Policy*

Instruments. IMF Staff Discussion Note 15, June 11, 2015, International Monetary Fund, Washington, DC.

Kolstad, Ivar. 2009. "The Resource Curse: Which Institutions Matter?" *Applied Economics Letters* 16(4):439–442.

Konar, Manaswita and Helen Ding. 2020. "A Sustainable Ocean Economy for 2050: Approximating Its Benefits and Costs." World Resources Institute, Washington, DC. www.oceanpanel.org/Economicanalysis.

Kuempel, Caitlin D., Kendall R. Jones, James E. M. Watson and Hugh P. Possingham. 2019."Quantifying Biases in Marine-Protected-Area Placement Relative to Abatable Threats." *Conservation Biology* 33(6):1350–1359.

Kummu, Matti, Joseph H. A. Guillaume, Hans de Moel et al. 2016. "The World's Road to Water Scarcity: Shortage and Stress in the 20th Century and Pathways towards Sustainability." *Scientific Reports* 6(1):1–16.

Lade, Steven J., Will Steffen, Wim De Vries et al. 2020. "Human Impacts on Planetary Boundaries Amplified by Earth System Interactions." *Nature Sustainability* 3(2):119–128.

Lai, Alessandro, Gaia Melloni and Riccardo Stacchezzini. 2014. "Corporate Sustainable Development: Is 'Integrated Reporting' a Legitimization Strategy?" *Business Strategy and the Environment* 25:165–177.

Lambin, Eric F. and Patrick Meyfroidt. 2011. "Global Land Use Change, Economic Globalization, and the Looming Land Scarcity." *Proceedings of the National Academy of Sciences* 108:3465–3472.

Larson, Donald F., Rie Murakoda and Keijiro Otsuka. 2016. "Why African Rural Development Strategies Must Depend on Small Farms." *Global Food Security* 10:39–51.

Lau, Jacqueline D., Christina C. Hicks, Georgina G. Gurney and Joshua E. Cinner. 2019. "What Matters to Whom and Why? Understanding the Importance of Coastal Ecosystem Services in Developing Coastal Communities." *Ecosystem Services* 35:219–230.

Laurence, W. F., J. Sayer and K. G. Cassman. 2014. "Agricultural Expansion and Its Impact on Tropical Nature." *Trends in Ecology & Evolution* 29:107–116.

Le Quéré, C., R. Jackson, M. Jones et al. 2020. "Temporary Reduction in Daily Global CO_2 Emissions during the COVID-19 Forced Fonfinement." *Nature Climate Change* 10:647–653.

Leblois, A., O. Damette and J. Wolfsberger. 2018. "What Has Driven Deforestation in Developing Countries Since the 2000s? Evidence from New Remote-Sensing Data." *World Development* 92:82–102.

Lebreton, Laurent, Matthias Egger and Boyan Slat. 2019. "A Global Mass Budget for Positively Buoyant Macroplastic Debris in the Ocean." *Scientific Reports* 9(1):1–10.

Leclére, David, Michael Obersteiner, Mike Barrett et al. 2020. "Bending the Curve of Terrestrial Biodiversity Needs an Integrated Strategy." *Nature* 585:551–556.

Lee, Eddy and Marco Vivarelli, eds. 2006. *Globalization, Employment, and Income Distribution in Developing Countries.* Palgrave Macmillan, London.

Lenton, Timothy M., Hermann Held, Elmar Kriegler et al. 2008. "Tipping Elements in the Earth's Climate System." *Proceedings of the National Academy of Sciences* 105(6):1786–1793.

Lenton, Timothy M. and Hywel T. P. Williams. 2013. "On the Origin of Planetary-Scale Tipping Points." *Trends in Ecology & Evolution* 28 (7):380–382.

Leonard, Bryan, Christopher Costello and Gary D. Libecap. 2019. "Expanding Water Markets in the Western United States: Barriers and Lessons from Other Natural Resource Markets." *Review of Environmental Economics and Policy* 13(1):43–61.

Lester, Sarah E., Benjamin S. Halpern, Kirsten Grorud-Colvert et al. 2009. "Biological Effects within No-Take Marine Reserves: A Global Synthesis." *Marine Ecology Progress Series* 384:33–46.

Lewis, David and Hang Zheng. 2019. "How Could Water Markets Like Australia's Work in China?" *International Journal of Water Resources Development* 35(2019):638–658.

Libecap, Gary D. 2011. "Institutional Path Dependence in Climate Adaptation: Coman's 'Some Unsettled Problems of Irrigation.'" *American Economic Review* 101:64–80.

Livi-Bacci, Massimo. 1997. *A Concise History of World Population,* 2nd ed. Blackwell Publishers, Oxford.

Long, Tony, Sjarief Widjaja, Hassan Wirajuda and Stephanie Juwana. 2020. "Approaches to Combatting Illegal, Unreported and Unregulated Fishing." *Nature Food* 1(7):389–391.

López-Feldman, Alejandro. 2014. Shocks, Income and Wealth: Do They Affect the Extraction of Natural Resources by Households? World Development 64: S91–S100.

Lotze, Heike K. and Inka Milewski. 2004. "Two Centuries of Multiple Human Impacts and Successive Changes in a North Atlantic Food Web." *Ecological Applications* 14(5):1428–1447.

Lotze, Heike K., Hunter S. Lenihan, Bruce J. Bourque et al. 2006. "Depletion, Degradation, and Recovery Potential of Estuaries and Coastal Seas." *Science* 312:1806–1809.

Lovelock, James E. 1988. *The Ages of Gaia: A Biography of Our Living Earth.* Oxford University Press, Oxford.

Lowder, Sarah K., Jakob Skoet and Terri Raney. 2016. "The Number, Size, and Distribution of Farms, Smallholder Farms, and Family Farms Worldwide." *World Development* 87:16–29.

Lubchenco, Jane, Elizabeth B. Cerny-Chipman, Jessica N. Reimer and Simon A. Levin. 2016. "The Right Incentives Enable Ocean Sustainability Successes and

Provide Hope for the Future." *Proceedings of the National Academy of Sciences* 113(51):14507–14514.

Mace, Georgina M., Belinda Reyers, Rob Alkemade et al. 2014. "Approaches to Defining a Planetary Boundary for Biodiversity." *Global Environmental Change* 28:289–297.

Mace, Georgina M., Mike Barrett, Neil D. Burgess et al. 2018. "Aiming Higher to Bend the Curve of Biodiversity Loss." *Nature Sustainability* 1:448–451.

Macedo, Marcia N., Ruth S. DeFries, Douglas C. Morton, Claudia M. Stickler, Gillian L. Galford and Yosio E. Shimabukuro. 2012. "Decoupling of Deforestation and Soy Production in the Southern Amazon during the Late 2000s." *Proceedings of the National Academy of Sciences* 109:1341–1346.

Maddison, Angus. 2003. *The World Economy: Historical Statistics.* Organization for Economic Cooperation and Development, Paris.

Madin, Joshua S. and Elizabeth M. P. Madin. 2015. "The Full Extent of the Global Coral Reef Crisis." *Conservation Biology* 29(6):1724–1726.

Maloney, William F. 2002. "Missed Opportunities: Innovation and Resource-Based Growth in Latin America." *Economía* 3(1):111–166.

Mangin, Tracey, Christopher Costello, James Anderson et al. 2018. "Are Fishery Management Upgrades Worth the Cost?" *PloS One* 13(9):e0204258.

Mannino, Marcello A. and Kenneth D. Thomas. 2002. "Depletion of a Resource? The Impact of Prehistoric Human Foraging on Intertidal Mollusc Communities and Its Significance for Human Settlement, Mobility and Dispersal." *World Archaeology* 33:452–474.

Matheson, Thornton. 2012. "Security Transaction Taxes: Issues and Evidence." *International Tax and Public Finance* 19(6):884–912.

Mathews, John A. 2012. "Green Growth Strategies – Korean Initiatives." *Futures* 44(8):761–769.

McDonald, Robert I., Katherine Weber, Julie Padowski et al. 2014. "Water on an Urban Planet: Urbanization and the Reach of Urban Water Infrastructure." *Global Environmental Change* 27:96–105.

McNeill, John R. 1998. "Chinese Environmental History in World Perspective." In Mark Elvin and Liu Ts'ui-jung, eds. *Sediments of Time: Environment and Society in Chinese History.* Cambridge University Press, Cambridge, pp. 31–49.

McNeill, John R. 2000. *Something New under the Sun: An Environmental History of the 20th-Century World.* W. W. Norton, New York.

McNeill, John R. 2005. "Modern Global Environmental History." *IHDP Update* 2:1–3.

McNeill, John R. and Peter Engelke. 2016. *The Great Acceleration: An Environmental History of the Anthropocene since 1945.* Belknap Press of Harvard University Press, Cambridge, MA.

McSweeney, Kendra. 2005. Natural Insurance, Forest Access, and Compound Misfortune: Forest Resources in Smallholder Coping Strategies before and after Hurricane Mitch in Northeastern Honduras. *World Development* 33(9):1453–1471.

Meadows, Dennis L., Donella H. Meadows, Jorgen Randers and William Behrens. 1972. *The Limits to Growth: A Report for the Club of Rome's Project on the Predicament of Man.* Universe Books, New York.

Medellí-Azuara, J., R. E. Howitt and J. J. Harou. 2012. "Predicting Farmer Responses to Water Pricing, Rationing and Subsidies Assuming Profit-Maximizing Investment in Irrigation Technology." *Agricultural Water Management* 108:73–82.

Mehlum, Halvor, Karl Moene and Ragnar Torvik. 2006. "Institutions and the Resource Curse." *Economic Journal* 116(508):1–20.

Mehrabi, Zia, Erle C. Ellis and Navin Rmankutty. 2018. "The Challenge of Feeding the World While Conserving Half the Planet." *Nature Sustainability* 1:409–412.

Meinig, Donald W. 2004 *The Shaping of America: A Geographical Perspective on 500 Years of History, Volume 4, Global America, 1915–2000.* Yale University Press, New Haven, CT.

Menéndez, Pelayo, Iñigo J. Losada, Saul Torres-Ortega, Siddharth Narayan and Michael W. Beck. 2020. "The Global Flood Protection Benefits of Mangroves." *Scientific Reports* 10(1):1–11.

Meschi, Elena and Marco Vivarelli. 2009. "Trade and Income Inequality in Developing Countries." *World Development* 37(2):287–302.

Metcalf, G. 2019. "On the Economics of a Carbon Tax for the United States." *Brookings Papers on Economic Activity* 49:405–458.

Metcalf, G. and Stock, J. 2020. "Measuring the Macroeconomic Impact of Carbon Taxes." *AEA Papers and Proceedings* 110:101–106.

Meyfroidt, Patrick, Kimberly M. Carlson, Matthew E. Fagan et al. 2014. "Multiple Pathways of Commodity Crop Expansion in Tropical Forest Landscapes." *Environmental and Research Letters* 9:074012.

Mittermeier, R. A., P. Robles-Gil and C. G. Mittermeier, eds. 1997. *Megadiversity: Earth's Biologically Wealthiest Earth's Biological Wealthiest Nations.* CEMEX/Agrupación Sierra Madre, Mexico City.

Montilla-López, Nazaret M., Carlos Gutiérrez-Martín and José A. Gómez-Limón. 2016. "Water Banks: What Have We Learnt from the International Experience?" *Water* 8:466.

Montoya, José M., Ian Donohue and Stuart L. Pimm. 2018. "Planetary Boundaries for Biodiversity: Implausible Science, Pernicious Policies." *Trends in Ecology & Evolution* 33(2):71–73.

Moore, Scott M. 2015. "The Development of Water Markets in China: Progress, Peril, and Prospects." *Water Policy* 17(2):253–267.

Moyer, Jonathan D. and Steve Hedden. 2020. "Are We on the Right Path to Achieve the Sustainable Development Goals." *World Development* 127:104749.

Murray, Nicholas J., Stuart R. Phinn, Michael DeWitt et al. 2019. "The Global Distribution and Trajectory of Tidal Flats." *Nature* 565(7738):222–225.

Nahuelhual, Laura, Gonzalo Saavedra, Gustavo Blanco, Esmee Wesselink, Gonzalo Campos and Ximena Vergara. 2018. "On Super Fishers and Black Capture: Images of Illegal Fishing in Artisanal Fisheries of Southern Chile." *Marine Policy* 95:36–45.

Narain, Urvashi, Shreekant Gupta and Klaas van 't Veld. 2008. "Poverty and Resource Dependence in Rural India." *Ecological Economics* 66(1):161–176.

Narloch, U. and M. Bangalore. 2018. "The Multifaceted Relationship between Environmental Risks and Poverty: New Insights from Vietnam." *Environment and Development Economics* 23:298–327.

Nauges, Celine and Dale Whittington. 2017. "Evaluating the Performance of Alternative Municipal Water Tariff Designs: Quantifying the Tradeoffs between Equity, Economic Efficiency, and Cost Recovery." *World Development* 91:125–143.

Navigant, The Generation Foundation and CDP. (2019). "Internal Carbon Pricing for Low-Carbon Investment" – a briefing paper on linking climate-related opportunities and risks to financing decisions for investors and banks, July 2019. Prepared under the Carbon Pricing Unlocked partnership. https://6fefcbb86e61af1b2fc4-c70d8ead6ced550b4d987d7c03fcdd1d.ssl.cf3.rackcdn.com/cms/reports/documents/000/004/655/original/carbon_pricing_unlocked_internal_carbon_pricing_low-carbon_finance.pdf?1563353352.

Nelson, Richard R. and Gavin Wright. 1992. "The Rise and Fall of American Technological Leadership: The Postwar Era in Historical Perspective." *Journal of Economic Literature* 30(4):1931–1964.

Network for Greening the Financial System (NGFS). 2021. *Annual Report 2020*. NGFS, Paris. March 2021. www.ngfs.net/en/annual-report-2020.

New Climate Economy (NCE). 2018. "Unlocking the Inclusive Growth Story of the 21st Century: Accelerating Climate Action in Urgent Times." https://newclimateeconomy.report/2018.

Newbold, Tim, Lawrence N. Hudson, Andrew P. Arnell et al. 2016. "Has Land Use Pushed Terrestrial Biodiversity beyond the Planetary Boundary? A Global Assessment." *Science* 353(6296):288–291.

Newton, Alice, John Icely, Sonia Cristina, Gerardo M.E. Perillo, R. Eugene Turner, Dewan Ashan, Simon Cragg, et al. 2020. "Anthropogenic, Direct Pressures on Coastal Wetlands." *Frontiers in Ecology and Evolution* 8:144.

Newton, Peter, Arun Agrawal and Lini Wollenberg. 2013. "Enhancing the Sustainability of Commodity Supply Chains in Tropical Forest and Agricultural Landscapes." *Global Environmental Change* 23:1761–1772.

Noack, Frederick, Marie-Catherine Riekhof and Salvatore Di Falco. 2019. "Droughts, Biodiversity, and Rural Incomes in the Tropics." *Journal of the Association of Environmental and Resource Economics* 6(4):823–852.

Nordhaus, William D. 2007. "A Review of the Stern Review on the Economics of Climate Change." *Journal of Economic Literature* 45:686–702.

Nordhaus, William D. 2015. *The Climate Casino: Risk, Uncertainty, and Economics for a Warming World.* Yale University Press, London.

Nülle, Grant Mark and Graham A. Davis. 2018. "Neither Dutch nor disease? Natural Resource Booms in Theory and Empirics." *Mineral Economics* 31:35–59.

O'Callaghan, Brian J. and Em Murdock (2021). "Are We Building Back Better? Evidence from 2020 and Pathways to Inclusive Green Recovery Spending?" United Nations Environment Programme (UNEP), Geneva. March 21, 2021. www.unep.org/resources/publication/are-we-building-back-better-evidence-2020-and-pathways-inclusive-green.

Olmstead Sheila M. 2010. "The Economics of Managing Scarce Water Resources." *Review of Environmental Economics and Policy* 4(2):179–198.

Olmstead, Sheila M. 2010. "The Economics of Water Quality." *Review of Environmental Economics and Policy* 4(1):44–62.

Organization for Economic Cooperation and Development (OECD). 2011. *An Overview of Growing Income Inequalities in OECD Countries: Main Findings. Divided We Stand: Why Inequality Keeps Rising.* OECD, Paris. www.oecd.org/social/soc/49499779.pdf.

Organization for Economic Cooperation and Development (OECD). 2012. *Meeting the Water Reform Challenge.* OECD, Paris. www.cawater-info.net/green-growth/files/oecd7.pdf.

Organization for Economic Cooperation and Development (OECD). 2016. *The Ocean Economy in 2030.* OECD, Paris. www.oecd.org/environment/the-ocean-economy-in-2030-9789264251724-en.htm.

Organization for Economic Cooperation and Development (OECD). 2017a. *Employment Implications of Green Growth: Linking Jobs, Growth, and Green Policies.* OECD, Paris. https://fsc-ccf.ca/references/employment-implications-of-green-growth-linking-jobs-growth-and-green-policies-oecd-report-for-the-g7-environment-ministers.

Organization for Economic Cooperation and Development (OECD). 2017b. *Water Risk Hotspots for Agriculture.* OECD, Paris. www.oecd-ilibrary.org/agriculture-and-food/water-risk-hotspots-for-agriculture_9789264279551-en.

Organization for Economic Cooperation and Development (OECD). 2019a. *Biodiversity: Finance and the Economic and Business Case for Action.* Report prepared for the G7 Environment Ministers' Meeting, May 5–6, 2019. OECD, Paris. www.oecd.org/environment/resources/biodiversity/G7-report-Biodiversity-Finance-and-the-Economic-and-Business-Case-for-Action.pdf.

Organization for Economic Cooperation and Development (OECD). 2019b. *Economic Policy Reforms 2019: Going for Growth*. OECD, Paris. www.oecd .org/economy/going-for-growth.

Organization for Economic Cooperation and Development (OECD). 2020a. *A Comprehensive Overview of Global Biodiversity Finance*. OECD, Paris. www.oecd.org/environment/resources/biodiversity/report-a-comprehensive-overview-of-global-biodiversity-finance.pdf.

Organization for Economic Cooperation and Development (OECD). 2020b. *Agricultural Policy Monitoring and Evaluation 2020*. OECD, Paris. www .oecd-ilibrary.org/agriculture-and-food/agricultural-policy-monitoring-and-evaluation_22217371.

Organization for Economic Cooperation and Development (OECD). 2020c. *Biodiversity and the Economic Response to COVID-19: Ensuring a Green and Resilient Recovery*. OECD, Paris. www.oecd.org/coronavirus/policy-responses/biodiversity-and-the-economic-response-to-covid-19-ensuring-a-green-and-resilient-recovery-d98b5a09.

Organization for Economic Cooperation and Development (OECD). 2020d. *Building Back Better: A Sustainable, Resilient Recovery after COVID-19*. OECD, Paris. www.oecd.org/coronavirus/policy-responses/building-back-better-a-sustainable-resilient-recovery-after-covid-19-52b869f5.

Organization for Economic Cooperation and Development (OECD). 2020e. *Tracking Economic Instruments and Finance for Biodiversity*. OECD, Paris. www.oecd.org/environment/resources/tracking-economic-instruments-and-finance-for-biodiversity-2020.pdf.

Organization of Economic Cooperation and Development (OECD) and International Energy Agency (IEA). 2019. "Update on Recent Progress in Reform of Inefficient Fossil-Fuel Subsidies That Encourage Wasteful Consumption." OECD, Paris. https://oecd.org/fossil-fuels/publication/OECD-IEA-G20-Fossil-Fuel-Subsidies-Reform-Update-2019.pdf.

Österblom, Henrik, Colette C. C. Wabnitz, Dire Tladi et al. 2020. *Towards Ocean Equity*. World Resources Institute, Washington, DC. www.oceanpanel .org/how-distribute-benefits-ocean-equitably.

Osterblöm, Henrik, Jean-Baptiste Jouffray, Carl Folke and Johan Rockström. 2017. "Emergence of a Global Science-Business Initiative for Ocean Stewardship." *Proceedings of the National Academy of Sciences* 114(34):9038–9034.

Oxfam. 2021. *The Inequality Virus: Bringing Together a World Torn Apart by Coronavirus through a Fair, Just and Sustainable Economy*. Oxfam, Oxford. https://policy-practice.oxfam.org/resources/the-inequality-virus-bringing-together-a-world-torn-apart-by-coronavirus-throug-621149.

Pahle, M., S. Pachauri and K. Steinbacher. 2016. "Can the Green Economy Deliver It All? Experiences of Renewable Energy Policies with Socio-economic Objectives." *Applied Energy* 179:1331–1341.

Palanisami, Kuppannan, Kadiri Mohan, Mark Giordano and Chris Charles. 2011. "Measuring Irrigation Subsidies in Andhra Pradesh and Southern India: An Application of the GSI Method for Quantifying Subsidies." Global Subsidies Initiative of the International Institute for Sustainable Development, Geneva.

Palanisami, Kuppannan, Krishna Reddy Kakumanu and Ravinder P. S. Malik. 2015. "Water Pricing Experiences in India: Emerging Issues." In A. Dinar et al., eds. *Water Pricing Experiences and Innovations*, Global Issues in Water Policy 9, Springer, Dordrecth, pp. 161–180.

Papyrakis, Elissaios. 2017. "The Resource Curse – What Have We Learned from Two Decades of Intensive Research: Introduction to the Special Issue." *Journal of Development Studies* 53(2):175–185.

Parker, Bradley J. 2002. "At the Edge of Empire: Conceptualizing Assyria's Anatolian Frontier ca. 700 BC." *Journal of Anthropological Archaeology* 21:371–395.

Pawariya, Vikash, R. C. Sharma and B. K. Sharma. 2017. "Factors Influencing Groundwater Markets in Rajasthan." *Agricultural Research Journal* 54 (4):572–577.

Pearce, David W. and Edward B. Barbier. 2000. *Blueprint for a Sustainable Economy*. Earthscan, London.

Pendrill, Florence, U. Martin Persson, Javier Godar et al. 2019. "Agricultural and Forestry Trade Drives Large Share of Tropical Deforestation Emissions." *Global Environmental Change* 56:1–10.

Pérez-López, Diego, Ana Moreno-Romero and Ralf Barkemeyer. 2015. "The Relationship between Sustainability Reporting and Sustainability Management Practices." *Business Strategy and the Environment* 24:720–734.

Peters, G., R. Andrew, J. Canadell et al. 2020. "Carbon Dioxide Emissions Continue to Grow amidst Slowly Emerging Climate Policies." *Nature Climate Change* 10:2–10.

Petrolia, Daniel R., Matthew G. Interis and Joonghyun Hwang. 2014. "America's Wetland? A National Survey of Willingness to Pay for Restoration of Louisiana's Coastal Wetlands." *Marine Resource Economics* 29(1):17–37.

Pezzey, J. C. V. 1989. "Economic Analysis of Sustainable Growth and Sustainable Development." Environment Department Working Paper No. 15. The World Bank, Washington, DC.

Piketty, Thomas. 2014. *Capital in the Twenty-First Century*. Harvard University Press, Cambridge, MA.

Piketty, Thomas and Gabriel Zucman. 2014. "Capital Is Back: Wealth-Income Ratios in Rich Countries, 1700–2010." *Quarterly Journal of Economics* 129:1255–1310.

Pimm, Stuart L., Gareth J. Russell, John L. Gittleman and Thomas M. Brooks. 1995. "The Future of Biodiversity." *Science* 269(5222):347–350.

Pingali, Prabhu L. 2012. "Green Revolution: Impacts, Limits, and the Path Ahead." *Proceedings of the National Academy of Sciences* 109:12302–12308.

Pitcher, Tony and Mimi E. Lam. 2015. "Fish Commoditization and the Historical Origins of Catching Fish for Profit." *Maritime Studies* 14(2).

Podgorski, Lauren. 2019. "From Wine to Water: Wet Markets for Dry Times." *Arizona State Law Journal* 51:821–844.

Raimi, Daniel, Neelesh Nerurkar and Jason Bordoff. 2020. *Green Stimulus for Oil and Gas Workers: Considering a Major Federal Effort to Plug Orphaned and Abandoned Wells*. Center on Global Energy Policy, Colombia University, New York. July 2020 www.energypolicy.columbia.edu/sites/default/files/file-uploads/OrphanWells_CGEP-Report_071620.pdf.

Ramankutty, Navin and Jonathon A. Foley. 1999. "Estimating Historical Changes in Global Land Cover: Croplands from 1700 to 1992." *Global Biogeochemical Cycles* 13:997–1027.

Randall, Alan. 2021. "Monitoring Sustainability and Targeting Interventions: Indicators, Planetary Boundaries, Benefits and Costs." *Sustainability* 12:3181. www.mdpi.com/2071-1050/13/6/3181.

Raubenheimer, Karen and Alistair McIlgorm. 2018. "Can a Global Fund Help Solve the Global Marine Plastic Debris Problem?" *Journal of Ocean and Coastal Economics* 5(1):6.

Resnick, Danielle, Finn Tarp and James Thurlow. 2012. "The Political Economy of Green Growth: Cases from Southern Africa." *Public Administration and Development* 32:215–228.

Revesz, R. L., P. H. Howard, L. H. Goulder et al. 2014. "Improve Economic Models of Climate Change." *Nature* 508:173–175.

Richards, Daniel R., Benjamin S. Thompson and Lahiru Wijedasa. 2020. "Quantifying Net Loss of Global Mangrove Carbon Stocks from 20 Years of Land Cover Change." *Nature Communications* 11(1):1–7.

Richards, John F. 2003. *The Unending Frontier: An Environmental History of the Early Modern World*. University of California Press, Berkeley.

Richards, Peter D. 2015. "What Drives Indirect Land Use Change? How Brazil's Agriculture Sector Influences Frontier Deforestation. *Annals of the Association of American Geographers* 105:1026–1040.

Richards, Peter D., Robert T. Walker and Eugenio Y. Arima. 2014. "Spatially Complex Land Change: The Indirect Effect of Brazil's Agricultural Sector on Land Use in Amazonia." *Global Environmental Change* 29:1–9.

Roberts, Callum. 2007. *The Unnatural History of the Sea*. Island Press, Washington, DC.

Robinson, Elizabeth J. Z. 2016. Resource-Dependent Livelihoods and the Natural Resource Base. *Annual Reviews of Resource Economics* 8:281–301.

Rockström, J., W. Steffen, K. Noone et al. 2009. "A Safe Operating Space for Humanity." *Nature* 461:472–475.

Rodrik, Dani. 2014. "Green Industrial Policy." *Oxford Review of Economic Policy* 30:469–491.

Roeflsema, Mark, Heleen L. van Soest, Mathijs Harmsen et al. 2020. "Taking Stock of National Climate Policies to Evaluate Implementation of the Paris Agreement." *Nature Communications* 11(1):1–12.

Rosegrant, Mark W., Claudia Ringler and Tingju Zhu. 2009. "Water for Agriculture: Maintaining Food Security under Growing Scarcity." *Annual Review of Environmental and Resources* 3–4:205–222.

Rulli, Maria Cristina, Antonio Saviori and Paolo D'Odorico. 2013. "Global Land and Water Grabbing." *Proceedings of the National Academy of Sciences* 110 (3):892–897.

Running, Steven W. 2012. "A Measurable Planetary Boundary for the Biosphere." *Science* 337(6101):1458–1459.

Sala, Enric, Juan Mayorga, Darcy Bradley et al. 2021. "Protecting the Global Ocean for Biodiversity, Food and Climate." *Nature* 592(7854):397–402.

Saleth. R. Maria. 2014. "Water Markets in India: Extent and Impact." In K. W. Easter and Q. Huang, eds. *Water Markets for the 21st Century: What Have We Learned?* Springer, Dordrecht, pp. 239–261.

Savenije, H. H. G., A. Y. Hoekstra and P. van der Zaag. 2014. "Evolving Water Science in the Anthropocene." *Hydrology and Earth System Sciences* 18:319–332.

Schellnhuber, Hans Joachim. 2009. "Tipping Elements in the Earth System." *Proceedings of the National Academy of Sciences* 106 (49):20561–20563.

Schneider, Anselm, Jennifer Hinton, David Collste, Taís Sonetti González, Sofia Valeria Cortes-Calderon and Ana Paula Dutra Aguiar. 2020. "Can Transnational Corporations Leverage Systemic Change towards a 'Sustainable' Future?" *Nature Ecology & Evolution* 4(4):491–492.

Schrijver, Nico. 2016. "Managing the Global Commons: Common Good or Common Sink?" *Third World Quarterly* 37(7):1252–1267.

Schuhbauer, Anna and U. Rashid Sumaila. 2016. "Economic Viability and Small-Scale Fisheries – A Review." *Ecological Economics* 124:69–75.

Schuhbauer, Anna, Ratana Chuenpagdee, William W. L. Cheung, Krista Greer and U. Rashid Sumaila. 2017. "How Subsidies Affect the Economic Viability of Small-Scale Fisheries." *Marine Policy* 82:114–121.

Shah, Hiral A., Paul Huxley, Jocelyn Elmes and Kris A. Murray. 2019. Agricultural Land-Uses Consistently Exacerbate Infectious Disease Risks in Southeast Asia. *Nature Communications* 10:4299.

Sharfman, Mark R. and Chitru S. Fernando. 2008. "Environmental Risk Management and the Cost of Capital." *Strategic Management Journal* 29:569–592.

Shen, Dajun and Juan Wu. 2017. "State of the Art Review: Water Pricing Reform in China." *International Journal of Water Resources Development* 33 (2):198–232.

Shiklomanov, Igor A. 1993. "World Fresh Water Resources." In Peter H. Gleick, ed. *Water in Crisis: A Guide to the World's Fresh Water Resources.* Oxford University Press, Oxford, pp. 13–24.

Shorrocks, Anthony, James Davies and Rodgrigo Lluberas. 2019. *Global Wealth Report 2019.* Credit Suisse Research Institute, Zurich.

Shorrocks, Anthony, James Davies and Rodgrigo Lluberas. 2020. *Global Wealth Report 2020.* Credit Suisse Research Institute, Zurich.

Shortle, James. 2013. "Economics and Environmental Markets: Lessons from Water-Quality Trading." *Agricultural and Resource Economics Review* 42(1):57–74

Shrubsole, Dan, Dan Walters, Barbara Veale and Bruce Mitchell. 2017. "Integrated Water Resources Management in Canada: The Experience of Watershed Agencies." *International Journal of Water Resources Development* 33(3):349–359.

Sierra-García, Laura, Ana Zorio-Grima and María A. García-Benau. 2015. "Stakeholder Engagement, Corporate Social Responsibility and Integrated Reporting: An Exploratory Study." *Corporate Social Responsibility and Environmental Management* 22:286–304.

Smil, Vaclav. 1994. *Energy in World History.* Westview Press, Boulder, CO.

Smil, Vaclav. 2005. *Creating the Twentieth Century: Technical Innovations of 1867–1914 and Their Lasting Impact.* Oxford University Press, Oxford.

Smil, Vaclav. 2006. *Transforming the Twentieth Century: Technical Innovations and Their Consequences.* Oxford University Press, Oxford.

Smil, Vaclav. 2010. *Energy Transitions: History, Requirements, Prospects.* Praeger, Santa Barbara, CA.

Smith, Eric Alden, Kim Hill, Frank W. Marlowe, David Nolin, Polly Wiessner, Michael Gurven, Samuel Bowles, Monique Borgerhoff Mulder, Tom Hertz and Adrian Bell. 2010. "Wealth Transmission and Inequality among Hunter-Gatherers." *Current Anthropology* 51(1):19–34.

Sommer, Jamie M., Michael Restivo and John M. Shandra. 2020. "The United States, Bilateral Debt-for-Nature Swaps, and Forest Loss: A Cross-National Analysis." *Journal of Development Studies* 56(4):748–764.

Song, Jennifer and Dale Whittington. 2004. "Why Have Some Countries on International Rivers Been Successful Negotiating Treaties? A Global Perspective." *Water Resources Research* 40:W05S06.

Spalding, Ana K. and Ricardo de Ycaza. 2020 "Navigating Shifting Regimes of Ocean Governance: From UNCLOS to Sustainable Development Goal 14." *Environment and Society* 11(1):5–26.

Springmann, Marco, Michael Clark, Daniel Mason-D'Croz et al. 2018. "Options for Keeping the Food System within Environmental Limits." *Nature* 562:519–524.

Standing, Guy. 2017. *Basic Income: A Guide for the Open-Minded.* Yale University Press, London.

Stavins, Robert N. 2011. "The Problem of the Commons: Still Unsettled after 100 Years." *American Economic Review* 101(1):81–108.

Steffen, Will, Angelina Sanderson, Peter Tyson et al. 2004. *Global Change and the Earth System: A Planet under Pressure*. Springer-Verlag, New York.

Steffen, Will, J. Rockström, Katherine Richardson et al. 2018. "Trajectories of the Earth System in the Anthropocene." *Proceedings of the National Academy of Sciences* 115(33):8252–8259.

Steffen, Will, Jacques Grinevald, Paul Crutzen and John McNeill. 2011. "The Anthropocene: Conceptual and Historical Perspectives." *Philosophical Transactions of the Royal Society A Mathematical, Physical and Engineering Sciences* 369:842–867.

Steffen, Will, Katherine Richardson, Johan Rockström et al. 2015b. "Planetary Boundaries: Guiding Human Development on a Changing Planet." *Science* 347:1259855.

Steffen, Will, Paul J. Crutzen and John R. McNeill. 2007. "The Anthropocene: Are Humans Now Overwhelming the Great Forces of Nature?" *Ambio* 36 (8):614–621.

Steffen, Will, Wendy Broadgate, Lisa Deutsch, Owen Gaffney and Cornelia Ludwig. 2015a. "The Trajectory of the Anthropocene: The Great Acceleration." *The Anthropocene Review* 2(1):81–98.

Stern, N. H., S. Peters, V. Bakhshi et al. 2006. *Stern Review: The Economics of Climate Change*. Cambridge: Cambridge University Press.

Sternberg, Troy. 2016. "Water Megaprojects in Deserts and Drylands." *International Journal of Water Resources Development* 32(2):301–320.

Sterner, T., E. B. Barbier, I. Bateman et al. 2019. "Policy Design for the Anthropocene." *Nature Sustainability* 2(1):14–21.

Stierli, Marcus, Anthony Shorrocks, James B. Davies, Rodrigo Lluberas and Antonios Koutsoukis. 2014. *Global Wealth Report 2014*. Credit Suisse Research Institute, Zurich.

Sukhdev, Pavan. 2012. *Corporation 2020: Transforming Business for Tomorrow's World*. Island Press, Washington, DC.

Sumaila, U. Rashid, D. Zeller, L. Hood, M. L. D. Palomares, Y. Li and D. Pauly. 2020a. "Illicit Trade in Marine Fish Catch and Its Effects on Ecosystems and People Worldwide." *Science Advances* 6(9):eaaz3801.

Sumaila, U. Rashid, Melissa Walsh, Kelly Hoareau, Anthony Cox et al. 2020b. *Ocean Finance: Financing the Transition to a Sustainable Ocean Economy*. World Resources Institute, Washington, DC. www.oceanpanel.org/ bluepapers/ocean-finance-financing-transition-sustainable-ocean-economy.

Sumaila, U. Rashid, Naazia Ebrahim, Anna Schuhbauer et al. 2019. "Updated Estimates and Analysis of Global Fishery Subsidies." *Marine Policy* 109:103695.

Svensson, Jesper, Dustin E. Garrick and Shaofeng Jia. 2019. "Water Markets as Coupled Infrastructure Systems: Comparing the Development of Water Rights and Water Markets in Heihe, Shiyang and Yellow Rivers." *Water International* 44(8):834–853.

Takasaki, Yoshito, Bradford L. Barham and Oliver T. Coomes. 2004. "Risk Coping Strategies in Tropical Forests: Floods, Illness, and Resource Extraction." *Environment and Development Economics* 9:203–224.

Task Force on Climate-Related Financial Disclosures (TCFD). 2020. *2020 Status Report*. Financial Stability Board, Bank for International Settlements, Basel. October 2020. https://assets.bbhub.io/company/sites/60/2020/09/2020-TCFD_Status-Report.pdf.

Task Force on Nature-Related Financial Disclosures (TNFD). 2021. *Proposed Technical Scope Recommendations for the TNFD*. Informal Technical Expert Group (ITEG) in support of the Informal Working Group (IWG) for TNFD. June 2021. https://tnfd.info/wp-content/uploads/2021/06/TNFD-%E2%80%93-Technical-Scope-1.pdf.

Thomas, Brinley. 1985. "Escaping from Constraints: The Industrial Revolution in a Malthusian Context." *Journal of Interdisciplinary History* 15:729–753.

Tilman, David, Christian Balzer, Jason Hill and Belinda L. Befort. 2011. "Global Food Demand and the Sustainable Intensification of Agriculture." *Proceedings of the National Academy of Sciences* 108(50):20260–20264.

Toan, Truong D. 2016. "Water Pricing Policy and Subsidies to Irrigation: A Review." *Environmental Processes* 3:1081–1098.

Tollefson, Jeffrey. 2021. "COVID Curbed Carbon Emissions in 2020 – But Not by Much." *Nature* 589:343.

Toynbee, Arnold J. 1978. *Mankind and Mother Earth*. Granada Publishing, London.

Tritsch, Isabelle and Damien Arvor. 2016. "Transition in Environmental Governance in the Brazilian Amazon: Emergence of a New Pattern of Socio-economic Development and Deforestation." *Land Use Policy* 59:446–455.

United Nations (UN). 2019. *The Sustainable Development Goals Report 2019*. United Nations, New York. Available at https://unstats.un.org/sdgs/report/2019/The-Sustainable-Development-Goals-Report-2019.pdf.

United Nations (UN). 2020. *Sustainable Development Goals Report 2020*. United Nations, New York. Available at https://unstats.un.org/sdgs/report/2020/The-Sustainable-Development-Goals-Report-2020.pdf.

United Nations (UN), Department of Economic and Social Affairs, Population Division. 2014. *World Urbanization Prospects: The 2014 Revision*. United Nations, New York. https://esa.un.org/unpd/wup.

United Nations Convention to Combat Desertification (UNCCD). 2017. *The Global Land Outlook*, 1st ed., Bonn.

United Nations Environment Programme (UNEP). 2011. *Towards a Green Economy: Pathways to Sustainable Development and Poverty Eradication.* UNEP, Nairobi.

United Nations Environment Programme (UNEP). 2019. *Emissions Gap Report 2019.* UNEP, Nairobi.

United Nations Environment Programme (UNEP). 2021. *State of Finance for Nature.* UNEP, Nairobi.

United Nations Environment Programme Finance Initiative (UNEP FI). 2015. *Towards including Natural Resource Risks in Cost of Capital, State of Play and the Way Forward, Natural Capital Declaration.* UNEP FI, Geneva. www.unepfi .org/fileadmin/documents/NCD-NaturalResourceRisksScopingStudy.pdf.

United Nations Environment Programme Finance Initiative (UNEP FI). 2020. *Turning the Tide: How to Finance a Sustainable Ocean Recovery–A Practical Guide for Financial Institutions.* UNEP FI, Geneva. www.unepfi.org/ publications/turning-the-tide.

United Nations Environment Programme Finance Initiative (UNEP FI). 2021. *The Climate Risk Landscape: Mapping Climate-Related Financial Risk Assessment Methodologies.* UNEP FI, Geneva. www.unepfi.org/publications/banking-publications/the-climate-risk-landscape.

van der Ploeg, Frederick. 2011. "Natural Resources: Curse or Blessing?" *Journal of Economic Literature* 49:366–420.

Van Dover, C. L., J. Aronson, L. Pendleton et al. 2014. "Ecological Restoration in the Deep Sea: Desiderata." *Marine Policy* 44:98–106.

Vardas, Giannis and Anastasios Xepapadeas. 2010. "Model Uncertainty, Ambiguity and the Precautionary Principle: Implications for Biodiversity Management." *Environmental and Resource Economics* 45(3):379–404.

Vedeld, Paul, Arild Angelsen, Jan Bojö, Espen Sjaastad and Gertrude Kobugabe Berg. 2007. "Forest Environmental Incomes and the Rural Poor." *Forest Policy and Economics* 9:869–879.

Venables, Anthony J. 2016. "Using Natural Resources for Development: Why Has It Proven So Difficult?" *Journal of Economic Perspectives* 30:161–184.

Verdone, Michael and Andrew Seidl. 2017. "Time, Space, Place, and the Bonn Challenge Forest Restoration Target." *Restoration Ecology* 26(6):903–911.

Victorero, Lissette, Les Watling, Maria L. Deng Palomares and Claire Nouvian. 2018. "Out of Sight, but within Reach: A Global History of Bottom-Trawled Deep-Sea Fisheries from> 400 m depth." *Frontiers in Marine Science* 5:98.

Vierros, Marjo K., Autumn-Lynn Harrison, Matthew R. Sloat et al. 2020. "Considering Indigenous Peoples and Local Communities in Governance of the Global Ocean Commons." *Marine Policy* 119:104039.

Vince, Joanna and Britta D. Hardesty. 2018. "Governance Solutions to the Tragedy of the Commons That Marine Plastics Have Become." *Frontiers in Marine Science* 5:214.

Virdin, J., T. Vegh, J-B. Jouffray et al. 2021. "The Ocean 100: Transnational Corporations in the Ocean Economy." *Science Advances* 7(3):eabc8041.

Volz, Ulrich, Shamshad Akhtar, Kevin P. Gallagher, Stephany Griffith-Jones, Jörg Haas and Moritz Kraemer. 2020. "Debt Relief for a Green and Inclusive Recovery: A Proposal." Heinrich-Böll-Stiftung; SOAS, University of London; and Boston University, Boston. November 2020. https://eprints.soas.ac.uk/34346/1/DRGR-report.pdf.

Wagner, Lorie A. 2002. *Materials in the Economy – Material Flows, Scarcity, and the Environment. US Geological Survey Circular 1221.* US Department of the Interior, US Geological Survey, Denver.

Waldron, Anthony, Daniel C. Miller, Dave Redding et al. 2017. "Reductions in Global Biodiversity Loss Predicted from Conservation Spending." *Nature* 551:364–367.

Walker, Robert T., John Browder, Eugenio Arima et al. 2009. "Ranching and the New Global Range: Amazônia in the 21st Century." *Geoforum* 40:732–745.

Ward, Frank A. 2010. "Financing Irrigation Water Management and Infrastructure: A Review." *Water Resources Development* 26(3):321–349.

Waters, Colin N., Jan Zalasiewicz, Colin Summerhayes et al. 2016. "The Anthropocene Is Functionally and Stratigraphically Distinct from the Holocene." *Science* 351(6269):aad2622.

Waycott, Michelle, Carlos M. Duarte, Tim J. B. Carruthers et al. 2009. "Accelerating Loss of Seagrasses across the Globe Threatens Coastal Ecosystems." *Proceedings of the National Academy of Sciences* 106 (30):12377–12381.

Wear, Stephanie L. 2016. "Missing the Boat: Critical Threats to Coral Reefs Are Neglected at Global Scale." *Marine Policy* 74:153–157.

Weitzman, Martin L. 2007. "A Review of the Stern Review on the Economics of Climate Change." *Journal of Economic Literature* 45(3):703–724.

Wheeler, Sarah Ann and Dustin E. Garrick. 2020. "A Tale of Two Water Markets in Australia: Lessons for Understanding Participation in Formal Water Markets." *Oxford Review of Economic Policy* 36(1):132–153.

White, Timothy D., Tiffany Ong, Francesco Ferretti et al. 2020. "Tracking the Response of Industrial Fishing Fleets to Large Marine Protected Areas in the Pacific Ocean." *Conservation Biology* 34(6):1571–1578.

Whittington, Dale, Mark Radin and Marc Jeuland. 2020. "Evidence-Based Policy Analysis? The Strange Case of the Randomized Controlled Trials of Community-Led Total Sanitation." *Oxford Review of Economic Policy* 36(1):191–221.

Whittington, Dale, W. Michael Hanemann, Claudia Sadoff and Marc Jeuland. 2008. "The Challenge of Improving Water and Sanitation Services in Less Developed Countries." *Foundations and Trends in Microeconomics* 4(6–7):469–609.

Widjaja, Sjarief, Tony Long, Hassan Wirajuda et al. 2020. "Illegal, Unreported and Unregulated Fishing and Associated Drivers." World Resources Institute, Washington, DC. www.oceanpanel.org/iuu-fishing-and-associated-drivers.

Wilson, Edward O. 2016. *Half-Earth: Our Planet's Fight for Life*. W. W. Norton & Co., New York.

Winther, Jan-Gunnar, Minhan Dai, Therese Rist et al. 2020. "Integrated Ocean Management for a Sustainable Ocean Economy." *Nature Ecology & Evolution* 4(11):1451–1458.

World Bank. 2019a. *Green Bond Impact Report 2019*. World Bank, Washington, DC. November 2019.

World Bank. 2019b. *State and Trends of Carbon Pricing 2019*. World Bank, Washington, DC. June 2019.

World Bank. 2020a. *Mobilizing Private Finance for Nature*. World Bank, Washington, DC. September 2020. www.worldbank.org/en/news/feature/2020/09/25/unlocking-private-finance-for-nature.

World Bank. 2020b. *Poverty and Shared Prosperity 2020: Reversals of Fortune*. World Bank, Washington, DC. www.worldbank.org/en/publication/poverty-and-shared-prosperity.

World Commission on Environment and Development (WCED). 1987. *Our Common Future*. Oxford University Press, New York.

World Economic Forum (WEF). 2020. *New Nature Economy Report II: The Future of Nature and Business*. World Economic Forum in Collaboration with AlphaBeta. WEF, Geneva. www3.weforum.org/docs/WEF_The_Future_Of_Nature_And_Business_2020.pdf.

World Economic Forum (WEF). 2021. *The Global Risks Report 2021*. World Economic Forum, Davos. www3.weforum.org/docs/WEF_The_Global_Risks_Report_2021.pdf.

Worm, Boris. 2016. "Averting a Global Fisheries Disaster." *Proceedings of the National Academy of Sciences* 113(18):4895–4897.

Worm, Boris and Trevor A. Branch. 2012. "The Future of Fish." *Trends in Ecology & Evolution* 27(11):594–599.

Worm, Boris, Edward B. Barbier, Beaumont Nicola et al. 2006. "Impacts of Biodiversity Loss on Ocean Ecosystem Services." *Science* 314(5800):787–790.

Wright, Gavin and Jesse Czelusta. 2004. "Why Economies Slow: The Myth of the Resource Curse." *Challenge* 47(2):6–38.

Wrigley, C. Anthony. 1988. *Continuity, Chance and Change: The Character of the Industrial Revolution in England*. Cambridge University Press, Cambridge.

Wunder, Sven, Jan Börner, Gerald Shively and Miriam Wyman. 2014. Safety Nets, Gap Filling and Forests: A Global-Comparative Perspective. *World Development* 64:S29–S42.

WWF. 2018. *Living Planet Report – 2018: Aiming Higher.* Grooten, M. and Almond, R. E. A. (eds.). WWF, Gland. www.worldwildlife.org/pages/living-planet-report-2018.

WWF. 2020. *Living Planet Report 2020 – Bending the Curve of Biodiversity Loss.* Almond, R. E. A., Grooten M. and Petersen, T. (eds.). WWF, Gland. www.zsl.org/sites/default/files/LPR%202020%20Full%20report.pdf.

Yamazaki, A. 2017. "Jobs and Climate Policy: Evidence from British Columbia's Revenue-Neutral Carbon Tax." *Journal of Environmental Economics and Management* 83:197–216.

Yamazaki, Satoshi, Eriko Hoshino and Budy P. Resosudarmo. 2015. "No-Take Marine Reserves and Illegal Fishing under Imperfect Enforcement." *Australian Journal of Agricultural and Resource Economics* 59(3):334–354.

Yoffee, Norman. 1988. "Orienting Collapse." In Norman Yoffee and George L. Cowgill, eds. 1988. *The Collapse of Ancient States and Civilizations.* University of Arizona Press, Tucson, AZ.

Zapana-Churata, Luis, Hug March and David Sauri. 2021. "Water Demand Management Strategies in Fast-Growing Cities: The Case of Arequipa, Perú." *International Journal of Water Resources Development* (April 2021):1–25.

Zeng, Yiwen, Daniel A. Friess, Tasya Vadya Sarira, Kelly Siman and Lian Pin Koh. 2021. "Global Potential and Limits of Mangrove Blue Carbon for Climate Change Mitigation." *Current Biology* 31(8):1737–1743.

INDEX

in low- and middle-income economies, 237

major economies' role in, 224–231

support for research and development in, 83–86

wage and education disparities and, 239–240

water management and, 150–153

water-saving innovations, 173–175

technology-push policies, 173–175

technology spillovers, 83–86

terrestrial realm, planetary boundaries and preservation of, 127–128

The Economics of Biodiversity (Dasgupta), 1–2

The Economics of Spaceship Earth (Boulding), 56–60

The Economist, 258–260, 274n.32

third-party fishery certification, 205–206

30 by 2030 biodiversity target, 127, 193, 202–203

timber crops, smallholder subsidies for, 122

tipping points

criticism of evidence on, 47–48

Earth climate systems, 3–4, 19n.13

Holocene period, 22

planetary boundaries and, 43–49

spaceship economy and, 58–59

Tobin, James, 238

Tobin tax, 238

Torvik, Ragnar, 112–113

total capital stock

defined, 59–60

environmental risk reduction and, 60–63

Toynbee, Arnold, 2, 19–20n.19, 32, 242–243n.18

tradeable water pollution permits, 167–170

transboundary water sources

collective action concerning, 175–179

water grabbing and, 178–179

transmission infrastructure, clean energy sources and lack of, 86

transnational corporations (TNCs)

market concentration and environmental exploitation by, 249–251

sustainability initiatives for, 251–252

transportation industry

fossil fuel impact on, 35

highway development and, 35–37

tropical carbon tax, 123–124, 234, 236

Tulare River Basin (California), 170–172

200 mile limit, 202–210

underfunding of nature

agriculture subsidies and, 115–120

coastal ecosystem underfunding, 198–202

green business practices and, 267–268

green economic transition and ending of, 226–227

land use and acquisition and, 118–120

underpricing of nature

business role in, 246–248, 271–272

ecological scarcity and, 67–69

elimination of, 6–10, 16, 55–56, 59–60, 69–72, 108–110, 115–120, 279–280

estimation and calculation of, 102n.19

of fisheries, 194–198

fossil fuel subsidies linked to, 15–16, 79–80

green business development and, 266–269

green economy and elimination of, 222–224, 226–227

of irrigation, 170–172

of land and natural resources, 111–113, 120–126

in low- and middle-income countries, 87–90, 234

major economies as leaders in, 80–86

of marine capital, 17, 184, 188–198, 203–205

poverty and inequity and, 113–115

revenue gains from abolition of, 95–99

suppression of technological innovation and, 79–80

Printed in the United States
by Baker & Taylor Publisher Services